thelightningpress.com

SMARTBOOK

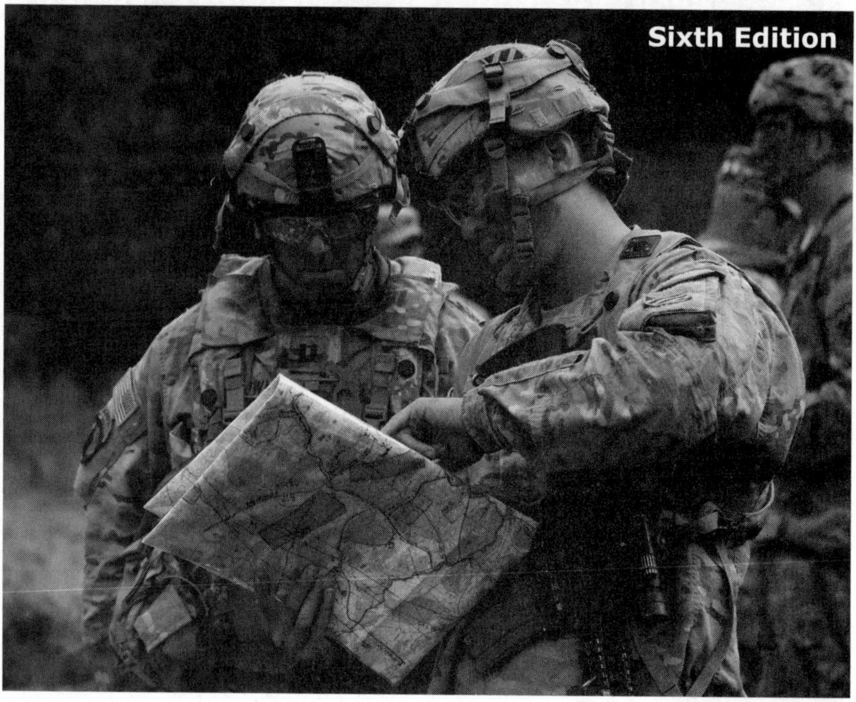

the BATTLE STAFF

Plan, Prepare, Execute, & Assess Military Operations

The Lightning Press
Norman M Wade

The Lightning Press

2227 Arrowhead Blvd.
Lakeland, FL 33813
24-hour Voicemail/Fax/Order: 1-800-997-8827
E-mail: SMARTbooks@TheLightningPress.com

www.TheLightningPress.com

(BSS6) The Battle Staff SMARTbook, 6th Ed.

Plan, Prepare, Execute, & Assess Military Operations

BSS6 is the sixth edition of The Battle Staff SMARTbook, completely updated for 2020. Updated material and references include the full scope of new material from ADP 5-0, The Operations Process (Jul '19); ADP 6-0, Mission Command (Jul '19); FM 3-0 (w/Change 1), Operations (Dec '17); FM 6-0 (w/change 2), Commander and Staff Organization and Operations (Apr '16); ATP 2-01.3, Intelligence Preparation of the Battlefield (Mar '19); ADP 3-19, Fires (Jul '19); ATP 3-60, Targeting (May '15); ATP 5-19 (w/change 1), Risk Management (Apr '14); and ADP 1-02, Terms and Military Symbols (Aug '19); and more.

ISBN: 978-1-935886-81-5

Notice of Liability

The information in this SMARTbook and quick reference guide is distributed on an "As Is" basis, without warranty. While every precaution has been taken to ensure the reliability and accuracy of all data and contents, neither the author nor The Lightning Press shall have any liability to any person or entity with respect to liability, loss, or damage caused directly or indirectly by the contents of this book. If there is a discrepancy, refer to the source document. This SMARTbook does not contain classified or sensitive information restricted from public release.

"The views presented in this publication are those of the author and do not necessarily represent the views of the Department of Defense or its components."

Photo Credits. Cover photo: U.S. Soldiers of the 3rd Infantry Division point at a map prior to conducting a 33rd Romanian Mountain Brigade Combined Arms Rehearsal during exercise Combined Resolve VII at the U.S. Army's Joint Multinational Readiness Center in Hohenfels Germany, Sept. 5, 2016. (U.S. Army photo by Spc. Nathaniel Nichols) Other photos courtesy of the Dept of Defense and Dept of Army.

Printed and bound in the United States of America.

[BSS6] Notes to Reader

Plan, Prepare, Execute, & Assess Military Operations

The Army's framework for organizing and putting command and control into action is the **operations process**—the major command and control activities performed during operations: **planning, preparing, executing, and continuously assessing** the operation. Commanders use the operations process to drive the conceptual and detailed planning necessary to **understand** their operational environment (OE); **visualize and describe** the operation's end state and operational approach; make and articulate decisions; and **direct, lead, and assess** operations.

Planning is the art and science of understanding a situation, envisioning a desired future, and laying out effective ways of bringing that future about. **Preparation** consists of those activities performed by units and Soldiers to improve their ability to execute an operation. **Execution** is the act of putting a plan into action by applying combat power to accomplish the mission and adjusting operations based on changes in the situation. **Assessment** is a continuous activity that supports decision making by ascertaining progress of the operation for the purpose of developing and refining plans and for making operations more effective.

The **Battle Staff SMARTbook** covers the operations process (ADP 5-0); commander's activities; Army planning methodologies; the military decisionmaking process and troop leading procedures (FM 6-0 w/Chg 2: MDMP & TLP); integrating processes (IPB, information collection, targeting, risk management, and knowledge management); plans and orders (WARNORDs/FRAGORDs/OPORDs); mission command, C2 warfighting function tasks, command posts, liaison (ADP 6-0); rehearsals & after action reviews; and operational terms and military symbols (ADP 1-02).

***BSS6** is the sixth edition of The Battle Staff SMARTbook, completely updated for 2020. Updated material includes the full scope of new material from ADP 5-0, The Operations Process (Jul '19); ADP 6-0, Mission Command (Jul '19); FM 3-0 (w/Change 1), Operations (Dec '17); FM 6-0 (w/change 2), Commander and Staff Organization and Operations (Apr '16); ATP 2-01.3, Intelligence Preparation of the Battlefield (Mar '19); ADP 3-19, Fires (Jul '19); ATP 3-60, Targeting (May '15); ATP 5-19 (w/change 1), Risk Management (Apr '14); and ADP 1-02, Terms and Military Symbols (Aug '19); and more.*

SMARTbooks - DIME is our DOMAIN!

SMARTbooks: Reference Essentials for the Instruments of National Power (D-I-M-E: Diplomatic, Informational, Military, Economic)! Recognized as a "whole of government" doctrinal reference standard by military, national security and government professionals around the world, SMARTbooks comprise a comprehensive professional library designed with all levels of Soldiers, Sailors, Airmen, Marines and Civilians in mind.

SMARTbooks can be used as quick reference guides during actual operations, as study guides at education and professional development courses, and as lesson plans and checklists in support of training. Visit **www.TheLightningPress.com**!

BSS6: The Battle Staff SMARTbook, 6th Ed.
(Plan, Prepare, Execute, & Assess Military Operations)

BSS6 is the sixth edition of The Battle Staff SMARTbook, completely updated for 2020. Updated material and references include the full scope of new material from ADP 5-0, The Operations Process (Jul '19); ADP 6-0, Mission Command (Jul '19); FM 3-0 (w/Change 1), Operations (Dec '17); FM 6-0 (w/change 2), Commander and Staff Organization and Operations (Apr '16); ATP 2-01.3, Intelligence Preparation of the Battlefield (Mar '19); ADP 3-19, Fires (Jul '19); ATP 3-60, Targeting (May '15); ATP 5-19 (w/change 1), Risk Management (Apr '14); and ADP 1-02, Terms and Military Symbols (Aug '19); and more.

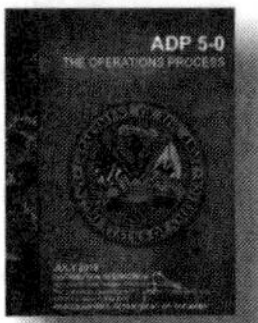

ADP 5-0

ADP 6-0

FM 3-0 (Chg 1)

FM 6-0 (Chg 2)

ATP 2-01.3

ADP 3-19

ADP 1-02

plus more!

The Battle Staff SMARTbook covers the operations process (ADP 5-0); commander's activities; Army planning methodologies; the military decisionmaking process and troop leading procedures (FM 6-0 w/Chg 2: MDMP & TLP); integrating processes (IPB, information collection, targeting, risk management, and knowledge management); plans and orders (WARNORDs/OPORDs/FRAGORDs); mission command, C2 warfighting function tasks, command posts, liaison (ADP 6-0); rehearsals & after action reviews; and operational terms and military symbols (ADP 1-02).

Chap 1: The Operations Process

The Army's framework for organizing and putting command and control into action is the **operations process**—the major command and control activities performed during operations: **planning, preparing, executing, and continuously assessing** the operation. Commanders use the operations process to drive the conceptual and detailed planning necessary to understand their operational environment (OE); visualize and describe the operation's end state and operational approach; make and articulate decisions; and direct, lead, and assess operations.

Commanders, staffs, and subordinate headquarters employ the operations process to organize efforts, integrate the warfighting functions across multiple domains, and synchronize forces to accomplish missions. This includes integrating numerous processes and activities such as information collection and targeting within the headquarters and with higher, subordinate, supporting, and supported units.

Commanders are the most important participants in the operations process. While staffs perform essential functions that amplify the effectiveness of operations, commanders drive the operations process through **understanding, visualizing, describing, directing, leading, and assessing** operations.

Chap 2: The Military Decisionmaking Process (MDMP & TLP)

The **military decisionmaking process (MDMP)** is an iterative planning methodology to understand the situation and mission develop a course of action, and produce an operation plan or order. The MDMP helps leaders apply thoroughness, clarity, sound judgment, logic, and professional knowledge to understand situations, develop options to solve problems, and reach decisions. This process, consisting of seven steps with inputs and outputs, helps commanders, staffs, and others think critically and creatively while planning.

Troop leading procedures extend the MDMP to the small-unit level. The MDMP and TLP are similar but not identical. They are both linked by the basic Army problem solving methodology explained. Commanders with a coordinating staff use the MDMP as their primary planning process. Company-level and smaller units lack formal staffs and use TLP to plan and prepare for operations. This places the responsibility for planning primarily on the commander or small-unit leader.

Chap 3: Integrating Processes

Commanders and staffs integrate the warfighting functions and synchronize the force to adapt to changing circumstances throughout the operations process. They use several **integrating processes** to do this. An integrating process consists of a series of steps that incorporate multiple disciplines to achieve a specific end. For example, during planning, the military decision-making process (MDMP) integrates the commander and staff in a series of steps to produce a plan or order. Key integrating processes that occur throughout the operations process include **intelligence preparation of the battlefield, information collection, targeting, risk management, and knowledge management**.

Chap 4: Plans & Orders

A product of planning is a **plan or order**—a directive for future action. Commanders issue plans and orders to subordinates to communicate their understanding of the situation and their visualization of an operation. Plans and orders direct, coordinate, and synchronize subordinate actions and inform those outside the unit how to cooperate and provide support.

Chap 5: Mission Command

Mission command is the Army's approach to command and control that empowers subordinate decision making and decentralized execution appropriate to the situation. Mission command supports the Army's operational concept of unified land operations and its emphasis on seizing, retaining, and exploiting the initiative. The **command and control warfighting function** is the related tasks and a system that enable commanders to synchronize and converge all elements of combat power. The primary purpose of the command and control warfighting function is to assist commanders in integrating the other elements of combat power to achieve objectives and accomplish missions.

Chap 6: Rehearsals & After Action Reviews (AARs)

Rehearsals allow leaders and their Soldiers to practice executing key aspects of the concept of operations. These actions help Soldiers orient themselves to their environment and other units before executing the operation. An **after action review (AAR)** is a guided analysis of an organization's performance, conducted at appropriate times during and at the conclusion of a training event or operation with the objective of improving future performance. The AAR provides valuable feedback essential to correcting training deficiencies. Feedback must be direct, on-the-spot and standards-based.

Chap 7: Operational Terms & Symbols

Terms and symbols provide a common language used to communicate during the conduct of operations. Terms are words defined in doctrinal publications specifically for Army use and codified in ADP 1-02 and the DOD Dictionary of Military and Associated Terms. Symbols are those graphics defined specifically for military use. They are codified in MIL-STD-2525D.

(BSS6) References

The following references were used to compile The Battle Staff SMARTbook. All references are considered public domain, available to the general public, and designated as "approved for public release; distribution is unlimited." The Battle Staff SMARTbook does not contain classified or sensitive material restricted from public release.

Army Doctrinal Publications (ADPs) and Army Doctrinal Reference Publications (ADRPs)

ADP 1-02*	Aug 2018	Terms and Military Symbols
ADP 2-0*	Jul 2019	Intelligence
ADP 3-19*	Jul 2019	Fires
ADP 3-90*	Jul 2019	Offense and Defense
ADP 5-0*	Jul 2019	The Operations Process
ADP 6-0*	Jul 2019	Mission Command

Army Techniques Publications (ATPs) and Army Tactics, Techniques and Procedures (ATTPs)

ATP 2-01.3*	Mar 2019	Intelligence Preparation of the Battlefield
ATP 3-60	May 2015	Targeting
ATP 5-19	Apr 2014	Risk Management (w/change 1)

Field Manuals (FMs)

FM 3-09	Apr 2014	Field Artillery Operations and Fire Support
FM 3-90-1	Mar 2013	Offense and Defense (Volume I)
FM 3-90-2	Mar 2013	Reconnaissance, Security, And Tactical Enabling Tasks (Volume 2)
FM 6-0*	Apr 2016	Commander and Staff Organization and Operations (w/change 2*)
FM 6-01.1*	Jul 2012	Knowledge Management Operations

Joint Publications (JPs)

JP 3-0*	Oct 2018	Joint Operations (w/Change 1)
JP 5-0*	Jun 2017	Joint Planning

** New or updated reference publication since last edition.*

[BSS6] Table of Contents

Chap 1 The Operations Process

Chap 2

Military Decision Making (MDMP &TLP)

Chap 3

Integrating Processes

Chap 4 Plans & Orders

Chap 5 Mission Command

Chap 6

Rehearsals & After Action Reviews (AARs)

Chap 7

Operational Terms, Acronyms & Symbols

Chap 1

I. Fundamentals of the Operations Process

Ref: ADP 5-0, The Operations Process (Jul '19), chap. I.

The Army's framework for organizing and putting command and control into action is the operations process—the major command and control activities performed during operations: planning, preparing, executing, and continuously assessing the operation. Commanders use the operations process to drive the conceptual and detailed planning necessary to understand their operational environment (OE); visualize and describe the operation's end state and operational approach; make and articulate decisions; and direct, lead, and assess operations.

The Operations Process

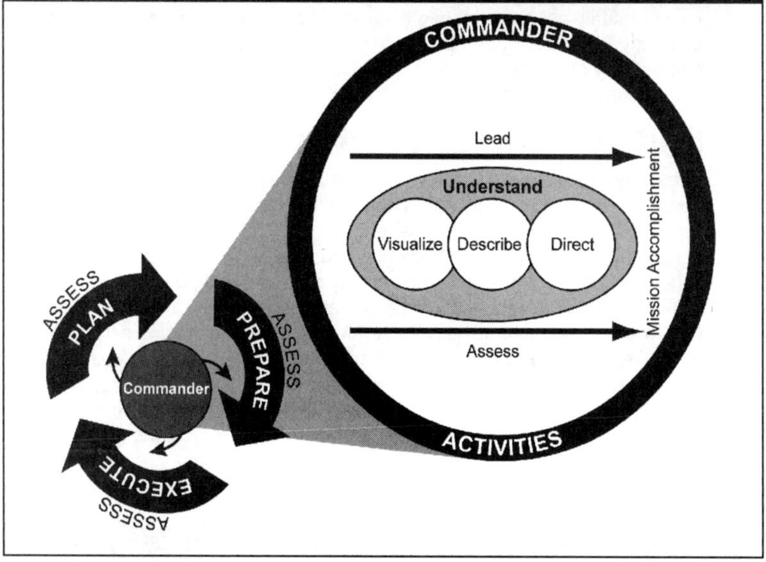

Ref: ADP 5-0, The Operations Process, fig. 1-1, p. 1-4.

Commanders, staffs, and subordinate headquarters employ the operations process to organize efforts, integrate the warfighting functions across multiple domains, and synchronize forces to accomplish missions. This includes integrating numerous processes and activities such as information collection and targeting within the headquarters and with higher, subordinate, supporting, and supported units. The unit's battle rhythm helps to integrate and synchronize the various processes and activities that occur within the operations process.

A goal of the operations process is to make timely and effective decisions and to act faster than the enemy. A tempo advantageous to friendly forces can place the enemy under the pressures of uncertainty and time. Throughout the operations process, making and communicating decisions faster than the enemy can react produces a tempo with which the enemy cannot compete. These decisions include assigning tasks; prioritizing, allocating, and organizing forces and resources; and selecting the critical times and places to act. Decision making during execution includes knowing how and when to adjust previous decisions. The speed and accuracy of a commander's actions to address a changing situation is a key contributor to agility.

I. The Nature of Operations

Understanding the doctrine on mission command and the operations process requires an appreciation of the nature of operations and the Army's vision of war. It is upon this appreciation that mission command— an approach to the exercise of command and control—is built. The principles of mission command guide commanders and staffs in planning, preparing, executing, and assessing operations.

Military operations fall along a competition continuum that spans cooperation to war. Between these extremes, societies maintain relationships. These relationships include economic competition, political or ideological tension, and at times armed conflict. Violent power struggles in failed states, along with the emergence of major regional powers like Russia, China, Iran, and North Korea seeking to gain strategic positions of advantage, present challenges to the joint force. Army forces must be prepared to meet these challenges across the range of military operations during periods of competition and war.

The range of military operations is a fundamental construct that helps relate military activities and operations in scope and purpose within a backdrop of the competition continuum. The potential range of military operations extends from military engagement, security cooperation, and deterrence in periods of competition to large-scale combat operations in periods of war. Whether fighting terrorists as part of a limited contingency operation or defeating a peer threat in large-scale combat, the nature of operations is constant.

II. Unified Land Operations

The Army's operational concept—the central idea that guides the conduct of Army operations—is unified land operations. Unified land operations is the simultaneous execution of offense, defense, stability, and defense support of civil authorities across multiple domains to shape operational environments, prevent conflict, prevail in large-scale ground combat, and consolidate gains as part of unified action (ADP 3-0). Army forces do this with combined arms formations possessing the mobility, firepower, protection, and sustainment to defeat an enemy and establish control of areas, resources, and populations. Army forces depend on the capabilities of the other Services as the joint force depends on Army capabilities across multiple domains. The goal of unified land operations is to achieve the joint force commander's end state by applying land power as part of unified action. During the conduct of unified land operations, Army forces support the joint force through four strategic roles: shape operational environments (OEs), prevent conflict, prevail in large-scale ground combat, and consolidate gains.

Army forces assist in shaping an operational environment (OE) by providing trained and ready forces to geographic combatant commanders (GCCs) in support of their campaign plan. Shaping activities include security cooperation, military engagement, and forward presence to promote U.S. interests and assure allies. Army operations to prevent are designed to deter undesirable actions of an adversary through positioning of friendly capabilities and demonstrating the will to use them. Army forces may have a significant role in the execution of flexible deterrent options or flexible response options. Additionally, Army prevent activities may include mobilization, force tailoring, and other pre-deployment activities; initial deployment into a theater of operations; and development of intelligence, communications, sustainment, and protection infrastructure to support the joint force commander. During large-scale combat operations, Army forces focus on the defeat of enemy ground forces. Army forces close with and destroy enemy forces, exploit success, and break their opponent's will to resist. While Army forces consolidate gains throughout an operation, consolidating gains become the focus of operations after large-scale combat operations have concluded.

A. Operations (Unified Logic Chart)

Ref: ADP 3-0, Operations (Jul '19), Introductory figure. ADP 3-0 unified logic chart.

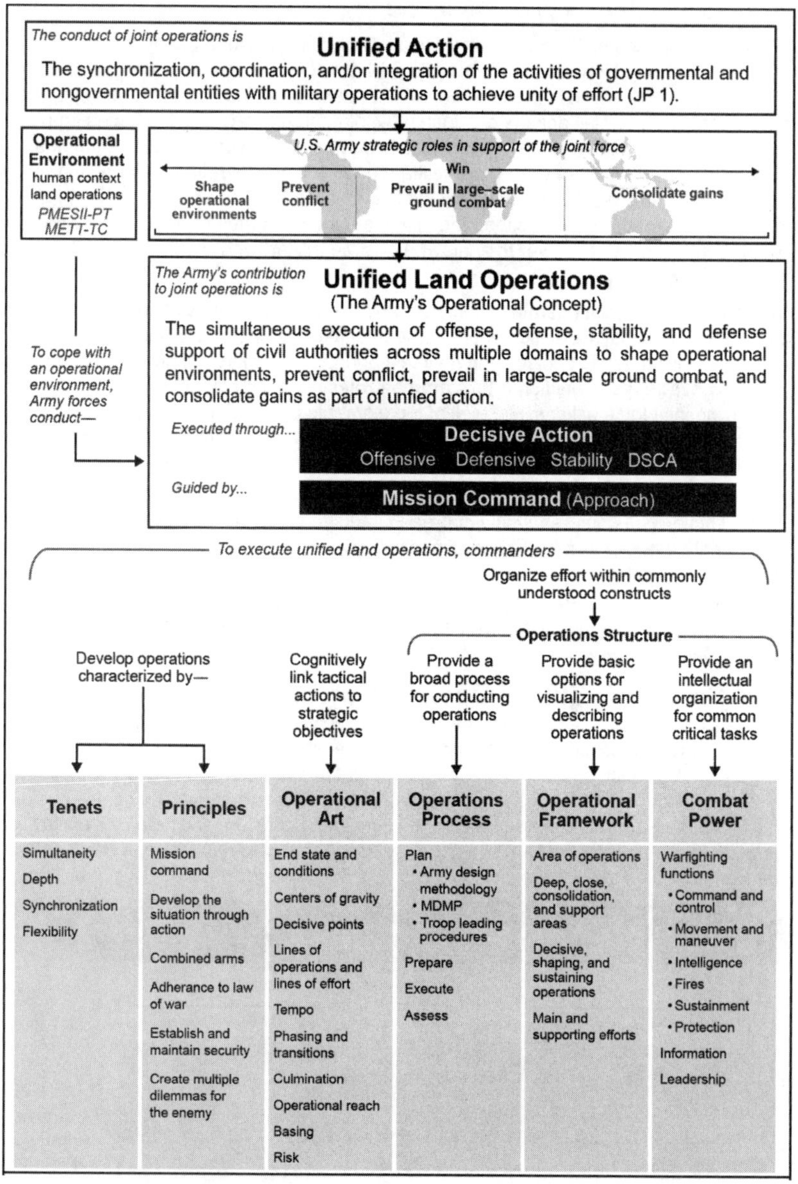
The conduct of joint operations is
Unified Action
The synchronization, coordination, and/or integration of the activities of governmental and nongovernmental entities with military operations to achieve unity of effort (JP 1).
Operational Environment
human context
land operations
PMESII-PT
METT-TC
U.S. Army strategic roles in support of the joint force
Win
Shape operational environments
Prevent conflict
Prevail in large-scale ground combat
Consolidate gains
To cope with an operational environment, Army forces conduct—
The Army's contribution to joint operations is
Unified Land Operations
(The Army's Operational Concept)
The simultaneous execution of offense, defense, stability, and defense support of civil authorities across multiple domains to shape operational environments, prevent conflict, prevail in large-scale ground combat, and consolidate gains as part of unfied action.
Executed through...
Decisive Action
Offensive Defensive Stability DSCA
Guided by...
Mission Command (Approach)
To execute unified land operations, commanders
Organize effort within commonly understood constructs
Operations Structure
Develop operations characterized by—
Cognitively link tactical actions to strategic objectives
Provide a broad process for conducting operations
Provide basic options for visualizing and describing operations
Provide an intellectual organization for common critical tasks
Tenets
Simultaneity
Depth
Synchronization
Flexibility
Principles
Mission command
Develop the situation through action
Combined arms
Adherence to law of war
Establish and maintain security
Create multiple dilemmas for the enemy
Operational Art
End state and conditions
Centers of gravity
Decisive points
Lines of operations and lines of effort
Tempo
Phasing and transitions
Culmination
Operational reach
Basing
Risk
Operations Process
Plan
• Army design methodology
• MDMP
• Troop leading procedures
Prepare
Execute
Assess
Operational Framework
Area of operations
Deep, close, consolidation, and support areas
Decisive, shaping, and sustaining operations
Main and supporting efforts
Combat Power
Warfighting functions
• Command and control
• Movement and maneuver
• Intelligence
• Fires
• Sustainment
• Protection
Information
Leadership

B. Joint Operations, Unified Action, & the Range of Military Operations (ROMO)

Ref: JP 3-0 (w/Chg 1), Joint Operations (Oct '18).

Services may accomplish tasks and missions in support of Department of Defense (DOD) objectives. However, the DOD primarily employs two or more services in a single operation, particularly in combat, through joint operations. The general term, joint operations, describes military actions conducted by joint forces or by Service forces employed under command relationships. A joint force is one composed of significant elements, assigned or attached, of two or more military departments operating under a single joint force commander. Joint operations exploit the advantages of interdependent Service capabilities through unified action, and joint planning integrates military power with other instruments of national power to achieve a desired military end state.

Unified Action

Whereas the term joint operations focuses on the integrated actions of the Armed Forces of the United States in a unified effort, the term unified action has a broader connotation. JFCs are challenged to achieve and maintain operational coherence given the requirement to operate in conjunction with interorganizational partners. CCDRs play a pivotal role in unifying joint force actions, since all of the elements and actions that comprise unified action normally are present at the CCDR's level. However, subordinate JFCs also integrate and synchronize their operations directly with the operations of other military forces and the activities of nonmilitary organizations in the operational area to promote unified action.

Unified action is a comprehensive approach that synchronizes, coordinates, and when appropriate, integrates military operations with the activities of other governmental and nongovernmental organizations to achieve unity of effort.

When conducting operations for a joint force commander, Army forces achieve unified action by synchronizing actions with the activities of components of the joint force and unified action partners.

The Range of Military Operations (ROMO)

The range of military operations is a fundamental construct that provides context. Military operations vary in scope, purpose, and conflict intensity across a range that extends from military engagement, security cooperation, and deterrence activities to crisis response and limited contingency operations and, if necessary, to major operations and campaigns. Use of joint capabilities in military engagement, security cooperation, and deterrence activities helps shape the operational environment and keep the day-to-day tensions between nations or groups below the threshold of armed conflict while maintaining US global influence.

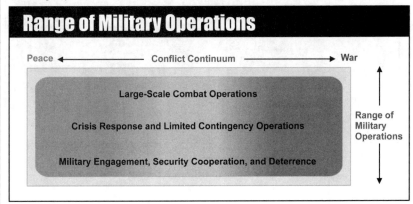

Range of Military Operations

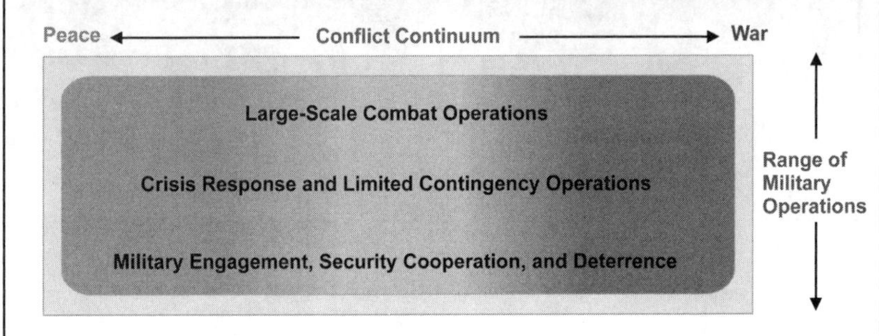

A. Military Engagement, Security Cooperation, and Deterrence

These ongoing activities establish, shape, maintain, and refine relations with other nations and domestic civil authorities (e.g., state governors or local law enforcement). The general strategic and operational objective is to protect US interests at home and abroad.

B. Crisis Response & Limited Contingency Operations

A crisis response or limited contingency operation can be a single small-scale, limited-duration operation or a significant part of a major operation of extended duration involving combat. The associated general strategic and operational objectives are to protect US interests and/or prevent surprise attack or further conflict.

C. Large-Scale Combat Operations

When required to achieve national strategic objectives or protect national interests, the US national leadership may decide to conduct a major operation or campaign normally involving large-scale combat. During **major operations**, joint force actions are conducted simultaneously or sequentially in accordance with a common plan and are controlled by a single commander. A **campaign** is a series of related major operations aimed at achieving strategic and operational objectives within a given time and space.

Joint Combat Operation Model (Notional)

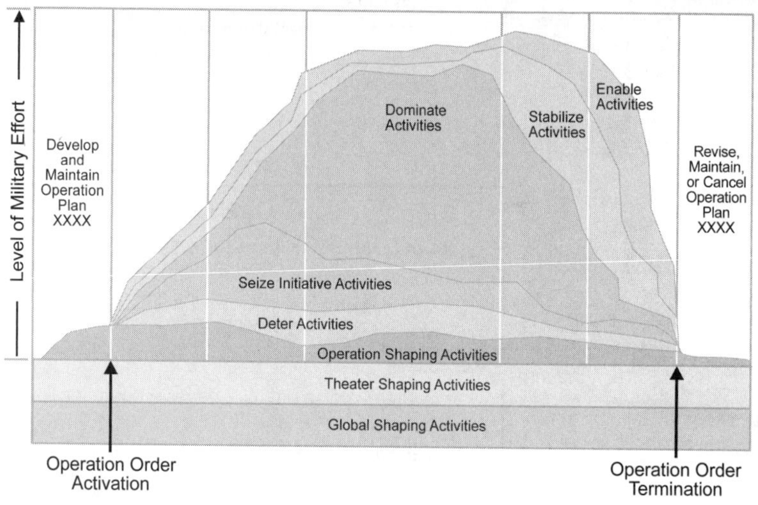

Refer to JFODS5-1: The Joint Forces Operations & Doctrine SMARTbook (Guide to Joint, Multinational & Interorganizational Operations). Updated for 2019, topics include joint doctrine fundamentals (JP 1), joint operations (JP 3-0 w/Chg 1), an expanded discussion of joint functions, joint planning (JP 5-0), joint logistics (JP 4-0), joint task forces (JP 3-33), joint force operations (JPs 3-30, 3-31, 3-32 & 3-05), multinational operations (JP 3-16), interorganizational cooperation (JP 3-08), & more!

C. Elements of Decisive Action

Ref: ADP 3-0, Operations (Jul '19), pp. 3-3 to 3-4 and table 3-1, p. 3-2.

Decisive action requires simultaneous combinations of offense, defense, and stability or defense support of civil authorities tasks.

1. Offensive Operations

An offensive operation is an operation to defeat or destroy enemy forces and gain control of terrain, resources, and population centers. Offensive operations impose the commander's will on an enemy.

The offense is the most direct means of seizing, retaining, and exploiting the initiative to gain a physical and psychological advantage. In the offense, the decisive operation is a sudden action directed toward enemy weaknesses and capitalizing on speed, surprise, and shock. If that operation fails to destroy an enemy, operations continue until enemy forces are defeated. The offense compels an enemy to react, creating new or larger weaknesses the attacking force can exploit.

Refer to SUTS3: The Small Unit Tactics SMARTbook, 3rd Ed. (ADP 3-90)

Offense

Types of Offensive Operations

- Movement to contact
- Attack
- Exploitation
- Pursuit

Purposes

- Dislocate, isolate, disrupt and destroy enemy forces
- Seize key terrain
- Deprive the enemy of resources
- Refine intelligence
- Deceive and divert the enemy
- Provide a secure environment for stability operations

2. Defensive Operations

A defensive operation is an operation to defeat an enemy attack, gain time, economize forces, and develop conditions favorable for offensive or stability operations. Normally the defense cannot achieve a decisive victory. However, it sets conditions for a counteroffensive or a counterattack that enables forces to regain the initiative. Defensive operations are a counter to an enemy offensive action, and they seek to destroy as much of the attacking enemy forces as possible. They preserve control over land, resources, and populations, and retain key terrain, protect lines of communications, and protect critical capabilities against attack. Commanders can conduct defensive operations in one area to free forces for offensive operations elsewhere.

Refer to SUTS3: The Small Unit Tactics SMARTbook, 3rd Ed. (ADP 3-90)

Defense

Types of Defensive Operations

- Mobile defense
- Area defense
- Retrograde

Purposes

- Deter or defeat enemy offensive operations
- Gain time
- Achieve economy of force
- Retain key terrain
- Protect the populace, critical assets and infrastructure
- Refine intelligence

3. Stability Operations

A stability operation is an operation conducted outside the United States in coordination with other instruments of national power to establish or maintain a secure environment and provide essential governmental services, emergency infrastructure reconstruction, and humanitarian relief. These operations support governance by a host nation, an interim government, or a military government. Stability involves coercive and constructive action. Stability helps in building relationships among unified action partners and promoting U.S. security interests. It can help establish political, legal, social, and economic institutions in an area while supporting transition of responsibility to a legitimate authority. Commanders are legally required to perform minimum-essential stability operations tasks when controlling populated areas of operations. These include security, food, water, shelter, and medical treatment.

Refer to TAA2: The Military Engagement, Security Cooperation & Stability SMARTbook, 2nd Ed. (ADP 3-07)

Stability

Stability Operations Tasks

- Establish civil security
- Establish civil control
- Restore essential services
- Support to governance
- Support to economic and infrastructure development
- Conduct security cooperation

Purposes

- Provide a secure environment
- Secure land areas
- Meet the critical needs of the populace
- Gain support for host-nation government
- Shape the environment for interagency and host-nation success
- Promote security, build partner capacity, and provide access
- Refine intelligence

Defense Support of Civil Authorities

Defense Support of Civil Authorities Tasks

- Provide support for domestic disasters
- Provide support for domestic CBRN incidents
- Provide support for domestic civilian law enforcement agencies
- Provide other designated support

Purposes

- Save lives
- Restore essential services
- Maintain or restore law and order
- Protect infrastructure and property
- Support maintenance or restoration of local government
- Shape the environment for interagency success

4. Defense Support of Civil Authority

Defense support of civil authorities is support provided by U.S. Federal military forces, DOD civilians, DOD contract personnel, DOD Component assets, and National Guard forces (when the Secretary of Defense, in coordination with the Governors of the affected States, elects and requests to use those forces in Title 32, United States Code status) in response to requests for assistance from civil authorities for domestic emergencies, law enforcement support, and other domestic activities, or from qualifying entities for special events. (DODD 3025.18). DSCA is a task executed in the homeland and U.S. territories. It is performed to support another primary agency, lead federal agency, or local authority. When DSCA is authorized, it consists of four types of operations. National Guard forces—Title 32 or state active forces under the command and control of the governor and the adjutant general—are usually the first forces to respond on behalf of state authorities. When Federal military forces are employed for DSCA activities, they remain under Federal military command and control at all times.

Refer to HDS1: Homeland Defense & DSCA SMARTbook. (JP 3-28)

III. Activities of the Operations Process

Ref: ADP 5-0, The Operations Process (Jul "19), pp. 1-4 to 1-7 (and intro fig. 1, p. vi).

The Army's framework for organizing and putting command and control into action is the operations process—the major command and control activities performed during operations: planning, preparing, executing, and continuously assessing the operation. Commanders use the operations process to drive the conceptual and detailed planning necessary to understand their operational environment (OE); visualize and describe the operation's end state and operational approach; make and articulate decisions; and direct, lead, and assess operations.

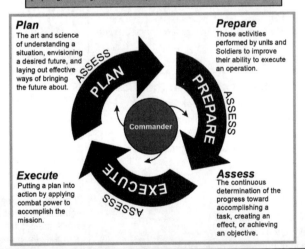

The Operations Process (Underlying Logic)

Nature of Operations
Military operations are inherently human endeavors representing a contest of wills, characterized by violence and continuous adaption by all participants, conducted in dynamic and uncertain operational environments to achieve a political purpose.

To account for the nature of operations, the Army's philosophy of command and control is...

Mission Command
The Army's approach to command and control that empowers subordinate decision making and decentralized execution appropriate to the situation.

The Army's framework for organizing and putting command and control into action is the...

Operations Process
The major command and control activities performed during operations: planning, preparing, executing, and continuously assessing the operation.

Plan
The art and science of understanding a situation, envisioning a desired future, and laying out effective ways of bringing the future about.

Prepare
Those activities performed by units and Soldiers to improve their ability to execute an operation.

Execute
Putting a plan into action by applying combat power to accomplish the mission.

Assess
The continuous determination of the progress toward accomplishing a task, creating an effect, or achieving an objective.

Central idea...
Commanders, supported by their staffs, use the operations process to drive the conceptual and detailed planning necessary to understand their operational environment; visualize and describe the operation's end state and operational approach; make and articulate decisions; and direct, lead, and assess military operations.

Guided by...

Principles
- Drive the operations process.
- Build and maintain situational understanding.
- Apply critical and creative thinking.

For further discussion of these activities, see planning (pp. 1-27 to 1-46), preparation (pp. 1-47 to 1-52), execution (pp. 1-53 to 1-64), and assessment (pp. 1-65 to 1-70).

The activities of the operations process are not discrete; they overlap and recur as circumstances demand. While **planning** may start an iteration of the operations process, planning does not stop with the production of an order. After the completion of the initial order, the commander and staff continuously revise the plan based on changing circumstances. **Preparation** for a specific mission begins early in planning and continues for some subordinate units during execution. **Execution** puts a plan into action and involves adjusting the plan based on changes in the situation and the assessment of progress.

Commanders Drive the Operations Process

Commanders are the most important participants in the operations process. While staffs perform essential functions that amplify the effectiveness of operations, commanders drive the operations process through understanding, visualizing, describing, directing, leading, and assessing operations. *See pp. 1-13 to 1-26 for further discussion.*

Understand *See p. 1-13.*

Understanding an OE and associated problems is fundamental to establishing a situation's context and visualizing operations. An operational environment is a composite of the conditions, circumstances, and influences that affect the employment of capabilities and bear on the decisions of the commander (JP 3-0). An OE encompasses the air, land, maritime, space, and cyberspace domains; the information environment; the electromagnetic spectrum; and other factors.

Visualize *See p. 1-14.*

As commanders build understanding about their OEs, they start to visualize solutions to solve the problems they identify. Collectively, this is known as commander's visualization—the mental process of developing situational understanding, determining a desired end state, and envisioning an operational approach by which the force will achieve that end state (ADP 6-0). Commanders complete their visualization by conceptualizing an operational approach—a broad description of the mission, operational concepts, tasks, and actions required to accomplish the mission (JP 5-0).

Describe *See p. 1-14.*

Commanders describe their visualization to their staffs and subordinate commanders to facilitate shared understanding and purpose throughout the force. During planning, commanders ensure subordinates understand their visualization well enough to begin course of action (COA) development. During execution, commanders describe modifications to their visualization in updated planning guidance and directives resulting in fragmentary orders (FRAGORDs) that adjust the original operation order (OPORD). Commanders describe their visualization in doctrinal terms, refining and clarifying it, as circumstances require. Commanders describe their visualization in terms of commander's intent, planning guidance, commander's critical information requirements (CCIRs), and essential elements of friendly information.

Direct *See p. 1-15.*

To direct is implicit in command. Commanders direct action to achieve results and lead forces to mission accomplishment. Commanders make decisions and direct action based on their situational understanding maintained by continuous assessment.

Lead *See p. 1-15.*

Leadership is the activity of influencing people by providing purpose, direction, and motivation to accomplish the mission and improve the organization (ADP 6-22). Leadership inspires Soldiers to accomplish things that they otherwise might not. Throughout the operations process, commanders make decisions and provide the purpose and motivation to follow through with the COA they chose. They must also possess the wisdom to know when to modify a COA when situations change.

Assess *See p. 1-15.*

Assessment involves deliberately comparing intended forecasted outcomes with actual events to determine the overall effectiveness of force employment. Assessment helps the commander determine progress toward attaining the desired end state, achieving objectives, and completing tasks. Commanders incorporate assessments by the staff, subordinate commanders, and unified action partners into their personal assessment of the situation.

See pp. 1-67 to 1-74 for further discussion.

IV. Mission Command

Command and control is the exercise of authority and direction by a properly designated commander over assigned and attached forces in the accomplishment of the mission (JP 1). Command and control is fundamental to all operations. By itself, however, command and control will not secure an objective, destroy an enemy target, or deliver supplies. Yet none of these activities could be coordinated towards a common objective, or synchronized to achieve maximum effect, without effective command and control. It is through command and control that the countless activities a military force must perform gain purpose and direction. The goal of command and control is effective mission accomplishment.

Mission command is the Army's approach to command and control that empowers subordinate decision making and decentralized execution appropriate to the situation (ADP 6-0). Mission command is based on the Army's view that war is inherently chaotic and uncertain. No plan can account for every possibility and most plans must change rapidly during execution if they are to succeed. No single person is ever well-enough informed to make every important decision, nor can a single person manage the number of decisions that need to be made during combat. As such, mission command empowers subordinate leaders to make decisions and act within the commander's intent to exploit opportunities and counter threats.

See chap. 5 for a detailed discussion of the mission command and the command and control warfighting function.

V. Principles of the Operations Process

The operations process, while simple in concept, is dynamic in execution. Commanders must organize and train their staffs and subordinates as an integrated team to simultaneously plan, prepare, execute, and assess operations. In addition to the principles of mission command, commanders and staffs consider the following principles for the effective employment of the operations process:

Principles of the Operations Process

- **Drive the operations process**
- **Build and maintain situational understanding**
- **Apply critical and creative thinking**

A. Drive the Operations Process

Commanders are the most important participants in the operations process. While staffs perform essential functions that amplify the effectiveness of operations, commanders drive the operations process through understanding, visualizing, describing, directing, leading, and assessing operations. Accurate and timely running estimates maintained by the staff, assist commanders in understanding situations and making decisions.

See pp. 1-13 to 1-26 for further discussion of commander's activities in terms of "Understand, Visualize, Describe, Direct, Lead and Assess."

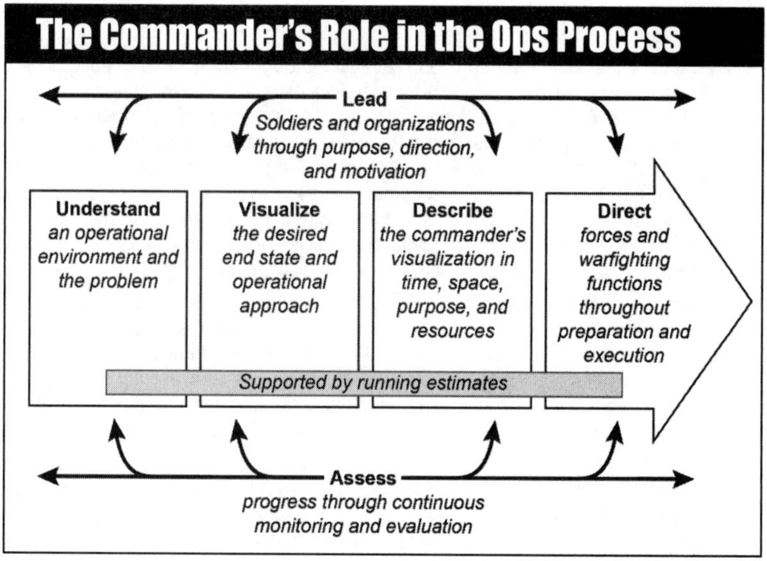
The Commander's Role in the Ops Process
Lead
Soldiers and organizations through purpose, direction, and motivation
Understand
an operational environment and the problem
Visualize
the desired end state and operational approach
Describe
the commander's visualization in time, space, purpose, and resources
Direct
forces and warfighting functions throughout preparation and execution
Supported by running estimates
Assess
progress through continuous monitoring and evaluation

Ref: ADP 5-0, The Operations Process (Jul '19), fig. 1-2, p. 1-8.

B. Build and Maintain Situational Understanding

Success in operations demands timely and effective decisions based on applying judgment to available information and knowledge. As such, commanders and staffs seek to build and maintain situational understanding throughout the operations process. Situational understanding is the product of applying analysis and judgment to relevant information to determine the relationships among the operational and mission variables (ADP 6-0). Commanders and staffs continually strive to maintain their situational understanding and work through periods of reduced understanding as a situation evolves. Effective commanders accept that uncertainty can never be eliminated and train their staffs and subordinates to function in uncertain environments.

As commanders build their situational understanding, they share their understanding across the forces and with unified action partners. Creating shared understanding is a principle of mission command and requires communication and information sharing from higher to lower and lower to higher. Higher headquarters ensure subordinates understand the larger situation to include the operation's end state, purpose, and objectives. Staffs from lower echelons share their understanding of their particular situation and provide feedback to the higher headquarters on the operation's progress. Communication and information sharing with adjacent units and unified action partners is also multi-directional. Several tools assist leaders in building situational understanding and creating a shared understanding across the force to include—

- Operational and mission variables *(see pp. 1-16 to 1-17)*
- Running estimates *(see pp. 2-4 to 2-5)*
- Intelligence *(see pp. 3-3 to 3-56)*
- Collaboration *(see pp. 3-78 and chap. 5)*
- Liaison *(see pp. 5-31 to 5-36)*

C. Apply Critical and Creative Thinking

Thinking includes awareness, perception, reasoning, and intuition. Thinking is naturally influenced by emotion, experience, and bias. As such, commanders and staffs apply critical and creative thinking throughout the operations process to assist them with understanding situations, making decisions, directing actions, and assessing operations.

Critical thinking is purposeful and reflective thought about what to believe or what to do in response to observations, experiences, verbal or written expressions, or arguments. By thinking critically, individuals formulate judgments about whether the information they encounter is true or false, or if it falls somewhere along a scale of plausibility between true or false. Critical thinking involves questioning information, assumptions, conclusions, and points of view to evaluate evidence, develop understanding, and clarify goals. Critical thinking helps commanders and staffs identify causes of problems, arrive at justifiable conclusions, and make good judgments. Critical thinking helps commanders counter their biases and avoid logic errors.

Creative thinking examines problems from a fresh perspective to develop innovative solutions. Creative thinking creates new and useful ideas, and reevaluates or combines old ideas to solve problems. Leaders face unfamiliar problems that require new or original approaches to solve them. This requires creativity and a willingness to accept change, newness, and a flexible outlook of new ideas and possibilities.

Breaking old habits of thought, questioning the status quo, visualizing a better future, and devising responses to new problems require creative thinking. During operations, leaders routinely face unfamiliar problems or old problems under new conditions. Leaders apply creative thinking to gain new insights, novel approaches, fresh perspectives, and new ways of understanding problems and conceiving ways to solve them.

Refer to ATP 5-0.1 for creative thinking tools and techniques.

Both critical and creative thinking must intentionally include ethical reasoning—the deliberate evaluation that decisions and actions conform to accepted standards of conduct. Ethical reasoning within critical and creative thinking helps commanders and staffs anticipate ethical hazards and consider options to prevent or mitigate the hazards within their proposed COAs.

Commanders may form red teams to help the staff think critically and creatively and to avoid groupthink, mirror imaging, cultural missteps, and tunnel vision. Red teaming enables commanders to explore alternative plans and operations in the context of an OE and from the perspective of unified action partners, adversaries, and others. Throughout the operations process, red team members help clarify the problem and explain how others (unified action partners, the population, and the enemy) potentially view the problem. Red team members challenge assumptions and the analysis used to build the plan.

Refer to JP 5-0 for a detailed discussion of red teams and red teaming.

VI. Battle Rhythm

Commanders and staffs must integrate and synchronize numerous activities, meetings, and reports within their headquarters, and with higher, subordinate, supporting, and adjacent units as part of the operations process. They do this by establishing the unit's battle rhythm. Battle rhythm is a deliberate, daily schedule of command, staff, and unit activities intended to maximize use of time and synchronize staff actions (JP 3-33). A unit's battle rhythm provides structure for managing a headquarters' most important internal resource—the time of the commander and staff. A headquarters' battle rhythm consists of a series of meetings, report requirements, and other activities synchronized by time and purpose. These activities may be daily, weekly, monthly, or quarterly depending on the echelon, type of operation, and planning horizon. An effective battle rhythm—

- Facilitates interaction among the commander, staff, and subordinate commanders
- Supports building and maintaining shared understanding throughout the hqs
- Establishes a routine for staff interaction and coordination

See chap. 5, Mission Command, for a discussion of command post operations to include establishing working groups and boards (pp. 5-26 to 5-27) and battle rhythm (p. 5-28).

II. Understand, Visualize Describe, Direct, Lead, Assess

Ref: ADP 5-0, The Operations Process (Jul '19), chap. I.

Commanders are the most important participants in the operations process. While staffs perform essential functions that amplify the effectiveness of operations, commanders drive the operations process through understanding, visualizing, describing, directing, leading, and assessing operations. Accurate and timely running estimates maintained by the staff, assist commanders in understanding situations and making decisions.

The Commander's Role in the Ops Process

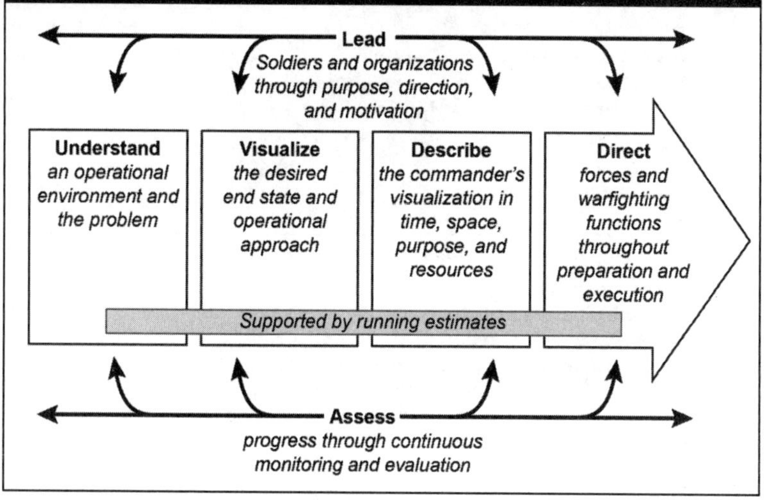
Lead
Soldiers and organizations through purpose, direction, and motivation
Understand an operational environment and the problem
Visualize the desired end state and operational approach
Describe the commander's visualization in time, space, purpose, and resources
Direct forces and warfighting functions throughout preparation and execution
Supported by running estimates
Assess
progress through continuous monitoring and evaluation

Ref: ADP 5-0, The Operations Process (Jul '19), fig. 1-2, p. 1-8.

I. Understand

Understanding an OE and associated problems is fundamental to establishing a situation's context and visualizing operations. An operational environment is a composite of the conditions, circumstances, and influences that affect the employment of capabilities and bear on the decisions of the commander (JP 3-0). An OE encompasses the air, land, maritime, space, and cyberspace domains; the information environment; the electromagnetic spectrum; and other factors. Included within these areas are the enemy, friendly, and neutral actors who are relevant to a specific operation.

Commanders collaborate with their staffs, other commanders, and unified action partners to build a shared understanding of their OEs and associated problems. Planning, intelligence preparation of the battlefield (IPB), and running estimates help commanders develop an initial understanding of their OEs. During execution, commanders direct reconnaissance and develop the situation through action to improve their understanding. Commanders circulate within the area of operations (AO) as often as possible, collaborating with subordinate commanders and speaking with Soldiers. Ideally, true understanding should be the basis for decisions.

See pp. 1-16 to 1-17 (operational and mission variables) and p. 1-26 (principles of joint operations).

II. Visualize

As commanders build understanding about their OEs, they start to visualize solutions to solve the problems they identify. Collectively, this is known as commander's visualization—the mental process of developing situational understanding, determining a desired end state, and envisioning an operational approach by which the force will achieve that end state (ADP 6-0).

In building their visualization, commanders first seek to understand those conditions that represent the current situation. Next, commanders envision a set of desired future conditions that represents the operation's end state. Commanders complete their visualization by conceptualizing an operational approach—a broad description of the mission, operational concepts, tasks, and actions required to accomplish the mission (JP 5-0). Figure 1-3 depicts activities associated with developing the commander's visualization.

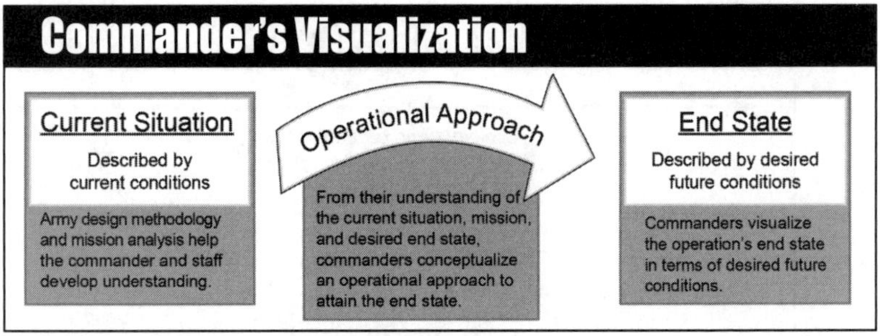

Ref: ADP 5-0, The Operations Process, fig. 1-3, p. 1-9.

Part of developing an operational approach includes visualizing an initial operational framework. The operational framework provides an organizing construct for how the commander intends to organize the AO geographically (deep, close, support, and consolidation areas), by purpose (decisive, shaping, and sustaining operations), and by effort (main and supporting). When establishing their operational framework, commanders consider the physical, temporal, virtual, and cognitive factors that impact on their AOs. Collectively, these considerations allow commanders and staffs to better account for the multi-domain capabilities of friendly and threat forces.

See p. 1-32 for discussion of the elements of operational design and art. See pp. 1-18 to 1-19 for related discussion of the operational framework, and pp. 1-22 to 1-23 for discussion of the elements of combat power and the six warfighting functions.

III. Describe

Commanders describe their visualization to their staffs and subordinate commanders to facilitate shared understanding and purpose throughout the force. During planning, commanders ensure subordinates understand their visualization well enough to begin course of action (COA) development. During execution, commanders describe modifications to their visualization in updated planning guidance and directives resulting in fragmentary orders (FRAGORDs) that adjust the original operation order (OPORD). Commanders describe their visualization in doctrinal terms, refining and clarifying it, as circumstances require. Commanders describe their visualization in terms of—

- Commander's intent
- Planning guidance, including an operational approach
- Commander's critical information requirements (CCIRs)
- Essential elements of friendly information

See pp. 1-20 to 1-21 for further discussion of these elements.

IV. Direct

To direct is implicit in command. Commanders direct action to achieve results and lead forces to mission accomplishment. Commanders make decisions and direct action based on their situational understanding maintained by continuous assessment. Throughout the operations process, commanders direct forces by—

- Approving plans and orders.
- Establishing command and support relationships.
- Assigning and adjusting tasks, control measures, and task organization.
- Positioning units to maximize combat power.
- Positioning key leaders at critical places and times to ensure supervision.
- Allocating resources to exploit opportunities and counter threats.
- Committing the reserve.

See pp. 1-22 to 1-23 for related discussion of the elements of combat power, and the six warfighting functions.

V. Lead

Leadership is the activity of influencing people by providing purpose, direction, and motivation to accomplish the mission and improve the organization (ADP 6-22). Leadership inspires Soldiers to accomplish things that they otherwise might not. Throughout the operations process, commanders make decisions and provide the purpose and motivation to follow through with the COA they chose. They must also possess the wisdom to know when to modify a COA when situations change.

Commanders lead by example through command presence. Command presence is creating a favorable impression in demeanor, appearance, and professional and personal conduct. Commanders use their presence to gather and communicate information and knowledge as well as to assess operations. Establishing a command presence makes the commander's knowledge and experience available to subordinates. It allows commanders to evaluate and provide direct feedback on their subordinates' performance.

Command occurs at the location of the commander. Where the commander locates within the AO is an important consideration for effective mission command. No standard pattern or simple prescription exists for the proper location of a commander on the battlefield; different commanders lead differently. Commanders balance their time among the command post and staff, subordinate commanders, forces, and other organizations to make the greatest contribution to success.

Refer to TLS5: The Leader's SMARTbook, 5th Ed. (Military Leadership & Training) for complete discussion of Military Leadership (ADP/ADRP 6-22); Leader Development (FM 6-22); Counsel, Coach, Mentor (ATP 6-22.1); Army Team Building (ATP 6-22.6); Military Training (ADP/ADRP 7-0); Train to Win in a Complex World (FM 7-0); Unit Training Plans, Meetings, Schedules, and Briefs; Conducting Training Events and Exercises; Training Assessments, After Action Reviews (AARs); and more!

VI. Assess

Assessment involves deliberately comparing intended forecasted outcomes with actual events to determine the overall effectiveness of force employment. Assessment helps the commander determine progress toward attaining the desired end state, achieving objectives, and completing tasks. Commanders incorporate assessments by the staff, subordinate commanders, and unified action partners into their personal assessment of the situation. Based on their assessment, commanders adjust their visualization and modify plans and orders to adapt the force to changing circumstances.

See pp. 1-65 to 1-72 for further discussion of "assessment" to include the assessment process activities, evaluation criteria, and formal assessment plans.

Operational/Mission Variables (Understand)

Ref: FM 6-0 (C2), Commander and Staff Organization and Operations (Apr '16), app. A.

Operational Variables (PMESII-PT)

The operational variables are fundamental to developing a comprehensive understanding of an operational environment.

Variable	Description
P - Political	Describes the distribution of responsibility and power at all levels of governance—formally constituted authorities, as well as informal or covert political powers
M - Military	Explores the military and paramilitary capabilities of all relevant actors (enemy, friendly, and neutral) in a given operational environment
E - Economic	Encompasses individual and group behaviors related to producing, distributing, and consuming resources
S - Social	Describes the cultural, religious, and ethnic makeup within an operational environment and the beliefs, values, customs, and behaviors of society members
I - Information	Describes the nature, scope, characteristics, and effects of individuals, organizations, and systems that collect, process, disseminate, or act on information
I - Infrastructure	Is composed of the basic facilities, services, and installations needed for the functioning of a community or society
P - Physical environment	Includes the geography and manmade structures, as well as the climate and weather in the area of operations
T - Time	Describes the timing and duration of activities, events, or conditions within an operational environment, as well as how the timing and duration are perceived by various actors in the operational environment

Ref: Adapted from ADRP 5-0, The Operations Process, table 1-1, p. 1-7.

Operational Subvariables

Each of the eight operational variables also has associated subvariables.

Political variable	Social variable	Physical Environment	Economic variable
Attitude toward the United States Centers of political power Type of government Government effectiveness and legitimacy Influential political groups International relationships	Demographic mix Social volatility Education level Ethnic diversity Religious diversity Population movement Common languages Criminal activity Human rights Centers of social power Basic cultural norms and values	Terrain ▪ Observation and fields of fire ▪ Avenues of approach ▪ Key terrain ▪ Obstacles ▪ Cover and concealment ▪ Landforms ▪ Vegetation ▪ Terrain complexity ▪ Mobility classification Natural Hazards Climate Weather ▪ Precipitation ▪ High temperature-heat index ▪ Low temperature-wind chill index ▪ Wind ▪ Visibility ▪ Cloud cover ▪ Relative humidity	Economic diversity Employment status Economic activity Illegal economic activity Banking and finance **Infrastructure variable** Construction pattern Urban zones Urbanized building density Utilities present Utility level Transportation architecture **Time variable** Cultural perception of time Information offset Tactical exploitation of time Key dates, time periods, or events
Military variable Military forces Government paramilitary forces Nonstate paramilitary forces Unarmed combatants Nonmilitary armed combatants Military functions ▪ Command and control (mission command) ▪ Maneuver ▪ Information warfare ▪ Reconnaissance, intelligence, surveillance, and target acquisition ▪ Fire support ▪ Protection ▪ Logistics	**Information variable** Public communications media Information warfare ▪ Electronic warfare ▪ Computer warfare ▪ Information attack ▪ Deception ▪ Physical destruction ▪ Protection and security measures ▪ Perception management Intelligence Information management		

Ref: Adapted from ADRP 5-0, The Operations Process, table 1-2, p. 1-8.

Mission Variables (METT-TC)

Mission variables describe characteristics of the area of operations, focusing on how they might affect a mission. Incorporating the analysis of the operational variables into METT–TC ensures Army leaders consider the best available relevant information about conditions that pertain to the mission. Using the operational variables as a source of relevant information for the mission variables allows commanders to refine their situational understanding of their operational environment and to visualize, describe, direct, lead and assess operations.

Variable		Description
Mission	**M**	Commanders and staffs view all of the mission variables in terms of their impact on mission accomplishment. The mission is the task, together with the purpose, that clearly indicates the action to be taken and the reason therefore. It is always the first variable commanders consider during decisionmaking. A mission statement contains the "who, what, when, where, and why" of the operation.
Enemy	**E**	The second variable to consider is the enemy—dispositions (including organization, strength, location, and tactical mobility), doctrine, equipment, capabilities, vulnerabilities, and probable courses of action.
Terrain and weather	**T**	Terrain and weather analysis are inseparable and directly influence each other's impact on military operations. Terrain includes natural features (such as rivers and mountains) and manmade features (such as cities, airfields, and bridges). Commanders analyze terrain using the five military aspects of terrain expressed in the memory aid **OAKOC**: observation and fields of fire, avenues of approach, key and decisive terrain, obstacles, cover and concealment. The military aspects of weather include visibility, wind, precipitation, cloud cover, temperature, humidity.
Troops and support available	**T**	This variable includes the number, type, capabilities, and condition of available friendly troops and support. These include supplies, services and support available from joint, host nation and unified action partners. They also include support from Civilians and contractors employed by military organizations, such as the Defense Logistics Agency and the Army Materiel Command.
Time available	**T**	Commanders assess the time available for planning, preparing, and executing tasks and operations. This includes the time required to assemble, deploy, and maneuver units in relationship to the enemy and conditions.
Civil consider-ations	**C**	Civil considerations are the influence of manmade infrastructure, civilian institutions, and cultures and activities of the civilian leaders, populations, and organizations within an area of operations on the conduct of military operations. Civil considerations comprise six characteristics, expressed in the memory aid **ASCOPE**: areas, structures, capabilities, organizations, people, and events.

Ref: Adapted from ADRP 5-0, The Operations Process, table 1-3, p. 1-9.

METT-TC is a memory aid that identifies the mission variables: Mission, Enemy, Terrain and weather, Troops and support available, Time available, and Civil considerations.

OAKOC - The Military Aspects of Terrain

For tactical operations, terrain is analyzed using the five military aspects of terrain, expressed in the memory aid, OAKOC: Observation and fields of fire, Avenues of approach, Key and decisive terrain, Obstacles, Cover and concealment.

See pp. 3-20 to 3-21 for further discussion of the military aspects of terrain (OAKOC).

ASCOPE - Civil Considerations

Commanders and staffs analyze civil considerations in terms of the categories expressed in the memory aid ASCOPE: Areas, Structures, Capabilities, Organizations, People, Events.

See pp. 3-30 to 3-31 for further discussion of civil considerations (ASCOPE).

Refer to FM 6-0 (C2), Commander and Staff Organization and Operations (Apr '16), app. A for further discussion of operational and mission variables.

Operational Framework (Visualize/Describe)

Ref: ADP 3-0, Operations (Jul '19), pp. 4-2 to 4-5. See also AODS6 pp. 2-14 to 2-21.

Army leaders are responsible for clearly articulating their concept of operations in time, space, purpose, and resources. They do this through an operational framework & associated vocabulary. An operational framework is a cognitive tool used to assist commanders and staffs in clearly visualizing and describing the application of combat power in time, space, purpose, and resources in the concept of operations (ADP 1-01).

Refer to AODS6 (w/SMARTupdate 1): The Army Operations & Doctrine SMARTbook (Guide to FM/ADP 3-0 Operations & the Elements of Combat Power). Completely updated with the Jul 2019 ADPs, Chg 1 to the 400-pg AODS6 includes operations (ADP 3-0), large-scale combat operations (FM 3-0 w/Chg 1), and refocused chapters on the elements of combat power: command & control (ADP 6-0), movement and maneuver (ADPs 3-90, 3-07, 3-28, 3-05), intelligence (ADP 2-0), fires (ADP 3-19), sustainment (ADP 4-0), & protection (ADP 3-37).

Area of Operations

An area of operations is an operational area defined by a commander for land and maritime forces that should be large enough to accomplish their missions and protect their forces (JP 3-0). For land operations, an area of operations includes subordinate areas of operations assigned by Army commanders to their subordinate echelons. In operations, commanders use control measures to assign responsibilities, coordinate fire and maneuver, and control combat operations. A control measure is a means of regulating forces or warfighting functions (ADP 6-0). One of the most important control measures is the assigned area of operations. The Army commander or joint force land component commander is the supported commander within an area of operations designated by the JFC for land operations. Within their areas of operations, commanders integrate and synchronize combat power. To facilitate this integration and synchronization, commanders designate targeting priorities, effects, and timing within their areas of operations.

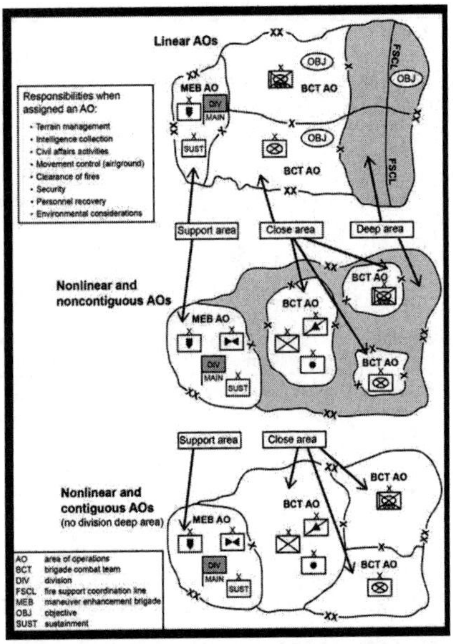

Understanding the area of influence helps the commander and staff plan branches to the current operation in which the force uses capabilities outside the area of operations.

Area of Influence

Commanders consider a unit's area of influence when assigning it an area of operations. An area of influence is a geographical area wherein a commander is directly capable of influencing operations by maneuver or fire support systems normally under the commander's command or control (JP 3-0).

Area of Interest

An area of interest is that area of concern to the commander, including the area of influence, areas adjacent thereto, and extending into enemy territory. This area also includes areas occupied by enemy forces who could jeopardize the accomplishment of the mission (JP 3-0). An area of interest for stability or DSCA tasks may be much larger than that area associated with the offense and defense.

Deep, Close, Support, and Consolidation Areas

- The **deep area** is where the commander sets conditions for future success in close combat. Operations in the deep area involve efforts to prevent uncommitted enemy forces from being committed in a coherent manner. A commander's deep area generally extends beyond subordinate unit boundaries out to the limits of the commander's designated area of operations. The purpose of operations in the deep area is often tied to setting conditions for future events in time and space.
- The **close area** is the portion of the commander's area of operations where the majority of subordinate maneuver forces conduct close combat. Operations in the close area are within a subordinate commander's area of operations. Commanders plan to conduct decisive operations using maneuver and fires in the close area, and they position most of the maneuver force in it.
- A **support area** is the portion of the commander's area of operations that is designated to facilitate the positioning, employment, and protection of base sustainment assets required to sustain, enable, and control operations.
- The **consolidation area** is the portion of the land commander's area of operations that may be designated to facilitate freedom of action, consolidate gains through decisive action, and set conditions to transition the area of operations to follow on forces or other legitimate authorities.

Decisive, Shaping, and Sustaining Operations

Decisive, shaping, and sustaining operations lend themselves to a broad conceptual orientation.

- The **decisive operation** is the operation that directly accomplishes the mission. The decisive operation is the focal point around which commanders design an entire operation. The decisive operation is designed to determine the outcome of a major operation, battle, or engagement. Multiple subordinate units may be engaged in the same decisive operation across multiple domains. Decisive operations lead directly to the accomplishment of the commander's intent.
- A **shaping operation** is an operation at any echelon that creates and preserves conditions for success of the decisive operation through effects on the enemy, other actors, and the terrain. Information operations, for example, may integrate engagement tasks into an operation to reduce tensions between Army units and different ethnic groups. In combat, synchronizing the effects of aircraft, artillery fires, and obscurants to delay or disrupt repositioning forces illustrates shaping operations. Shaping operations may occur throughout the area of operations and involve any combination of forces and capabilities across multiple domains. Shaping operations set conditions for the success of the decisive operation. Commanders may designate more than one shaping operation.
- A **sustaining operation** is an operation at any echelon that enables the decisive operation or shaping operations by generating and maintaining combat power. Sustaining operations differ from decisive and shaping operations in that they focus internally (on friendly forces) rather than externally (on the enemy or environment).

Throughout decisive, shaping, and sustaining operations, commanders and their staffs need to ensure that forces maintain **positions of relative advantage**, operations are **integrated with unified action partners**, and **continuity** is maintained throughout operations.

Main and Supporting Efforts

Commanders designate main and supporting efforts to establish clear priorities of support and resources among subordinate units.

- The **main effort** is a designated subordinate unit whose mission at a given point in time is most critical to overall mission success. It is usually weighted with the preponderance of combat power. Typically, commanders shift the main effort one or more times during execution. Designating a main effort temporarily prioritizes resource allocation. When commanders designate a unit as the main effort, it receives priority of support and resources in order to maximize combat power.
- A **supporting effort** is a designated subordinate unit with a mission that supports the success of the main effort. Commanders resource supporting efforts with the minimum assets necessary to accomplish the mission. Forces often realize success of the main effort through success of supporting efforts.

3. Describe

Ref: ADP 5-0, The Operations Process (Jul '19), pp. 1-9 to 1-10.

Commanders describe their visualization to their staffs and subordinate commanders to facilitate shared understanding and purpose throughout the force. During planning, commanders ensure subordinates understand their visualization well enough to begin course of action (COA) development. During execution, commanders describe modifications to their visualization in updated planning guidance and directives resulting in fragmentary orders (FRAGORDs) that adjust the original operation order (OPORD). Commanders describe their visualization in doctrinal terms, refining and clarifying it, as circumstances require. Commanders describe their visualization in terms of—

- Commander's intent
- Planning guidance, including an operational approach
- Commander's critical information requirements (CCIRs)
- Essential elements of friendly information

A. Commander's Intent *See p. 2-26.*

The commander's intent is a clear and concise expression of the purpose of the operation and the desired military end state that supports mission command, provides focus to the staff, and helps subordinate and supporting commanders act to achieve the commander's desired results without further orders, even when the operation does not unfold as planned (JP 3-0). During planning, the initial commander's intent guides COA development. In execution, the commander's intent guides initiative as subordinates make decisions and take action when unforeseen opportunities arise or when countering threats. Commanders develop their intent statement personally. It must be easy to remember and clearly understood by commanders and staffs two echelons lower in the chain of command. The more concise the commander's intent, the easier it is to understand and recall.

B. Planning Guidance *See p. 2-27.*

Commanders provide planning guidance to the staff based upon their visualization of the operation. Planning guidance conveys the essence of the commander's visualization, including a description of the operational approach. Effective planning guidance reflects how the commander sees the operation unfolding. The commander's planning guidance broadly describes when, where, and how the commander intends to employ combat power to accomplish the mission within the higher commander's intent. Broad and general guidance gives the staff and subordinate leaders maximum latitude; it lets proficient staffs develop flexible and effective options. Commanders modify planning guidance based on staff and subordinate input and changing conditions during different stages of planning and throughout the operations process.

Refer to FM 6-0 for sample planning guidance by warfighting function.

C. Commander's Critical Information Requirements (CCIR) *See p. 2-21.*

A commander's critical information requirement is an information requirement identified by the commander as being critical to facilitating timely decision making (JP 3-0). Commanders decide to designate an information requirement as a CCIR based on likely decisions during the conduct of an operation. A CCIR may support one or more decision points. During planning, staffs recommend information requirements for commanders to designate as CCIRs. During preparation and execution, they recommend changes to CCIRs based on their assessments of the operation.

Always promulgated by a plan or order, commanders limit the number of CCIRs to focus their staff and subordinate unit information collection and assessment efforts. The fewer the CCIRs, the easier it is for staffs to remember, recognize, and act on each one. As such, the rapid reporting of CCIRs to the commander is essential to adjusting operations. CCIR falls into one of two categories: priority intelligence requirements (known as PIRs) and friendly force information requirements (known as FFIRs).

Priority Intelligence Requirement (PIR) *See p. 2-21*

A priority intelligence requirement is an intelligence requirement that the commander and staff need to understand the threat and other aspects of the operational environment (JP 2-01). Priority intelligence requirements identify the information about the enemy and other aspects of an OE that the commander considers most important. Intelligence about civil considerations may be as critical as intelligence about the enemy. In coordination with the staff, the intelligence officer manages priority intelligence requirements for the commander as part of the intelligence process.

Friendly Force Information Requirement (FFIR) *See p. 2-21*

A friendly force information requirement is information the commander and staff need to understand the status of friendly force and supporting capabilities (JP 3-0). Friendly force information requirements identify the information about the mission, troops and support available, and time available for friendly forces that the commander considers most important. In coordination with the staff, the operations officer manages friendly force information requirements for the commander.

D. Essential Elements of Friendly Information (EEFI) *See p. 2-21.*

Commanders also describe information they want protected as essential elements of friendly information. An essential element of friendly information is a critical aspect of a friendly operation that, if known by a threat would subsequently compromise, lead to failure, or limit success of the operation and therefore should be protected from enemy detection (ADP 6-0). Although essential elements of friendly information (known as EEFIs) are not CCIRs, they have the same priority. Essential elements of friendly information establish elements of information to protect rather than elements to collect. Their identification is the first step in the operations security process and central to the protection of information.

Elements of Combat Power (Direct)

Ref: ADP 3-0, Operations (Jul '19), chap. 5 (and figure 5-1).

Combat power is the total means of destructive, constructive, and information capabilities that a military unit or formation can apply at a given time. Operations executed through simultaneous offensive, defensive, stability, or DSCA operations require the continuous generation and application of combat power. To an Army commander, Army forces generate combat power by converting potential into effective action. Combat power includes all capabilities provided by unified action partners that are integrated and synchronized with the commander's objectives to achieve unity of effort in sustained operations.

Elements of Combat Power

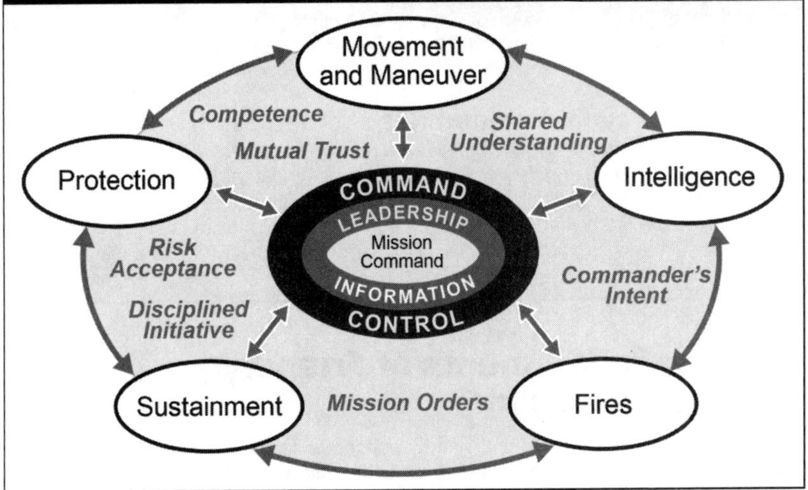

To execute combined arms operations, commanders conceptualize capabilities in terms of combat power. Combat power has eight elements: leadership, information, command and control, movement and maneuver, intelligence, fires, sustainment, and protection. The elements facilitate Army forces accessing joint and multinational fires and assets. The Army collectively describes the last six elements as **warfighting functions.** Commanders apply combat power through the warfighting functions using **leadership and information**.

Generating and maintaining combat power throughout an operation is essential. Factors that contribute to generating and maintaining combat power include reserves, force rotation, network viability, access to cyberspace and space enablers, and joint support. Commanders balance the ability to mass lethal and nonlethal effects with the need to deploy and sustain the units that produce those effects.

Leadership & Information

Commanders apply leadership through mission command. **Leadership** is the multiplying and unifying element of combat power. The Army defines leadership as the process of influencing people by providing purpose, direction, and motivation to accomplish the mission and improve the organization (ADP 6-22). An Army commander, by virtue of assumed role or assigned responsibility, inspires and influences people to accomplish organizational goals. **Information** enables commanders at all levels to make informed decisions on how best to apply combat power.

See pp. 5-10 to 5-11 for discussion of information operations from FM 3-0.

The Six Warfighting Functions

1. Command and Control

The command and control warfighting function is the related tasks and a system that enable commanders to synchronize and converge all elements of combat power. The primary purpose of the command and control warfighting function is to assist commanders in integrating the other elements of combat power (leadership, information, movement and maneuver, intelligence, fires, sustainment, and protection) to achieve objectives and accomplish missions.

Refer to AODS6, chap. 3 for further discussion.

2. Movement and Maneuver

The movement and maneuver warfighting function is the related tasks and systems that move and employ forces to achieve a position of relative advantage over the enemy and other threats. Direct fire and close combat are inherent in maneuver. The movement and maneuver warfighting function includes tasks associated with force projection. Movement is necessary to disperse and displace the force as a whole or in part when maneuvering. Maneuver directly gains or exploits positions of relative advantage. Commanders use maneuver for massing effects to achieve surprise, shock, and momentum

Refer to AODS6, chap. 4 for further discussion.

3. Intelligence

The intelligence warfighting function is the related tasks and systems that facilitate understanding the enemy, terrain, weather, civil considerations, and other significant aspects of the operational environment. Other significant aspects of an operational environment include threats, adversaries, and operational variables, which vary with the nature of operations. The intelligence warfighting function synchronizes information collection with primary tactical tasks of reconnaissance, surveillance, security, and intelligence operations. Intelligence is driven by commanders, and it involves analyzing information from all sources and conducting operations to develop the situation.

Refer to AODS6, chap. 5 for further discussion.

4. Fires

The fires warfighting function is the related tasks and systems that create and converge effects in all domains against the adversary or enemy to enable operations across the range of military operations (ADP 3-0). These tasks and systems create lethal and nonlethal effects delivered from both Army and joint forces, as well as other unified action partners.

Refer to AODS6, chap. 6 for further discussion.

5. Sustainment

The sustainment warfighting function is the related tasks and systems that provide support and services to ensure freedom of action, extended operational reach, and prolong endurance. Sustainment determines the depth and duration of Army operations. Successful sustainment enables freedom of action by increasing the number of options available to the commander. Sustainment is essential for retaining and exploiting the initiative.

Refer to AODS6, chap. 7 for further discussion.

6. Protection

The protection warfighting function is the related tasks and systems that preserve the force so the commander can apply maximum combat power to accomplish the mission. Commanders incorporate protection when they understand and visualize threats and hazards in an operational environment. This allows them to synchronize and integrate all protection capabilities to safeguard bases, secure routes, and protect forces. Preserving the force includes protecting personnel (combatants and noncombatants) and physical assets of the United States, unified action partners, and host nations.

Refer to AODS6, chap. 8 for further discussion.

Integrating Processes (Direct)

Ref: ADP 5-0, The Operations Process (Jul '19), pp. 1-15 to 1-17.

Commanders and staffs integrate the warfighting functions and synchronize the force to adapt to changing circumstances throughout the operations process. They use several integrating processes to do this. An integrating process consists of a series of steps that incorporate multiple disciplines to achieve a specific end. For example, during planning, the military decision-making process (MDMP) integrates the commander and staff in a series of steps to produce a plan or order. Key integrating processes that occur throughout the operations process include—

- Intelligence preparation of the battlefield
- Information collection
- Targeting
- Risk management
- Knowledge management

Intelligence Preparation of the Battlefield (IPB) *See pp. 3-3 to 3-52.*

Intelligence preparation of the battlefield is the systematic process of analyzing the mission variables of enemy, terrain, weather, and civil considerations in an area of interest to determine their effect on operations (ATP 2-01.3). Led by the intelligence officer, the entire staff participates in IPB to develop and sustain an understanding of the enemy, terrain and weather, and civil considerations. IPB helps identify options available to friendly and threat forces.

IPB consists of four steps. Each step is performed or assessed and refined to ensure that IPB products remain complete and relevant. The four IPB steps are—

- Define the Operational Environment
- Describe Environmental Effects on Operations
- Evaluate the Threat
- Determine Threat Courses of Action

IPB begins in planning and continues throughout the operations process. IPB results in intelligence products used to aid in developing friendly COAs and decision points for the commander. Additionally, the conclusions reached and the products created during IPB are critical to planning information collection and targeting. .

Refer to ATP 2-01.3 for a detailed discussion of IPB.

Information Collection *See pp. 3-53 to 3-56.*

Information collection is an activity that synchronizes and integrates the planning and employment of sensors and assets as well as the processing, exploitation, and dissemination systems in direct support of current and future operations (FM 3-55). It integrates the functions of the intelligence and operations staffs that focus on answering CCIRs. Information collection includes acquiring information and providing it to processing elements. It has three steps:

- Collection management
- Task and direct collection
- Execute collection

Information collection helps the commander understand and visualize the operation by identifying gaps in information and aligning reconnaissance, surveillance, security, and intelligence assets to collect information on those gaps. The "decide" and "detect" steps of targeting tie heavily to information collection.

Refer to FM 3-55 for a detailed discussion of information collection to include the relationship between the duties of intelligence and operations staffs.

Targeting *See pp. 3-57 to 3-70.*

Targeting is the process of selecting and prioritizing targets and matching the appropriate response to them, considering operational requirements and capabilities (JP 3-0). Targeting seeks to create specific desired effects through lethal and nonlethal actions. The emphasis of targeting is on identifying enemy resources (targets) that if destroyed or degraded will contribute to the success of the friendly mission. Targeting begins in planning and continues throughout the operations process. The steps of the Army's targeting process are—

- Decide
- Detect
- Deliver
- Assess

This methodology facilitates engagement of the right target, at the right time, with the most appropriate assets using the commander's targeting guidance.

Targeting is a multidiscipline effort that requires coordinated interaction among the commander and several staff sections that together form the targeting working group. The chief of staff (executive officer) or the chief of fires (fire support officer) leads the staff through the targeting process. Based on the commander's targeting guidance and priorities, the staff determines which targets to engage and how, where, and when to engage them. The staff then assigns friendly capabilities best suited to produce the desired effect on each target, while ensuring compliance with the rules of engagement.

See pp. 6-26 to 6-27 for discussion of fires and targeting (D3A). Refer to ATP 3-60 for a detailed discussion of Army targeting to include how Army targeting nest within the joint targeting cycle.

Risk Management *See pp. 3-71 to 3-74.*

Risk—the exposure of someone or something valued to danger, harm, or loss—is inherent in all operations. Because risk is part of all military operations, it cannot be avoided. Identifying, mitigating, and accepting risk is a function of command and a key consideration during planning and execution.

Risk management is the process to identify, assess, and control risks and make decisions that balance risk cost with mission benefits (JP 3-0). Commanders and staffs use risk management throughout the operations process to identify and mitigate risks associated with hazards (to include ethical risk and moral hazards) that have the potential to cause friendly and civilian casualties, damage or destroy equipment, or otherwise impact mission effectiveness. Like targeting, risk management begins in planning and continues through preparation and execution. Risk management consists of the following steps:

- Identify hazards
- Assess hazards to determine risks
- Develop controls and make risk decisions
- Implement controls
- Supervise and evaluate

Knowledge Management *See pp. 3-75 to 3-78.*

Knowledge management is the process of enabling knowledge flow to enhance shared understanding, learning, and decision making (ADP 6-0). It facilitates the transfer of knowledge among commanders, staffs, and forces to build and maintain situational understanding. Knowledge management helps get the right information to the right person at the right time to facilitate decision making. Knowledge management uses a five-step process to create shared understanding. The steps of knowledge management include—

- Assess
- Design
- Develop
- Pilot
- Implement

Refer to ATP 6-01.1 for discussion on knowledge management.

Principles of Joint Operations (Understand)

Ref: ADP 3-0, Operations (Jul '19), table 2-1 and JP 3-0 (w/Chg 1), Joint Operations (Oct '18), pp. I-2 to I-3 and app. A.

Objective
Direct every military operation toward a clearly defined, decisive, and achievable goal.

Offensive
Seize, retain, and exploit the initiative.

Mass
Concentrate the effects of combat power at the most advantageous place and time to produce decisive results.

Maneuver
Place the enemy in a position of disadvantage through the flexible application of combat power.

Economy of Force
Expend minimum essential combat power on secondary efforts in order to allocate the maximum possible combat power on primary efforts.

Unity of Command
Ensure unity of effort under one responsible commander for every objective.

Security
Prevent the enemy from acquiring unexpected advantage.

Surprise
Strike at a time or place or in a manner for which the enemy is unprepared.

Simplicity
Increase the probability that plans and operations will be executed as intended by preparing clear, uncomplicated plans and concise orders.

Restraint
Limit collateral damage and prevent the unnecessary use of force.

Perseverance
Ensure the commitment necessary to attain the national strategic end state.

Legitimacy
Maintain legal and moral authority in the conduct of operations.

Refer to JFODS5-1: The Joint Forces Operations & Doctrine SMARTbook (Guide to Joint, Multinational & Interorganizational Operations). Updated for 2019, topics include joint doctrine fundamentals (JP 1), joint operations (JP 3-0 w/Chg 1), an expanded discussion of joint functions, joint planning (JP 5-0), joint logistics (JP 4-0), joint task forces (JP 3-33), joint force operations (JPs 3-30, 3-31, 3-32 & 3-05), multinational operations (JP 3-16), interorganizational cooperation (JP 3-08), & more!

Chap 1

(The Operations Process)
A. Planning

Ref: ADP 5-0, The Operations Process (Jul '19), chap. 2.

Planning is the art and science of understanding a situation, envisioning a desired future, and determining effective ways to bring that future about. Planning helps leaders understand situations; develop solutions to problems; direct, coordinate, and synchronize actions; prioritize efforts; and anticipate events. In its simplest form, planning helps leaders determine how to move from the current state of affairs to a more desirable future state while identifying potential opportunities and threats along the way.

Planning Methodologies

A **Army Design Methodology**
See pp. 1-36 to 1-39.

B **The Military Decisionmaking Process (MDMP)** *See pp. 2-1 to 2-58.*

C **Troop Leading Procedures (TLP)**
See pp. 2-59 to 2-62.

D **Rapid Decision-Making and Synchronization Process (RDSP)** *See pp. 1-60 to 1-63.*

E **Army Problem Solving**
See pp. 1-40 to 1-41.

Ref: ADP 5-0, The Operations Process, p. 2-16.

Planning is a continuous learning activity. While planning may start an iteration of the operations process, planning does not stop with the production of an order. During preparation and execution, the commander and staff continuously refine the order to account for changes in the situation. Subordinates and others provide assessments about what works, what does not work, and how the force can do things better. In some circumstances, commanders may determine that the current order (to include associated branches and sequels) no longer applies. In these instances, instead of modifying the current order, commanders reframe the problem and develop a new plan.

Planning may be highly structured, involving the commander, staff, subordinate commanders, and others who develop a fully synchronized plan or order. Planning may also be less structured, involving a commander and selected staff who quickly determine a scheme of maneuver for a hasty attack. Planning is conducted along various planning horizons, depending on the echelon and circumstances. Some units may plan out to years and months, others out to days and hours.

Planning techniques and methods vary based on circumstances. Planners may plan forward, starting with the present conditions and laying out potential decisions and actions forward in time. Planners also plan in reverse, starting with the envisioned end state and working backward in time to the present. Planning methods may be analytical, as in the MDMP, or more systemic, as in the Army design methodology (ADM).

Plans and Orders

A product of planning is a plan or order—a directive for future action. Commanders issue plans and orders to subordinates to communicate their visualization of the operations and to direct action. Plans and orders synchronize the action of forces in time, space, and purpose to achieve objectives and accomplish the mission. They inform others outside the organization on how to cooperate and provide support.

See chap. 4 for further discussion of plans and orders.

I. The Science and Art of Planning

Planning is both a science and an art. Many aspects of military operations, such as movement rates, fuel consumption, and weapons effects, are quantifiable. They are part of the science of planning. The combination of forces, choice of tactics, and arrangement of activities belong to the art of planning. Soldiers often gain knowledge of the science of planning through institutional training and study. They gain understanding of the art of planning primarily through operational training and experience. Effective planners are grounded in both the science and the art of planning.

The science of planning encompasses aspects of operations that can be measured and analyzed. These aspects include the physical capabilities of friendly and enemy organizations. The science of planning includes a realistic appreciation for time-distance factors; an understanding of how long it takes to initiate certain actions; the techniques and procedures used to accomplish planning tasks; and the terms and graphics that compose the language of military operations. While not easy, the science of planning is fairly straightforward.

Mastery of the science of planning is necessary for military professionals to understand the physical and procedural constraints under which units operate. These constraints include the effects of terrain, weather, and time on friendly and enemy forces. However—because combat is an intensely human activity—the solution to problems cannot be reduced to a formula. This realization necessitates the study of the art of planning.

The art of planning requires understanding the dynamic relationships among friendly forces, the threat, and other aspects of an OE during operations. It includes making decisions based on skilled judgment acquired from experience, training, study, imagination, and critical and creative thinking. Commanders apply judgment based on their knowledge and experience to select the right time and place to act, assign tasks, prioritize actions, and allocate resources. The art of planning involves the commander's willingness to accept risk.

Planning requires creative application of doctrine, units, and resources. It requires a thorough knowledge and application of the fundamentals of unified land operations (see ADP 3-0) and the fundamentals of tactics (see ADP 3-90). The art of planning involves developing plans within the commander's intent and planning guidance by choosing from interrelated options, including—

- Arrangement of activities in time, space, and purpose.
- Assignment of tactical mission tasks and tactical enabling tasks.
- Task organization of available forces and resource allocation.
- Choice and arrangement of control measures.
- Tempo.
- The risk the commander is willing to take.

II. The Functions of Planning

Ref: ADP 5-0, The Operations Process (Jul '19), pp. 2-3 to 2-7.

Imperfect knowledge and assumptions about the future are inherent in all planning. Planning cannot predict with precision how enemies will react or how civilians will respond during operations. Nonetheless, the understanding and learning that occurs during planning have great value. Even if units do not execute the plan exactly as envisioned—and few ever do—planning results in an improved understanding of the situation that facilitates future decision making. Planning and plans help leaders—

A. Understand and Develop Solutions to Problems

Planning helps commanders and staffs understand situations to include discerning the relationship of the operational and mission variable. Effective planning not only helps leaders understand the land domain, but it helps leaders understand how capabilities in the air, maritime, space, and cyberspace domains and the information environment impact operations on land and vice versa. Planning also helps leaders identify problems and develop solutions to solve or manage those problems. Not all problems require the same level of planning. Leaders often identify simple problems immediately and quickly decide on a solution—sometimes on the spot. Planning is critical, however, when a problem is actually a set of interrelated issues, and the solution to each affects the others. For unfamiliar situations, planning offers ways to solve the complete set of problems as a whole. In general, the more complex a situation is, the more important and involved the planning effort becomes.

B. Task-Organize the Force and Prioritize Efforts

When developing their concept of operations, commanders first visualize the decisive operation that directly accomplishes the mission. They then visualize how shaping and sustaining operations support the decisive operation. The decisive operation prioritizes effort and is the focal point around which the plan is developed. When developing associated tasks to subordinate units, commanders ensure subordinates have the capabilities and resources to accomplish their assigned tasks. They do this by task-organizing the force and establishing priorities of support.

In addition to task-organizing, commanders establish priorities of support during planning and shift priorities during execution as the situation requires. A priority of support is a priority set by the commander to ensure a subordinate unit has support in accordance with its relative importance to accomplish the mission.

C. Direct, Coordinate, and Synchronize Action

Plans and orders are the principle means commanders use to direct, coordinate, and synchronize actions. Plans and orders also inform those outside the unit how to cooperate and provide support. Good plans direct subordinates by stating what is required (the task) and why (the purpose); they leave how (the method) up to subordinates. They contain the minimum number of control measures needed to coordinate actions and synchronize the warfighting functions to mass the effects of combat power at the decisive point and time.

D. Anticipate Events & Adapt to Changing Circumstances

A fundamental tension exists between the desire to plan far into the future to facilitate preparation and coordination and the fact that the farther into the future the commander plans, the less certain the plan will remain relevant. Given the fundamentally uncertain nature of operations, the object of planning is not to eliminate uncertainty but to develop a framework for action in the midst of such uncertainty. Planning provides an informed forecast of how future events may unfold. It entails identifying and evaluating potential decisions and actions in advance to include thinking through consequences of certain actions. Planning involves thinking about ways to influence the future as well as ways to respond to potential events.

III. Planning and the Levels of Warfare

Ref: ADP 5-0, The Operations Process (Jul '19), pp. 2-7 to 2-10.

It is important to understand how Army planning nests with joint planning and how planning differs at the levels of warfare. The levels of warfare are a framework for defining and clarifying the relationship among national objectives, the operational approach, and tactical tasks (ADP 1-01). The three levels are strategic, operational, and tactical. There is no hard boundary between levels of warfare, nor fixed echelon responsible for a particular level.

The levels of warfare focus a headquarters on one of three broad roles—creating strategy; conducting campaigns and major operations; or sequencing battles, engagements, and actions. The levels of warfare correspond to specific levels of responsibility and planning with decisions at one level affecting other levels. They help commanders visualize a logical arrangement and synchronization of operations, allocate resources, and assign tasks to the appropriate command. Among the levels of warfare, planning horizons differ greatly.

Strategic Level

The strategic level of warfare is the level of warfare at which a nation, often as a member of a group of nations, determines national or multinational (alliance or coalition) strategic security objectives and guidance, then develops and uses national resources to achieve those objectives (JP 3-0). The focus at this level is the development of strategy—a foundational idea or set of ideas for employing the instruments of national power in a synchronized and integrated fashion to achieve national and multinational objectives. The strategic level of war is primarily the province of national leadership in coordination with combatant commanders.

The National Security Council develops and recommends national security policy options for Presidential approval. The President, the Secretary of Defense, and the Chairman of the Joint Chiefs of Staff provide their orders, intent, strategy, direction, and guidance via strategic direction to the military (Services and combatant commands) to pursue national interest. They communicate strategic direction to the military through written documents referred to as strategic guidance. Key strategic guidance documents include—

- National Security Strategy of the United States.
- National Defense Strategy of the United States.
- National Military Strategy of the United States.
- Joint Strategic Campaign Plan.
- Unified Command Plan.
- Guidance for Employment of the Force.
- Global Force Management Implementation Guidance.

Based on strategic guidance, GCCs and staffs—with input from subordinate commands (to include the theater army) and supporting commands and agencies—update their strategic estimates and develop theater strategies. A theater strategy is a broad statement of a GCC's long-term vision that bridges national strategic guidance and the joint planning required to achieve national and theater objectives. The theater strategy prioritizes the ends, ways, and means within the limitations established by the budget, global force management processes, and strategic guidance.

Operational Level

The operational level of warfare is the level of warfare at which campaigns and major operations are planned, conducted, and sustained to achieve strategic objectives within theaters or other operational areas (JP 3-0). Operational-level planning focuses on developing plans for campaigns and other joint operations. A campaign plan is a joint operation plan for a series of related major operations aimed at achieving strategic or operational objectives within a given time and space (JP 5-0). Joint force commanders (combatant commanders and their subordinate joint task force commanders) and their component commanders (Service and functional) conduct operational-level planning. Planning at the operational level requires operational art to integrate ends, ways, and means while balancing risk. Operational-level planners use operational design and the joint planning process to develop campaign plans, OPLANs, OPORDs, and supporting plans.

The combatant command campaign plan (CCP) operationalizes the GCC's strategy by organizing and aligning operations and activities with resources to achieve objectives in an area of responsibility. The CCP provides a framework within which the GCC conducts security cooperation activities and military engagement with regional partners. The CCP contains contingency plans that are viewed as branches within the campaign. Contingency plans identify how the command might respond in the event of a crisis. Contingency plans are often phased and have specified end states that seek to re-establish conditions favorable to the United States. Contingency plans have an identified military objective and termination criteria. They may address limited contingency operations or large-scale combat operations.

The theater army develops a support plan to the CCP. This support plan includes methods to achieve security cooperation, training and exercise programs, and ongoing Army activities within the theater including intelligence, air and missile defense, sustainment, and communications. The theater army also develops supporting plans for contingencies identified by the GCC. These include OPLANs for large-scale ground combat, noncombatant evacuation operations, humanitarian assistance and disaster relief, and other crises response activities. Theater army planners routinely develop, review, and update supporting plans to numbered OPLANs to ensure they remain feasible. This includes a review of Army force structure as well as time-phased force and deployment data.

Corps and below Army units normally conduct Army tactical planning. However, corps and divisions serving as the base headquarters for a joint task force or land component headquarters employ joint planning and develop joint formatted plans and orders. Corps or divisions receive joint formatted plans and orders when directly subordinate to a joint task force or joint land component command. It is important for these headquarters to be familiar with joint Adaptive Planning and Execution.

Tactical Level

The tactical level of warfare is the level of warfare at which battles and engagements are planned and executed to achieve military objectives assigned to tactical units or task forces (JP 3-0). Tactical-level planning revolves around how best to achieve objectives and accomplish tasks assigned by higher headquarters. Planning horizons for tactical-level planning are relatively shorter than planning horizons for operational-level planning. Tactical-level planning works within the framework of an operational-level plan and is addressed in Service doctrine or, in the case of multinational operations, the lead nation's doctrine. Army tactical planning is guided by the MDMP for units with a staff and TLP for small-units without a staff.

IV. Operational Art

Ref: ADP 5-0, The Operations Process (Mar '12), p. 2-10 to 2-17.

Operational art is the cognitive approach by commanders and staffs—supported by their skill, knowledge, experience, creativity, and judgment—to develop strategies, campaigns, and operations to organize and employ military forces by integrating ends, ways, and means (JP 3-0). Operational art applies to all types and aspects of operations. It integrates ends, ways, and means while accounting for risk. Applying operational art requires commanders to answer the following questions:

- What conditions, when established, constitute the desired end state (*ends*)?
- How will the force achieve these desired conditions (*ways*)?
- What sequence of actions helps attain these conditions (*ways*)?
- What resources are required to accomplish that sequence of actions (*means*)?
- What risks are associated with that sequence of actions and how can they be mitigated (*risks*)?

Operational art encompasses all levels of warfare. It requires creative vision, broad experience, and a knowledge of capabilities, tactics, and techniques across multiple domains. Commanders and staffs employ operational art during ADM and the MDMP.

Elements of *Operational Design*

Within operational art, joint force commanders and staffs consider elements of operational design. Elements of operational design are individual tools that help the joint force commander and staff visualize and describe the broad operational approach.

- Termination
- Military end state
- Objective
- Effects
- Center of gravity
- Decisive point
- Lines of operations and lines of effort
- Direct and indirect approach
- Anticipation
- Operational reach
- Culmination
- Arranging operations
- Force and functions

Elements of *Operational Art*

As some elements of operational design apply only to joint force commanders, the Army modifies the elements of operational design into elements of operational art, adding Army specific elements. During the planning and execution of Army operations, Army commanders and staffs consider the elements of operational art as they assess the situation.

- End state and conditions
- Center of gravity
- Decisive points
- Lines of operations and lines of effort
- Operational reach
- Basing
- Tempo
- Phasing and transitions
- Culmination
- Risk

Refer to AODS6 (w/SMARTupdate 1): The Army Operations & Doctrine SMARTbook (Guide to FM/ADP 3-0 Operations & the Elements of Combat Power). Completely updated with the Jul 2019 ADPs, Chg 1 to the 400-pg AODS6 includes operations (ADP 3-0), large-scale combat operations (FM 3-0 w/Chg 1), and refocused chapters on the elements of combat power: command & control (ADP 6-0), movement and maneuver (ADPs 3-90, 3-07, 3-28, 3-05), intelligence (ADP 2-0), fires (ADP 3-19), sustainment (ADP 4-0), & protection (ADP 3-37).

V. Army Planning Methodologies

Planning activities occupy a continuum ranging from conceptual to detailed as shown in figure 2-3 below. Understanding an OE and its problems, determining the operation's end state, establishing objectives, and sequencing the operation in broad terms all illustrate conceptual planning. Conceptual planning generally corresponds to the art of operations and is the focus of a commander with staff support.

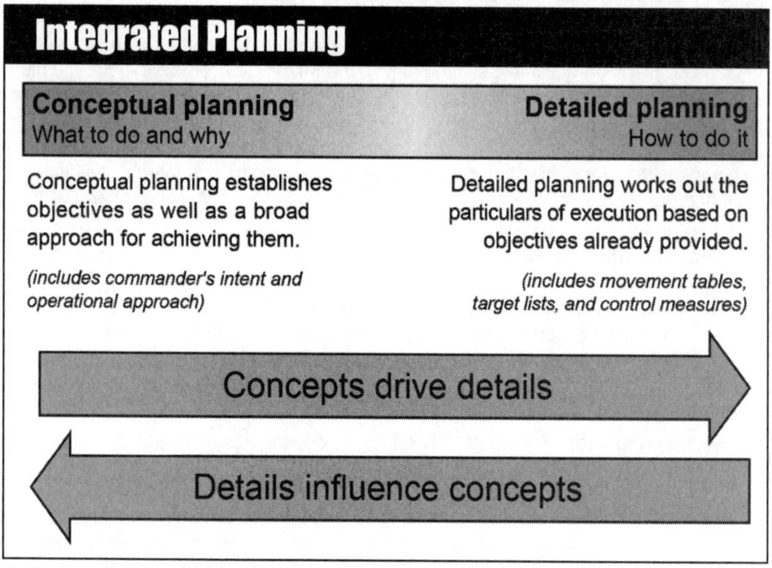

Integrated Planning
Conceptual planning
What to do and why
Detailed planning
How to do it
Conceptual planning establishes objectives as well as a broad approach for achieving them.
(includes commander's intent and operational approach)
Detailed planning works out the particulars of execution based on objectives already provided.
(includes movement tables, target lists, and control measures)
Concepts drive details
Details influence concepts

Ref: ADP 5-0, The Operations Process (Jul '19), fig. 2-3, p. 2-16.

Detailed planning translates the broad operational approach into a complete and practical plan. Generally, detailed planning is associated with aspects of science, such as movement tables, fuel consumption, target list, weapon effects, and time-distance factors. Detailed planning falls under the purview of the staff, focusing on specifics of execution. Detailed planning works out the scheduling, coordination, or technical problems involved with moving, sustaining, synchronizing, and directing the force. Detailed planning does not mean developing plans with excessive control measures that impede subordinate freedom of action. Planners develop mission orders that establish those controls necessary to coordinate and synchronize the force as a whole. They leave much of the how to accomplish tasks to the subordinate.

The commander personally leads the conceptual component of planning. While they are engaged in parts of detailed planning, commanders leave most specifics to the staff. **Conceptual planning** provides the basis for all subsequent planning. The commander's intent and operational approach provide the framework for the entire plan. This framework leads to a concept of operations and associated schemes of support, such as schemes of intelligence, maneuver, fires, protection, and sustainment. In turn, the schemes of support lead to the specifics of execution, including tasks to subordinate units and detailed annexes to the OPLAN or OPORD. However, the dynamic does not operate in only one direction. Conceptual planning must respond to detailed constraints.

Successful planning requires the integration of both conceptual and detailed thinking. Army leaders employ several methodologies for planning, determining the appropriate mix based on the scope of the problem, time available, and availability of a staff.

See following pages (pp. 1-34 to 1-35) for an overview and further discussion of the five Army planning methodologies.

Army Planning Methodologies

Ref: ADP 5-0, The Operations Process (Jul '19), pp. 2-16 to 2-19.

A. Army Design Methodology (ADM)

Army design methodology is a methodology for applying critical and creative thinking to understand, visualize, and describe problems and approaches to solving them. ADM is particularly useful as an aid to conceptual planning, but it must be integrated with the detailed planning typically associated with the MDMP to produce executable plans and orders. There is no one way or prescribed set of steps to employ the ADM. There are, however, several activities associated with ADM including framing an OE, framing problems, developing an operational approach, and reframing when necessary. While planners complete some activities before others, the understanding and learning within one activity may require revisiting the learning from another activity. Thus, ADM is iterative in nature.

When problems are difficult to identify, the operation's end state is unclear, or a COA is not self-evident, commanders employ ADM. This is often the case when developing long-range plans for extended operation or developing supporting plans to the CCP and associated contingencies. The results of ADM include an understanding of an OE and problem, the initial commander's intent, and an operational approach that serves as the link between conceptual and detailed planning. Based on their understanding and learning gained during ADM, commanders issue planning guidance—to include an operational approach—to guide more detailed planning using the MDMP.

See following pages (pp. 1-36 to 1-39) for an overview and discussion from ATP 5-0.1.

B. The Military Decision-Making Process (MDMP)

The military decision-making process is an iterative planning methodology to understand the situation and mission, develop a course of action, and produce an operation plan or order. It is an orderly, analytical process that integrates the activities of the commander, staff, and subordinate headquarters in the development of a plan or order. The MDMP helps leaders apply thoroughness, clarity, sound judgement, logic, and professional knowledge to develop situational understanding and produce a plan or order that best accomplishes the mission.

The MDMP consists of seven steps. Each step of the MDMP has inputs, a series of substeps, and outputs. The outputs lead to an increased understanding of the situation facilitating the next step of the MDMP. Commanders and staffs generally perform these steps sequentially; however, before producing the plan or order, they may revisit several steps in an iterative fashion as they learn more about the situation. The seven steps are—

- Step 1 – Receipt of mission.
- Step 2 – Mission analysis.
- Step 3 – COA development.
- Step 4 – COA analysis.
- Step 5 – COA comparison.
- Step 6 – COA approval.
- Step 7 – Orders production, dissemination, and transition.

Commanders initiate the MDMP upon receipt of, or in anticipation of, a mission. Commanders and staffs often begin planning in the absence of an approved higher headquarters' OPLAN or OPORD. In these instances, they start planning based on a warning order (WARNORD), a planning order, or an alert order from higher headquarters. This requires active collaboration with the higher headquarters and parallel planning among echelons as the plan or order is developed.

See chap. 2, Military Decision-Making Process (MDMP), for complete discussion.

C. Troop Leading Procedures (TLP)

The MDMP and TLP are similar but not identical. Troop leading procedures are a dynamic process used by small-unit leaders to analyze a mission, develop a plan, and prepare for an operation. TLP extend the MDMP to the small-unit level. Commanders with a coordinating staff use the MDMP as their primary planning process. Company-level and smaller units lack formal staffs and use TLP to plan and prepare for operations. This places the responsibility for planning primarily on the commander or small-unit leader with assistance from forward observers, supply sergeants, and other specialists in the unit.

- Step 1 – Receive the mission.
- Step 2 – Issue a warning order.
- Step 3 – Make a tentative plan.
- Step 4 – Initiate movement.
- Step 5 – Conduct reconnaissance.
- Step 6 – Complete the plan.
- Step 7 – Issue the order.
- Step 8 – Supervise and refine.

See pp. 2-59 to 2-62 for discussion of the troop leading procedures from FM 6-0.

D. Rapid Decision-Making and Synchronization Process (RDSP)

The rapid decision-making and synchronization process (RDSP) is a decision-making and planning technique that commanders and staffs commonly use during execution when available planning time is limited. While the MDMP seeks an optimal solution, the RDSP seeks a timely and effective solution within the commander's intent. Using the RDSP lets leaders avoid the time-consuming requirements of developing decision criteria and multiple COAs. Under the RDSP, leaders combine their experiences and intuition to quickly understand the situation and develop a COA. The RDSP includes five steps:

- Step 1 – Compare the current situation to the order.
- Step 2 – Determine that a decision, and what type, is required.
- Step 3 – Develop a course of action.
- Step 4 – Refine and validate the course of action.
- Step 5 – Issue the implement the order.

See pp. 1-60 to 1-63 for an overview and further discussion of RDSP from FM 6-0.

E. Army Problem Solving

The ability to recognize and effectively solve problems is an essential skill for Army leaders. Where the previous methodologies are designed for planning operations, Army problem solving is a methodology available for leaders in identifying and solving a variety of problems. Similar in logic to the MDMP, Army problem solving is an analytical approach to defining a problem, developing possible solutions to solve the problem, arriving at the best solution, developing a plan, and implementing that plan to solve the problem. The steps to Army problem solving are—

- Step 1 – Gather information.
- Step 2 – Identify the problem.
- Step 3 – Develop criteria.
- Step 4 – Generate possible solutions.
- Step 4 – Analyze possible solutions.
- Step 6 – Compare possible solutions.
- Step 7 – Make and implement the decision.

See pp. 1-40 to 1-41 for an overview and further discussion from FM 6-0.

A. Army Design Methodology (ADM)

Ref: ADP 5-0, The Operations Process (Jul '19), pp. 2-16 to 2-19 and ATP 5-0.1, Army Design Methodology (Jul '15).

Army design methodology is a methodology for applying critical and creative thinking to understand, visualize, and describe problems and approaches to solving them. ADM is particularly useful as an aid to conceptual planning, but it must be integrated with the detailed planning typically associated with the MDMP to produce executable plans and orders. There is no one way or prescribed set of steps to employ the ADM. There are, however, several activities associated with ADM including framing an OE, framing problems, developing an operational approach, and reframing when necessary as shown in figure 2-4. While planners complete some activities before others, the understanding and learning within one activity may require revisiting the learning from another activity. Thus, ADM is iterative in nature.

Activities of the Army Design Methodology

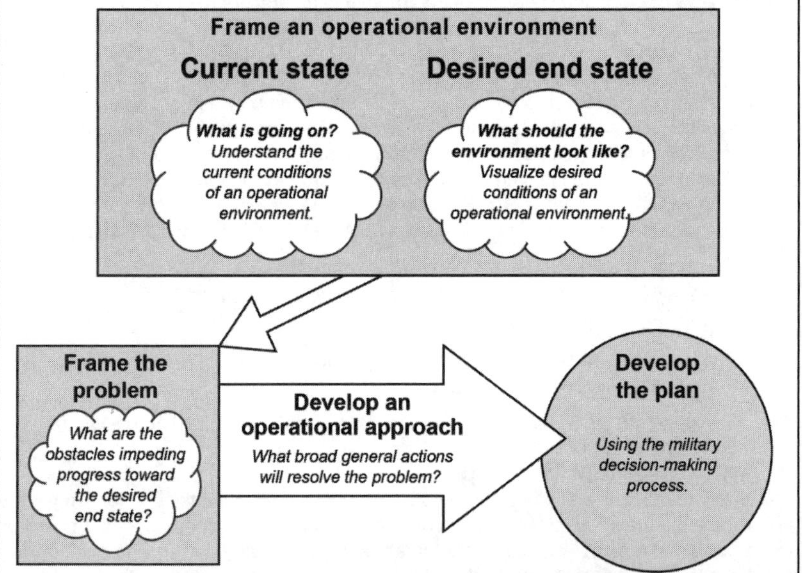
Frame an operational environment
Current state
What is going on? Understand the current conditions of an operational environment.
Desired end state
What should the environment look like? Visualize desired conditions of an operational environment.
Frame the problem
What are the obstacles impeding progress toward the desired end state?
Develop an operational approach
What broad general actions will resolve the problem?
Develop the plan
Using the military decision-making process.
Continuous assessment and reframing as required

Ref: ADP 5-0, The Operations Process (Jul '19), fig. 2-4, p. 2-17.

When problems are difficult to identify, the operation's end state is unclear, or a COA is not self-evident, commanders employ ADM. This is often the case when developing long-range plans for extended operation or developing supporting plans to the CCP and associated contingencies. The results of ADM include an understanding of an OE and problem, the initial commander's intent, and an operational approach that serves as the link between conceptual and detailed planning. Based on their understanding and learning gained during ADM, commanders issue planning guidance—to include an operational approach—to guide more detailed planning using the MDMP.

1. Framing Operational Environments

Ref: ATP 5-0.1, Army Design Methodology (Jul '15), chap. 3.

An operational environment is a composite of the conditions, circumstances, and influences that affect the employment of capabilities and bear on the decisions of the commander (JP 3-0). An operational environment includes physical areas (air, land, maritime, and space domains) and cyberspace. It also includes the information that shapes conditions in those areas and enemy, friendly, and neutral aspects relevant to operations. An operational environment is not isolated or independent but interconnected by various influences (for example, information and economics) from around the globe. No two operational environments are the same.

Commanders and staffs employ systems thinking and use the operational variables to help understand, visualize, and describe an operational environment. Operational variables are those aspects of an operational environment, both military and nonmilitary, that differ from one operational area to another and affect operations. Operational variables describe not only the military aspects of an operational environment but also the population's influence on it. The eight interrelated operational variables are political, military, economic, social, information, infrastructure, physical environment, and time (PMESII-PT). The operational variables are broad information categories that help the commander analyze and develop a comprehensive understanding of an operational environment. The operational variables are information categories used to describe an operational environment.

See pp. 1-16 to 1-17 for discussion of operational and mission variables (PMESII-PT and METT-TC.

Framing Activities

Military operation occurs in a context larger than a unit's mission. As such, the staff supports commanders in developing a contextual understanding of an operational environment through framing—the act of constructing models that seek to describe reality. Framing involves selecting, organizing, interpreting, and making sense of interrelated variables and relevant actors in an operational environment. When framing an operational environment, the commander and planning team understand the current state and visualize a desired future state of an operational environment.

Understanding current conditions and desired future conditions of an operational environment helps commanders identify problems and develop approaches to solve or manage those problems.

A product of framing an operational environment is an environmental frame. The environmental frame describes and depicts the context of the operational environment—how the context developed (historical and cultural perspective), how the context currently exists (current conditions), and how the context could trend in the future (projected future conditions). The environmental frame also includes a description of what the operational environment should look like at the conclusion of an operation (desired end state conditions).

There is no "one- way" or set of steps for framing an operational environment. There are, however, several activities that help the commander and staff develop an environmental frame including:

- Understand higher guidance and direction.
- Understand the current state of an operational environment.
- Project how an operational environment may trend in the future.
- Discern desired future states of other actors.
- Envision a desired end state.

Continued on next page

Army Design Methodology (Cont.)

2. Framing Problems

Ref: ATP 5-0.1, Army Design Methodology (Jul '15), chap. 4.

Continued from previous page

A problem is an issue or obstacle that makes it difficult to achieve a desired goal or objective. In a broad sense, a problem exists when an individual notices a difference between the current state and desired end state. In the context of operations, an operational problem is a discrepancy between the state of affairs as it is and the state of affairs as it ought to be that compels military actions to resolve it. An operational problem includes those issues that impede commanders from accomplishing missions, achieving objectives, and attaining the desired end state.

Army leaders are problem solvers and the complexity of problems they address range from well-structured problems to those extremely complex and ill-structured. The degree of interactive complexity (see chapter 3) of a given situation is the primary factor that determines the problem's structure. Another factor determining problem structure is an individual perception of a problem. Perception of whether a problem is well, medium, or ill-structured depends on the perceived familiarity and understanding of the problem.

Framing Activities

Identifying and understanding problems is essential to solving them. As the planning team understands an operational environment and the desired end state, the planning team shifts their efforts to identifying and understanding those issues that may impede progress toward achieving the desired end state. These interrelated issues represent the problem situation or "system of problems" the command will need to address. During problem framing, commanders and staffs answer questions such as:

- What is the difference between the current state of an operational environment and the desired endstate?
- What is the difference between the natural tendency of an operational environment and the desired end state?
- What is the difference between the desired end state of other actors and the desired end state?
- What is preventing the command from reaching the desired end state?
- What needs to change?
- What does not need to change?
- What are the opportunities and threats from a friendly perspective?
- What are the opportunities and threats from an enemy and other actor's perspective?

Continued from previous page

The planning team captures its work in a problem frame that describes the set of interrelated problems or system of problems in a narrative supported by visual models. The problem frame supports the commander's dialogue with higher commanders and unified action partners in defining problems and developing common expectations regarding resolution. This is vital to develop an effective operational approach to solve or manage identified problems.

Like framing an operational environment, there is no "one way" or set of steps for framing problems. There are three activities that help the commander and staff develop a problem frame.

- Review the environmental frame.
- Identify problems and map out their relationships.
- Capture the problem frame in text and graphics.

3. Framing Solutions

Ref: ATP 5-0.1, Army Design Methodology (Jul '15), chap. 5.

Operational Approach

Once commanders and planners agree on the problem or set of problems, they develop ways to address them. They do this by developing an operational approach—a description of the broad actions the force must take to transform current conditions into those desired at end state (JP 5-0). An operational approach is the commander's visualization of what needs to be done to solve or manage identified problems. It is the main idea that informs detailed planning. The operational approach promotes mutual understanding and unity of effort between the force and unified action partner on the way ahead.

The operational approach reflects understanding of the operational environment and the problem while describing the commander's visualization of ways to achieve the desired end state as shown in figure 5-1.

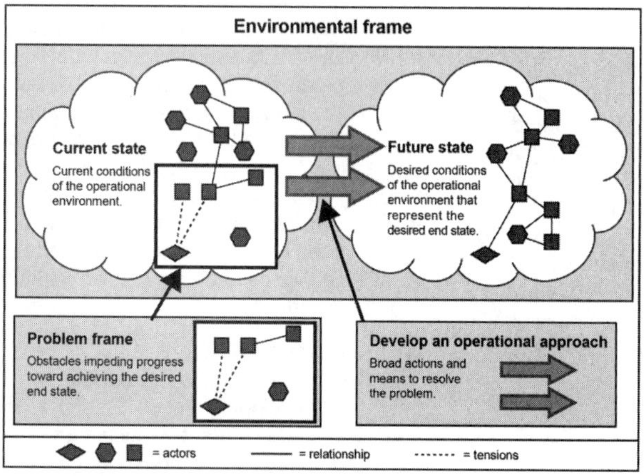

Note: An operational approach is not a course of action. An operational approach provides focus and boundaries for the development of COAs during the MDMP. A COA is more detailed than an operational approach, including details such as task organization, unit boundaries, and tasks to accomplish.

Ref: ATP 5-0.1, fig. 5-1. Operational approach.

The operational approach is a conceptualization of "what needs to be done" to solve or manage identified problems. Like the other activities of ADM, commanders collaborate and dialogue with their staffs, other commanders, and unified action partners as they formulate their operational approach. In developing their operational approach, the commander and planning team synthesize early work concerning the operational environment, problem, and desired end state and seek to answer questions such as:

- How do we go from the existing conditions to the desired end state?
- What obstacles or tensions exist between the two?
- What broad actions help attain these conditions?
- What type of resources are required?
- What are the risks?

Activities

As with the other activities of ADM, there is no prescribed format for developing an operational approach. Several activities help the commander and staffs develop an operational approach and translate that operational approach into a plan or order for execution. Activities include:

- Review the environmental and problem frames.
- Formulate an operational approach.
- Document results.

E. Problem Solving Steps

Ref: FM 6-0 (C2), Commander and Staff Organization and Operations (Apr '16), chap. 4.

The ability to recognize and effectively solve problems is an essential skill for leaders. A problem is an issue or obstacle that makes it difficult to achieve a desired goal or end state. . Troop leading procedures and the MDMP are specifically designed for planning and problem solving for conducting operations. For situations when operational planning is not appropriate, the Army's approach to problem solving involves the following steps:

1. Gather Information and Knowledge

Gathering information and knowledge and is an important first step in problem solving. Leaders cannot understand or identify the problem without first gathering information and knowledge. While described as a step, gathering information and knowledge continues throughout the problem solving process. It helps leaders understand the situation and determine what the problem is by defining its limitations and scope. Leaders never stop acquiring and assessing the impact of new or additional information relevant to the problem.

Leaders require facts and assumptions to solve problems. Understanding facts and assumptions is critical to understanding problem solving. In addition, leaders need to know how to handle opinions and organize information.

- **Facts**. Facts are verifiable pieces of information or information presented that has objective reality.
- **Assumptions**. An assumption is a supposition on the current situation or a presupposition on the future course of events, either or both assumed to be true in the absence of positive proof, necessary to enable the commander in the process of planning to complete an estimate of the situation and make a decision on the course of action (JP 5-0).
- **Opinions**. An opinion is a personal judgment that the leader or another individual makes. Opinions cannot be totally discounted.

2. Identify the Problem

A problem exists when the current state or condition differs from or impedes achieving the desired end state or condition. Leaders identify problems from a variety of sources. These include—

- Higher headquarters' directives or guidance.
- Decisionmaker's guidance.
- Subordinates.
- Personal observations.

When identifying a problem, leaders actively seek to identify its root cause, not merely the symptoms on the surface. Symptoms may be the reason that the problem became visible. They are often the first things noticed and frequently require attention. However, focusing on the symptoms of a problem may lead to false conclusions or inappropriate solutions. Using a systematic approach to identifying the real problem helps avoid the "solving symptoms" pitfall.

3. Develop Criteria

The third step in the problem-solving process is developing criteria. A criterion is a standard, rule, or test by which something can be judged—a measure of value. Problem solvers develop criteria to assist them in formulating and evaluating possible solutions to a problem. Criteria are based on facts or assumptions. Problem solvers develop two types of criteria:

- **Screening Criteria**. Screening criteria defines the limits of an acceptable solution. As such, they are tools to establish the baseline products for analysis.
- **Evaluation Criteria**. After developing screening criteria, the problem solver develops the evaluation criteria in order to differentiate among possible solutions.

In practice, the criteria by which choices are made are almost never of equal importance. Because of this, it is often convenient to assign weights to each evaluation criterion. Weighting criteria establishes the relative importance of each one with respect to the others.

4. Generate Possible Solutions

After gathering information relevant to the problem and developing criteria, leaders formulate possible solutions. They carefully consider the guidance provided by the commander or their superiors, and develop several alternatives to solve the problem. Several alternatives should be considered, however too many possible solutions may result in wasted time. Experience and time available determine how many solutions to consider. Leaders should consider at least two solutions. Doing this enables the problem solver to use both analysis and comparison as problem solving tools. Developing only one solution to "save time" may produce a faster solution, but risks creating more problems from factors not considered. Generating solutions has two steps:

- Generate Options. The basic technique for developing new ideas in a group setting is brainstorming.
- Summarize the Solution in Writing and Sketches

5. Analyze Possible Solutions

Having identified possible solutions, leaders analyze each one to determine its merits and drawbacks. If criteria are well defined, to include careful selection of benchmarks, analysis is greatly simplified.

Leaders use screening criteria and benchmarks to analyze possible solutions. They apply screening criteria to judge whether a solution meets minimum requirements. For quantitative criteria, they measure, compute, or estimate the raw data values for each solution and each criterion. In analyzing solutions, which involve predicting future events, it is useful to have a process for visualizing those events. Wargaming, models, and simulations are examples of tools that can help problem solvers visualize events and estimate raw data values for use in analysis. Once raw data values have been determined, the leader judges them against applicable screening criteria to determine if a possible solution merits further consideration. A solution that fails to meet or exceed the set threshold of one or more screening criteria is screened out.

6. Compare Possible Solutions

During this step, leaders compare each solution against the others to determine the optimum one. Comparing solutions identifies which solution best solves the problem based on the evaluation criteria. Leaders use any comparison technique that helps reach the best recommendation. The most common technique is a decision matrix.

The most common technique is a decision matrix (see p. 2-51).

7. Make and Implement the Decision

After completing their analysis and comparison, leaders identify the preferred solution. If a superior assigned the problem, leaders prepare the necessary products (verbal, written, or both) needed to present the recommendation to the decisionmaker. Before presenting the findings and a recommendation, leaders coordinate their recommendation with those affected by the problem or the solutions. In formal situations, leaders present their findings and recommendations to the decisionmaker as staff studies, decision papers, or decision briefings.

A good solution can be lost if the leader cannot persuade the audience that it is correct. Every problem requires both a solution and the ability to communicate the solution clearly. The writing and briefing skills a leader possesses may ultimately be as important as good problem-solving skills.

Based on the decisionmaker's decision and final guidance, leaders refine the solution and prepare necessary implementing instructions. Formal implementing instructions can be issued as a memorandum of instruction, policy letter, or command directive. Once leaders have given instructions, they monitor their implementation and compare results to the measure of success and the desired end state established in the approved solution. When necessary, they issue additional instructions.

A feedback system that provides timely and accurate information, periodic review, and the flexibility to adjust must also be built into the implementation plan.

VI. Key Components of a Plan

Ref: ADRP 5-0, The Operations Process (Jul '19), pp. 2-19 to 2-20.

The mission statement, commander's intent, and concept of operations are key components of a plan that serve as the framework for an operation. Commanders ensure their mission and commander's intent nest with those of their higher headquarters. While the commander's intent focuses on the end state, the concept of operations focuses on the way or sequence of actions by which the force will achieve the end state. The concept of operations expands on the mission statement and commander's intent. Within the concept of operations, commanders establish objectives as intermediate goals toward achieving the operation's end state.

A. Mission Statement *See pp. 2-24 and 2-25.*

The mission is the task, together with the purpose, that clearly indicates the action to be taken and the reason therefore (JP 3-0). Commanders analyze a mission based on their higher commander's intent, specified tasks, and implied tasks. Results of that analysis yield the essential task—the task that when executed accomplishes the mission. The essential task becomes the "what" of the mission statement—a clear statement of the action to be taken and the reason for taking it. The five elements of a mission statement answer these questions:

- *Who* will execute the operation (unit or organization)?
- *What* is the unit's essential task (normally a tactical mission task or tactical enabling task)?
- *Where* will the operation occur (AO, objective, engagement areas, or grid coordinates)?
- *When* will the operation begin (by time or event)?
- *Why* will the force conduct the operation (for what purpose)?

The "who,""where," and "when"of a mission statement are straightforward. The "what" and "why" are more challenging to write and can confuse subordinates if not stated clearly. The "what"is a task and is expressed in terms of action verbs. These tasks are defined and measurable and can be grouped as "actions by friendly forces" or "effects on enemy forces." The "why" puts the task into context by describing the reason for performing it. The mission's purpose facilitates initiative in changing circumstances.

See pp. 7-35 to 7-38 for a list and discussion of tactical mission tasks from ADP 1-02.

B. Commander's Intent *See p. 2-26.*

The commander's intent succinctly describes what constitutes success for the operation. It includes the operation's purpose, key tasks, and conditions that define the end state. When describing the purpose of the operation, the commander's intent does not restate the "why"of the mission statement. Rather, it describes the broader purpose of the unit's operation in relationship to the higher commander's intent and concept of operations.

Key Tasks

Key tasks are those activities the force must perform as a whole to achieve the desired end state (ADP 6-0). During execution—when significant opportunities present themselves or the concept of operations no longer fits the situation—subordinates use key tasks to keep their efforts focused on achieving the desired end state. Examples of key tasks include terrain the force must control or an effect the force must have on the enemy.

End State

The end state is a set of desired future conditions the commander wants to exist when an operation ends. Commanders describe the operation's end state by stating the desired conditions of the friendly force in relationship to desired conditions of the enemy, terrain, and civil considerations. A clearly defined end state promotes unity of effort among the force and with unified action partners.

C. Concept of Operations

The concept of operations is a statement that directs the manner in which subordinate units cooperate to accomplish the mission and establishes the sequence of actions the force will use to achieve the end state. The concept of operations describes how the commander sees the actions of subordinate units fitting together to accomplish the mission. At a minimum, it includes a scheme of maneuver and scheme of fires. Where the commander's intent focuses on the end state, the concept of operations focuses on the method by which the operation uses and synchronizes the warfighting functions to translate the vision and end state into action.

The concept of operations describes the combination of offensive, defensive, or stability operations and how these tasks complement each other. It describes the deep, close, support, and consolidation areas; decisive, shaping, and sustaining operations within those areas; and main and supporting efforts.

In developing the concept of operations, commanders and staffs ensure their concepts nest with that of their higher headquarters. Nested concepts is a planning technique to achieve unity of purpose whereby each succeeding echelon's concept of operations is aligned by purpose with the higher echelons' concept of operations. An effective concept of operations describes how the forces will support a mission of the higher headquarters and how the actions of subordinate units fit together to accomplish a mission.

The operations overlay—part of Annex C (Operations) to an OPLAN or OPORD—supplements the concept of operations by depicting graphic control measures used to direct operations. A graphic control measure is a symbol used on maps and displays to regulate forces and warfighting functions (ADP 6-0). Graphic control measures include symbols for boundaries, fire support coordination measures, some airspace control measures, air defense areas, and obstacles. Commanders establish them to regulate maneuver, movement, airspace use, fires, and other aspects of operations.

See chap. 7, Operational Terms and Symbols, for instructions on depicting graphic control measures from ADP 1-02.

VII. Guides to Effective Planning

Ref: ADRP 5-0, The Operations Process (Mar '12), pp. 2-21 to 2-25.

Planning is an inherent and fundamental part of command and control, and commanders are the single most important factor in effective planning. Effective planning requires dedication, study, and practice. Planners must be technically and tactically competent within their areas of expertise and understand basic planning concepts. The following aids in effective planning:

Incorporate the Tenets of Unified Land Operations

Tenets of operations are desirable attributes that should be built into all plans and operations and are directly related to the Army's operational concept (ADP 1-01). Tenets of unified land operations describe the Army's approach to generating and applying combat power across the range of military operations. Commanders and staffs consider and incorporate the following tenets into all plans:

- Simultaneity
- Depth
- Synchronization
- Flexibility

Commanders Focus Planning

The responsibility for planning is inherent in command. Commanders are planners—they are the central figure to effective planning. Often with the most experience, commanders are ultimately responsible for the execution of the plan. As such, the plan must reflect how commanders intend to conduct operations. Commanders ensure the approaches to planning meet the requirements of time, planning horizons, level of detail, and desired outcomes. Commanders ensure that all plans and orders comply with domestic and international laws as well as the Army Ethic. They confirm that the plan or order is relevant and suitable for subordinates. Generally, the more involved commanders are in planning, the faster staffs can plan. Through personal involvement, commanders learn from the staff and others about a situation and ensure the plan reflects their commander's intent.

Develop Simple, Flexible Plans through Mission Orders

Simplicity—prepare clear, uncomplicated plans and clear, concise orders to ensure thorough understanding—is a principle of war. Effective plans and orders are simple and direct. Staffs prepare clear, concise orders that communicate understanding of the operation by using doctrinally correct military terms and symbols. Using the correct terms and symbols minimizes chances of misunderstanding and aids with brevity. Developing shorter plans helps maintain simplicity. Shorter plans are easier to disseminate, read, and remember.

Commanders stress the importance of using mission orders as a way of building simple, flexible plans. Mission orders are directives that emphasize to subordinates the results to be attained, not how they are to achieve them (ADP 6-0). Mission orders are not a specific type of order but a reflected style or technique for writing OPLANs, OPORDs, and FRAGORDs. In developing mission orders, commanders focus subordinates on what to do and why to do it without prescribing exactly how to do it. Commanders establish control measures to aid cooperation among forces without imposing needless restrictions on freedom of action.

Optimize Available Planning Time

Time is a critical variable in operations. Therefore, time management is important in planning. Whether done deliberately or rapidly, all planning requires the skillful use of available time to optimize planning and preparation throughout the unit. Taking more time to plan often results in greater synchronization; however, any delay in execution risks yielding the initiative—with more time to prepare and act—to the enemy. When allocating planning time to staffs, commanders must ensure subordinates have enough time to plan and prepare their own actions prior to execution. Commanders follow the **"one-third—two-thirds rule"** as a guide to allocate time available. They use one-third of the time available before execution for their planning and allocate the remaining two-thirds of the time available before execution to their subordinates for planning and preparation.

Both collaborative and parallel planning help optimize available planning time. **Collaborative planning** is several echelons developing plans and orders together. Commanders, subordinate commanders, and staffs share their understanding of the situation and participate in course of action development and decisionmaking for development of the higher headquarters plan or order.

Parallel planning is two or more echelons planning for the same operation through the sequential sharing of information through warning orders from the higher headquarters prior to the higher headquarters publishing their operation plan or operation order. Since several echelons develop their plans simultaneously, parallel planning can significantly shorten planning time. The higher headquarters continuously shares information concerning future operations with subordinate units through warning orders and other means. Frequent communication between commanders and staffs and sharing of information (such as intelligence preparation of the battlefield products) help subordinate headquarters plan. Parallel planning requires significant interaction among echelons. During parallel planning, subordinate units do not wait for their higher headquarters to publish an order to begin developing their own plans and orders.

Commanders are sensitive not to overload subordinates with planning requirements. Generally, the higher the headquarters, the more time and staff resources are available to plan and explore options. Higher headquarters involve subordinates with developing those plans and concepts that have the highest likelihood of being adopted or fully developed.

Focus on the Right Planning Horizon

The defining challenges to effective planning are uncertainty and time. Tension exists when commanders determine how far ahead to plan effectively without preparation and coordination becoming irrelevant. Planning too far into the future may overwhelm the capabilities of planning staffs, especially subordinate staffs. Not planning far enough ahead may result in losing the initiative and being unprepared. Understanding this tension is key to ensuring that the command focuses on the right planning horizon.

A planning horizon is a point in time commanders use to focus the organization's planning efforts to shape future events. Planning horizons may be measured in weeks or months or in hours and days depending on the echelon and situation. Organizations often plan simultaneously in several different horizons, especially division and above. To guide their planning efforts, commanders use three planning horizons—short-range, mid-range, and long-range.

Determine Relevant Facts and Develop Assumptions

Commanders and staffs gather key facts and develop assumptions as they build their plan. A fact is something known to exist or have happened—a statement known to be true. Facts concerning the operational and mission variables serve as the basis for developing situational understanding during planning. When listing facts, planners are careful they are directly relevant to a COA or help commanders make a decision. Any captured, recorded, and most importantly briefed fact must add value to the planning conversation.

An assumption provides a supposition about the current situation or future course of events, presumed to be true in the absence of facts. Assumptions must be valid (logical and realistic) and necessary for planning to continue. Assumptions address gaps in knowledge that are critical for the planning process to continue. Staffs continually review assumptions to ensure validity and to challenge if they appear unrealistic.

VIII. Planning Pitfalls

Commanders and staffs recognize the value of planning and avoid common planning pitfalls. These pitfalls generally stem from a common cause: the failure to appreciate the unpredictability and uncertainty of military operations. Pointing these out is not a criticism of planning, but of planning improperly. Common planning pitfalls include—

- Attempting to forecast and dictate events too far into the future.
- Trying to plan in too much detail.
- Using the plan as a script for execution.
- Institutionalizing rigid planning methods.

The first pitfall, attempting to forecast and dictate events too far into the future, may result from believing a plan can control the future. Planners tend to plan based on assumptions that the future will be a linear continuation of the present. These plans often underestimate the scope of changes in directions that may occur and the results of second- and third-order effects. Even the most effective plans cannot anticipate all the unexpected events. Often, events overcome plans much sooner than anticipated. Effective plans include sufficient branches and sequels to account for the nonlinear nature of events.

The second pitfall consists of trying to plan in too much detail. Sound plans include necessary details; however, planning in unnecessary detail consumes limited time and resources that subordinates need. This pitfall often stems from the desire to leave as little as possible to chance. In general, the less certain the situation, the fewer details a plan should include. However, planners often respond to uncertainty by planning in more detail to try to account for every possibility. Preparing detailed plans under uncertain conditions generates even more anxiety, which leads to even more detailed planning. Often this over planning results in an extremely detailed plan that does not survive the friction of the situation and constricts effective action. A good plan only includes details needed to coordinate or synchronize actions of two or more subordinate units.

The third pitfall, using the plan as a script for execution, tries to prescribe the course of events with precision. When planners fail to recognize the limits of foresight and control, the plan can become a coercive and overly regulatory mechanism. Commanders, staffs, and subordinates mistakenly focus on meeting the requirements of the plan rather than deciding and acting effectively.

The fourth pitfall is the danger of institutionalizing rigid planning methods that leads to inflexible or overly structured thinking. This pitfall tends to make planning rigidly focused on the process and produces plans that overly emphasize detailed procedures. Effective planning provides a disciplined framework for approaching and solving complex problems. Taking that discipline to the extreme often results in subordinates not getting plans on time or getting overly detailed plans.

Chap 1

(The Operations Process) B. Preparation

Ref: ADP 5-0, The Operations Process (Jul '19), chap. 3.

Preparation consists of those activities performed by units and Soldiers to improve their ability to execute an operation. Preparation creates conditions that improve friendly forces' opportunities for success and include activities such as rehearsals, training, and inspections. It requires commander, staff, unit, and Soldier actions to ensure the force is ready to execute operations.

Preparation helps the force transition from planning to execution. Preparation normally begins during planning and continues into execution by uncommitted units. Like the other activities of the operations process, commanders drive preparation activities with a focus on leading and assessing.

Preparation Activities

- Coordinate and establish liaison
- Initiate information collection
- Initiate security operations
- Initiate troop movements
- Complete task organization
- Integrate new units and Soldiers
- Train
- Conduct pre-operations checks and inspections
- Initiate sustainment preparation
- Initiate network preparations
- Manage terrain
- Prepare terrain
- Conduct confirmation briefs
- Conduct rehearsals
- Conduct plans-to-operations transition
- Revise and refine the plan
- Supervise

Ref: ADP 5-0, The Operations Process (Jul '19), table 3-1, p. 3-4.

Guides to Effective Preparation

Like the other activities of the operations process, commanders drive preparation. They continue to understand, visualize, describe, direct, lead, and assess. They gather additional information to improve their situational understanding, revise the plan as required, coordinate with other units and partners, and supervise preparation activities to ensure their forces are ready to execute operations. The following guides aid commanders and leaders in effectively preparing for operations:

- Allocate time and prioritize preparation efforts.
- Protect the force.
- Supervise.

See following pages (pp. 1-48 to 1-51) for discussion of activities Commanders, units, and Soldiers conduct to ensure the force is protected and prepared for execution. See also p. 1- 52 for discussion of preparation fundamentals.

I. Preparation Activities

Ref: ADP 5-0, The Operations Process (Jul '19), pp. 3-4 to 3-9.

Commanders, units, and Soldiers conduct the following activities to ensure the force is protected and prepared for execution.

Coordinate and Conduct Liaison

Units and organizations establish liaison in planning and preparation. Establishing liaison helps leaders internal and external to the headquarters understand their unit's role in upcoming operations and prepare to perform that role. In addition to military forces, many civilian organizations may operate in the operational area. Their presence can both affect and be affected by the commander's operations. Continuous liaison between the command and unified action partners helps to build unity of effort.

Liaison is most commonly used for establishing and maintaining close communications. It continuously enables direct, physical communications between commands. Establishing and maintaining liaison is vital to external coordination. Liaison enables direct communications between the sending and receiving headquarters. It may begin with planning and continue through preparing and executing, or it may start as late as execution. Available resources and the need for direct contact between sending and receiving headquarters determine when to establish liaison.

Establishing liaisons with civilian organizations is especially important in stability operations because of various external organizations and the inherent coordination challenges. Civil affairs units (to include LNOs) are particularly important in coordination with civilian organizations.

See pp. 5-29 to 5-34 for further discussion.

Initiate Information Collection

During planning and preparation, commanders take every opportunity to improve their situational understanding prior to execution. This requires aggressive and continuous information collection. Commanders often direct information collection (to include reconnaissance operations) early in planning that continues in preparation and execution. Through information collection, commanders and staffs continuously plan, task, and employ collection assets and forces to collect timely and accurate information to help satisfy CCIRs and other information requirements. *(Refer to FM 3-55).*

Initiate Security Operations

Security operations—screen, guard, cover, area security, and local security—are essential during preparation. During preparation, the force is vulnerable to surprise and enemy attacks. Leaders are often away from their units and concentrated together during rehearsals. Parts of the force could be moving to task-organize. Required supplies may be unavailable or being repositioned. Units assigned security missions execute these missions while the rest of the force prepares for the overall operation. Every unit provides local security to its own forces and resources.

Refer to SUTS3: The Small Unit Tactics SMARTbook, 3rd Ed. for further discussion.

Initiate Troop Movements

The repositioning of forces prior to execution makes up a significant portion of activities of preparation. Commanders position or reposition units to the correct starting places before execution. Commanders integrate operations security measures with troop movements to ensure these movements do not reveal any intentions to the enemy. Troop movements include assembly area reconnaissance by advance parties and route reconnaissance. They also include movements required by changes to the task organization. Commanders can use WARNORDs to direct troop movements before they issue the OPORD.

Complete Task Organization

During preparation, commanders complete task-organizing their force to obtain the right mix of capabilities to accomplish a specific mission. The commander may direct task organization to occur immediately before the OPORD is issued. This task-organizing is done with a WARNORD. Doing this gives units more time to execute the tasks needed to affect the new task organization. Task-organizing early allows affected units to become better integrated and more familiar with all elements involved. This is especially important with inherently time-consuming tasks, such as planning technical network support for the organization.

See pp. 4-7 to -14 for further discussion.

Integrate New Units and Soldiers

Commanders, command sergeants major, and staffs help assimilate new units into the force and new Soldiers into their units. They also prepare new units and Soldiers in performing their duties properly and integrating into an upcoming operation smoothly. Integration for new Soldiers includes training on unit SOPs and mission-essential tasks for the operation. It also means orienting new Soldiers on their places and roles in the force and during the operation. This integration for units includes, but is not limited to—

- Receiving and introducing new units to the force and the AO.
- Exchanging SOPs.
- Conducting briefs and rehearsals.
- Establishing communications links.
- Exchanging liaison teams (if required).

Refer to TLS5: The Leader's SMARTbook, 5th Ed.

Train

Training prepares forces and Soldiers to conduct operations according to doctrine, SOPs, and the unit's mission. Training develops the teamwork, trust, and mutual understanding that commanders need to exercise mission command and that forces need to achieve unity of effort. Training does not stop when a unit deploys. If the unit is not conducting operations or recovering from operations, it is training. While deployed, unit training focuses on fundamental skills, current SOPs, and skills for a specific mission.

Refer to TLS5: The Leader's SMARTbook, 5th Ed.

Conduct Pre-Operations Checks and Inspections

Unit preparation includes completing pre-operations checks and inspections. These checks ensure units, Soldiers, and systems are as fully capable and ready to execute the mission as time and resources permit. The inspections ensure the force has the resources necessary to accomplish the mission. During pre-operations checks and inspections, leaders also check Soldiers' ability to perform crew drills that may not be directly related to the mission. Some examples of these include drills that respond to a vehicle rollover or an onboard fire.

Initiate Sustainment Preparation

Resupplying, maintaining, and issuing supplies or equipment are major activities during preparation. Repositioning of sustainment assets can also occur. During preparation, sustainment personnel at all levels take action to optimize means (force structure and resources) for supporting the commander's plan. These actions include, but are not limited to, identification and preparation of bases, coordinating for host-nation support, and improving lines of communications.

Refer to SMFLS4: The Sustainment & Multifunctional Logistics SMARTbook, 4th Ed.

Continued on next page

Preparation Activities (Cont.)

Ref: ADP 5-0, The Operations Process (Jul '19), pp. 3-1 to 3-5.

Continued from previous page

Initiate Network Preparations

During preparation, units must tailor the information network to meet the specific needs of each operation. This includes not only the communications, but also how the commander expects information to move between and be available for units and leaders in an AO.

Manage Terrain

Terrain management includes allocating terrain by establishing AOs, designating assembly areas, and specifying locations for units. Terrain management is an important activity during preparation as units reposition and stage prior to execution. Commanders assigned an AO manage terrain within their boundaries. Through terrain management, commanders identify and locate units in the area. The operations officer, with support from others in the staff, can then de-conflict operations, control movements, and deter fratricide as units get in position to execute planned missions. Commanders also consider unified action partners located in their AO and coordinate with them for the use of terrain.

Prepare Terrain

Commanders must understand the terrain and the infrastructure of their AO as early as possible to identify potential for improvement, establish priorities of work, and begin preparing the area. Terrain preparation involves shaping the terrain to gain an advantage, such as building fighting and protective positions, improving cover and concealment, and reinforcing obstacles. Engineer units are critical in assisting units in preparing terrain to include building and maintaining roads, trails, airfields, and bases camps prior to and during operations. (Refer to FM 3-34 for a detailed discussion of engineer operations.)

Conduct Confirmation Briefs

A confirmation brief is a brief subordinate leaders give to the higher commander immediately after the operation order is given to confirm understanding. It is their understanding of the higher commander's intent, their specific tasks, and the relationship between their mission and the other units' missions in the operation. The confirmation brief is a tool used to ensure subordinate leaders understand—

- The commander's intent, mission, and concept of operations.
- Their unit's tasks and associated purposes.
- The relationship between their unit's mission and those of other units in the operation.

Continued from previous page

Conduct Rehearsals

A rehearsal is a session in which the commander and staff or unit practices expected actions to improve performance during execution. Commanders use rehearsals to ensure staffs and subordinates understand the concept of operations and commander's intent. Rehearsals also allow leaders to practice synchronizing operations at times and places critical to mission accomplishment. Effective rehearsals imprint a mental picture of the sequence of the operation's key actions and improve mutual understanding among subordinate and supporting units and leaders. The extent of rehearsals depends on available time. In cases of short-notice requirements, detailed rehearsals may not be possible. In these instances, subordinate leaders backbrief their higher commander on how they intend to accomplish the mission. Leaders conduct rehearsals to—

- Practice essential tasks.
- Identify weaknesses or problems in the plan.
- Coordinate subordinate element actions.

- Improve Soldier understanding of the concept of operations.
- Foster confidence among Soldiers.

See pp. 6-1 to 6-12 for further discussion.

Conduct Plans-to-Operations Transition

The plans-to-operations transition is a preparation activity that occurs within the headquarters. It_ ensures members of the current operations integration cell fully understand the plan before execution. During_ preparation, the responsibility for maintaining the plan shifts from the plans (or future operations integrating_ cell for division and above headquarters) integrating cell to the current operations integration cell (see_ figure 3-1). This transition is the point at which the current operations integration cell becomes responsible for short-term planning and controlling execution of the OPORD. This responsibility includes answering requests for information concerning the order and maintaining the order through FRAGORDs._This transition enables the plans and future operations integrating cells to focus their planning efforts on_ sequels, branches,_and other planning requirements directed by the commander.

See p. 2-56 for further discussion.

The timing of the plans-to-operations transition requires careful consideration. It must allow enough time for members of the current operations integration cell to understand the plan well enough to coordinate and synchronize its execution. Ideally, the plans or future operations cell briefs members of the current operations integration cell on the transition before the combined arms rehearsal. This brief enables members of the current operations integration cell to understand the upcoming operation as well as identify friction points and issues to solve prior to its execution. The transition brief is a mission brief that generally follows the five-paragraph OPORD format. Additional areas addressed, include—

- Decision support products (execution matrixes, decision support templates, decision support matrixes, and risk assessment matrixes).
- Known friction points.
- Branches and sequels under considerations.
- Outstanding requests for information and issues.

Following the combined arms rehearsal, planners and members of the current operations integration cell review additional planning guidance issued by the commander and modify the plan as necessary. Significant changes may require assistance from the plans cell to include moving a lead planner to the current operations integration cell. The plans cell continues planning for branches and sequels.

Revise and Refine the Plan

Revising and refining the plan is a key activity of preparation. During preparation, assumptions made during planning may be proven true or false. Intelligence analysis and reconnaissance may confirm or deny enemy actions or show changed conditions in the AO because of shaping operations. The status of friendly forces may change as the situation changes. Rehearsals may identify coordination issues or other problems needing adjusted. In any of these cases, commanders identify the changed conditions, refine the plan, and issue FRAGORDs.

Supervise

When leaders supervise, they check details critical to effective preparation. Leaders monitor and supervise activities to ensure the unit is ready for the mission. Leaders supervise subordinates and inspect their personnel and equipment. Rehearsals allow leaders to assess their subordinates' preparations. They may identify areas that require more supervision.

II. Fundamentals of Preparation

Ref: ADP 5-0, The Operations Process (Jul '19), pp. 3-1 to 3-2.

Preparation helps the force transition from planning to execution. Preparation normally begins during planning and continues into execution by uncommitted units. Like the other activities of the operations process, commanders drive preparation activities with a focus on leading and assessing. The functions of preparation include the following:

Improve Situational Understanding

Developing and maintaining situational understanding requires continuous effort throughout the operations process as discussed in chapter 1. During preparation, commanders continue to improve their understanding of a situation. They realize that the initial understanding developed during planning may be neither accurate nor complete. As such, commanders strive to validate assumptions and improve their situational understanding as they prepare for operations. Information collection helps leaders better understand the enemy, terrain, and civil considerations. Inspections, rehearsals, and liaison help leaders improve their understanding of the friendly force. Based on new information gained from various preparation activities, commanders refine the plan prior to execution.

Develop a Common Understanding of the Plan

A successful transition from planning to execution requires those charged with executing the order to understand the plan fully. The transition between planning and execution takes place both internally in the headquarters and externally between the commander and subordinate commanders. Several preparation activities help leaders develop a common understanding of the plan. Confirmation briefs, rehearsals, and the plans-to-operations transition brief help improve understanding of the concept of operations, control measures, decision points, and command and support relationships. They assist the force with understanding the plan prior to execution.

Train and Become Proficient on Critical Tasks

Units train to become proficient in those tasks critical to success for a specific operation. Commanders issue guidance about which tasks to train on and rehearse. They emphasize training that incorporates attached units to ensure they are integrated and to mitigate interoperability challenges prior to execution. Commanders also allocate time during preparation for units and Soldiers to train on unfamiliar tasks prior to execution. For example, a unit unfamiliar with a wet-gap crossing requires significant training and familiarization on employing small boats. Leaders also allocate time for attaining and maintaining proficiency on individual Soldier skills.

Task-Organize and Integrate the Force

Task-organizing the force is an important part of planning. During preparation, commanders allocate time to put the new task organization into effect. This includes detaching units, moving forces, and receiving and integrating new units and Soldiers into the force. When units change task organization, they need preparation time to learn the gaining unit's SOPs and learn their role in the gaining unit's plan. The gaining unit needs preparation time to assess the new unit's capabilities and limitations and to integrate new capabilities. Properly integrating units and Soldiers into the force builds trust and improves performance in execution.

Ensure Forces and Resources are Positioned

Effective preparation ensures the right forces are in the right place at the right time with the right equipment and other resources ready to execute the operation. Concurrent with task organization, commanders use troop movement to position or reposition forces to the correct locations prior to execution. This includes positioning sustainment units and supplies. Pre-operations checks confirm that the force has the proper and functional equipment before execution.

Chap 1

(The Operations Process) C. Execution

Ref: ADP 5-0, The Operations Process (Jul '19), chap. 4.

Execution is the act of putting a plan into action by applying combat power to accomplish the mission and adjusting operations based on changes in the situation. In execution, commanders, staffs, and subordinate commanders focus their efforts on translating decisions into actions. They direct action to apply combat power at decisive points and times to achieve objectives and accomplish missions. Inherent in execution is deciding whether to execute planned actions (such as phases, branches, and sequels) or to modify the plan based on unforeseen opportunities or threats.

Commanders fight the enemy, not the plan. Moltke's dictum above, rather than condemning the value of planning, reminds commanders, staffs, and subordinate unit leaders the proper relationship between planning and execution. A plan provides a reasonably forecast of execution. However, it remains a starting point, not an exact script to follow. As General George S. Patton, Jr. cautioned, "...one makes plans to fit circumstances and does not try to create circumstances to fit plans."

During execution, the situation may change rapidly. Operations the commander envisioned in the plan may bear little resemblance to actual events in execution. Subordinate commanders need maximum latitude to take advantage of situations and meet the higher commander's intent when the original order no longer applies. Effective execution requires leaders trained in independent decision making, aggressiveness, and risk taking in an environment of mission command.

I. Guides to Effective Execution

Execution is a concerted effort to seize and retain the initiative, maintain momentum, and exploit success. Initiative is fundamental to success in any operation, yet simply seizing the initiative is not enough. A sudden barrage of precision munitions may surprise and disorganize the enemy, but if not followed by swift and relentless action, the friendly advantage diminishes and disappears. Successful operations maintain the momentum generated by initiative and exploit successes within the commander's intent. Guides to effective execution include—

- Seize and retain the initiative.
- Build and maintain momentum.
- Exploit success.

A. Seize and Retain the Initiative

Operationally, initiative is setting or dictating the terms of action during operations. Army forces do this by forcing the enemy to respond to friendly actions. By presenting the enemy with multiple cross-domain dilemmas, commanders force the enemy to react continuously until the enemy is finally driven into untenable positions. Seizing the initiative pressures enemy commanders into abandoning their preferred options and making costly mistakes. As enemy mistakes occur, friendly forces apply continuous pressure to prevent the enemy from recovering. These actions enable friendly forces to seize opportunities and create new avenues for an exploitation.

Seizing the initiative ultimately results from forcing an enemy reaction. Commanders identify times and places where they can mass the effects of combat power to relative advantage. To compel a reaction, they threaten something the enemy cares about such as its center of gravity or decisive points leading to it. By forcing the enemy to react, commanders initiate an action-to-reaction sequence that ultimately reduces enemy options to zero. Each action develops the situation further and reduces the number of possibilities to be considered, thereby reducing friendly uncertainty. Each time the enemy must react, its uncertainty increases. Developing the situation by forcing the enemy to react is the essence of seizing the initiative.

Retaining the initiative involves applying unrelenting pressure on the enemy. Commanders do this by synchronizing the warfighting functions to present enemy commanders with continuously changing combinations of combat power at a tempo they cannot effectively counter. Commanders and staffs use information collection assets to identify enemy attempts to regain the initiative. During execution, commanders create a seamless, uninterrupted series of actions that forces enemies to react immediately and does not allow them to regain synchronization. Ideally, these actions present enemies with multiple dilemmas, the solutions to any one of which increases the enemy's vulnerability to other elements of combat power.

Take Action

Commanders and their subordinate leaders create conditions for seizing the initiative with action. Without action, seizing the initiative is impossible. Faced with an uncertain situation, there is a natural tendency to hesitate and gather more information to reduce the uncertainty. Although waiting and gathering information might reduce uncertainty, such inaction will not eliminate it. Waiting may even increase uncertainty by providing the enemy with time to seize the initiative. Effective leaders can manage uncertainty by acting and developing the situation. When the immediate situation is unclear, commanders clarify it by action, not by sitting and gathering information.

Create and Exploit Opportunities

Events that offer better ways to success are opportunities. Commanders recognize opportunities by continuously monitoring and evaluating the situation. Failure to understand the opportunities inherent in an enemy's action can surrender the initiative. CCIRs must include information requirements that support exploiting opportunities. Commanders encourage subordinates to act within the commander's intent as opportunities occur. Shared understanding of the commander's intent creates an atmosphere conducive to subordinates exercising initiative.

Accept Risk

Uncertainty and risk are inherent in all military operations. Recognizing and acting on opportunity means taking risks. Reasonably estimating and intentionally accepting risk is not gambling. Carefully determining the risks, analyzing and minimizing as many hazards as possible, and executing a plan that accounts for those hazards contributes to successfully applying military force. Gambling, in contrast, is imprudently staking the success of an entire action on a single, improbable event. Commanders assess risk by answering three questions:

- Am I minimizing the risk of friendly losses?
- Am I risking the success of the operation?
- Am I minimizing the risk of civilian casualties and collateral damage?

When commanders embrace opportunity, they accept risk. It is counterproductive to wait for perfect preparation and synchronization. The time taken to fully synchronize forces and warfighting functions in a detailed order could mean a lost opportunity. It is far better to quickly summarize the essentials, get things moving, and send the details later. Leaders optimize the use of time with WARNORDs, FRAGORDs, and verbal updates.

Commanders exercise the art of command when deciding how much risk to accept. As shown in figure 4-1, the commander has several techniques available to reduce the risk associated in a specific operation.

See facing page.

Risk Reduction Factors

Ref: ADP 5-0, The Operations Process (Jul '19), pp. 4-2 to 4-3.

Uncertainty and risk are inherent in all military operations. Recognizing and acting on opportunity means taking risks. Reasonably estimating and intentionally accepting risk is not gambling. Carefully determining the risks, analyzing and minimizing as many hazards as possible, and executing a plan that accounts for those hazards contributes to successfully applying military force. Gambling, in contrast, is imprudently staking the success of an entire action on a single, improbable event. Commanders assess risk by answering three questions:

- Am I minimizing the risk of friendly losses?
- Am I risking the success of the operation?
- Am I minimizing the risk of civilian casualties and collateral damage?

When commanders embrace opportunity, they accept risk. It is counterproductive to wait for perfect preparation and synchronization. The time taken to fully synchronize forces and warfighting functions in a detailed order could mean a lost opportunity. It is far better to quickly summarize the essentials, get things moving, and send the details later. Leaders optimize the use of time with WARNORDs, FRAGORDs, and verbal updates.

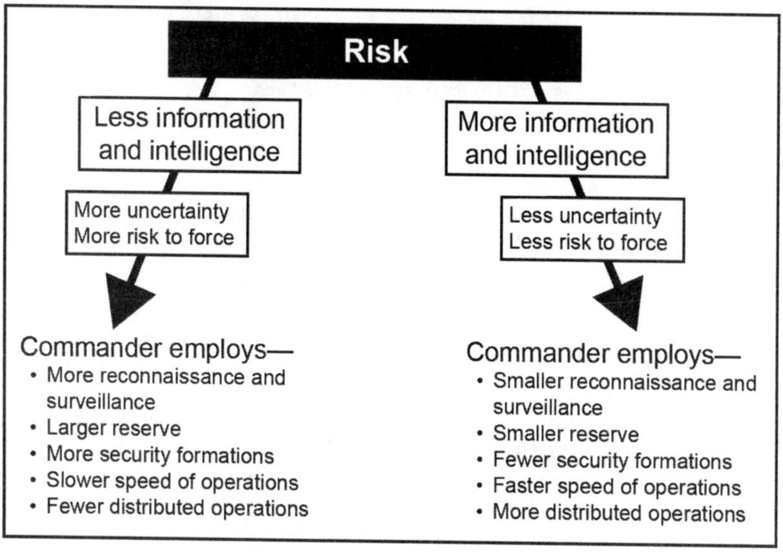

Ref: ADP 5-0, fig. 4-1. Risk reduction factors.

Commanders exercise the art of command when deciding how much risk to accept. As shown above in figure 4-1, the commander has several techniques available to reduce the risk associated in a specific operation. Some techniques for reducing risk take resources from the decisive operation, which reduces the concentration of effects at the decisive point.

See pp. 3-71 to 3-74 for discussion of risk management (from ATP 5-19) as an integrating process. Refer to ADP 3-90 for a detailed discussion of the art of tactics and risk reduction.

B. Build and Maintain Momentum

Momentum comes from seizing the initiative and executing decisive, shaping, and sustaining operations at a rapid and sustainable tempo. Momentum allows commanders to create opportunities to engage the enemy from unexpected directions with unanticipated capabilities. Having seized the initiative, commanders continue to control the relative momentum by maintaining focus and pressure and controlling the tempo. They ensure that they maintain momentum by anticipating transitions and moving rapidly between types of operations.

Speed promotes surprise and can compensate for lack of forces. It magnifies the impact of success in seizing the initiative. By executing at a rapid tempo, Army forces present the enemy with new problems before it can solve current ones. Rapid tempo should not degenerate into haste. Ill-informed and hasty action usually precludes effective combinations of combat power; it may lead to unnecessary casualties.

The condition of the enemy force dictates the degree of synchronization necessary. When confronted by a coherent and disciplined enemy, commanders may slow the tempo to deliver synchronized attacks. As the enemy force loses cohesion, commanders increase the tempo, seeking to accelerate the enemy's morale and physical collapse.

C. Exploit Success

Ultimately, only successes that achieve the end state count. To determine how to exploit tactical and operational successes, commanders assess them in terms of the higher commander's intent. However, success will likely occur in ways unanticipated in the plan. Commanders may gain an objective in an unexpected way. Success signals a rapid assessment to answer these questions:

- Does the success generate opportunities that more easily accomplish the objectives?
- Does it suggest other lines of operations or lines of effort?
- Does it cause commanders to change their overall intent?
- Should the force transition to a sequel?
- Should the force accelerate the phasing of the operation?

An exploitation demands assessment and understanding of the impact on sustaining operations. Sustainment provides the means to exploit success and convert it into decisive results. Sustainment preserves the freedom of action necessary to take advantage of opportunity. Commanders remain fully aware of the status of units and anticipate sustainment requirements; they recognize that sustainment often determines the depth to which Army forces exploit success.

II. Responsibilities during Execution

Ref: ADP 5-0, The Operations Process (Jul '19), pp. 4-4 to 4-5.

During execution, commanders focus their activities on directing, assessing, and leading while improving their understanding and modifying their visualization. Initially, commanders direct the transition from planning to execution as the order is issued and the responsibility for integration passes from the plans cell to the current operations integration cell. During execution, the staff directs units, within delegated authority, to keep the operation progressing successfully. Assessing allows the commander and staff to determine the existence and significance of variances from the operations as envisioned in the initial plan. The staff makes recommendations to the commander about what action to take concerning identified variances in the plan. During execution, leading is as important as decision making, since commanders influence subordinates by providing purpose, direction, and motivation.

Commanders, Seconds in Command, and Command Sergeants Major

During execution, commanders locate where they can best exercise command and sense the operations. Sometimes this is at the command post. Other times, it is forward with a command group. Effective commanders balance the need to make personal observations, provide command presence, and sense the mood of subordinates from forward locations with their ability to maintain command and control continuity with the entire force. No matter where they are located, commanders are always looking beyond the current operation to anticipate the next operation.

Seconds in command (deputy commanders, executive officers) are a key command resource during execution. First, they can serve as senior advisors to their commander. Second, they may oversee a specific warfighting function (for example, sustainment). Finally, they can command a specific operation (such as a gap crossing), area, or part of the unit (such as the covering force) for the commander.

The command sergeant major provides another set of senior eyes to assist the commander. The command sergeant major assists the commander with assessing operations as well as assessing the condition and morale of forces. In addition, the command sergeant major provides leadership and expertise to units and Soldiers at critical locations and times during execution.

Staff

The chief of staff or executive officer is the commander's principal assistant for directing, coordinating, and supervising the staff. During execution, the chief of staff or executive officer must anticipate events and integrate the efforts of the whole staff to ensure operations are proceeding in accordance with the commander's intent and visualization. The chief of staff or executive officer assists the commander with coordinating efforts among the plans, future operations, and current operations integration cells.

In execution, the staff—primarily through the current operations integration cell—integrates forces and warfighting functions to accomplish the mission. The current operations integration cell is the integrating cell in the command post with primary responsibility for coordinating and directing execution. Staff members in the current operations integration cell actively assist the commander and subordinate units in controlling the current operation. They provide information, synchronize staff and subordinate unit or echelon activities, and coordinate support requests from subordinates. The current operations integration cell solves problems and acts within the authority delegated by the commander. It also performs some short-range planning using the rapid decision-making and synchronization process.

III. Execution Activities

Ref: ADP 5-0, The Operations Process (Jul '19), pp. 4-5 to 4-9.

Execution entails putting the plan into action, and adjusting the plan based on changing circumstances. Friction and uncertainty, especially enemy actions, dynamically affect plans. An accurate situational understanding that accounts for new realties that affect plans provides the basis for commanders to exploit opportunities or counter threats. Major activities of execution include—

A. Assessment

During execution, assessment helps commanders visualize probable outcomes and determine whether they need to change the plan to accomplish the mission, take advantage of opportunities, or react to unexpected threats. Assessment includes both monitoring the situation and evaluating progress. Monitoring—the continuous observation of those conditions relevant to the current operation—allows commanders and staffs to improve their understanding of the situation. Evaluation—using indicators to measure change in the situation and judge progress—allows commanders to identify variances, their significance, and if a decision is required to alter the plan.

A variance is a difference between the actual situation during an operation and the forecasted plan for the situation at that time or event. A variance can be categorized as an opportunity or threat as shown with the vertical lines in figure 4-2. The first form of variance is an opportunity to accomplish the mission more effectively. Opportunities result from forecasted or unexpected success. When commanders recognize an opportunity, they alter the order to exploit it if the change achieves the end state more effectively or efficiently. The second form of variance is a threat to mission accomplishment or survival of the force. When recognizing a threat, the commander adjusts the order to eliminate the enemy advantage, restore the friendly advantage, and regain the initiative.

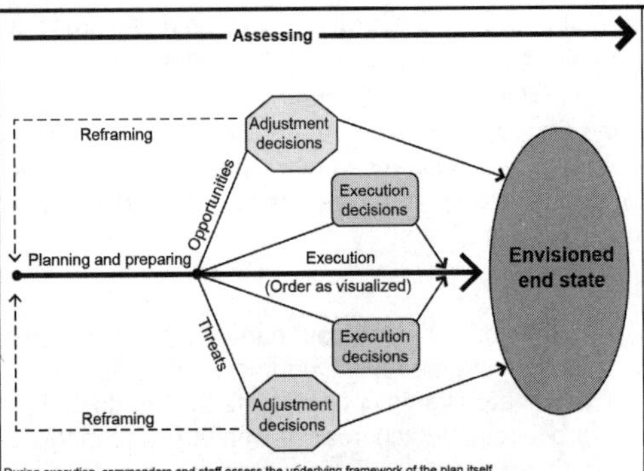

During execution, commanders and staff assess the underlying framework of the plan itself. This involves reexamining the original operational approach and determining if it is still relevant to the situation.

B. Decisionmaking

When operations are progressing satisfactorily, variances are minor and within acceptable levels. Commanders who make this evaluation—explicitly or implicitly—allow operations to continue according to the plan. Plans usually identify some decision points; however, unexpected enemy actions or other changes often present situations that require unanticipated decisions. Commanders act when these decisions are required. As commanders assess the operation, they describe their impressions to staffs and subordinates and then discuss the desirability of choices available. Once commanders make decisions, their staffs transmit the necessary directives, normally in a FRAGORD. Decisions made during execution are either **execution decisions** or **adjustment decisions** *(facing page)* as shown in figure 4-2's lightly shaded boxes above.

Execution Decisions

Execution decisions implement a planned action under circumstances anticipated in the order such as changing a boundary, committing the reserve, or executing a branch plan. In their most basic form, execution decisions are decisions the commander foresees and identifies for execution during an operation. Commanders are responsible for those decisions but may direct the chief of staff, executive officer, or staff officer to supervise implementation. The current operations integration cell oversees the synchronization and integration needed to implement execution decisions.

Adjustment Decisions

Adjustment decisions modify the operation to respond to unanticipated opportunities and threats. They often require implementing unanticipated operations and resynchronizing the warfighting functions. Commanders make these decisions, delegating implementing authority only after directing the major change themselves. Adjustments may take one of three forms: reallocating resources, changing the concept of operations, or changing the mission.

	Decision types	Actions
Execution decisions	Minor variances from the plan Operation proceeding according to plan. Variances are within acceptable limits.	To execute planned actions • Commander or designee decides which planned actions best meet the situation and directs their execution. • Staff issues fragmentary order. • Staff completes follow-up actions.
Execution decisions	Anticipated situation Operation encountering variances within the limits for one or more branches or sequels anticipated in the plan.	To execute a branch or sequel • Commander or staff reviews branch or sequel plan. • Commander receives assessments and recommendations for modifications to the plan, determines the time available to refine it, and either issues guidance for further actions or directs execution of a branch or sequel. • Staff issues fragmentary order. • Staff completes follow-up actions.
Adjustment decisions	Unanticipated situation —friendly success Significant, unanticipated positive variances result in opportunities to achieve the end state in ways that differ significantly from the plan.	To make an adjustment decision • Commander recognizes the opportunity or threat and determines time available for decision making. • Commander selects a decision-making method. If there is not enough time for a complete military decision-making process, the commander may direct a single course of action or conduct the rapid decision-making and synchronization process with select staff members. • Depending on time available, commanders may issue verbal fragmentary orders to subordinates followed by a written fragmentary order to counter the threat or exploit an opportunity. • In rare situations, commanders may reframe the problem, change the mission, and develop an entirely new plan to address significant changes in the situation.
Adjustment decisions	Unanticipated situation —enemy threat Significant, unanticipated negative variances impede mission accomplishment.	

Several decision support tools assist the commander and staff during execution. See p. 1-64 for an overview and further discussion of the DST and execution matrix.

C. Directing Action

To implement execution or adjustment decisions, commanders direct actions that apply combat power. Based on the commander's decision and guidance, the staff resynchronizes the operation to mass the maximum effects of combat power to seize, retain, and exploit the initiative. This involves synchronizing the operations in time, space, and purpose and issuing directives to subordinates. When modifying the plan, commander and staffs seek to make the fewest changes possible and facilitate future operations.

IV. Rapid Decisionmaking and Synchronization Process (RDSP)

Ref: FM 6-0 (C2), Commander and Staff Organization and Operations (Apr '16), pp. 14-3 to 14-8.

The rapid decisionmaking and synchronization process is a technique that commanders and staffs commonly use during execution. While identified here with a specific name and method, the approach is not new; its use in the Army is well established. Commanders and staffs develop this capability through training and practice. When using this technique, the following considerations apply: rapid is often more important than process, much of it may be mental rather than written, and it should become a battle drill for the current operations integration cells, future operations cells, or both.

While the military decisionmaking process (MDMP) seeks the optimal solution, the rapid decisionmaking and synchronization process seeks a timely and effective solution within the commander's intent, mission, and concept of operations. Using the rapid decisionmaking and synchronization process lets leaders avoid the time-consuming requirements of developing decision criteria and comparing courses of action (COAs). Operational and mission variables continually change during execution. This often invalidates or weakens COAs and decision criteria before leaders can make a decision. Under the rapid decisionmaking and synchronization process, leaders combine their experience and intuition to quickly reach situational understanding. Based on this, they develop and refine workable COAs.

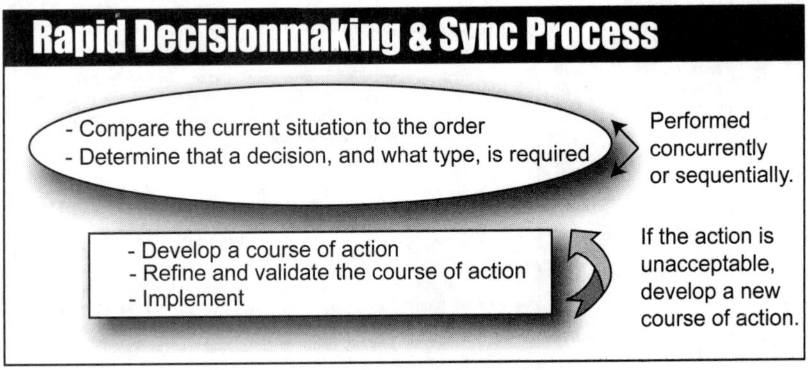

Rapid Decisionmaking & Sync Process
- Compare the current situation to the order
- Determine that a decision, and what type, is required
Performed concurrently or sequentially.
- Develop a course of action
- Refine and validate the course of action
- Implement
If the action is unacceptable, develop a new course of action.

A. Compare the Current Situation to the Order

Commanders and staffs identify likely variances during planning and identify options that will be present and actions that will be available when each variance occurs. During execution, commanders and staffs monitor the situation to identify changes in conditions. Then they ask if these changes affect the overall conduct of operations or their part in them and if the changes are significant. Finally, they identify if the changed conditions represent variances from the order—especially opportunities and risks. Staff members use running estimates to look for indicators of variances that affect their areas of expertise.

When performing the rapid decisionmaking and synchronization process, the current operations integration cell first compares the current situation to the one envisioned in the order. It may obtain assistance from the assessment section or the red team section in this analysis. If the situation requires greater analysis, the chief of staff or executive officer (COS [XO]) may task the future operations cell (where authorized) or the plans cell to perform this analysis. At echelons with no future operations cell, the plans cell or the current operations integration cell performs this function.

See facing page for examples of change indicators (table 14-2).

Change Indicators

Types	Indicators	
General	• Answer to a commander's critical information requirement. • Identification of an information requirement. • Change in mission. • Change in organization of unit. • Change in leadership of unit. • Signing or implementation of peace treaty or other key political arrangement.	• Change in capabilities of subordinate unit. • Change in role of host-nation military force. • Climate changes or natural disasters impacting on the population, agriculture, industry. • Upcoming local election. • Changes in key civilian leadership.
Intelligence	• Identification of enemy main effort. • Identification of enemy reserves or counterattack. • Indications of unexpected enemy action or preparation. • Increase in enemy solicitation of civilians for intelligence operations. • Identification of an information requirement. • Insertion of manned surveillance teams. • Disruption of primary and secondary education system. • Unexplained disappearance of key members of intelligence community.	• Enemy electronic attack use. • Indicators of illicit economic activity. • Identification of threats from within the population. • Increased unemployment within the population. • Interference with freedom of religious worship. • Identification of high-value targets. • Unmanned aircraft system launch. • Answer to a priority intelligence requirement. • Enemy rotary-wing or unmanned aircraft system use.
Movement and Maneuver	• Success or failure in breaching or gap crossing operations. • Capture of significant numbers of enemy prisoners of war, enemy command posts, supply points, or artillery units. • Establishment of road blocks along major traffic routes. • Unexplained displacement of neighborhoods within a given sector.	• Success or failure of a subordinate unit task. • Modification of an airspace control measure. • Numbers of dislocated civilians sufficient to affect friendly operations. • Damages to civilian infrastructure affecting friendly mobility. • Loss of one or more critical transportation systems.
Fires	• Receipt of an air tasking order. • Battle damage assessment results. • Unplanned repositioning of firing units. • Identification of high-payoff targets. • Identification of an information requirement.	• Execution of planned fires. • Modification of a fire support coordination measure. • Effective enemy counterfire. • Negative effects of fires on civilians. • Destruction of any place of worship by friendly fire.
Protection	• Chemical, biological, radiological, nuclear report or other indicators of enemy chemical, biological, radiological, nuclear use. • Report or other indicators of enemy improvised explosive device use. • Indicators of coordinated enemy actions against civilians or friendly forces. • Increased criminal activity in a given sector. • Increase in organized protests or riots.	• Identification of threats to communications or computer systems. • Reports of enemy targeting critical host-nation infrastructure. • Identification of threat to base or sustainment facilities. • Escalation of force incidents. • Loss of border security.
Sustainment	• Significant loss of capability in any class of supply. • Opening or closing of civilian businesses within a given area. • Identification of significant incidences of disease and nonbattle injury casualties. • Closing of major financial institutions. • Mass casualties. • Receipt of significant resupply. • Disruption of one or more essential civil services (such as water or electricity). • Contact on a supply route. • Answer to a friendly force information requirement. • Mass detainees.	• Degradations to essential civilian infrastructure by threat actions. • Civilian mass casualty event beyond capability of host-nation resources. • Identification of significant shortage in any class of supply. • Outbreak of epidemic or famine within the civilian population. • Medical evacuation launch. • Dislocated civilian event beyond capability of host-nation resources. • Disruption of key logistics lines of communication. • Changes in availability of host-nation support.
Mission Command	• Impending changes in key military leadership. • Interference with freedom of the press or news media. • Receipt of a fragmentary order or warning order from higher headquarters.	• Effective adversary information efforts on civilians. • Loss of civilian communications nodes. • Loss of contact with a command post or commander. • Jamming or interference.

Ref: FM 6-0 (C2), Commander and Staff Organization and Operations (Apr '16), table 14-2.

Continued on next page

Continued on next page

Continued from previous page

B. Determine the Type of Decision Required

When a variance is identified, the commander directs action while the chief of operations leads chiefs of the current operations integration cell and selected functional cells in quickly comparing the current situation to the expected situation. This assessment accomplishes the following:

- Describes the variance
- Determines if the variance provides a significant opportunity or threat and examines the potential of either
- Determines if a decision is needed by identifying if the variance:
- Indicates an opportunity that can be exploited to accomplish the mission faster or with fewer resources Directly threatens the decisive operation's success
- Threatens a shaping operation such that it may threaten the decisive operation directly or in the near future
- Can be addressed within the commander's intent and concept of operations. (If so, determine what execution decision is needed.)
- Requires changing the concept of operations substantially (If so, determine what adjustment decision or new approach will best suit the circumstances.)

For minor variances, the chief of operations works with other cell chiefs to determine whether changes to control measures are needed. If so, they determine how those changes affect other warfighting functions. They direct changes within their authority (execution decisions) and notify the COS (XO) and the affected command post cells and staff elements.

Commanders intervene directly in cases that affect the overall direction of the unit. They describe the situation, direct their subordinates to provide any additional information they need, and order either implementation of planned responses or development of an order to redirect the force.

C. Develop a Course of Action

If the variance requires an adjustment decision, the designated integrating cell and affected command post cell chiefs recommend implementation of a COA or obtain the commander's guidance for developing one. They use the following conditions to screen possible COAs:

- Mission
- Commander's intent
- Current dispositions and freedom of action
- CCIRs
- Limiting factors, such as supply constraints, boundaries, and combat strength

The new options must conform to the commander's intent. Possible COAs may alter the concept of operations and CCIRs, if they remain within the commander's intent. However, the commander approves changes to the CCIRs. Functional cell chiefs and other staff section leaders identify areas that may be affected within their areas of expertise by proposed changes to the order or mission. The commander is as likely as anyone else to detect the need for change and to sketch out the options. Whether the commander, COS (XO), or chief of operations does this, the future operations cell is often directed to further develop the concept and draft the order. The chief of operations and the current operations integration cell normally lead this effort, especially if the response is needed promptly or the situation is not complex. The commander or COS (XO) is usually the decision-making authority, depending on the commander's delegation of authority.

Commanders normally direct the future operations cell or the current operations integration cell to prepare a fragmentary order (FRAGORD) setting conditions for executing a new COA. When lacking time to perform the MDMP, or quickness of action is desirable, commanders make an immediate adjustment decision—using intuitive decisionmaking—in the form of a focused COA

Continued from previous page

D. Refine and Validate the Course of Action

Once commanders describe the new COA, the current operations integration cell conducts an analysis to validate its feasibility, suitability, and acceptability. If acceptable, the COA is refined to resynchronize the war fighting functions enough to generate and apply the needed combat power. Staffs with a future operations cell may assign that cell responsibility for developing the details of the new COA and drafting a fragmentary order to implement it. The commander or COS (XO) may direct an "on-call" operations synchronization meeting to perform this task and ensure rapid resynchronization.

Validation and refinement are done quickly. Normally, the commander and staff officers conduct a mental war game of the new COA. They consider potential enemy reactions, the unit's counteractions, and secondary effects that might affect the force's synchronization:

- Is the new COA feasible in terms of my area of expertise?
- How will this action affect my area of expertise?
- Does it require changing my information requirements?
  - Should any of the information requirements be nominated as a CCIR?
  - What actions within my area of expertise does this change require?
  - Will this COA require changing objectives or targets nominated by the staff section?
- What other command post cells and elements does this action affect?
- What are potential enemy reactions?
- What are the possible friendly counteractions?
  - Does this counteraction affect my area of expertise?
  - Will it require changing my information requirements?
  - Are any of my information requirements potential CCIRs?
  - What actions within my area of expertise does this counteraction require?
  - Will it require changing objectives or targets nominated by the staff section?
  - What other command post cells and elements does this counteraction affect?

The validation and refinement will show if the COA will acceptably solve the problem. If it does not, the COS or chief of operations modifies it through additional analysis or develops a new COA. The COS (XO) informs the commander of any changes made to the COA.

E. Implement

When a COA is acceptable, the COS (XO) recommends implementation to the commander or implements it directly, if the commander has delegated that authority. Implementation normally requires a fragmentary order; in exceptional circumstances, it may require a new operation order. That order changes the concept of operations (in adjustment decisions), resynchronizes the war fighting functions, and disseminates changes to control measures. The staff uses warning orders to alert subordinates to a pending change. The staff also establishes sufficient time for the unit to implement the change without losing integration or being exposed to unnecessary tactical risk.

Commanders often issue orders to subordinates verbally in situations requiring quick reactions. At battalion and higher levels, written fragmentary orders confirm verbal orders to ensure synchronization, integration, and notification of all parts of the force. If time permits, leaders verify that subordinates understand critical tasks. Methods for doing this include the confirmation brief and back brief. These are conducted both between commanders and within staff elements to ensure mutual understanding.

After the analysis is complete, the current operations integration cell and command post cell chiefs update decision support templates and synchronization matrixes. When time is available, the operations officer or chief of operations continues this analysis to the operation's end to complete combat power integration. Staff members begin the synchronization needed to implement the decision. This synchronization involves collaboration with other command post cells and subordinate staffs.

V. Decision-Making Tools

Ref: ADP 5-0, The Operations Process (Jul '19), pp. 4-7 to 4-8.

Several decision support tools assist the commander and staff during execution. Among the most important are the decision support template, decision support matrix, execution matrix, and execution checklist. The current operations integration cell uses these tools, among others, to help control operations and to determine when anticipated decisions are coming up for execution.

Decision Support Template (DST)

The decision support template depicts decision points, timelines associated with movement of forces and the flow of the operation, and other key items of information required to execute a specific friendly COA. Part of the decision support template is the decision support matrix—a written record of a war-gamed course of action that describes decision points and associated actions at those decision points. The decision support matrix lists decision points, locations of decision points, criteria to be evaluated at decision points, actions that occur at decision points, and the units responsible to act on the decision points.

See p. 3-51 for related discussion of the DST from ATP 2-01.3.

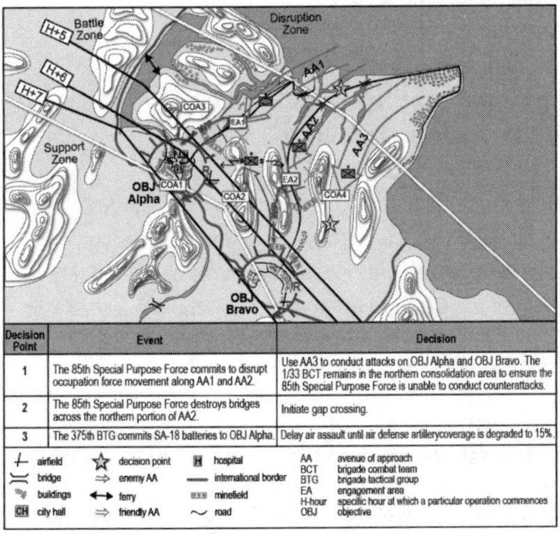

Decision Point	Event	Decision
1	The 85th Special Purpose Force commits to disrupt occupation force movement along AA1 and AA2.	Use AA3 to conduct attacks on OBJ Alpha and OBJ Bravo. The 1/33 BCT remains in the northern consolidation area to ensure the 85th Special Purpose Force is unable to conduct counterattacks.
2	The 85th Special Purpose Force destroys bridges across the northern portion of AA2.	Initiate gap crossing.
3	The 375th BTG commits SA-18 batteries to OBJ Alpha.	Delay air assault until air defense artillerycoverage is degraded to 15%.

airfield; decision point; hospital; AA avenue of approach
bridge; enemy AA; international border; BCT brigade combat team
buildings; ferry; minefield; BTG brigade tactical group
CH city hall; friendly AA; road; EA engagement area
H-hour specific hour at which a particular operation commences
OBJ objective

The DST provides the commander with a structured basis for deploying fires, maneuver, and jamming assets and for reducing the enemy's defensive capability with these assets. Simply stated, it provides commanders with the specific points on the battlefield where they will be required to make decisions regarding the employment of assets. These decisions can be keyed to phase lines, events on the ground, or to specific enemy actions. (ATP 2-01.3, fig. 6-14. DST and matrix example.)

Execution Matrix

An execution matrix is a visual representation of subordinate tasks in relationship to each other over time. An operation can have multiple execution matrices. An execution matrix can cover the entire force for the duration of an operation; a specific portion of an operation (such as an air assault execution matrix); or for a specific warfighting function (such as a fire support execution matrix). Commanders and staffs use the execution matrix to control, synchronize, and adjust operations as required. An execution checklist is a distillation of the execution matrix that list key actions sequentially, units responsible for the action, and an associated code word to quickly provide shared understanding among the commander, staff, and subordinate units on initiation or completion of the action.

See p. 3-51 for related discussion of the execution matrix from ATP 2-01.3.

Chap 1

(The Operations Process) D. Assessment

Ref: ADP 5-0, The Operations Process (Jul '19), chap. 5.

Assessment is the determination of the progress toward accomplishing a task, creating a condition, or achieving an objective (JP 3-0). Assessment is a continuous activity of the operations process that supports decision making by ascertaining progress of the operation for the purpose of developing and refining plans and for making operations more effective. Assessment results enhance the commander's decision making and help the commander and the staff to keep pace with constantly changing situations.

Assessment Process Activities

A Monitoring

B Evaluating

C Recommending or Directing Action

Assessment involves deliberately comparing intended outcomes with actual events to determine the overall effectiveness of force employment. More specifically, assessment helps the commander determine progress toward attaining the desired end state, achieving objectives, and performing tasks. Through professional military judgment, assessment helps answer the following questions:

- Where are we?
- What happened?
- Why do we think it happened?
- So what?
- What are the likely future opportunities and risks?
- What do we need to do?

Assessment precedes and guides the other activities of the operations process. During planning, assessment focuses on understanding an OE and building an assessment plan. During preparation, the focus of assessment switches to discerning changes in the situation and the force's readiness to execute operations. During execution, assessment involves deliberately comparing forecasted outcomes to actual events while using indicators to judge operational progress towards success. Assessment during execution helps commanders determine whether changes in the operation are necessary to take advantage of opportunities or to counter unexpected threats.

The situation and echelon dictate the focus and methods leaders use to assess. Assessment occurs at all echelons. Normally, commanders assess those specific operations or tasks that they were directed to accomplish. This properly focuses collection and assessment at each echelon, reduces redundancy, and enhances the efficiency of the overall assessment process.

I. Assessment Activities

Ref: ADP 5-0, The Operations Process (Jul '19), pp. 5-2 to 5-4.

The situation and type of operations affect the characteristics of assessment. During large-scale combat, assessment tends to be rapid, focused on the level of destruction of enemy units, terrain gained or lost, objectives secured, and the status of the friendly force to include sustainment. In other situations, such as counterinsurgency, assessment is less tangible. Assessing the level of security in an area or the level of the population's support for the government is challenging. Identifying what and how to assess requires significant effort from the commander and staff.

A. Monitoring

Monitoring is continuous observation of those conditions relevant to the current operation. Monitoring allows staffs to collect relevant information, specifically that information about the current situation described in the commander's intent and concept of operations. Commanders cannot judge progress nor make effective decisions without an accurate understanding of the current situation.

CCIRs and associated information requirements focus the staff's monitoring activities and prioritize the unit's collection efforts. Information requirements concerning the enemy, terrain and weather, and civil considerations are identified and assigned priorities through reconnaissance and surveillance. Operations officers use friendly reports to coordinate other assessment-related information requirements.

Staffs monitor and collect information from the common operational picture and friendly reports. This information includes operational and intelligence summaries from subordinate, higher, and adjacent headquarters and communications and reports from liaison teams. Staffs also identify information sources outside military channels and monitor their reports. These other channels might include products from civilian, host-nation, and other government agencies. Staffs apply information management and knowledge management to facilitate disseminating this information to the right people at the right time.

Staff sections record relevant information in running estimates. Staff sections maintain a continuous assessment of current operations as a basis to determine if operations are proceeding according to the commander's intent, mission, and concept of operations. In their running estimates, staff sections use this new information and these updated facts and assumptions as the basis for evaluation.

B. Evaluating

The staff analyzes relevant information collected through monitoring to evaluate the operation's progress. Evaluating is using indicators to judge progress toward desired conditions and determining why the current degree of progress exists. Evaluation is at the heart of the assessment process where most of the analysis occurs. Evaluation helps commanders determine what is working and what is not working, and it helps them gain insights into how to better accomplish the mission.

In the context of assessment, an indicator is a specific piece of information that infers the condition, state, or existence of something, and provides a reliable means to ascertain performance or effectiveness (JP 5-0). Indicators should be—

- **Relevant**—bear a direct relationship to a task, effect, object, or end state condition.
- **Observable**—collectable so that changes can be detected and measured or evaluated.
- **Responsive**—signify changes in the OE in time to enable effective decision making.
- **Resourced**—collection assets and staff resources are identified to observe and evaluate.

The two types of indicators commonly used in assessment include measures of performance (MOPs) and measures of effectiveness (MOEs):

Measure of Performance (MOPs)

A measure of performance is an indicator used to measure a friendly action that is tied to measuring task accomplishment (JP 5-0). MOPs help answer questions such as "Was the action taken?" or "Were the tasks completed to standard?" A MOP confirms or denies that a task has been properly performed. MOPs are commonly found and tracked at all levels in execution matrixes. MOPs help to answer the question "Are we doing things right?"

At the most basic level, every Soldier assigned a task maintains a formal or informal checklist to track task completion. The status of those tasks and subtasks are MOPs. Similarly, operations consist of a series of collective tasks sequenced in time, space, and purpose to accomplish missions. Current operations integration cells use MOPs in execution matrixes, checklists, and running estimates to track completed tasks. Staffs use MOPs as a primary element of battle tracking with a focus on the friendly force. Evaluating task accomplishment using MOPs is relatively straightforward and often results in a "yes" or "no" answer.

Measure of Effectiveness (MOEs)

A measure of effectiveness is an indicator used to measure a current system state, with change indicated by comparing multiple observations over time (JP 5-0). MOEs help measure changes in conditions, both positive and negative. MOEs help to answer the question "Are we doing the right things?" MOEs are commonly found and tracked in formal assessment plans.

Evaluation includes analysis of why progress is or is not being made. Commanders and staffs propose and consider possible causes. In particular, they address the question of whether or not changes in the situation can be attributed to friendly actions. Commanders consult subject matter experts, both internal and external to the staff, on whether their staffs have correctly identified the underlying causes for specific changes in the situation. These experts challenge key facts and assumptions identified in the planning process to determine if the facts and assumptions are still relevant or valid.

Evaluating also includes considering whether the desired conditions have changed, are no longer achievable, or are not achievable through the current operational approach. Staffs continually challenge the key assumptions made when framing the problem. When an assumption is invalidated, then reframing may be in order.

C. Recommending or Directing Action

Monitoring and evaluating are critical activities; however, assessment is incomplete without recommending or directing action. Assessment may reveal problems, but unless it results in recommended adjustments, its use to the commander is limited. Ideally, recommendations highlight ways to improve the effectiveness of operations and plans by informing all decisions.

Based on the evaluation of progress, the staff brainstorms possible improvements to the plan and makes preliminary judgments about the relative merit of those changes. Staff members identify those changes possessing sufficient merit and provide them as recommendations to the commander or make adjustments within their delegated authority. Recommendations to the commander range from continuing the operation as planned, to executing a branch, or to making unanticipated adjustments. Making adjustments includes assigning new tasks to subordinates, reprioritizing support, adjusting information collection assets, and significantly modifying the COA. Commanders integrate recommendations from the staff, subordinate commanders, and other partners with their personal assessments. Using those recommendations, they decide if and how to modify the operation to better accomplish the mission. Assessment helps identify threats, suggests improvements to effectiveness, and reveals opportunities. The staff presents the results and conclusions of its assessments and recommendations to the commander as an operation develops.

II. Assessment Process

Ref: ADP 5-0, The Operations Process (Jul '19), pp. 5-4 to 5-6. Refer to ATP 5-0.3 for a detailed discussion of each step of the assessment process.

For units with a staff, assessment becomes more formal at each higher echelon. Assessment resources (to include staff officer expertise and time available) proportionally increase from battalion to brigade, division, corps, and theater army. The analytic resources and level of expertise of staffs available at higher echelon headquarters include a dedicated core group of analysts. This group specializes in operations research and systems analysis, formal assessment plans, and various assessment products. Division, corps, and theater army headquarters, for example, have dedicated plans, future operations, and current operations integration cells. They have larger intelligence staffs and more staff officers trained in operations research and systems analysis. Assessment at brigade echelon and lower is usually less formal, often relying on direct observations and the judgment of commanders and their staffs.

For small units (those without a staff), assessment is mostly informal. Small-unit leaders focus on assessing their unit's readiness—personnel, equipment, supplies, and morale—and their unit's ability to perform assigned tasks. Leaders also determine whether the unit has attained task proficiency. If those tasks have not produced the desired results, leaders explore why they have not and consider what improvements could be made for unit operations. As they assess and learn, small units change their tactics, techniques, and procedures based on their experiences. In this way, even the lowest echelons in the Army follow the assessment process.

There is no single way to conduct assessment. Every situation has its own distinctive challenges, making every assessment unique. The following steps can help guide the development of an effective assessment plan and assessment activities during preparation and execution:

Step 1 – Develop the Assessment Approach

Assessment begins in planning as the commander identifies the operation's end state, operational approach, and associated objectives and tasks. Concurrently, the staff begins to develop an assessment approach by identifying specific information needed to monitor and analyze conditions associated with attaining the operation's end state, achieving objectives, and accomplishing tasks. In doing so, the staff tries to answer the following questions:

- How will we know we are creating the desired conditions?
- What information do we need?
- Who is best postured to provide that information?

If a higher headquarters assessment plan exists, the staff aligns applicable elements of that assessment plan to the plan they are developing. The assessment approach becomes the framework for the assessment plan and will continue to mature through plan development. The assessment approach should identify the information and intelligence needed to assess progress and inform decision making.

Step 2 – Develop the Assessment Plan

This step overlaps Step 1. It focuses on developing a plan to monitor and collect necessary information and intelligence to inform decision making throughout execution. The assessment plan should link end state conditions, objectives, and tasks to observable key indicators. This plan also should include specific staff responsibilities to monitor, collect, and analyze information as well as develop recommendations and assessment products as required.

Step 3 – Collect Information

Staffs collect relevant information throughout planning and execution. They refine and adapt information collection requirements as the operations progresses. Staffs and subordinate commands provide information during execution through applicable battle rhythm events and reports. Intelligence staffs continually provide updates about the situation to include information about the enemy, terrain, and civil considerations.

Step 4 – Analyze Information and Intelligence

Analysis seeks to identify positive or negative movement toward achieving objectives or attaining end state conditions. Accurate analysis seeks to identify trends and changes that significantly impact the operation. Based on this analysis, the staff estimates the effects of force employment and resource allocation; determines whether forces have achieved their objectives; or realizes that a decision point has emerged.

Recommendations generated by staff analyses regarding achievement of the objective or attainment of the desired end state conditions, force employment, resource allocation, validity of planning assumptions, and decision points should enable the staff to develop recommendations for consideration. Recommendations can include the following:

- Update, change, add, or remove critical assumptions.
- Transition between phases.
- Execute branches or sequels.
- Change resource allocation.
- Adjust objectives or end state conditions.
- Change or add tasks to subordinate units.
- Adjust priorities.
- Change priorities of effort.
- Change command relationships.
- Change task organizations.
- Adjust decision points.
- Refine or adapt the assessment plan.

Step 5 – Communicate Feedback and Recommendations

Assessment products contain recommendations for the commander based upon the commander's guidance. Regardless of quality and effort, the assessment process is limited if the communication of its results is deficient or inconsistent with the commander's personal style of assimilating information and making decisions. Additionally, there may be a requirement to provide input to higher headquarters assessments in which the requirements and feedback could be within a different construct.

Step 6 – Adapt Plans or Operations

Commanders direct changes or provide additional guidance that dictate updates or modifications to operations to drive progress of operations to objectives and end state conditions. Staffs capture the commander's decisions and guidance to ensure forces take necessary actions. As the operation evolves, the assessment plan will evolve as well.

III. Guides to Effective Assessment

Ref: ADP 5-0, The Operations Process (Jul '19), pp. 5-6 to 5-8.

Throughout the conduct of operations, commanders integrate their own assessments with those of the staff, subordinate commanders, and other unified action partners in the AO. The following guides aid in effective assessment:

Commander Involvement

The commander's involvement in operation assessment is essential. The assessment plan should focus on the information and intelligence that directly support the commander's decision making. Commanders establish priorities for assessment in their planning guidance and CCIRs. By prioritizing the effort, commanders guide the staff's analysis efforts. Committing valuable time and energy to developing excessive and time-consuming assessment schemes squanders resources better devoted to other operations process activities. Commanders reject the tendency to measure something just because it is measurable. Effective commanders avoid burdening subordinates and staffs with overly detailed assessments and collection tasks. Generally, the echelon at which a specific operation, task, or action is conducted should be the echelon at which it is assessed.

Integration

Assessment requires integration. Assessing progress is the responsibility of all staff sections and not the purview of any one staff section or command post cell. Each staff section assesses the operation from its specific area of expertise. However, these staff sections must coordinate and integrate their individual assessments and associated recommendations across the warfighting functions to produce comprehensive assessments for the commander, particularly in protracted operations. They do this in the assessment working group.

Most assessment working groups are at higher echelons (division and above) and are more likely to be required in protracted operations. Normally, the frequency of meetings is part of a unit's battle rhythm. The staff, however, does not wait for a scheduled working group to inform the commander on issues that require immediate attention. Nor does the staff wait to take action in those areas within its delegated authority.

Developing an assessment plan occurs concurrently within the steps of the MDMP. The resulting assessment plan should support the command's battle rhythm. The frequency with which the assessment working group meets depends on the situation. Additionally, the assessment working group may present its findings and recommendations to the commander for decision. Subordinate commanders may participate and provide their assessments of operations and recommendations along with the staff. Commanders combine these assessments with their personal assessment, consider recommendations, and then direct changes to improve performance and better accomplish the mission.

Incorporation of the Logic of the Plan

Effective assessment relies on an accurate understanding of the logic (reasoning) used to build the plan. Each plan is built on assumptions and an operational approach. The reasons or logic as to why the commander believes the plan will produce the desired results become important considerations when staffs determine how to assess operations. Recording, understanding, and making this logic explicit helps the staffs recommend the appropriate MOEs and MOPs for assessing the operation.

Caution when Establishing Cause and Effect

Although establishing cause and effect is sometimes difficult, it is crucial to effective assessment. Sometimes, establishing causality between actions and their effects can be relatively straightforward, such as in observing a bomb destroy a bridge. In other instances, especially regarding changes in human behavior, attitudes, and perception, establishing links between cause and effect proves difficult. Commanders and staffs must guard against drawing erroneous conclusions in these instances.

Chap 2

The Military Decision-making Process (MDMP)

Ref: FM 6-0 (C2), Commander and Staff Organization and Operations (Apr '16), chap. 9.

The military decisionmaking process is an iterative planning methodology to understand the situation and mission develop a course of action, and produce an operation plan or order (ADP 5-0).

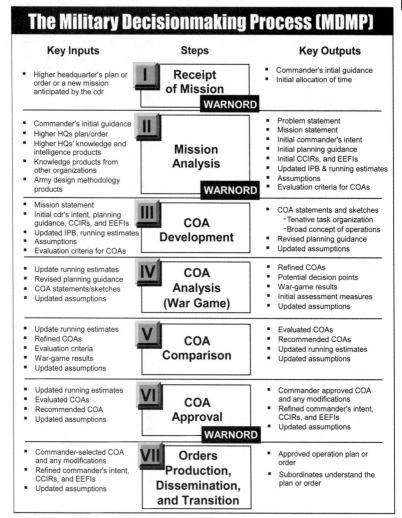

The Military Decisionmaking Process (MDMP)

Key Inputs	Steps	Key Outputs
▪ Higher headquarter's plan or order or a new mission anticipated by the cdr	I Receipt of Mission (WARNORD)	▪ Commander's intial guidance ▪ Initial allocation of time
▪ Commander's initial guidance ▪ Higher HQs plan/order ▪ Higher HQs' knowledge and intelligence products ▪ Knowledge products from other organizations ▪ Army design methodology products	II Mission Analysis (WARNORD)	▪ Problem statement ▪ Mission statement ▪ Initial commander's intent ▪ Initial planning guidance ▪ Initial CCIRs, and EEFIs ▪ Updated IPB & running estimates ▪ Assumptions ▪ Evaluation criteria for COAs
▪ Mission statement ▪ Initial cdr's intent, planning guidance, CCIRs, and EEFIs ▪ Updated IPB, running estimates ▪ Assumptions ▪ Evaluation criteria for COAs	III COA Development	▪ COA statements and sketches -Tenative task organization -Broad concept of operations ▪ Revised planning guidance ▪ Updated assumptions
▪ Update running estimates ▪ Revised planning guidance ▪ COA statements/sketches ▪ Updated assumptions	IV COA Analysis (War Game)	▪ Refined COAs ▪ Potential decision points ▪ War-game results ▪ Initial assessment measures ▪ Updated assumptions
▪ Update running estimates ▪ Refined COAs ▪ Evaluation criteria ▪ War-game results ▪ Updated assumptions	V COA Comparison	▪ Evaluated COAs ▪ Recommended COAs ▪ Updated running estimates ▪ Updated assumptions
▪ Updated running estimates ▪ Evaluated COAs ▪ Recommended COA ▪ Updated assumptions	VI COA Approval (WARNORD)	▪ Commander approved COA and any modifications ▪ Refined commander's intent, CCIRs, and EEFIs ▪ Updated assumptions
▪ Commander-selected COA and any modifications ▪ Refined commander's intent, CCIRs, and EEFIs ▪ Updated assumptions	VII Orders Production, Dissemination, and Transition	▪ Approved operation plan or order ▪ Subordinates understand the plan or order

Ref: FM 6-0 (C2), Commander and Staff Organization and Operations, fig. 9-1, p. 9-3.

The military decision making process (MDMP) helps leaders apply thoroughness, clarity, sound judgment, logic, and professional knowledge to understand situations, develop options to solve problems, and reach decisions. This process helps commanders, staffs, and others think critically and creatively while planning.

MDMP & TLP

Collaborative Planning

The MDMP facilitates collaborative planning. The higher headquarters solicits input and continuously shares information concerning future operations through planning meetings, warning orders, and other means. It shares information with subordinate and adjacent units, supporting and supported units, and other military and civilian partners. Commanders encourage active collaboration among all organizations affected by the pending operations to build a shared understanding of the situation, participate in course of action development and decision making, and resolve conflicts before publishing the plan or order.

Assessment

During planning, assessment focuses on developing an understanding of the current situation and determining what to assess and how to assess progress using measures of effectiveness and measures of performance. Developing the unit's assessment plan occurs during the MDMP—not after developing the plan or order.

See pp. 1-65 to 1-70 for further discussion of assessment.

Preparation

The MDMP also drives preparation. Since time is a factor in all operations, commanders and staffs conduct a time analysis early in the planning process. This analysis helps them determine what actions they need and when to begin those actions to ensure forces are ready and in position before execution. This may require the commander to direct subordinates to start necessary movements, conduct task organization changes, begin surveillance and reconnaissance operations, and execute other preparation activities before completing the plan. As the commander and staff conduct the MDMP, they direct the tasks in a series of warning orders (WARNORDs).

See pp. 1-47 to 1-52 for further discussion of preparation.

Army Design Methodology and the Military Decision-making Process (MDMP)

See pp. 1-36 to 1-39 for further discussion of the Army design methodology.

Depending on the situation—to include the familiarity of the problem—commanders conduct Army design methodology before, in parallel with, or after the MDMP. When faced with an unfamiliar problem or when developing initial plans for extended operations, commanders often initiate the Army design methodology before the MDMP. This sequence helps them better understand the operational environment, frame the problem, and develop an operational approach to guide more detailed planning.

Commanders may also elect to conduct the Army design methodology in parallel with the MDMP. In this instance, members of the staff conduct mission analysis as the commander and other staff members engage in framing the operational environment and the problem. Knowledge products—such as results from intelligence preparation of the battlefield and running estimates—help inform the Army design methodology team about the operational environment. Commanders may direct some staff members to focus their mission analysis on certain areas. This focus helps commanders better understand aspects of the operational environment. The results of mission analysis (to include intelligence preparation of the battlefield and running estimates) inform commanders as they develop their operational approach that, in turn, facilitates course of action development during the MDMP.

In time-constrained conditions requiring immediate action, or if the problem is familiar, commanders may conduct the MDMP and publish an operation order without formally conducting Army design methodology. As time becomes available during execution, commanders may then initiate Army design methodology to help refine their commander's visualization and the initial plan developed using the MDMP.

Steps of the Military Decisionmaking Process

The MDMP consists of seven steps. Each step of the MDMP has various inputs, a method (step) to conduct, and outputs. The outputs lead to an increased understanding of the situation facilitating the next step of the MDMP. Commanders and staffs generally perform these steps sequentially; however, they may revisit several steps in an iterative fashion as they learn more about the situation before producing the plan or order.

Commanders initiate the MDMP upon receipt of or in anticipation of a mission. Commanders and staffs often begin planning in the absence of a complete and approved higher headquarters' operation plan (OPLAN) or operation order (OPORD). In these instances, the headquarters begins a new planning effort based on a WARNORD and other directives, such as a planning order or an alert order from their higher headquarters. This requires active collaboration with the higher headquarters and parallel planning among echelons as the plan or order is developed.

This chapter describes the methods and provides techniques for conducting each step of the MDMP. This section also describes how the following processes are integrated throughout the MDMP:

- Intelligence preparation of the battlefield *(see pp. 3-3 to 3-52)*
- Targeting *(see pp. 3-57 to 3-70)*
- Risk management *(see pp. 3-71 to 3-74)*

Modifying the MDMP

The MDMP can be as detailed as time, resources, experience, and the situation permit. Conducting all steps of the MDMP is detailed, deliberate, and time-consuming. Commanders use the full MDMP when they have enough planning time and staff support to thoroughly examine two or more COAs and develop a fully synchronized plan or order. This typically occurs when planning for an entirely new mission.

Commanders may alter the steps of the MDMP to fit time-constrained circumstances and produce a satisfactory plan. In time-constrained conditions, commanders assess the situation, update the commander's visualization, and direct the staff to perform the MDMP activities that support the required decisions. In extremely compressed situations, commanders rely on more intuitive decision making techniques, such as the rapid decision making and synchronization process.

See pp. 2-57 to 2-58 for discussion of planning in a time-constrained environment.

An Army headquarters (battalion through Army Service component command) uses the MDMP and publishes plans and orders in accordance with the Army plans and orders format. An Army headquarters that forms the base of a joint task force uses the joint operation planning process (JOPP) and publishes plans and orders in accordance with the joint format. An Army headquarters (such as Army Corps) that provides the base of a joint force or coalition forces land component command headquarters will participate in joint planning and receive a joint formatted plan or order. This headquarters then has the option to use the MDMP or JOPP to develop its own supporting plan or order written in the proper Army or joint format to distribute to subordinate commands.

Refer to JFODS5-1: The Joint Forces Operations & Doctrine SMARTbook, 5th Ed (w/Change 1) for further discussion.

II. Running Estimates

Ref: FM 6-0 (C2), Commander and Staff Organization and Operations (Apr '16), chap. 8.

A running estimate is the continuous assessment of the current situation and future operations used to determine if the current operation is proceeding according to the commander's intent and if future operations are supportable. The commander and each staff section maintain a running estimate. In their running estimates, the commander and each staff section continuously consider the effects of new information and update the following:

- Facts
- Assumptions
- Friendly force status
- Enemy activities and capabilities
- Civil considerations
- Conclusions and recommendations

Commanders maintain their running estimates to consolidate their understanding and visualization of an operation. The commander's running estimate includes a summary of the problem and integrates information and knowledge of the staff's and subordinate commanders' running estimates.

Each staff element builds and maintains running estimates. The running estimate helps the staff to track and record pertinent information and provide recommendations to commanders. Running estimates represent the analysis and expert opinion of each staff element by functional area. Staffs maintain running estimates throughout the operations process to assist commanders in the exercise of mission command.

Each staff element and command post functional cell maintains a running estimate focused on how its specific areas of expertise are postured to support future operations. Because an estimate may be needed at any time, running estimates must be developed, revised, updated, and maintained continuously while in garrison and during operations. While in garrison, staffs must maintain a running estimate on friendly capabilities. Running estimates can be presented verbally or in writing.

A comprehensive running estimate addresses all aspects of operations and contains both facts and assumptions based on the staff's experience within a specific area of expertise. Each staff element modifies it to account for its specific functional areas. All running estimates cover essential facts and assumptions, including a summary of the current situation by the mission variables, conclusions, and recommendations. Once they complete the plan, commanders and staff elements continuously update their estimates.

See pp. 2-14 to 2-17 for sample staff guidelines for mission analysis.

The base running estimate addresses information unique to each functional area. It serves as the staff's initial assessment of the current readiness of equipment and personnel and how the factors considered in the running estimate affect their ability to accomplish the mission. The staff identifies functional area friendly and enemy strengths, systems, training, morale, leadership, weather and terrain effects, and how all these factors define both the operational environment and area of operations. Because the running estimate is a picture relative to time, facts, and assumptions, it is constantly updated as new information arises, as assumptions become facts or are invalidated, when the mission changes, or when the commander requires additional input.

Running Estimates in the Operations Process

Commanders and staff elements immediately begin updating their running estimates upon receipt of a mission. They continue to build and maintain their running estimates throughout the operations process in planning, preparation, execution, and assessment. Running estimates can be presented verbally or in writing.

Generic Base Running Estimate Format

1. SITUATION AND CONSIDERATIONS.

a. Area of Interest. Identify and describe the area of interest that impact or affect functional area considerations.

b. Characteristics of the Area of Operations.

(1) Terrain. State how terrain affects staff functional area's capabilities.

(2) Weather. State how weather affects staff functional area's capabilities.

(3) Enemy Forces. Describe enemy disposition, composition, strength, capabilities, systems, and possible courses of action (COAs) with respect to their effect on functional area.

(4) Friendly Forces. List current functional area resources in terms of equipment, personnel, and systems. Identify additional resources available for functional area located at higher, adjacent, or other units. Compare requirements to current capabilities and suggest solutions for satisfying discrepancies.

(5) Civilian Considerations. Describe additional personnel, groups, or associations that cannot be categorized as friendly or enemy. Discuss possible impact these entities may have on functional area.

c. Assumptions. List all assumptions that affect the functional area.

2. MISSION. Show the restated mission resulting from mission analysis.

3. COURSES OF ACTION.

a. List friendly COAs that were war-gamed.

b. List enemy actions or COAs that were templated that impact functional area.

c. List the evaluation criteria identified during COA analysis. All staff use the same criteria.

4. ANALYSIS. Analyze each COA using the evaluation criteria from COA analysis. Review enemy actions that impact functional area as they relate to COAs. Identify issues, risks, and deficiencies these enemy actions may create with respect to functional area.

5. COMPARISON. Compare COAs. Rank order COAs for each key consideration. Use a decision matrix to aid the comparison process.

6. RECOMMENDATION AND CONCLUSIONS.

a. Recommend the most supportable COAs from the perspective of the functional area.

b. Prioritize and list issues, deficiencies, and risks and make recommendations on how to mitigate them.

Each staff element continuously analyzes new information during operations to create knowledge and to understand if operations are progressing according to plan. During planning, staffs develop measures of effectiveness and measures of performance to support assessment, including analysis of anticipated decisions during preparation and execution. The assessment of current operations also supports validation or rejection of additional information that will help update the estimates and support further planning. At a minimum, a staff element's running estimate assesses the following::

- Friendly force capabilities with respect to ongoing and planned operations.
- Enemy capabilities as they affect the staff element's area of expertise for current operations and plans for future operations.
- Civil considerations as they affect the staff element's area of expertise for current operations and plans for future operations.

III. The Role of Commanders and Staff

Ref: FM 6-0 (C2), Commander and Staff Organization and Operations (Apr '16), p. 9-2.

The **commander** is the most important participant in the MDMP. More than simply the decision makers in this process, commanders use their experience, knowledge, and judgment to guide staff planning efforts. While unable to devote all their time to the MDMP, commanders remain aware of the current status of the planning effort, participate during critical periods of the process, and make sound decisions based upon the detailed work of the staff. During the MDMP, commanders focus their battle command activities on understanding, visualizing, and describing.

The **chief of staff (COS)** or **executive officer (XO)** is a key participant in the MDMP. The COS or XO manages and coordinates the staff's work and provides quality control during the MDMP. The COS or XO must clearly understand the commander's intent and guidance because COS's or Sox supervise the entire process. They provide timelines to the staff, establish briefing times and locations, and provide any instructions necessary to complete the plan.

The **staff's** effort during the MDMP focuses on helping the commander understand the situation, making decisions, and synchronizing those decisions into a fully developed plan or order. Staff activities during planning initially focus on mission analysis. The products developed during mission analysis help commanders understand the situation and develop the commander's visualization. During course of action (COA) development and COA comparison, the staff provides recommendations to support the commander in selecting a COA. After the commander makes a decision, the staff prepares the plan or order that reflects the commander's intent, coordinating all necessary details.

	Cdr	Staff Officers	Staff NCOs	RTOs	Clerks/ Typists
Mission Analysis					
Prepare charts for msn analysis				x	x
Prepare terrain sketches				x	x
Update/post unit reports/status			x	x	
Prepare TOC for planning			x	x	x
Conduct mission analysis		x	x		
Serve as recorder			x	x	x
Brief commander and staff	x	x	x		
Commander's Guidance					
Assist cdr in developing guidance		x	x		
Issue guidance	x				
Record/post cdr's guidance		x	x	x	x
COA Development					
Prepare charts				x	x
Sketch COAs				x	x
Develop COAs	x	x	x		
COA Analysis					
Collect and prepare tools/charts				x	x
Serve as war-game recorders			x	x	x
Conduct war-game session	x	x	x		
COA Approval					
Make recommendation to cdr		x	x		
Decide	x				
Record/post cdr's guidance		x	x	x	x
Orders Preparation					
Write annexes		x	x		
Consolidate annexes			x	x	
Type order			x	x	x
Reproduce order/graphics				x	x
Review order	x	x	x		
Approve order	x				

Ref: Adapted from FM 101-5, fig. K-1 (not found in FM 6-0).

MDMP Step I. Receipt of Mission

Ref: FM 6-0 (C2), Commander and Staff Organization and Operations (Apr '16), pp. 9-4 to 9-6.

Commanders initiate the MDMP upon receipt or in anticipation of a mission. This step alerts all participants of the pending planning requirements, enabling them to determine the amount of time available for planning and preparation and decide on a planning approach, including guidance on design and how to abbreviate the MDMP, if required. When commanders identify a new mission, commanders and staffs perform the actions and produce the expected key outputs.

I. Receipt of Mission

Key Inputs	Key Outputs
▪ **Higher headquarters plan or order or a new mission anticipated by the commander**	▪ **Commander's initial guidance** ▪ **Initial allocation of time** WARNORD

1. **Alert the Staff and Other Key Participants**
2. **Gather the Tools**
3. **Update Running Estimates**
4. **Conduct Initial Assessment**
5. **Issue the Commander's Initial Guidance**
6. **Issue the Initial Warning Order**

Ref: FM 6-0 (C2), Commander and Staff Organization and Operations, fig. 9-2, p. 9-4.

1. Alert the Staff and Other Key Participants

As soon as a unit receives a new mission (or when the commander directs), the current operations integration cell alerts the staff of the pending planning requirement. Unit standard operating procedures (SOPs) should identify members of the planning staff who participate in mission analysis. In addition, the current operations integration cell also notifies other military, civilian, and host-nation organizations of pending planning events as required.

MDMP & TLP

2. Gather the Tools

Once notified of the new planning requirement, the staff prepares for mission analysis by gathering the needed tools. These tools include, but are not limited to:

- Appropriate publications, including ADRP 1-02
- All documents related to the mission and area of operations, including the higher headquarters' OPLAN and OPORD, maps and terrain products, and operational graphics
- Higher headquarters' and other organizations' intelligence and assessment products
- Estimates and products of other military and civilian agencies and organizations
- Both their own and the higher headquarters' SOPs
- Current running estimates
- Any Army design methodology products

The gathering of knowledge products continues throughout the MDMP. Staff officers carefully review the reference sections (located before paragraph 1. Situation) of the higher headquarters' OPLANs and OPORDs to identify documents (such as theater policies and memoranda) related to the upcoming operation. If the MDMP occurs while in the process of replacing another unit, the staff begins collecting relevant documents—such as the current OPORD, branch plans, current assessments, operations and intelligence summaries, and SOPs—from that unit.

3. Update Running Estimates

While gathering the necessary tools for planning, each staff section begins updating its running estimate—especially the status of friendly units and resources and key civil considerations that affect each functional area. Running estimates compile critical facts and assumptions not only from the perspective of each staff section, but also include information from other staff sections and other military and civilian organizations. While this task is listed at the beginning of the MDMP, developing and updating running estimates is continuous throughout the MDMP and the operations process.

See pp. 2-4 to 2-5 for further discussion of running estimates.

4. Conduct Initial Assessment

During receipt of mission, the commander and staff conduct an initial assessment of time and resources available to plan, prepare, and begin execution of an operation. This initial assessment helps commanders determine:

- The time needed to plan and prepare for the mission for both headquarters and subordinate units
- Guidance on conducting the Army design methodology and abbreviating the MDMP, if required
- Which outside agencies and organizations to contact and incorporate into the planning process
- The staff's experience, cohesiveness, and level of rest or stress

This assessment primarily identifies an initial allocation of available time. The commander and staff balance the desire for detailed planning against the need for immediate action. The commander provides guidance to subordinate units as early as possible to allow subordinates the maximum time for their own planning and preparation of operations. As a rule, commanders allocate a minimum of two-thirds of available time for subordinate units to conduct their planning and preparation. This leaves one-third of the time for commanders and their staff to do their planning. They use the other two-thirds for their own preparation. Time, more than any other factor, determines the detail to which the commander and staff can plan.

Initial Allocation of Available Time

Ref: Adapted from FM 5-0, The Operations Process (Mar '10), pp. B-5 (not found in FM 6-0).

A key product of this assessment is an initial allocation of available time. The commander and staff balance the desire for detailed planning against the need for immediate action. The commander provides guidance to subordinate units as early as possible to allow subordinates the maximum time for their own planning and preparation of operations. As a rule, the commander allocates a minimum of two-thirds of available time for subordinate units to conduct their planning and preparation. This leaves one-third of the time for commanders and their staff to do their planning. They use the other two-thirds for their own preparation. Time, more than any other factor, determines the detail in which the commander and staff can plan.

Based on the commander's initial allocation of time, the COS or XO develops a staff planning timeline that outlines how long the headquarters can spend on each step of the MDMP. The staff planning timeline indicates what products are due, who is responsible for them, and who receives them. It includes times and locations for meetings and briefings. It serves as a benchmark for the commander and staff throughout the MDMP.

A generic time line could be based on the one-third/two-thirds rule:

• Mission analysis	30%
• COA development	20%
• COA analysis/comparison/decision	30%
• Orders production	20%

One-Third, Two-Thirds Rule

Effective execution requires issuing timely plans and orders to subordinates. Timely plans are those issued soon enough to allow subordinates enough time to plan, issue their orders, and prepare for operations. At a minimum, commanders follow the "one-third–two-thirds rule" to allocate time available. They use one-third of the time available before execution for their planning and allocate the remaining two-thirds to their subordinates for planning and preparation.

Parallel and Collaborative Planning

Commanders ensure that plans are sent to subordinates in enough time to allow them to adequately plan and prepare their own operations. To accomplish this, echelons plan in parallel as much as possible. Additionally, new information systems (INFOSYS) enable echelons to plan collaboratively without being co-located.

Parallel planning is two or more echelons planning for the same operation nearly simultaneously. Since several echelons develop their plans simultaneously, parallel planning can significantly shorten planning time. The higher headquarters continuously shares information concerning future operations with subordinate units through warning orders and other means. Frequent communication between commanders and staff and sharing of information, such as intelligence preparation of the battlefield products, helps subordinate headquarters plan. Parallel planning requires significant interaction among echelons.

Collaborative planning is when commanders, subordinate commanders, staffs and other partners share information, knowledge, perceptions, ideas, and concepts regardless of physical location throughout the planning process. Collaboration occurs during all operations process activities, not just planning. During planning, commanders, subordinate commanders, and others in the area of operations share assessments, statuses, and ideas.

See pp. 2-57 to 2-58 for discussion of planning in a time-constrained environment.

Based on the commander's initial allocation of time, the COS (XO) develops a staff planning timeline that outlines how long the headquarters can spend on each step of the MDMP. The staff planning timeline indicates what products are due, who is responsible for them, and who receives them. It includes times and locations for meetings and briefings. It serves as a benchmark for the commander and staff throughout the MDMP.

5. Issue the Commander's Initial Guidance

Once time is allocated, the commander determines whether to initiate Army design methodology, perform Army design methodology in parallel with the MDMP, or proceed directly into the MDMP without the benefits of formal Army design methodology activities. In time-sensitive situations where commanders decide to proceed directly into the MDMP, they may also issue guidance on how to abbreviate the process. Having determined the time available together with the scope and scale of the planning effort, commanders issue initial planning guidance. Although brief, the initial guidance includes, but is not limited to:

- Initial time allocations
- A decision to initiate Army design methodology or go straight into the MDMP
- How to abbreviate the MDMP, if required
- Necessary coordination to exchange liaison officers
- Authorized movements and initiation of information collection
- Collaborative planning times and locations
- Initial information requirements
- Additional staff tasks

6. Issue the Initial Warning Order

The last task in receipt of mission is to issue a WARNORD to subordinate and supporting units. This order includes at a minimum the type of operation, the general location of the operation, the initial timeline, and any movement or reconnaissance to initiate.

See p. 4-21 for a sample warning order format.

MDMP Step II. Mission Analysis

Ref: FM 6-0 (C2), Commander and Staff Organization and Operations (Apr '16), pp. 9-6 to 9-16.

The MDMP continues with an assessment of the situation called mission analysis. Commanders (supported by their staffs and informed by subordinate and adjacent commanders and by other partners) gather, analyze, and synthesize information to orient themselves on the current conditions of the operational environment. The commander and staff conduct mission analysis to better understand the situation and problem, and identify *what* the command must accomplish, *when* and *where* it must be done, and most importantly *why*—the purpose of the operation.

II. Mission Analysis

Key Inputs	Key Outputs
▪ Commander's initial guidance ▪ Higher headquarters plan or order ▪ Higher headquarters knowledge and intelligence products ▪ Knowledge products from other organizations ▪ Updated running estimates ▪ Army design methodology products	▪ Problem statement ▪ Mission statement ▪ Initial commander's intent ▪ Initial planning guidance ▪ Initial CCIRs, and EEFIs ▪ Updated IPB products and running estimates ▪ Assumptions ▪ Evaluation criteria for COAs WARNORD

1. Analyze the Higher HQ Plan or Order
2. Perform Initial IPB
3. Determine Specified, Implied and Essential Tasks
4. Review Available Assets and Identify Resource Shortfalls
5. Determine Constraints
6. Identify Critical Facts and Develop Assumptions
7. Begin Risk Management
8. Develop Initial CCIR and EEFI
9. Develop the Initial Information Collection Plan
10. Update Plan for Use of Available Time
11. Develop Initial Themes and Messages
12. Develop a Proposed Problem Statement
13. Develop a Proposed Mission Statement
14. Present the Mission Analysis Briefing
15. Develop and Issue Initial Commander's Intent
16. Develop and Issue Initial Planning Guidance
17. Develop COA Evaluation Criteria
18. Issue a Warning Order

Ref: FM 6-0 (C2), Commander and Staff Organization and Operations, fig. 9-3, p. 9-7.

Since no amount of subsequent planning can solve an insufficiently understood problem, mission analysis is the most important step in the MDMP. This understanding of the situation and the problem allows commanders to visualize and describe how the operation may unfold in their initial commander's intent and planning guidance. During mission analysis, the commander and staff perform the process actions and produce the outputs.

Commanders and staffs may also begin the development of evaluation criteria during this step. These evaluation criteria are continually developed and refined throughout the MDMP and become a key input during Step 5—Course of Action Comparison.

1. Analyze the Higher Headquarters Plan or Order

Commanders and staffs thoroughly analyze the higher headquarters' plan or order. They determine how their unit—by task and purpose—contributes to the mission, commander's intent, and concept of operations of the higher headquarters. The commander and staff seek to completely understand:

- The higher headquarters'
  - Commander's intent
  - Mission
  - Concept of operations
  - Available assets
  - Timeline
- The missions of adjacent, supporting, and supported units and their relationships to the higher headquarters' plan
- The missions or goals of unified action partners that work in the operational areas
- Their assigned area of operations

If the commander misinterprets the higher headquarters' plan, time is wasted. Additionally, when analyzing the higher order, the commander and staff may identify difficulties and contradictions in the higher order. Therefore, if confused by the higher headquarters' order or guidance, commanders must seek immediate clarification. Liaison officers familiar with the higher headquarters' plan can help clarify issues. Collaborative planning with the higher headquarters also facilitates this task. Staffs use requests for information to clarify or obtain additional information from the higher headquarters.

2. Perform Initial Intelligence Preparation of the Battlefield (IPB)

IPB is the systematic process of analyzing the mission variables of enemy, terrain, weather, and civil considerations in an area of interest to determine their effect on operations. The IPB process identifies critical gaps in the commander's knowledge of an operational environment. As a part of the initial planning guidance, commanders use these gaps as a guide to establish their initial intelligence requirements. IPB products enable the commander to assess facts about the operational environment and make assumptions about how friendly and threat forces will interact in the operational environment. The description of the operational environment's effects identifies constraints on potential friendly COAs. It also identifies key aspects of the operational environment, such as avenues of approach, engagement areas, and landing zones, which the staff integrates into potential friendly COAs and their running estimates. For mission analysis, the intelligence staff, along with the other staff elements, will use IPB to develop detailed threat COA models, which depict a COA available to the threat. The threat COA models provide a basis for formulating friendly COAs and completing the intelligence estimate.

See facing page for an overview, and pp. 3-3 to 3-52 for a discussion of the IPB process from ATP 2-01.3.

IPB and the MDMP (Overview)

Ref: ATP 2-01.3, Intelligence Preparation of the Battlefield (Mar '19), pp. 2-1 to 2-3.

The intelligence staff, in collaboration with other staffs, develops other IPB products during mission analysis. That collaboration should result in the drafting of initial priority intelligence requirements (PIRs), the production of a complete modified combined obstacles overlay, a list of high value targets, and unrefined event templates and matrices. IPB should provide an understanding of the threat's center of gravity, which then can be exploited by friendly forces.

Figure 2-1 shows the relationship between IPB and the steps of MDMP.

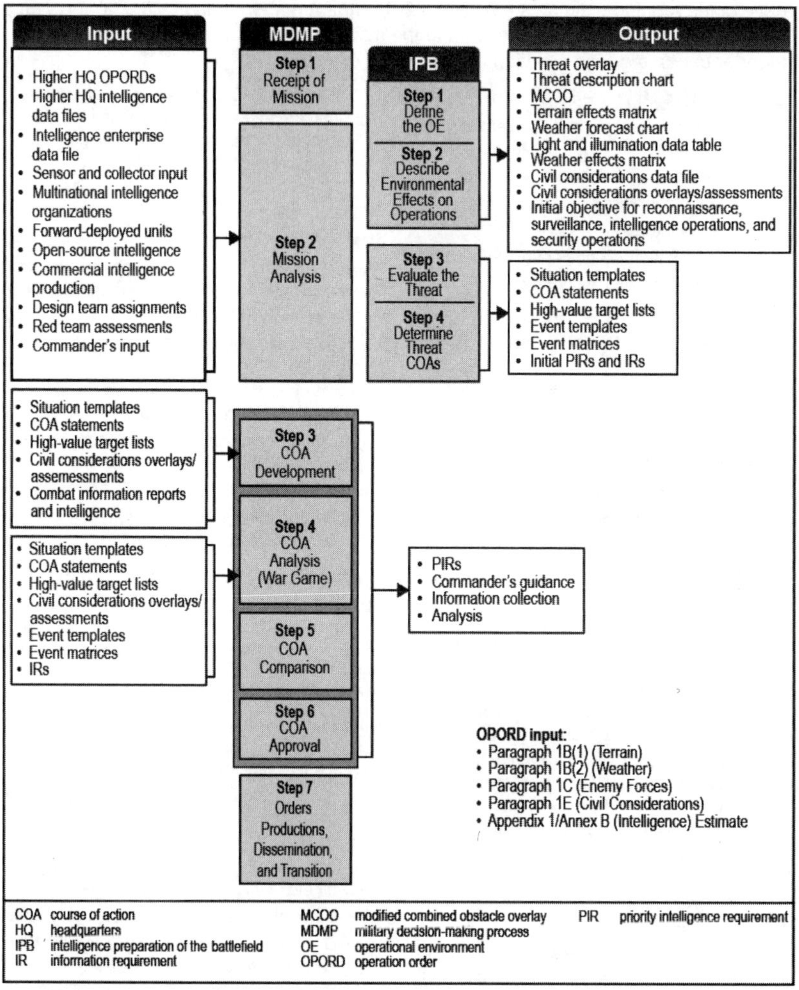

Ref: ATP 2-01.3, fig. 2-1. IPB and the MDMP steps.

See pp. 3-6 to 3-7 for further discussion of the relationship between IPB and the steps of the MDMP. See pp. 3-3 to 3-52 for a discussion of the IPB process from ATP 2-01.3.

Staff Guidelines for Mission Analysis

Ref: Adapted from previous references (not provided in FM 6-0, C2).

During mission analysis, the commander and staff thoroughly analyze the higher headquarters plan or order and any planning directives pertaining to the situation. Their goal is to determine how their unit, by task and purpose, contributes to the mission, commander's intent, and concept of operations of the higher headquarters. They analyze their own unit capabilities and limitations, those of the enemy, and the terrain and weather. They also analyze civil considerations through the memory aid ASCOPE -- areas, structures, capabilities, organizations, people, and events. These considerations are also used when developing running estimates *(pp. 2-4 to 2-5)*. Staff members bring technical knowledge, running estimates, and historical data to the mission analysis briefing to help the commander understand the situation and the unit's mission.

All Staff Officers

- Mission and commander's intent of higher headquarters one and two levels up
- Specified, implied, and essential tasks
- Area of operations
- Area of interest
- Enemy situation and capabilities
- Critical facts and assumptions
- Status of subordinate units
- Weapon systems capabilities and limitations
- Status of available assets within their functional area
- Constraints
- Risk considerations
- Time considerations
- Recommended commander's critical information requirements (CCIRs) and information requirements

Intelligence

ACOS, G-2 (S-2), Intelligence

- Managing intelligence preparation of the battlefield (IPB), to include integrating the IPB efforts of the rest of the staff and other echelons and supporting parallel planning during dynamic situations
- Performing situation development, to include updating the enemy, terrain and weather, and civil consideration portions of the common operational picture
- Conducting ISR synchronization, to include:
- Developing and continuously updating a list of intelligence gaps
- Recommending CCIR's and information requirements to develop initial collection tasks and requests for support from higher and adjacent commands
- Determining collection capabilities and limitations
- Determining unit intelligence production capabilities and limitations
- Facilitating ISR integration by giving the commander and G-3 (S-3) the initial ISR synchronization plan and helping the G-3 (S-3) develop the initial ISR plan
- Identifying enemy intelligence collection capabilities

Staff Weather Officer

The staff weather officer conducts mission analysis on how weather and the natural environment affect both the enemy and friendly forces:

- Developing and continuously updating current weather data
- Determining and continuously updating a long-term weather forecast
- Coordinating with the geospatial engineer to combine terrain and weather reports

Foreign Disclosure Officer

The foreign disclosure officer determines what may and may not be released to foreign partners.

Movement and Maneuver

ACOS, G-3 (S-3), Operations

The ACOS, G-3 (S-3), is the principal staff officer for operations and is the chief of movement and maneuver. This officer conducts mission analysis on all matters concerning training, operations, and plan:

- Managing the overall mission analysis effort of the staff to include:
- Consolidating facts and assumptions, specific and implied tasks, constraints, risk considerations, unit status, and recommended CCIR's
- Summarizing the current situation of subordinate units and activities
- Determining status of the task organization
- Developing the intelligence, surveillance, and reconnaissance (ISR) plan (with G-2 [S-2] and the rest of the staff). The ISR plan produces an initial ISR order to answer initial CCIRs and information requirements
- Developing the unit's recommended mission statement
- Developing the unit's operational timeline

ACOS, G-5 (S-5), Plans

The ACOS, G-5 (S-5), is the chief of plans, and conducts mission analysis on all matters concerning plans to include integration of all higher, lower, and supporting plans.

Aviation Coordinator

The aviation coordinator conducts mission analysis on all matters concerning Army aviation:

- Determining the status of the task organization
- Determining the current status of subordinate Army aviation units

Engineer Coordinator

- Identifying available information on routes and key facilities. Evaluate requirements for lines of communications, aerial ports of debarkation, and sea ports of debarkation
- Determining availability of construction and other engineering materials
- Reviewing availability of all engineer capabilities both civilian and military
- Identifying any obvious shortfalls in engineer forces or equipment and initiating requests for information or augmentation as early as possible
- Identifying available information on major roads, bridges, and key facilities in the area of operations
- Determining bed down requirements for supported force. Reviewing theater construction standards and base camp master planning.
- Reviewing existing geospatial data on potential sites; conducting site reconnaissance; and determining the threat (to include environmental)
- Obtaining necessary geologic, hydrologic, and climatic data
- Determining the level of interagency cooperation required
- Determining funding sources
- Determining terrain and mobility restraints, obstacle intelligence, threat engineer capabilities, and critical infrastructure
- Coordinating the integration of geospatial engineering into the MDMP
- Monitoring the production and distribution of maps and terrain products based on established priorities
- Integrating engineer reconnaissance
- Identifying gaps in geospatial data and nominating collection
- Synchronizing with the G-2 or S-2 and the geospatial information technician to prioritize requirements
- Coordinating engineer-related ISR requirements with the intel officer

Military Deception Officer

- Determining opportunities for military deception
- Identifying potential deception targets, objectives, and stories

Space Officer

- Identifying theater, strategic, national, and commercial space assets
- Determining global positioning system satellite coverage and accuracy data
- Providing Department of Defense and commercial satellite terrain and weather imagery
- Identifying the capabilities and vulnerabilities of enemy satellite systems
- Estimating the effects of space weather activities
- Identifying adversarial ground stations for possible targeting

Special Operations Coordinator

- Identifying status and capabilities of SOF available to the commander
- Identifying the status and capabilities of host-nation security forces
- Determining enemy SOF capabilities
- Identifying SOF aviation assets and status
- Determining SOF support requirements

Fires

Chief of Fires/Fire Support Officer (FSO)

- Higher HQ's specified and implied tasks
- A fires running estimate to identify capabilities and limitations including the status of: field artillery weapons, field artillery ammunition, field artillery target acquisition radars , close air support (CAS) and other related fixed-wing support, other assets allocated from higher headquarters
- Field artillery and mortar survey support
- Established and recommended fire support coordination measures
- The impact of rules of engagement
- The impact of geometry, terrain, and weather on friendly and enemy fires (such as smoke, CAS, and air interdiction)
- ISR support and requirements
- Initial high-payoff target list
- Fire support input to the IPB analysis
- Fire support tasks and purposes

Air Liaison Officer

The air liaison officer conducts mission analysis with regard to the availability and status of CAS, air interdiction, air reconnaissance, airlift, and joint suppression of enemy air defenses.

Electronic Warfare Officer

- Identifying enemy's electronic warfare capabilities and vulnerabilities
- Determining friendly electronic warfare capabilities and vulnerabilities
- Identifying electronic warfare targets
- Identifying electronic attack targets
- Determining electronic protection requirements

Continued on next page

Staff Guidelines (CONT)

Ref: Adapted from previous references (not provided in FM 6-0, C2).

Continued from previous page

Protection

Chief of Protection

The chief of protection is responsible for all mission analysis conducted by the protection section:

Air and Missile Defense Coordinator

- Air defense rules of engagement
- Weapons control status
- Current airspace control measures (current, planned, and required)
- Enemy air and missile capabilities (most likely air avenues of approach, types and numbers of sorties, and high-value target lists)
- Offensive counter-air, defensive counter-air, and theater missile defense targets and priorities
- Active and passive air defense measures
- Status of air and missile defense systems, air and missile defense sensor assets, and air defense artillery ammunition available

Chemical Officer

- Assets available, including reconnaissance, decontamination, and smoke
- Constraints related to CBRNE
- Mission-oriented protective posture status
- Troop safety criteria
- Enemy CBRNE capabilities and friendly vulnerabilities

Explosive Ordnance Disposal Officer

- Status of explosive ordnance disposal units
- Identifying the status of explosive ordnance disposal tools, equipment, and demolition materials
- Enemy explosive threats and capabilities

Operations Security Officer

- Assessing the commander's posture on operations security
- Determining essential elements of friendly information and OPSEC vulnerabilities
- Determining appropriate OPSEC measures
- Evaluating the potential effect of compromise to friendly information system, functions, and data

Personnel Recovery Officer

- Determining the time-distance relationship to interned, missing, detained, and captured for all units
- Assessing status of personnel recovery equipment
- Assessing ISR operations for effects on personnel recovery
- Assessing civilian and diplomatic capabilities to support personnel recovery
- Assessing how civilians and local security forces support and disrupt personnel recovery
- Identifying medical support to personnel recovery

Provost Marshal

- Route reconnaissance
- Dislocated civilian and straggler movement control
- Traffic regulation and enforcement
- Main supply route regulation
- Populace and resource control
- Tactical and police intelligence collecting and reporting

The provost marshal also considers area security operations, including activities associated with:

- Area and base security operations
- Command post access control
- Physical security procedures for critical assets, nodes, and sensitive materials
- Counter reconnaissance
- Protective services for key personnel
- Response force operations
- Antiterrorism
- Tactical and police intelligence collecting and reporting
- Criminal activity and trends within the operational area
- Host-nation law enforcement organization and capabilities
- Internment and resettlement of enemy prisoners of war and civilian internees, dislocated civilians, and U.S. military prisoners
- Law and order operations

Safety Officer

The safety officer provides technical advice and assistance to the staff as they complete their functional area risk assessments.

Sustainment

Chief of Sustainment

The chief of sustainment leads the mission analysis effort for the sustainment section.

ACOS, G-1/AG (S-1), Personnel

- Analyzing personnel strength data to determine current capabilities and project future requirements
- Analyzing unit strength maintenance, including monitoring, collecting, and analyzing data affecting Soldier readiness
- Preparing estimates for personnel replacement requirements based on estimated casualties, non-battle losses, and foreseeable administrative losses to include critical

military occupational skill requirements
- Determining personnel services available to the force (current and projected)
- Determining personnel support available to the force (current and projected)

ACOS, G-4 (S-4), Logistics
- Determining current and projected supply status (classes I, II, III, IV, V, VII, and IX)
- Providing current equipment readiness status of the force and projected maintenance timelines
- Forecasting combat vehicle and weapons status
- Identifying availability of transportation assets
- Identifying availability and status of services
- Identifying contracted and host-nation support
- Reviewing availability of general engineer assets that enable logistics, to include units, host-nation support, and contract support

ACOS, G-8, Financial Management
- Determining current and projected funding levels, by type of appropriated funding
- Ensuring funding complies with laws and financial management regulations
- Determining current and projected currency requirements (U.S. and foreign) to support the procurement process
- Developing cost estimates and providing cost analyses (cost alternatives)
- Determining resource impact of contract and host-nation support

Command Surgeon
- Civilian and military medical assets available (treatment, evacuation, critical medical equipment, and personnel)
- Class VIII supply status including blood management, medical equipment maintenance and repair, and drug supply issues
- Environmental health effects on military forces
- Medical threats (to include occupational and environment health hazards)
- Patient estimates (medical workload)
- Theater evacuation policy
- Medical troop ceiling and availability of health service support medical treatment and evaluation resources
- Force health protection

Command and Control

ACOS, G-6 (S-6), Signal
- Determining communication and information systems operational status
- Determining available communications assets, including higher and host-nation support
- Ensuring integration with the higher headquarters communications plan

ACOS, G-7 (S-7), Information Engagement
- Identify higher themes and messages
- Analyze internal and external audience to inform, educate, and influence

ACOS, G-8, Financial Management
- Determining current and projected funding levels, by type of appropriated funding
- Ensuring funding complies with laws and financial management regulations
- Determining current and projected currency requirements (U.S. and foreign) to support the procurement process
- Developing cost estimates and providing cost analyses (cost alternatives)
- Determining resource impact of contract and host-nation support

ACOS, G-9 (S-9), Civil Affairs Operations
- Analyzing how civilian populations affect military operations
- Analyzing how military operations affect the host nation and its populace
- Determining dislocated civilian movement, routes, and assembly areas
- Identifying the host-nation ability to care for civilians
- Identifying host-nation resources to support military operations
- Determining a no-strike list, including cultural, religious, historical, and high-density civilian population areas
- Identifying NGO & other independent organizations in the operational area

Public Affairs Officer (PAO)
- The operation and information environment
- Level of U.S. public, host-nation, and international support
- The media presence and facilitation in the operational area
- Public affairs support to counter deception and counterpropaganda
- The status of public affairs units

Knowledge Management Officer
- Identifies knowledge gaps and additional knowledge requirements
- Identifies sources and solutions to fill knowledge gaps
- Determines what information and knowledge needs to be shared, who it needs to be shared with, and how best to share it
- Captures, organizes, and transfers new knowledge created by the staff

Chaplain
- The status of available unit ministry teams to include identified religious preferences
- Effects of indigenous religions on military operations

MDMP & TLP

3. Determine Specified, Implied, and Essential Tasks

The staff analyzes the higher headquarters order and the higher commander's guidance to determine their specified and implied tasks. In the context of operations, a task is a clearly defined and measurable activity accomplished by Soldiers, units, and organizations that may support or be supported by other tasks. The "what" of a mission statement is always a task. From the list of specified and implied tasks, the staff determines essential tasks for inclusion in the recommended mission statement.

A. Specified Tasks

A specified task is a task specifically assigned to a unit by its higher headquarters. Paragraphs 2 and 3 of the higher headquarters' order or plan state specified tasks. Some tasks may be in paragraphs 4 and 5. Specified tasks may be listed in annexes and overlays. They may also be assigned verbally during collaborative planning sessions or in directives from the higher commander.

B. Implied Tasks

An implied task is a task that must be performed to accomplish a specified task or mission but is not stated in the higher headquarters' order. Implied tasks are derived from a detailed analysis of the higher headquarters' order, the enemy situation, the terrain, and civil considerations. Additionally, analysis of doctrinal requirements for each specified task might disclose implied tasks.

When analyzing the higher order for specified and implied tasks, the staff also identifies any be-prepared or on-order missions.

- A **be-prepared mission** is a mission assigned to a unit that might be executed. Generally a contingency mission, commanders execute it because something planned has or has not been successful. In planning priorities, commanders plan a be-prepared mission after any on-order mission.
- An **on-order mission** is a mission to be executed at an unspecified time. A unit with an on-order mission is a committed force. Commanders envisions task execution in the concept of operations; however, they may not know the exact time or place of execution. Subordinate commanders develop plans and orders and allocate resources, task-organize, and position forces for execution.

C. Essential Tasks

Once staff members have identified specified and implied tasks, they ensure they understand each task's requirements and purpose. The staff then identifies essential tasks. An essential task is a specified or implied task that must be executed to accomplish the mission. Essential tasks are always included in the unit's mission statement.

4. Review Available Assets and Identify Resource Shortfalls

The commander and staff examine additions to and deletions from the current task organization, command and support relationships, and status (current capabilities and limitations) of all units. This analysis also includes capabilities of civilian and military organizations (joint, special operations, and multinational) that operate within their unit's AO. They consider relationships among specified, implied, and essential tasks, and between them and available assets. From this analysis, staffs determine if they have the assets needed to complete all tasks. If shortages occur, they identify additional resources needed for mission success to the higher headquarters. Staffs also identify any deviations from the normal task organization and provide them to the commander to consider when developing the planning guidance. A more detailed analysis of available assets occurs during COA development.

5. Determine Constraints

The commander and staff identify any constraints placed on their command. A constraint is a restriction placed on the command by a higher command. A constraint dictates an action or inaction, thus restricting the freedom of action of a subordinate commander. Constraints are found in paragraph 3 of the OPLAN or OPORD. Annexes to the order may also include constraints. The operation overlay, for example, may contain a restrictive fire line or a no fire area. Constraints may also be issued verbally, in WARNORDs, or in policy memoranda.

Constraints may also be based on resource limitations within the command, such as organic fuel transport capacity, or physical characteristics of the operational environment, such as the number of vehicles that can cross a bridge in a specified time.

The commander and staff should coordinate with the Staff Judge Advocate for a legal review of perceived or obvious constraints, restraints, or limitations in the OPLAN, OPORD, or related documents.

6. Identify Critical Facts and Develop Assumptions

Plans and orders are based on facts and assumptions. Commanders and staffs gather facts and develop assumptions as they build their plan.

A. Facts

A fact is a statement of truth or a statement thought to be true at the time. Facts concerning the operational and mission variables serve as the basis for developing situational understanding, for continued planning, and when assessing progress during preparation and execution.

B. Assumptions

An assumption is a supposition on the current situation or a presupposition on the future course of events, either or both assumed to be true in the absence of positive proof, necessary to enable the commander in the process of planning to complete an estimate of the situation and make a decision on the course of action. In the absence of facts, the commander and staff consider assumptions from their higher headquarters. They then develop their own assumptions necessary for continued planning.

Having assumptions requires commanders and staffs to continually attempt to replace those assumptions with facts. The commander and staff should list and review the key assumptions on which fundamental judgments rest throughout the MDMP. Rechecking assumptions is valuable at any time during the operations process prior to rendering judgments and making decisions.

7. Begin Risk Management

Risk management is the process of identifying, assessing, and controlling risks arising from operational factors and making decisions that balance risk cost with mission benefits (JP 3-0). During mission analysis, the commander and staff focus on identifying and assessing hazards. Developing specific control measures to mitigate those hazards occurs during course of action development.

The chief of protection (or operations staff officer [S-3] in units without a protection cell) in coordination with the safety officer integrates risk management into the MDMP. All staff sections integrate risk management for hazards within their functional areas. Units conduct the first four steps of risk management in the MDMP.

See following page and pp. 3-71 to 3-74 for further discussion of risk management from ATP 5-19.

Risk Management Process

Ref: ATP 5-19 (w/C1), Risk Management (Apr '2014), chap. 1. *See also pp. 3-71 to 3-74.*

Risk Management is the process of identifying, assessing, and controlling risks arising from operational factors and making decisions that balance risk cost with mission benefits. (JP 3-0) *The Army no longer uses the term "composite risk management." Term replaced with joint term "risk management."*

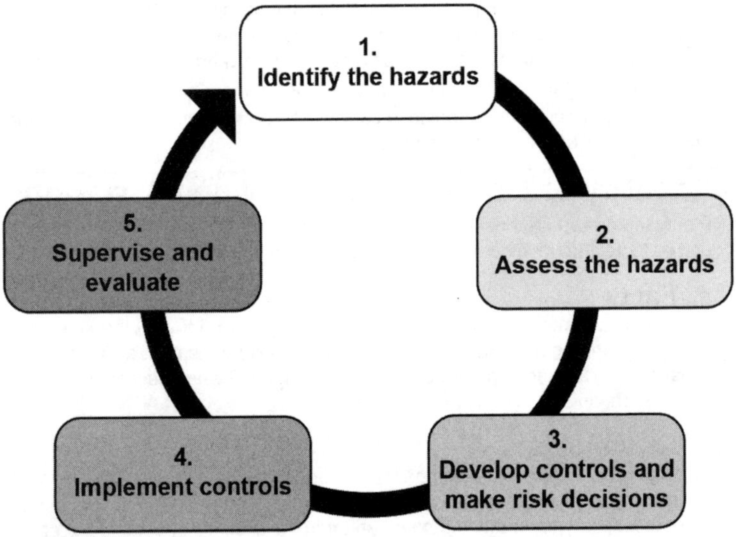

Ref: ATP 5-19, fig. 1-1. A cyclical, continuous process for managing risk.

1. Identify the hazards

A hazard is a condition with the potential to cause injury, illness, or death of personnel; damage to or loss of equipment or property; or mission degradation. Hazards exist in all environments—combat operations, stability operations, base support operations, training, garrison activities, and off-duty activities. The factors of mission, enemy, terrain and weather, troops and support available, time available, and civil considerations (METT-TC) serve as a standard format for identification of hazards, on-duty or off-duty.

2. Assess the hazards

This process is systematic in nature and uses charts, codes and numbers to present a methodology to assess probability and severity to obtain a standardized level of risk. Hazards are assessed and risk is assigned in terms of probability and severity of adverse impact of an event/occurrence.

3. Develop controls and make risk decisions

The process of developing and applying controls and reassessing risk continues until an acceptable level of risk is achieved or until all risks are reduced to a level where benefits outweigh the potential cost.

4. Implement controls

Leaders and staffs ensure that controls are integrated into SOPs, written and verbal orders, mission briefings, and staff estimates.

5. Supervise and evaluate

8. Develop Initial CCIR and EEFI

The mission analysis process identifies gaps in information required for further planning and decisionmaking during preparation and execution. During mission analysis, the staff develops information requirements (IRs). Some information requirements are of such importance to the commander that staffs nominate them to the commander to become a commander's critical information requirement (CCIR).

MDMP & TLP

Commander's Critical Information Requirements (CCIR)

Commanders consider staff input when determining their CCIRs. CCIRs are situation-dependent and specified by the commander for each operation. Commanders continuously review CCIRs during the planning process and adjust them as situations change. The initial CCIRs developed during mission analysis normally focus on decisions the commander needs to make to focus planning. Once the commander selects a COA, the CCIRs shift to information the commander needs in order to make decisions during preparation and execution. Commanders designate CCIRs to inform the staff and subordinates what they deem essential for making decisions. Typically, commanders identify ten or fewer CCIRs; minimizing the number of CCIRs assists in prioritizing the allocation of limited resources. CCIR fall into one of two categories: PIRs and friendly force information requirements (FFIRs).

See pp. 1-20 to 1-21 for further discussion of CCIRs, to include FFIRs and PIRs.

- **Priority Intelligence Requirements (PIRs).** A PIR is an intelligence requirement, stated as a priority for intelligence support, that the commander and staff need to understand the adversary or the operational environment. PIRs identify the information about the enemy and other aspects of the operational environment that the commander considers most important. Lessons from recent operations show that intelligence about civil considerations may be as critical as intelligence about the enemy. Thus, all staff sections may recommend information about civil considerations as PIRs. The intelligence officer manages PIRs for the commander through planning requirements and assessing collection.
- **Friendly Force Information Requirements (FFIRs).** An FFIR is information the commander and staff need to understand the status of friendly force and supporting capabilities. FFIRs identify the information about the mission, troops and support available, and time available for friendly forces that the commander considers most important. In coordination with the staff, the operations officer manages FFIRs for the commander.

Essential Elements of Friendly Information (EEFI)

In addition to nominating CCIRs to the commander, the staff also identifies and nominates essential elements of friendly information (EEFIs). Although EEFIs are not CCIRs, they have the same priority as CCIRs and require approval by the commander. An EEFI establishes an element of information to protect rather than one to collect. EEFIs identify those elements of friendly force information that, if compromised, would jeopardize mission success. Like CCIRs, EEFIs change as an operation progresses.

See p. 1-21 for further discussion of EEFI.

Depending on the situation, the commander and selected staff members meet prior to the mission analysis brief to approve the initial CCIRs and EEFIs. This is especially important if the commander intends to conduct reconnaissance and collect information early in the planning process. The approval of the initial CCIRs early in planning assist the staff in developing the initial reconnaissance and surveillance synchronization plan and the subsequent reconnaissance and surveillance plan. Approval of an EEFI allows the staff to begin planning and implementing measures to protect friendly force information, such as military deception and operations security.

9. Develop the Initial Information Collection Plan

The initial information collection plan is crucial to begin or adjust the information collection effort to help answer information requirements necessary in developing effective plans. The initial information collection plan sets reconnaissance, surveillance, and intelligence operations in motion. It may be issued as part of a WARNORD, a fragmentary order (FRAGORD), or an OPORD. As more information becomes available, it is incorporated into a complete information collection plan (Annex L) to the OPORD.

The intelligence staff creates the requirements management tools for the information collection plan. The operations staff is responsible for the information collection plan. During this step, the operations and intelligence staff work closely to ensure they fully synchronize and integrate information collection activities into the overall plan.

The operations officer considers several factors when developing the initial information collection plan, including:

- Requirements for collection assets in subsequent missions.
- The time available to develop and refine the initial information collection plan.
- The risk the commander is willing to accept if information collection missions are begun before the information collection plan is fully integrated into the scheme of maneuver.
- Insertion and extraction methods for reconnaissance, security, surveillance, and intelligence collection assets.
- Contingencies for inclement weather to ensure coverage of key named areas of interest or target areas of interest.
- The communications plan for transmission of reports from assets to command posts.
- The inclusion of collection asset locations and movements into the fire support plan.
- The reconnaissance handover with higher or subordinate echelons.
- The sustainment support.
- Legal support requirements.

See pp. 3-53 to 3-56 for discussion of information collection as an integrating process from FM 3-55.

10. Update Plan for the Use of Available Time

As more information becomes available, the commander and staff refine their initial plan for the use of available time. They compare the time needed to accomplish tasks to the higher headquarters' timeline to ensure mission accomplishment is possible in the allotted time. They compare the timeline to the assumed enemy timeline or the projected timelines within the civil sector with how they anticipate conditions will unfold. From this, they determine windows of opportunity for exploitation, times when the unit will be at risk for enemy activity, or when action to arrest deterioration in the civil sector is required.

The commander and COS (XO) also refine the staff planning timeline. The refined timeline includes the:

- Subject, time, and location of briefings the commander requires
- Times of collaborative planning sessions and the medium over which they will take place
- Times, locations, and forms of rehearsals

11. Develop Initial Themes and Messages

Gaining and maintaining the trust of key actors is an important aspect of operations. Faced with the many different actors (individuals, organizations, and the public) connected with the operation, commanders identify and engage those actors who matter to operational success. These actors' behaviors can help solve or complicate the friendly forces' challenges as commanders strive to accomplish missions.

Themes and messages support operations and military actions:

- A **theme** is a unifying or dominant idea or image that expresses the purpose for military action. Themes tie to objectives, lines of effort, and end state conditions. They are overarching and apply to capabilities of public affairs, military information support operations, and Soldier and leader engagements.
- A **message** is a verbal, written, or electronic communications that supports an information theme focused on a specific actor or the public and in support of a specific action (task).

Units transmit information themes and messages to those actors or the public whose perceptions, attitudes, beliefs, and behaviors matter to the success of an operation.

The public affairs officer adjusts and refines themes and messages received from higher headquarters for use by the command. These themes and messages are designed to inform specific domestic and foreign audiences about current or planned military operations. The military information support operations element receives approved themes and messages. This element adjusts or refines depending on the situation. It employs themes and messages as part of planned activities designed to influence specific foreign audiences for various purposes that support current or planned operations. The commander and the chief of staff approve all themes and messages used to support operations. The information operations officer assists the G-3 (S-3) and the commander to de-conflict and synchronize the use of information-related capabilities used specifically to disseminate approved themes and messages during operations.

12. Develop a Proposed Problem Statement

A problem is an issue or obstacle that makes it difficult to achieve a desired goal or objective. As such, a problem statement is the description of the primary issue or issues that may impede commanders from achieving their desired end states.

Note: The commander, staff, and other partners develop the problem statement as part of Army design methodology. During mission analysis, the commander and staff review the problem statement and revise it as necessary based on the increased understanding of the situation. If Army design methodology activities do not precede mission analysis, then the commander and staff develop a problem statement prior to moving to Step 3—COA Development.

How the problem is formulated leads to particular solutions. It is important that commanders dedicate the time in identifying the right problem to solve and describe it clearly in a problem statement. Ideally, the commander and members of the staff meet to share their analysis of the situation. They talk with each other, synthesize the results of the current mission analysis, and determine the problem. If the commander is not available, the staff members talk among themselves.

As part of the discussion to help identify and understand the problem, the staff:

- Compares the current situation to the desired end state
- Brainstorms and lists issues that impede the commander from achieving the desired end state

Based on this analysis, the staff develops a proposed problem statement—a statement of the problem to be solved—for the commander's approval.

13. Develop a Proposed Mission Statement

The COS (XO) or operations officer prepares a proposed mission statement for the unit based on the mission analysis. The commander receives and approves the unit's mission statement normally during the mission analysis brief. A mission statement is a short sentence or paragraph that describes the organization's essential task (or tasks) and purpose—a clear statement of the action to be taken and the reason for doing so. The mission statement contains the elements of who, what, when, where, and why, but seldom specifies how (JP 5-0). The five elements of a mission statement answer the questions:

- **Who** will execute the operation (unit or organization)?
- **What** is the unit's essential task (tactical mission task)?
- **When** will the operation begin (by time or event) or what is the duration of the operation?
- **Where** will the operation occur (area of operations, objective, grid coordinates)?
- **Why** will the force conduct the operations (for what purpose)?

The who, where, and when of a mission statement are straightforward. The what and why are more challenging to write and can confuse subordinates if not stated clearly. The what is a task and is expressed in terms of action verbs. These tasks are measurable and can be grouped as "actions by friendly forces" or "effects on enemy forces." The why puts the task into context by describing the reason for performing it. The why provides the mission's purpose—the reason the unit is to perform the task. It is extremely important to mission command and mission orders.

See facing page for further discussion.

14. Present the Mission Analysis Briefing

The mission analysis briefing informs the commander of the results of the staff's analysis of the situation. It helps the commander understand, visualize, and describe the operations. Throughout the mission analysis briefing, the commander, staff, and other partners discuss the various facts and assumptions about the situation. Staff officers present a summary of their running estimates from their specific functional area and how their findings impact or are impacted by other areas. This helps the commander and staff as a whole to focus on the interrelationships among the mission variables and to develop a deeper understanding of the situation. The commander issues guidance to the staff for continued planning based on situational understanding gained from the mission analysis briefing.

Ideally, the commander holds several informal meetings with key staff members before the mission analysis briefing, including meetings to assist the commander in developing CCIRs, the mission statement, and themes and messages. These meetings enable commanders to issue guidance for activities (such as reconnaissance, surveillance, security, and intelligence operations) and develop their initial commander's intent and planning guidance.

A comprehensive mission analysis briefing helps the commander, staff, subordinates, and other partners develop a shared understanding of the requirements of the upcoming operation. Time permitting, the staff briefs the commander on its mission analysis:

- Mission and commander's intent of the headquarters two levels up
- Mission, commander's intent, and concept of operations of the headquarters one level up
- A proposed problem statement
- A proposed mission statement
- Review of the commander's initial guidance

Proposed Mission Statement

Ref: FM 6-0 (C2), Commander and Staff Organization and Operations (Apr '16), pp. 9-12 to 9-13.

The mission statement contains the elements of who, what, when, where, and why, but seldom specifies how. The five elements of a mission statement answer the questions:

- **Who** will execute the operation (unit or organization)?
- **What** is the unit's essential task (tactical mission task)?
- **When** will the operation begin (by time or event) or what is the duration of the operation?
- **Where** will the operation occur (area of operations, objective, grid coordinates)?
- **Why** will the force conduct the operations (for what purpose or reason)?

The what is a task and is expressed in terms of action verbs. These tasks are measurable and can be grouped as "actions by friendly forces" or "effects on enemy forces." The why puts the task into context by describing the reason for performing it. The why provides the mission's purpose—the reason the unit is to perform the task. It is extremely important to mission command and mission orders.

Example 1. *Not later than 220400 Aug 09 (when), 1st Brigade (who) secures ROUTE SOUTH DAKOTA (what/task) in AREA OF OPERATIONS JACKRABBIT (where) to enable the movement of humanitarian assistance materials (why/purpose).*

Example 2. *1-505th Parachute Infantry Regiment (who) seizes (what/task) JACKSON INTERNATIONAL AIRPORT (where) not later than D-day, H+3 (when) to allow follow-on forces to air-land into AREA OF OPERATIONS SPARTAN (why/ purpose).*

The mission statement may have more than one essential task:

Example. *1-509th Parachute Infantry Regiment (who) seizes (what/task) JACKSON INTERNATIONAL AIRPORT (where) not later than D-day, H+3 (when) to allow follow-on forces to air-land into AREA OF OPERATIONS SPARTAN (why/purpose). On order (when), secures (what/task) OBJECTIVE GOLD (where) to prevent the 2nd Pandor Guards Brigade from crossing the BLUE RIVER and disrupting operations in AREA OF OPERATIONS SPARTAN (why/purpose).*

Tactical Mission Tasks

Commanders should use tactical mission tasks or other doctrinally approved tasks contained in combined arms field manuals or mission training plans in mission statements. These tasks have specific military definitions that differ from dictionary definitions. A tactical mission task is a specific activity performed by a unit while executing a form of tactical operation or form of maneuver. It may be expressed as either an action by a friendly force or effects on an enemy force (FM 7-15). FM 3-90-1 describes each tactical task. FM 3-07 provides a list of primary stability tasks which military forces must be prepared to execute. Commanders and planners should carefully choose the task that best describes the commander's intent and planning guidance.

The following is a list of commonly used tactical mission tasks; see pp. 7-35 to 7-38 for a listing of tactical mission tasks to include symbols and definitions:

- attack by fire
- block
- breach
- bypass
- canalize
- clear
- contain
- control
- counter reconnaissance
- defeat
- destroy
- disengage
- disrupt
- exfiltrate
- fix
- follow and assume
- follow and support
- interdict
- isolate
- neutralize
- occupy
- reduce
- retain
- secure
- seize
- support-by-fire
- suppress
- turn

- Initial IPB products, including civil considerations that impact the conduct of operations
- Specified, implied, and essential tasks
- Pertinent facts and assumptions
- Constraints
- Forces available and resource shortfalls
- Initial risk assessment
- Proposed themes and messages
- Proposed CCIRs and EEFIs
- Initial information collection plan
- Recommended timeline
- Recommended collaborative planning sessions

During the mission analysis briefing or shortly thereafter, commanders approve the mission statement and CCIRs. They then develop and issue their initial commander's intent and planning guidance.

15. Develop and Issue Initial Commander's Intent

The commander's intent is a clear and concise expression of the purpose of the operation and the desired military end state that supports mission command, provides focus to the staff, and helps subordinate and supporting commanders act to achieve the commander's desired results without further orders, even when the operation does not unfold as planned (JP 3-0). The initial commander's intent describes the purpose of the operation, initial key tasks, and the desired end state

See p. 1-20 for further discussion of commander's intent.

The higher commander's intent provides the basis for unity of effort throughout the force. Each commander's intent nests within the higher commander's intent. The commander's intent explains the broader purpose of the operation beyond that of the mission statement. This explanation allows subordinate commanders and Soldiers to gain insight into what is expected of them, what constraints apply, and most importantly, why the mission is being conducted.

Based on their situational understanding, commanders summarize their visualization in their initial commander's intent statement. The initial commander's intent links the operation's purpose with conditions that define the desired end state. Commanders may change their intent statement as planning progresses and more information becomes available. The commander's intent must be easy to remember and clearly understood by leaders two echelons lower in the chain of command. The shorter the commander's intent, the better it serves these purposes. Typically, the commander's intent statement is three to five sentences long and contains the purpose, key tasks, and end state.

16. Develop and Issue Initial Planning Guidance

Commanders provide planning guidance along with their initial commander's intent. Planning guidance conveys the essence of the commander's visualization. This guidance may be broad or detailed, depending on the situation. The initial planning guidance outlines an operational approach—a description of the broad actions the force must take to transform current conditions into those desired at end state (JP 5-0). The initial planning guidance outlines specific COAs the commander desires the staff to look at as well as rules out any COAs the commander will not accept. That clear guidance allows the staff to develop several COAs without wasting effort on things that the commander will not consider. It reflects how the commander sees the operation unfolding. It broadly describes when, where, and how the commander intends to employ combat power to accomplish the mission within the higher commander's intent.

Commander's Planning Guidance by Warfighting Function

Ref: FM 6-0 (C2), Commander and Staff Organization and Operations (Apr '16), table 9-1, p. 9-15.

The following list is not intended to meet the need of all situations. Commanders tailor planning guidance to meet specific needs based on the situation rather than address each item.

Mission Command	**Commander's critical information requirements** **Rules of engagement** **Command post positioning** **Commander's location** **Initial themes and messages** **Succession of command**	**Liaison officer guidance** **Planning and operational guidance timeline** **Type of order and rehearsal** **Communications guidance** **Civil affairs operations** **Cyber electromagnetic considerations**
Intelligence	**Information collection guidance** **Information gaps** **Most likely and most dangerous enemy courses of action** **Priority intelligence requirements** **Most critical terrain and weather factors**	**Most critical local environment and civil considerations** **Intelligence requests for information** **Intelligence focus during phased operations** **Desired enemy perception of friendly forces**
Movement and Maneuver	**Commander's intent** **Course of action development guidance** **Number of courses of action to consider or not consider** **Critical events** **Task organization** **Task and purpose of subordinate units** **Forms of maneuver** **Reserve composition, mission, priorities, and control measures**	**Security and counterreconnaissance** **Friendly decision points** **Branches and sequels** **Task and direct collection** **Military deception** **Risk to friendly forces** **Collateral damage or civilian casualties** **Any condition that affects achievement of endstate** **Informationoperations**
Fires	**Synchronization and focus of fires with maneuver** **Priority of fires** **High priority targets** **Special munitions** **Target acquisition zones** **Observer plan** **Air and missile defense positioning** **High-value targets**	**Task and purpose of fires** **Scheme of fires** **Suppression of enemy air defenses** **Fire support coordination measures** **Attack guidance** **Branches and sequels** **No strike list** **Restricted target list**
Protection	**Protection priorities** **Priorities for survivability assets** **Terrain and weather factors** **Intelligence focus and limitations for security** **Acceptable risk** **Protected targets and areas**	**Vehicle and equipment safety or security constraints** **Environmental considerations** **Unexploded ordnance** **Operations security risk tolerance** **Rules of engagement** **Escalation of force and nonlethal weapons** **Counterintelligence**
Sustainment	**Sustainment priorities—manning, fueling, fixing, arming, moving the force, and sustaining Soldiers and systems** **Health system support** **Sustainment of detainee and resettlement operations**	**Construction and provision of facilities and installations** **Detainee movement** **Anticipated requirements of Classes III, IV, V** **Controlled supply rates**

Refer to AODS6-1: The Army Operations & Doctrine SMARTbook, 6th Ed. (w/SMARTupdate 1) for discussion of the fundamentals, principles and tenets of Army operations, plus chapters on each of the six warfighting functions: command & control, movement and maneuver, intelligence, fires, sustainment, and protection.

Commanders use their experience and judgment to add depth and clarity to their planning guidance. They ensure staffs understand the broad outline of their visualization while allowing the latitude necessary to explore different options. This guidance provides the basis for a detailed concept of operations without dictating the specifics of the final plan. As with their intent, commanders may modify planning guidance based on staff and subordinate input and changing conditions.

Commanders issue planning guidance initially after mission analysis. They continue to consider additional guidance throughout the MDMP including, but not limited, to the following::

- Upon receipt of or in anticipation of a mission (initial planning guidance)
- Following mission analysis (planning guidance for COA development)
- Following COA development (revised planning guidance for COAs)
- COA approval (revised planning guidance to complete the plan)

See previous page for a listing of commander's planning guidance by warfighting function.

17. Develop Course of Action Evaluation Criteria

Evaluation criteria are standards the commander and staff will later use to measure the relative effectiveness and efficiency of one COA relative to other COAs. Developing these criteria during mission analysis helps to eliminate a source of bias prior to COA analysis and comparison. Evaluation criteria address factors that affect success and those that can cause failure. Criteria change from mission to mission and must be clearly defined and understood by all staff members before starting the war game to test the proposed COAs. Normally, the COS (XO) initially determines each proposed criterion with weights based on the assessment of its relative importance and the commander's guidance. Commanders adjust criteria selection and weighting according to their own experience and vision. Higher weights are assigned to more important criteria. The staff member responsible for a functional area ranks each COA using those criteria. The staff presents the proposed evaluation criteria to the commander at the mission analysis brief for approval.

18. Issue a Warning Order

Immediately after the commander gives the planning guidance, the staff sends subordinate and supporting units a WARNORD. It contains, at a minimum:

- The approved mission statement
- The commander's intent
- Changes to task organization
- The unit area of operations (sketch, overlay, or some other description)
- CCIRs and EEFIs
- Risk guidance
- Priorities by warfighting functions
- Military deception guidance
- Essential stability tasks
- Initial information collection plan
- Specific priorities
- Updated operational timeline
- Movements

See p. 4-21 for a sample warning order format.

Chap 2

MDMP Step III. COA Development

Ref: FM 6-0 (C2), Commander and Staff Organization and Operations (Apr '16), pp. 9-16 to 9-25.

A COA is a broad potential solution to an identified problem. The COA development step generates options for follow-on analysis and comparison that satisfy the commander's intent and planning guidance. During COA development, planners use the problem statement, mission statement, commander's intent, planning guidance, and various knowledge products developed during mission analysis.

III. COA Development

Key Inputs	Key Outputs
▪ Mission statement ▪ Initial commander's intent, planning guidance, CCIRs, and EEFIs ▪ Updated IPB and running estimates ▪ Assumptions ▪ Evaluation Criteria for COAs	▪ COA statements and sketches - Tentative task organization - Broad concept of operations ▪ Revised planning guidance ▪ Updated assumptions

1. Assess Relative Combat Power
2. Generate Options
3. Array Forces
4. Develop a Broad Concept
5. Assign Headquarters
6. Prepare COA Statements & Sketches
7. Conduct COA Briefing
8. Select or Modify COAs for Continued Analysis

Ref: FM 6-0 (C2), Commander and Staff Organization and Operations, fig. 9-4, p. 9-16.

1. Assess Relative Combat Power

Combat power is the total means of destructive, constructive, and information capabilities that a military unit/formation can apply at a given time. Army forces generate combat power by converting potential into effective action (ADP 3-0). Combat power is the effect created by combining the elements of intelligence, movement and maneuver, fires, sustainment, protection, mission command, information, and leadership. The goal is to generate overwhelming combat power to accomplish the mission at minimal cost.

To assess relative combat power, planners initially make a rough estimate of force ratios of maneuver units two levels down. For example, at division level, planners compare all types of maneuver battalions with enemy maneuver battalion equivalents. Planners then compare friendly strengths against enemy weaknesses, and vice versa, for each element of combat power. From these comparisons, they may deduce particular vulnerabilities for each force that may be exploited or may need protection. These comparisons provide planners insight into effective force employment.

In troop-to-task analysis for stability and defense support of civil authorities, staffs determine relative combat power by comparing available resources to specified or implied stability or civil support tasks. This analysis provides insight as available options and needed resources. In such operations, the elements of sustainment, movement and maneuver, non-lethal effects, and information may dominate. By analyzing force ratios and determining and comparing each force's strengths and weaknesses as a function of combat power, planners can gain insight into:

- Friendly capabilities that pertain to the operation
- The types of operations possible from both friendly and enemy perspectives
- How and where the enemy may be vulnerable
- How and where friendly forces are vulnerable
- Additional resources needed to execute the mission
- How to allocate existing resources

Planners must not develop and recommend COAs based solely on mathematical analysis of force ratios. Although the process uses some numerical relationships, the estimate is largely subjective. Assessing combat power requires assessing both tangible and intangible factors, such as morale and levels of training. A relative combat power assessment identifies exploitable enemy weaknesses, identifies unprotected friendly weaknesses, and determines the combat power necessary to conduct essential stability or defense support of civil authorities tasks.

2. Generate Options

Based on the commander's guidance and the initial results of the relative combat power assessment, the staff generates options. A good COA can defeat all feasible enemy COAs while accounting for essential stability tasks. In an unconstrained environment, planners aim to develop several possible COAs. Depending on available time, commanders may limit the options in the commander's guidance. Options focus on enemy COAs arranged in order of their probable adoption or on those stability tasks that are most essential to prevent the situation from deteriorating further.

Brainstorming is the preferred technique for generating options. It requires time, imagination, and creativity, but it produces the widest range of choices. The staff (and members of organizations outside the headquarters) remains unbiased and open-minded when developing proposed options.

In developing COAs, staff members determine the doctrinal requirements for each proposed operation, including doctrinal tasks for subordinate units. For example, a deliberate breach requires a breach force, a support force, and an assault force. Essential stability tasks require the ability to provide a level of civil security, civil control, and certain essential services. In addition, the staff considers the potential capabilities of attachments and other organizations and agencies outside military channels.

Course of Action (COA) Development

Ref: FM 6-0 (C2), Commander and Staff Organization and Operations (Apr '16), p. 9-17.

Embedded in COA development is the application of operational and tactical art. Planners develop different COAs by varying combinations of the elements of operational design, such as phasing, lines of effort, and tempo. (See ADRP 3-0.) Planners convert the approved COA into the concept of operations.

COA Screening Criteria

The commander's direct involvement in COA development greatly aids in producing comprehensive and flexible COA's within the available time. To save time, the commander may also limit the number of COA's to be developed or specify particular COA's not to explore. Planners examine each prospective COA for validity using the following screening criteria:

Feasible

The COA can accomplish the mission within the established time, space, and resource limitations

Acceptable

The COA must balance cost and risk with the advantage gained

Suitable

The COA can accomplish the mission within the commander's intent and planning guidance

Distinguishable

Each COA must differ significantly from the others (such as scheme or form of maneuver, lines of effort, phasing, day or night operations, use of reserves, and task organization)

Complete

A COA must incorporate:

- How the decisive operation or effort leads to mission accomplishment
- How shaping operations or efforts create and preserve conditions for success of the decisive operation or effort
- How sustaining operations enable shaping and decisive operations or efforts
- How offensive, defensive, and stability tasks are accounted for
- How to account for offensive, defensive, and stability or defense support of civil authorities tasks.
- Tasks to be performed and conditions to be achieved.

It is important in COA development that commanders and staffs appreciate the unpredictable and uncertain nature of the operational environment, and understand how to cope with ambiguity. Some problems that commanders face are straightforward, as when clearly defined guidance is provided from higher headquarters, or when resources required for a mission are available and can easily be allocated. In such cases, the COA is often self evident. However, for problems that are unfamiliar or ambiguous, Army design methodology may assist commanders in better understanding the nature of the problem, and afford both the commander and staff a level of comfort necessary to effectively advance through COA development. Commanders and staffs that are comfortable with ambiguity will often find that the Army design methodology provides flexibility in developing COAs that contain multiple options for dealing with changing circumstances. Staffs tend to focus on specific COAs for specific sets of circumstances, when it is usually best to focus on flexible COAs that provide the greatest options to account for the widest range of circumstances.

Army leaders are responsible for clearly articulating their visualization of operations in time, space, purpose, and resources in order to generate options. ADRP 3-0 describes in detail three established operational frameworks. Army leaders are not bound by any specific framework in organizing operations, but three operational frameworks, mentioned below, have proven valuable in the past. The higher headquarters will direct the specific framework or frameworks to be used by subordinate headquarters; the frameworks should be consistent throughout all echelons. The three operational frameworks are—

- Deep-close-security
- Main and supporting effort
- Decisive-shaping-sustaining

For example, when generating options for a decisive-shaping-sustaining operation, the staff starts with the decisive operation identified in the commander's planning guidance. The staff checks that the decisive operation nests within the higher headquarters' concept of operations. The staff clarifies the decisive operation's purpose and considers ways to mass the effects (lethal and nonlethal) of overwhelming combat power to achieve it.

Next, the staff considers shaping operations. The staff establishes a purpose for each shaping operation tied to creating or preserving a condition for the decisive operation's success. Shaping operations may occur before, concurrently with, or after the decisive operation. A shaping operation may be designated as the main effort if executed before or after the decisive operation.

The staff then determines sustaining operations necessary to create and maintain the combat power required for the decisive operation and shaping operation. After developing the basic operational organization for a given COA, the staff then determines the essential tasks for each decisive, shaping, and sustaining operation.

Once staff members have explored possibilities for each COA, they examine each COA to determine if it satisfies the pre-determined screening criteria. In doing so, they change, add, or eliminate COAs as appropriate. During this process, staffs avoid focusing on the development of one good COA among several throwaway COAs.

3. Array Forces

After determining the decisive and shaping operations and their related tasks and purposes, planners determine the relative combat power required to accomplish each task. Planners may use minimum historical planning ratios as a starting point:

Historical Minimum Planning Data

Friendly Mission	*Position*	*Friendly:Enemy*
Delay		1:6
Defend	Prepared or fortified	1:3
Defend	Hasty	1:2.5
Attack	Prepared or fortified	3:1
Attack	Hasty	2.5:1
Counterattack	Flank	1:1

FM 6-0 (C2), Commander & Staff Organization & Operations, table 9-2, p. 4-20.

For example, historically defenders have over a 50% probability of defeating an attacking force approximately three times their equivalent strength. Therefore, as a starting point, commanders may defend on each avenue of approach with roughly a 1:3 force ratio.

Planners determine whether these and other intangibles increase the relative combat power of the unit assigned the task to the point that it exceeds the historical planning ratio for that task. If it does not, planners determine how to reinforce the unit. Combat power comparisons are provisional at best. Arraying forces is tricky, inexact work, affected by factors that are difficult to gauge, such as impact of past engagements, quality of leaders, morale, maintenance of equipment, and time in position. Levels of electronic warfare support, fire support, close air support, civilian support, and many other factors also affect arraying forces.

In counterinsurgency operations, planners can develop force requirements by gauging troop density—the ratio of security forces (including host-nation military and police forces as well as foreign counterinsurgents) to inhabitants. Most density recommendations fall within a range of 20 to 25 counterinsurgents for every 1,000 residents in an AO. Twenty counterinsurgents per 1,000 residents are often considered the minimum troop density required for effective counterinsurgency operations; however, as with any fixed ratio, such calculations strongly depend on the situation.

Planners also determine relative combat power with regard to civilian requirements and conditions that require attention and then array forces and capabilities for stability tasks. For example, a COA may require a follow-on force to establish civil security, maintain civil control, and restore essential services in a densely populated urban area over an extended period. Planners conduct a troop-to-task analysis to determine the type of units and capabilities needed to accomplish these tasks.

Planners then proceed to initially array friendly forces starting with the decisive operation and continuing with all shaping and sustaining operations. Planners normally array ground forces two levels down. The initial array focuses on generic ground maneuver units without regard to specific type or task organization and then considers all appropriate intangible factors. During this step, planners do not assign missions to specific units; they only consider which forces are necessary to accomplish its task. In this step, planners also array assets to accomplish essential stability tasks.

The initial array identifies the total number of units needed and identifies possible methods of dealing with the enemy and stability tasks. If the number arrayed is less than the number available, planners place additional units in a pool for use when they develop the initial concept of the operation. If the number of units arrayed exceeds the number available and the difference cannot be compensated for with intangible factors, the staff determines whether the COA is feasible. Ways to make up the shortfall include requesting additional resources, accepting risk in that portion of the area of operations, or executing tasks required for the COA sequentially rather than simultaneously. Commanders should also consider requirements to minimize and relieve civilian suffering. Establishing civil security and providing essential services such as medical care, water, food, and shelter are implied tasks for commanders during any combat operation.

4. Develop a Broad Concept

In developing the broad concept of the operation, the commander describes how arrayed forces will accomplish the mission within the commander's intent. The broad concept concisely expresses the how of the commander's visualization and will eventually provide the framework for the concept of operations and summarizes the contributions of all warfighting functions. The staff develops the initial concept of the operation for each COA expressed in both narrative and graphic forms. A sound COA is more than the arraying of forces. It presents an overall combined arms idea that will accomplish the mission. The initial concept of the operation includes, but is not limited to, the following:

- The purpose of the operation
- A statement of where the commander will accept risk
- Identification of critical friendly events and transitions between phases (if the operation is phased)

- Designation of the reserve, including its location and composition
- Information collection activities
- Essential stability tasks
- Identification of maneuver options that may develop during an operation
- Assignment of subordinate areas of operations
- Scheme of fires
- Themes, messages, and means of delivery
- Military deception operations (on a need to know basis)
- Key control measures
- Designate the operational framework for this operation: deep-close-security, main and supporting effort, or decisive-shaping-sustaining
- Designation of the decisive operation, along with its task and purpose, linked to how it supports the higher headquarters' concept

Planners select control measures, including graphics, to control subordinate units during an operation. These establish responsibilities and limits that prevent subordinate units' actions from impeding one another. These measures also foster coordination and cooperation between forces without unnecessarily restricting freedom of action. Good control measures foster decision making and individual initiative.

Planners may use both lines of operations and lines of effort to build their broad concept. Lines of operations portray the more traditional links among objectives, decisive points, and centers of gravity. A line of effort, however, helps planners link multiple tasks with goals, objectives, and end state conditions. Combining lines of operations with lines of efforts allows planners to include nonmilitary activities in their broad concept. This combination helps commanders incorporate stability or defense support of civil authorities tasks that, when accomplished, help set end state conditions of the operation. Based on the commander's planning guidance (informed by the design concept if design preceded the MDMP), planners develop lines of effort by:

- Confirming end state conditions from the initial commander's intent and planning guidance
- Determining and describing each line of effort
- Identifying objectives (intermediate goals) and determining tasks along each line of effort

During COA development, lines of efforts are general and lack specifics, such as tasks to subordinate units associated to objectives along each line of effort. Units develop and refine lines of effort, to include specific tasks to subordinate units, during war-gaming. As planning progresses, commanders may modify lines of effort and add details while war-gaming. Operations with other instruments of national power support a broader, comprehensive approach to stability operations. Each operation, however, differs. Commanders develop and modify lines of effort to focus operations on achieving the end state, even as the situation evolves.

5. Assign Headquarters

After determining the broad concept, planners create a task organization by assigning headquarters to groupings of forces. They consider the types of units to be assigned to a headquarters and the ability of that headquarters to control those units. Generally, a headquarters controls at least two subordinate maneuver units (but not more than five) for fast-paced offensive or defensive operations. The number and type of units assigned to a headquarters for stability operations vary based on factors of the mission variables (known as METT-TC). If planners need additional headquarters, they note the shortage and resolve it later. Task organization takes into account the entire operational organization. It also accounts for the special mission command requirements for operations, such as a passage of lines, or air assault.

Sample COA Sketch and Statement

Ref: FM 6-0 (C2), Commander and Staff Organization and Operations (Apr '16), fig. 9-5, pp. 9-24 to 9-25.

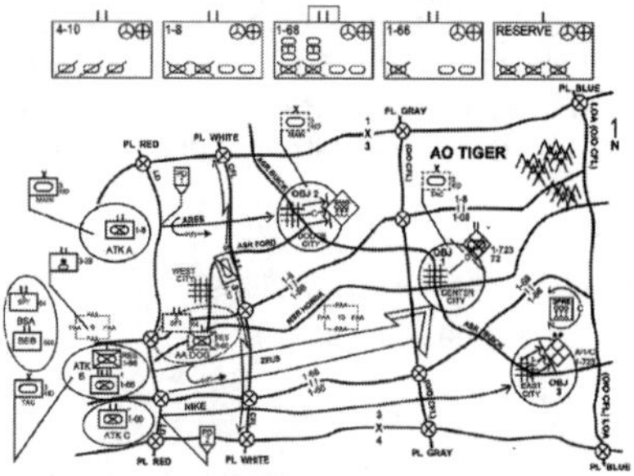

MISSION: On order, 3d ABCT clears remnants of the 72d Brigade in AO TIGER to establish security and enable the host-nation in reestablishing civil control in the region.

COMMANDER'S INTENT: The purpose of this operation is to provide a safe and secure environment in AO TIGER to enable the host-nation and other civilian organizations to reestablish civil control, restore essential services, and reestablish local governance within the area. The **key tasks** are: 1) destroy remnants of the 72nd BDE; 2) secure population centers vic OBHs 1, 2, and 3; 3) transition authority to the host nation. At **end state**, the BCT has destroyed remnant enemy forces in AO TIGER, secured population centers, and is prepared to transition responsibility for security to hostnnation authority.

INFORMATION COLLECTION: Priority of reconnaissance initially to locate enemy forces between PL RED (LD) and PL WHITE. Information collection operations subsequently focus on: 1) Identifying the location and disposition of enemy forces vic OBJ 1; 2) Observation of MSR HONDA between PL WHITE and PL BLUE; 3) observation of dislocated civilian traffic from CENTER CITY to EAST CITY.

SHAPING OPERATIONS:

4-10 CAV (ME) initially screens along PL WHITE IOT deny enemy reconnaissance and provide freedom of maneuver to follow on operations. On order, conducts FPOL at PL WHITE IOT move 1-8 CAB and 1-66 CAB(-) foward to conduct operations while maintaining contact with enemy.

O/O, **1-8 CAB (SE)** in the north moves from ATK A, crosses LD at PD1 on DIRECTION OF ATTACK ARES, conducts FPOL, and clears hostile gang vic OBJ 2 IOT enable NGO delivery of humanitarian assistance to WEST CITY and DODGE CITY.

TF 1-68 (SE) in the center occupies ATK B IOT prepare for follow on operations. On order, 1-66 CAB(-) (SE) in the south moves from ATK C, crosses LD at PD2, attacks along DIRECTION OF ATTACK NIKE, and clears enemy vic OBJ 3 IOT prevent disruption of DO vic OBJ 1.

588 BEB (SE) occupies BSA IOT set conditions for follow on operations.

RESERVE initially establishes vic ATK B. On order, displace to AA DOG (east). Priority of commitment to DO vic OBJ 1.

DECISIVE OPERATION:

4-10 CAV (SE) conducts FPOL vic PL WHITE IOT move 1-68 CAB (ME) forward to conduct operations while maintaining enemy contact. On order, occupy AA DOG (south) IOT prepare for future operations. BPT conduct security operations in northeastern portion of AO TIGER IOT provide early and accurate warning of enemy or hostile threats to the security of the population centers.

1-8 CAB (SE) controls ASRs BUICK and FORD in assigned AO IOT facilitate sustaining operations and prevent civilians interference with DO vic OBJ 1.

O/O, TF -68 (ME) moves from ATK B along AXIS ZEUS, conducts FPOL, and attacks to destroy elements of 72nd BDE vic OBJ 1 IOT provide a secure environment for the CENTER CITY population. Bypass criteria is platoon-size or smaller.

1-66 CAB(-) (SE) controls DPRE camp vic EAST CITY IOT provide a secure environment and controls ASR BUICK in assigned AO IOT facilitate sustaining operations and prevent civilian intereference with DO vic OBJ 1.

588 BEB (SE) conducts operations as required IOT support DO.

RESERVE establishes in AA DOG (east). Priority of commitment is to reinforce DO vic OBJ 1.

FIRES:

(Shaping Operations): Priority of fires to 4-10 CAV, 1-8 CAB, 1-66 CAB, and TF 1-68 initially from PAA 9. O/O displace to PAA 10. HPTs are enemy reconnaissance forces, indirect fire systems, and mechanized enemy forces.

(Decisive Operations): Priority of fires to TF 1-68 (ME), 1-66 CAB, 1-8 CAB, and 4-10 CAB from PAA 10. HPTs are enemy armor, mechanized enemy forces, and indirect fire systems.

FSCM: CFL initially PL WHITE, O/O PL Gray, O/O PL BLUE (LOA).

SUSTAINING OPERATIONS:

(Shaping Operations): 64 BSB will initially establish operations in BSA. O/O, establish BSA in AA DOG vic WEST CITY using MSR HONDA, ASR FORD, and ASR BUICK as primary routes IOT sustain operations. Establish FLEs as required to support operations. Priority of support to 4-10 CAV (ME) will be class III, V, maintenance, and medical.

(Decisive Operations): Priority of support to TF 1-68 (ME) will be class III, V, maintenance, and medical. Coordinate with humanitarian relief agencies IOT facilitate rapid restoration of essential services in AO TIGER.

MISSION COMMAND:

(Command): 3rd ABCT commander located with TAC CP and executive officer located with MAIN CP throughout mission.

(Control/Signal): 3rd ABCT **MAIN CP** initially located vic ATK A. O/O displaces vic OBJ 2. 3rd ABCT **TAC CP** initially located vic ATK B. O/O, displaces vic OBJ 1.

RISK: Based on intelligence reports of negative enemy activity in the northeast mountainous portion of AO TIGER, risk is assumed with no ground maneuver forces initially allocated to conduct reconnaissance or surveillance operations. Mitigation will be accomplished by assigning a BPT mission to 4-10 CAV to conduct security operations IOT provide early and accurate warning of enemy or hostile threats to security of population centers.

MDMP & TLP

6. Prepare COA Statements and Sketches

The G-3 (S-3) prepares a COA statement and supporting sketch for each COA. The COA statement clearly portrays how the unit will accomplish the mission. The COA statement briefly expresses how the unit will conduct the combined arms concept. The sketch provides a picture of the movement and maneuver aspects of the concept, including the positioning of forces. Together, the statement and sketch cover the who (generic task organization), what (tasks), when, where, and why (purpose) for each subordinate unit. The COA sketch includes the array of generic forces and control measures, such as:

- The unit and subordinate unit boundaries
- Unit movement formations (but not subordinate unit formations)
- The line of departure or line of contact and phase lines, if used
- Information collection graphics
- Ground and air axes of advance
- Assembly areas, battle positions, strong points, engagement areas, and objectives
- Obstacle control measures and tactical mission graphics
- Fire support coordination and airspace coordinating measures
- Main effort
- Location of command posts and critical information systems nodes
- Known or templated enemy locations
- Population concentrations

Planners can include identifying features (such as cities, rivers, and roads) to help orient users. The sketch may be on any medium. What it portrays is more important than its form.

7. Conduct a Course of Action Briefing

After developing COAs, the staff briefs them to the commander. A collaborative session may facilitate subordinate planning. The COA briefing includes:

- An updated IPB (if there are significant changes).
- As many threat COAs as necessary (or specified by the commander). At a minimum the most likely and most dangerous threat COAs must be developed.
- The approved problem statement and mission statement.
- The commander's and higher commander's intents.
- COA statements and sketches, including lines of effort if used.
- The rationale for each COA, including:
  - Considerations that might affect enemy COAs
  - Critical events for each COA
  - Deductions resulting from the relative combat power analysis
  - The reason units are arrayed as shown on the sketch *(refer to ADP 1-02 for doctrine on COA*)*
  - The reason the staff used the selected control measures
  - The impact on civilians
  - How the COA accounts for minimum essential stability tasks
  - New facts and new or updated assumptions
  - Refined COA evaluation criteria

8. Select or Modify COAs for Continued Analysis

After the COA briefing, the commander selects or modifies those COAs for continued analysis. The commander also issues planning guidance. If commanders reject all COAs, the staff begins again. If commanders accept one or more of the COAs, staff members begin COA analysis. The commander may create a new COA by incorporating elements of one or more COAs developed by the staff. The staff then prepares to war-game this new COA. The staff incorporates those modifications and ensures all staff members understand the changed COA.

Chap 2

MDMP Step IV. COA Analysis & War-Gaming

Ref: FM 6-0 (C2), Commander and Staff Organization and Operations (Apr '16), pp. 9-26 to 9-39.

COA analysis enables commanders and staffs to identify difficulties or coordination problems as well as probable consequences of planned actions for each COA being considered. It helps them think through the tentative plan. COA analysis may require commanders and staffs to revisit parts of a COA as discrepancies arise. COA analysis not only appraises the quality of each COA, but it also uncovers potential execution problems, decisions, and contingencies. In addition, COA analysis influences how commanders and staffs understand a problem and may require the planning process to restart.

IV. COA Analysis (War Game)

Key Inputs	Key Outputs
▪ Updated running estimates ▪ Revised planning guidance ▪ COA statements and sketches ▪ Updated assumptions	▪ Refined COAs ▪ Potential decision points ▪ War-game results ▪ Initial assessment measures ▪ Updated assumptions

1. Gather the Tools
2. List all Friendly Forces
3. List Assumptions
4. List Known Critical Events & Decision Points
5. Select the War-Gaming Method
6. Select a Technique to Record and Display Results
7. War-Game the Operation and Assess the Results
8. Conduct a War-Game Briefing (Optional)

Ref: FM 6-0 (C2), Commander and Staff Organization and Operations, fig. 9-6, p. 9-26.

War-gaming is a disciplined process, with rules and steps that attempt to visualize the flow of the operation, given the force's strengths and dispositions, enemy's capabilities and possible COAs, impact and requirements of civilians in the AO, and other aspects of the situation. The simplest form of war-gaming is the manual method, often utilizing a tabletop approach with blowups of matrixes and templates. The most sophisticated form of war-gaming is modern, computer-aided modeling and simulation. Regardless of the form used, each critical event within a proposed COA should be war-gamed using the action, reaction, and counteraction methods of friendly and enemy forces interaction. This basic war-gaming method (modified to fit the specific mission and environment) applies to offensive, defensive, and stability or defense support of civil authorities operations. When conducting COA analysis, commanders and staffs perform the process actions and produce the outputs .

War-gaming results in refined COAs, a completed synchronization matrix, and decision support templates and matrixes for each COA. A synchronization matrix records the results of a war game. It depicts how friendly forces for a particular COA are synchronized in time, space, and purpose in relation to an enemy COA or other events in stability or defense support of civil authorities operations. The decision support template and matrix portray key decisions and potential actions that are likely to arise during the execution of each COA.

COA analysis allows the staff to synchronize the six war fighting functions for each COA. It also helps the commander and staff to:

- Determine how to maximize the effects of combat power while protecting friendly forces and minimizing collateral damage
- Further develop a visualization of the operation
- Anticipate operational events
- Determine conditions and resources required for success
- Determine when and where to apply force capabilities
- Identify coordination needed to produce synchronized results
- Determine the most flexible COA

During the war game, the staff takes each COA and begins to develop a detailed plan while determining its strengths or weaknesses. War-gaming tests and improves COAs. The commander, staff, and other available partners (and subordinate commanders and staffs if the war game is conducted collaboratively) may change an existing COA or develop a new COA after identifying unforeseen events, tasks, requirements, or problems.

General War-Gaming Rules

War gamers need to:

- Remain objective, not allowing personality or their sense of "what the commander wants" to influence them
- Avoid defending a COA just because they personally developed it
- Record advantages and disadvantages of each COA accurately as they emerge
- Continually assess feasibility, acceptability, and suitability of each COA. If a COA fails any of these tests, reject it
- Avoid drawing premature conclusions and gathering facts to support such conclusions
- Avoid comparing one COA with another during the war game. This occurs during Step 5—COA Comparison.

1. Gather the Tools

The first task for COA analysis is to gather the necessary tools to conduct the war game. The chief of staff or executive officer directs the staff to gather tools, materials, and data for the war game. Units war-game with maps, sand tables, computer simulations, or other tools that accurately reflect the terrain. The staff posts the COA on a map displaying the AO. Tools required include, but are not limited to:

- Running estimates
- Threat templates and models
- Civil considerations overlays, databases, and data files
- Modified combined obstacle overlays and terrain effects matrices
- A recording method
- Completed COAs, including graphics
- A means to post or display enemy and friendly unit symbols and other organizations
- A map of the area of operations

2. List All Friendly Forces

The commander and staff consider all units that can be committed to the operation, paying special attention to support relationships and constraints. This list must include assets from all participants operating in the AO. The friendly force list remains constant for all COA's.

3. List Assumptions

The commander and staff review previous assumptions for continued validity and necessity. Any changes resulting from this review are noted for record.

4. List Known Critical Events and Decision Points

A. Critical Events

A critical event is an event that directly influences mission accomplishment. Critical events include events that trigger significant actions or decisions (such as commitment of an enemy reserve), complicated actions requiring detailed study (such as a passage of lines), and essential tasks. The list of critical events includes major events from the unit's current position through mission accomplishment. It includes reactions by civilians that potentially affect operations or require allocation of significant assets to account for essential stability tasks.

B. Decision Points (DPs)

A decision point is a point in space and time when the commander or staff anticipates making a key decision concerning a specific course of action. Decision points may also be associated with the friendly force and the status of ongoing operations. A decision point will be associated with CCIRs that describe what information the commander requires to make the anticipated decision. The PIR describes what must be known about the enemy or the environment and often is associated with a named area of interest. A decision point requires a decision by the commander. It does not dictate what the decision is, only that the commander must make one, and when and where it should be made to maximally impact friendly or enemy COA's or the accomplishment of stability tasks.

MDMP & TLP

War-Gaming Responsibilities

Ref: FM 6-0 (C2), Commander and Staff Organization and Operations (Apr '16), pp. 9-36 to 9-39.

Mission Command Responsibilities

The commander has overall responsibility for the war-gaming process, and the commander can determine the staff members who are involved in war-gaming. Traditionally, certain staff members have key and specific roles.

The COS (XO) coordinates actions of the staff during the war game. This officer is the unbiased controller of the process, ensuring the staff stays on a timeline and achieves the goals of the war-gaming session. In a time-constrained environment, this officer ensures that, at a minimum, the decisive operation is war-gamed.

The G-3 (S-3) assists the commander with the rehearsal. The G-3 (S-3)—

- Portrays the friendly scheme of maneuver, including the employment of information-related capabilities.
- Ensures subordinate unit actions comply with the commander's intent.
- Normally provides the recorder.

The assistant chief of staff, signal (G-6 [S-6]) assesses network operations, spectrum management operations, network defense, and information protection feasibility of each war-gamed COA. The G-6 (S-6) determines communications systems requirements and compares them to available assets, identifies potential shortfalls, and recommends actions to eliminate or reduce their effects The information operations officer assesses the information operations concept of support against the ability of information-related capabilities to execute tasks in support of each war-gamed COA and the effectiveness of integrated information-related capabilities to impact various audiences and populations in and outside the area of operations. The information operations officer, in coordination with the electronic warfare officer, also integrates information operations with cyber electromagnetic activities.

The assistant chief of staff, civil affairs operations (G-9 [S-9]) ensures each war-gamed COA effectively integrates civil considerations (the "C" of METT-TC). The civil affairs operations officer considers not only tactical issues but also sustainment issues. This officer assesses how operations affect civilians and estimates the requirements for essential stability tasks commanders might have to undertake based on the ability of the unified action partners. Host-nation support and care of dislocated civilians are of particular concern. The civil affairs operations officer's analysis considers how operations affect public order and safety, the potential for disaster relief requirements, noncombatant evacuation operations, emergency services, and the protection of culturally significant sites. This officer provides feedback on how the culture in the area of operations affects each COA. If the unit lacks an assigned civil affairs officer, the commander assigns these responsibilities to another staff member.

The red team staff section provides the commander and assistant chief of staff, intelligence (G-2) with an independent capability to fully explore alternatives. The staff looks at plans, operations, concepts, organizations, and capabilities of the operational environment from the perspectives of enemies, unified action partners, and others.

The electronic warfare officer provides information on the electronic warfare target list, electronic attack taskings, electronic attack requests, and the electronic warfare portion of the collection matrix and the attack guidance matrix. Additionally, the electronic warfare officer assesses threat vulnerabilities, friendly electronic warfare capabilities, and friendly actions relative to electronic warfare activities and other cyber electromagnetic activities not covered by the G-6 or G-2.

The staff judge advocate advises the commander on all matters pertaining to law, policy, regulation, good order, and discipline for each war-gamed COA. This officer provides legal advice across the range of military operations on law of war, rules of engagement, international agreements, Geneva Conventions, treatment and disposition of noncombatants, and the legal aspects of targeting.

The operations research and systems analysis staff section provides analytic support to the commander for planning and assessment of operations. The safety officer provides input to influence accident and incident reductions by implementing risk management procedures throughout the mission planning and execution process. The knowledge management officer assesses the effectiveness of the knowledge management plan for each course of action. The space operations officer provides and represents friendly, threat, and non-aligned space capabilities.

Intelligence Responsibilities

During the war game the G-2 (S-2) role-plays the enemy commander, other threat organizations in the area of operations, and critical civil considerations in the area of operations. This officer develops critical enemy decision points in relation to the friendly COAs, projects enemy reactions to friendly actions, and projects enemy losses. The intelligence officer assigns different responsibilities to available staff members within the section (such as the enemy commander, friendly intelligence officer, and enemy recorder) for war-gaming. The intelligence officer captures the results of each enemy, threat group, and civil considerations action and counteraction as well as the corresponding friendly and enemy strengths and vulnerabilities. By trying to realistically win the war game for the enemy, the intelligence officer ensures that the staff fully addresses friendly responses for each enemy COA.

Movement and Maneuver Responsibilities

During the war game, the G-3 (S-3) and assistant chief of staff, plans (G-5 [S-5]) are responsible for movement and maneuver. The G-3 (S-3) normally selects the technique for the war game and role-plays the friendly maneuver commander. Various staff officers assist the G-3 (S-3), such as the aviation officer and engineer officer. The G-3 (S-3) executes friendly maneuver as outlined in the COA sketch and COA statement. The G-5 (S-5) assesses warfighting function requirements, solutions, and concepts for each COA; develops plans and orders; and determines potential branches and sequels arising from various war-gamed COAs. The G-5 (S-5) also coordinates and synchronizes warfighting functions in all plans and orders. The planning staff ensures that the war game of each COA covers every operational aspect of the mission. The members of the staff record each event's strengths and weaknesses and the rationale for each action. They complete the decision support template and matrix for each COA. They annotate the rationale for actions during the war game and use it later with the commander's guidance to compare COAs.

Fires Responsibilities

The chief of fires (fire support officer) assesses the fire support feasibility of each war-gamed COA. This officer develops a proposed high-payoff target list, target selection standards, and attack guidance matrix. The chief of fires works with the intelligence officer to identify named and target areas of interest for enemy indirect fire weapon systems, and identifies high-payoff targets and additional events that may influence the positioning of field artillery and air defense artillery assets. The chief of fires should also offer a list of possible defended assets for air defense artillery forces and assist the commander in making a final determination about asset priority.

Protection Responsibilities

The chief of protection assesses protection element requirements, refines EEFIs, and develops a scheme of protection for each war-gamed COA.

Sustainment Responsibilities

During the war game, the assistant chief of staff, personnel (G-1 [S-1]) assesses the personnel aspect of building and maintaining the combat power of units. This officer identifies potential shortfalls and recommends COAs to ensure units maintain adequate manning to accomplish their mission. As the primary staff officer assessing the human resources planning considerations to support sustainment operations, the G-1 (S-1) provides human resources support for the operation.

The assistant chief of staff, logistics (G-4 [S-4]) assesses the logistics feasibility of each war-gamed COA. This officer determines critical requirements for each logistics function (classes I through VII, IX, and X) and identifies potential problems and deficiencies. The G-4 (S-4) assesses the status of all logistics functions required to support the COA, including potential support required to provide essential services to the civilians, and compares it to available assets. This officer identifies potential shortfalls and recommends actions to eliminate or reduce their effects. While improvising can contribute to responsiveness, only accurately predicting requirements for each logistics function can ensure continuous sustainment. The logistics officer ensures that available movement times and assets support each COA.

During the war game, the assistant chief of staff, financial management (G-8) assesses the commander's area of operations to determine the best COA for use of resources. This assessment includes both core functions of financial management: resource management and finance operations. This officer determines partner relationships (joint, interagency, intergovernmental, and multinational), requirements for special funding, and support to the procurement process.

The surgeon section coordinates, monitors, and synchronizes the execution of the health system activities for the command for each war-gamed COA to ensure a fit and healthy force.

Recorders

The use of recorders is particularly important. Recorders capture coordinating instructions, subunit tasks and purposes, and information required to synchronize the operation. Recorders allow the staff to write part of the order before they complete the planning. Automated information systems enable recorders to enter information into preformatted forms that represent either briefing charts or appendixes to orders. Each staff section keeps formats available to facilitate networked orders production.

5. Select the War-Game Method

Three recommended war-game methods exist: belt, avenue-in-depth, and box. Each considers the area of interest and all enemy forces that can affect the outcome of the operation. Planners can use the methods separately or in combination and modified for long-term operations dominated by stability.

See facing page (p. 2-43) for further discussion of the three war-game methods.

A. The Belt Method

The belt method divides the AO into belts (areas) running the width of the AO. The shape of each belt is based on the factors of METT-TC. The belt method works best when conducting offensive and defensive operations on terrain divided into well-defined cross-compartments, during phased operations (such as river crossings, air assaults, or airborne operations), or when the enemy is deployed in clearly defined belts or echelons. Belts can be adjacent to or overlap each other.

This method is based on a sequential analysis of events in each belt. It is preferred because it focuses simultaneously on all forces affecting a particular event. A belt might include more than one critical event. Under time-constrained conditions, the commander can use a modified belt method. The modified belt method divides the AO into not more than three sequential belts. These belts are not necessarily adjacent or overlapping but focus on the critical actions throughout the depth of the AO.

In stability tasks, the belt method can divide the COA by events, objectives (goals not geographic location), or events and objectives in a selected slice across all lines of effort. It consists of war-gaming relationships among events or objectives on all lines of effort in the belt.

B. Avenue-in-Depth Method

The avenue-in-depth method focuses on one avenue of approach at a time, beginning with the decisive operation. This method is good for offensive COA's or in the defense when canalizing terrain inhibits mutual support.

In stability tasks, planners can modify the avenue-in-depth method. Instead of focusing on a geographic avenue, the staff war-games a line of effort. This method focuses on one line of effort at a time, beginning with the decisive line. The avenue-in-depth method includes not only war-gaming events and objectives in the selected line, but also war-gaming relationships among events or objectives on all lines of effort with respect to events in the selected line.

C. The Box Method

The box method is a detailed analysis of a critical area, such as an engagement area, a river-crossing site, or a landing zone. It works best in a time-constrained environment, such as a hasty attack. It is particularly useful when planning operations in noncontiguous areas of operation. When using this method, the staff isolates the area and focuses on critical events in it. Staff members assume that friendly units can handle most situations in the AO's and focus their attention on essential tasks.

In stability tasks, the box method may focus analysis on a specific objective along a line of effort, such as development of local security forces as part of improving civil security.

War-Game Methods

Ref: FM 6-0 (C2), Commander and Staff Organization and Operations (Apr '16), pp. 9-28 to 9-31.

Belt Method

The belt method divides the AO into belts (areas) running the width of the AO. The shape of each belt is based on the factors of METT-TC. The belt method works best when conducting offensive and defensive operations on terrain divided into well-defined cross-compartments, during phased operations or when the enemy is deployed in clearly defined belts or echelons.

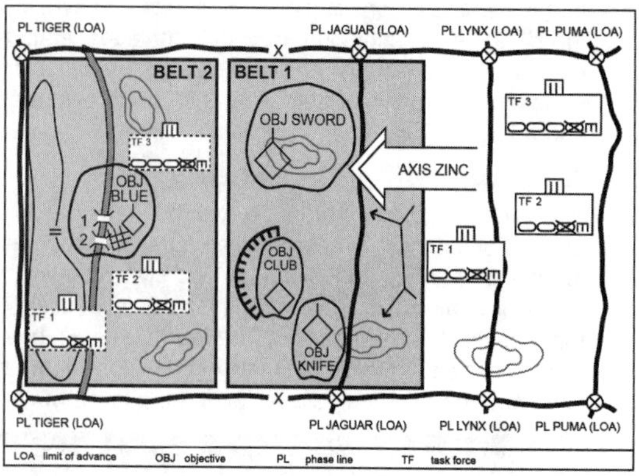

Avenue-in-Depth Method

The avenue-in-depth method focuses on one avenue of approach at a time, beginning with the decisive operation. This method is good for offensive COA's or in the defense when canalizing terrain inhibits mutual support. In stability operations, this method can be modified. Instead of focusing on a geographic avenue, the staff war-games a line of effort.

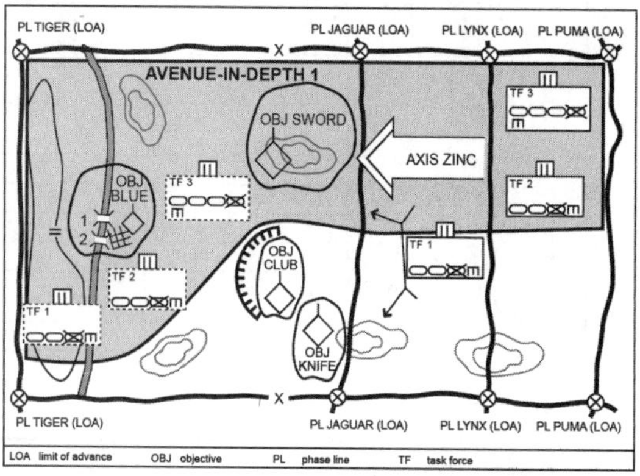

Box Method

The box method is a detailed analysis of a critical area, such as an engagement area, a river-crossing site, or a landing zone. It is used when time is constrained. It is particularly useful when planning operations in noncontiguous AOs. The staff isolates the area and focuses on critical events in it. Staff members assume friendly units can handle most situations on the battlefield and focus on essential tasks.

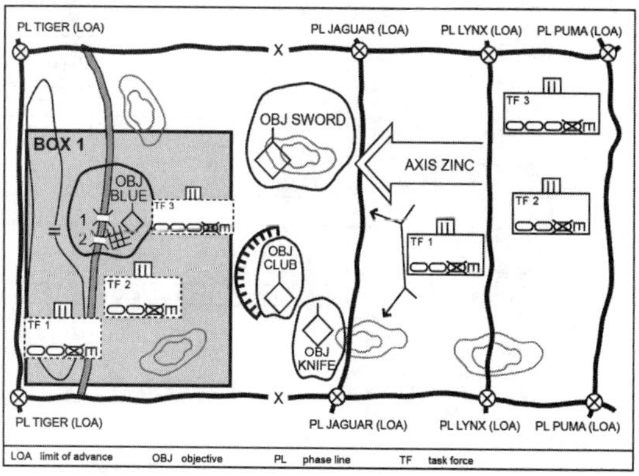

6. Select a Technique to Record and Display Results

The war-game results provide a record from which to build task organizations, synchronize activities, develop decision support templates, confirm and refine event templates, prepare plans or orders, and compare COA's. Two techniques are commonly used to record and display results: the synchronization matrix technique and the sketch note technique. In both techniques, staff members record any remarks regarding the strengths and weaknesses they discover. The amount of detail depends on the time available. Unit SOPs address details and methods of recording and displaying war-gaming results.

A. Synchronization Matrix

The synchronization matrix is a tool the staff uses to record the results of war-gaming and helps them synchronize a course of action across time, space, and purpose in relationship to potential enemy and civil actions. The first entry is time or phase of the operation. The second entry is the most likely enemy action. The third entry is the most likely civilian action. The fourth entry is the decision points for the friendly COA. The remainder of the matrix is developed around selected war fighting functions and their subordinate tasks and the unit's major subordinate commands.

Sample Synchronization Matrix

Time/Event		***H – 24 hours***	***H-hour***	***H + 24***
Enemy Action		Monitors movements	Defends from security zone	Commits reserve
Population		Orderly evacuation from area continues		
Decision Points		Conduct aviation attack of OBJ Irene		
Control Measures				
Movement and Maneuver	***1st BCT***	Move on Route Irish	Cross LD	Seize on OBJ Irene
	2d BCT	Move on Route Longstreet	Cross LD	Seize on OBJ Rose
	3d BCT			FPOL with 1st BCT
	Avn Bde	Attack enemy reserve on OBJ Irene		
	R&S			
Reserve				
Information Collection				
Fires		Prep fires initiated at H-5		
Protection	***Engineer***			
	PMO			
	CBRNE			
Sustainment				
Mission Command			MAIN CP with 1st BCT	
Close Air Support				
Electronic Warfare			Enemy C2 jammed	
Nonlethal Effects		Surrender broadcasts and leaflets		
Host Nation				
Interagency				
NGOs			Begins refugee relief	

Note: The first column is representative only and can be modified to fit formation needs.

AMD	air and missile defense
Avn Bde	aviation brigade
BCT	brigade combat team
C2	command and control
CBRNE	chemical, biological, radiological, nuclear, and high-yield explosives
CP	command post
FPOL	forward passage of lines
LD	line of departure
NGO	nongovernmental organization
OBJ	objective
PMO	provost marshal office
R&S	reconnaissance and surveillance

Ref: FM 6-0 (C2), Commander & Staff Organization & Operations, table 9-3, p. 9-32.

B. Sketch Note Technique

The sketch note technique uses brief notes concerning critical locations or tasks and purposes. These notes refer to specific locations or relate to general considerations covering broad areas. The commander and staff mark locations on the map and on a separate war-game work sheet. Staff members use sequence numbers to link the notes to the corresponding locations on the map or overlay. Staff members also identify actions by placing them in sequential action groups, giving each subtask a separate number. They use the war-game work sheet to identify all pertinent data for a critical event. They assign each event a number and title and use the columns on the work sheet to identify and list in sequence:

- Units and assigned tasks
- Expected enemy actions and reactions
- Friendly counteractions and assets
- Total assets needed for the task
- Estimated time to accomplish the task
- The decision point tied to executing the task
- CCIR's
- Control measures
- Remarks

Sample Sketch Note Technique

Critical Event	*Seize OBJ Sword*
Sequence number	*1*
Action	*TF 3 attacks to destroy enemy company on OBJ Sword*
Reaction	*Enemy company on OBJ Club counterattacks*
Counteraction	*TF 1 suppresses enemy company on OBJ Club*
Assets	*TF 3, TF 1, and 1-78 FA (155-SP)*
Time	*H+1 to H+4*
Decision point	*DP 3a and 3b*
Commander's Critical information Requirements	*Location of enemy armor reserve west of PL Jaguar*
Control measures	*Axis Zinc and support by fire position 1*
Remarks	

Ref: FM 6-0 (C2), Commander & Staff Organization & Operations, table 9-4, p. 9-33.

MDMP & TLP

7. War-Game the Operation and Assess the Results

War-gaming is a conscious attempt to visualize the flow of operations, given the friendly force's strengths and disposition, enemy's capabilities and possible COA's, and civilians. During the war game, the commander and staff try to foresee the actions, reactions, and counteractions of all participants to include civilians. The staff analyzes each selected event. They identify tasks that the force must accomplish one echelon down, using assets two echelons down. Identifying strengths and weaknesses of each COA allows the staff to adjust the COA's as necessary.

The war game focuses not so much on the tools used but on the people who participate. Staff members who participate in war-gaming should be the individuals deeply involved in developing COA's. Red team members (who can provide alternative points of view) provide insight on each COA. In stability operations, subject matter experts in areas such as economic or local governance can also help assess results of planned actions to include identifying possible unintended effects.

The war game follows an action-reaction-counteraction cycle. Actions are those events initiated by the side with the initiative. Reactions are the opposing side's actions in response. With regard to stability operations, the war game tests the effects of actions including intended and unintended effects as they stimulate anticipated responses from civilians and civil institutions. Counteractions are the first side's responses to reactions. This sequence of action-reaction-counteraction continues until the critical event is completed or until the commander decides to use another COA to accomplish the mission.

The staff considers all possible forces, including templated enemy forces outside the AO, which can influence the operation. The staff also considers the actions of civilians in the AO and the diverse kinds of coverage of unfolding events and their consequences in the global media. The staff evaluates each friendly move to determine the assets and actions required to defeat the enemy at that point or to accomplish stability tasks. Then the staff continually considers branches to the plan that promote success against likely enemy counteractions or unexpected civilian reactions. Lastly, the staff lists assets used in the appropriate columns of the work sheet and lists the totals in the assets column (not considering any assets lower than two command levels down).

The commander and staff examine many areas in detail during the war game:

- All friendly capabilities
- All enemy capabilities and critical civil considerations that impact operations
- Global media responses to proposed actions
- Movement considerations
- Closure rates
- Lengths of columns
- Formation depths
- Ranges and capabilities of weapon systems
- Desired effects of fires

The commander and staff consider how to create conditions for success, protect the force, and shape the operational environment. Experience, historical data, SOPs, and doctrinal literature provide much of the necessary information. During the war game, staff officers perform a risk assessment for their functional area for each COA. They then propose appropriate controls. They continually assess the risk of adverse population and media reactions that result from actions taken by all sides in the operation. Staff officers develop ways to mitigate those risks.

The staff continually assesses the risk to friendly forces, balancing between mass and dispersion. When assessing the risk of weapons of mass destruction to friendly

Effective War Game Results

Ref: FM 6-0 (C2), Commander and Staff Organization and Operations (Apr '16), table 9-5, p. 9-35.

The commander and staff refine (or modify):

- Each course of action, to include identifying branches and sequels that become on-order or be-prepared missions.
- The locations and times of decisive points.
- The enemy event template and matrix.
- The task organization, including forces retained in general support.
- Control requirements, including control measures & updated operational graphics.
- CCIR and other information requirements—including the latest time information is of value—and incorporate them into the information collection plan.

The commander and staff identify:

- Key or decisive terrain and determining how to use it.
- Tasks the unit retains and tasks assigned to subordinates.
- Likely times and areas for enemy use of weapons of mass destruction and friendly chemical, biological, radiological, and nuclear defense requirements.
- Potential times or locations for committing the reserve.
- The most dangerous enemy course of action.
- The most likely enemy course of action.
- The most dangerous civilian reaction.
- Locations for the commander and command posts.
- Critical events.
- Requirements for support of each warfighting function.
- Effects of friendly and enemy actions on civilians and infrastructure and on military operations.
- Or confirming the locations of named areas of interest, target areas of interest, decision points, and intelligence requirements needed to support them.
- Analyzing, and evaluating strengths and weaknesses of each course of action.
- Hazards, assessing their risk, developing control measures for them, and determining residual risk.
- The coordination required for integrating and synchronizing interagency, host-nation, and nongovernmental organization involvement.

The commander and staff analyze:

- Potential civilian reactions to operations.
- Potential media reaction to operations.
- Potential impacts on civil security, civil control, and essential services in the area of operations.

The commander and staff develop:

- Decision points.
- A synchronization matrix.
- A decision support template and matrix.
- Solutions to achieving minimum essential stability tasks in the area of operations.
- The information collection plan and graphics.
- Themes and messages.
- Fires, protection, and sustainment plans and graphic control measures.

The commander and staff determine:

- The requirements for military deception and surprise.
- The timing for concentrating forces and starting the attack or counterattack.
- The movement times & tables for critical assets, including information systems nodes.
- The estimated the duration of the entire operation and each critical event.
- The projected percentage of enemy forces defeated in each critical event & overall.
- The percentage of minimum essential tasks that the unit can or must accomplish.
- The media coverage and impact on key audiences.
- The targeting requirements in the operation, to include identifying or confirming high-payoff targets and establishing attack guidance.
- The allocation of assets to subordinate commanders to accomplish their missions.

forces, planners view the target that the force presents through the eyes of an enemy target analyst. They consider ways to reduce vulnerability and determine the appropriate level of mission-oriented protective posture consistent with mission accomplishment.

The staff identifies the required assets of the warfighting functions to support the concept of operations, including those needed to synchronize sustaining operations. If requirements exceed available assets, the staff recommends priorities based on the situation, commander's intent, and planning guidance. To maintain flexibility, the commander may decide to create a reserve to maintain assets for unforeseen tasks or opportunities.

The commander can modify any COA based on how things develop during the war game. When doing this, the commander validates the composition and location of the decisive operation, shaping operations, and reserve forces. Control measures are adjusted as necessary. The commander may also identify situations, opportunities, or additional critical events that require more analysis. The staff performs this analysis quickly and incorporates the results into the war-gaming record.

An effective war game results in the commander and staff refining, identifying, analyzing, developing, and determining several effects.

See previous page for discussion of effective war game results.

8. Conduct a War-Game Briefing (Optional)

Time permitting, the staff delivers a briefing to all affected elements to ensure everyone understands the results of the war game. The staff uses the briefing for review and ensures that it captures all relevant points of the war game for presentation to the commander, COS (XO), or deputy or assistant commander. In a collaborative environment, the briefing may include selected subordinate staffs. A war-game briefing format includes the following:

- Higher headquarters mission, commander's intent, and military deception plan
- Updated IPB
- Assumptions
- Friendly and enemy COA's that were war-gamed, to include:
  - Critical events
  - Possible enemy actions and reactions
  - Possible impact on civilians
  - Possible media impacts
  - Modifications to the COA's
  - Strengths and weaknesses
  - Results of the war game
- War-gaming technique used

MDMP Step V. COA Comparison

Ref: FM 6-0 (C2), Commander and Staff Organization and Operations (Apr '16), pp. 9-39 to 9-41.

COA comparison is an objective process to evaluate COA's independently of each other and against set evaluation criteria approved by the commander and staff. The goal to identify the strengths and weaknesses of COA's enable selecting a COA with the highest probability of success and further developing it in an OPLAN or OPORD. The commander and staff perform certain actions and processes that lead to the key outputs.

V. COA Comparison

Key Inputs	Key Outputs
▪ Updated running estimates ▪ Refined COAs ▪ Evaluation criteria ▪ War-game results ▪ Updated assumptions	▪ Evaluated COAs ▪ Recommended COAs ▪ Update running estimates ▪ Updated assumptions

1. Conduct Advantages and Disadvantages Analysis
2. Compare COAs
3. Conduct COA Decision Briefing

Ref: FM 6-0 (C2), Commander and Staff Organization and Operations, fig. 9-13, p. 9-39.

1. Conduct Advantages and Disadvantages Analysis

The COA comparison starts with all staff members analyzing and evaluating the advantages and disadvantages of each COA from their perspectives. Staff members each present their findings for the others' consideration. Using the evaluation criteria developed before the war game, the staff outlines each COA, highlighting its advantages and disadvantages. Comparing the strengths and weaknesses of the COAs identifies their advantages and disadvantages with respect to each other.

See following page (p. 2-51) for a sample advantages and disadvantages analysis.

Sample Advantages and Disadvantages

Course of Action	Advantages	Disadvantages
Course of action 1	Decisive operation avoids major terrain obstacles. Adequate maneuver space available for units conducting the decisive operation and the reserve.	Units conducting the decisive operation face stronger resistance at the start of the operation. Limited resources available to establishing civil control to town X.
Course of action 2	Shaping operations provide excellent flank protection of the decisive operations. Upon completion of decisive operations, units conducting shaping operations can quickly transition to establish civil control and provide civil security to the population in town X.	Operation may require the early employment of the division's reserve.

*Ref: FM 6-0 (C2), Commander and Staff Organization and Operations, table 9-6, p. 9-40.**

2. Compare Courses of Action

Comparison of COAs is critical. The staff uses any technique that helps develop those key outputs and recommendations and assists the commander to make the best decision. A common technique is the decision matrix. This matrix uses evaluation criteria developed during mission analysis and refined during COA development to help assess the effectiveness and efficiency of each COA.

See facing page for a sample decision matrix.

Commanders and staffs cannot solely rely on the outcome of a decision matrix, as it only provides a partial basis for a solution. During the decision matrix process, planners carefully avoid reaching conclusions from a quantitative analysis of subjective weights. Comparing and evaluating COAs by criterion is probably more useful than merely comparing totaled ranks. Judgments often change with regard to the relative weighting of criteria during close analysis of COAs, which will change weighted rank totals and possibly the most preferred COA.

The staff compares feasible COAs to identify the one with the highest probability of success against the most likely enemy COA, the most dangerous enemy COA, the most important stability task, or the most damaging environmental impact. The selected COA should also:

- Pose the minimum risk to the force and mission accomplishment
- Place the force in the best posture for future operations
- Provide maximum latitude for initiative by subordinates
- Provide the most flexibility to meet unexpected threats and opportunities
- Provide the most secure and stable environment for civilians in the AO
- Best facilitate information themes and messages

Staff officers often use their own matrix to compare COAs with respect to their functional areas. Matrixes use the evaluation criteria developed before the war game. Their greatest value is providing a method to compare COAs against criteria that, when met, produce operational success. Staff officers use these analytical tools to prepare recommendations. Commanders provide the solution by applying their judgment to staff recommendations and making a decision.

Sample Decision Matrix

Ref: FM 6-0 (C2), Commander and Staff Organization and Operations (Apr '16), pp. 9-40 to 9-41.

The decision matrix is a tool to compare and evaluate COAs thoroughly and logically. However, the process is based on highly subjective judgments that may change dramatically during the course of evaluation.

Sample Decision Matrix

Weight[1]	1	2	1	1	2	
Criteria[2]						
Course of Action	Simplicity	Maneuver	Fires	Civil control	Mass	Total
COA 1[3]	2	2 (4)	2	1	1 (2)	8 (11)
COA 2[3]	1	1 (2)	1	2	2 (4)	7 (10)

Notes:
[1] The COS (XO) may emphasize one or more criteria by assigning weights to them based on a determination of their relative importance. Higher weights correspond to emphasized or more important criteria.
[2] Criteria are those approved by the commander during the mission analysis brief.
[3] COAs selected for war-gaming have rankings assigned with regards to each criteria based on relative advantages and disadvantages of each COA. For example, when compared for relative simplicity, COA 2 is simpler than COA 1 and is therefore ranked 1, with COA 1 ranked 2.

*Ref: FM 6-0 (C2), Commander & Staff Organization & Operations, table 9-7, p. 9-40.**

* The decision matrix is a tool to compare and evaluate COAs thoroughly and logically. However, the process may be based on highly subjective judgments that can change dramatically during the course of evaluation. In table 9-7, the weights reflect the relative importance of each criterion as initially estimated by a COS (XO) during mission analysis and adjusted or approved by the commander. During COA comparison, rankings are assigned from 1 to however many COAs exist. Lower rankings are more preferred. After assigning ranks to COAs, the staff adds the unweighted ranks in each row horizontally and records the sum in the Total column on the far right of each COA. The staff then multiplies the same ranks by the weights associated with each criterion and notes the product in parenthesis underneath the unweighted rank. No notation is required if the weight is 1. The staff adds these weighted ranks horizontally and records the sum in parenthesis underneath the unweighted total in the Total column to the right of each COA. The staff then compares the totals to determine the most preferred (lowest total) COA based on both unweighted and weighted ranks. Although the lowest total denotes a most preferred solution, the process for estimating relative COA ranks and relative criteria weighting may be highly subjective. Upon review and consideration, the commander—based on personal judgment—may accept the results of the decision matrix or elect to execute one of the other COAs.

Commanders and staffs cannot solely rely on the outcome of a decision matrix, as it only provides a partial basis for a solution. During the decision matrix process, planners carefully avoid reaching conclusions from a quantitative analysis of subjective weights. Comparing and evaluating COAs by criterion is probably more useful than merely comparing totaled ranks. Judgments often change with regard to the relative weighting of criteria during close analysis of COAs, which will change weighted rank totals and possibly the most preferred COA.

MDMP & TLP

3. Conduct a COA Decision Briefing

After completing its analysis and comparison, the staff identifies its preferred COA and makes a recommendation. If the staff cannot reach a decision, the COS (XO) decides which COA to recommend. The staff then delivers a decision briefing to the commander. The COS (XO) highlights any changes to each COA resulting from the war game. The decision briefing includes:

- The commander's intent of the higher and next higher commanders
- The status of the force and its components
- The current IPB
- The COAs considered, including:
  - Assumptions used
  - Results of running estimates
  - A summary of the war game for each COA, including critical events, modifications to any COA, and war-game results
  - Advantages and disadvantages (including risks) of each COA
  - The recommended COA. If a significant disagreement exists, then the staff should inform the commander and, if necessary, discuss the disagreement

MDMP Step VI. COA Approval

Ref: FM 6-0 (C2), Commander and Staff Organization and Operations (Apr '16), pp. 9-41 to 9-42.

After the decision briefing, the commander selects the COA to best accomplish the mission. If the commander rejects all COAs, the staff starts COA development again. If the commander modifies a proposed COA or gives the staff an entirely different one, the staff war-games the new COA and presents the results to the commander with a recommendation.

Note: These sub-steps are not delineated specifically in FM 6-0.

VI. COA Approval

Key Inputs	Key Outputs
▪ Updated running estimates ▪ Evaluated COAs ▪ Recommended COA ▪ Updated assumptions	▪ Commander approved COA and any modifications ▪ Refined commander's intent, CCIRs, and EEFIs ▪ Updated assumptions WARNORD

(Commander Approves a COA)

1 **Commander's Decision**

2 **Issue Final Commander's Plannning Guidance**

3 **Issue Final Warning Order**

Ref: FM 6-0 (C2), Commander and Staff Organization and Operations, fig. 9-14, p. 9-42.

1. Commander's Decision

After the decision briefing, the commander selects the COA to best accomplish the mission. If the commander rejects all COAs, the staff starts COA development again. If the commander modifies a proposed COA or gives the staff an entirely different one, the staff war-games the new COA and presents the results to the commander with a recommendation.

2. Issue Final Commander's Planning Guidance

After approves a COA, the commander issues the final planning guidance. The final planning guidance includes a refined commander's intent (if necessary) and new CCIRs to support execution. It also includes any additional guidance on priorities for the war fighting functions, orders preparation, rehearsal, and preparation. This guidance includes priorities for resources needed to preserve freedom of action and ensure continuous sustainment.

Commanders include the risk they are willing to accept in the final planning guidance. If there is time, commanders use a video teleconference to discuss acceptable risk with adjacent, subordinate, and senior commanders. However, commanders still obtain the higher commander's approval to accept any risk that might imperil accomplishing the higher commander's mission.

MDMP & TLP

3. Issue Final Warning Order

Based on the commander's decision and final planning guidance, the staff issues a WARNORD to subordinate headquarters. This WARNORD contains the information subordinate units need to refine their plans. It confirms guidance issued in person or by video teleconference and expands on details not covered by the commander personally. The WARNORD issued after COA approval normally contains:

- The area of operations
- Mission
- Commander's intent
- Updated CCIRs and EEFIs
- Concept of operations
- Principal tasks assigned to subordinate units
- Preparation and rehearsal instructions not included in the SOPs
- A final timeline for the operations

See p. 4-21 for a sample warning order format.

MDMP Step VII. Orders Production

Ref: FM 6-0 (C2), Commander and Staff Organization and Operations (Apr '16), pp. 9-42 to 9-44.

VII. Orders Production, Dissemination & Transition

Key Inputs	Key Outputs
▪ **Commander approved COA and any modifications** ▪ **Refined commander's intent, CCIRs, and EEFIs** ▪ **Updated assumptions**	▪ **Approved operation plan or order** ▪ **Subordinates understand the plan or order**

1 Produce and Disseminate Orders

2 Transition from Planning to Operations

Ref: FM 6-0 (C2), Commander and Staff Organization and Operations, fig. 9-15, p. 9-43.

1. Produce and Disseminate Orders

The staff prepares the order or plan by turning the selected COA into a clear, concise concept of operations and the required supporting information. The COA statement becomes the concept of operations for the plan. The COA sketch becomes the basis for the operation overlay. If time permits, the staff may conduct a more detailed war game of the selected COA to more fully synchronize the operation and complete the plan. The staff writes the OPORD or OPLAN using the Army's operation order format.

See chap. 4, Plans & Orders.

Normally, the COS (XO) coordinates with staff principals to assist the G-3 (S-3) in developing the plan or order. Based on the commander's planning guidance, the COS (XO) dictates the type of order, sets and enforces the time limits and development sequence, and determines which staff section publishes which attachments.

Prior to the commander approving the plan or order, the staff ensures the plan or order is internally consistent and is nested with the higher commander's intent. They do this through—

- Plans and orders reconciliation
- Plans and orders crosswalk

Plans and Orders Reconciliation

Plans and orders reconciliation occurs internally as the staff conducts a detailed review of the entire plan or order. This reconciliation ensures that the base plan or order and all attachments are complete and in agreement. It identifies discrepancies or gaps in planning. If staff members find discrepancies or gaps, they take corrective actions. Specifically, the staff compares the commander's intent, mission, and commander's CCIRs against the concept of operations and the different schemes of support (such as scheme of fires or scheme of sustainment). The staff ensures attachments are consistent with the information in the base plan or order.

MDMP & TLP

Plans and Orders Crosswalk

During the plans and orders crosswalk, the staff compares the plan or order with that of the higher and adjacent commanders to achieve unity of effort and ensure the plan meets the superior commander's intent. The crosswalk identifies discrepancies or gaps in planning. If staff members find discrepancies or gaps, they take corrective action.

Approving the Plan or Order

The final action in plan and order development is the approval of the plan or order by the commander. Commanders normally do not sign attachments; however, they should review them before signing the base plan or order.

2. Plans-to-Operations Transition

Step 7 bridges the transition between planning and preparations. The plans-to-operations transition is a preparation activity that occurs within the headquarters. It ensures members of the current operations cell fully understand the plan before execution. During preparation, the responsibility for developing and maintaining the plan shifts from the plans (or future operations) cell to the current operations cell. This transition is the point at which the current operations cell becomes responsible for controlling execution of the operation order. This responsibility includes answering requests for information concerning the order and maintaining the order through fragmentary orders. This transition enables the plans cell to focus its planning efforts on sequels, branches, and other planning requirements directed by the commander.

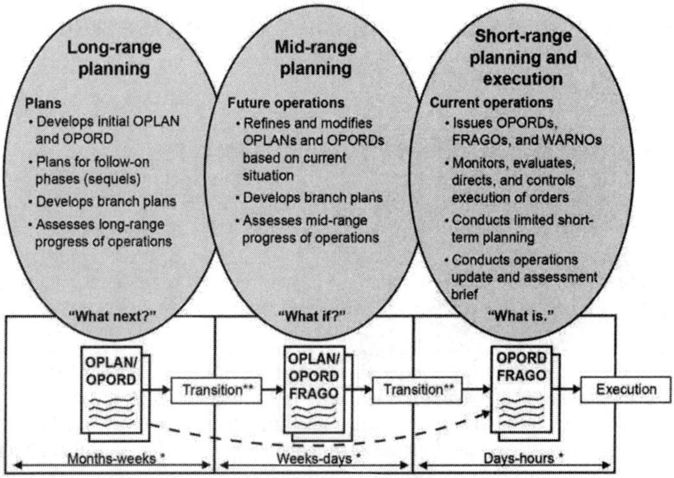

Long-range planning
Plans
• Develops initial OPLAN and OPORD
• Plans for follow-on phases (sequels)
• Develops branch plans
• Assesses long-range progress of operations
"What next?"
Mid-range planning
Future operations
• Refines and modifies OPLANs and OPORDs based on current situation
• Develops branch plans
• Assesses mid-range progress of operations
"What if?"
Short-range planning and execution
Current operations
• Issues OPORDs, FRAGOs, and WARNOs
• Monitors, evaluates, directs, and controls execution of orders
• Conducts limited short-term planning
• Conducts operations update and assessment brief
"What is."
OPLAN/ OPORD
Transition**
OPLAN/ OPORD FRAGO
Transition**
OPORD FRAGO
Execution
Months-weeks *
Weeks-days *
Days-hours *

Ref: ADP 5-0, The Operations Process (Jul '19), fig. 3-1, p. 3-8.

The timing of the plans-to-operations transition requires careful consideration. It must allow enough time for members of the current operations cell to understand the plan well enough to coordinate and synchronize its execution. Ideally, the plans cell briefs the members of the current operations cell on the plans-to-operations transition before the combined arms rehearsal. This briefing enables members of the current operations cell to understand the upcoming operation as well as identify friction points and issues to solve prior to its execution. The transition briefing is a mission briefing that generally follows the five-paragraph operation order format.

Following the combined arms rehearsal, planners and members of the current operations cell review additional planning guidance issued by the commander and modify the plan as necessary. Significant changes may require assistance from the plans cell to include moving a lead planner to the current operations cell. The plans cell continues planning for branches and sequels.

Planning in a Time-Constrained Environment

Ref: FM 6-0 (C2), Commander and Staff Organization and Operations (Apr '16), pp. 9-44 to 9-46.

Any planning process aims to quickly develop a flexible, sound, and fully integrated and synchronized plan. However, any operation may "outrun" the initial plan. The most detailed estimates cannot anticipate every possible branch or sequel, enemy action, unexpected opportunity, or change in mission directed from higher headquarters. Fleeting opportunities or unexpected enemy action may require a quick decision to implement a new or modified plan. When this occurs, units often find themselves pressed for time in developing a new plan.

Quality staffs produce simple, flexible, and tactically sound plans in a time-constrained environment. Any METT-TC factor, but especially limited time, may make it difficult to complete every step of the MDMP in detail. Applying an inflexible process to all situations does not work. Anticipation, organization, and prior preparation are the keys to successful planning under time-constrained conditions. Staff can use the time saved on any step of the MDMP to:

- Refine the plan more thoroughly
- Conduct a more deliberate and detailed war game
- Consider potential branches and sequels in detail
- Focus more on rehearsing and preparing the plan
- Allow subordinate units more planning and preparation time

The Commander's Responsibility

The commander decides how to adjust the MDMP, giving specific guidance to the staff to focus on the process and save time. Commanders shorten the MDMP when they lack time to perform each step in detail. The most significant factor to consider is time. It is the only nonrenewable, and often the most critical, resource. Commanders (who have access to only a small portion of the staff or none at all) rely even more than normal on their own expertise, intuition, and creativity as well as on their understanding of the environment and of the art and science of warfare. They may have to select a COA, mentally war-game it, and confirm their decision to the staff in a short time. If so, they base their decision more on experience than on a formal, integrated staff process.

Effective commanders avoid changing their guidance unless a significantly changed situation requires major revisions. Commanders consult with subordinate commanders before making a decision, if possible. In situations where commanders must decide quickly, they advise their higher headquarters of the selected COA, if possible. However, commanders do not let an opportunity pass just because they cannot report.

The Staff's Responsibility

Staff members keep their running estimates current. When time constraints exist, they can provide accurate, up-to-date assessments quickly and move directly into COA development. Under time-constrained conditions, commanders and staffs use as much of the previously analyzed information and as many of the previously created products as possible. The importance of running estimates increases as time decreases. Decisionmaking in a time-constrained environment usually occurs after a unit has entered the area of operations and begun operations. Detailed planning provides the basis for information that the commander and staff need to make decisions during execution.

Time-Saving Techniques

Ref: FM 6-0 (C2), Commander and Staff Organization and Operations (Apr '16), pp. 9-45 to 9-46.

The following paragraphs discuss time-saving techniques to speed the planning process.

Increase Commander's Involvement

While commanders cannot spend all their time with the planning staff, the greater the commander's involvement in planning, the faster the staff can plan. In time-constrained conditions, commanders who participate in the planning process can make decisions (such as COA selection) without waiting for a detailed briefing from the staff.

Limit the Number of COAs to Develop

Limiting the number of COAs developed and war-gamed can save planning time. If time is extremely short, the commander can direct development of only one COA. In this case, the goal is an acceptable COA that meets mission requirements in the time available. This technique saves the most time. The fastest way to develop a plan has the commander directing development of one COA with branches against the most likely enemy COA or most damaging civil situation or condition. However, this technique should be used only when time is severely limited. In such cases, this choice of COA is often intuitive, relying on the commander's experience and judgment. The commander determines which staff officers are essential to assist in COA development. Normally commanders require the intelligence officer, operations officer, plans officer, chief of fires (fire support officer), engineer officer, civil affairs operations officer, inform and influence activities officer, and COS (XO). They may also include subordinate commanders, if available, either in person or by video teleconference. This team quickly develops a flexible COA that it feels will accomplish the mission. The commander mentally war-games this COA and gives it to the staff to refine.

Maximize Parallel Planning

Although parallel planning is the norm, maximizing its use in time-constrained environments is critical. In a time-constrained environment, the importance of WARNORDs increases as available time decreases. A verbal WARNORD now followed by a written order later saves more time than a written order one hour from now. The staff issues the same WARNORDs used in the full MDMP when abbreviating the process. In addition to WARNORDs, units must share all available information with subordinates, especially IPB products, as early as possible. The staff uses every opportunity to perform parallel planning with the higher headquarters and to share information with subordinates.

Increase Collaborative Planning

Planning in real time with higher headquarters and subordinates improves the overall planning effort of the organization. Modern information systems and a common operational picture shared electronically allow collaboration with subordinates from distant locations, can increase information sharing, and can improve the commander's visualization. Additionally, taking advantage of subordinates' input and knowledge of the situation in their AOs often results in developing better COAs quickly.

Use Liaison Officers (LNOs)

Liaison officers posted to higher headquarters allow the commander to have representation in their higher headquarters' planning session. These officers assist in passing timely information to their parent headquarters and directly to the commander. Effective liaison officers have the commander's full confidence and the necessary rank and experience for the mission. Commanders may elect to use a single individual or a liaison team.

See pp. 5-31 to 5-36 for discussion of liaison.

Troop Leading Procedures (TLP)

Ref: FM 6-0 (C2), Commander and Staff Organization and Operations (Apr '16), chap. 10.

Troop leading procedures extend the MDMP to the small-unit level. The MDMP and TLP are similar but not identical. They are both linked by the basic Army problem solving methodology explained. Commanders with a coordinating staff use the MDMP as their primary planning process. Company-level and smaller units lack formal staffs and use TLP to plan and prepare for operations. This places the responsibility for planning primarily on the commander or small-unit leader.

TLP - Planning at Company and Below

Troop Leading Procedures

1. Receive Mission
2. Issue Warning Order
3. Make Tentative Plan
4. Initiate Movement
5. Conduct Recon
6. Complete Plan
7. Issue OPORD
8. Supervise and Refine

METT-TC

Plan Development

Mission Analysis
- Analysis of the Mission
  - Purpose
  - Tasks – Specified, Implied, Essential
  - Constraints
  - Written Restated Mission
- Enemy Analysis
- Terrain and Weather Analysis
- Troops Available
- Time Available
- Risk Assessment

Course of Action Development
- Analyze Relative Combat Power
- Generate Options
- Develop a Concept of Operations
- Assign Responsibilities
- Prepare COA Statement and Sketch

COA Analysis
- Hasty War Game

COA Comparison

COA Selection

Troop leading procedures are a dynamic process used by small-unit leaders to analyze a mission, develop a plan, and prepare for an operation (ADP 5-0). These procedures enable leaders to maximize available planning time while developing effective plans and preparing their units for an operation. TLP consist of eight steps. The sequence of the steps of TLP is not rigid. Leaders modify the sequence to meet the mission, situation, and available time. Leaders perform some steps concurrently, while other steps may be performed continuously throughout the operation.

Leaders use TLP when working alone or with a small group to solve tactical problems. For example, a company commander may use the executive officer, first sergeant, fire support officer, supply sergeant, and communications sergeant to assist during TLP.

Refer to SUTS3: The Small Unit Tactics SMARTbook, 3rd Ed. for further discussion of troop leading procedures and related activities/ topics -- such as combat orders, preparation and pre-combat inspections (PCIs), and rehearsals -- from a small unit perspective.

Troop Leading Procedures (TLP)

Ref: FM 6-0 (C2), Commander and Staff Organization and Operations (Apr '16), pp. 10-3 to 10-9. Refer to SUTS3:The Small Unit Tactics SMARTbook, 3rd Ed. for further discussion.

TLP provide small-unit leaders a framework for planning and preparing for operations. This occurs in steps 1 and 2 of TLP and is refined in plan development. Plan development occurs in step 3 and is completed in 6 of TLP. These tasks are similar to the steps of the military decisionmaking process (MDMP).

1. Receive the Mission

Receive the mission may occur in several ways. It may begin with the initial WARNORD or OPORD from higher headquarters or when a leader anticipates a new mission. Frequently, leaders receive a mission in a FRAGORD over the radio. Ideally, they receive a series of WARNORD's, the OPORD, and a briefing from their commander. Normally after receiving an OPORD, leaders give a confirmation brief to their higher commander to ensure they understand the higher commander's intent and concept of operations. The leader obtains clarification on any portions of the higher headquarters plan as required.

When they receive the mission, leaders perform an initial assessment of the situation (METT-TC analysis) and allocate the time available for planning and preparation. (Preparation includes rehearsals and movement.) This initial assessment and time allocation forms the basis of their initial WARNORD's.

Leaders complete a formal mission statement during TLP step 3 (make a tentative plan) and step 6 (complete the plan).

Based on what they know, leaders estimate the time available to plan and prepare for the mission. They begin by identifying the times at which major planning and preparation events, including rehearsals, must be complete. Reverse planning helps them do this. Leaders identify the critical times specified by higher headquarters and work back from them. Critical times might include aircraft loading times, the line of departure time, or the start point for movement.

Leaders ensure that all subordinate echelons have sufficient time for their own planning and preparation needs. A general rule of thumb for leaders at all levels is to use no more than one-third of the available time for planning and issuing the OPORD.

2. Issue a Warning Order

As soon as leaders finish their initial assessment of the situation and available time, they issue a WARNORD. Leaders do not wait for more information. They issue the best WARNORD possible with the information at hand and update it as needed with additional WARNORD's.

The WARNORD contains as much detail as possible. It informs subordinates of the unit mission and gives them the leader's timeline. Leaders may also pass on any other instructions or information they think will help subordinates prepare for the new mission. This includes information on the enemy, the nature of the higher headquarters' plan, and any specific instructions for preparing their units. The most important thing is that leaders not delay in issuing the initial WARNORD. As more information becomes available, leaders can—and should—issue additional WARNORD's. By issuing the initial WARNORD as quickly as possible, leaders enable their subordinates to begin their own planning and preparation.

WARNORD's follow the five-paragraph OPORD format. Normally an initial WARNORD issued below battalion level includes:

- Mission or nature of the operation
- Time and place for issuing the OPORD
- Units or elements participating in the operation
- Specific tasks not addressed by unit SOPs
- Timeline for the operation

3. Make a Tentative Plan

Once they have issued the initial WARNORD, leaders develop a tentative plan. This step combines the MDMP steps 2 through 6: mission analysis, COA development, COA analysis, COA comparison, and COA approval. At levels below battalion, these steps are less structured than for units with staffs. Often, leaders perform them mentally. They may include their principal subordinates—especially during COA development, analysis, and comparison:

- Mission analysis
- Course of action development
- Analyze courses of action (war game)
- Compare COA's & make a decision

4. Initiate Movement

Leaders initiate any movement necessary to continue mission preparation or position the unit for execution, sometimes before making a tentative plan. They do this as soon as they have enough information to do so, or when the unit is required to move to position itself for a task. This is also essential when time is short. Movements may be to an assembly area, a battle position, a new AO, or an attack position. They may include movement of reconnaissance elements, guides, or quartering parties. Leaders often initiate movement based on their tentative plan and issue the order to subordinates in the new location.

5. Conduct Reconnaissance

Whenever time and circumstances allow, leaders personally observe the AO for the mission prior to execution. No amount of intelligence preparation of the battlefield can substitute for firsthand assessment of METT-TC from within the AO. Unfortunately, many factors can keep leaders from performing a personal reconnaissance. The minimum action necessary is a thorough map reconnaissance, supplemented by imagery and intelligence products.

Leaders use results of the war game to identify information requirements. Reconnaissance operations seek to confirm or deny information that supports the tentative plan. They focus first on information gaps identified during mission analysis.

6. Complete the Plan

During this step, leaders incorporate the result of reconnaissance into their selected COA to complete the plan or order. This includes preparing overlays, refining the indirect fire target list, coordinating sustainment with command and control requirements, and updating the tentative plan as a result of the reconnaissance. At lower levels, this step may entail only confirming or updating information contained in the tentative plan. If time allows, leaders make final coordination with adjacent units and higher HQs before issuing the order.

7. Issue the Order

Small-unit orders are normally issued verbally and supplemented by graphics and other control measures. The order follows the standard five paragraph format OPORD format. Typically, leaders below company level do not issue a commander's intent. They reiterate the intent of their higher and next higher commander.

The ideal location for issuing the order is a point in the AO with a view of the objective and other aspects of the terrain. The leader may perform a leader's reconnaissance, complete the order, and then summon subordinates to a specified location to receive it. Sometimes security or other constraints make it infeasible to issue the order on the terrain. Then leaders use a sand table, detailed sketch, maps, and other products to depict the AO and situation.

8. Supervise and Refine

Throughout TLP, leaders monitor mission preparations, refine the plan, coordinate with adjacent units, and supervise and assess preparations. Normally unit SOPs state individual responsibilities and the sequence of preparation activities. Leaders supervise subordinates and inspect their personnel and equipment to ensure the unit is ready for the mission. A crucial component of preparation is the rehearsal:

- Practice essential tasks
- Identify weaknesses or problems in the plan
- Coordinate subordinate element actions
- Improve Soldier understanding of the concept of operations
- Foster confidence among Soldiers

Company and smaller sized units use four types of rehearsals:

- Back brief
- Combined arms rehearsal
- Support rehearsal
- Battle drill or SOP rehearsal

Troop Leading Procedures and the MDMP

Ref: FM 6-0 (C2), Commander and Staff Organization and Operations (Apr '16), chap. 10.

Troop leading procedures extend the MDMP to the small-unit level. The MDMP and TLP are similar but not identical. The type, amount, and timeliness of information passed from higher to lower headquarters directly impact the lower unit leader's TLP. The solid arrows depict when a higher headquarters' planning event could start TLP of a subordinate unit. However, events do not always occur in the order shown. For example, TLP may start with receipt of a warning order (WARNORD), or they may not start until the higher headquarters has completed the MDMP and issues an operation order (OPORD). WARNORD's from higher headquarters may arrive at any time during TLP. Leaders remain flexible. They adapt TLP to fit the situation rather than try to alter the situation to fit a preconceived idea of how events should flow.

Parallel Planning

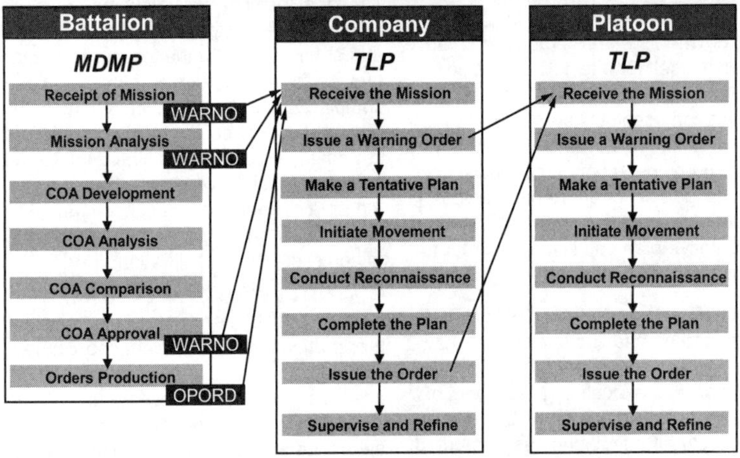

Ref: FM 6-0, Commander and Staff Organization and Operations, fig. 10-1, p. 10-2.

Normally, the first three steps (receive the mission, issue a WARNORD, and make a tentative plan) of TLP occur in order. However, the sequence of subsequent steps is based on the situation. The tasks involved in some steps (for example, initiate movement and conduct reconnaissance) may occur several times. The last step, supervise and refine, occurs throughout.

A tension exists between executing current operations and planning for future operations. The small-unit leader must balance both. If engaged in a current operation, there is less time for TLP. If in a lull, transition, or an assembly area, there is more time to use TLP thoroughly. In some situations, time constraints or other factors may prevent leaders from performing each step of TLP as thoroughly as they would like. For example, during the step make a tentative plan, small-unit leaders often develop only one acceptable course of action (COA) vice multiple COA's. If time permits, leaders may develop, compare, and analyze several COA's before arriving at a decision on which one to execute.

Chap 3

Integrating Processes

Ref: ADP 5-0, The Operations Process (Jul '19), pp. 1-15 to 1-17.

Commanders and staffs integrate the warfighting functions and synchronize the force to adapt to changing circumstances throughout the operations process. They use several integrating processes to do this. An integrating process consists of a series of steps that incorporate multiple disciplines to achieve a specific end. For example, during planning, the military decision-making process (MDMP) integrates the commander and staff in a series of steps to produce a plan or order. Key integrating processes that occur throughout the operations process include—

- Intelligence preparation of the battlefield
- Information collection
- Targeting
- Risk management
- Knowledge management

I. Intelligence Preparation of the Battlefield (IPB) *See p. 3-3.*

Intelligence preparation of the battlefield is the systematic process of analyzing the mission variables of enemy, terrain, weather, and civil considerations in an area of interest to determine their effect on operations (ATP 2-01.3). Led by the intelligence officer, the entire staff participates in IPB to develop and sustain an understanding of the enemy, terrain and weather, and civil considerations. IPB helps identify options available to friendly and threat forces.

IPB consists of four steps. Each step is performed or assessed and refined to ensure that IPB products remain complete and relevant:

- Define the Operational Environment
- Describe Environmental Effects on Operations
- Evaluate the Threat
- Determine Threat Courses of Action

IPB begins in planning and continues throughout the operations process. IPB results in intelligence products used to aid in developing friendly COAs and decision points for the commander. Additionally, the conclusions reached and the products created during IPB are critical to planning information collection and targeting.

II. Information Collection *See pp. 3-53 to 3-56.*

Information collection is an activity that synchronizes and integrates the planning and employment of sensors and assets as well as the processing, exploitation, and dissemination systems in direct support of current and future operations (FM 3-55). It integrates the functions of the intelligence and operations staffs that focus on answering CCIRs. Information collection includes acquiring information and providing it to processing elements. It has three steps:

- Collection management
- Task and direct collection
- Execute collection

III. Targeting *See pp. 3-57 to 3-70.*

Targeting is the process of selecting and prioritizing targets and matching the appropriate response to them, considering operational requirements and capabilities (JP 3-0). Targeting seeks to create specific desired effects through lethal and nonlethal actions. The emphasis of targeting is on identifying enemy resources (targets) that if destroyed or degraded will contribute to the success of the friendly mission. Targeting begins in planning and continues throughout the operations process. The steps of the Army's targeting process are—

- Decide
- Detect
- Deliver
- Assess

This methodology facilitates engagement of the right target, at the right time, with the most appropriate assets using the commander's targeting guidance.

IV. Risk Management *See pp. 3-71 to 3-74.*

Risk—the exposure of someone or something valued to danger, harm, or loss—is inherent in all operations. Because risk is part of all military operations, it cannot be avoided. Identifying, mitigating, and accepting risk is a function of command and a key consideration during planning and execution.

Risk management is the process to identify, assess, and control risks and make decisions that balance risk cost with mission benefits (JP 3-0). Commanders and staffs use risk management throughout the operations process to identify and mitigate risks associated with hazards (to include ethical risk and moral hazards) that have the potential to cause friendly and civilian casualties, damage or destroy equipment, or otherwise impact mission effectiveness. Like targeting, risk management begins in planning and continues through preparation and execution. Risk management consists of the following steps:

- Identify hazards
- Assess hazards to determine risks
- Develop controls and make risk decisions
- Implement controls
- Supervise and evaluate

V. Knowledge Management *See pp. 3-75 to 3-78.*

Knowledge management is the process of enabling knowledge flow to enhance shared understanding, learning, and decision making (ADP 6-0). It facilitates the transfer of knowledge among commanders, staffs, and forces to build and maintain situational understanding. Knowledge management helps get the right information to the right person at the right time to facilitate decision making. Knowledge management uses a five-step process to create shared understanding. The steps of knowledge management include—

- Assess
- Design
- Develop
- Pilot
- Implement

I. Intelligence Preparation of the Battlefield (IPB)

Ref: ATP 2-01.3, Intelligence Preparation of the Battlefield (Mar '19).

Intelligence preparation of the battlefield is the systematic process of analyzing the mission variables of enemy, terrain, weather, and civil considerations in an area of interest to determine their effect on operations.

I. IPB Process

1 Define the Operational Environment
(See p. 3-16.)

2 Describe Environmental Effects on Operations
(See p. 3-23.)

3 Evaluate the Threat
(See p. 3-32.)

4 Determine Threat Courses of Action
(See p. 3-42.)

IPB allows commanders and staffs to take a holistic approach to analyzing the operational environment (OE). A holistic approach—

- Describes the totality of relevant aspects of the OE that may impact friendly, threat, and neutral forces.
- Accounts for all relevant domains that may impact friendly and threat operations.
- Identifies windows of opportunity to leverage friendly capabilities against threat forces.
- Allows commanders to leverage positions of relative advantage at a time and place most advantageous for mission success with the most accurate information available.

IPB results in intelligence products that are used during the military decision-making process (MDMP)to assist in developing friendly courses of action (COAs) and decision points for the commander. Additionally, the conclusions reached and the products (which are included in the intelligence estimate)developed during IPB are critical to planning information collection and targeting operations. IPB products include—

- Threat situation templates with associated COA statements and high-value target (HVT) lists.
- Event templates and associated event matrices.
- Modified combined obstacle overlays (MCOOs), terrain effects matrices, and terrain assessments.
- Weather effects work aids—weather forecast charts, weather effects matrices, light and illumination tables, and weather estimates.
- Civil considerations overlays and assessments.

The J-2/G-2/S-2 leads the staff effort and begins preparing for IPB during generate intelligence knowledge, which is associated with the intelligence support to force generation task of the intelligence warfighting function and incorporated into the Army design methodology.

During generate intelligence knowledge, intelligence staffs create data files for their OE based on existing information and their evaluation of the information and intelligence related to the operational variables (political, military, economic, social, information, infrastructure, physical environment, and time[PMESII-PT]). The intelligence staff can also access holdings maintained by the military intelligence brigade-theater (also called MIB-T). This theater-aligned unit processes, refines, and stores intelligence products daily, which benefit nonregionally aligned units.

When generating intelligence knowledge, the intelligence staff should begin by determining the information needed to collect on the OE. As the staff begins to collect data on the OE, the data should be organized into baseline data files in accordance with the commander's guidance. These files must be compatible with the unit's mission command information systems. Generally, tactical echelons create primary data files based on the enemy, terrain and weather, and civil considerations. Strategic and operational echelons create data files based on the commander's operational requirements.

Given the limited time available to collect and evaluate information and intelligence on the operational variables, the information obtained from these data files may not be specific enough to support the IPB process and the MDMP. However, the commander and staff can use the information to assist in framing the OE during the Army design methodology.

Throughout the operations process, the commander and staff continually collect information and analyze the operational variables in order to provide increased situational understanding due to possible contingency operations. Situational understanding is the product of applying analysis and judgment to relevant information to determine the relationship among the operational and mission variables to facilitate decision making (ADP 5-0).

Upon receipt of a warning order or mission, the commander and staff draw relevant information categorized by the operational variables and filter it into the mission variables used during mission analysis. The mission variables are mission, enemy, terrain and weather, troops and support available, time available,and civil considerations (METT-TC). During IPB, the staff focuses on the relevant aspects of the OE as they pertain to the staff's warfighting function. The staff focuses primarily on the mission variables of enemy,terrain and weather, and civil considerations. However, depending on the staff's echelon, the type of OE, the type of operation, and changes in the OE, the staff may need to update its analysis to ensure the mission focus is both relevant and accurate.

Commanders conduct planning to—

- Understand a problem or situation.
- Envision a desired future.
- Develop COAs, with assistance from their staffs, that can bring about that desired future.

During planning, commanders focus their activities on understanding, visualizing, and describing the OE, while directing and assessing operations. IPB is one of the processes commanders use to assist in planning. IPB supports the MDMP and troop leading procedures—two of the three methodologies that assist commanders and staffs in planning.

See following pages for an overview and discussion of IPB in relation to the military decisionmaking process (pp. 3-6 to 3-7), troop leading procedures (pp. 3-8 to 3-9), and rapid decisionmaking and synchronization process (pp. 3-10 to 3-11).

A. Products of the IPB Process

Ref: ATP 2-01.3, Intelligence Preparation of the Battlefield (Mar '19), p. xi.

IPB is a collaborative staff effort led by the J-2/G-2/S-2 and the intelligence staff. IPB products developed and continuously updated facilitate situational understanding and assist commanders and staffs in identifying relevant aspects within the area of operations and area of interest that can affect mission accomplishment. The introductory figure lists and summarizes the relevant IPB products.

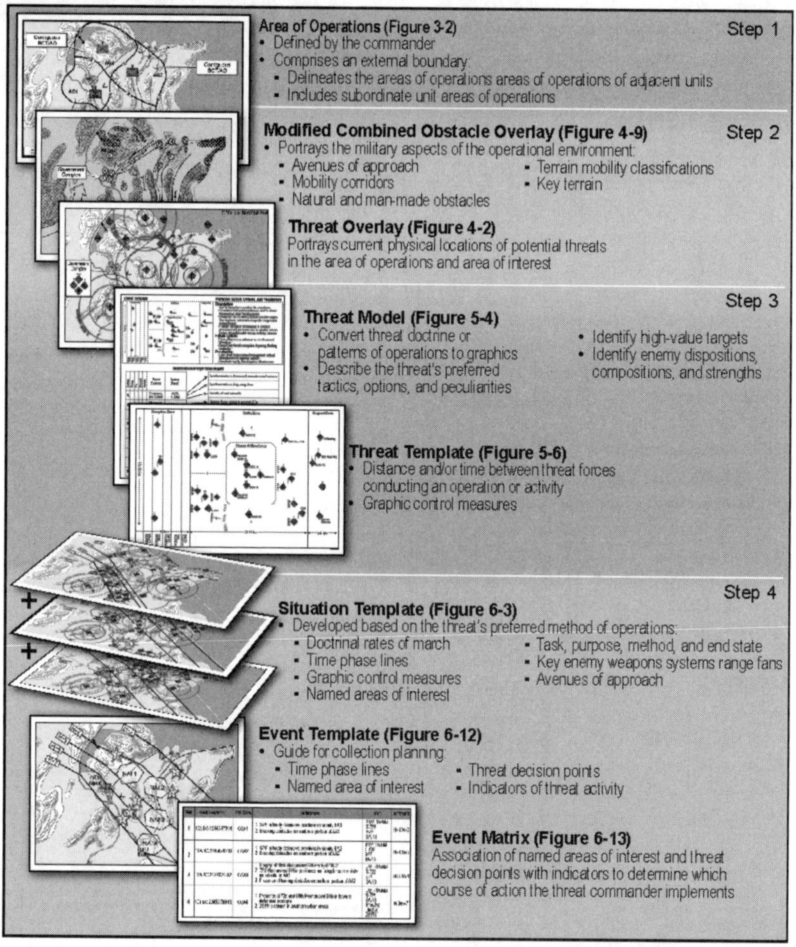

Area of Operations (Figure 3-2)
Step 1
• Defined by the commander
• Comprises an external boundary:
- Delineates the areas of operations areas of operations of adjacent units
- Includes subordinate unit areas of operations
Modified Combined Obstacle Overlay (Figure 4-9)
Step 2
• Portrays the military aspects of the operational environment:
- Avenues of approach
- Mobility corridors
- Natural and man-made obstacles
- Terrain mobility classifications
- Key terrain
Threat Overlay (Figure 4-2)
Portrays current physical locations of potential threats in the area of operations and area of interest
Step 3
Threat Model (Figure 5-4)
• Convert threat doctrine or patterns of operations to graphics
• Describe the threat's preferred tactics, options, and peculiarities
• Identify high-value targets
• Identify enemy dispositions, compositions, and strengths
Threat Template (Figure 5-6)
• Distance and/or time between threat forces conducting an operation or activity
• Graphic control measures
Step 4
Situation Template (Figure 6-3)
• Developed based on the threat's preferred method of operations:
- Doctrinal rates of march
- Time phase lines
- Graphic control measures
- Named areas of interest
- Task, purpose, method, and end state
- Key enemy weapons systems range fans
- Avenues of approach
Event Template (Figure 6-12)
• Guide for collection planning:
- Time phase lines
- Named area of interest
- Threat decision points
- Indicators of threat activity
Event Matrix (Figure 6-13)
Association of named areas of interest and threat decision points with indicators to determine which course of action the threat commander implements

Ref: Introductory figure. Products of the IPB process.

The IPB process is unique—it impacts the range of military operations, is relevant across all echelons, and is the fundamental element used in all planning and decision making. IPB serves as the initial framework for analysis of the battlefield in all operations.

B. IPB and the MDMP

Ref: ATP 2-01.3, Intelligence Preparation of the Battlefield (Mar '19), pp. 2-1 to 2-3.

The military decision-making process is an interactive planning methodology to understand the situation and mission, develop a course of action, and produce an operation plan or order (ADP 5-0).

See chap. 2 for detailed discussion of the MDMP.

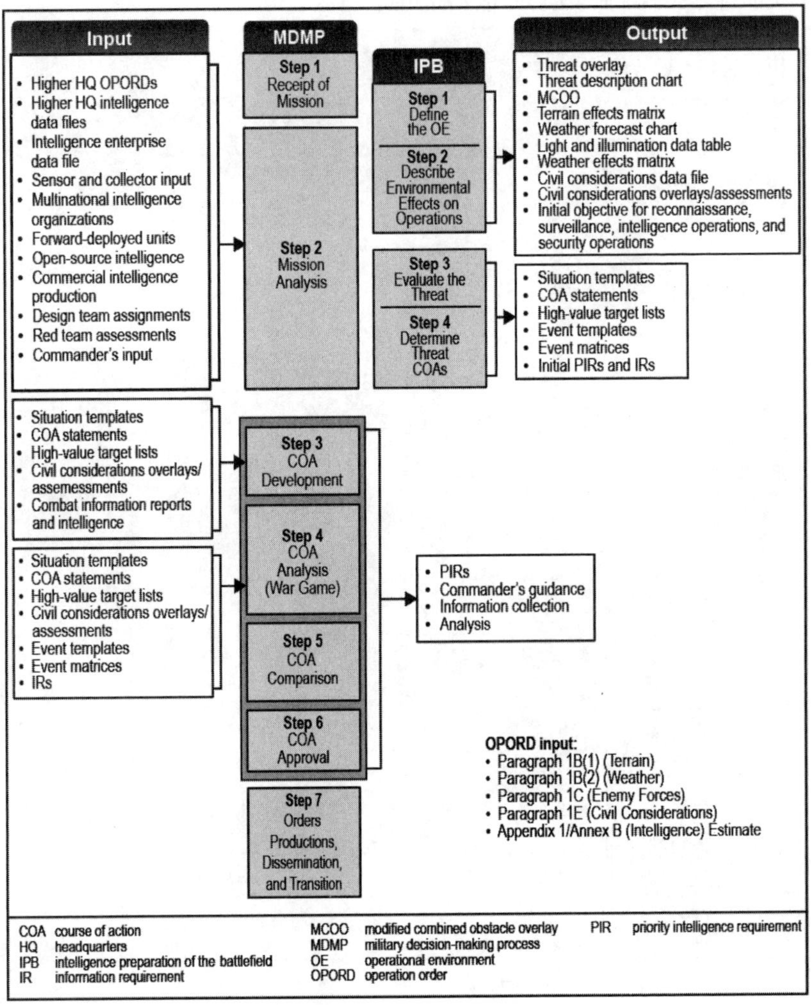

Ref: Figure 2-1. IPB and the MDMP steps.

Understand the Situation and Mission

During the mission analysis step of the MDMP, the staff conducts IPB to understand the situation and mission. The IPB products developed during this step are discussed fully in ATP 2-01.3, chapters 3 through 6. The products listed below are critical to developing and comparing COAs, deciding on a COA, and producing an operation order:

- Intelligence gaps.
- Information requirements.
- Threat situation templates with associated COA statements and HVT lists.
- Event templates with associated event matrices.
- Relative combat power matrices for threat forces.
- Geospatial intelligence tactical decision aids required to support continual planning (terrain effects).
- Weather tactical decision aids required to support continued planning (operational climatology or weather forecast chart and weather effects matrix).
- Civil considerations tactical decision aids required to support continued planning (civil considerations effects).
- Estimates on how other significant variables may affect the mission.
- Reconnaissance objectives.
- The tempo and focus of reconnaissance, surveillance, security operations, and intelligence operations to answer PIRs and meet other requirements.

Develop and Compare Courses of Action

In the COA development step of the MDMP, friendly COAs are broad potential solutions to an identified problem. These solutions are based on conclusions reached during initial IPB and any refinement of those conclusions that occurs between the conclusion of mission analysis and the beginning of COA development. The primary IPB product required for COA development is the threat situation template with the associated COA statement.

Decide on a Course of Action that Best Accomplishes the Mission

In the COA analysis step of the MDMP, deciding on a COA enables commanders and staffs to identify difficulties or coordination problems and probable consequences of planned actions for each COA being considered. The primary IPB products required for deciding a COA are—

- Threat situation templates with associated COA statements.
- Event templates with associated event matrices.
- Relative combat power matrices for threat forces.

During stability tasks, additional products may be required, such as civil considerations overlays and assessments. Information collection operations conducted during the mission analysis step of the MDMP provide pertinent combat information that informs COA development. This information confirms or denies the threat situation template and the associated COA statement.

Produce an Operation Plan or Operation Order for Execution

At the conclusion of the MDMP, the staff prepares the operation plan or order by turning the selected COA into a clear, concise concept of operations and required supporting material. The results of IPB are included within the base order and appropriate annexes.

Integrating Processes

C. IPB and Troop Leading Procedures (TLP)

Ref: ATP 2-01.3, Intelligence Preparation of the Battlefield (Mar '19), pp. 2-3 to 2-5.

The troop leading procedures extend the MDMP to the small-unit level. The MDMP and troop leading procedures are similar but not identical. Troop leading procedures is a dynamic process used by small-unit leaders to analyze a mission, develop a plan, and prepare for an operation (ADP 5-0). These procedures enable leaders to maximize available planning time while developing effective plans and preparing their units for an operation.

The sequence of actions assists leaders in effectively using available time to issue orders and execute tactical operations. Troop leading procedures consist of eight steps. The sequence of the steps is not rigid. Leaders modify the sequence to meet the mission, situation, and available time. Some of the following steps may be performed concurrently while other steps may be performed continuously throughout the operation:

- Step 1—Receive the mission.
- Step 2—Issue a warning order.
- Step 3—Make a tentative plan.
- Step 4—Initiate movement.
- Step 5—Conduct reconnaissance.
- Step 6—Complete the plan.
- Step 7—Issue the order.
- Step 8—Supervise and refine.

The intelligence staff at the battalion intelligence cell develops and provides the IPB products required by the company commander to use troop leading procedures. Commanders should not need to do any other refinement of these products. The following includes standard IPB products provided by the battalion to assist the commander in using the troop leading procedures:

- Threat situation templates and COA statements.
- Terrain and weather products.
- Tactical decision aids (such as MCOOs and terrain effects evaluations, weather forecast charts,weather effects matrices, and light and illumination data tables).
- Civil considerations tools and products.

Note. Company commanders coordinate with the battalion intelligence cell for any IPB products or tools they may need.

Due to the lack of a staff and resources, as well as time constraints, the small-unit leader depends on the timely delivery of IPB products developed by higher headquarters tailored to support small-unit planning. Specifically, the components of IPB inform steps 2 through 5 and actions within the troop leading procedures.

Step 2—Issue a Warning Order

The battalion intelligence cell provides IPB products to the company commander on what to include in warning orders for areas such as but not limited to—

- Terrain analysis.
- Enemy forces.
- AOs and AOIs.
- Commander's critical information requirements and essential elements of friendly information.
- Risk guidance.

- Surveillance and reconnaissance to initiate.
- Security measures.
- Deception guidance.
- Mobility and countermobility.
- Guidance on rehearsals.

Step 3—Make a Tentative Plan

When developing a tentative plan, the company commander relies on the battalion intelligence cell to provide IPB tools as the leader conducts mission analysis, COA development, COA analysis, and COA comparison and selection.

Mission Analysis

The battalion intelligence cell provides IPB tools and products on mission analysis by evaluating enemy, terrain and weather, and civil considerations. This includes providing information and analysis on the terrain and friendly and enemy forces that most affect tactical operations.

Course of Action Development

IPB products assist the leader in constructing a solid COA. The purpose of COA development is determining one or more ways to accomplish the mission that is consistent with the immediate higher commander's intent. A COA describes how the unit might generate the effects of overwhelming combat power against the enemy at the decisive point with the least friendly casualties.

Course of Action Analysis

The battalion intelligence cell provides IPB tools the leader can use to determine how the enemy will likely react during war gaming. War gaming assists the leader in synchronizing friendly actions while considering the enemy's likely reactions. COA analysis begins with both friendly and threat COAs and, using a method of action-reaction-counteraction war game, results in a synchronized friendly plan, identified strengths and vulnerabilities, and an updated risk assessment. After developing the COA, the leader analyzes it to determine its strengths and vulnerabilities and gains insights into actions at the decisive point of the mission. COA analysis (war game) unites friendly and enemy forces on the actual terrain to visualize how the operation will unfold.

Course of Action Comparison and Selection

The battalion intelligence cell provides products from IPB to leaders to determine PIRs, friendly force information requirements, and essential elements of friendly information. Although essential elements of friendly information are not part of the commander's critical information requirements, they still become priorities, and this information must be protected from enemy identification.

Step 4—Initiate Movement

The battalion intelligence cell provides IPB products to leaders on any movement necessary to continue mission preparation or to posture the unit for the start of the mission.

Step 5—Conduct Reconnaissance

If time permits, leaders verify intelligence from higher headquarters by reconnoitering to seek to confirm PIRs that support their tentative plans. These PIRs usually consist of assumptions or critical facts about the enemy (including strength and location). The PIRs can also include information on the terrain (to verify that a tentative support-by-fire position can suppress the enemy, or an AA is usable).

See pp. 2-59 to 2-62 for complete discussion of troop leading procedures from FM 6-0.

D. IPB and Decision Making

Ref: ATP 2-01.3, Intelligence Preparation of the Battlefield (Mar '19), pp. 2-5 to 2-6.

Decision making refers to selecting a COA as the one most favorable to accomplish the mission. Decision making is knowing whether to decide or not, then when and what to decide, and finally understanding the consequences. Commanders make decisions in part based on the intelligence developed during initial IPB and on the refinement of that intelligence throughout the operations process.

For more information on the operations process, see chap. 1.

Commanders require accurate and timely intelligence about the OE to make informed and good decisions. Through IPB, the staff aids the commander's understanding of how the mission variables of enemy, terrain and weather, and civil considerations influence the OE and affect operations. IPB also assists the commander in understanding how to influence, use, or employ these variables to achieve the desired conditions and end state. IPB is essential in assisting the commander to—

- Understand, visualize, and describe the OE:
  - **Understand**. Understanding involves analyzing the mission variables in a given OE. IPB defines and describes the mission variables of enemy, terrain and weather, and civil considerations but more importantly, concludes how the interrelationships, dynamics, and interactions of these variables cause changes in the OE.
  - **Visualize**. Visualization involves developing situational understanding, determining an end state, and envisioning the sequence of events the force must ensure to achieve the end state. Every product developed during IPB is essential in assisting the commander to visualize the situation. These products must be produced on time and in accordance with unit standard operating procedures.
  - **Describe**. After commanders visualize an operation, they communicate their vision to the staffs and subordinate commands using staff products developed during IPB.
- Make and articulate decisions.
- Direct, lead, and assess military operations.

See pp. 1-13 to 1-26 for related discussion of understanding, visualizing, describing, directing, leading, and assessing operations from ADP 5-0.

Rapid Decisionmaking and Synchronization Process (RDSP)

One technique commanders and staffs commonly use during execution is the rapid decisionmaking and synchronization process. Throughout mission execution, continuous information collection is conducted to answer information requirements and to close intelligence gaps. The process is usually conducted based on an existing operation order that includes the IPB products and estimates produced during the MDMP. The rapid decisionmaking and synchronization process has five steps:

- **Compare the current situation to the order**. During execution, the staff looks for indicators of change that may affect the overall operation. These changes must be identified for the commander to the make necessary modifications to the operation plan. The event template and event matrix (developed during step 4 of IPB) and the DST (a critical output of step 4 of the MDMP) are the primary staff tools used to identify variances and alert the commander to situations that require a decision. These products are updated as changes occur.
- **Determine the type of decision required**. When a variance is identified, the staff describes the variance and determines if it provides a significant opportunity to friendly forces or the enemy.
- **Develop a COA**. If the situation warrants the development of a new friendly COA, it may result in the creation of new or modified PIRs and HVTs. It may also require the creation of a new or modified event template and event matrix.
- **Refine and validate the COA**. The commander and staff conduct a mental war game of the new COA. At a minimum the enemy situation template and COA statement, along with the friendly operations graphics and COA statement, are required to focus the mental war game.
- **Implement**. The commander normally implements the new COA by issuing a fragmentary order. The following are issued as part of that fragmentary order:
- **IPB products,** including the enemy situation template with COA statement and HPT list, and terrain, weather, and civil considerations products.
- **Updated PIRs**.

See pp. 1-60 to 1-63 for an overview and further discussion on the rapid decision-making and synchronization process from FM 6-0.

II. IPB Process Activities (Overview)

Ref: ATP 2-01.3, Intelligence Preparation of the Battlefield (Mar '19), pp. 1-3 to 1-4.

Although there are four steps to the IPB process, it is important to note that IPB is a continuous process. Continuous analysis and assessment are necessary to maintain situational understanding of an OE in constant flux.

Step 1—Define the Operational Environment (OE) *See p. 3-16.*

An operational environment is a composite of the conditions, circumstances, and influences that affect the employment of capabilities and bear on the decisions of the commander (JP 3-0). An OE for any specific operation comprises more than the interacting variables that exist within a specific physical area. It also involves interconnected influences from the global or regional perspective (such as politics, economics) that affect OE conditions and operations. Thus, each commander's OE is part of a higher commander's OE. Defining the OE results in the identification of—

- Significant characteristics of the OE that can affect friendly and threat operations.
- Gaps in current intelligence holdings.

Step 1 is important because it assists the commander in defining relative aspects of the OE in time and space. This is equally important when considering characteristics of multi-domain OEs. Aspects of these OEs may act simultaneously across the battlefield but may only factor in friendly or threat operations at specific times and locations.

During step 1, the intelligence staff must identify those significant characteristics related to the mission variables of enemy, terrain and weather, and civil considerations that are relevant to the mission. The intelligence staff evaluates significant characteristics to identify gaps and initiate information collection. The intelligence staff then justifies the analysis to the commander. Failure to identify or misidentifying the effect these variables may have on operations at a given time and place can hinder decision making and result in the development of an ineffective information collection strategy. During step 1, the area of operations (AO), AOI, and area of influence must also be identified and established.

Understanding friendly and threat forces is not enough; other factors, such as culture, languages, tribal affiliations, and operational and mission variables, can be equally important. Identifying the significant characteristics of the OE is essential in identifying the additional information needed to complete IPB. Once approved by the commander, this information becomes the commander's initial intelligence requirements—which focus the commander's initial information collection efforts and the remaining steps of the IPB process.

Additionally, where a unit will be assigned and how its operations will synchronize with other associated operations must be considered. For example, the G-2/S-2 should be forming questions regarding where the unit will deploy within the entire theater of operations and the specific logistics requirements needed to handle the operation's contingency plans.

Step 2—Describe Environmental Effects on Operations *See p. 3-23.*

During step 2 of the IPB process, the intelligence staff describes how significant characteristics affect friendly operations. The intelligence staff also describes how terrain, weather, civil considerations, and friendly forces affect threat forces. This evaluation focuses on the general capabilities of each force until the development of threat COAs in step 4 of IPB and friendly COAs later in the MDMP. The entire staff determines the effects of friendly and threat force actions on the population.

If the intelligence staff does not have the information required to form conclusions, it uses assumptions to fill information gaps—always careful to ensure the commander understands when assumptions are used in place of facts to form conclusions.

Step 3—Evaluate The Threat *See p. 3-32.*

The purpose of evaluating the threat is to understand how a threat can affect friendly operations. Although threat forces may conform to some of the fundamental principles of warfare that guide Army operations, these forces will have obvious, as well as subtle, differences in how they approach situations and problem solving. Understanding these differences is essential to understanding how a threat force will react in a given situation.

Threat evaluation does not begin with IPB. The intelligence staff conducts threat evaluations and creates threat models during generate intelligence knowledge of the intelligence support to force generation task. Using this information, the intelligence staff refines threat models, as necessary, to support IPB. When analyzing a well-known threat, the intelligence staff may be able to rely on previously developed threat models. When analyzing a new or less well-known threat, the intelligence staff may need to evaluate the threat and develop threat models during the MDMP's mission analysis step. When this occurs, the intelligence staff relies heavily on the threat evaluation conducted by higher headquarters and other intelligence agencies.

In situations where there is no threat force, the intelligence analysis conducted and the products developed relating to terrain, weather, and civil considerations may be sufficient to support planning. An example of this type of situation is a natural disaster.

Step 4—Determine Threat Courses Of Action *See p. 3-42.*

During step 4, the intelligence staff identifies and develops possible threat COAs that can affect accomplishing the friendly mission. The staff uses the products associated with determining threat COAs to assist in developing and selecting friendly COAs during COA steps of the MDMP. Identifying and developing all valid threat COAs minimize the potential of surprise to the commander by an unanticipated threat action.

Failure to fully identify and develop all valid threat COAs may lead to the development of an information collection strategy that does not provide the information necessary to confirm what COA the threat has taken and may result in friendly forces being surprised and possibly defeated. When needed, the staff should identify all significant civil considerations (this refers to those civil considerations identified as OE significant characteristics) to portray the interrelationship of the threat, friendly forces, and population activities.

The staff develops threat COAs in the same manner friendly COAs are developed. The COA development discussion in ADRP 5-0 is an excellent model for developing valid threat COAs that are suitable, feasible, acceptable, unique, and consistent with threat doctrine or patterns of operation. Although the intelligence staff has the primary responsibility for developing threat COAs, it needs assistance from the rest of the staff to present the most accurate and complete analysis to the commander.

Staff Collaboration

Precise intelligence is critical to targeting threat capabilities at the right time and place to open windows of opportunity across domains. Commanders and staffs receive effective intelligence when they direct and participate in intelligence warfighting function activities. Close interaction between the commander, G-2/S-2,G-3/S-3, and the rest of the staff is essential, as the entire staff supports unit planning and preparation through the integrating processes and continuing activities.

G-2/S-2s facilitate the IPB effort; however, G-2/S-2s and their staffs cannot provide all of the information the commander requires for situational understanding. Other staff sections or supporting elements must assist the intelligence staff in producing and continuously refining all IPB products. Total staff integration ensures a holistic view of the OE, reduces the initial time required for IPB development, and assists the commander in timely decision making. This coordination also improves the quality and accuracy of IPB products.

See following pages for an overview and discussion of additional intelligence products.

III. Types of Intelligence Products

Ref: Adapted from ADRP 2-0, Intelligence (Aug '12), pp. 5-9 to 5-12.

In addition to IPB, the G-2/S-2 staff produces and maintains a broad variety of products tailored to its consumers. These products are developed and maintained in accordance with the commander's guidance. For all of these products, the primary focus of the G-2/S-2 staff's analysis is presenting predictive intelligence to support operations.

A. Intelligence Estimate

An intelligence estimate is the appraisal, expressed in writing or orally, of available intelligence relating to a specific situation or condition with a view to determining the courses of action open to the threat and the order of probability of their adoption. The G-2/S-2 staff develops and maintains the intelligence estimate. The primary purpose is to—

- Determine the full set of COAs open to the threat and the probable order of their adoption
- Disseminate information and intelligence
- Determine requirements concerning threats and other relevant aspects of the operational environment

The intelligence estimate is a logical and orderly examination of intelligence factors affecting the accomplishment of a mission (threats, terrain and weather, and civil considerations). It provides commanders with an analysis of the area of interest and threat strengths and capabilities that can influence their mission. An intelligence estimate may be prepared at any level. It may be formal or informal and detailed or summarized. It is normally written at division and higher levels and briefed down to the battalion level. The following is an example of the basic information and intelligence that could be included:

- **Mission.**
- **Analysis of the AO.** This analysis of the terrain is based on—
  - The military aspects of terrain (OAKOC)
  - Other significant characteristics
  - The effects of the terrain on friendly and threat operations and civil considerations
  - The effects of weather on friendly and threat operations and civil considerations:
    - Operational climatology data and information, light data, and predictive weather effects based on specific weather sensitivity thresholds
    - The current weather conditions based on the military aspects of weather (visibility, wind, precipitation, cloud cover, temperature, and humidity)
    - Projected weather forecasts with significant seasonal trends for that specific geographic location
  - An analysis of the civil considerations and projected effects of civil considerations on friendly and threat operations, and vice versa.
- **Current threat situation.** This is based on the threat characteristics (see FM 2-01.3) and includes estimates of the strength of threat forces, recent significant threat activities and trends, and threat peculiarities and weaknesses.
- **Threat capabilities.** These are the broad COAs and supporting operations that threats can take to achieve their goals and objectives. The G-2/S-2 staff considers each threat's ability to conduct each operation based on the mission variables (METT-TC) related to the current situation.
- **Threat characteristics.** These provide a framework for the consistent evaluation of any force. The G-2/S-2 staff considers composition, disposition, strengths, weaknesses, combat effectiveness, doctrine and tactics, command and support relationships, electronic technical data, capabilities and limitations, current operations, and historical data when analyzing threat characteristics.
- **Summary of the most significant points.** This includes:
  - The most significant terrain and weather and civil considerations effects on operations.
  - Potential impacts of operations on terrain and civil considerations.
  - At a minimum, the most likely and most dangerous threat COAs.
  - The most significant threat strengths and vulnerabilities.

The intelligence estimate also includes four tabs: Tab A (Terrain), Tab B (Weather), Tab C (Civil Considerations), and Tab D (IPB).

B. Intelligence Summary (INTSUM)

INTSUMs provide the context for commander's situational understanding. The INTSUM reflects the G-2's/S-2's interpretation and conclusions regarding threats, terrain and weather, and civil considerations over a designated period of time. This period will vary with the desires of the commander and the requirements of the situation. The INTSUM provides a summary of the threat situation, threat capabilities, the characteristics of terrain and weather and civil considerations, and COAs.

The INTSUM can be presented in written, graphic, or oral format, as directed by the commander. The INTSUM assists in assessing the current situation and updating other intelligence reports. It is disseminated to higher, lower, and adjacent units. The INTSUM has no prescribed format. The following is an example of the basic information and intelligence that should be included in an INTSUM:

- **Date-time group (DTG)** of the INTSUM and the period of time the INTSUM covers.
- **Weather and weather effects** that include current and forecast meteorological parameters and analysis based on the military aspects of weather and weather sensitivity thresholds.
- **Significant threat activities** over the reporting period and a near-term analysis of threat intent and activity.
- **Significant impacts of civil considerations** on operations and vice versa.
- **Subunit assessments of significant threat activities and civil considerations** in the AO over the reporting period and a near-term analysis of threat intent and activity.
- **Notable trends in threat activity** over a designated period of time (such as the previous 14 days). This may be presented as an all-source analysis product or focused on specific threat activities of interest to the commander—or both. This portion of the INTSUM should highlight new or emerging threats and the level of impact that each threat may present to the unit's operations.
- **Combat damage assessment roll-up** includes known or estimated threat unit strengths, significant threat systems degraded or destroyed, and all known captured, wounded, or killed threat personnel during the reporting period.
- **Written threat situation or situation template** (as of a specific DTG).
- **Assessments** include a near-term and long-term assessment of threat activities with as much detail as possible based on available information and current intelligence analysis. INTSUMs are predictive in nature. When specific intelligence or information is not available, INTSUMs must contain the G-2/S-2's best assessment of probabilities of threat actions based on experience and professional military judgment.
- **HVTLs** (in coordination with the targeting officer) may include high-value individuals, depending on the unit mission.
- **Current PIRs and projected PIRs** by phase.
- **Planning requirements tools and products.**
- **Special assessments** are developed for any unique circumstance that requires additional analysis.

C. Intelligence Running Estimate

Effective plans and successful execution hinge on accurate and current running estimates. A running estimate is the continuous assessment of the current situation used to determine if the current operation is proceeding according to the commander's intent and if the planned future operations are supportable (ADP 5-0). Failure to maintain accurate running estimates may lead to errors or omissions that result in flawed plans or bad decisions during execution. Running estimates are principal knowledge management tools used by the commander and staff throughout the operations process. In their running estimates, the commander and each staff section continuously consider the effect of new information and update the following: facts, assumptions, friendly force status, threat activities and capabilities, civil considerations, recommendations and conclusions.

D. Common Operational Picture (COP)

A common operational picture is a single display of relevant information within a commander's area of interest tailored to the user's requirements and based on common data and information shared by more than one command (ADRP 6-0). The COP is the primary tool for supporting the commander's situational understanding. All staff sections provide input from their area of expertise to the COP.

Step 1—Define the Operational Environment

During step 1 of the IPB process, the intelligence staff identifies for further analysis the significant characteristics of or activities within the OE that may influence friendly and threat COAs and command decisions, as well as the physical space the mission will occupy. Within an OE, Army forces may face large-scale combat operations, which simultaneously encompass multiple domains, military engagements, and populations.

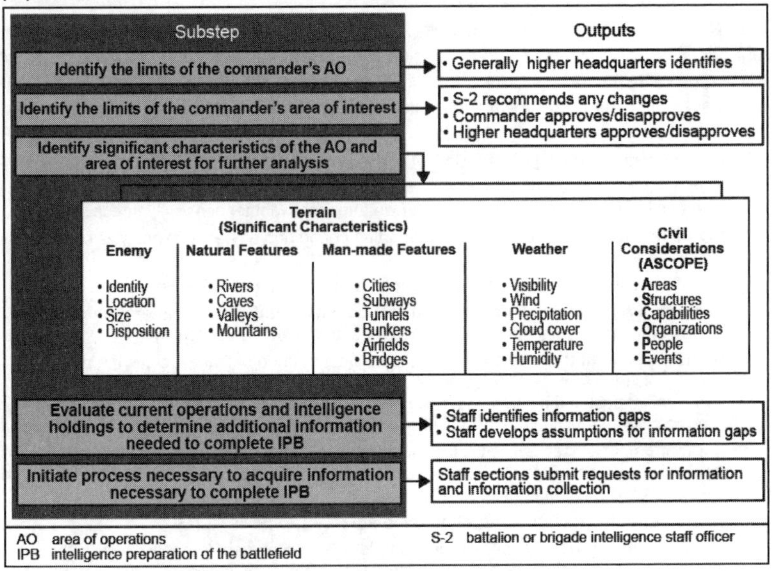

Ref: Figure 3-1. Substeps and outputs of step 1 of the IPB process.

So What?

The "so what" of step 1 is to clearly define for commanders the relevant characteristics of their AOIs:

- Success results in time and effort saved by focusing only on those characteristics that influence friendly COAs and command decisions.

Consequences of failure:

- Failure to focus on only the significant characteristics leads to wasted time and effort collecting and evaluating intelligence on OE characteristics that do not influence the operation.
- Staff failure to identify all significant characteristics in all domains relevant to the OE may lead to the command's surprise and unpreparedness when some overlooked feature of the OE affects the operation for which the commander did not plan.

A. Identify the Limits of the Commander's Area of Operations

Area of operations is an operational area defined by a commander for land and maritime forces that should be large enough to accomplish their missions and protect their forces (JP 3-0). The AO comprises an external boundary that delineates adjacent units AOs and includes subordinate unit AOs. Subordinate unit AOs may be contiguous or noncontiguous.

Within an AO, commanders conduct decisive, shaping, and sustaining operations to articulate an operation in terms of purpose. Commanders designate main and supporting efforts to establish the shifting and prioritization of resources. The AO may be impacted due to political boundaries and/or other civil considerations. Once assigned, an AO can be subdivided by that command, as necessary, to support mission requirements. Figure 3-2 illustrates contiguous AOs.

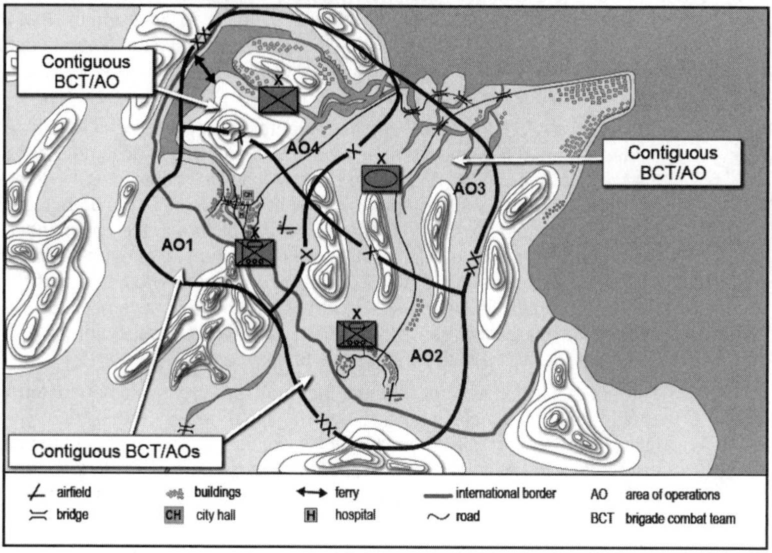

Ref: Figure 3-2. Area of operations examples.

B. Identify the Limits of the Commander's Area of Interest

An area of interest is that area of concern to the commander, including the area of influence, areas adjacent thereto, and extending into enemy territory (JP 3-0). The AOI also includes areas occupied by threat forces who could jeopardize mission accomplishment. An area of influence is a geographical area wherein a commander is directly capable of influencing operations by maneuver or fire support systems normally under the commander's command or control (JP 3-0). The area of influence includes terrain inside and outside the AO and is determined by both the G-2/S-2 and G-3/S-3.

The AOI is—

- Established by the commander with input from the G-2/S-2 or G-3/S-3. The operational and mission variables must be considered.
- An area normally larger than or outside the area of influence that directly impacts the AO;therefore, possibly requiring more intelligence assets to monitor. It may include staging areas.
- An area that may be irregular in shape or noncontiguous and can overlap the areas of adjacent and subordinate unit AOs.
- An area that assists in determining NAIs during step 4 of the IPB process.

An AOI is the geographical area from which information is required to facilitate planning and the successful conduct of the command's operation. The area changes as the situation changes and as commanders determine new information requirements. It includes any threat forces or characteristics that significantly influence accomplishing the command's mission. In combat operations, the AOI extends into threat territory to the objectives of current or planned friendly operations if those objectives are located outside the assigned AO. In stability or defense support of civil authorities tasks, the AOI is typically much larger than that defined for combat operations.

In establishing the limits of an AOI, time is one of the primary considerations. Time limits should be based not only on the threat's mobility but also on the amount of time needed to accomplish the friendly mission. For example, if the command estimates that it will take two days to accomplish the friendly mission,the AOI must encompass all threat forces and activities that could influence accomplishing the command's mission within the two days. Additional considerations when establishing AOI limits include but are not limited to—

- Dividing the AOI into several components (for example, ground AOI, air AOI, subterranean AOI, and cyberspace AOI). Such a division accommodates the types of information relevant to each AOI as well as each AOI's different geographical limits. At some point, it may be necessary to integrate the various AOIs into a whole in order to present a holistic picture to the commander. One method of illustrating and articulating the AOI is the use of overlays to depict the relevant aspects of the AOI. For example, a threat force outside the AO may have capabilities that reside in or are employed in each of the domains. An overlay depicting this threat's capabilities (one relevant aspect of the AOI) can be layered with other relevant aspects to show a holistic view.
- Threats to mission accomplishment that may also cross into neutral terrain countries. For example, if political decisions in a neutral terrain country may influence the accomplishment of a unit's mission, include that country within the limits of the AOI. Likewise, if a segment of the population in a neutral terrain country provides a support base to forces that oppose the command's mission, include that country within the AOI.
- Technological advances. Due to technological advances in communications, such as social media and global media organizations, commanders are likely to witness increased visibility of friendly operations. This may lead to an increase in neutral and threat actions caused by friendly operations. Considering this, it is important to analyze how civil considerations and the dissemination of information may affect operations

C. Identify Significant Characteristics of the Area of Operations and Area of Interest for Further Analysis

In order to focus IPB and what is important to the commander, the staff identifies and defines the characteristics of the enemy, terrain and weather, and civil considerations of the OE to determine the significance of each in relation to the mission—essentially building an environmental model as the framework for conducting and then presenting analysis to the commander. This prevents unnecessary analysis and allows the staff to dedicate and maximize resources in critical areas. The initial analysis that occurs in this substep determines the amount of time and resources the intelligence staff commits to the detailed analysis that occurs in step 2 of the IPB process.

When identifying significant characteristics of the OE, the staff may be faced with analyzing aspects that transcend the AO—for example, analyzing a threat located outside the AO (and potentially outside the geographic combatant commander's area of responsibility) who will likely use cyberspace capabilities to affect friendly operations in the AO across multiple domains. Accounting for these actors and their capabilities and determining their relationships and interdependencies with systems and other actors in the OE significantly increase the effectiveness of analysis in subsequent IPB steps and provide commanders with multiple options during the MDMP.

Additionally, the intelligence staff and other staff sections must consider threat forces and other aspects of the environment that may affect accomplishing the friendly mission. These include but are not limited to—

- The area's geography, terrain, and weather.
- Population demographics (ethnic groups, religious groups, age distribution, income groups).
- Political or socioeconomic factors, including the role of clans, tribes, religious organizations,criminal organizations, corruption, rule of law, gender, age, cultural groups, and ethnicity.
- Infrastructures such as transportation or telecommunications.
- Rules of engagement or legal restrictions such as international treaties, status of forces agreements,international sanctions, or United Nations charters.
- Threat force capabilities, including, military, other foreign security forces, as well as paramilitary forces, criminal and terrorist organizations (transnational and local), and antigovernment groups.

The intelligence staff should—

- Inspect each characteristic briefly to identify those of significance to the command and its mission.
- Further evaluate effects of each characteristic in later steps of the IPB process.
- Analyze characteristics that may impact decisive, shaping, and sustaining operations.
- Evaluate each threat's specific capabilities and determine probable COAs during later steps of the IPB process.

Enemy

Analysis of the enemy includes not only the known enemy but also other threats to mission success,such as multiple threats posing with a wide array of political, economic, religious, and personal motivations. Additionally, threats may wear uniforms and be easily identifiable, blend into the population, and use either traditional threat capabilities (such as rifles or mortars) or nontraditional capabilities (such as computer networks and social media).

Terrain and Weather

It is important to identify the types of environments in which a unit will conduct operations. Terrain and weather are natural conditions of the environment that profoundly influence operations and the type of information collected. Terrain and weather favor neither the friendly nor the threat force, unless one is more familiar with or better prepared to operate in the physical environment.

- **Terrain**. Terrain includes natural features (such as rivers, caves, valleys, and mountains) and man-made features(such as cities, subway tunnels, bunkers, airfields, and bridges). Terrain directly affects how commanders select objectives and locate, move, and control forces. Terrain also influences protective measures and the effectiveness of weapons and other systems. The effective use of terrain reduces the effects of threat fires, increases the effects of friendly fires, and facilitates surprise. Terrain appreciation—the ability to predict its impact on operations—is an important skill for every leader. For tactical operations, commanders and staffs analyze terrain using the five military aspects of terrain (observation and fields of fire, avenues of approach, key terrain, obstacles, and cover and concealment [OAKOC]), as performed during step 2 of the IPB process.
- **Weather**. Climate refers to the average weather conditions of a location, area, or region for a specific time of the year as recorded for a period of years. Operational climatology is used to assess effects on weapon systems,collection systems, ground forces, tactics and procedures, threat TTP, and other capabilities based on specific weather sensitivity thresholds when operational planning occurs more than 10 days before the execution. Climatological data is important at both the operational and tactical levels. Actual weather forecasts and/or predictions, using weather models and other tools, are used to assess weather effects on weapon systems,collection systems, ground forces, TTP, and other capabilities when operations occur within 10 days of operational planning.

OAKOC - Military Aspects of the Terrain

Ref: ATP 2-01.3, Intelligence Preparation of the Battlefield (Mar '19), pp. 4-6 to 4-12.

The military aspects of terrain are often described using the acronym OAKOC:

O - Observation and Fields of Fire

A - Avenues of Approach (AA)

K - Key Terrain

O - Obstacles

C - Concealment and Cover

This section provides broad aspects of the terrain analysis essential to intelligence analysts conducting terrain analysis to support threat analysis. For more information on the military aspects of terrain, refer to ATP 3-34.80 and JP 2-03.

O - Observation and Fields of Fire

Observation. Observation is the condition of weather and terrain that permits a force to see the friendly, enemy, and neutral personnel and systems, and key aspects of the environment (ADP 1-02).

Fields of fire. Field of fire is the area that a weapon or group of weapons may cover effectively from a given position (FM 3-90-1). A unit's field of fire is directly related to its ability to observe.

Evaluation of observation and fields of fire identifies:

- Potential engagement areas.
- Defensible terrain, which offers good observation and fields of fire.
- Specific equipment or positions.
- Areas where forces are most vulnerable to observation and fires.
- Visual dead space.

Analysis of fields of fire includes an evaluation of all direct and indirect fire weapon systems in a command's inventory. An ideal field of fire for direct fire weapon systems is an open area where the threat can be seen and has no protection out to the maximum effective range of that weapon.

Both observation and fields of fire are based on LOSs. Line of sight is the unobstructed path from a Soldier's weapon, weapon sight, electronic sending and receiving antennas, or piece of reconnaissance equipment from one point to another. In other words, a LOS is a straight line from one point to another.

There are two types of LOSs normally evaluated during terrain analysis:

- **Horizontal LOS** is an unobstructed path from a Soldier's weapon, weapon sight, laser designator, and electronic sending and receiving antennas.
- **Oblique (or vertical) LOS** assists in planning ADA system locations, selecting landing zones and drop zones, and selecting forward arming and refueling points.

An effective technique for analyzing observation and fields of fire is the production of a map displaying observation and fields of fire

A - Avenue of Approach (AA)

An ***Avenue of Approach (AA)*** is a path used by an attacking force leading to its objective or to key terrain. Avenues of approach exist in all domains (ADP 3-90). Identifying AAs is important because all COAs that involve maneuver depend on available AAs.

AAs consist of a series of mobility corridors through which a maneuvering force must pass to reach its objective. AAs must provide ease of movement and enough width for dispersion of a force large enough to affect the outcome of the operation significantly. AAs are developed by identifying, categorizing, and grouping mobility corridors and evaluating AAs.

K - Key Terrain

Key terrain is an identifiable characteristic whose seizure or retention affords a marked advantage to either combatant (ADP 3-90). In natural terrain environments dominated by restrictive terrain features, high ground can be key terrain because it dominates an area with good observation and fields of fire. In an open or arid environment, a dry riverbed, channel, or valley can be key terrain because it offers good cover and concealment.

A common technique is to depict key terrain on overlays and sketches with a large "K" within a circle or curve that encloses and follows the contours of the designated terrain. On transparent overlays use a color, such as purple, that stands out.

In urban areas, infrastructure (such as bridges, medical facilities, choke points, intersections, industrial complexes, and economic, social, and government institutions) can be considered key terrain.

In the offense, key terrain features are usually forward of friendly dispositions and are often assigned as objectives. Adjacent terrain features may be key terrain if their control is necessary for the continuation of the attack or the accomplishment of the mission.

In the defense, In the defense, key terrain is usually within and/or behind the defensive area, such as—

- Terrain that gives good observation over AAs to and through the defensive position.
- Terrain that permits the defender to cover an obstacle by fire.
- Areas along a LOC that affect the use of reserves or sustainment operations.

In stability tasks, key terrain may include portions of the population, such as—

- Political, tribal, or religious groups or leaders.
- A local population.
- Governmental organizations.

Decisive terrain is key terrain whose seizure and retention is mandatory for successful mission accomplishment (ADP 3-90). Key terrain is not necessarily decisive terrain. Decisive terrain has an extraordinary impact on the mission. The successful accomplishment of the mission depends on seizing, retaining, or denying the use of the terrain to a threat force. Commanders designate decisive terrain to communicate to the staff and subordinate commanders about the importance of the terrain to the concept of operations.

O - Obstacles

An ***obstacle*** is any natural or man-made obstruction designed or employed to disrupt, fix, turn, or block the movement of an opposing force, and to impose additional losses in personnel, time, and equipment on the opposing force (JP 3-15).

Obstacles affect certain types of mobility differently:

- **Mounted mobility.** Obstacles such as rivers, lakes, swamps, dense forested areas, road craters,rubble in the street, or densely populated urban areas may have a greater effect on mounted mobility than on dismounted mobility.
- **Dismounted mobility**. Antipersonnel minefields, concertina wire, or steep slopes may be more effective against dismounted mobility.

Obstacles may decrease the effectiveness of information-related capabilities to influence threat operations and activities, as well as friendly and neutral populations. For example, mountains may block terrestrial-based signals used to broadcast surrender appeals to a threat-held territory, or messages to populations explaining the intent of U.S. operations.

C - Concealment and Cover

Cover is protection from the effects of fires (FM 3-96). Cover is the physical protection from bullets, fragments of exploding rounds, flame, nuclear effects, and biological and chemical agents. Cover and concealment can be provided by (but are not limited to) ditches, caves, riverbanks, folds in the ground, shell craters, buildings, walls, and embankments. Cover does not necessarily provide concealment. An example of cover without concealment is a bunker in plain sight that is intended for personnel survivability.

Refer to ATP 2-01.3 , appendix B for examples of cover and ATP 3-37.34 for information on hardening infrastructure and creating survivability positions.

Concealment is protection from observation or surveillance (FM 3-96). It degrades the threat's ability to observe forces, equipment, or positions. Concealment can be provided by trees, underbrush, tall grass, cultivated vegetation, weather conditions (such as snow, fog, or rain), as well as man-made camouflage. Concealment does not necessarily provide cover.

LOS analysis determines the observation, fields of fire, and cover and concealment the terrain will provide to both friendly and threat forces.

Civil Considerations

Civil considerations is the influence of man-made infrastructure, civilian institutions, and activities of civilian leaders, populations, and organizations within an area of operations on the conduct of military operations (ADRP 5-0). Commanders and staffs analyze civil considerations in terms of these characteristics: areas, structures, capabilities, organizations, people, and events (ASCOPE).

Civil considerations assist commanders in refining their understanding of the operational and mission variables within the AO and effects on the mission. Understanding the relationship between military operations and populations is critical in conducting operations and essential in developing effective plans. Operations often involve stabilizing the situation, securing the peace, building partner capacity, and transitioning authority to civilian control. Combat operations directly affect the populace, infrastructure, and the force's ability to transition to host-nation authority. The degree to which the populace is expected to support or resist U.S. and friendly forces also affects the offensive and defensive operational design.

Commanders and staffs use personal knowledge and running estimates to assess social, economic, and political factors. Commanders consider how these factors may relate to potential lawlessness, subversion, or insurgency. Their goal is to develop an understanding to the level of cultural awareness. At this level,commanders can estimate the effects of friendly actions and direct subordinates with confidence. Cultural awareness improves how Soldiers interact with the populace and deters false or unrealistic expectations by both sides. Soldiers have more knowledge of the society's common practices, perceptions, assumptions,customs, and values, giving better insight into the intent of individuals and groups. This allows staffs to better understand how friendly actions may affect the OE and assist in planning for possible branches and sequels.

To improve commanders' sociocultural understanding, intelligence staffs can use sociocultural databases and repositories, when available, to aid the intelligence analysis conducted as part of assessing civil considerations. Additionally, commanders and staffs should continually seek to improve cultural understanding to improve their roles in IPB.

D. Evaluate Current Operations and Intelligence Holdings to Determine Additional Information Needed to Complete IPB

Not all information needed to complete IPB will be in the command's or higher headquarters' data files and databases. Information gaps should be identified early and prioritized based on the commander's initial guidance and intent for intelligence and information collection. The staff should ensure the commander is aware of any information gaps that cannot be answered within the time allotted for IPB, develop reasonable assumptions to use in place of these answers, and explain to the commander how it arrived at these assumptions.

E. Initiate Processes Necessary to Acquire the Information Needed to Complete IPB

After determining that the information necessary to complete IPB is not contained within local and searchable external data files and databases, staff sections submit requests for information or requests for collection to obtain the information necessary to complete IPB. As information is received, IPB products are updated and intelligence gaps eliminated. New intelligence gaps and information requirements may be developed as IPB continues.

See pp. 3-53 to 3-56 for discussion of information collection and ATP 2-01 for more information on collection management.

Step 2. Describe Environmental Effects on Operations

Step 2 of the IPB process determines how significant characteristics of the OE can affect friendly and threat operations. The staff begins evaluation by analyzing existing and projected conditions in the AO and AOI, and then determining effects on both friendly and threat operations. The example shows how significant characteristics of the OE (specifically the terrain) impact friendly operations.

> ***Example***
>
> *A brigade S-2 informs the commander that the terrain the brigade must attack through will canalize friendly forces into platoon-sized mobility corridors that will prevent the friendly forces from supporting each other. The brigade S-2 also informs the commander that the terrain favors enemy use of obstacles, small antitank ambushes, and indirect fire throughout its security zone.*

Describing environmental effects on operations consists of the substeps and outputs shown in figure 4-1.

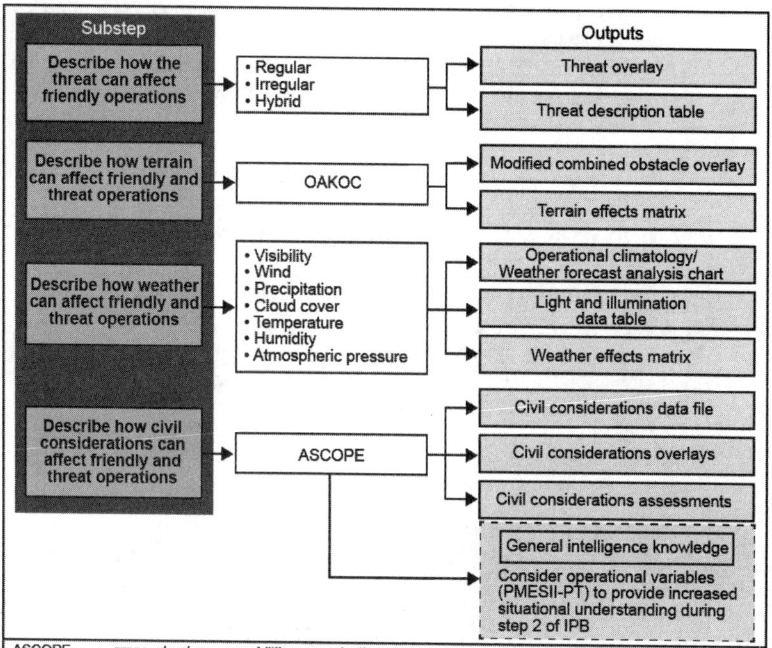

ASCOPE	areas, structures, capabilities, organizations, people, and events
IPB	intelligence preparation of the battlefield
OAKOC	observation and fields of fire, avenues of approach, key terrain, obstacles, and cover and concealment
PMESII-PT	political, military, economic, social, information, infrastructure, physical environment, and time

Ref: Figure 4-1. Substeps and outputs of step 2 of the IPB process.

So What?

The "so what" of step 2 is to identify how relevant characteristics of the AOI affect friendly and threat operations:

- Success results in the commander being able to quickly choose and exploit terrain, weather, and civil considerations to best support the mission during decisive, shaping, and sustaining operations.

Consequences of failure:

- The commander may not have the information needed to exploit the opportunities the OE provides at a given time and place.
- The threat commander may have the information needed to exploit the opportunities the OE provides in a way the friendly commander did not anticipate.

A. Describe How the Threat Can Affect Friendly Operations

Threats are part of the OE; therefore, commanders need to understand all threats that can potentially affect operations within the AO and AOI. They may face one unified threat force or several disparate threat forces that must be engaged to accomplish the mission. Although detailed analysis of threat forces occurs during steps 3 and 4 of the IPB process, the type of threat force and its general capabilities must be defined during step 2. This places the threat force in context with other variables in order to understand its relative importance as a characteristic of the OE. For example—

- When facing a **regular threat** in combat operations, regardless of where the engagement occurs, that threat is likely the most important characteristic in that OE.
- When facing an **irregular threat** conducting operations as part of an insurgency in a failing nation-state, the state of governance and other civil considerations may be more significant than the threat posed by the irregular threat.
- When facing a **hybrid threat i**n combat operations, the hybrid threat will likely be equipped with capabilities that can be used to exploit perceived friendly vulnerabilities. The mixture of regular and irregular threat capabilities expands threat COA possibilities and can create significant impacts outside friendly force decision cycles.

The threat overlay and the threat description table focus the analysis of the threat and assist in communicating that analysis to the commander.

Threat Overlay

The threat overlay depicts the current physical location of all potential threats in the AO and the AOI. The overlay includes the identity, size, location, strength, and AO for each known threat location. The date-time group of the threat activity should be annotated on the threat overlay or maintained in intelligence reference files. Maintaining a threat overlay provides a reference to past threat activity and assists in determining patterns of threat movement and dispositions. During step 4 of the IPB process, this reference assists in determining threat COAs.

Threat Description Table

The threat description table supports the threat overlay by classifying the types of threats identified on the overlay and describing the broad capabilities of each threat.

B. Describe How Terrain Can Affect Friendly and Threat Operations

Terrain analysis is the collection, analysis, evaluation, and interpretation of geographic information on the natural and man-made features of the terrain, combined with other relevant factors, to predict the effect of the terrain on military operations (JP 2-03). It also involves the study and interpretation of natural and man-made features within an area, their effects on military operations, and the effects of weather and climate on these features. Terrain analysis is a continual process since changes in the OE may alter the analysis of terrain effects on operations.

A command may operate in two types of terrain—natural and complex—which are analyzed based on the military aspects of terrain (OAKOC):

- **Natural terrain** analysis focuses on airspace and surface and subsurface areas.
- **Complex terrain** analysis also focuses on airspace, surface and subsurface areas, but it must also consider internal, external, and super surface areas.

Analyze the Military Aspects of Terrain

Geospatial intelligence cells generally conduct detailed terrain analysis. These cells are assigned to theater army, corps, and division headquarters and to brigade combat teams based on priorities established by the S-2. These cells have digital mapping tools and access to national-level support from agencies such as the National Geospatial-Intelligence Agency. The geospatial intelligence cell, along with the G-2/S-2,collaborates with an Air Force staff weather officer to leverage the appropriate weather capabilities in order to incorporate the effects of current and future weather conditions into terrain analysis. Terrain analysis results in the evaluation of the military aspects of terrain (OAKOC) on operations.

See pp. 3-20 to 3-21 for an overview of the military aspects of terrain (OAKOC).

Evaluate Terrain Effects on Military Operations

The staff determines terrain effects on friendly and threat operations. The MCOO and the terrain effects matrix are the primary analytic tools used to determine these effects.

Modified Combined Obstacle Overlay (MCOO)

The modified combined obstacle overlay is a joint intelligence preparation of the operational environment product used to portray the militarily significant aspects of the operational environment, such as obstacles restricting military movement, key geography, and military objectives (JP 2-01.3). The MCOO is tailored to the mission and is a collaborative effort involving input from the entire staff. The staff uses its warfighting function expertise to determine how the terrain will impact that function. Specific aspects of the MCOO include but are not limited to AAs, key terrain, mobility corridors, natural and man-made obstacles, and terrain mobility classifications.

See following pages (pp. 3-26 to 3-27) for further discussion of the MCOO.

Terrain Effects Matrix

Using the MCOO as a guide, a terrain effects matrix describes OAKOC factor effects on friendly and threat operations.

OAKOC factors (military aspects of terrain)	*Terrain effects*
Observation and fields of fire	• Sparse vegetation on generally flat desert terrain with observation of 3 to 5 kilometers. • There are 10 kilometers between intervisibility lines. • Limited air support observation due to sparse terrain and the Earth's curvature. • Fields of fire for direct fire are 300 to 500 meters for small arms. • Intermediate breaks in observation and fields of fire due to runoffs and cuts. • Likely engagement area at Julian pass. • Likely engagement area 1000 meters north of the major city.
Avenues of approach (AAs)	• Primary and secondary road systems for high AAs. • Generally flat terrain with brigade-sized mobility corridors between small villages. • Railroad in the north running east to west. • AA2 is the recommended AA as it enables the placement of organic weapon systems in range before observation from the threat in the defense.
Key terrain	• Airfield used as resupply and troop movements. • Dam controls water flow on the river and is the primary objective of the threat.
Obstacles	• Restrictive runoffs and cuts run throughout the area of operations with an average depth of 5 to 10 feet and an average width of 20 feet that runs 6 to 10 kilometers long. • Aboveground oil and transport pipeline (which is severely restrictive terrain) that runs through the central width of the area of operations.
Cover and concealment	• Cover by direct fire systems is provided by intervisibility lines. • Concealment is limited by the open terrain and sparse vegetation.

Table 4-5. Terrain effects matrix example.

Modified Combined Obstacle Overlay (MCOO)

Ref: ATP 2-01.3, Intelligence Preparation of the Battlefield (Mar '19), pp. 4-13 to 4-16.

The combined obstacle overlay provides a basis for identifying ground AAs and mobility corridors. Unlike the cross-country mobility, the combined obstacle overlay integrates all impediments to mobility, such as built-up areas, slope, soils, vegetation, and hydrology into one overlay. This overlay also allows the staff to visualize impediments to mobility for both friendly and threat forces. The overlay depicts areas that impede mobility (severely restricted and restricted areas) and areas where friendly and threat forces can move unimpeded (unrestricted areas).

The modified combined obstacle overlay is a joint intelligence preparation of the operational environment product used to portray the militarily significant aspects of the operational environment, such as obstacles restricting military movement, key geography, and military objectives (JP 2-01.3). The MCOO is tailored to the mission and is a collaborative effort involving input from the entire staff. The staff uses its warfighting function expertise to determine how the terrain will impact that function.

Specific aspects of the MCOO include but are not limited to:

- AAs
- Key terrain
- Mobility corridors
- Natural and man-made obstacles
- Terrain mobility classifications

The MCOO depicts the terrain according to the mobility classification. These classifications are severely restricted, restricted, and unrestricted:

- **Severely restricted terrain** severely hinders or slows movement in combat formations unless some effort is made to enhance mobility, such as committing engineer assets to improving mobility or deviating from doctrinal tactics (moving in columns instead of line formations or at speeds much lower than those preferred). For example, severely restricted terrain for armored and mechanized forces is typically characterized by steep slopes and large or dense obstacle compositions with few bypasses. A common technique to depict this type of terrain on overlays and sketches is marking the areas with green crosshatched diagonal lines.
- **Restricted terrain** hinders movement to some degree. Little effort is needed to enhance mobility, but units may have difficulty maintaining preferred speeds, moving in combat formations, or transitioning from one formation to another. Restricted terrain slows movement by requiring zigzagging or frequent detours. Restricted terrain for armored or mechanized forces typically consists of moderate-to-steep slopes or moderate-to-dense obstacle compositions, such as restrictive slopes or curves. Swamps or rugged terrain are examples of restricted terrain for dismounted infantry forces. Logistical or sustainment area movement may be supported by poorly developed road systems. A common and useful technique to depict restricted terrain on overlays and sketches is marking the areas with green diagonal lines.
- **Unrestricted terrain** is free from any restriction to movement. Nothing is required to enhance mobility. Unrestricted terrain for armored or mechanized forces is typically flat to moderately sloping terrain with few obstacles such as limiting slopes or curves. This terrain allows wide maneuver by the forces under consideration and unlimited travel supported by well-developed road networks. No symbology is needed to show unrestricted terrain on overlays and sketches.

Terrain mobility classifications are not absolute but reflect the relative effect of terrain on the different types and sizes of movement formations. They are based on the force's ability to maneuver in combat formations or transition from one type of formation to another.

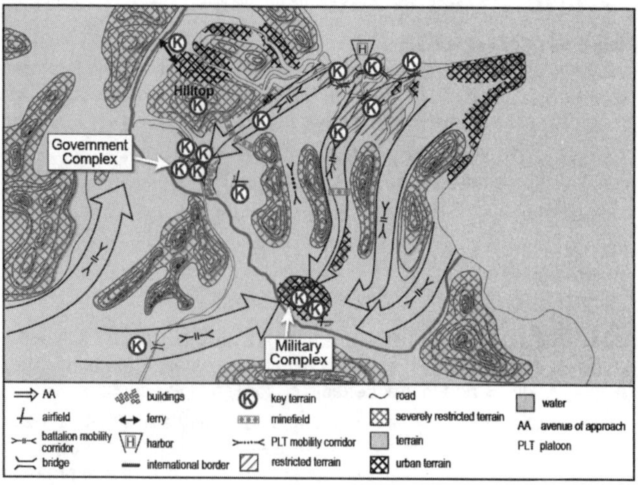

Figure 4-9. Modified combined obstacle overlay example.

The staff should consider the following:

- Obstacles are only effective if covered by observation and fields of fire. However, even undefended obstacles may canalize an attacker into concentrations, which are easier to detect and target or defend. Obstacles are green on map overlays.
- When evaluating the terrain's effects on more than one type of organization (for example, mounted or dismounted), obstacle overlays reflect an impact on mobility of a particular force.
- The cumulative effects of individual obstacles should be considered in the final evaluation. For example, individually, a gentle slope or a moderately dense forest may prove to be an unrestrictive obstacle to vehicular traffic; together, the slope and dense forest may prove to be restrictive.
- The staff should account for the weather's effects on factors that affect mobility.
- The classification of terrain into various obstacle types reflects only its relative impact on force mobility.

For urban areas, graphics typically depict population status overlays (dense population centers, political boundaries), logistics sustainability overlays, LOCs, route overlays (street names, patterns, widths),bridges (underpass and overpass information), potential sniper and ambush locations (will likely be a separate overlay), and key navigational landmarks. In developing urban area and complex terrain overlays, the following should be depicted:

- **Natural terrain**. The underlying terrain on which man-made terrain is superimposed, such as rivers, streams, hills, valleys, forests, desert, bogs, swamps.
- **Man-made terrain**. Streets, bridges, buildings, railways, canals, sewer systems, subway systems, military bunkers, traffic control points; building density, construct, dimensions; functional zone disposition; street construct, materials, disposition, dimensions.
- **Key facilities, targets and/or terrain**. Banks, hospitals, police stations, industrial plants and factories, media and information facilities, bridges, airports, seaports, electric power grids, oil facilities, military facilities, key residences and places of employment, waterways; tall structures(skyscrapers); choke points; street patterns, intersections; industrial complexes; other facilities; density of construction or population.
- **Obstacles**. Rubble and vehicles on the road; fixed barriers; masking of fires, burning of buildings, and other fire hazards; rivers and lakes; power lines and cell phone towers; population; trenches and minefields; certain religious or cultural sites; wire obstacles (concertina wire, barb wire).

C. Describe How Weather Can Affect Friendly and Threat Operations

Weather analysis is the collection, processing, evaluation, and interpretation of relevant military aspects of weather. It is the evaluation of forecasted weather effects on operations. There are two substeps in weather analysis:

Analyze the Military Aspects of Weather

The following are military aspects of weather:

- Visibility
- Wind
- Precipitation
- Cloud cover
- Temperature
- Humidity
- Atmospheric pressure (as required)

Evaluate the Weather's Effects on Military Operations

Weather has both direct and indirect effects on military operations. The following are examples of direct and indirect effects on military operations:

- Temperature inversions might cause some battle positions to be more at risk to the effects of chemical agents because of atmospheric ducting, a process that occurs when strong high pressure influences an area and prevents particulates from dispersing into the upper atmosphere.
- Local visibility restrictions, such as fog, affect observation for both friendly and threat forces. Severe restrictions to visibility often restrict aviation operations.
- Hot, dry weather might force friendly and threat forces to consider water sources as key terrain.
- Dense, humid air limits the range of loudspeaker broadcasts, affecting sonic deception, surrender appeals to threat forces, and the ability to provide instruction to friendly or neutral audiences.
- Sandstorms with high silica content may decrease the strength and clarity of radio and television signals.

Weather and climate effects can impact seasonal outlooks, which affect seasonal decision making—for example, giving crop selection and rotation advice in a particular area that boosts plant growth. Knowing that a particular area may be susceptible to locust swarms may enable pesticide application to prevent such a swarm. If a drought is expected, civil affairs personnel may advise planting another crop that raises the benefit to the farmer.

The G-2/S-2 coordinates with the Air Force staff weather officer to provide weather effects to support operations. The following work aids assist in analyzing and describing weather effects on operations:

- Weather forecast charts are guides for determining the weather information needed for planning and operations.
- Light and illumination data tables are guides for determining the light and illumination data needed for planning and operations.
- Weather effects matrices are guides for determining the weather effects on personnel, weapons, and equipment needed for planning and operations.

D. Describe How Civil Considerations Can Affect Friendly and Threat Operations

An understanding of civil considerations—the ability to analyze their impact on operations—enhances several aspects of operations, including the selection of objectives; location, movement, and control of forces; use of weapons; and protection measures. The intelligence staff should leverage the rest of the staff, as well as outside agencies, who have expertise in civil considerations, to aid the intelligence analysis in this area. Generating intelligence knowledge is an opportunity to leverage nonorganic units, agencies, academia, other organizations, or other Services that are not deploying with the unit but have relevant regional knowledge. This is especially true when accounting for cyberspace considerations, which may not be an organic expertise at the G-2/S-2 levels.

Civil considerations assist commanders in understanding the social, political, and cultural variables within the AO and their effects on the mission. Tactical Army staffs use ASCOPE characteristics to analyze civil considerations that are essential in supporting the development of effective plans for operations.

See following pages (pp. 3-30 to 3-31) for an overview and further discussion of one method by cross-walking civil considerations (including examples for each ASCOPE characteristic) with the operational variables (PMESII).

Due to the complexity and volume of data involving civil considerations, there is no simple model for presenting civil considerations analysis. The intelligence staff maintains this information in the civil considerations data file and constructs intelligence products comprising overlays and assessments areas overlay to assist in planning.

Civil Considerations Data Files, Overlays, & Assessments

The intelligence staff maintains a civil considerations data file that organizes the information it has collected and analyzed based on the ASCOPE characteristics. This data file organizes the raw data the intelligence staff uses to assess civil considerations during IPB, as well as to support targeting and civil affairs operations.

Civil considerations overlays are graphic depictions of the data file. They assist in planning throughout the MDMP, developing the situation during operations, and the intelligence staff in describing civil considerations effects, as assessed in the data file, to the commander and the rest of the staff. For example, the civil considerations overlay may assist in identifying areas or routes likely to be used if conflict creates conditions for refugees or displaced persons. This information can permit the prepositioning of capabilities, materials, and assets to mitigate impacts to ongoing friendly operations and to assist in humanitarian assistance efforts.

The civil considerations data file and associated overlays assist the commander and staff in identifying information and intelligence requirements not normally identified through the event templating process associated with determining threat COAs. In contingency operations, or when conducting stability tasks, these work aids assist the intelligence staff in determining and assessing threat COAs.

Civil considerations assessments are used throughout the MDMP. They use both the civil considerations data file and overlays to provide the supported commander with a detailed analysis of the civil component of the AOI in accordance with ASCOPE characteristics. Potential areas of investigation in the civil considerations assessment include mapping social and political patterns (formal and informal leadership and identifying key societal friction points.

Understanding the relationship between military operations and civilians, culture, and society is critical to operations and essential in developing effective plans. The development of the civil considerations data file, overlays, and assessments can be augmented by regional civil considerations data repositories maintained at national and theater levels.

Civil and foreign affairs officers can also provide detailed information and analysis pertaining to sociocultural factors as aspects of civil considerations. The insights these personnel provide often fill multiple information gaps concerning those areas unfamiliar to both the intelligence and other staff sections.

There is no standard set of subcharacteristics and overlays produced by the intelligence staff. Determining what is needed is based on the intelligence staff's assessment of the situation and complexity of the AO. Each staff section may have pertinent information to add to the overlays.

Civil Considerations (PMESII and ASCOPE)

Ref: ATP 2-01.3, Intelligence Preparation of the Battlefield (Mar '19), table 4-6. Crosswalk of civil considerations (ASCOPE) with operational variables (PMESII) pp. 4-29 to 4-30.

Civil considerations assist commanders in understanding the social, political, and cultural variables within the AO and their effects on the mission. Tactical Army staffs use ASCOPE characteristics to analyze civil considerations that are essential in supporting the development of effective plans for operations. Table 4-6 below presents one method by cross-walking civil considerations (including examples for each ASCOPE characteristic) with the operational variables (PMESII). *See also pp. 1-16 to 1-17.*

	Areas	*Structures*	*Capabilities*	*Organizations*	*People*	*Events*
POLITICAL	• Enclaves • Municipalities • Provinces • Districts • Political districts • Voting • Party affiliation areas • Shadow government influence areas	• Courts (court house, mobile courts) • Government centers • Provincial/District centers • Meeting halls • Polling sites • Police stations • Prisons	• Public administration: ▪ Civil authority, practices, and rights ▪ Political system, stability, traditions ▪ Standards and effectiveness • Executive and Legislative: ▪ Administration ▪ Policies ▪ Powers ▪ Organization • Judicial/Legal: ▪ Administration ▪ Capacity ▪ Policies ▪ Civil and criminal codes ▪ Powers ▪ Organization ▪ Law enforcement • Dispute resolution, grievances • Local leadership • Degrees of legitimacy • Corrections	• Banks • Business organizations • Cooperatives • Economic nongovernment organizations • Guilds • Labor unions • Major illicit industries • Large landholders • Volunteer groups	• United Nations representatives • Political leaders • Governors • Councils • Elders • Community leaders • Paramilitary members • Judges • Prosecutors • Law enforcement officers • Corrections officers	• Elections • Council meetings • Speeches (significant) • Security and military training sessions • Significant trials • Political Motivation • Treaties • Will
MILITARY	• Areas of influence • Areas of interest • Areas of operations • Safe havens or sanctuaries • Multinational/local nation bases • Historic data on operations by the opposition	• Bases • Headquarters (police) • Known leader houses/businesses	• Doctrine • Organization • Training • Materiel • Leadership • Personnel manpower • Facilities • History • Nature of civil-military relationships • Resource constraints • Local security forces • Quick-reaction forces • Insurgent strength • Enemy recruiting	• Host-nation forces present • Insurgent groups present and networks • Multinational forces present • Paramilitary organizations • Fraternal organizations • Civic organizations	• Key leaders • Multinational, insurgent, military	• Combat • Historical • Noncombat • Kinetic events • Unit reliefs • Loss of leadership
ECONOMIC	• Commercial • Fishery • Forestry • Industrial • Livestock dealers • Markets • Mining • Movement of goods/ services • Smuggling routes • Trade routes • Black market areas	• Banking • Fuel: distribution, refining, source • Industrial plants • Manufacturing • Mining • Warehousing • Markets • Silos, granaries, warehouses • Farms/Ranches • Auto repair shops	• Fiscal: access to banks, currency, monetary policy • Can tolerate drought • Black market • Energy • Imports/Exports • External support/aid • Food: distributing, marketing, production, processing, rationing, security, storing, transporting • Inflation • Market prices • Raw materials • Tariffs	• Banks • Business organizations • Cooperatives • Economic nongovernment organizations • Guilds • Labor unions • Major illicit industries • Large landholders • Volunteer groups • Police departments	• Bankers • Police • Employers/ Employees • Labor occupations • Consumption patterns • Unemployment rate (if exists) • Job lines • Landholders • Merchants • Money lenders • Black marketers • Gang members • Smuggling chain	• Drought, harvest, yield, domestic animals, livestock (cattle, sheep), market cycles • Labor migration events • Market days • Payday • Business openings • Loss of business

An understanding of civil considerations—the ability to analyze their impact on operations—enhances several aspects of operations, including the selection of objectives; location, movement, and control of forces; use of weapons; and protection measures. The intelligence staff should leverage the rest of the staff, as well as outside agencies, who have expertise in civil considerations, to aid the intelligence analysis in this area. Generating intelligence knowledge is an opportunity to leverage nonorganic units, agencies, academia, other organizations, or other Services that are not deploying with the unit but have relevant regional knowledge. This is especially true when accounting for cyberspace considerations, which may not be an organic expertise at the G-2/S-2 levels.

	Areas	*Structures*	*Capabilities*	*Organizations*	*People*	*Events*
SOCIAL	• Refugee camps • Enclaves: ethnic, religious, social, tribal, families or clans • Neighborhoods • Boundaries of influence • School districts • Parks • Traditional picnic areas • Markets • Outdoor religious sites	• Clubs • Jails • Historical buildings/houses • Libraries • Religious buildings • Schools/ Universities • Stadiums • Cemeteries • Bars and tea shops • Social gathering places (meeting places) • Restaurants • Police stations	• Medical: Traditional, modern • Social networks, including those on websites • Academic • Strength of tribal/ village traditional structures • Judicial • Police	• Clan • Community councils and organizations • School councils • Familial • Patriotic/Service organizations • Religious groups • Tribes • Police departments	• Community leaders, councils, and members • Education • Ethnicity/Racial: biases, dominant group, percentages, role in conflict • Key figures: criminals, entertainment, religious leaders, chiefs/elders • Languages/ Dialects • Vulnerable populations • Displaced persons • Sports • Influential families • Migration patterns • Culture: Artifacts, behaviors, customs, shared beliefs/value • Police	• Celebrations • Civil disturbance • National holidays • Religious holidays and observance days • Food lines • Weddings • Birthdays • Funerals • Sports events • Market days • Family gatherings • History: major wars/ conflicts • Police engagement
INFORMATION	• Broadcast coverage area (newspaper, radio, television) • Word of mouth • Gathering points • Graffiti • Posters	• Communications: Lines, towers (cell, radio, television) • Internet service: satellite, hard wire, cafes • Cellular phone • Postal service • Print shops • Telephone • Television stations • Radio stations	• Availability of electronic media • Local communications networks • Internet access • Intelligence services • Printed material: flyers, journals, newspapers • Propaganda • Radio • Television • Social media • Literacy rate • Word of mouth	• Media groups, news organizations • Religious groups • Insurgent inform and influence activity groups • Government groups • Public relations and advertising groups	• Decision makers • Media personalities • Media groups, news organizations • Community leaders • Elders • Heads of families	• Disruption of services • Censorship • Religious observance days • Publishing dates • Inform and influence activity campaigns • Project openings
INFRASTRUCTURE	• Commercial • Industrial • Residential • Rural • Urban • Road systems • Power grids • Irrigation networks • Water tables	• Emergency shelters • Energy: distribution system, electrical lines, natural gas, power plants • Medical: hospitals, veterinary • Public buildings • Transportation: airfields, bridges, bus stations, ports and harbors, railroads, roadways, subways • Waste distribution, storage, and treatment: dams, sewage, solid • Construction sites	• Construction • Clean water • Communications systems • Law enforcement • Fire fighting • Medical: basic, intensive, urgent • Sanitation • Maintenance of roads, dams, irrigation, sewage systems • Environmental management	• Construction companies: government, contract	• Builders • Road contractors • Local development councils	• Scheduled maintenance (road/bridge construction) • Natural/Man-made disasters • Well digging • Community center construction • School construction

Step 3—Evaluate the Threat

Step 3 of the IPB process determines threat force capabilities and the doctrinal principles and TTP threat forces prefer to employ. This may include threats that create multiple dilemmas for U.S. maneuver forces by simultaneously employing regular, irregular, and terrorist forces and criminal elements, using a variety of traditional and nontraditional tactics.

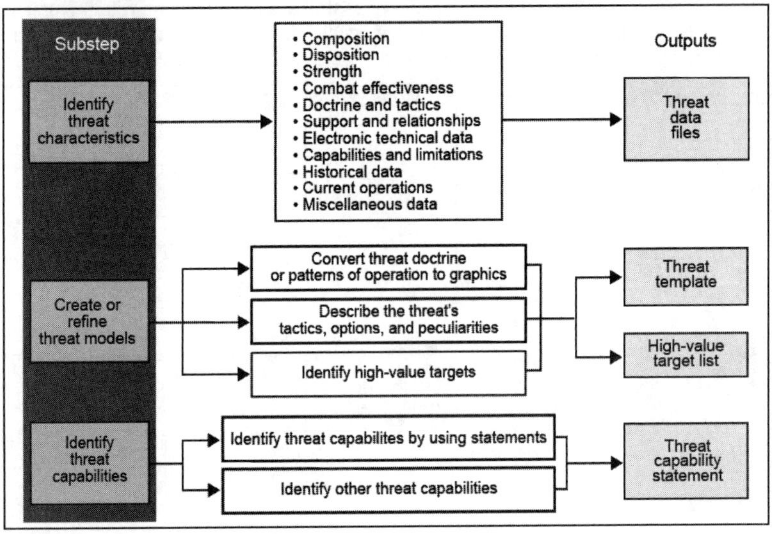

Figure 5-1. Substeps and outputs of step 3 of the IPB.

So What?

The "so what" of step 3 is to enhance commanders' understanding of the regular, irregular, and hybrid threats within their AOI:

- Threat COAs developed in the next step of IPB reflect what the threat is capable of and trained to do in similar situations.

Consequences of failure:

- The staff may lack the intelligence needed for planning.
- The threat may surprise the friendly force with capabilities not accounted for by the G-2/S-2.
- The staff may waste time & effort planning against nonexistent threat capabilities.
- The friendly force's ability to exploit threat windows of vulnerability may be degraded.

Evaluating the threat should begin with identifying all threats based on their characteristics and ultimately creating the threat model (regular, irregular, or hybrid structure). At the tactical level, threat characteristics are often referred to as order of battle. The tactical-level evaluation of a military threat should concentrate on standard threat characteristics/order of battle factors, such as the composition, disposition, strength, TTP, and training status of specific tactical units or factional groups that could interfere with mission accomplishment. Order of battle is the identification, strength, command structure, and disposition of the personnel, units, and equipment of any military force (JP 2-01.3).

Note. When operating against a new or emerging threat not identified and described in the unit's threat data files, the intelligence staff must develop new data files for each of these threats. Other units' and organizations' data files may also assist in developing threat products.

The Threat

Ref: ATP 2-01.3, Intelligence Preparation of the Battlefield (Mar '19), pp. 5-1 to 5-3.

Over the past three decades, threats have studied the manner in which U.S. forces have deployed and conducted operations. Several have adapted, modernized, and developed capabilities to counter U.S. advantages in the air, land, maritime, space, and cyberspace domains. Military advances by Russia, China, North Korea, and Iran most clearly portray this changing threat. Therefore, understanding threat capabilities is critical to developing COAs.

Threats, large and small, increasingly operate in an indeterminate zone between peace and war. They seek to avoid U.S. strengths and, instead, take advantage of U.S. laws and policies regarding the use of information and cyberspace capabilities. Coupled with the Nation's initial reluctance to engage in major combat operations, threats achieve incremental gains that advance their agenda and narrative. They use a range of techniques, including nonattribution, innuendo, propaganda, disinformation, and misinformation, to sway global opinion favorable to their aims.

For the Army, threats are a fundamental part of an overall OE for any operation, but they are discussed separately here simply for emphasis. A threat is any combination of actors, entities, or forces that have the capability and intent to harm United States forces, United States national interests, or the homeland (ADRP 3-0). Threats may include paramilitary or military forces, nation-states, national alliances, individuals, groups of individuals (organized or not organized), or conditions that can damage or destroy life,vital resources, or institutions.

While the Army must be manned, equipped, and trained to operate across the range of military operations, large-scale ground combat against a peer threat represents the most significant readiness requirement. FM 3-0 focuses on peer threats in large-scale combat operations. It describes peer threats as adversaries or enemies with capabilities and capacity to oppose U.S. forces across multiple domains worldwide or in a specific region where they enjoy a position of relative advantage. Peer threats possess roughly equal combat power in geographical proximity to a conflict area with U.S. forces. Peer threats generate tactical, operational, and strategic challenges of an order of magnitude more challenging militarily than those the Army has faced since the end of the Cold War.

Regular threats from peer competitors with significant ability to act in all domains are considered multi-domain threats. These **peer threats** are only peer in the military or economic elements of power.

Irregular threats are opponents employing unconventional, asymmetric methods and means to counter U.S. advantages, such as overwhelming firepower and technological overmatch.

A **hybrid threat** is the diverse and dynamic combination of regular forces, irregular forces, terrorist forces, or criminal elements unified to achieve mutually benefitting threat effects.

Refer to AODS6 (w/SMARTupdate 1): The Army Operations & Doctrine SMARTbook (Guide to FM/ADP 3-0 Operations & the Elements of Combat Power). Completely updated with the Jul 2019 ADPs, Chg 1 to the 400-pg AODS6 includes operations (ADP 3-0), large-scale combat operations (FM 3-0 w/Chg 1), and refocused chapters on the elements of combat power: command & control (ADP 6-0), movement and maneuver (ADPs 3-90, 3-07, 3-28, 3-05), intelligence (ADP 2-0), fires (ADP 3-19), sustainment (ADP 4-0), & protection (ADP 3-37).

A commander's understanding of the threat is based in part on the intelligence staff's research and analysis of the threat characteristics, as part of generating intelligence knowledge. The intelligence staff considers broad characteristics when analyzing the threat, such as composition, disposition, strength, combat effectiveness, doctrine and tactics, support and relationships, electronic technical data, capabilities and limitations, current operations, historical data, and miscellaneous data. To ensure this understanding is as complete as possible, the intelligence staff considers the following when assessing these characteristics:

- Threat characteristics form a framework for the consistent evaluation of any force.
- The threat characteristics evaluation framework should be adapted to the threat mission and the unit's needs.
- Properly maintained files at multiple echelons and organizations are sources of information on threat operations, capabilities, and vulnerabilities.
- Threat characteristics are analyzed as a whole

Although threat forces may conform to some of the fundamental principles of warfare that guide Army operations, these forces have obvious and subtle differences in how they approach situations and problem solving. Understanding these differences is essential to understanding how a threat force reacts in a given situation.

A. Identify Threat Characteristics

During steps 1 and 2 of the IPB process, the intelligence staff identifies and defines each individual threat within the commander's AOI. During step 3, the intelligence staff analyzes the characteristics associated with each of these threats as well as develops threat models for each of these threats.

See following pages (pp. 3-36 to 3-37) for discussion and an overview of broad threat characteristics. Refer to ATP 2-01.3, appendix C for threat characteristics associated with regular, irregular, and hybrid threats.

B. Create or Refine Threat Models

Threat models accurately portray how threat forces normally execute operations and how they have reacted to similar situations in the past. This also includes knowledge of threat capabilities based on the current situation. Threat models are initially created by analyzing information in various databases concerning threat organizations, equipment, doctrine, and TTP. Higher agencies and organizations create some threat models; but in immature OEs or when a new threat emerges, analysts develop threat models.

Analysts must use all available sources to update and refine threat models. The most useful sources are threat characteristic files with information that assists analysts in making conclusions about threat operations, capabilities, and vulnerabilities. Staff integration during threat model development is essential in achieving the most accurate depiction of how the threat conducts operations in ideal situations with no terrain constraints.

A threat model is an analytical tool that assists analysts in developing situation templates during step 4 of the IPB process. See facing page.

Threat Models

Ref: ATP 2-01.3, Intelligence Preparation of the Battlefield (Mar '19), pp. 5-9 to 5-16.

A threat model is an analytical tool that assists analysts in developing situation templates during step 4 of the IPB process. Threat models consist of three activities:

1. Convert Threat Doctrine or Patterns of Operation to Graphics

Threat templates graphically portray how the threat might use its capabilities to perform the functions required to accomplish its objectives when not constrained by the effects of the OE. Threat templates are scaled to depict the threat's disposition and actions for a type of operation (for example, offense, defense, ambush, personnel movement, clandestine sustainment operations or kidnapping). When possible, templates should be depicted graphically as an overlay, on a supporting system, or through some other means. Threat templates are tailored to the needs of the unit or staff creating them. Some threat templates consider threat forces, while others focus on a single warfighting function, such as intelligence or fire support. Other products depict pattern analysis, time event charts, and association matrices. Threat templates may depict, but are not limited to, unit frontages, unit depths, boundaries, engagement areas, and obstacles.

Refer to ATP 2-33.4 for more on pattern analysis and association matrices.

2. Describe the Threat's Tactics, Options, and Peculiarities

The threat model includes a description of the threat's preferred **tactics** (including but not limited to attack, defend, reinforce, and retrograde). A description is still required even if the preferred tactics are depicted in graphic form. This allows the template to become more than a "snapshot in time" of the operation being depicted.

Options are described by listing items such as identified threat capabilities and branches and sequels. Branches and sequels are used primarily for changing deployments or direction of movement and for accepting or declining combat. Analysts research and annotate any threat peculiarities about the operation.

Peculiarities can provide insights into threat strengths and vulnerabilities, as well as assist friendly forces in addressing them.

3. Identify High-Value Targets (HVTs)

Identifying HVTs assists the staff in creating HPTs during the COA development step of the MDMP. The following techniques may be useful in identifying/evaluating HVTs:

- Identify HVTs from existing intelligence studies; the evaluation of the databases; size, activity, location, unit, time, and equipment (also called SALUTE) reports; patrol debriefs; the threat template and its associated threat capability statement; and the use of tactical judgment.
- Review threat TTP and previous threat operations as well as understand the threat's task, purpose, method, and end state.
- Consider that HVTs usually fall within non maneuver elements (command and control [C2],intelligence, fires, sustainment, and protection).
- Identify assets that are key to executing the primary operation or sequels.
- Determine how the threat might react to losing each identified HVT. Consider the threat's ability to substitute other assets as well as adopt branches or sequels.
- Conduct mental war gaming and think through the operation under consideration and how the threat will use assets from each of the elements (such as fire support, engineers).

Target Value Analysis. HVTs should be prioritized by their relative value to the threat's operation. Target value analysis assists in prioritizing HVTs. Target value analysis is a process led by the fires cell as part of targeting that quantifies the relative value of HVTs with each other in relation to a threat operation.

Threat Characteristics

Ref: ATP 2-01.3, Intelligence Preparation of the Battlefield (Mar '19), pp. 5-5 to 5-9.

Composition

Composition is the identification and organization of a threat. It describes how an entity is organized and equipped—essentially the number and types of personnel, weapons, and equipment available for a given operation. Composition applies to specific units or commands as opposed to types of units. Understanding a threat's composition—

- Is essential in determining the threat's capabilities and limitations.
- To help construct threat models that assist in developing valid threat COAs and friendly counteractions.
- Assists in determining a threat's combat effectiveness and conducting combat assessment.

Regular threats are normally self-identified and organized similarly to friendly forces. Irregular threats may follow similar rules but are mostly organized mostly based on a cellular structure. The staff uses line and block chart products to depict the threat's composition.

Composition also refers to how an entity is commanded and controlled. Military forces have distinct and well-defined organizational structures generally built around a linear chain of command. Regardless of the threat type, knowing its structure assists in understanding its capabilities and limitations.

Disposition

Disposition refers to how threat forces are arrayed on the battlefield. It includes the recent, current, and projected movements or locations of tactical forces. Regular threats generally conduct some form of offensive or defensive maneuver. Irregular threats are generally in part of the plan, prepare, execute, and assess activities of an operation, such as a raid or ambush. In a hybrid threat scenario, irregular threats may have the capability to mass and be the main effort or fixing force on the battlefield. Understanding how the threat doctrinally arrays on the battlefield is essential in developing threat models in step 3 of IPB and threat situation templates in step 4 of IPB. The intelligence staff becomes familiar with graphic training aids to illustrate range fans with weapon fire limits and direct and indirect weapon capabilities. This provides a better understanding of threat weapon systems.

Strength

Strength describes a unit in terms of personnel, weapons, and equipment. Information concerning strength provides commanders with an indication of threat capabilities and assists in determining the probable COAs or options open to threat commanders. A lack of strength or a preponderance of strength has the effect lowering or raising the estimate of the threat's capabilities. Likewise, a marked concentration or build-up of units in an area gives commanders certain indications of threat objectives and probable COAs. During peacetime, changes in the strength of potential threats are important factors as they may indicate changes in the threat's intention. Strength is determined by comparing how a threat organization is doctrinally staffed and equipped with what the organization has on hand.

Combat Effectiveness

Combat effectiveness, the readiness of a military unit to engage in combat based on behavioral, operational, and leadership considerations. Combat effectiveness measures the ability of a military force to accomplish its objective—it describes a unit's abilities and fighting quality. Numerous tangible and intangible factors affect combat effectiveness, including but not limited to the number of personnel or equipment losses and replacements, reinforcements (tangibles), and operational experience and morale(intangibles). The simple fact that a military has large numbers does not ensure a unit is combat effective.

Doctrine and Tactics

Doctrine and tactics include tactical doctrine as well as tactics employed by specific units. While tactical doctrine refers to the threat's accepted organization and employment principles, tactics refer to the threat force's conduct of operations. Based on knowledge of a threat's tactical doctrine, the intelligence staff can determine how the threat may employ its forces in the offense and defense under various conditions. Analysts integrate tactics in threat templates and other intelligence products.

Support and Relationships

The threat's adoption of a COA should depend on its support system's ability to support that action. However, depending on the threat's objectives, possible time constraints, and/or willingness to assume risk—especially as dictated by political leaders or dynamics of political-military circumstances—this could substantially alter adoption of a COA. With knowledge of these factors, analysts can better evaluate the threat's combat effectiveness, strength, and capabilities.

Electronic Technical Data

Electronic technical data is required to conduct EW. For the Army, this data is also derived from cyberspace electromagnetic activities, signals intelligence (SIGINT), and measurement and signature intelligence. This data includes communications and noncommunications equipment parameters, such as emitter type and nomenclature, modulation, multiplex capability, pulse duration, pulse repetition frequency, bandwidth, associated weapon systems, and other technical characteristics of electronic emissions. This information can be developed into an overlay. To produce the overlay, SIGINT personnel require the targeting and EW staffs' assistance and input.

Capabilities and Limitations

Capabilities are the broad COAs and supporting operations that the threat can take to achieve its goals and objectives. The following tactical COAs are generally open to military forces in conventional operations: attack, defend, reinforce, and retrograde. Each of these broad COAs can be divided into specific COAs.

Current Operations

Current operations are those operations in which an enemy force is currently engaged. This includes operations against U.S. military forces or interests or against the military forces or interests of other nation-states. Analyzing current operations provides up-to-date information on other threat characteristics.

Historical Data

Compiling the history of any threat organization involves conducting the research necessary to gather all relevant information regarding the threat and producing the materials needed to communicate that information to the commander and staff. Information briefings and papers are the two most common methods used for this purpose. These methods support intelligence training, officer professional development, and noncommissioned officer professional development. The history component of the threat data file includes the original sources of information used to compile information briefings and papers. These sources form part of the professional readings required by the unit's intelligence personnel.

Miscellaneous Data

Intelligence staffs use supporting information to develop threat force characteristics and to construct comprehensive intelligence estimates. This information includes but is not limited to biographic and personality data, culture, biometric and forensic data, as well as other information important to mission accomplishment.

Integrating Processes

C. Identify Threat Capabilities

Threat capabilities are broad options and supporting operations that the threat can take to influence accomplishing friendly missions. They provide the means for accomplishing goals, attacking friendly vulnerabilities, and degrading or neutralizing strengths. Threat actors employ a combination of four major capabilities:

Conventional capabilities are those military assets employed by states in identifiable formations. International law, military tradition, and custom govern conventional capabilities. Nearly every recognized nation-state maintains some conventional forces.

Irregular capabilities are those means of employing unconventional methods, including asymmetric ways to counter U.S. advantages. Irregular capabilities are unregulated; they can act without legal restrictions on the use of violence. Additionally, they are used to create conditions for a protracted conflict in order to exhaust U.S. political will. Targeting economic or political centers with irregular capabilities or exacerbating cultural differences to promote instability are often the preferred means of attack on the U.S. influence.

Disruptive capabilities involve the use of technologies to reduce friendly advantages. Disruptive capabilities use technology to provide the threat with an advantage over similar technology used by friendly forces.

Weapons of mass destruction (WMD) capabilities involve the acquisition, possession, and use of CBRN weapons—also referred to as WMD. The likelihood of the threat's use of WMD increases during large-scale combat operations. The proliferation of these weapons provides potential threats the capability to inflict sudden and catastrophic effects likely to have significant military and political impact today more so than in the past.

When identifying threat capabilities and COAs, analysts start with a full set of threat models and consider the threat's ability to conduct each operation based on the current situation and the threat's METT-TC conditions. Most situations do not present the threat with ideal conditions envisioned by its doctrine. Therefore, the threat's actual capabilities usually do not mirror the ideal capabilities represented by the complete set of threat models. This, in turn, causes the threat to use certain capabilities during friendly windows of vulnerability.

The threat could be under strength in personnel and equipment or may be lacking in logistical support,or threat personnel may be inexperienced or poorly trained. For example, a terrorist group's normal tactics may call for the use of car bombs as a diversionary tactic to conduct other operations elsewhere. The evaluation of the threat's logistics might indicate a critical shortage of explosives. Analysts should consider the following:

- Avoid limiting threat models and capabilities strictly to the threat's conventional forces. For example, student rioters during a noncombatant evacuation operation may be or may become a threat during the operation. By not limiting threat capabilities, intelligence staffs have a more holistic view of all possible COAs when conducting step 4 of the IPB process.
- Avoid overstating threat models and capabilities. The proper use of findings and recommendations developed from threat assessments develops realistic threat models and reserves valuable time and resources for the commander and staff.
- During any discussion of the threat, be culturally aware; this is an important factor. By developing an awareness of the culture, friendly units can identify groups or individual members of the population that may be friendly, a threat, somewhere in between, or both.

Identify Threat Capabilities (Examples)

Identify Threat Capabilities By Using Statements

Analysts identify threat capabilities by using statements such as the following:

- "The threat has the capability to attack with up to eight divisions supported by 150 daily sorties of fixed-wing aircraft."
- "The criminal organization has the ability to pay off local law enforcement agencies."
- "The terrorists have the capability to send destructive viruses over the internet that can destroy computer files and archives."
- "The threat has ADA capabilities to counter rotary-wing support during infiltration operations."
- "The threat can establish a prepared defense by 14 May."
- "The terrorists have the capability of using CBRN weapons."
- "The threat has the capability to conduct information warfare from Site X."
- "The drug smugglers have the ability to conduct three drug-smuggling operations simultaneously."
- "The terrorists have the ability to conduct multiple car bombings simultaneously."
- "The threat has the ability to target friendly convoys along main supply routes using remotely detonated improvised explosive devices (IEDs)."
- "The threat has the ability to counter friendly UASs before crossing Phase Line Green."

Identify Other Threat Capabilities

Other threat capabilities include support to COAs, which may include attack, defend, reinforce, retrograde, or specific types of operations, as well as operations that would allow threat forces to use a COA that would not normally be available or would be severely hindered if the supporting operation were not conducted. Examples of these types of operations include—

- Use of CBRN weapons.
- Intelligence collection.
- EW operations.
- Use of air assets (fixed-wing and rotary-wing).
- Engineering operations.
- Air assault or airborne operations.
- Amphibious operations.
- River operations.
- Propaganda.
- Recruitment.
- Deception operations.
- Car bombings, bomb scares, and suicide bombers.
- Raids on weapons storage facilities.
- Carjacking or hijacking of vehicles used in transporting personnel, weapons, or drugs.
- Theft of chemicals related to drug manufacturing.
- Counter-UAS assets.
- Offensive cyberspace operations.
- Ant access and area denial assets.
- Social media exploitation.

Outputs from IPB Step 3

Ref: ATP 2-01.3, Intelligence Preparation of the Battlefield (Mar '19), pp. 5-18 to 5-22.

The following IPB products are developed based on outcomes from step 3 of the IPB process:

1. Threat Template

As operations begin, it is imperative to develop foundationally sound and accurate threat models through careful analysis. The analyst analyzes a threat's capabilities, vulnerabilities, doctrinal principles, and preferred TTP. It is from the threat's doctrine, training practices, and observed patterns and activities that analysts construct threat templates.

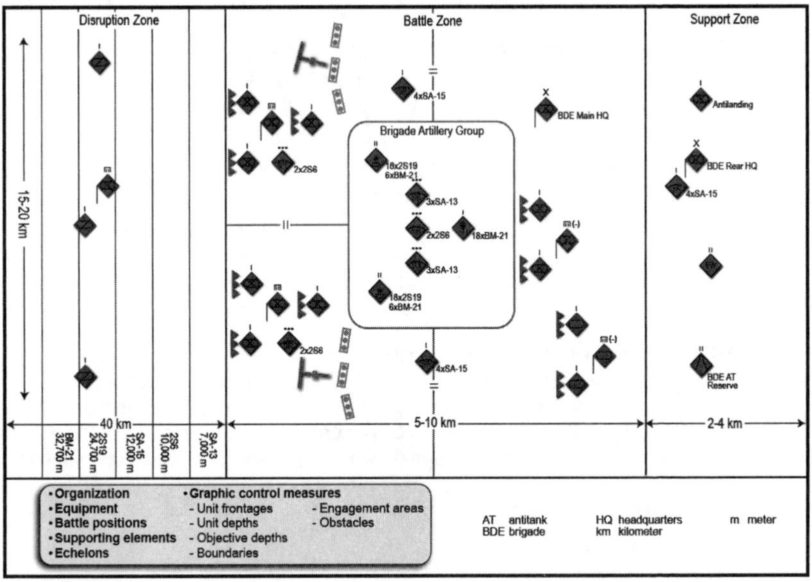

Figure 5-6. Threat template example.

Threat templates graphically portray how the threat prefers to use its capabilities to perform the functions required to accomplish its objectives. They are scaled depictions of threat deployment patterns and dispositions for a particular operation (for example, offense, defense, ambush, or terrorist kidnapping operation) when not constrained by OE effects. Depending on the mission variables, developing templates can be time intensive.

Note. Analysts should create as many threat templates as time allows. This assists in creating situation templates during step 4 of the IPB process.

Threat templates are tailored to the needs of the unit or staff creating them. When possible, they should be depicted graphically as an overlay, on a supporting system, or through some other means. Threat templates do not include environmental effects, such as terrain and weather. They include—

- The location of all threat units two levels down. For example, an infantry battalion in the defense template would depict platoon and specialty team locations.
- The distance and/or time between threat forces conducting a specific operation or activity.
- Graphic control measures associated with the operation, including but not limited to unit frontages, unit depths, boundaries, engagement areas, and obstacles.

Threat templates allow analysts and the staff to—

- Fuse all relevant combat information.
- Assist in identifying intelligence gaps.
- Predict threat activities and adapt COAs.
- Synchronize information collection.

2. High-Value Target List

The HVTs identified during step 3 of IPB are initially refined during step 4 of IPB. They are refined again during the COA analysis step of the MDMP. The HVT list is developed based on identified HVTs.

Threat element	*High-value targets*	
Command and control	• Commander's variant main battle tank (T-72 BK) • Command and staff vehicle (BMP-1KShM) • SAM system fire control (SA-15b)	• Artillery command and reconnaissance vehicle (1V14-3) • Command infantry fighting vehicle (BMP-3K)
Movement and maneuver	• Main battle tank (T-72B) • Excavating vehicle (MDK-3) • Tracked minelaying vehicle (GMZ-3) • Infantry fighting vehicle (BMP-3)	• Towed mechanical minelayer (PMZ-4) • Mine-clearing plow attached (KMT-8) • Armored personnel carrier (BTR-80)
Protection	• NBC reconnaissance vehicle (RKhm-4-01)	• NBC reconnaissance vehicle (BRDM-2RKh)
Fires	• 122-mm multiple rocket launcher (BM-21) • 30-mm self-propelled antiaircraft gun/missile system (2S6M1) • 152-mm self-propelled howitzer (2S19M1)	• 120-mm self-propelled mortar (2S12) • Man-portable SAM system (SA-18) • SAM system (SA-15b) • SAM system (SA-13b)
Intelligence	• Signal van (GAZ-66) • Battlefield surveillance radar (SNAR-10) • Armored scout car (BRDM)	• Short range drone (ORLAN-10) • SAM system radar system (SA-15b) • Artillery locating radar (ARK-1M)
Sustainment	• Tactical utility vehicle (UAZ-469) • 2-mT 4x4 cargo truck (GAZ-66)	• 4.5-mT 6x6 cargo truck (URAL-4320)

mm	millimeter	NBC	nuclear, biological, chemical
mT	metric ton	SAM	surface-to-air missile

Figure 5-7. High-value target list developed during step 3 of IPB (example)

3. Threat Capability Statement

A threat capability statement can be a narrative, table, or visual representation of the data. It identifies a particular action the threat has the capability to complete, and the tactics the threat prefers to accomplish its objectives. It addresses a major unit's operations portrayed on the threat template and the activities of each threat capability.

Threat element	*Statement*
Command and control	The threat can establish commands across the country based on communications capabilities. The threat has constant communications to maintain control of subordinate units from corps down to team echelons.
Movement and maneuver	Corps can provide defensive positions for the forward line of own troops, as well as necessary reinforcement operations to the forward division tactical groups via blocking and ambush operations. The groups will delay United States (U.S.) operations to the eastern border.
Protection	Corps will maintain constant communications to establish air corridor denial of U.S. forces within their respective areas of operations: coordinate with the 9th Corps to ensure successful capture of the capital while denying U.S. forces control of airspace and delaying U.S. forces arrival.
Fires	Division tactical groups will use SS26s and 2S19s to delay U.S. force advancements to the country capital while canalizing U.S. forces through constant fires operations. Division tactical groups will only retaliate with CBRN capability when U.S. forces first use CBRN or U.S. forces approach the capital before division tactical group control is imminent.
Intelligence	The threat uses special purpose forces for early warning systems and can establish terror organizations. It uses guerilla warfare and insurgency tactics against U.S. forces to delay advancement.
Sustainment	Protection and fires will ensure routes are established for resupply opportunities and will establish consolidation areas for refit of forward elements.
CBRN	chemical, biological, radiological, and nuclear

Figure 5-8. Threat capability statement example (narrative format). (Fig 5-9, not depicted, provides a table format example.)

Step 4—Determine Threat Courses of Action

Step 4 of the IPB process identifies and describes threat COAs that can influence friendly operations.

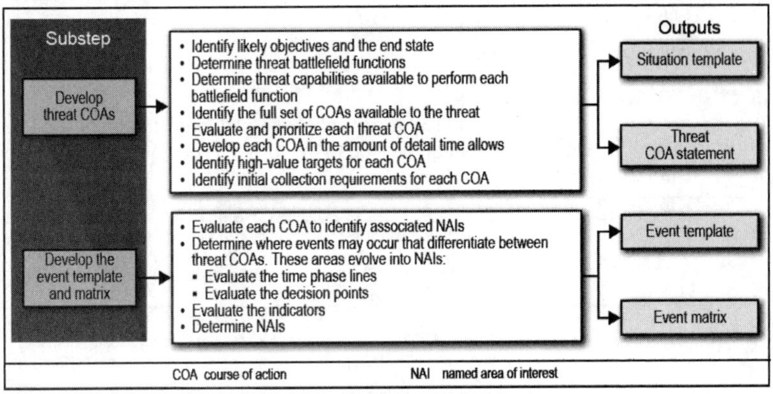

Figure 6-1. Substeps and outputs of step 4 of the IPB process.

So What?

The "so what" is to determine the threat COAs necessary to aid the development of friendly COAs:

- The friendly commander will avoid being surprised with an unanticipated threat action, thus quickly narrowing the set of possible threat COAs to the one the threat has chosen.

Consequences of failure:

- Failure to identify which of the possible COAs the threat has chosen, leading to surprise of the friendly command.
- The threat commander may have the information needed to exploit the opportunities the OE provides in a way the friendly commander did not anticipate.

Determining threat COAs is a two-step process:

A. Develop Threat Courses Of Action

Developing a threat COA requires an understanding of the threat characteristics discussed earlier, as well as the effects of terrain, weather, and civil considerations on operations. Population effects on operations must be clearly annotated with full details. This ensures population effects and threat actions are portrayed during the war game.

The most important element in determining threat COAs is understanding threat operational art and tactics. U.S. forces may encounter regular, irregular, and hybrid threats. The process for determining the COAs these threat forces may employ mirrors friendly COA development and consists of the following:

- Identify likely objectives and the end state.
- Determine threat battlefield functions.
- Determine threat capabilities available to perform each battlefield function.
- Identify the full set of COAs available to the threat.
- Evaluate and prioritize each threat COA.
- Develop each COA in the amount of detail time allows.
- Identify HVTs for each COA.
- Identify initial collection requirements for each COA.

See following pages (pp. 3-43 to 3-45) for an overview and further discussion.

Develop Threat COAs (Overview)

Ref: ATP 2-01.3, Intelligence Preparation of the Battlefield (Mar '19), pp. 6-2 to 6-19.

Developing a threat COA requires an understanding of the threat characteristics discussed earlier, as well as the effects of terrain, weather, and civil considerations on operations. Population effects on operations must be clearly annotated with full details. This ensures population effects and threat actions are portrayed during the war game.

The most important element in determining threat COAs is understanding threat operational art and tactics. U.S. forces may encounter regular, irregular, and hybrid threats. The process for determining the COAs these threat forces may employ mirrors friendly COA development and consists of the following:

Continued on next page

1. Identify Likely Objectives and End State

Based on the results of the mission variables analysis conducted earlier in the IPB process, the staff now identifies the threat's likely immediate and subsequent objectives and desired end state. These elements are included in the threat COA statement developed for each COA.

An **objective** is the clearly defined, decisive, and attainable goal toward which an operation is directed (JP 5-0). Threat objectives are normally terrain- or force-oriented. For example, an enemy may attack to destroy a friendly force or to seize key terrain; defend to delay a friendly force or retain control of key terrain; or conduct guerrilla operations to disrupt friendly operations.

The **end state** is the set of required conditions that defines achievement of the commander's objectives(JP 3-0). The end state, if achieved, meets the conditions of policy, orders, guidance, and directives issued by the commander. For example, the end state for an attack to destroy may be the destruction of all friendly forces down to the platoon level and friendly forces incapable of conducting a coordinated defense.

2. Determine Threat Battlefield Functions

The threat executes several different battlefield functions each time a threat attempts to accomplish a mission. Threat commanders identify the specific functions they intend their various subordinate forces or elements to perform. The functions do not change, regardless of the forces' or elements' location on the battlefield. While the various functions required to accomplish any given mission can be quite diverse, they can be divided into two very broad categories: action and enabling.

3. Determine Threat Capabilities Available to Perform each Battlefield Function

Upon determining which battlefield functions the threat needs to perform and what objective or goal the threat commander seeks to accomplish through the performance of those functions, analysts must then determine what capabilities the threat has in order to execute each function.

While the functions required for a high chance of success in achieving a military objective or goal are universal, the means to accomplish them depend on the location, threat, and environment. For example, in one battlefield, the threat may employ an infantry platoon equipped with infantry-fighting vehicles and sophisticated thermal sensors to execute the security function. In another example, a civillan in a third-floor apartment window using a cellular phone may perform the same function.

Functional analysis is an analytical technique that depicts graphically how the threat might use its capabilities to perform the functions required to accomplish its objectives. It is based on the concept—while every action or battle is unique, certain functions are performed to bring about mission accomplishment. When analysts apply their knowledge of common and necessary military functions to specific threat capabilities, they are performing functional analysis. *Refer to ATP 2-33.4 for more information about functional analysis.*

Continued on next page

Develop Threat COAs (Cont.)

Ref: ATP 2-01.3, Intelligence Preparation of the Battlefield (Mar '19), pp. 6-2 to 6-19.

Continued from previous page

Integrating Processes

4. Identify the Full Set of COAs Available to the Threat

Each threat capability has unique COAs available at any given time. Regardless of the threat category and the capability employed, the threat plans the employment of specific capabilities based on a task, purpose, method, and end state. The intelligence staff identifies the task, purpose, method, and end state for each potential COA developed by the threat for each threat capability. By identifying these for each COA, the intelligence staff can better determine the chosen threat COA during the conduct of operations.

When determining a threat COA, the intelligence staff accounts for all relevant threat activity. For threat offensive tasks, the staff focuses on determining the main, supporting, and reinforcing efforts; use of reserves; use of special munitions; use of air support; and use of UASs to support fires. For threat defensive tasks, the staff focuses on determining the location of engagement areas and obstacles; the location, type, and size of security zone forces and counterattack forces; and the use of special munitions, air support, UASs, and ant access and area denial systems.

5. Evaluate and Prioritize each Threat COA

To plan for all possible contingencies, the commander understands all COAs a threat commander can use to accomplish objectives. The staff assists in this understanding by determining all valid threat Coarsened prioritizing them from most likely to least likely. The staff also determines which threat COA is the most dangerous to friendly forces. To be valid, threat COAs should be feasible, acceptable, suitable, distinguishable, and complete—the same criteria used to validate friendly COAs.

The commander approves a plan optimized to counter the most likely threat COA, while allowing for contingency options should the threat choose another COA. Therefore, the staff evaluates each threat and prioritizes it according to how likely it is that the threat will adopt that option. Generally, threat forces are more likely to use a COA that offers the greatest advantage while minimizing risk. However, based on the situation and its objectives, the threat may choose to accept risk to achieve a desired end state. It is impossible to predict what COA the threat will choose. Therefore, the staff develops and prioritizes as many valid COAs as time allows but, at a minimum, develops the most likely and most dangerous COAs.

Upon identifying all valid threat COAs, the staff compares each COA to the others and prioritizes them by number. For example, if four COAs have been developed, COA 1 is the threat's most likely COA, COA 4 is the least likely. Additionally, the staff determines which COA is the most dangerous; however, the designation of the most dangerous COA largely depends on how much each threat COA threatens the selected friendly COA. The most likely COA may also be the most dangerous. Additionally, a COA needs to answer six basic questions:

- **Who** (the organizational structure of the threat organization, including external organizations providing support)?
- **What** (type of tactical mission task such as defeat, destroy, seize)?
- **When** (the earliest time the action can begin)?
- **Where** (the battlefield geometry that frames the COA [boundaries, objectives, routes, other])?
- **How** (the threat attacks, defends)?
- **Why** (the threat's objectives)?

Continued from previous page

6. Develop Each COA in the Amount of Detail Time Allows

A threat COA consists of the following products:

- **Situation Template for the Threat Course of Action**. A situation template is a depiction of assumed adversary dispositions, based on that adversary's preferred method of operations and the impact of the operational environment if the adversary should adopt a particular course of action (JP 2-01.3). A situation template graphic depicts a potential threat COA as part of a particular threat operation. It usually depicts the most critical point in the operation as agreed upon by the commander, the operations officer, and the intelligence officer. However, the operation may require the preparation of several templates as overlays representing different "snapshots in time," starting with the threat's initial array of forces. *See following pages (pp. 3-46 to 3-47) for further discussion of the situation template.*
- **Threat COA statement**. Every threat COA includes a threat COA statement, which is a narrative that describes the situation template as an overlay. *See p. 3-50.*

Integrating Processes

7. Identify High-Value Targets for each COA

Identifying HVTs involves mentally war gaming a threat COA to determine the assets required to complete the mission. This process involves using as a guide the HVT list developed based on HVTs identified as part of the threat model in step 3 of the IPB process, determining the effect on the threat COA if the target is lost, and identifying possible threat responses if the target is lost.

Based on the situation, one or more of the targets from the threat model may be validated as HVTs. Additionally, targets that were not identified in the threat model may be HVTs. During planning, the staff uses the HVT list developed for each threat COA to develop the HPT list during the COA development step of the MDMP.

Once identified and nominated, HPTs are grouped into a list—identified for a specific time and space in the battle and prioritized based on the commander's approval for formal targeting. The HPT list is continually refined during execution by targeting groups. HPTs can include various threat considerations potentially detrimental to the success of friendly missions. HPTs are incorporated into the scheme of fires and used to create target selection standards and attack guidance matrices.

8. Identify Initial Collection Requirements for each COA

After identifying the full set of potential threat COAs, the staff develops the tools necessary to determine which COA the threat may implement. Because the threat has not acted yet, this determination cannot be made during IPB. However, the staff can develop the information requirements and indicators necessary to support the construction of the information collection plan that can provide the information necessary to confirm or deny threat COAs and locate threat targets.

Information requirements are, in intelligence usage, those items of information regarding the adversary and other relevant aspects of the operational environment that need to be collected and processed in order to meet the intelligence requirements of a commander (JP 2-0).

An **indicator** is, in intelligence usage, an item of information which reflects the intention or capability of an adversary to adopt or reject a course of action (JP 2-0). Identifying and monitoring indicators are fundamental tasks of intelligence analysis, as they are the principal means of avoiding surprise. Indicators are often described as forward looking of predictive indicators.

Situation Template for the Threat COA

Ref: ATP 2-01.3, Intelligence Preparation of the Battlefield (Mar '19), pp. 6-7 to 6-11.

A situation template is a depiction of assumed adversary dispositions, based on that adversary's preferred method of operations and the impact of the operational environment if the adversary should adopt a particular course of action (JP 2-01.3). A situation template graphic depicts a potential threat COA as part of a particular threat operation. It usually depicts the most critical point in the operation as agreed upon by the commander, the operations officer, and the intelligence officer. However, the operation may require the preparation of several templates as overlays representing different "snapshots in time," starting with the threat's initial array of forces. These snapshots in time are useful in depicting—

- Points where the threat might adopt branches or sequels to the main COA.
- Places where the threat is especially vulnerable.
- Other key points in the battle, such as initial contact with friendly forces.

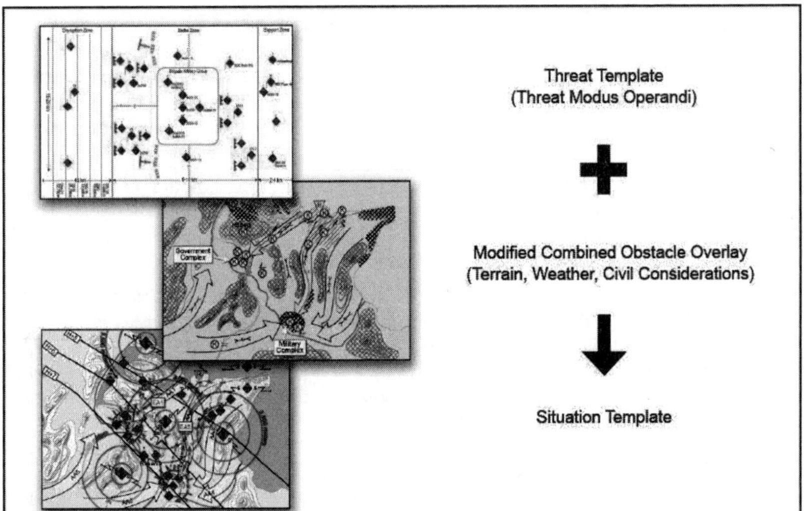

Figure 6-2. Developing a situation template.

Situation templates are developed using the threat's current situation, based on threat doctrine and the effects of terrain, weather, and civil considerations. The situation template may include—

- Doctrinal rates of march. *(Refer to appendix B and ATP 3-34.80 for examples.)*
- Time phase lines.
- Graphic control measures, including but not limited to—
- Obstacles (natural and reinforcing). *(Refer to ATP 3-34.80 for examples.)*
- Engagement areas.
- Threat composition, disposition, and strength.
- Task, purpose, method, and end state.
- Key threat weapon systems range fans.
- AAs.
- NAIs.

The basis for modifying a threat situation template is the significant effects the OE may have on the threat COA. For example, the threat may prefer to establish battle positions 1 to 1.5 kilometers apart. However, the terrain may force it to increase this distance to protect its flanks. As another example, the threat prefers to attack on high speed AAs but also prefers to avoid complex terrain. Therefore, the location of an urban area along a high speed, optimal AA may force the threat to use a suboptimal approach.

Analysts can prepare as many graphics as necessary to depict the COA in enough detail to support staff war gaming and collection planning. For example, a COA may begin as a movement to contact, transition to a hasty attack, followed by pursuit operations that include a river crossing. Each of these phases may require a separate template.

Analysts should tailor situation templates to their needs by focusing on factors important to the commander or mission area. For example, the situation might focus only on the threat's reconnaissance assets when determining and developing threat COAs. Situation templates produced might show only the location and movement routes of these assets, their likely employment areas, and their likely NAIs. An aviation unit,for example, might develop situation templates that depict details such as specific radar and ADA weapon locations and their range fans or areas of coverage.

At higher echelons, situation templates usually focus on culminating points and installations or activities associated with decisive points rather than specific military units. Some situation templates are better presented in a matrix format. Figure 6-4 illustrates a situation template in a matrix format that shows one threat COA for area defense. The timeline indicates when the threat is most likely to use assets to reach a desired end state, as well as the time threat assets or effects are expected within each NAI.

Generally, there is not enough minimum, the staff may develop overlays for the threat's most likely and most dangerous COAs. The overlays are used during friendly COA analysis.

Note. Sometimes, situation templates are replaced by other products, such as a key facilities and targets overlay. Analysts should use whatever technique best graphically depicts the threat's COAs.

There are three primary types of enemy situation templates the staff may need to develop as overlays:

- Enemy in the offense.
- Enemy in the defense.
- Irregular forces.

During IPB, these overlays are largely based on assumption and depict enemy locations and activities that are usually templated. This is especially true of overlays depicting enemy offensive tasks or guerilla and/or terrorist activities. Because the enemy is more static in defensive tasks, the staff may have information related to enemy locations that may assist in developing the overlay.

When developing an overlay depicting regular forces conducting offensive or defensive tasks, the staff should depict enemy locations and activities two levels down. For example, a friendly brigade combat team would construct an overlay showing maneuver companies and specialty platoons. One of the brigade's battalions would refine that overlay for its zone or sector showing maneuver platoons and specialty teams.

When developing an overlay depicting irregular enemies, the staff at every echelon depicts enemy locations and activities at the cellular level. For example, whether at corps, division, brigade, or battalion the staff templates enemy cells where these cells are believed to be operating. Staffs template where they believe the activity associated with each cell can occur. This activity is determined by evaluating enemy activity through predictive and pattern analysis.

See following pages (pp. 3-48 to 3-49) for further discussion of preparing overlays.

Preparing Overlays

Ref: ATP 2-01.3, Intelligence Preparation of the Battlefield (Mar '19), pp. 6-11 to 6-15.

Integrating Processes

Overlays Depicting the Enemy in Offensive Tasks

The staff constructs an enemy offensive task overlay using a five-step process that includes the following steps:

Step 1—Determine the enemy's end state to make U.S. forces combat ineffective. Visualize enemy success and how the enemy force achieved those objectives given the forces available. Most enemy offensive objectives are force-orientated.

- **Step 1A**: Review the U.S. forces' defensive plan. Even if the commander has not have approved the plan, the planning staff should have a rough idea of the friendly force defense based on the IPB process thus far.
- **Step 1B**: Identify the U.S. forces' key targets on the battlefield that the enemy commander would attack (enemy commander HPTs).
- **Step 1C** (brigade and above): Determine the vulnerability of this operation based on the operational variables gathered from previous IPB process steps.
- **Step 1D**: Review the enemy commander's purpose for the offense: gain freedom of movement; restrict freedom of movement; gain control of key terrain, personnel, or equipment; gain information; dislocate; and disrupt.

Step 2—Identify the functions used by the enemy to reach the end state:

- **Step 2A**: Determine the action element (what the enemy uses to accomplish the mission).
- **Step 2B**: Determine the enabling elements (what makes it possible for the action element to accomplish the mission).
- **Step 2C**: Display the action form, task, and purpose for each element (for example, action form: enabling element, task: fix U.S. battalion, purpose: prevent U.S. forces from maneuvering).

Step 3—Allocate the enemy's resources:

- **Step 3A**: How many enemy units are required to accomplish the mission?
- **Step 3B**: What types of capabilities are required to support the enemy's mission?
  - **Step 3B1**: Determine locations of enemy reconnaissance assets needed to support the offensive mission.
  - **Step 3B2**: Determine initial and subsequent artillery and air defense firing positions and display the range fans for each type of enemy direct fire system and indirect fire system required to support the mission.
  - **Step 3B3**: Determine potential locations where the enemy may employ special munitions to isolate part of the friendly defense.
  - **Step 3B4**: Determine enemy air AAs that enable the enemy's use of close air support (CAS) to support the mission.

Step 4—Synchronize the enemy mission:

- **Step 4A**: Determine enemy attack sequence and movement formations.
- **Step 4B**: Determine the enemy commander's decision points.

Step 5—Continue refining the enemy COA; collaborating with staff sections, review staff estimates and changes to the U.S. forces' array.

Overlays Depicting the Enemy in Defensive Tasks

The staff constructs an enemy defensive overlay using a five-step process that includes the following steps:

Step 1—Determine the enemy's end state to make U.S. forces combat ineffective. Visualize enemy success and how the enemy force achieved those objectives given the forces available.

- **Step 1A**: Review the U.S. forces' offensive plan. Although the commander may not have approved the plan, the planning staff should already have a rough idea of the friendly force plan for an attack based on the IPB process thus far.
- **Step 1B**: Identify the U.S. forces' key targets on the battlefield that the enemy commander would attack (enemy commander HPTs).
- **Step 1C**: (brigade and above) Determine the vulnerability of this operation based on the operational variables gathered from previous IPB process steps.
- **Step 1D**: Review the enemy commander's purpose for the defense: protect personnel and equipment, restrict freedom of movement, control key terrain, gain time.

Step 2—Identify the functions used by the enemy to reach the end state:

- **Step 2A**: Determine the action element (what the enemy uses to accomplish the mission).
- **Step 2B**: Determine the enabling elements (what makes it possible for the action element to accomplish the mission).
- **Step 2C**: Display the action form, task, and purpose for each element (for example: action form: enabling element, task: fix U.S. battalion, purpose: prevent U.S. forces from maneuvering).

Step 3—Allocate the enemy's resources:

- **Step 3A**: How many enemy units are required to accomplish the mission?
- **Step 3B**: What types of capabilities are required to support the enemy's mission?
  - **Step 3B1**: Determine locations of enemy reconnaissance assets needed to support the defensive mission. This is normally associated with the enemy commander's decision points and locations where reconnaissance assets can provide observation to support targeting.
  - **Step 3B2**: Determine initial and subsequent artillery and air defense firing positions and display the range fans for each type of enemy direct fire system and indirect fire system required to support the mission.
  - **Step 3B3**: Determine potential locations where the enemy may employ special munitions to isolate part of the friendly offense.
  - **Step 3B4:** Determine enemy air AAs that enable the enemy's use of CAS to support the mission.
  - **Step 3B5**: Determine the locations of enemy disruption zones, battle zones, and support zones with suspected unit boundaries. Add time phase lines, supplementary and primary simple battle positions, ambush locations, and observation posts.
  - **Step 3B6**: Determine enemy obstacle locations and intents for each obstacle.

Step 4—Synchronize the enemy mission:

- **Step 4A**: Determine enemy attack sequence and movement formations.
- **Step 4B**: Determine the enemy commander's decision points.

Step 5—Continue refining the enemy COA; collaborating with staff sections, review staff estimates and changes to the U.S. forces' array.

Overlays Depicting Irregular Forces

Overlays depicting irregular forces conducting operations typically focus on armed forces in a tactical array. The staff should consider whether to create overlays that depict the enemy's less visible elements, such as leadership, enemy external relationships, support networks, as well as the activities in which the enemy engages. Additionally, the staff should capture the process used to template the overlay,so the staff and subordinate staffs can replicate the process as required. *The techniques in ATP 5-0.6 can facilitate this analysis.*

Integrating Processes

Threat Course of Action Statement

Ref: ATP 2-01.3, Intelligence Preparation of the Battlefield (Mar '19), p. 6-16.

Every threat COA includes a threat COA statement, which is a narrative that describes the situation template as an overlay. Figure 6-8 illustrates a threat COA statement.

Mission: The 375th Brigade Tactical Group conducts an area defense at OBJ Alpha and OBJ Bravo no later than 110900ZNOV16 to prevent occupation force seizure of government and military infrastructure.

Enemy Commander's Intent: Retain control of OBJ Alpha and OBJ Bravo with minimal key infrastructure losses.

End State:
Enemy: Occupation force denied seizure of OBJ Alpha and OBJ Bravo.
Friendly: Maintain combat effectiveness of 75% until negotiations or regional partner assistance obtained.
Terrain: Key coastal and inland infrastructure remain intact.

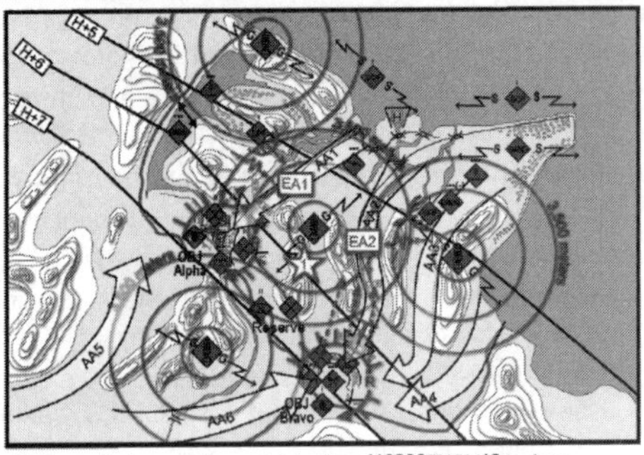

Decisive Operations: The 65th and 72d Mechanized BNs conduct area defense no later than 110900ZNOV16 to deny occupation force seizure of OBJ Alpha and OBJ Bravo.

Shaping Operations:
Shaping Operation 1: Special purpose forces conduct ambushes along high-speed AAs to disrupt occupation force freedom of movement toward southern infrastructure.
Shaping Operation 2: Engineer emplacement of minefields along high-speed AAs to block occupation force.

Movement and Maneuver
Disruption Zone:
85th Special Purpose Force
Task: Disrupt occupation force in vicinity EA1 and EA2.
Purpose: Delay occupation force movement to the south.
Method: Conduct ambushes on occupation force using complex terrain features and hasty defensive positions.
End State: Occupation force ground movement is delayed in vicinity EA1 and EA2.

Battle Zone:
65th Mechanized BN
Task: Prevent western movement of occupation force.
Purpose: Protect southern flank of the 72d Mechanized BN.
Method: Use of obstacle belts and attack by fire positions.
End State: Occupation force is unable to turn west to OBJ Alpha.

72d Mechanized BN
Task: Prevent occupation of OBJ Alpha.
Purpose: Retain control of government.
Method: Use of obstacle belts and attack by fire position.
End State: Government status quo is maintained.

Support Zone:
97th Mechanized BN and 10th Infantry BN (Reserve)
Task: Reinforce the 65th and 72d Mechanized BNs.
Purpose: Prevent occupation force flanking of the 65th and 72d Mechanized BNs.
Method: Conduct a counterattack.
End State: Occupation force is prevented from seizing OBJ Alpha and OBJ Bravo.

AA	avenue of approach	EA	engagement area
BN	battalion	OBJ	objective
C2	command and control		

Fires
Disruption Zone:
Task: Disrupt occupation force coastal lodgement.
Purpose: Delay movement to the south.
Method: Long-range precision fires.
End State: The 65th and 72d Mechanized BNs are afforded additional time to prepare defenses.

Battle Zone:
Task: Disrupt air AAs.
Purpose: Prevent light infantry air assault in vicinity OBJ Alpha and OBJ Bravo.
Method: Use SA-13s to close air corridors.
End State: Occupation force unable to control friendly rear.

Sustainment:
Task: Conduct resupply operations across all zones.
Purpose: Maintain the initiative.
Method: Support echelons aligned to support main and supporting efforts.
End State: Friendly forces are able to maintain momentum of the battle to repel occupation force.

Reconnaissance
Disruption Zone:
Task: Identify coastal landing areas.
Purpose: Direct long-range precision fires.
Method: Special purpose forces.
End State: Occupation force lodgement is contested and delayed.

Battle Zone:
Task: Identify occupation force AAs.
Purpose: Direct long-range precision fires.
Method: Special purpose forces.
End State: C2 elements are able to direct the main effort.

Figure 6-8. Threat course of action statement example.

B. Develop the Event Template and Matrix

Intelligence analysts develop event templates and event matrices as analytical planning tools. The initial event template and event matrix are normally developed before COA analysis, refined during COA analysis, and further refined during execution as the situation changes. In addition to using the event template and matrix to support its own planning, the staff normally disseminates the event template to subordinate units to assist in developing subordinate unit information collection plans.

Event Template

An event template is a guide for collection planning that depicts the named areas of interest where activity, or its lack of activity, will indicate which course of action the adversary has adopted (JP 2-01.3). It is a graphic overlay used during the COA analysis step of the MDMP to confirm or deny threat COAs throughout war gaming. Additionally, the event template is used to develop the information collection overlay *(refer to FM 3-55)* and/or matrix and the DST during COA analysis. The event template is used during the execution activity of the operations process to assist in determining which COA the threat has adopted. An event template is accompanied by an event matrix.

Figure 6-11 and figure 6-12 on the following page (p. 3-52) illustrate the basic mechanics of this process.

Event Matrix

An event matrix is a cross-referenced description of the indicators and activity expected to occur in each named area of interest (JP 2-01.3). Constructing an event matrix table is an analytical process that involves associating NAIs and threat decision points identified on the event template with indicators to assist in determining which COA the threat commander is implementing. To create an event matrix—

- Using the event template, examine the events associated with each NAI and restate the events as indicators.
- Enter the indicators into the event matrix along with the associated times they are likely to occur. Use the time phase lines from the event template to establish the expected times in the event matrix.
- Take the threat decision points from the event template and list them in the event matrix.

Decision Support Template and Information Collection Matrix

The completed event template and event matrix form the basis for planning collection strategies, synchronizing intelligence with friendly operations, and developing the DST and matrix and information collection matrix. In some instances, the staff might disseminate the event template as a collection graphic to support intelligence planning and collection by other units.

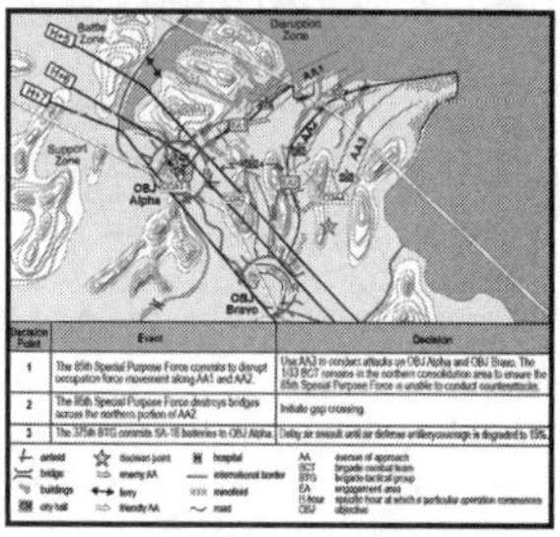

The DST provides the commander with a structured basis for deploying fires, maneuver, and jamming assets and for reducing the enemy's defensive capability with these assets. Simply stated, it provides commanders with the specific points on the battlefield where they will be required to make decisions regarding the employment of assets. These decisions can be keyed to phase lines, events on the ground, or to specific enemy actions. (Figure 6-14. DST and matrix example.)

Constructing an Event Template

Ref: ATP 2-01.3, Intelligence Preparation of the Battlefield (Mar '19), pp. 6-20 to 6-21.

An event template is accompanied by an event matrix. The event template comprises:

- Time phase lines
- NAIs
- Decision points.

Constructing an event template is an analytical process that involves comparing the multiple threat COAs developed earlier in step 4 of the IPB process to determine the time or event and the place or condition where the threat commander must decide on a particular COA. Figure 6-11 below illustrates the basic mechanics of this process. The figure displays minimal information for what is included on the **event template**.

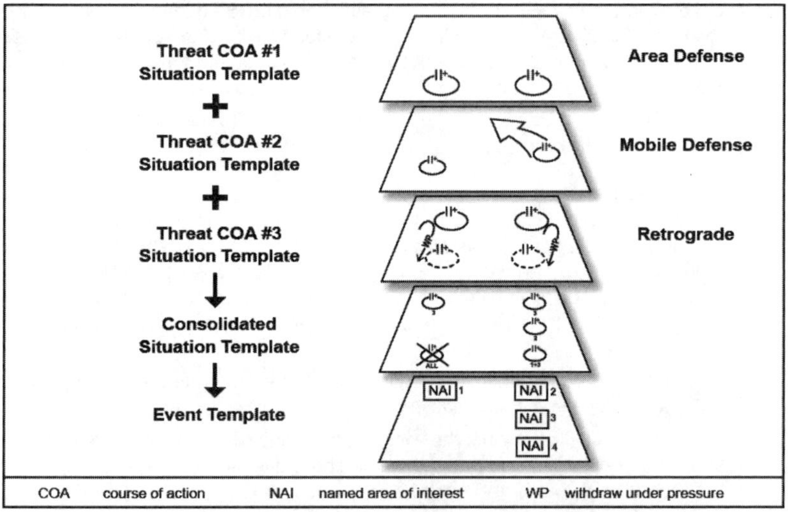

Figure 6-12 below illustrates a completed **event template** based on the consolidation of the area, mobile, and retrograde defensive tasks. In threat doctrine, these types of defensive tasks are tactical methods and guides for designing operational COAs.

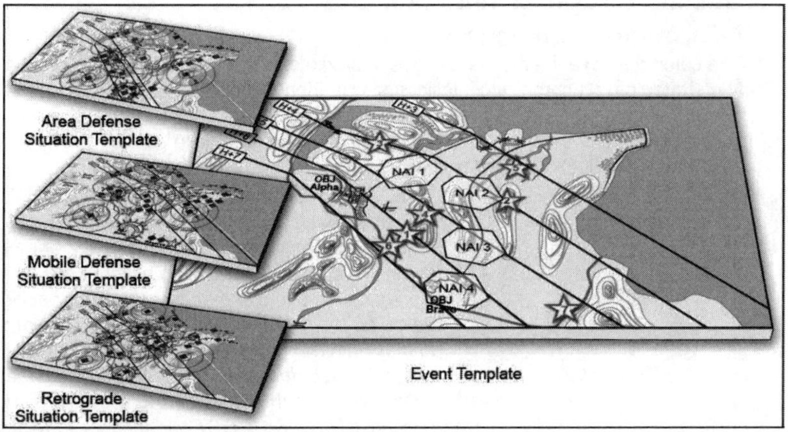

II. Information Collection

Ref: FM 3-55, Information Collection (May '13).

Knowledge is the precursor to effective action in the informational or physical domains. Knowledge about an operational environment requires aggressive and continuous operations to acquire information. Information collected from multiple sources and analyzed becomes intelligence that provides answers to commander's critical information requirements (CCIRs). Commanders use reconnaissance and surveillance to provide intelligence to reduce the inherent uncertainty of war.

Information collection is an activity that synchronizes and integrates the planning and employment of sensors and assets as well as the processing, exploitation, and dissemination systems in direct support of current and future operations.

Information Collection Activities

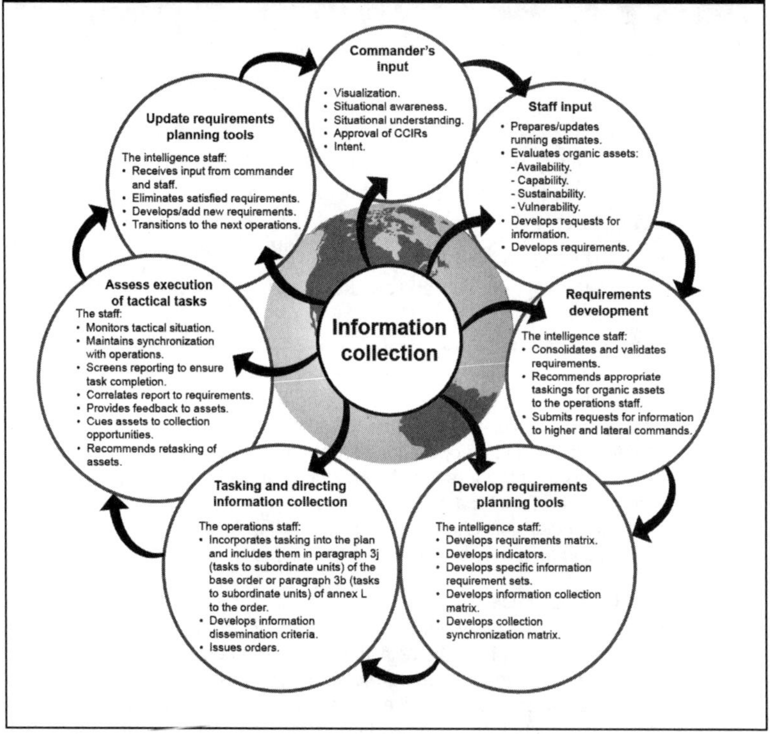

Ref: FM 3-55, fig. 1-1. Information collection activities.

Information collection is the acquisition of information and the provision of this information to processing elements. This includes the following:

- Plan requirements and assess collection.
- Task and direct collection.
- Execute collection.

Integrating Processes

I. Primary Information Collection Tasks and Operations

Ref: FM 3-55, Information Collection (May '13), pp. 1-4 to 1-14.

Information collection activities help the commander understand and visualize the operation by identifying gaps in information, aligning assets and resources against those gaps, and assessing the collected information and intelligence to inform the commander's decisions. These activities also support the staff's integrating processes during planning and execution. The direct result of the information collection effort is a coordinated plan that supports the operation. The staff assesses information and intelligence, refines the plan, and issues fragmentary orders to the plan to retask or assign a new mission to assets and units.

Information Collection Purpose

Information collection activities provide commanders with detailed, timely, and accurate intelligence. By answering the CCIRs, information collection activities help commanders make informed decisions. For effective information collection activities to occur, the staff must—

- Provide relevant information and intelligence products to commanders and staffs.
- Provide combat information to commanders.
- Contribute to situational awareness and facilitate continuous situational understanding.
- Develop a significant portion of the common operational picture (COP) vertically and horizontally among organizations, commanders, and staffs.
- Support the commander's visualization, permitting more effective mission command.
- Answer the CCIRs.
- Facilitate intelligence preparation of the battlefield (IPB).
- Support effective, efficient, and accurate targeting.
- Decrease risk for the unit.

Information collection includes all activities and operations that gather data and information used to create knowledge and support the commander's requirements, situational understanding, and visualization. Commanders achieve information collection when they employ all collection tasks and operations together in an operation. This appropriate mix of collection tasks and operations helps satisfy many different requirements. It also ensures that the operations and intelligence working group does not favor or become too reliant on one particular unit, discipline, or system. The Army has four tasks or operations it primarily conducts as a part of the information collection plan:

A. Reconnaissance

Reconnaissance is a mission undertaken to obtain, by visual observation or other detection methods, information about the activities and resources of an enemy or adversary, or to secure data concerning the meteorological, hydrographic, or geographic characteristics of a particular area (JP 2-0). Reconnaissance primarily relies on the human dynamic rather than technical means and it is a focused collection effort. A combined arms operation, reconnaissance actively collects information against targets for a specified time based on mission objectives.

Successful and effective units combine three methods to perform reconnaissance: dismounted, mounted, and aerial. Sensors can augment each method. To gain information on the enemy or a particular area, units use passive surveillance, technical means, and human interaction or they fight for information.

The five forms of reconnaissance are—

- Area reconnaissance
- Route reconnaissance
- Zone reconnaissance
- Reconnaissance in force
- Special reconnaissance

B. Surveillance

Surveillance is the systematic observation of aerospace, surface, or subsurface areas, places, persons, or things, by visual, aural, electronic, photographic, or other means (JP 3-0). Surveillance involves observing an area to collect information.

In the observation of a given area, the focus and tempo of the collection effort primarily comes from the commander's intent and guidance. Surveillance involves observing the threat and local populace in a NAI or target area of interest (TAI). Surveillance may be a stand-alone mission or part of a reconnaissance mission (particularly area reconnaissance). Elements conducting surveillance must maximize assets, maintain continuous surveillance on all NAIs and TAIs, and report all information rapidly and accurately.

Surveillance tasks can be performed by a variety of assets (ground, air, sea, and space), means (Soldier and systems), and mediums (throughout the electromagnetic spectrum).

Generally, surveillance is a "task" when performed as part of a reconnaissance mission. However, many Army, joint, and national systems are designed to conduct only surveillance. These are surveillance missions. Army military intelligence organizations typically conduct surveillance missions. Reconnaissance units can conduct surveillance tasks as part of reconnaissance, security, or other missions. Reconnaissance and surveillance both include observation and reporting.

Surveillance is distinct from reconnaissance. Surveillance is tiered and layered with technical assets that collect information. It is passive and continuous. Reconnaissance is active in the collection of information (such as maneuver) and usually includes human participation. Additionally, reconnaissance may involve fighting for information. Sometimes these operations are deliberate, as in a reconnaissance in force; however, the purpose of reconnaissance is to collect information, not initiate combat. Reconnaissance involves many tactics, techniques, and procedures throughout the course of a mission. An extended period of surveillance may be a tactic or technique. Commanders complement surveillance with frequent reconnaissance. Surveillance, in turn, increases the efficiency of reconnaissance by focusing those missions while reducing the risk to Soldiers.

Effective surveillance—

- Maintains continuous observations of all assigned NAIs and TAIs
- Provides early warning
- Detects, tracks, and assesses key targets
- Provides mixed, redundant, and overlapping coverage

The types of surveillance are—

- Zone surveillance
- Area surveillance
- Point surveillance
- Network surveillance

C. Security Operations

Security operations are those operations undertaken by a commander to provide early and accurate warning of enemy operations, to provide the force being protected with time and maneuver space within which to react to the enemy, and to develop the situation to

Continued on next page
Continued on next page

Primary Information Collection Tasks and Operations (Cont.)

Ref: FM 3-55, Information Collection (May '13), pp. 1-4 to 1-14.

Continued from previous page

allow the commander to effectively use the protected force (ADRP 3-90). Security operations are shaping operations that can occur during all operations. Other collection assets provide the commander with early warning and information on the strength and disposition of enemy forces. The availability of information collection assets enables greater flexibility in the employment of the security force.

Security operations aim to protect the force from surprise and reduce the unknowns in any situation. A commander undertakes these operations to provide early and accurate warning of enemy operations, to provide the force being protected with time and maneuver space to react to the enemy, and to develop the situation to allow the commander to use the protected force. Commanders may conduct security operations to the front, flanks, and rear of their forces. The main difference between security operations and reconnaissance is that security operations orient on the force or facility protected, while reconnaissance is enemy, populace, and terrain oriented.

The five tasks of security operations commanders may employ are screen, guard, cover, area security, and local security.

Successful security operations depends on properly applying the following five fundamentals:

- Provide early and accurate warning
- Provide reaction time and maneuver space
- Orient on the force or facility to be secured
- Perform continuous reconnaissance
- Maintain enemy contact

To collect information and apply the fundamentals for security operations, the security force aggressively and continuously seeks the enemy, interacts with the populace, and reconnoiters key terrain.

D. Intelligence Operations

Intelligence operations are the tasks undertaken by military intelligence units and Soldiers to obtain information to satisfy validated requirements (ADP 2-0). Intelligence operations align intelligence assets and resources against requirements to collect information and intelligence to inform the commander's decisions. Conducting intelligence operations requires an organic collection and analysis capability. Successful intelligence operations support the unit's ability to conduct focused intelligence analysis. Data and information collected during the course of intelligence operations is essential to the development of timely, relevant, accurate, predictive, and tailored intelligence products. Those units without resources must rely on augmentation from within the intelligence enterprise for intelligence. Although the focus is normally on tactical intelligence, the Army draws on both strategic and operational intelligence resources.

Continued from previous page

III. Targeting (D3A)

Ref: ADP 3-19, Fires (Jul '19); ATP 3-60, Targeting (May '15); and FM 3-09, Field Artillery Operations and Fire Support (Apr '14).

Army targeting uses the functions decide, detect, deliver, and assess (D3A) as its methodology. Its functions complement the planning, preparing, executing, and assessing stages of the operations process. Army targeting addresses two targeting categories—deliberate and dynamic.

Targeting Methodology

I Decide	II Detect	III Deliver	IV Assess
▪ Target Development ▪ TVA ▪ HPT and HVT ▪ TSS ▪ Attack Options ▪ Attack Guidance	▪ Target Deception Means ▪ Detection Procedures ▪ Target Tracking	▪ Attack ▪ Planned Targets ▪ Targets of Opportunity ▪ Desired Effects ▪ Attack Systems	▪ Tactical Level ▪ Operational Level ▪ Restrike ▪ Feedback

Deliberate Targeting

Deliberate targeting prosecutes planned targets. These targets are known to exist in an operational area and have actions scheduled against them. There are two types:

- **Scheduled targets** exist in the operational environment and are located in sufficient time or prosecuted at a specific, planned time.
- **On-call targets** have actions planned, but not for a specific delivery time. The commander expects to locate these targets in sufficient time to execute planned actions. These targets are unique in that actions are planned against them using deliberate targeting, but execution will normally be conducted using dynamic targeting such as close air support missions and time-sensitive targets (TST).

Dynamic Targeting

Dynamic targeting prosecutes targets of opportunity and changes to planned targets or objectives. Targets of opportunity are targets identified too late, or not selected for action in time, to be included in deliberate targeting. Targets prosecuted as part of dynamic targeting are previously unanticipated, unplanned, or newly detected. There are two types:

- **Unplanned targets** are known to exist in the operational environment, but no action has been planned against them. The target may not have been detected or located in sufficient time to meet planning deadlines, or alternatively not previously considered of sufficient importance to engage.
- **Unanticipated targets** are unknown or not expected to exist in the operational environment.

Army Targeting Process (D3A)

Ref: ADP 3-19, Fires (Jul '19), pp. 3-7 to 3-9.

The Army targeting process organizes the efforts of the commander and staff to accomplish key targeting requirements. This methodology is referred to as the D3A. D3A assists the commander and staff decide which targets must be acquired and engaged and to help develop options to engage those targets. Options may include lethal or nonlethal, organic or supporting assets at all levels, including maneuver, electronic attack, psychological operations, attack aircraft, surface-to-surface fires, air to surface fires, other information-related capabilities, or a combination of these options.

The D3A methodology is an integral part of the MDMP. As the MDMP is conducted, targeting becomes more focused based on the commander's guidance and intent. Certain targets may require special considerations or caution, because engaging them improperly could create unintended effects. Examples include targets that should be handled with sensitivity due to potential political and or diplomatic repercussions and targets located in areas with a high risks of collateral damage, to include weapons of mass destruction facilities. These measures are incorporated in the coordinating instructions and appropriate annexes of the operation plan or operation order.

Integrating Processes

I. Decide

Decide is the first function in targeting and occurs during the planning portion of the operations process. It is the most important function, requiring close interaction between the commander, intelligence, plans, operations, the fires cell, and staff judge advocate. It begins during the mission analysis portion of the MDMP and continues throughout the operation.

II. Detect

Detect is the second function in targeting and occurs initially during the prepare portion of the operations process, continuing throughout the operation. A key resource for fires planning and targeting is the intelligence generated through information collection to answer the targeting information requirements. Commanders express requirements for target detection and action as priority intelligence and information requirements. During large-scale combat operations, it might be challenging to prioritize the detection of targets and could require the opening of windows of opportunity for specific collection capabilities in support of fires. High-payoff targets must be integrated and support associated priority intelligence requirements. Their priority depends on the importance of the target to the friendly course of action and target acquisition requirements. Targets are prioritized through a quantitative and qualitative valuation methodology. An example of a valuation methodology is the target value analysis process that prioritizes targets based on the target's criticality, accessibility, recuperability, vulnerability, effect, and recognizability. Targeting working groups incorporate priority intelligence and information requirements that support acquisition of high-payoff targets into the overall information collection plan along with named areas of interest, target areas of interest, and engagement areas.

III. Deliver

Deliver is the third function in targeting and occurs primarily during the execution portion of the operations process. The main objective is to engage targets in accordance with the commander's guidance or engagement authority's direction. The selection of a weapon system or a combination of weapons systems leads to the tactical decision of time of engagement and then the technical solution for the selected weapon.

IV. Assess

Assess is the fourth function of targeting and occurs throughout the operations process. The commander and staff assess the results of mission execution. The assessment process is continuous and directly tied to the commander's decisions throughout planning, preparation, and execution of operations.

Operations Process & Targeting Relationship

Fires are an integral part of the operations process—the major mission command activities performed during operations: planning, preparing, executing, and continuously assessing the operation (ADP 5-0). The commander drives the operations process.

Army targeting uses the functions decide, detect, deliver, and assess (D3A) as its methodology. Its functions complement the planning, preparing, executing, and assessing stages of the operations process. Army targeting addresses two targeting categories—deliberate and dynamic.

Operations Process		D3A	Targeting Task
Continuous Assessment	Planning	Decide	• Perform target value analysis to develop fire support, high-value targets, and critical asset list. • Provide fires running estimates and information/influence to the commander's targeting guidance and desired effects.
			• Designate potential high-payoff targets. • Deconflict and coordinate potential high-payoff targets. • Develop high-payoff target list/defended asset list. • Establish target selection standards and identification matrix (air and missile defense). • Develop attack guidance matrix, fire support, and cyber/electromagnetic activities tasks. • Develop associated measures of performance and measures of effectiveness.
			• Refine high-payoff target list. • Refine target selection standards. • Refine attack guidance matrix and surface-to-air-missile tactical order. • Refine fire support tasks. • Refine associated measures of performance and measures of effectiveness. • Develop the target synchronization matrix. • Draft airspace control means requests.
			• Finalize the high-payoff target list. • Finalize target selection standards. • Finalize the attack guidance matrix. • Finalize the targeting synchronization matrix. • Finalize fire support tasks. • Finalize associated measures of performance and measures of effectiveness. • Submit information requirements to staff and subordinate units.
	Preparation	Detect	• Collect information (surveillance, reconnaissance). • Report and disseminate information. • Update information requirements as they are answered. • Focus sensors, locate, identify, maintain track, and determine time available. • Update the high-payoff target list, attack guidance matrix, targeting synchronization matrix, identification matrix (air and missile defense) and surface-to-air-missile tactical order as necessary. • Update fire support tasks. • Update associated measures of performance and measures of effectiveness. • Target validated, deconfliction and target area clearance resolved, target execution/engagement approval.
	Execution	Deliver	• Order engagement. • Execute fires in accordance with the attack guidance matrix, the targeting synchronization matrix, identification matrix (air and missile defense), and surface-to-air-missile tactical order. • Monitor/manage engagement.
	Assess	Assess	• Assess task accomplishment (as determined by measures of performance). • Assess effects (as determined by measures of effectiveness). • Reporting results. • Reattack/reengagement recommendations.

Legend: D3A – decide, detect, deliver, and assess

Ref: Adapted from ADRP 3-09, Fires (Aug '12), table 3-2, p. 3-2 (not provided in ADP 3-19).

Refer to AODS6-1: The Army Operations & Doctrine SMARTbook, 6th Ed. (w/SMARTupdate 1) for complete discussion of the fires warfighting function from ADP 3-19 (Jul '19). Sections include fires as a warfighting function; fires in unified land operations, execution of fires across the domains; and integrating Army, joint & multinational fires (to include airspace planning/integration and air and missile defense planning/integration).

Joint Targeting

Ref: ADP 3-19, Fires (Jul '19), pp. 3-9 to 3-11.

Joint targeting is dependent in part on joint planning through publication of the campaign or contingency plan, operation order, or fragmentary order. Plans and orders provide the context for targeting. Geographic combatant commands maintain a database for targets within their areas of responsibility that relate to their campaign plans and contingency plans. Detailed foundational intelligence products to include dynamic threat assessments, joint intelligence preparation of the operational environment, and country assessments facilitate detailed targeting, beginning with target systems analysis. Many products used to support a contingency or military operation are developed, maintained, and continuously updated as foundational information for specific targets. A combatant command can normally provide a subordinate JFC with a list of targets, and perhaps target folders, applicable to a plan for a joint operations area within their area of responsibility.

The joint targeting cycle is a six-phase iterative process:

- **Phase 1—Commander's objectives, Targeting guidance, and intent**. The JFC develops and issues targeting guidance. This guidance includes targeting priorities, time-sensitive targets criteria and procedures, component critical targets, target acquisition and identification criteria, authorized.
- **Phase 2—Target development and prioritization**. Target development is the systematic examination of potential target systems and their components, individual targets, and even elements of targets to determine the necessary type and duration of the action that must be exerted on each target to create an effect that is consistent with the commander's specific objectives.
- **Phase 3—Capabilities analysis**. This phase of the joint targeting cycle involves evaluating all available capabilities against targets' critical target elements to determine the appropriate options available to the component commander for target engagement and developing the best possible solution under given circumstances.
- **Phase 4—Commander's decision and force assignment**. The force assignment process at the component level integrates previous phases of joint targeting and fuses capabilities analysis with available forces, sensors, and weapons systems.
- **Phase 5—Mission planning and force execution**. Upon receipt of component tasking orders, detailed unit-level planning must be performed for the execution of operations. The joint targeting process supports this planning by providing component planners with direct access to detailed information on the targets, supported by the nominating component's analytical reasoning that linked the target with the desired effect (phase 2).
- **Phase 6—Combat assessment**. The combat assessment phase is a continuous process that assesses the effectiveness of the activities that occurred during the first five phases of the joint targeting cycle.

Integrating Army Targeting with Joint Targeting

LCCs contribute to the joint targeting cycle by assisting the JFC in formulating guidance, integrating land component fires with other joint fires to support JFC operations, conducting target development, synchronizing and coordinating the use of collection assets, engaging targets, and providing feedback as part of the assessment process. These functions remain constant regardless of how the joint force is organized (functional or Service components). Coordination and communication between the components, theater analyst, and multinational partners is critical executing fire plans and engaging targets of opportunity.

The LCC HQ is responsible for integrating the D3A targeting processes into the joint targeting cycle. Additional target development steps are required when nominating a target into the joint targeting cycle.

The LCC HQ consolidates subordinate tactical level targeting nominations (developed through D3A) for inclusion into the joint targeting cycle while bridging the target development gaps required for phases II and III of the joint targeting cycle (see JP 3-60 and also see figure 3-1 for more information). A critical intelligence gap between D3A and joint targeting cycle is the capability to conduct intermediate, and advanced target development on tactical target nominations in accordance with CJCSI 3370.01C. Target nominations must meet the JFC's target validation criteria through the joint targeting decision board. The joint integrated prioritize target list is used by all components to task assets available to best create the desired effects against targets.

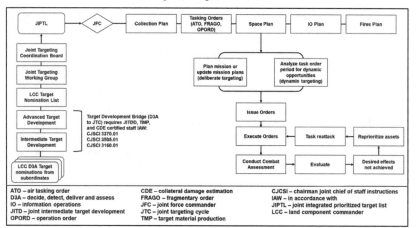

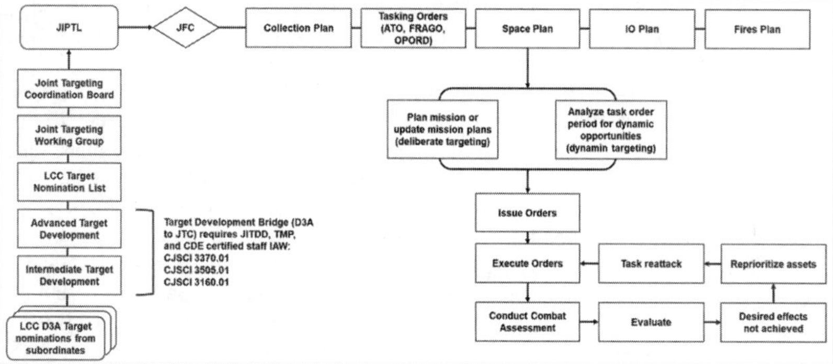

ATO – air tasking order
D3A – decide, detect, deliver and assess
IO – information operations
JITD – joint intermediate target development
OPORD – operation order
CDE – collateral damage estimation
FRAGO – fragmentary order
JFC – joint force commander
JTC – joint targeting cycle
TMP – target material production
CJCSI – chairman joint chief of staff instructions
IAW – in accordance with
JIPTL – joint integrated prioritized target list
LCC – land component commander

Ref: ADP 3-19, Fires (Jul '19), fig. 3-1. Example LCC D3A Target nominated to joint targeting cycle.

In order to meet the requirement for intermediate target development within phase II of the joint targeting cycle the LCC staff must certify intelligence staff in joint intermediate target development (JITD) guidance as defined by the current updated Chairman of the Joint Chiefs of Staff Instruction on target development.

In order to meet the requirement for advanced target development within phase III of the joint targeting cycle the LCC staff must certify intelligence staff and establish accredited target material production work centers according to guidance defined by the current updated CJCSIs on target development and collateral damage methodology.

Target development in a joint environment generally requires the following things:

- Component analysts trained and certified in joint intermediate target development, target material production, collateral damage estimation, weaponeering, and battle damage assessment. Component analysts require training and require access to intelligence and targeting databases and repositories (many found only on Top Secret architecture). This includes training on the creation and maintenance of electronic target folders which are databased in the Modernized Integrated Database (referred to as the MIDB). The two interfaces for the Modernized Integrated Database are the National production Workshop and the Joint Targeting Toolbox.
- Training on all three steps in target development:
  - Target system analysis
  - Entity level target development
  - Target list management

For more on Joint Target Development, reference CJCSI 3370.01 Target Development Standards and JP 3-60 Joint Targeting.

I. Decide

Decide is the first function in targeting and occurs during the planning portion of the operations process. The "decide" function continues throughout the operation. The staff develops "decide" information to address:

- What targets should be acquired and attacked/engaged?
- When and where are the targets likely to be found?
- How do the rules of engagement impact target selection?
- How long will the target remain once acquired?
- Who or what can locate/track the targets?
- What accuracy of target location will be required to attack/engage the target?
- What are the priorities for reconnaissance, surveillance, target acquisition, sensor allocation, and employment?
- What intelligence requirements are essential to the targeting effort and how and by when must the information be collected, processed, and disseminated?
- When, where, how, and in what priority should the targets be attacked/engaged?
- What are the measures of performance and measure of effectiveness that determine whether the target has been successfully attacked/engaged and whether the commander's desired effects have been generated by doing so?
- Who or what can attack/engage the targets, and how should the attack/engagement be conducted (for example, number/type of attack/engagement assets, ammunition to be used) to generate desired effects and what are the required assets/resources based on commander's guidance?
- What or who will obtain assessment or other information required for determining the success or failure of each attack/engagement? Who must receive and process that information, how rapidly, and in what format?
- Who has the decisionmaking authority to determine success or failure, and how rapidly must the decision be made and disseminated?
- What actions will be required if an attack/engagement is unsuccessful and who has the authority to direct those actions?

Decide Products

1. High-Payoff Target List (HPTL)
2. Intelligence Collection Plan
3. Target Selection Standards (TSSs)
4. Attack Guidance Matrix (AGM)

A. High-Payoff Target List (HPTL)

The high-payoff target list (HPTL) is a prioritized list of high-payoff targets (HPTs) whose loss to the enemy will contribute to the success of the friendly course of action. Target value is usually the greatest factor contributing to target payoff. However, other things to be considered include the following:

- The sequence or order of appearance
- The ability to detect identify, classify, locate, and track the target. (This decision must include sensor availability and processing time-line considerations.)
- The degree of accuracy available from the acquisition system(s)
- The ability to engage the target
- The ability to suppress, neutralize, or destroy on the basis of attack guidance
- The resources required to do all of the above

High-Payoff Target List (HPTL) Example

Event or Phase:		
Priority	Category	Target

Ref: FM 34-8-2, Intelligence Officer's Handbook, fig. F-5, p. F-9.

Integrating Processes

B. Intelligence Collection Plan

The intelligence collection plan answers the commander's PIRs, to include those HPTs designated as PIR. The plan, within the availability of additional collection assets, supports the acquisition of more HPTs. Determining the intelligence requirements is the first step in the collection management process.

The collection plan provides a framework that collection managers use to determine, evaluate, and satisfy intelligence needs. Because of the diversity of missions, capabilities, and requirements, the collection plan has no prescribed doctrinal format. However, a dynamic collection plan should:

- Have as its basis the commander's priority intelligence requirements, to include those HPTs approved as PIRs
- Help the commander see his area of interest
- Provides synchronized coverage of the commander's area of operations
- Have a five-dimensional battlefield approach: width, length, depth or altitude, time, and electromagnetic spectrum
- Cover the collection capabilities of higher and adjacent units. Identify assets for acquiring and tracking HPTs and determining BDA on HPTs
- Be flexible enough to allow response to changes as they occur
- Cover only priority requirements
- Be a working document
- Contain precise and concise information

See pp. 3-53 to 3-56 for discussion of information collection from FM 3-55.

C. Target Selection Standards (TSS)

Target selection standards address accuracy or other specific criteria that must be met before targets can be attacked. TSS are criteria applied to enemy activity (acquisitions and battlefield information) used in deciding whether the activity is a target. TSS break nominations into two categories: targets, which meet accuracy and timeliness requirements for attack; and suspected targets, which must be confirmed before any attack.

- **HPT**. This refers to the designated HPTs which the collection manager is tasked to acquire.
- **Timeliness**. Valid targets are reported to attack systems within the designated timeliness criteria.
- **Accuracy**. Valid targets must be reported to the attack system meeting the required TLE criteria. The criteria is the least restrictive TLE considering the capabilities of available attack systems.

Example TSS Matrix

Target Selections Standards		
HPT	Timeliness	Accuracy
COPs	3 hr	150 m
RISTA	30 min	150 m
2S3	30 min	500 m
M-46	30 min	500 m
ADA	15 min	500 m
CPs	3 hr	500 m
Ammunition	6 hr	1 km
Maneuver	1 hr	150 m

Ref: FM 34-8-2, Intelligence Officer's Handbook, fig. F-6, p. F-10.

Considering these factors, different TSS may exist for a given enemy activity on the basis of different attack systems. For example, an enemy artillery battery may have a 150-meter TLE requirement for attack by cannon artillery and a 1 km requirement for attack helicopters. TSS are developed by the FSE in conjunction with MI personnel. Intelligence analysts use TSS to quickly determine targets from battlefield information and pass the targets to the FSE.

Attack system managers, such as FSEs, FCEs, or FDCs, use TSS to quickly identify targets for attack. Commands can develop standard TSS based on anticipated enemy OB and doctrine matched with the normally available attack systems.

D. Attack Guidance Matrix (AGM)

The attack guidance matrix (AGM), approved by the commander, addresses which targets will be attacked, how, when, and the desired effects. The products of the decide function are briefed to the commander. Upon his approval, his decisions are translated into the OPORD with annexes.

Knowing target vulnerabilities and the effect an attack will have on enemy operations allows a staff to propose the most efficient available attack option. Key guidance is whether the commander wishes to disrupt, delay, limit damage, or destroy the enemy. During wargaming, DPs linked to events, areas (NAIs and TAIs), or points on the battlefield are developed. These DPs cue the command decisions and staff actions where tactical decisions are needed.

On the basis of commander's guidance, the targeting team recommends how each target should be engaged in terms of the effects of fire and attack options to use. Effects of fire *(see Joint Pub 1-02)* can be to **harass, suppress, neutralize,** or **destroy** the target. The subjective nature of what is meant by these terms means the commander must ensure the targeting team understands his use of them. Applying FS automation system default values further complicates this understanding.

Example Attack Guidance Matrix (AGM)

PHASE/EVENT: ATTACK THROUGH THE SECURITY ZONE				
HPTL	**WHEN**	**HOW**	**EFFECT**	**REMARKS**
COPs	P	GS ARTY	N	PLAN IN INITIAL PREP
RISTA and OPs	P	GS ARTY	N	P
2S1 and 2S3	P	MLRS	N	
2S6, S9 and SA13	P	GS ARTY	S	SEAD FOR AVN OPS
REGT CP	A	MLRS	N	
RESERVE BN	P	AVN BDE	D	INTENT TO ATTACK RESERVE BN IN EA HOT

LEGEND
I = IMMEDIATE
A = AS ACQUIRED
P = PLANNED
S = SUPPRESS
N = NEUTRALIZE
D = DESTROY

Ref: FM 34-8-2, Intelligence Officer's Handbook, fig. F-7, p. F-13.

1. Harassing Fire

Harassing fire is designed to disturb the rest of the enemy troops, to curtail movement, and, by threat of losses, to lower morale. The decision to employ harassing fires needs careful consideration. Harassing fire has little real effect on the enemy, subjects gun crews to an additional workload, and increases the threat of counter-battery fires. ROE or the potential for adverse public opinion may prohibit its use. However, harassing fires may be a combat multiplier in some situations. Consider their use in SASO , delaying actions, and economy of force operations.

2. Suppressive Fire

Suppressive fire on or about a weapons system degrades its performance below the level needed to fulfill its mission objectives. Suppression lasts only as long as the fires continue. The duration of suppressive fires is either specified in the call for fire or established by SOP. Suppression is used to prevent effective fire on friendly forces. It is typically used to support a specified movement of forces. The FSCOORD needs to ask or calculate the *when* and *how long* questions.

3. Neutralization Fire

Neutralization fire is delivered to render the target ineffective or unusable temporarily. Neutralization fire results in enemy personnel or material becoming incapable of interfering with an operation or COA. Key questions the FSCOORD must ask are when and how long does the commander want the target to be neutralized. Most planned missions are neutralization fires.

4. Destructive Fire

Destruction fire is delivered for the sole purpose of destroying material objects. It physically renders the target permanently combat-ineffective unless it is restored, reconstituted, or rebuilt. Setting automated FS default values for destruction of 30 percent does not guarantee achieving the commander's intent. The surviving 70 percent may still influence the operation. Destruction missions are expensive in terms of time and material. Consider whether neutralization or suppression may be more efficient.

Which Attack System to Use?

The decision of what attack system to use is made at the same time as the decision on when to acquire and attack the target. Coordination is required when deciding to attack with two different means (such as EW and combat air operations). Coordination requirements are recorded during the wargame process.

The attack guidance must be approved by the commander and detail the following:

- A prioritized list of HPTs
- When, how, and desired effects of attack
- Any special instructions
- HPTs that require BDA

This information is developed during the wargame. Attack guidance:

- Applies to planned targets and targets of opportunity
- May address specific or general target descriptions
- Is provided to attack system managers via the AGM
- May change as the operation progresses

The AGM must be updated during staff planning meetings and as the enemy situation changes. Consider separate AGMs for each phase of an operation.

II. Detect

Detect is the second function in targeting and occurs primarily during the prepare portion of the operations process. A key resource for fires planning and targeting is the intelligence generated through reconnaissance, surveillance, and intelligence operations to answer the targeting information requirements. Requirements for target detection and action are expressed as PIR and information requirements. Their priority depends on the importance of the target to the friendly course of action and tracking requirements. PIR and information requirements that support detection of HPTs are incorporated into the overall unit information collection plan. Named areas of interest and target areas of interest are focal points particularly for this effort and are integrated into the information collection plan.

The detect function continues during the execution of the operations order (OPORD). Target acquisition assets gather information and report their findings back to their controlling headquarters, which in turn pass pertinent information to the tasking agency. Some collection assets provide actual targets, while other assets must have their information processed to produce valid targets. The target priorities developed in the decide function are used to expedite the processing of targets. Situations arise where the attack, upon location and identification, of a target is either impossible (for example out of range) or undesirable (outside of but moving toward an advantageous location for the attack). Critical targets that we cannot or choose not to attack in accordance with the attack guidance must be tracked to ensure they are not lost. Tracking suspected targets expedites execution of the attack guidance. Tracking suspected targets keeps them in view while they are validated. Planners and executors must keep in mind that assets used for target tracking may be unavailable for target acquisition. As targets are developed, appropriate weapon systems are tasked in accordance with the attack guidance and location requirements of the system.

III. Deliver

Deliver is the third function in targeting and occurs primarily during the execution stage of the operations process. The main objective is to attack/engage targets in accordance with the commander's guidance. The selection of a weapon system or a combination of weapons systems leads to a technical solution for the selected weapon.

Attack of Targets

The attack of targets must satisfy the attack guidance developed in the decide function. Target attack requires several decisions and actions. These decisions fall into two categories—tactical and technical.

Attack of Targets (Decision Categories)

A. Tactical Decisions
- The time of attack
- The desired effect, or degree of damage
- The attack system to be used

B. Technical Decisions
- Number and type of munitions
- Unit to conduct the attack
- Response time of the attacking unit

A. Tactical Decisions

1. Time of Attack

The time of attack is determined according to the type of target-planned target or target of opportunity.

2. Planned Targets

Some targets will not appear as anticipated. Target attack takes place only when the forecasted enemy activity occurs in the projected time or place. The detection and tracking of activities associated with the target becomes the trigger for target attack. Once the designated activity is detected the targeting team does the following:

- The G2 verifies the enemy activity as the planned target to be attacked. This is done by monitoring decision points and TAIs/NAIs associated with HPTs.
- The G2 validates the target by conducting a final check of the reliability of the source and the accuracy (time and location) of the target. Then he passes the target to the FSE.
- The current operations officer checks the legality of the target in terms of the rules of engagement (ROE)
- The FSE determines if the attack system(s) planned is available and still the best system for the attack
- The FSE coordinates as required with higher, lower, and adjacent units, other services, allies, and host nation. This is particularly important where potential fratricide situations are identified.

- The FSE issues the fire mission request to the appropriate executing unit(s)
- The FSE informs the G2 of target attack
- The G2 alerts the appropriate system responsible for BDA (when applicable)

3. Targets of Opportunity

High-payoff targets of opportunity are processed the same as planned HPTs. Targets of opportunity not on the HPTL are first evaluated to determine when or if they should be attacked. The decision to attack targets of opportunity follows the attack guidance and is based on a number of factors such as the following:

- Activity of the target
- Dwell time
- Target payoff compared to other targets currently being processed for engagement

If the decision is made to attack immediately, the target is processed further. The availability and capabilities of attack systems to engage the target are assessed. If the target exceeds the capabilities or availability of the unit attack systems, the target should be sent to a higher headquarters for immediate attack. If the decision is to defer the attack, continue tracking, determine decision point(s) for attack, and modify collection taskings as appropriate.

4. Desired Effects

Effects of fires can only be properly assessed by an observer or with an analysts. At brigade and TF, it is important that each target has a primary and alternate observer. The observers must understand the desired effects, when and for how long they are required. When in doubt about the commander's intent, ask—never assume. Emphasis on this issue during training will enhance the effectiveness and efficiency of fire support.

5. Attack System

The last tactical decision to be made is the selection of the appropriate attack system. For planned targets, this decision should have been made during the decide function of the targeting process. A check must be made to ensure that the selected attack system is available and can conduct the attack. If not, the targeting team must determine the best system available to attack the target. All available attack assets should be considered. In some cases, the target attach must be coordinated among two or more attack systems.

B. Technical Decisions

Once the tactical decisions have been made, the FS cell directs the attack system to attack the target. The FS cell provides the attack system manager with the following:

- Selected time of attack
- Effects desired in accordance with previous discussion
- Any special restraints or requests for particular munitions types

The attack system manager (FSCOORD, ALO, avn bde LO, NGLO, and so on) determines if his system can meet the requirements. If his system is unable to meet the requirements, he notifies the FS cell. There are various reasons an attack system may not be able to meet the requirements. Some are:

- System not available at the specified time
- Required munitions not available
- Target out of range

The FS cell must decide if the selected system should attack under different criteria or if a different system should be used.

IV. Assess

Assess is the fourth function of targeting and occurs throughout the operations process. The commander and staff assess the results of mission execution. If assessment reveals that the commander's guidance has not been met, the targeting must continue to focus on the target(s) involved. This feedback may result in changes to original decisions made during the target selection. These changes may influence the continued execution of the plan.

Combat assessment is the determination of the effectiveness of force employment during military operations. Combat assessment is composed of three elements:

Combat Assessment

- **A** Battle Damage Assessment (BDA)
- **B** Munitions Effects Assessment (MEA)
- **C** Reattack Recommendation

A. Battle Damage Assessment (BDA)

In combination, BDA and MEA inform the commander of effects against targets and target sets. Based on this, the threat's ability to make and sustain war and centers of gravity are continuously estimated. During the review of the effects of the campaign, restrike recommendations are proposed or executed. BDA pertains to the results of attacks on targets designated by the commander.

B. Munitions Effectiveness Assessment (MEA)

The G3 through the targeting team conducts MEA concurrently and interactively with BDA as a function of combat assessment. MEA is used as the basis for recommending changes to increase effectiveness in:

- Methodology
- Tactics
- Weapon systems
- Munitions
- Weapon delivery parameters

The G3 develops MEA by determining the effectiveness of tactics, weapons systems, and munitions. Munitions effect on targets can be calculated by obtaining rounds fired on specific targets by artillery assets. The targeting team may generate modified commander's guidance concerning:

- Unit Basic Load (UBL)
- Required Supply Rate (RSR)
- Controlled Supply Rate (CSR)

The need for BDA for specific HPTs is determined during the decide function. Record BDA on the AGM and intelligence collection plan. The resources used for BDA are the same resources used for target development and TA. An asset used for BDA may not be available for target development and TA. The ACE receives, processes, and disseminates the results of attack (in terms of desired effects).

Each BDA has three assessment components:

1. Physical Damage Assessment

Physical damage assessment estimates the quantitative extent of physical damage through munitions blast, fragmentation, and/or fire damage effects to a target. This assessment is based on observed or interpreted damage.

2. Functional Damage Assessment

Functional damage assessment estimates the effect of attack on the target to perform its intended mission compared to the operational objective established against the target. This assessment is inferred on the basis of all-source intelligence and includes an estimate of the time needed to replace the target function. A functional damage assessment is a temporary assessment (compared to target system assessment) used for specific missions.

3. Target System Assessment

Target system assessment is a broad assessment of the overall impact and effectiveness of all types of attack against an entire target systems capability; for example, enemy ADA systems. It may also be applied against enemy unit combat effectiveness. A target system assessment may also look at subdivisions of the system compared to the commander's stated operational objectives. It is a relatively permanent assessment (compared to a functional damage assessment) that will be used for more than one mission.

BDA is more than determining the number of casualties or the amount of equipment destroyed. The targeting team can use other information, such as:

- Whether the targets are moving or hardening in response to the attack
- Changes in deception efforts and techniques
- Increased communication efforts as the result of jamming
- Whether the damage achieved is affecting the enemy's combat effectiveness as expected

BDA may also be passive by compiling information regarding a particular target or area (e.g., the cessation of fires from an area). If BDA is to be made, the targeting team must give intelligence acquisition systems adequate warning for sensors to be directed at the target at the proper time. BDA results may change plans and earlier decisions. The targeting team must periodically update the decisions made during the decide function concerning:

- IPB products
- HPTLs
- TSS
- AGMs
- Intelligence collection plans
- OPLANs

C. Reattack Recommendation

Based on BDA and MEA, the G2/G3 consider the level to which operational objectives have been achieved and make recommendations to the commander. Reattack and other recommendations should address operational objectives relative to the:

- Target
- Target critical elements
- Target systems
- Enemy combat force strengths

IV. Risk Management (RM)

Ref: ATP 5-19 (w/C1), Risk Management (Sept '14).

Risk management is the process of identifying, assessing, and controlling risks arising from operational factors and making decisions that balance risk cost with mission benefits (JP 3-0). The Army uses risk management (RM) to help maintain combat power while ensuring mission accomplishment in current and future operations. RM applies to operations and to nonoperational activities.

RM is the Army's process for helping organizations and individuals make informed decisions to reduce or offset risk. Using this process increases operational effectiveness and the probability of mission accomplishment. It is a systematic way of identifying hazards, assessing them, and managing the associated risks.

Commanders, staffs, Army leaders, Soldiers, and Army civilians integrate RM into all planning, preparing, executing, and assessing of operations. The process applies to all types of operations, tasks, and activities.

RM outlines a disciplined approach to express a risk level in terms readily understood at all echelons. Except in time-constrained situations, planners complete the process in a deliberate manner—systematically applying all the steps and recording the results on the prescribed form (*see DD Form 2977 on following pages*).

RM Principles

The principles of RM are—

- Integrate RM into all phases of missions and operations
- Make risk decisions at the appropriate level
- Accept no unnecessary risk
- Apply RM cyclically and continuously

Army forces must integrate RM throughout planning, preparation, execution, and assessment activities. Army units should use RM for on- and off-duty activities. Commanders must emphasize RM in planning processes; they must dedicate sufficient time and other resources to RM during planning to ensure Army forces manage risk effectively throughout all phases of missions and operations.

A *risk decision* is a commander, leader, or individual's determination to accept or not accept the risk(s) associated with an action he or she will take or will direct others to take. RM is only effective when the specific information about hazards and risks is passed to the appropriate level of command for a risk decision. Subordinates must pass specific risk information up the chain of command. Conversely, the higher command must provide subordinates making risk decisions or implementing controls with the established *risk tolerance*—the level of risk the responsible commander is willing to accept. RM application must be inclusive; those executing an operation and those directing it participate in an integrated process.

In the context of RM, a *control* is an action taken to eliminate a hazard or to reduce its risk. If a commander, Army leader, or any individual responsible for executing a task determines that the controls available will not reduce risk to a level within the risk tolerance, that person must elevate the risk decision to the next level in the chain of command.

See following pages (pp. 3-72 to 3-73) for sample notional examples of a completed DD Form 2977.

Risk Management Worksheet (DD Form 2977)

Ref: ATP 5-19 (w/C1), Risk Management (Sept '14), app. A.

DD Form 2977 is the Army's standard form for deliberate risk assessment. Aviation; explosive; chemical, biological, radiological, or nuclear; and other highly technical activities may require additional specialized documentation. However, when coordination may occur across sections or commands, DD Form 2977 is the standard for the majority of Army operations. It allows units to track hazards and risks in a logical manner. Army forces use this form to document risk management (RM) steps taken during planning, preparation, and execution of any type of operation, including training and combat.

DELIBERATE RISK ASSESSMENT WORKSHEET

1. MISSION/TASK DESCRIPTION	2. DATE *(DD/MM/YYYY)*

3. PREPARED BY

a. Name *(Last, First, Middle Initial)*	b. Rank/Grade	c. Duty Title/Position
d. Unit	e. Work Email	f. Telephone *(DSN/Commercial (Include Area Code))*
g. UIC/CIN *(as required)*	h. Training Support/Lesson Plan or OPORD *(as required)*	i. Signature of Preparer

Five steps of Risk Management: (1) Identify the hazards (2) Assess the hazards (3) Develop controls & make decisions (4) Implement controls (5) Supervise and evaluate *(Step numbers not equal to numbered items on form)*

4. SUBTASK/SUBSTEP OF MISSION/TASK	5. HAZARD	6. INITIAL RISK LEVEL	7. CONTROL	8. HOW TO IMPLEMENT/ WHO WILL IMPLEMENT	9. RESIDUAL RISK LEVEL
				How: Who:	
				How: Who:	
				How: Who:	
				How: Who:	
				How: Who:	

Additional entries for items 5 through 9 are provided on page 2.

10. OVERALL RESIDUAL RISK LEVEL *(All controls implemented)*:
☐ EXTREMELY HIGH ☐ HIGH ☐ MEDIUM ☐ LOW

11. OVERALL SUPERVISION PLAN AND RECOMMENDED COURSE OF ACTION

12. APPROVAL OR DISAPPROVAL OF MISSION OR TASK ☐ APPROVE ☐ DISAPPROVE

a. Name *(Last, First, Middle Initial)*	b. Rank/Grade	c. Duty Title/Position	d. Signature of Approval Authority

e. Additional Guidance:

DD FORM 2977, JAN 2014

Page 1 of ____ Pages

Adobe Professional X

DD Form 2977 is designed for the entire Army and the other Services. It provides standardization for joint operations and assignments. It may be filled out electronically or free hand. It is the standard way of capturing the information analyzed during the five steps of RM. It helps the user in thinking through the five steps and then sharing the resulting assessment. It is a living document. Pen and pencil changes on hard copies are acceptable and encouraged since changes will occur during operations.

RM is a universal process used for managing risk at every level of effort from the individual to large units or organizations. Its application is blind to the cause of the hazard.

Refer to ATP 5-19, app. A for sample general, notional examples of completed DD Form 2977.

DELIBERATE RISK ASSESSMENT WORKSHEET

Risk Assessment Matrix		Probability *(expected frequency)*				
		Frequent: Continuous, regular, or inevitable occurrences	Likely: Several or numerous occurrences	Occasional: Sporadic or intermittent occurrences	Seldom: Infrequent occurrences	Unlikely: Possible occurrences but improbable
Severity *(expected consequence)*		A	B	C	D	E
Catastrophic: *Death, unacceptable loss or damage, mission failure, or unit readiness eliminated*	I	EH	EH	H	H	M
Critical: *Severe injury, illness, loss, or damage; significantly degraded unit readiness or mission capability*	II	EH	H	H	M	L
Moderate: *Minor injury, illness, loss, or damage; somewhat degraded unit readiness or mission capability*	III	H	M	M	L	L
Negligible: *Minimal injury, loss, or damage; little or no impact to unit readiness or mission capability*	IV	M	L	L	L	L

Legend*:*
EH – extremely high risk H – high risk M – medium risk L – low risk

13. RISK ASSESSMENT REVIEW *(Required when assessment applies to ongoing operations or activities)*

a. Date	b. Last Name	c. Rank/Grade	d. Duty Title/Position	e. Signature of Reviewer

14. FEEDBACK AND LESSONS LEARNED

15. ADDITIONAL COMMENTS OR REMARKS

DD FORM 2977, JAN 2014 Page ____ of ____ Pages

Integrating Processes

Risk Management Process

Ref: ATP 5-19 (w/C1), Risk Management (Sept '14), chap. 1.

Risk Management is the process of identifying, assessing, and controlling risks arising from operational factors and making decisions that balance risk cost with mission benefits. (JP 3-0) *The Army no longer uses the term "composite risk management." Term replaced with joint term "risk management."*

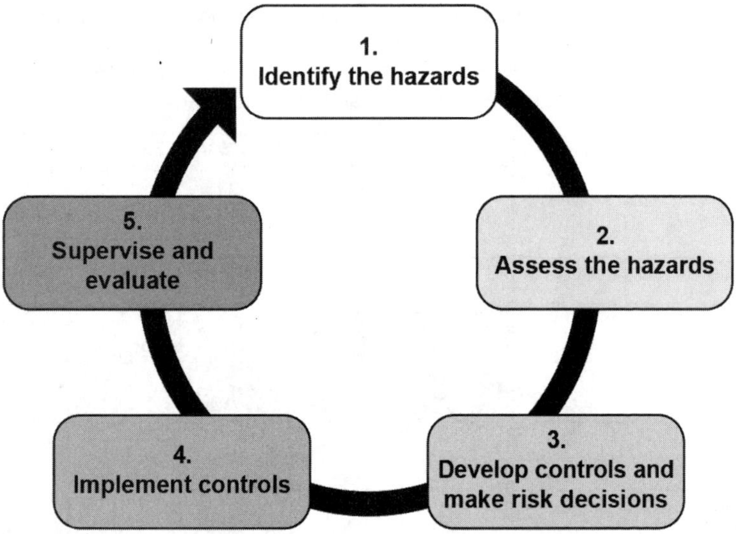

Ref: ATP 5-19, fig. 1-1. A cyclical, continuous process for managing risk.

1. Identify the hazards

A hazard is a condition with the potential to cause injury, illness, or death of personnel; damage to or loss of equipment or property; or mission degradation. Hazards exist in all environments—combat operations, stability operations, base support operations, training, garrison activities, and off-duty activities. The factors of mission, enemy, terrain and weather, troops and support available, time available, and civil considerations (METT-TC) serve as a standard format for identification of hazards, on-duty or off-duty.

2. Assess the hazards

This process is systematic in nature and uses charts, codes and numbers to present a methodology to assess probability and severity to obtain a standardized level of risk. Hazards are assessed and risk is assigned in terms of probability and severity of adverse impact of an event/occurrence.

3. Develop controls and make risk decisions

The process of developing and applying controls and reassessing risk continues until an acceptable level of risk is achieved or until all risks are reduced to a level where benefits outweigh the potential cost.

4. Implement controls

Leaders and staffs ensure that controls are integrated into SOPs, written and verbal orders, mission briefings, and staff estimates.

5. Supervise and evaluate

Chap 3

V. Knowledge Management (KM)

Ref: ATP 6-01.1, Techniques for Effective Knowledge Management (Mar '15).

Knowledge management is the process of enabling knowledge flow to enhance shared understanding, learning, and decisionmaking (ADRP 6-0). Knowledge flow is the ease of movement of knowledge in organizations. Knowledge management uses a five-step process to create shared understanding. The steps of knowledge management include:

Knowledge Management

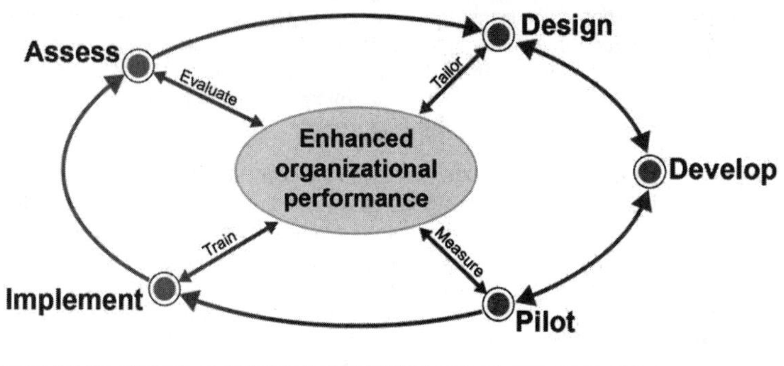

Ref: ATP 6-01.1, fig. 1-1. Knowledge management – an iterative cycle.

The five-step knowledge management process in figure 1-1 aligns people, processes, and tools in the organization and culture for leaders and subordinates to collaborate and share understanding. The four components of knowledge management include: people, processes, tools, organization.

I. Types of Knowledge

Knowledge provides meaning or value for the operation. It is gained through study, experience, practice, and human interaction and is the basis for expertise and skilled judgment. In ATP 6-01.1, knowledge is differentiated into tacit knowledge and explicit knowledge. *(Refer to FM 6-22, Army Leadership, for discussion on tactical knowledge, technical knowledge, joint knowledge and cultural and geopolitical knowledge.)*

- **Tacit Knowledge**. Tacit knowledge is what individuals know; a unique, personal store of knowledge gained from life experiences, training, and networks of friends, acquaintances, and professional colleagues. It includes learned nuances, subtleties, and workarounds. Intuition, mental agility, and response to crises are also forms of tacit knowledge.
- **Explicit Knowledge**. Explicit knowledge is codified or formally documented knowledge organized and transferred to others through digital or non-digital means. Explicit knowledge has rules, limits, and precise meanings. Examples include computer files, dictionaries, textbooks, and Army and joint doctrinal publications.

Integrating Processes

II. KM and Mission Command

Ref: ATP 6-01.1, Techniques for Effective Knowledge Management (Mar '15), pp. 1-5 to 1-7.

Executing the mission command staff task of "perform knowledge management and information management" provides commanders the information and knowledge to create and maintain understanding and make decisions. The staff studies the operational environment, identifies information gaps, and helps the commander develop and answer information requirements. The staff performs information management to organize and process collected data into information and applies analysis to develop information into knowledge.

The commander is the central figure in mission command. Commanders drive operations through understanding, visualizing, describing, directing, leading, and assessing operations. The staff supports the commander by performing operations. Knowledge management is integral to commanders and staffs as they perform these tasks.

During operations, knowledge flows between individuals and organizations. Staffs manage this exchange and use knowledge management practices to enable knowledge transfer. Knowledge transfer occurs formally through processes and procedures and informally through collaboration and dialogue. Army-wide knowledge management implementation enables the Army, through mission command, to execute decisive action. Shared understanding creates adaptive learning organizations. This helps the commander achieve a relative advantage on the battlefield.

Supporting Commander's Decisionmaking

The knowledge management staff helps units implement processes and practices to provide commanders with the knowledge and understanding to make decisions. Staffs use various information and knowledge management practices to help commander's process information. They piece together data and information and produce knowledge through analysis and evaluation. Staffs provide collective knowledge to the commander. Commanders apply judgment to transform knowledge into understanding Table 1-3 shows how knowledge management enhances decisionmaking.

Enabling the unit to focus and direct	
Element	Examples
The right information	• Commanders critical information requirements • Significant activity reports • Situation reports • Medical evacuation • Requests
To the right person	• Commanders • Staffs • Action officers
At the right time	• Latest time information of value • Battle rhythm
In the right form	• Significant activities • Spot reports • Ground intelligence summaries • Size activity location unit time equipment
In the right place	• Command posts • Boards • Battlefield update briefs • Commander's updates • Situation reports
In order to enable informed decisionmaking based on shared understanding	

Ref: ATP 6-01.1, table 1-3. How knowledge management enhances decisionmaking.

Facilitating Dialogue and Interaction

Knowledge management has many collaborative tools and processes to facilitate dialogue and interaction. These include tools to help units perform and record virtual meetings, share documents and presentations, brainstorm via white boarding; and collaborate through tools such as SharePoint and a variety of Army professional forums, communities of purpose, and knowledge networks. The knowledge management working group enables collaboration in units, sets up processes and facilitates training so organizations collaborate and interact. The resulting dialogue enhances critical and creative thinking essential to successful mission command.

Facilitating the Capture and Transfer of Knowledge

Knowledge is a transferable asset that grows with use and application. Linking sources of tacit knowledge and encouraging interaction at all levels (individual to enterprise) helps the Army acquire and share knowledge to support the mission. Knowledge management tools that facilitate collaboration and the exchange of knowledge enable staffs to capture tacit knowledge. Tacit knowledge provides part of the foundation for intuition. It is a component of knowledge commanders use to exercise mission command. Commanders combine their tacit and explicit knowledge to visualize an operation or battle. When commanders have tacit and explicit knowledge, their situational understanding improves and they make more effective decisions. Effective knowledge management makes both tacit and explicit knowledge from a wide range of sources available to those who need it and when they need it so they can operate more effectively.

Providing Timely and Relevant Information and Knowledge

Effective knowledge management identifies the information the unit needs and its importance. Staffs use processes to produce information from data and analyze and evaluate that information to produce knowledge. Staffs provide collective knowledge to commanders who apply experience and judgment to transform that knowledge into understanding. Knowledge management, supported by information management, helps do this more effectively. Information management helps staffs extract relevant information from the vast amounts of data and available information so they can provide timely and relevant information and analysis to help commanders build and maintain situational understanding. Through analysis, staffs develop and provide knowledge to commanders by running estimates and providing recommendations to help commanders understand situations, make and implement decisions, control operations, collaborate with peers, and assess progress on the operation.

Enabling Adaptive and Learning Organizations

Knowledge management helps Soldiers and organizations learn and adapt. The increased collaboration and interaction between commanders and Soldiers across the force improves flexibility, adaptability, and integration of the warfighting functions. Knowledge management connects leaders, subordinates, and organizations and facilitates sharing and integration of information and knowledge. It integrates informal and organizational learning strategies to foster learning. Together, these contribute to developing adaptive learning organizations. Leaders who promote initiative and innovation foster learning. It involves knowledge transfer during interaction and collaboration and leverages resources inside and outside the organization. Organizations and Soldiers adapt faster than enemies and adversaries when they foster learning.

Supporting Mission Command Warfighting Function Tasks

Commanders exercise mission command through the commander tasks and the staff supports the commander in the exercise of mission command by performing the staff tasks. For commanders, creating shared understanding through knowledge management is an important principle of mission command. Staffs perform knowledge management as a part of mission command.

III. KM and Operations Principles

Ref: ATP 6-01.1, Techniques for Effective Knowledge Management (Mar '15), pp. 1-10 to 1-11.

Commanders Drive Operations

Commanders are the central figure in mission command. They drive operations through execution of their tasks of understand, visualize, describe, direct, lead, and assess. The knowledge management staff supports the commander's understanding and visualization by facilitating access to sources of knowledge including those that support the staff to prepare running estimates for the commander. Knowledge management collaboration tools help commanders share their own understanding as they describe their visualization and direct actions of staff and subordinate commanders. Collaboration and dialogue leads to shared understanding of the commander's intent and enables commanders to effectively lead.

Build and Maintain Situational Understanding

Staffs perform knowledge management and information management to find relevant information from large amounts of data and available information. They provide timely and relevant information and analysis to help commanders build and maintain situational understanding. Through analysis, staffs develop knowledge for commanders and run estimates and recommendations to help commanders understand situations, make and implement decisions, control operations, and assess progress.

Knowledge management tools and processes facilitate the commander's situational understanding. The staff executes knowledge management and information management to help a commander's situational understanding, and makes and implements decisions, controls operations, and assesses progress. Knowledge management enhances the staff's ability to help subordinate units (commanders and staffs) and keep units and organizations outside the headquarters informed throughout an operation. This requires connecting people and knowledge. Knowledge management transfers tacit knowledge between individuals, teams, and units through collaboration.

The product of shared understanding is better decisionmaking at every level. Collaboration and interaction help subordinate leaders understand the commander's guidance and intent. This enables them to make appropriate decisions when circumstances change. They communicate and reinforce the commander's intent to Soldiers whose individual decisions and actions reflect their understanding of it.

Apply Critical and Creative Thinking

Collaboration and dialogue helps with critical and creative thinking as participants share knowledge and insights. They question each other's assumptions and exchange ideas. This exchange helps commanders and staffs understand situations, make decisions, and direct action. When commanders encourage a collaborative environment where knowledge and ideas are freely shared, the resulting creative thinking leads to new insights, novel approaches, fresh perspectives, and new ways of to understand and conceive situations.

Encourage Collaboration and Dialogue

Knowledge management aligns people, processes, and tools in an organization to facilitate collaboration and interaction between leaders and subordinates. Collaboration, dialogue, and other forms of interaction occur with commander and staff, commander, and/or staff with subordinate commanders, in working groups, during battle update briefings, in communities of purpose via Army professional forums, centers of excellence or other means. Through collaboration and dialogue, participants share their knowledge, perspectives, and understanding of a situation. This exchange increases shared understanding of the enemy and the operational environment, problems to be solved, and approaches to solving them. This exchange contributes to the overall Army knowledge base.

Chap 4

I. Plans & Orders

Ref: FM 6-0 (C2), Commander and Staff Organization and Operations (Apr '16), app. C.

Planning is the art and science of understanding a situation, envisioning a desired future, and laying out an operational approach to achieve that future. Based on this understanding and operational approach, planning continues with the development of a fully synchronized operation plan or order that arranges potential actions in time, space, and purpose to guide the force during execution (see ADP 5-0).

A product of planning is a plan or order—a directive for future action. Commanders issue plans and orders to subordinates to communicate their understanding of the situation and their visualization of an operation. Plans and orders direct, coordinate, and synchronize subordinate actions and inform those outside the unit how to cooperate and provide support.

Prepare the Order or Plan

The staff prepares the order or plan by turning the selected COA into a clear, concise concept of operations and the required supporting information. The COA statement becomes the concept of operations for the plan. The COA sketch becomes the basis for the operation overlay. If time permits, the staff may conduct a more detailed war game of the selected COA to more fully synchronize the operation and complete the plan. The staff writes the OPORD or OPLAN using the Army's operation order format.

See pp. 2-55 to 2-56, step VII of the MDMP, Orders Production.

Normally, the COS (XO) coordinates with staff principals to assist the G-3 (S-3) in developing the plan or order. Based on the commander's planning guidance, the COS (XO) dictates the type of order, sets and enforces the time limits and development sequence, and determines which staff section publishes which attachments.

Prior to the commander approving the plan or order, the staff ensures the plan or order is internally consistent and is nested with the higher commander's intent through—

- Plans and orders reconciliation
- Plans and orders crosswalk

Verbal Orders

Commanders use verbal orders when operating in an extremely time-constrained environment. These orders offer the advantage of being distributed quickly but risk important information being overlooked or misunderstood. Verbal orders are usually followed by written FRAGORDs.

Written Orders

Commanders issue written plans and orders that contain both text and graphics. Graphics convey information and instructions through military symbols. (FM 1-02 lists approved symbols.) They complement the written portion of a plan or an order and promote clarity, accuracy, and brevity. Staffs often develop and disseminate written orders electronically to shorten the time needed to gather and brief the orders group. Staffs can easily edit and modify electronically produced orders. They can send the same order to multiple recipients simultaneously. Using computer programs to develop and disseminate precise, corresponding graphics adds to the efficiency and clarity of the orders process. Electronic editing makes importing text and graphics into orders easy. Unfortunately, such ease can result in orders becoming unnecessarily large without added operational value.

I. Guidance for Plans

Planning is the art and science of understanding a situation, envisioning a desired future, and laying out an operational approach to achieve that future. Based on this understanding and operational approach, planning continues with the development of a fully synchronized operation plan or order that arranges potential actions in time, space, and purpose to guide the force during execution (see FM 5-0).

A product of planning is a plan or order—a directive for future action. Commanders issue plans and orders to subordinates to communicate their understanding of the situation and their visualization of an operation. Plans and orders direct, coordinate, and synchronize subordinate actions and inform those outside the unit how to cooperate and provide support. To properly understand and execute the joint commander's plan, Army commanders and staffs must be familiar with joint planning processes, procedures, and orders formats. (Refer to JP 3-33 and JP 5-0.)

Building Simple, Flexible Plans

Simplicity is a principle of war and vital to effective planning. Effective plans and orders are simple and direct. Staffs prepare clear, concise, and complete plans and orders to ensure thorough understanding. They use doctrinally correct operational terms and graphics. Doing this minimizes chances of misunderstanding. Shorter rather than longer plans aid in simplicity. Shorter plans are easier to disseminate, read, and remember.

Complex plans have a greater potential to fail in execution since they often rely on intricate coordination. Operations are always subject to the fog of war and friction. The more detailed the plan, the greater the chances it will no longer be applicable as friendly, enemy, and civilian actions change the situation throughout an operation.

Simple plans require an easily understood concept of operations. Planners also promote simplicity by minimizing details where possible and by limiting the actions or tasks to what the situation requires. Subordinates can then develop specifics within the commander's intent. For example, instead of assigning a direction of attack, planners can designate an axis of advance.

Simple plans are not simplistic plans. Simplistic refers to something made overly simple by ignoring the situation's complexity. Good plans simplify complicated situations. However, some situations require more complex plans than others do. Commanders at all levels weigh the apparent benefits of a complex concept of operations against the risk that subordinates will be unable to understand or follow it adequately. Commanders prefer simple plans that are easy to understand and execute.

Flexible plans help units adapt quickly to changing circumstances. Commanders and planners build opportunities for initiative into plans by anticipating events that allow them to operate inside of the enemy's decision cycle or react promptly to deteriorating situations. Identifying decision points and designing branches ahead of time—combined with a clear commander's intent—help create flexible plans. Incorporating control measures to reduce risk also makes plans more flexible. For example, a commander may hold a large, mobile reserve to compensate for the lack of information concerning an anticipated enemy attack.

II. Mission Orders

Ref: FM 6-0 (C2), Commander and Staff Organization and Operations (Apr '16), p. C-2.

Commanders stress the importance of mission orders as a way of building simple, flexible plans. Mission orders are directives that emphasize to subordinates the results to be attained, not how they are to achieve them (ADP 6-0). Mission orders focus on what to do and the purpose of doing it without prescribing exactly how to do it. Commanders establish control measures to aid cooperation among forces without imposing needless restrictions on freedom of action. Mission orders contribute to flexibility by allowing subordinates the freedom to seize opportunities or react effectively to unforeseen enemy actions and capabilities.

Mission orders follow the five-paragraph format (situation, mission, execution, sustainment, and command and signal) and are as brief and simple as possible. Mission orders clearly convey the unit's mission and commander's intent. They summarize the situation (current or anticipated starting conditions), describe the operation's objectives and end state (desired conditions), and provide a simple concept of operations to accomplish the unit's mission. When assigning tasks to subordinate units, mission orders include all components of a task statement: who, what, when, where, and why. However, commanders particularly emphasize the purpose (why) of the tasks to guide (along with the commander's intent) individual initiative. Effective plans and orders foster mission command by:

- Describing the situation to create a common situational understanding
- Conveying the commander's intent and concept of operations
- Assigning tasks to subordinate units and stating the purpose for conducting the task
- Providing the control measures necessary to synchronize the operation while retaining the maximum freedom of action for subordinates
- Task-organizing forces and allocating resources
- Directing preparation activities and establishing times or conditions for execution

Mission orders contain the proper level of detail; they are neither so detailed that they stifle initiative nor so general that they provide insufficient direction. The proper level depends on each situation and is not easy to determine. Some phases of operations require tighter control over subordinate elements than others require. An air assault's air movement and landing phases, for example, require precise synchronization. Its ground maneuver plan requires less detail. As a rule, the base plan or order contains only the specific information required to provide the guidance to synchronize combat power at the decisive time and place while allowing subordinates as much freedom of action as possible. Commanders rely on individual initiative and coordination to act within the commander's intent and concept of operations. The attachments to the plan or order contain details regarding the situation and instructions necessary for synchronization.

III. Types of Plans and Orders

Ref: FM 6-0 (C2), Commander and Staff Organization and Operations (Apr '16)), pp. C-3 to C-4.

Plans

Plans come in many forms and vary in scope, complexity, and length of planning horizons. Strategic plans establish national and multinational military objectives and include ways to achieve those objectives. Operational-level or campaign plans cover a series of related military operations aimed at accomplishing a strategic or operational objective within a given time and space. Tactical plans cover the employment of units in operations, including the ordered arrangement and maneuver of units in relation to each other and to the enemy within the framework of an operational-level or campaign plan. There are several types of plans:

1. Campaign Plan

A campaign plan is a joint operation plan for a series of related major operations aimed at achieving strategic or operational objectives within a given time and space (JP 5-0). Developing and issuing a campaign plan is appropriate when the contemplated simultaneous or sequential military operations exceed the scope of a single major operation. Only joint force commanders develop campaign plans.

2. Operation Plan (OPLAN)

An operation plan is 1. Any plan for the conduct of military operations prepared in response to actual and potential contingencies. 2. A complete and detailed joint plan containing a full description of the concept of operations, all annexes applicable to the plan, and a time-phased force and deployment data. (JP 5-0). An OPLAN may address an extended period connecting a series of objectives and operations, or it may be developed for a single part or phase of a long-term operation. An OPLAN becomes an operation order when the commander sets an execution time or designates an event that triggers the operation.

3. Supporting Plan

A supporting plan is an operation plan prepared by a supporting commander, a subordinate commander, or an agency to satisfy the requests or requirements of the supported commander's plan (JP 5-0). For example, the ARFOR commander develops a supporting plan as to how Army forces will support the joint force commander's campaign plan or OPLAN.

4. Concept Plan

In the context of joint operation planning level 3 planning detail, a concept plan is an operation plan in an abbreviated format that may require considerable expansion or alteration to convert it into a complete operation plan or operation order (JP 5-0). Often branches and sequels are written as concept plans. As time and the potential allow for executing a particular branch or sequel, these concept plans are developed in detail into OPLANs.

5. Branch

A branch describes the contingency options built into the base plan. A branch is used for changing the mission, orientation, or direction of movement of a force to aid success of the operation based on anticipated events, opportunities, or disruptions caused by enemy actions and reactions. Branches are also used in stability operations to address potential actions and reactions of populations.

6. Sequel

A sequel is the subsequent major operation or phase based on the possible outcomes (success, stalemate, or defeat) of the current major operation or phase (JP 5-0). For every action or major operation that does not accomplish a strategic or operational objective, there should be a sequel for each possible outcome, such as win, lose, draw, or decisive win.

Orders

An order is a communication—verbal, written, or signaled—which conveys instructions from a superior to a subordinate. Commanders issue orders verbally or in writing. The five-paragraph format (situation, mission, execution, sustainment, and command and signal) remains the standard for issuing orders. The technique used to issue orders (verbal or written) is at the discretion of the commander; each technique depends on time and the situation. Army organizations use three types of orders:

1. Operation Order (OPORD)

An operation order is a directive issued by a commander to subordinate commanders for the purpose of effecting the coordinated execution of an operation (JP 5-0). Commanders issue OPORDs to direct the execution of long-term operations as well as the execution of discrete short-term operations within the framework of a long-range OPORD.

See pp. 4-22 to 4-27 for a sample format.

2. Fragmentary Order (FRAGORD)

A fragmentary order is an abbreviated form of an operation order issued as needed after an operation order to change or modify that order or to execute a branch or sequel to that order (JP 5-0). FRAGORDs include all five OPORD paragraph headings and differ from OPORDs only in the degree of detail provided. An example of the proper naming convention for a FRAGORD to an OPORD is "FRAGORD 11 to OPORD 3411 (OPERATION DESERT DRAGON) (UNCLASSIFIED)." If a FRAGORD contains an entire annex, then the proper naming convention for the annex would be "Annex A (Task Organization) to FRAGORD 12 to OPORD 3411 (OPERATION DESERT DRAGON) (UNCLASSIFIED)."

See p. 4-32 for a sample format.

3. Warning Order (WARNORD)

A warning order is a preliminary notice of an order or action that is to follow (JP 3-33). WARNORDs help subordinate units and staffs prepare for new missions by describing the situation, providing initial planning guidance, and directing preparation activities. For example, the proper naming convention for WARNORD number 8 is "WARNORD #8."

See p. 4-21 for a sample format.

In addition to these types of orders, Army forces may receive the following types of orders from a joint headquarters:

- Planning order
- Alert order
- Execute order
- Prepare-to-deploy order

Joint Planning Processes, Procedures and Orders

To properly understand and execute the joint commander's plan, Army commanders and staffs must be familiar with joint planning processes, procedures, and orders formats. An Army headquarters that forms the base of a joint task force uses the joint operation planning process and publishes plans and orders in accordance with the joint format. An Army HQs that provides the base of a joint force or coalition forces land component command headquarters will participate in joint planning and receive a joint formatted plan or order. This headquarters then has the option to use the MDMP or joint operations planning process to develop its own supporting plan or order. Refer to JFODS5-1: The Joint Forces Operations & Doctrine SMARTbook.

IV. Characteristics of Plans and Orders

The amount of detail provided in a plan or order depends on several factors, including the cohesion and experience of subordinate units and complexity of the operation. Effective plans and orders encourage subordinates' initiative by providing the "what" and "why" of tasks to subordinate units; they leave how to perform the tasks to subordinates. To maintain clarity and simplicity, planners keep the base plan or order as short and concise as possible. They address detailed information and instructions in attachments as required.

Effective plans and orders are simple and direct to reduce misunderstanding and confusion. The situation determines the degree of simplicity required. Simple plans executed on time are better than detailed plans executed late. Commanders at all echelons weigh potential benefits of a complex concept of operations against the risk that subordinates will fail to understand it. Multinational operations mandate simplicity due to the differences in language, doctrine, and culture. The same applies to operations involving interagency and nongovernmental organizations.

Effective plans and orders reflect authoritative and positive expression through the commander's intent. As such, the language is direct and affirmative. An example of this is, "The combat trains will remain in the assembly area" instead of "The combat trains will not accompany the unit." Effective plans and orders directly and positively state what the commander wants the unit and its subordinate units to do and why.

Effective plans and orders avoid meaningless expressions, such as "as soon as possible." Indecisive, vague, and ambiguous language leads to uncertainty and lack of confidence.

Effective plans and orders possess brevity and clarity. These plans use short words, sentences, and paragraphs. Plans use acronyms unless clarity is hindered. They do not include material covered in SOPs, but refer to those SOPs instead. Brief and clear orders use doctrinally correct terms and symbols, avoid jargon, and eliminate every opportunity for misunderstanding the commander's exact, intended meaning.

Effective plans and orders contain assumptions. This helps subordinates and others better understand the logic behind a plan or order and facilitates the preparation of branches and sequels.

Effective plans and orders incorporate flexibility. There is room built into the plan to adapt and make adjustments to counter unexpected challenges and seize opportunities. Effective plans and orders identify decision points and proposed options at those decision points to build flexibility.

Effective plans and orders exercise timeliness. Plans and orders sent to subordinates promptly allow subordinates to collaborate, plan, and prepare their own actions.

II. Task Organization (Annex A)

Ref: FM 6-0 (C2), Commander and Staff Organization and Operations (Apr '16), app. D.

This section discusses the fundamentals of task organization and provides the format and instructions for developing Annex A (Task Organization) to the base plan or order. This annex does not follow the five-paragraph attachment format. Unit standard operating procedures (SOPs) will dictate development and format for this annex.

Task-organizing is the act of designing an operating force, support staff, or sustainment package of specific size and composition to meet a unique task or mission (ADRP 3-0). Characteristics to examine when task-organizing the force include, but are not limited to, training, experience, equipment, sustainability, operational environment, (including enemy threat), and mobility. For Army forces, it includes allocating available assets to subordinate commanders and establishing their command and support relationships. Command and support relationships provide the basis for unity of command in operations. The assistant chief of staff, plans (G-5) or assistant chief of staff, operations (G-3 [S-3]) develops Annex A (Task Organization).

I. Fundamental Considerations

Military units consist of organic components. Organic parts of a unit are those forming an essential part of the unit and are listed in its table of organization and equipment (TOE). Commanders can alter organizations' organic unit relationships to better allocate assets to subordinate commanders. They also can establish temporary command and support relationships to facilitate exercising mission command.

Establishing clear command and support relationships is fundamental to organizing any operation. These relationships establish clear responsibilities and authorities between subordinate and supporting units. Some command and support relationships (for example, tactical control) limit the commander's authority to prescribe additional relationships. Knowing the inherent responsibilities of each command and support relationship allows commanders to effectively organize their forces and helps supporting commanders to understand their unit's role in the organizational structure.

Commanders designate command and support relationships to weight the decisive operation and support the concept of operations. Task organization also helps subordinate and supporting commanders support the commander's intent. These relationships carry with them varying responsibilities to the subordinate unit by the parent and gaining units. Commanders consider two organizational principles when task-organizing forces:

1. **When possible, commanders maintain cohesive mission teams.** They organize forces based on standing headquarters, their assigned forces, and habitual associations when possible. When not feasible and ad hoc organizations are created, commanders arrange time for training and establishing functional working relationships and procedures. Once commanders have organized and committed a force, they keep its task organization unless the benefits of a change clearly outweigh the disadvantages.
2. Commanders carefully avoid exceeding the span of control capabilities of subordinates. Span of control refers to the number of subordinate units under a single commander. This number is situation dependent and may vary. As a rule, commanders can effectively command two to six subordinate units. Allocating subordinate commanders more units gives them greater flexibility and increases options and combinations. However, increasing the number of subordinate units increases the number of decisions for commanders to make in a timely fashion. This slows down the reaction time among decisionmakers.

Running Estimates and Course of Action (COA) Analysis

Running estimates and course of action (COA) analysis of the military decisionmaking process provide information that helps commanders determine the best task organization. An effective task organization:

- Facilitates the commander's intent and concept of operations
- Retains flexibility within the concept of operations
- Adapts to conditions imposed by mission variables
- Accounts for the requirements to conduct essential stability tasks for populations within an area of operations
- Creates effective combined arms teams
- Provides mutual support among units
- Ensures flexibility to meet unforeseen events and to support future operations
- Allocates resources with minimum restrictions on their employment
- Promotes unity of command
- Offsets limitations and maximizes the potential of all forces available
- Exploits enemy vulnerabilities

Creating an appropriate task organization requires understanding:

- The mission, including the higher commander's intent and concept of operations
- The fundamentals of offense, defense, stability, and defense support of civil authorities tasks (ADRP 3-0) and basic tactical concepts (ADRP 3-90)
- The roles and relationships among the warfighting functions
- The status of available forces, including morale, training, and equipment capabilities
- Specific unit capabilities, limitations, strengths, and weaknesses
- The risks inherent in the plan

During COA analysis, commanders identify what resources they need, and where, when, and how frequently they will need them. Formal task organization and the change from generic to specific units begin after COA analysis when commanders assign tasks to subordinate commanders. The staffs assign tasks to subordinate headquarters and determine if subordinate headquarters have enough combat power, reallocating combat power as necessary. They then refine command and support relationships for subordinate units and decide the priorities of support. Commanders approve or modify the staff's recommended task organization based on their evaluation of the factors and information from running estimates and COA analysis.

In allocating assets, the commander and staff consider the:

- Task organization for the ongoing operation
- Potential adverse effects of breaking up cohesive teams by changing the task organization
- Time necessary to realign the organization after receipt of the task organization
- Limits on control over supporting units provided by higher headquarters

II. Army Command and Support Relationships

Ref: FM 6-0 (C2), Commander and Staff Organization and Operations (Apr '16), app. B.

Establishing clear command and support relationships is a key task in task organizing for any operation. (See ADRP 5-0.) These relationships establish clear responsibilities and authorities between subordinate and supporting units. Some command and support relationships limit the commander's authority to prescribe additional relationships.

Army commanders build combined arms organizations using command and support relationships.

- **Command relationships** define command responsibility and authority.
- **Support relationships** define the desired purpose, scope, and effect when one capability supports another.

Refer to The Joint Forces Operations & Doctrine SMARTbook and/or JP1 for discussion of the four types of joint command relationships (combatant command, operational control, tactical control, and support).

Army Command Relationships

Command relationships define superior and subordinate relationships between unit commanders. By specifying a chain of command, command relationships unify effort and enable commanders to use subordinate forces with maximum flexibility. Army command relationships identify the degree of control of the gaining Army commander. The type of command relationship often relates to the expected longevity of the relationship between the headquarters involved and quickly identifies the degree of support that the gaining and losing Army commanders provide. Army command relationships include:

See table B-1 on the following pages for Army command relationships.

Organic. Organic forces are those assigned to and forming an essential part of a military organization as listed in its table of organization for the Army, Air Force, and Marine Corps, and are assigned to the operating forces for the Navy (JP 1). Joint command relationships do not include organic because a joint force commander is not responsible for the organizational structure of units. That is a Service responsibility. The Army establishes organic command relationships through organizational documents such as tables of organization and equipment and tables of distribution and allowances. If temporarily task-organized with another headquarters, organic units return to the control of their organic headquarters after completing the mission.

Assigned. Assign is to place units or personnel in an organization where such placement is relatively permanent, and/or where such organization controls and administers the units or personnel for the primary function, or greater portion of the functions, of the unit or personnel (JP 3-0). Unless specifically stated, this relationship includes administrative control.

Attached. Attach is the placement of units or personnel in an organization where such placement is relatively temporary (JP 3-0). A unit that is temporarily placed into an organization is attached.

Operational Control. Operational control is the authority to perform those functions of command over subordinate forces involving organizing and employing commands and forces, assigning tasks, designating objectives, and giving authoritative direction necessary to accomplish the mission (JP 1).

Tactical Control. Tactical control is the authority over forces that is limited to the detailed direction and control of movements or maneuvers within the operational area necessary to accomplish missions or tasks assigned (JP 1). Tactical control allows commanders below combatant command level to apply force and direct tactical use of logistic assets but does not provide authority to change organizational structure or direct administrative and logistical support.

Army Command & Support Relationships

Ref: FM 6-0 (C2), Commander and Staff Organization and Operations (Apr '16), app. B.

Army command and support relationships are similar but not identical to joint command authorities and relationships. Differences stem from the way Army forces task-organize internally and the need for a system of support relationships between Army forces. Another important difference is the requirement for Army commanders to handle the administrative support requirements that meet the needs of Soldiers

A. Command Relationships

Army command relationships define superior and subordinate relationships between unit commanders. By specifying a chain of command, command relationships unify effort and enable commanders to use subordinate forces with maximum flexibility. Army command relationships identify the degree of control of the gaining Army commander. The type of command relationship often relates to the expected longevity of the relationship between the headquarters involved and quickly identifies the degree of support that the gaining and losing Army commanders provide.

If relationship is:	Then inherent responsibilities:							
	Have command relationship with:	May be task-organized by: [1]	Unless modified, ADCON have responsibility through:	Are assigned position or AO by:	Provide liaison to:	Establish/ maintain communications with:	Have priorities established by:	Can impose on gaining unit further command or support relationship of:
Organic	All organic forces organized with the HQ	Organic HQ	Army HQ specified in organizing document	Organic HQ	N/A	N/A	Organic HQ	Attached; OPCON; TACON; GS; GSR; R; DS
Assigned	Combatant command	Gaining HQ	Gaining Army HQ	OPCON chain of command	As required by OPCON	As required by OPCON	ASCC or Service-assigned HQ	As required by OPCON HQ
Attached	Gaining unit	Gaining unit	Gaining Army HQ	Gaining unit	As required by gaining unit	Unit to which attached	Gaining unit	Attached; OPCON; TACON; GS; GSR; R; DS
OPCON	Gaining unit	Parent unit and gaining unit; gaining unit may pass OPCON to lower HQ[1]	Parent unit	Gaining unit	As required by gaining unit	As required by gaining unit and parent unit	Gaining unit	OPCON; TACON; GS; GSR; R; DS
TACON	Gaining unit	Parent unit	Parent unit	Gaining unit	As required by gaining unit	As required by gaining unit and parent unit	Gaining unit	TACON;GS GSR; R; DS

Note: [1] In NATO, the gaining unit may not task-organize a multinational force. (See TACON.)

ADCON administrative control
AO area of operations
ASCC Army Service component command
DS direct support
GS general support
GSR general support–reinforcing
HQ headquarters
N/A not applicable
NATO North Atlantic Treaty Organization
OPCON operational control
R reinforcing
TACON tactical control

Ref: FM 6-0 (C2), Commander and Staff Organization and Operations, table B-2, p. B-5.

B. Support Relationships

Table B-3 on the following page lists Army support relationships. Army support relationships are not a command authority and are more specific than the joint support relationships. Commanders establish support relationships when subordination of one unit to another is inappropriate. Commanders assign a support relationship when—

- The support is more effective if a commander with the requisite technical and tactical expertise controls the supporting unit, rather than the supported commander. The echelon of the supporting unit is the same as or higher than that of the supported unit. For example, the supporting unit may be a brigade, and the supported unit may be a battalion. It would be inappropriate for the brigade to be subordinated to the battalion, hence the use of an support relationship.
- The supporting unit supports several units simultaneously. The requirement to set support priorities to allocate resources to supported units exists. Assigning support relationships is one aspect of mission command.

If relationship is:	Then inherent responsibilities:							
	Have command relationship with:	May be task-organized by:	Receive sustainment from:	Are assigned position or an area of operations by:	Provide liaison to:	Establish/ maintain communications with:	Have priorities established by:	Can impose on gaining unit further command or support relationship by:
Direct support[1]	Parent unit	Parent unit	Parent unit	Supported unit	Supported unit	Parent unit; supported unit	Supported unit	See note[1]
Reinforcing	Parent unit	Parent unit	Parent unit	Reinforced unit	Reinforced unit	Parent unit; reinforced unit	Reinforced unit; then parent unit	Not applicable
General support–reinforcing	Parent unit	Parent unit	Parent unit	Parent unit	Reinforced unit and as required by parent unit	Reinforced unit and as required by parent unit	Parent unit; then reinforced unit	Not applicable
General support	Parent unit	Parent unit	Parent unit	Parent unit	As required by parent unit	As required by parent unit	Parent unit	Not applicable

Note: [1] Commanders of units in direct support may further assign support relationships between their subordinate units and elements of the supported unit after coordination with the supported commander.

Ref: FM 6-0 (C2), Commander and Staff Organization and Operations, table B-3, p. B-6.

Army support relationships allow supporting commanders to employ their units' capabilities to achieve results required by supported commanders. Support relationships are graduated from an exclusive supported and supporting relationship between two units—as in direct support—to a broad level of support extended to all units under the control of the higher headquarters—as in general support. Support relationships do not alter administrative control. Commanders specify and change support relationships through task organization.

Direct support is a support relationship requiring a force to support another specific force and authorizing it to answer directly to the supported force's request for assistance (ADRP 5-0). A unit assigned a direct support relationship retains its command relationship with its parent unit, but is positioned by and has priorities of support established by the supported unit.

General support is that support which is given to the supported force as a whole and not to any particular subdivision thereof (JP 3-09.3). Units assigned a GS relationship are positioned and have priorities established by their parent unit.

Reinforcing is a support relationship requiring a force to support another supporting unit (ADRP 5-0). Only like units (for example, artillery to artillery) can be given a reinforcing mission. A unit assigned a reinforcing support relationship retains its command relationship with its parent unit, but is positioned by the reinforced unit. A unit that is reinforcing has priorities of support established by the reinforced unit, then the parent unit.

General support-reinforcing is a support relationship assigned to a unit to support the force as a whole and to reinforce another similar-type unit (ADRP 5-0). A unit assigned a general support-reinforcing (GSR) support relationship is positioned and has priorities established by its parent unit and secondly by the reinforced unit.

III. Unit Listing Sequence

Ref: FM 6-0 (C2), Commander and Staff Organization and Operations (Apr '16), pp. D-3 to D-6.

Order writers group units by headquarters. They list major subordinate maneuver units first (for example, 2d ABCT; 1-77th IN; A/4-52d CAV). Order writers place them by size in numerical order. They list brigade combat teams (BCTs) ahead of combat aviation brigades. In cases where two BCTs are numbered the same, order writers use the division number (by type). For example, 1st ABCT (armored brigade combat team) 1st Infantry Division (Mechanized) is listed before the 1st ABCT 1st Armored Division (AD). In turn, the 1st ABCT 1st Armored Division is listed before the 1st ABCT 1st Cavalry Division. Combined arms battalions are listed before battalions, and company teams before companies. Order writers follow maneuver units with multifunctional supporting units in the following order: fires, battlefield surveillance, maneuver enhancement, and sustainment. Supporting units (in alpha-numerical order) follow multifunctional supporting units. The last listing should be any special troops units under the command of the force headquarters.

Order writers use a plus (+) symbol when attaching one or more subordinate elements of a similar function to a headquarters. They use a minus symbol (–) when deleting one or more subordinate elements of a similar function to a headquarters. Order writers always show the symbols in parenthesis. They do not use a plus symbol when the receiving headquarters is a combined arms task force or company team. Order writers do not use plus and minus symbols together (as when a headquarters detaches one element and receives attachment of another); they use the symbol that portrays the element's combat power with respect to other similar elements. Order writers do not use either symbol when two units swap subordinate elements and their combat power is unchanged.

If applicable, order writers list task organizations according to phases of the operation. When the effective attachment time of a nonorganic unit to another unit differs from the effective time of the plan or order, order writers add the effective attachment time in parentheses after the attached unit—for example, 1-80 IN (OPCON 2 ABCT Phase II). They list this information either in the task organization (preferred) or in paragraph 1c of the plan or order, but not both. For clarity, order writers list subsequent command or support relationships under the task organization in parentheses following the affected unit—for example, "...on order, OPCON (operational control) to 2 ABCT" is written (O/O OPCON 2 ABCT).

Long or complex task organizations are displayed in outline format in Annex A (Task Organization) of the OPLAN or OPORD in lieu of being placed in the base plan or order. Units are listed under the headquarters to which they are allocated or that they support in accordance with the organizational taxonomy previously provided in this chapter. The complete unit task organization for each major subordinate unit should be shown on the same page. Order writers only show command or support relationships if they are other than organic or attached. Other Services and multinational forces recognize and understand this format. Planners should use it during joint and multinational operations.

Order writers list subordinate units under the higher headquarters to which they are assigned, attached, or in support. They place direct support (DS) units below the units they support. Order writers indent subordinate and supporting units two spaces. They identify relationships other than attached with parenthetical terms—for example, (GS) or (DS).

Order writers provide the numerical designations of units as Arabic numerals, unless they are shown as Roman numerals. For example, an Army corps is numbered in series beginning with Roman numeral "I"—for example, I Corps or XVIII Airborne Corps.

During multinational operations, order writers insert the country code between the numeric designation and the unit name—for example, 3d (DE) Corps. (Here, DE designates that the corps is German. ADRP 1-02 contains authorized country codes.)

Order writers use abbreviated designations for organic units. They use the full designation for nonorganic units—for example, 1-52 FA (MLRS) (GS), rather than 1-52 FA. They specify a unit's command or support relationship only if it differs from that of its higher headquarters.

Order writers designate task forces with the last name of the task force (TF) commander (for example, TF WILLIAMS), a code name (for example, TF DESERT DRAGON), or a number.

For unit designation at theater army level, order writers list major subordinate maneuver units first, placing them in alpha-numerical order, followed by multifunctional brigades in the following order: fires, intelligence, maneuver enhancement, sustainment, then followed by functional brigades in alpha-numerical order, and any units under the command of the force headquarters. For each function following maneuver, they list headquarters in the order of commands, brigades, groups, battalions, squadrons, companies, detachments, and teams.

Plans & Orders

	Corps	Division	Brigade	Battalion	Company
Movement and Maneuver	Divisions Separate maneuver brigades or battalions Combat aviation brigades or battalions Special operations forces - Ranger - Special forces MISO	Brigade-size ground units in alpha-numerical order - Infantry - Armor - Stryker Battalion TF - Named TFs in alphabetical order - Numbered TFs in numerical order MISO Combat aviation brigade Special operations forces - Ranger - Special forces	Battalion TFs Battalions or squadrons - Combined arms - Infantry - Reconnaissance Company teams Companies Air cavalry squadrons MISO	Company teams - Named teams in alphabetical order - Letter designated teams in alphabetical order Companies or troops (in alphabetical order) - Infantry - Armor - Stryker MISO	Platoons - Organic platoons - Attached platoons - Weapons squads
Fires	Fires brigade USAF air support unit - Air defense	Fires brigade USAF air support unit - Air defense	Fires battalion USAF air support unit - Air defense	FA batteries Fire support team Mortar platoon USAF air support unit - Air defense	FA firing platoons Fire support team Mortar section - Air defense
Intelligence	Battlefield surveillance brigade - MI - Recon squads - Human terrain team	Battlefield surveillance brigade - MI - Recon squads - Human terrain team	CI teams Ground sensor teams Human terrain team HUMINT teams Scout platoon TUAS platoon	CI teams Ground sensor teams HUMINT teams Scout platoon TUAS platoon	CI teams Ground sensor teams HUMINT teams
Protection	MEB Functional brigades - Air defense - CBRN - Engineer - EOD - Military police	MEB Functional brigades - Air defense - CBRN - Engineer - EOD - Military police	Functional battalions or companies or batteries and detachments - Air defense - CBRN - Engineer - EOD - Military police	Functional companies or batteries and detachments - Air defense - CBRN - Engineer - EOD - Military police	Functional platoons and detachments - Air defense - CBRN - Engineer - EOD - Military police
Sustainment	Sustainment brigade (attached functional units are listed in alpha-numerical order) - Contracting - Finance - Ordnance - Personnel services - Transportation - Quartermaster Medical brigade (support)	Sustainment brigade (attached functional units are listed in alpha-numerical order) - Contracting - Finance - Ordnance - Personnel services - Transportation - Quartermaster Medical brigade (support)	Brigade support battalion (attached or supporting functional units are listed first by branch in alphabetical order and then in numerical order)	Forward support company (attached or supporting functional units are listed first by branch in alphabetical order and then in numerical order)	Attached or supporting functional platoons and teams listed in alpha-numerical order

Ref: FM 6-0 (C2), Commander and Staff Organization and Operations (Apr '16), table D-1, pp. D-3 to D-4.

IV. Outline Format (Sample)

Ref: FM 6-0 (C2), Commander and Staff Organization and Operations (Apr '16), pp. D-8 to D-9.

Use the outline format for listing units as shown in the example below. (An acronym list is helpful if attached units are unfamiliar with Army acronyms.) If applicable, list task organization according to the phases of the operation during which it applies.

[CLASSIFICATION]

ANNEX A (TASK ORGANIZATION) TO OPERATION PLAN/ORDER [number] [(code name)]—[issuing headquarters] [(classification of title)]

(sample task organization)

- 2/52 ABCT
  - 1-31 IN (-)
  - 1-30 AR (-)
  - 1-20 CAV
  - A/4-52 CAV (ARS) (DS)
  - 2-606 FA (2x8)
    - TACP/52 ASOS (USAF)
  - 521 BSB
    - 2/2/311 QM CO (MA)
    - 1/B/2-52 AV (GSAB) (TACON)
    - 2/577 MED CO (GRD AMB) (attached)
    - 842 FST
  - 2 BSTB
    - 31 EN CO (MRBC) (DS)
    - 63 EOD
    - 2/244 EN CO (RTE CL) (DS)
    - 1/2/1/55 SIG CO (COMCAM)
  - 2D MP PLT
    - RTS TM 1/A/52 BSTB
    - RTS TM 2/A/52 BSTB
    - RTS TM 3/A/52 BSTB
    - RTS TM
- 87 IBCT
  - 1-80 IN
  - 2-80 IN
  - 3-13 CAV
  - A/3-52 AV (ASLT) (DS)
  - B/1-52 AV (ARB) (DS)
  - C/4-52 CAV (ARS) (-) (DS)
  - 2-636 FA
    - A/3-52 FA (+)
    - TACP/52 ASOS (USAF)
    - Q37 52 FA BDE (GS)
  - 99 BSB
    - 845 FST
    - 1/577 MED CO (GRD AMB)
    - 3/B/2-52 AV (GSAB) (TACON)
    - 1/2/311 QM CO (MA)
  - 87 BSTB
    - 53 EOD
    - 3/2/1/55 SIG CO (COMCAM)
    - B/420 CA BN
    - 2 HCT/3/B/52 BSTB
    - 745 EN CO (MAC) (DS)
    - 1/1/52 CM CO (R/D) (R)
    - 2/467 CM CO (MX) (S)
    - 1/1102 MP CO (DS)
- 4/A/52 BSTB

- 2/54 ABCT
  - 4-77 IN
  - 8-40 AR
  - 3-20 CAV
  - 2/C/4-52 CAV (ARS) (DS)
  - 2-607 FA
    - TACP/52 ASOS (USAF)
  - 105 BSB
    - 3/2/311 QM CO (MA)
    - 2/B/2-52 AV (GSAB) (TACON)
    - 843 FST
    - 3/577 MED CO (GRD AMB)
  - 3 BSTB
    - A 388 CA BN
    - 1/244 EN CO (RTE CL) (DS)
    - 763 EOD
    - 2/2/1/55 SIG CO (COMCAM)
  - 3D MP PLT
- 52 CAB AASLT
  - HHC/52 CAB
    - 1/B/1-31 IN (DIV QRF) (OPCON)
  - 1-52 AV (ARB) (-)
  - 4-52 CAV (ARS) (-)
  - 3-52 AV (ASLT) (-)
  - 2-52 AV (GSAB)
  - 1 (TUAS)/B/52 BSTB (-) (GS)
  - 2/694 EN CO (HORIZ) (DS)
- 52 FIRES BDE
  - HHB
  - TAB (-)
  - 1-52 FA (MLRS)
  - 3-52 FA (-) (M109A6)
  - 1/694 EN CO (HORIZ) (DS)
- 17 MEB 52 ID
  - 25 CM BN (-)
  - 700 MP BN
  - 7 EN BN
  - 2/2/1/55 SIG CO (COMCAM)
  - 11 ASOS (USAF)

- 116 ABCT (+)
  - 3-116 AR
  - 1-163 IN
  - 2-116 AR
  - 1-148 FA
  - 145 BSB
    - 4/B/2-52 AV (GSAB) (TACON)
    - 4/2/311 QM CO (MA)
    - 4/577 MED CO (GRD AMB)
    - 844 FST
  - 116 BSTB
    - 366 EN CO (SAPPER) (DS)
    - 1/401 EN CO (ESC) (DS)
    - 2/244 EN CO (RTE CL) (DS)
    - 52 EOD
    - 1/301 MP CO
    - 1/3/1/55 SIG CO (COMCAM)
    - 1/467 CM CO (MX) (S)
    - C/388 CA BN
  - 116 MP PLT
- 52 SUST BDE
  - 52 BTB
  - 520 CSSB
  - 521 CSSB
  - 10 CSH
    - 168 MMB
- 52 HHB
  - A/1-30 AR (DIV RES)
  - 35 SIG CO (-) (DS)
  - 154 LTF
  - 2/1/55 SIG CO (-)
  - 14 PAD
  - 388 CA BN (-) (DS)

[page number]

[CLASSIFICATION]

Ref: FM 6-0 (C2), Commander and Staff Organization and Operations, fig. D-1, p. D-8.

III. Administrative Instructions & Examples

Ref: FM 6-0 (C2), Commander and Staff Organization and Operations (Apr '16), pp. C-5 to C-10.

I. Administrative Instructions

The following information pertains to administrative instructions for preparing all plans and orders. Unless otherwise stated, the term order refers to both plans and orders. The term base order refers to the main body of a plan or order without annexes.

Regardless of echelon, all orders adhere to the same guidance. Show all paragraph headings on written orders. A paragraph heading with no text will state "None" or "See [attachment type] [attachment letter or number]." In this context, attachment is a collective term for annex, appendix, tab, and exhibit.

The base order and all attachments follow a specific template for the paragraph layout. The paragraph title begins with a capital letter and is underlined. For example, "situation" is <u>Situation</u>. All subparagraphs and subtitles begin with capital letters and are underlined. For example, "concept of operations" is <u>Concept of Operations</u>.

When a paragraph is subdivided, it must have at least two subdivisions. The tabs are 0.25 inches and the space is doubled between paragraphs. Subsequent lines of text for each paragraph may be flush left or equally indented at the option of the chief of staff or executive officer, as long as consistency is maintained throughout the order.

A. Acronyms and Abbreviations

Order writers use acronyms and abbreviations to save time and space, if these acronyms and abbreviations do not cause confusion. However, order writers do not sacrifice clarity for brevity. Order writers keep acronyms and abbreviations consistent throughout the order and its attachments. They do not use acronyms and abbreviations not found in ADP 1-02 or JP 1-02. Before using an entire acronym or abbreviation, at its first use in the document order writers use the full form of the term and then place the acronym or abbreviation between parentheses immediately after the term. After this first use, they use the acronym or abbreviation throughout the document.

B. Digital Display and Common Access to Information

To ensure standardization and the ability to understand the common operational picture (COP), commanders must designate the standardized system to display, access, and share information. Commanders also designate which COP the command will use to gain shared understanding.

B. Place and Direction Designations

Order writers describe locations or points on the ground by:

- Providing the map datum used throughout the order
- Referring to military grid reference system coordinates.
- Referring to longitude and latitude, if available maps do not have the military grid reference system.

Order writers designate directions in one of two ways:

- As a point of the compass. For example, north or northeast
- As a magnetic, grid, or true bearing, stating the unit of measure. For example, 85 degrees (magnetic)

When first mentioning a place or feature on a map, order writers print the name in capital letters exactly as spelled on the map and show its complete grid coordinates (grid zone designator, 100-kilometer grid square, and four-, six-, eight-, or ten-digit grid coordinates) in parentheses after it. When first using a control measure (such as a contact point), order writers print the name or designation of the point followed by its complete grid coordinates in parentheses. Thereafter, they repeat the coordinates only for clarity.

Order writers describe areas by naming the northernmost (12 o'clock) point first and the remaining points in clockwise order. They describe positions from left to right and from front to rear, facing the enemy. To avoid confusion, order writers identify flanks by compass directions, rather than right or left of the friendly force.

If the possibility of confusion exists when describing a route, order writers add a compass direction for clarity (for example, "The route is northwest along the road LAPRAIRIE–DELSON."). If a particular route already has a planning name, such as main supply route SPARTAN, order writers refer to the route using only that designator.

Order writers designate trails, roads, and railroads by the names of places along them or with grid coordinates. They precede place names with a trail, road, or railroad (for example, "road GRANT– CODY"). Order writers designate the route for a movement by listing a sequence of grids from the start point to the release point. Otherwise, they list the sequence of points from left to right or front to rear, facing the enemy.

Order writers identify riverbanks as north, south, east, or west. In wet gap-crossing operations, they identify riverbanks as either near or far.

Plans & Orders

C. Naming Conventions

Unit SOPs normally designate naming conventions for graphics. Otherwise, planners select them. For clarity, avoid multiword names, such as "Junction City." Simple names are better than complex ones. To ensure operations security, avoid assigning names that could reveal unit identities, such as the commander's name or the unit's home station. Do not name sequential phase lines and objectives in alphabetical order. For memory aids, use sets of names designated by the type of control measure or subordinate unit. For example, the division might use colors for objective names and minerals for phase line names.

D. Classification Markings

AR 380-5 contains a detailed description of marking techniques, transmitting procedures, and other classification instructions. Each page and portions of the text on that page will be marked with the appropriate abbreviation ("TS" for TOP SECRET, "S" for SECRET, "C" for CONFIDENTIAL, or "U for UNCLASSIFIED). Place classification markings at the top and bottom of each page. All paragraphs must have the appropriate classification marking immediately following the alphanumeric designation of the paragraph (preceding the first word if the paragraph is not numbered).

The abbreviation "FOUO" will be used in place of "U" when a portion is UNCLASSIFIED but contains "For Official Use Only" information. AR 25-55 contains the definition and policy application of FOUO markings.

Leaders may have to handle Department of State information. Sensitive But Unclassified (SBU) information is information originating from within the Department of State.

The Army continues its involvement in numerous multinational commitments and operations. This involves an understanding of how commanders may release to or withhold information from select unified action partners. Intelligence information previously marked "Not Releasable To Foreign Nationals" (NOFORN) continues to be non-releasable to foreigners and must be referred to the originator. NOFORN is not authorized for new classification decisions. A limited amount of information will contain the marking "U.S. ONLY". This information cannot be shared with any foreign government.

E. Expressing Unnamed Dates and Hours

Ref: FM 6-0 (C2), Commander and Staff Organization and Operations (Apr '16), pp. C-6 to C-9.

Order writers use specific letters to designate unnamed dates and times in plans and orders.

Term	Designates
C-Day	The unnamed day on which a deployment operation commences or is to commence (JP 5-0).
D-day	The unnamed day on which a particular operation commences or is to commence (JP 3-02).
F-hour	The effective time of announcement by the Secretary of Defense to the Military Departments of a decision to mobilize reserve units (JP 3-02).
H-hour	The specific hour on D-Day at which a particular operation commences (JP 5-0).
L-hour	The specific hour on C-day at which a deployment operation commences or is to commence (JP 5-0).
M-day	The term used to designate the unnamed day on which full mobilization commences or is due to commence (JP 3-02).
N-day	The unnamed day an active duty unit is notified for deployment or redeployment (JP 3-02).
P-hour	The specific hour on D-day at which a parachute assault commences with the exit of the first Soldier from an aircraft over a designated drop zone. P-hour may or may not coincide with H-hour.
R-day	Redeployment day. The day on which redeployment of major combat, combat support, and combat service support forces begins in an operation (JP 3-02).
S-day	The day the President authorizes Selective reserve callup (not more than 200,000) (JP 3-02).
T-day	The effective day coincident with Presidential declaration of national emergency and authorization of partial mobilization (not more than 1,000,000 personnel exclusive of the 200,000 callup) (JP 3-02).
W-day	Declared by the President, W-day is associated with an adversary decision to prepare for war (unambiguous strategic warning) (JP 3-02).

Ref: FM 6-0 (C2), Commander and Staff Organization & Operations, table C-1, p. C-8.

The effective time for implementing the plan or order is the same as the date-time group of the order. Order writers express the date and time as a six-digit date-time group. The first two digits indicate the day of the month; the next four digits indicate the time. The letter at the end of the time indicates the time zone. Staffs add the month and year to the date-time group to avoid confusion. For example, a complete date-time group for 6 August 20XX at 1145 appears as 061145Z August 20XX.

If the effective time of any portion of the order differs from that of the order, staffs identify those portions at the beginning of the coordinating instructions (in paragraph 3). For example, order writers may use "Effective only for planning on receipt" or "Task organization effective 261300Z May 20XX."

Order writers express all times in a plan or order in terms of one time zone, for example ZULU (Z) or LOCAL. (Order writers do not abbreviate local time as [L]. The abbreviation for the LIMA time is L.) Staffs include the appropriate time zone indicator in the heading data and mission statement. For example, the time zone indicator for Central Standard Time in the continental United States is SIERRA. When daylight savings time is in effect, the time zone indicator for Central Standard Time is ROMEO. The relationship of local time to ZULU time, not the geographic location, determines the time zone indicator to use.

When using inclusive dates, staffs express them by writing both dates separated by a dash (6–9 August 20XX or 6 August–6 September 20XX). They express times in the 24-hour clock system by means of four-digit Arabic numbers, including the time zone indicator.

F. Attachments (Annexes, Appendixes, Tabs, and Exhibits)

Ref: FM 6-0 (C2), Commander and Staff Organization and Operations (Apr '16), pp. C-6 to C-9 and table C-2, pp. C-17 to C-21.

Attachments (annexes, appendixes, tabs, and exhibits) are information management tools. They simplify orders by providing a structure for organizing information. However, even when attachments are used, an effective base order contains enough information to be executed without them. The organizational structure for attachments to Army OPLANs and OPORDs is in table C-2 on page C-17 through C-21.

Attachments are part of an order. Using them increases the base order's clarity and usefulness by keeping the base order or plan short. Attachments include information (such as sustainment), administrative support details, and instructions that expand upon the base order.

Commanders and staffs are not required to develop all attachments listed in table C-2. The number and type of attachments depend on the commander, level of command, and complexity or needs of a particular operation. Minimizing the number of attachments keeps the order consistent with completeness and clarity. If the information relating to an attachment's subject is brief, the order writer places the information in the base order and "omits" the attachment. (See paragraph C-64 for information on omitting attachments.)

Staffs list attachments under an appropriate heading at the end of the document they expand. For example, they list annexes at the end of the base order, appendixes at the end of annexes, and so forth.

Army OPLANs or OPORDs do not use Annexes I and O as attachments. Army orders label these annexes "Not Used." Annexes T, X, and Y are available for use and are labeled as "Spare." If the commander needs to use any of these three spare annexes (T, X, Y), orders writers use the same attachment format as described as figure C-3 on page C-22 and C-23. When an attachment required by doctrine or an SOP is unnecessary, staffs indicate this by stating, "Type of attachment and its alphanumeric identifier omitted."

Staffs refer to attachments by letter or number and title using the following naming conventions:

Annexes. Staffs designate annexes with capital letters, for example, Annex D (Fires) to OPORD 09 06—1 ID.

Appendixes. Staffs designate appendixes with Arabic numbers, for example, Appendix 1 (Intelligence Estimate) to Annex B (Intelligence) to OPORD 09-06—1 ID.

Tabs. Staffs designate tabs with capital letters, for example, Tab B (Target Synchronization Matrix) to Appendix 3 (Targeting) to Annex D (Fires) to OPORD 09-06—1 ID.

Exhibits. Staffs designate exhibits with Arabic numbers, for example, Exhibit 1 (Traffic Circulation and Control) to Tab C (Transportation) to Appendix 1 (Logistics) to Annex F (Sustainment) to OPORD 09-06—1 ID.

If an attachment has wider distribution than the base order or is issued separately, the attachment requires a complete heading and acknowledgment instructions. When staffs distribute attachments with the base order, these elements are not required.

ANNEX A – TASK ORGANIZATION (G-5 or G-3 [S-3])
ANNEX B – INTELLIGENCE (G-2 [S-2])
- Appendix 1 – Intelligence Estimate
  - Tab A – Terrain (Engineer Officer)
  - Tab B – Weather (Staff Weather Officer)
  - Tab C – Civil Considerations
  - Tab D – Intelligence Preparation of the Battlefield Products
- Appendix 2 – Counterintelligence
- Appendix 3 – Signals Intelligence
- Appendix 4 – Human Intelligence
- Appendix 5 – Geospatial Intelligence
- Appendix 6 – Measurement and Signature Intelligence
- Appendix 7 – Open Source Intelligence

ANNEX C – OPERATIONS (G-5 or G-3 [S-3])
- Appendix 1 – Army Design Methodology Products
- Appendix 2 – Operation Overlay
- Appendix 3 – Decision Support Products
  - Tab A – Execution Matrix
  - Tab B – Decision Support Template and Matrix
- Appendix 4 – Gap Crossing Operations
  - Tab A – Traffic Control Overlay
- Appendix 5 – Air Assault Operations
  - Tab A – Pickup Zone Diagram
  - Tab B – Air Movement Table
  - Tab C – Landing Zone Diagram
- Appendix 6 – Airborne Operations
  - Tab A – Marshalling Plan
  - Tab B – Air Movement Plan
  - Tab C – Drop Zone/Extraction Zone Diagram
- Appendix 7 – Amphibious Operations
  - Tab A – Advance Force Operations
  - Tab B – Embarkation Plan
  - Tab C – Landing Plan

Plans & Orders

Tab D – Rehearsal Plan
Appendix 8 – Special Operations (G-3 [S-3])
Appendix 9 – Battlefield Obscuration (CBRN Officer)
Appendix 10 – Airspace (G-3 [S-3] or Airspace Control Officer)
Tab A – Air Traffic Services
Appendix 11 – Rules of Engagement (Staff Judge Advocate)
Tab A – No Strike List
Tab B – Restricted Target List (G-3 [S-3] with Staff Judge Advocate)
Appendix 12–Cyber Electromagnetic Activities (Electronic Warfare Officer)
Tab A–Offensive Cyberspace Operations
Tab B–Defensive Cyberspace Operations–Response Actions
Tab C–Electronic Attack
Tab D–Electronic Protection
Tab E–Electronic Warfare Support
Appendix 13–Military Information Support Operations (Military Information Support Officer)
Appendix 14–Military Deception (Military Deception Officer)
Appendix 15–Information Operations (Information Operations Officer)
ANNEX D – FIRES (Chief of Fires/Fire Support Officer)
Appendix 1 – Fire Support Overlay
Appendix 2 – Fire Support Execution Matrix
Appendix 3 – Targeting
Tab A – Target Selection Standards
Tab B – Target Synchronization Matrix
Tab C – Attack Guidance Matrix
Tab D – Target List Worksheets
Tab E – Battle Damage Assessment (G-2 [S-2])
Appendix 4 – Field Artillery Support
Appendix 5 – Air Support
Appendix 6 – Naval Fire Support
Appendix 7–Air and Missile Defense (Air and Missile Defense Officer)
Tab A–Enemy Air Avenues of Approach
Tab B–Enemy Air Order of Battle
Tab C–Enemy Theater Ballistic Missile Overlay
Tab D–Air and Missile Defense Protection Overlay
ANNEX E – PROTECTION (Chief of Protection/Protection Officer as designated by the commander)
Appendix 1–Operational Area Security
Appendix 2–Safety (Safety Officer)
Appendix 3–Operations Security
Appendix 4–Intelligence Support to Protection
Appendix 5–Physical Security
Appendix 6–Antiterrorism
Appendix 7–Police Operations (Provost Marshal)
Appendix 8–Survivability Operations
Appendix 9–Force Health Protection (Surgeon)
Appendix 10–Chemical, Biological, Radiological, and Nuclear Defense (CBRN Officer)
Appendix 11–Explosive Ordnance Disposal (EOD Officer)
Appendix 12–Coordinate Air and Missile Defense (Air Defense Officer)
Appendix 13–Personnel Recovery (Personnel Recovery Officer)
Appendix 14–Detainee and Resettlement
ANNEX F – SUSTAINMENT (Chief of Sustainment [S-4])
Appendix 1 – Logistics (G-4 [S-4])
Tab A – Sustainment Overlay
Tab B – Maintenance
Tab C – Transportation
Exhibit 1 – Traffic Circulation and Control (Provost Marshal)
Exhibit 2 – Traffic Circulation Overlay
Exhibit 3 – Road Movement Table
Exhibit 4 – Highway Regulation (Provost Marshal)
Tab D – Supply
Tab E – Field Services
Tab F – Distribution
Tab G – Contract Support Integration
Tab H – Mortuary Affairs
Tab I – Internment and Resettlement Support
Appendix 2 – Personnel Services Support (G-1 [S-1])
Tab A – Human Resources Support (G-1 [S-1])
Tab B – Financial Management (G-8)
Tab C – Legal Support (Staff Judge Advocate)
Tab D – Religious Support (Chaplain)
Tab E – Band Operations (G-1 [S-1])
Appendix 3 – Army Heath System Support (Surgeon)
ANNEX G – Engineer (Engineer Officer)
Appendix 1 – Mobility/Countermobility
Tab A – Obstacle Overlay
Appendix 2 – Survivability (Engineer Officer)
Appendix 3 – General Engineering
Appendix 4 – Geospatial Engineering
Appendix 5 – Environmental Considerations
Tab A – Environmental Assessments
Tab B – Environmental Assessment Exemptions
Tab C – Environmental Baseline Survey
ANNEX H – SIGNAL (G-6 [S-6])
Appendix 1–Defensive Cyberspace Operations
Appendix 2–Information Network Operations
Appendix 3–Voice, Video, and Data Network Diagrams
Appendix 4–Satellite Communications
Appendix 5–Foreign Data Exchanges
Appendix 6–Spectrum Management Operations
Appendix 7–Information Services
ANNEX I – Not Used
ANNEX J – PUBLIC AFFAIRS
Appendix 1–Public Affairs Running Estimate
Appendix 2–Public Affairs Guidance
ANNEX K – CIVIL AFFAIRS OPERATIONS (G-9 [S-9])
Appendix 1 – Execution Matrix
Appendix 2 – Populace and Resources Control Plan
Appendix 3 – Civil Information Management Plan
ANNEX L – INFORMATION COLLECTION (G-3 [S-3])
Appendix 1–Information Collection Plan
Appendix 2–Information Collection Overlay
ANNEX M – ASSESSMENT (G-5 [S-5] or G-3 [S-3])
Appendix 1 – Nesting of Assessment Efforts
Appendix 2 – Assessment Framework
Appendix 3 – Assessment Working Group
ANNEX N – SPACE OPERATIONS
ANNEX O – Not Used
ANNEX P – HOST-NATION SUPPORT (G-4 [S-4])
ANNEX Q – KNOWLEDGE MANAGEMENT (Knowledge Management Officer)
Appendix 1–Knowledge Management Decision Support Matrix
Appendix 2–Common Operational Picture Configuration Matrix
Appendix 3–Mission Command Information Systems Integration Matrix
Appendix 4–Content Management
Appendix 5–Battle Rhythm
ANNEX R – REPORTS (G-3 [S-3], G-5 [S-5], G-7, and Knowledge Management Officer)
ANNEX S – SPECIAL TECHNICAL OPERATIONS
Appendix 1 – Special Technical Operations Capabilities Integration Matrix
Appendix 2 – Functional Area I Program and Objectives
Appendix 3 – Functional Area II Program and Objectives
ANNEX T – Spare
ANNEX U – INSPECTOR GENERAL
ANNEX V – INTERAGENCY COORDINATION (G-3 [S-3] and G-9 [S-9])
ANNEX W – OPERATIONAL CONTRACT SUPPORT (G-4 [S-4])
ANNEX X – Spare
ANNEX Y –Spare
ANNEX Z – DISTRIBUTION (G-3 [S-3] and Knowledge Management Officer)

G. Expressing Time

The effective time for implementing the plan or order is the same as the date-time group of the order. Order writers express the date and time as a six-digit date-time group. The first two digits indicate the day of the month; the next four digits indicate the time. The letter at the end of the time indicates the time zone. Staffs add the month and year to the date-time group to avoid confusion. For example, a complete date-time group for 6 August 20XX at 1145 appears as 061145Z August 20XX.

If the effective time of any portion of the order differs from that of the order, staffs identify those portions at the beginning of the coordinating instructions (in paragraph 3). For example, order writers may use "Effective only for planning on receipt" or "Task organization effective 261300Z May 20XX."

Order writers express all times in a plan or order in terms of one time zone, for example ZULU (Z) or LOCAL. (Order writers do not abbreviate local time as [L]. The abbreviation for the LIMA time is L.) Staffs include the appropriate time zone indicator in the heading data and mission statement. For example, the time zone indicator for Central Standard Time in the continental United States is SIERRA. When daylight savings time is in effect, the time zone indicator for Central Standard Time is ROMEO. The relationship of local time to ZULU time, not the geographic location, determines the time zone indicator to use.

When using inclusive dates, staffs express them by writing both dates separated by a dash (6–9 August 20XX or 6 August–6 September 20XX). They express times in the 24-hour clock system by means of four-digit Arabic numbers, including the time zone indicator.

H. Identifying Pages

Staffs identify pages following the first page of plans and orders with a short title identification heading located two spaces under the classification marking. They include the number (or letter) designation of the plan, and the issuing headquarters. For example, OPLAN 09-15–23d AD (U) or Annex B (Intelligence) to OPLAN 09-15–23rd AD (U).

I. Numbering Pages

Order writers use the following convention to indicate page numbers:

- Order writers number the pages of the base order and each attachment separately beginning on the first page of each attachment. They use a combination of alphanumeric designations to identify each attachment.
- Order writers use Arabic numbers only to indicate page numbers. They place page numbers after the alphanumeric designation that identifies the attachment. (Use Arabic numbers without any proceeding alphanumeric designation for base order page numbers.) For example, the designation of the third page to Annex C is C-3. Order writers assign each attachment either a letter or Arabic number that corresponds to the letter or number in the attachment's short title. They assign letters to annexes, Arabic numbers to appendixes, letters to tabs, and Arabic numbers to exhibits. For example, the designation of the third page to Appendix 5 to Annex C is C-5-3.
- Order writers separate elements of the alphanumeric designation with hyphens. For example, the designation of the third page of exhibit 2 to Tab B to Appendix 5 to Annex C is C-5-B-2-3.

II. Example Plan & Order Formats

All plans and orders follow the five-paragraph order format. Attachments also follow the five-paragraph format except matrixes, overlays, and lists.

See following pages for examples.

Warning Order (WARNORD) Format

Ref: FM 6-0 (C2), Commander and Staff Organization and Operations (Apr '16), fig. C-4, p. C-24.

[Classification]
(Change from verbal orders, if any) (Optional)

Copy ## of ## copies
Issuing headquarters
Place of issue
Date-time group of signature
Message reference number

WARNING ORDER [number] Example: **WARNING ORDER #8**

(U) References: *Refer to higher headquarters' OPLAN/OPORD and identify map sheets for operation (Optional).*

(U) Time Zone Used Throughout the OPLAN/OPORD: (Optional)

(U) Task Organization: (Optional)

1. (U) Situation. *The situation paragraph describes the conditions and circumstances of the operational environment that impact operations in the following subparagraphs:*

a. (U) Area of Interest.

b. (U) Area of Operations.

c. (U) Enemy Forces.

d. (U) Friendly Forces.

e. (U) Interagency, Intergovernmental, and Nongovernmental Organizations.

f. (U) Civil Considerations.

g. (U) Attachments and Detachments. *Provide initial task organization.*

h. (U) Assumptions. *List any significant assumptions for order development.*

2. (U) Mission. *State the issuing headquarters' mission.*

3. (U) Execution.

a. (U) Initial Commander's Intent. *Provide brief commander's intent statement.*

b. (U) Concept of Operations. *This may be "to be determined" for an initial WARNORD.*

c. (U) Task to Subordinate Units. *Include any known tasks at time of issuance of WARNORD.*

d. (U) Coordinating Instructions.

4. (U) Sustainment. *Include known logistics, personnel, or health system prep tasks.*

5. (U) Command and Signal. *Include changes to existing order or state "no change."*

ACKNOWLEDGE:

[Commander's last name]
[Commander's rank]

OFFICIAL:
[Authenticator's name]
[Authenticator's position]

ANNEXES: *List annexes by letter and title.*

DISTRIBUTION: *List recipients.*

[page number]
[CLASSIFICATION]

Plans & Orders

Annotated OPLAN/OPORD Format

Ref: FM 6-0 (C2), Commander and Staff Organization and Operations (Apr '16), fig. C-2, pp. C-11 to C-17.

[CLASSIFICATION]

Place the classification at the top and bottom of every page of the OPLAN or OPORD. Place the classification marking at the front of each paragraph and subparagraph in parentheses. Refer to AR 380-5 for classification and release marking instructions.

Copy ## of ## copies
Issuing headquarters
Place of issue
Date-time group of signature
Message reference number

The first line of the heading is the copy number assigned by the issuing headquarters. A log is maintained of specific copies issued to addressees. The second line is the official designation of the issuing headquarters (for example, 1st Infantry Division). The third line is the place of issue. It may be a code name, postal designation, or geographic location. The fourth line is the date or date-time group that the plan or order was signed or issued and becomes effective unless specified otherwise in the coordinating instructions. The fifth line is a headquarters internal control number assigned to all plans and orders in accordance with unit standing operating procedures (SOPs).

OPERATION PLAN/ORDER [number] [(code name)] [(classification of title)]
Example: **OPORD 3411 (OPERATION DESERT DRAGON) (UNCLASSIFIED)**

Number plans and orders consecutively by calendar year. Include code name, if any.

(U) References: *List documents essential to understanding the OPLAN/OPORD. List references concerning a specific function in the appropriate attachments.*

(a) List maps and charts first. Map entries include series number, country, sheet names, or numbers, edition, and scale.

(b) List other references in subparagraphs labeled as shown.

(U) Time Zone Used Throughout the OPLAN/OPORD: *State the time zone used in the area of operations during execution. When the OPLAN/OPORD applies to units in different time zones, use Greenwich Mean (ZULU) Time.*

(U) Task Organization: *Describe the organization of forces available to the issuing headquarters and their command and support relationships. Refer to Annex A (Task Organization) if long or complicated.*

1. (U) Situation. *The situation paragraph describes the conditions of the operational environment that impact operations in the following subparagraphs:*

a. (U) Area of Interest. *Describe the area of interest. Refer to Annex B (Intelligence) as required.*

b. (U) Area of Operations. *Describe the area of operations (AO). Refer to the appropriate map by its subparagraph under references, for example, "Map, reference (b)." Refer to the Appendix 2 (Operation Overlay) to Annex C (Operations).*

(1) (U) Terrain. *Describe the aspects of terrain that impact operations. Refer to Annex B (Intelligence) as required.*

(2) (U) Weather. *Describe the aspects of weather that impact operations. Refer to Annex B (Intelligence) as required.*

[page number]
[CLASSIFICATION]

Plans & Orders

[CLASSIFICATION]

OPLAN/OPORD [number] [(code name)]—[issuing headquarters] [(classification of title)]
Place the classification and title of the OPLAN/OPORD and the issuing headquarters at the top of the second and any subsequent pages of the base plan or order.

c. (U) Enemy Forces. *Identify enemy forces and appraise their general capabilities. Describe the enemy's disposition, location, strength, and probable courses of action. Identify known or potential terrorist threats and adversaries within the AO. Refer to Annex B (Intelligence) as required.*

d. (U) Friendly Forces. *Briefly identify the missions of friendly forces and the objectives, goals, and missions of civilian organizations that impact the issuing headquarters in following subparagraphs:*

(1) (U) Higher Headquarters' Mission and Intent. *Identify and state the mission and commander's intent for headquarters two levels up and one level up from the issuing headquarters.*

(a) (U) Higher Headquarters Two Levels Up. *Identify the higher headquarters two levels up the paragraph heading (for example, Joint Task Force-18).*

1 (U) Mission.

2 (U) Commander's Intent.

(b) (U) Higher Headquarters. *Identify the higher headquarters one level up in the paragraph heading (for example, 1st (US) Armored Division).*

1 (U) Mission.

2 (U) Commander's Intent.

(2) (U) Missions of Adjacent Units. *Identify and state the missions of adjacent units and other units whose actions have a significant impact on the issuing headquarters.*

e. (U) Interagency, Intergovernmental, and Nongovernmental Organizations. *Identify and state the objective or goals and primary tasks of those non-Department of Defense organizations that have a significant role within the AO. Refer to Annex V (Interagency Coordination) as required.*

f. (U) Civil Considerations. *Describe the critical aspects of the civil situation that impact operations. Refer to Appepndix 1 (Intelligence Estimate) to Annex B (Intelligence) as required.*

g. (U) Attachments and Detachments. *List units attached to or detached from the issuing headquarters. State when each attachment or detachment is effective (for example, on order, on commitment of the reserve) if different from the effective time of the OPLAN/OPORD. Do not repeat information already listed in Annex A (Task Organization).*

h. (U) Assumptions. *List assumptions used in the development of the OPLAN/OPORD*

2. (U) Mission. *State the unit's mission—a short description of the who, what (task), when, where, and why (purpose) that clearly indicates the action to be taken and the reason for doing so.*

3. (U) Execution. *Describe how the commander intends to accomplish the mission in terms of the commander's intent, an overarching concept of operations, schemes of employment for each warfighting function, assessment, specified tasks to subordinate units, and key coordinating instructions in the subparagraphs below.*

[page number]
[CLASSIFICATION]

Continued on next page

Continued from previous page

a. (U) Commander's Intent. *Commanders develop their intent statement personally. The commander's intent is a clear, concise statement of what the force must do and the conditions the force must establish with respect to the enemy, terrain, and civil considerations that represent the desired end state. It succinctly describes what constitutes the success of an operation and provides the purpose and conditions that define that desired end state. The commander's intent must be easy to remember and clearly understood two echelons down. The commander's intent includes:*

Purpose–an expanded description of the operation's purpose beyond the "why" of the mission statement.

Key tasks–those significant activities the force as a whole must perform to achieve the desired end state.

End state–a description of the desired future conditions that represent success.

b. (U) Concept of Operations. *The concept of operations is a statement that directs the manner in which subordinate units cooperate to accomplish the mission and establishes the sequence of actions the force will use to achieve the end state. It is normally expressed in terms of the commander's desired operational framework as discussed in ADRP 3-0. It states the principal tasks required, the responsible subordinate units, and how the principal tasks complement one another. Normally, the concept of operations projects the status of the force at the end of the operation. If the mission dictates a significant change in tasks during the operation, the commander may phase the operation. The concept of operations may be a single paragraph, divided into two or more subparagraphs, or if unusually lengthy, summarize here with details located in Annex C (Operations). If the concept of operations is phased, describe each phase in a subparagraph. Label these subparagraphs as "Phase" followed by the appropriate Roman numeral, for example, "Phase I." If the operation is phased, all paragraphs and subparagraphs of the base order and all annexes must mirror the phasing established in the concept of operations. The operation overlay and graphic depictions of lines of effort help portray the concept of operations and are located in Annex C (Operations).*

c. (U) Scheme of Movement and Maneuver. *Describe the employment of maneuver units in accordance with the concept of operations. Provide the primary tasks of maneuver units conducting the decisive operation and the purpose of each. Next, state the primary tasks of maneuver units conducting shaping operations, including security operations, and the purpose of each. For offensive tasks, identify the form of maneuver. For defensive tasks, identify the type of defense. For stability tasks, describe the role of maneuver units by primary stability tasks. If the operation is phased, identify the main effort.*

(1) (U) Scheme of Mobility/Countermobility. *State the scheme of mobility/countermobility including priorities by unit or area. Refer to Annex G (Engineer) as required.*

(2) (U) Scheme of Battlefield Obscuration. *State the scheme of battlefield obscuration, including priorities by unit or area. Refer to Appendix 9 (Battlefield Obscuration) to Annex C (Operations) as required.*

(3) (U) Scheme of Information Collection. *Describe how the commander intends to use reconnaissance missions and surveillance tasks to support the concept of operations. Include the primary reconnaissance objectives. Refer to Annex L (Information Collection) as required.*

(Note: Army forces do not conduct reconnaissance and surveillance within the United States and its territories. For domestic operations, this paragraph is titled "Information Awareness and Assessment" and the contents of this paragraph comply with Executive Order 12333.)

Continued from previous page

d. (U) Scheme of Intelligence. *Describe how the commander envisions intelligence supporting the concept of operations. Include the priority of effort to situation development, targeting, and assessment. State the priority of intelligence support to units and areas. Refer to Annex B (Intelligence) as required.*

e. (U) Scheme of Fires. *Describe how the commander intends to use fires (lethal and nonlethal) to support the concept of operations with emphasis on the scheme of maneuver. State the fire support tasks and the purpose of each task. State the priorities for, allocation of, and restrictions on fires. Refer to Annex D (Fires) as required.*

f. (U) Scheme of Protection. *Describe how the commander envisions protection supporting the concept of operations. Include the priorities of protection by unit and area. Include survivability. Address the scheme of operational area security, including security for routes, bases, and critical infrastructure. Identify tactical combat forces and other reaction forces. Use subparagraphs for protection categories (for example, air and missile defense and explosive ordnance disposal) based on the situation. Refer to Annex E (Protection) as required.*

g. (U) Cyber Electromagnetic Activities. *Describe how cyber electromagnetic activities (including cyberspace operations, electronic warfare and spectrum management operations), supports the concept of operations. Refer to Appendix 12 (Cyber Electromagnetic Activities) to Annex C (Operations) as required. Refer to Annex H (Signal) for defensive cyberspace operations, network operations and spectrum management operations as required.*

h. (U) Stability Tasks. *Describe how stability tasks support the concept of operations. Describe how the commander envisions the conduct of stability tasks in coordination with other organizations. (See ADRP 3-07.) If other organizations or the host nation cannot provide for civil security, restoration of essential services, and civil control, then commanders with an assigned area of operations must do so with available resources, request additional resources, or request relief for these requirements from higher headquarters. Commanders assign specific responsibilities for stability tasks to subordinate units in paragraph 3j (Tasks to Subordinate Units) and paragraph 3k (Coordinating Instructions). Refer to Annex C (Operations) and Annex K (Civil Affairs Operations) as required.*

i. (U) Assessment. *Describe the priorities for assessment and identify the measures of effectiveness used to assess end state conditions and objectives. Refer to Annex M (Assessment) as required.*

j. (U) Tasks to Subordinate Units. *State the task assigned to each unit that reports directly to the headquarters issuing the order. Each task must include who (the subordinate unit assigned the task), what (the task itself), when, where, and why (purpose). Use a separate subparagraph for each unit. List units in task organization sequence. Place tasks that affect two or more units in paragraph 3k (Coordinating Instructions).*

k. (U) Coordinating Instructions. *List only instructions and tasks applicable to two or more units not covered in unit SOPs.*

(1) (U) Time or condition when the OPORD becomes effective.

(2) (U) Commander's Critical Information Requirements. *List commander's critical information requirements (CCIRs) here.*

(3) (U) Essential Elements of Friendly Information. *List essential elements of friendly information (EEFIs) here.*

(4) (U) Fire Support Coordination Measures. *List critical fire support coordination or control measures.*

Continued on next page

Plans & Orders

[Classification]

OPLAN/OPORD [number] [(code name)]—[issuing headquarters] [(classification of title)]

(5) (U) Airspace Coordinating Measures. *List critical airspace coordinating or control measures.*

(6) (U) Rules of Engagement. *List rules of engagement here. Refer to Appendix 11 (Rules of Engagement) to Annex C (Operations) as required.*

(Note: For operations within the United States and its territories, title this paragraph "Rules for the Use of Force").

(7) (U) Risk Reduction Control Measures. *State measures specific to this operation not included in unit SOPs. They may include mission-oriented protective posture, operational exposure guidance, troop-safety criteria, and fratricide prevention measures. Refer to Annex E (Protection) as required.*

(8) (U) Personnel Recovery Coordination Measures. *Refer to Appendix 13 (Personnel Recovery) to Annex E (Protection) as required.*

(9) (U) Environmental Considerations. *Refer to Appendix 5 (Environmental Considerations) to Annex G (Engineer) as required.*

(10) (U) Soldier and Leader Engagement. *State commander's guidance for target audiences and reporting requirements.*

(11) (U) Other Coordinating Instructions. *List in subparagraphs any additional coordinating instructions and tasks that apply to two or more units, such as the operational timeline and any other critical timing or events.*

4. (U) Sustainment. *Describe the concept of sustainment, including priorities of sustainment by unit or area. Include instructions for administrative movements, deployments, and transportation—or references to applicable appendixes—if appropriate. Use the following subparagraphs to provide the broad concept of support for logistics, personnel, and health service support. Provide detailed instructions for each sustainment subfunction in the appendixes to Annex F (Sustainment).*

a. (U) Logistics. *Refer to Annex F (Sustainment) as required.*

b. (U) Personnel. *Refer to Annex F (Sustainment) as required.*

c. (U) Health System Support. *Refer to Annex F (Sustainment) as required.*

5. (U) Command and Signal.

a. (U) Command.

(1) (U) Location of Commander and Key Leaders. *State where the commander and key leaders intend to be during the operation, by phase if the operation is phased.*

(2) (U) Succession of Command. *State the succession of command if not covered in the unit's SOPs.*

(3) (U) Liaison Requirements. *State liaison requirements not covered in the unit's SOPs.*

b. (U) Control.

(1) (U) Command Posts. *Describe the employment of command posts (CPs), including the location of each CP and its time of opening and closing, as appropriate. State the primary controlling CP for specific tasks or phases of the operation (for example, "Division tactical command post will control the air assault").*

(2) (U) Reports. *List reports not covered in SOPs. Refer to Annex R (Reports) as required.*

c. (U) Signal. *Describe the concept of signal support, including location and movement of key signal nodes and critical electromagnetic spectrum considerations throughout the operation. Refer to Annex H (Signal) as required.*

[page number]

[CLASSIFICATION]

Continued from previous page

[Classification]

OPLAN/OPORD [number] [(code name)]—[issuing headquarters] [(classification of title)]

ACKNOWLEDGE: *Include instructions for the acknowledgement of the OPLAN/OPORD by addressees. The word "acknowledge" may suffice. Refer to the message reference number if necessary. Acknowledgement of a plan or order means that it has been received and understood.*

[Commander's last name]
[Commander's rank]

The commander or authorized representative signs the original copy. If the representative signs the original, add the phrase "For the Commander." The signed copy is the historical copy and remains in the headquarters' files.

OFFICIAL:

[Authenticator's name]
[Authenticator's position]

Use only if the commander does not sign the original order. If the commander signs the original, no further authentication is required. If the commander does not sign, the signature of the preparing staff officer requires authentication and only the last name and rank of the commander appear in the signature block.

ANNEXES: *List annexes by letter and title. Army and joint OPLANs or OPORDs do not use Annexes I and O as attachments and in Army orders label these annexes "Not Used." Annexes T, X, and Y are available for use in Army OPLANs or OPORDs and are labeled as "Spare." When an attachment required by doctrine or an SOP is unnecessary, label it "Omitted."* *(See pp. 4-18 to 4-19 for further discussion of annexes).*

Annex A–Task Organization
Annex B –Intelligence
Annex C –Operations
Annex D–Fires
Annex E –Protection
Annex F –Sustainment
Annex G–Engineer
Annex H–Signal
Annex I–Not Used
Annex J–Public Affairs
Annex K–Civil Affairs Operations
Annex L –Information Collection
Annex M–Assessment
Annex N–Space Operations
Annex O–Not Used
Annex P –Host-Nation Support
Annex Q–Knowledge Management
Annex R –Reports
Annex S –Special Technical Operations
Annex T –Spare
Annex U–Inspector General
Annex V–Interagency Coordination
Annex W–Operational Contract Support
Annex X–Spare
Annex Y–Spare
Annex Z –Distribution

DISTRIBUTION: *Furnish distribution copies either for action or for information. List in detail those who are to receive the plan or order. Refer to Annex Z (Distribution) if lengthy.*

[page number]
[CLASSIFICATION]

Plans & Orders

Attachment Format (OPLANS/OPORDS)

Ref: FM 6-0 (C2), Commander and Staff Organization and Operations (Apr '16), fig. C-3, pp. C-22 to C-23. See pp. 4-16 to 4-17 for discussion of attachments (annexes, appendixes, tabs, and exhibits).

[CLASSIFICATION]

(Change from verbal orders, if any)

Copy ## of ## copies
Issuing headquarters
Place of issue
Date-time group of signature
Message reference number

Include heading if attachment is distributed separately from the base order or higher-level attachment.

[Attachment type and number/letter] [(attachment title)] TO [higher-level attachment type and number/letter, if applicable] [(higher-level attachment title, if applicable)] TO OPERATION PLAN/ORDER [number] [(code name)] [(classification of title)]

References: *Refer to higher headquarters' OPLAN or OPORD and identify map sheets for operation (Optional).*

Time Zone Used Throughout the Order:

1. (U) Situation. *Include information affecting the functional area that paragraph 1 of the OPLAN/OPORD does not cover or that needs to be expanded.*

a. (U) Area of Interest. *Refer to Annex B (Intelligence) as required.*

b. (U) Area of Operations. *Refer to Appendix 2 (Operation Overlay) to Annex C (Operations).*

(1) (U) Terrain. *Describe aspects of terrain that impact functional area operations. Refer to Annex B (Intelligence) as required.*

(2) (U) Weather. *Describe aspects of weather that impact functional area operations. Refer to Annex B (Intelligence) as required.*

c. (U) Enemy Forces. *List known and templated locations and activities of enemy functional area units for one echelon up and two echelons down. List enemy maneuver and other area capabilities that will impact friendly operations. State expected enemy courses of action and employment of enemy functional area assets. Refer to Annex B (Intelligence) as required.*

d. (U) Friendly Forces. *Outline the higher headquarters' plan as it pertains to the functional area. List designation, location, and outline of plan of higher, adjacent, and other functional area assets that support or impact the issuing headquarters or require coordination and additional support.*

e. (U) Interagency, Intergovernmental, and Nongovernmental Organizations. *Identify and describe other organizations in the area of operations that may impact the conduct of functional area operations or implementation of functional area-specific equipment and tactics.*

f. (U) Civil Considerations. *Describe critical aspects of the civil situation that impact functional area operations. Refer to Annex K (Civil Affairs Operations) as required.*

g. (U) Attachments and Detachments. *List units attached or detached only as necessary to clarify task organization. Refer to Annex A (Task Organization) as required.*

h. (U) Assumptions. *List any functional area-specific assumptions that support the annex development.*

[page number]
[CLASSIFICATION]

[CLASSIFICATION]

[Attachment type and number/letter] [(attachment title)] TO [higher-level attachment type and number/letter, if applicable] [(higher-level attachment title, if applicable)] TO OPERATION PLAN/ORDER [number] [(code name)]—[issuing headquarters] [(classification of title)]

2. (U) Mission. *State the mission of the functional area in support of the base plan or order.*

3. (U) Execution.

a. (U) Scheme of Support. *Describe how the functional area supports the commander's intent and concept of operations. Establish the priorities of support to units for each phase of the operation. Refer to Annex C (Operations) as required.*

b. (U) Tasks to Subordinate Units. *List functional area tasks assigned to specific subordinate units not contained in the base order.*

c. (U) Coordinating Instructions. *List only instructions applicable to two or more subordinate units not covered in the base order.*

4. (U) Sustainment. *Identify priorities of sustainment for functional area key tasks and specify additional instructions as required. Refer to Annex F (Sustainment) as required.*

5. (U) Command and Signal.

a. (U) Command. *State the location of key leaders.*

b. (U) Control. *State the functional area liaison requirements not covered in the base order.*

c. (U) Signal. *Address any functional area-specific communications requirements or reports. Refer to Annex H (Signal) as required.*

ACKNOWLEDGE: *Include only if attachment is distributed separately from the base order.*

OFFICIAL:

[Authenticator's name]

[Authenticator's position]

Either the commander or coordinating staff officer responsible for the functional area may sign attachments.

ATTACHMENT: *List lower-level attachments.*

DISTRIBUTION: *Show only if distributed separately from the base order or higher-level attachments.*

Note. See pp. 4-18 to 4-19 for discussion of administrative instructions for preparing attachments (annexes, appendixes, tabs, and exhibits).

[page number]
[CLASSIFICATION]

Overlay Order Format (Example)

Ref: FM 6-0 (C2), Commander and Staff Organization and Operations (Apr '16), fig. C-6, p. C-27.

An overlay order is a technique used to issue an order (normally a FRAGO) that has abbreviated instructions written on an overlay. Overlay orders combine a five-paragraph order with an operation overlay. Commanders may issue an overlay order when planning and preparation time is severely constrained and they must get the order to subordinate commanders as soon as possible. Commanders issue overlay orders by any suitable graphic method. An overlay order may consist of more than one overlay. A separate overlay or written annex can contain the service support coordination and organizations.

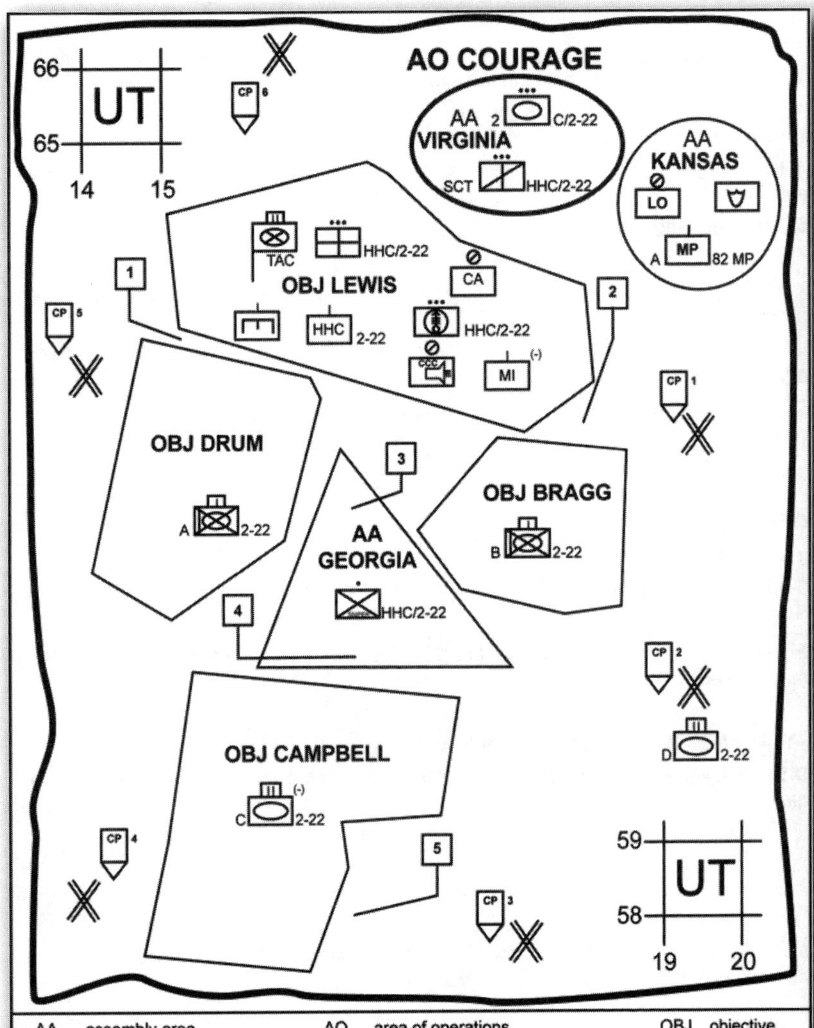

AA assembly area AO area of operations OBJ objective

TASK ORGANIZATION

TF Control	A/2-22 IN	B/2-22 IN	C/2-22 AR	D/2-22 AR
Sniper Sqd/HHC/2-22	1/A/2-22 IN 2/A/2-22 IN 3/C/2-22 AR	1/B/2-22 IN 2/B/2-22 IN 3/D/2-22 AR	1/C/2-22 AR 2/C/2-22 AR 3/A/2-22 IN	1/D/2-22 AR 2/D/2-22 AR 3/B/2-22 IN
HHC	HN Civil Authorities (DIRLAUTH)			
Scout PLT/2-22 IN Mortars/HHC/2-22 Medical/HHC/2-22	None			

MISSION:

TF 2-22 conducts a cordon and search in AO COURAGE NLT 120900ZJAN07 to capture anti-coalition forces (ACF) and seize weapons caches in order to limit the attacks on coalition forces.

COMMANDER'S INTENT:

Simultaneous occupation of outer cordon checkpoints (CKPs) to isolate search objectives and prevent ACF exfiltration or infiltration. Lead with information dissemination of information themes and messages. Exercise patience, discipline, and respect for host-nation population and property while conducting thorough searches. Immediate evacuation of ACF personnel to BCT Detainee Collection Point for processing and evacuation. End state is OBJ's LEWIS, DRUM, BRAGG and CAMPBELL free of ACF and companies postured for future operations.

EXECUTION – TASKS TO SUBORDINATE UNITS:

A/2-22 IN	**TF Decisive Operation:** Secure OBJ DRUM (inner cordon) and conduct search to capture ACF and seize weapons caches in order to limit the attacks on coalition forces.
B/2-22 IN	Secure OBJ BRAGG (inner cordon) and conduct search to capture ACF and seize weapons caches in order to limit the attacks on coalition forces.
C/2-22 AR	1. Secure OBJ CAMPBELL (inner cordon) and conduct search to capture ACF and seize weapons caches in order to limit the attacks on coalition forces.
D/2-22 AR	1. Secure the outer cordon at CKPs 1-6. 2. Secure AA KANSAS, for HNCA occupation.
HHC (-)/2-22	1. Secure TF tactical command post and TF Forward Aid Station in OBJ LEWIS.
Sniper/HHC/2-22	1. Occupy AA GEORGIA and provide observation and surveillance of OBJs DRUM, BRAGG, and CAMPBELL. 2. O/O deliver precision fires to destroy ACF.

Acknowledge: A/2-22 IN, B/2-22 IN, C/2-22 AR, D/2-22 AR, HHC/2-22, Sniper/2-22 IN

Fragmentary Order (FRAGORD) Format

Ref: FM 6-0 (C2), Commander and Staff Organization and Operations (Apr '16), fig. C-5, p. C-25.

[CLASSIFICATION]

(Change from verbal orders, if any) (Optional)

Copy ## of ## copies
Issuing headquarters
Place of issue
Date-time group of signature
Message reference number

FRAGMENTARY ORDER [number] to OPERATION PLAN/ORDER [number] [(code name)]—[(classification of title)]

(U) References: *Refer to higher the order being modified.*

(U) Time Zone Used Throughout the OPLAN/OPORD: *(Optional)*

1. (U) Situation. *Include any changes to the existing order or state "No change." For example, "No change to OPORD 03-XX."*

2. (U) Mission. *State "No change."*

3. (U) Execution. *Include any changes or state "No change."*

a. (U) Commander's Intent. *Include any changes or state "No change."*

b. (U) Concept of Operations. *Include any changes or state "No change."*

c. (U) Scheme Movement and Maneuver. *Include changes or state "No change."*

d. (U) Scheme of Intelligence. *Include any changes or state "No change."*

e. (U) Scheme of Fires. *Include any changes or state "No change."*

f. (U) Scheme of Protection. *Include any changes or state "No change."*

g. (U) Cyber Electromagnetic Activities. *Include changes or state "No change."*

h. (U) Stability Tasks. *Include any changes or state "No change."*

i. (U) Assessment. *Include any changes or state "No change."*

j. (U) Tasks to Subordinate Units. *Include any changes or state "No change."*

k. (U) Coordinating Instructions. *Include any changes or state "No change"*

4. (U) Sustainment. *Include any changes or state "No change."*

5. (U) Command and Signal. *Include any changes or state "No change."*

ACKNOWLEDGE:

[Commander's last name]
[Commander's rank]

OFFICIAL:

[Authenticator's name]

[Authenticator's position]

ANNEXES: *List annexes by letter and title. Army and joint OPLANs or OPORDs do not use Annexes I and O as attachments and in Army orders label these annexes "Not Used." Annexes T, X, and Y are available for use in Army OPLANs or OPORDs and are labeled as "Spare." When an attachment required by doctrine or an SOP is unnecessary, label it "Omitted."*

DISTRIBUTION:

[page number]
[CLASSIFICATION]

Plans & Orders

I. Mission Command

Ref: ADP 6-0, Mission Command (Jul '19) and ADP 3-0, Operations (Jul '19), p. 5-3.

I. Command & Control Warfighting Function

The command and control warfighting function is the related tasks and a system that enable commanders to synchronize and converge all elements of combat power (ADP 3-0). The primary purpose of the command and control warfighting function is to assist commanders in integrating the other elements of combat power to achieve objectives and accomplish missions. The command and control warfighting function consists of the command and control warfighting function tasks and the command and control system.

Command and Control Warfighting Function

The related tasks and a system that enables commanders to synchronize and converge all elements of combat power.

Tasks

- Command forces
- Control operations
- Drive the operations process
- Establish the command and control system

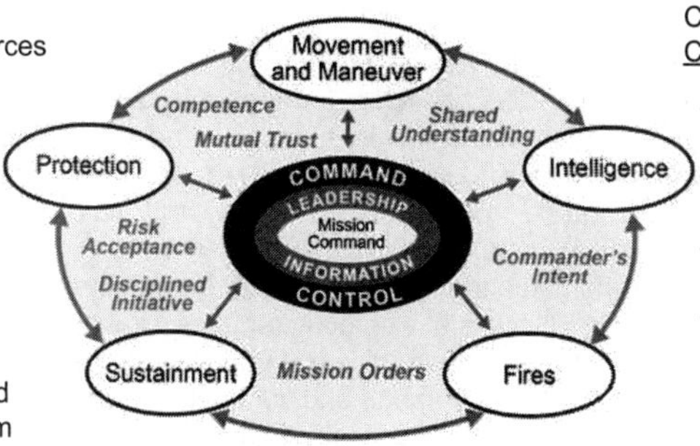

Command and Control System

- People
- Processes
- Networks
- Command posts

Ref: ADP 6-0 (Jul '19), Figure 1-2. Combat power model.

The command and control warfighting function tasks focus on integrating the activities of the other elements of combat power to accomplish missions. Commanders, assisted by their staffs, integrate numerous processes and activities within their headquarters and across the force through the mission command warfighting function:

- Command forces
- Control operations
- Drive the operations process *(see pp. 5-8 to 5-9)*
- Establish the command and control system

See p. 5-7 for discussion of specific warfighting function tasks as described in FM 3-0.

Mission Command: Command and Control of Army Forces

Ref: ADP 6-0, Mission Command (Jul '19), preface and introduction.

ADP 6-0, Mission Command: Command and Control of Army Forces, provides a discussion of the fundamentals of mission command, command and control, and the command and control warfighting function. It describes how commanders, supported by their staffs, combine the art and science of command and control to understand situations, make decisions, direct actions, and lead forces toward mission accomplishment.

This revision to ADP 6-0 represents an evolution of mission command doctrine based upon lessons learned since 2012. The use of the term mission command to describe multiple things—the warfighting function, the system, and a philosophy—created unforeseen ambiguity. Mission command replaced command and control, but in practical application it often meant the same thing. This led to differing expectations among leadership cohorts regarding the appropriate application of mission command during operations and garrison activities. Labeling multiple things mission command unintentionally eroded the importance of mission command, which is critical to the command and control of Army forces across the range of military operations. Differentiating mission command from command and control provides clarity, allows leaders to focus on mission command in the context of the missions they execute, and aligns the Army with joint and multinational partners, all of whom use the term command and control.

Command and control—the exercise of authority and direction by a properly designated commander over assigned and attached forces—is fundamental to the art and science of warfare. No single specialized military function, either by itself or combined with others, has a purpose without it. Commanders are responsible for command and control. Through command and control, commanders provide purpose and direction to integrate all military activities towards a common goal—mission accomplishment. Military operations are inherently human endeavors, characterized by violence and continuous adaptation by all participants. Successful execution requires Army forces to make and implement effective decisions faster than enemy forces. Therefore, the Army has adopted mission command as its approach to command and control that empowers subordinate decision making and decentralized execution appropriate to the situation.

Mission command requires tactically and technically competent commanders, staffs, and subordinates operating in an environment of mutual trust and shared understanding. It requires building effective teams and a command climate in which commanders encourage subordinates to take risks and exercise disciplined initiative to seize opportunities and counter threats within the commander's intent. Through mission orders, commanders focus their subordinates on the purpose of an operation rather than on the details of how to perform assigned tasks. This allows subordinates the greatest possible freedom of action in the context of a particular situation. Finally, when delegating authority to subordinates, commanders set the necessary conditions for success by allocating resources to subordinates based on assigned tasks.

Commanders need support to exercise command and control effectively. At every echelon of command, commanders are supported by the command and control warfighting function—the related tasks and a system that enables commanders to synchronize and converge all elements of combat power. Commanders execute command and control through their staffs and subordinate leaders.

ADP 6-0 provides fundamental principles on mission command, command and control, and the command and control warfighting function. Key updates and changes to this version of ADP 6-0 include—

- Combined information from ADP 6-0 and ADRP 6-0 into a single document.
- Command and control reintroduced into Army doctrine.

- An expanded discussion of command and control and its relationship to mission command.
- Revised mission command principles.
- Command and control system reintroduced, along with new tasks, and an updated system description.
- Expanded discussion of the command and control system.

Mission Command (Logic Map)

Nature of War

Military operations are inherently human endeavors representing a contest of wills, characterized by violence and continuous adaption by all participants, conducted in dynamic and uncertain operational environments to achieve a political purpose.

Operations must account for the nature of war. As such the Army's operational concept is...

Unified Land Operations

The simultaneous execution of offense, defense, stability, and defense support of civil authorities across multiple domains to shape operational environments, prevent conflict, prevail in large-scale ground combat, and consolidate gains as part of unified action.

The Army's operational concept is enabled by....

Mission Command

The Army's approach to command and control that empowers subordinate decision making and decentralized execution appropriate to the situation.

Enabled by the principles of...

Competence | Mutual trust | Shared understanding | Commander's intent
Mission orders | Disciplined initiative | Risk acceptance

Command and control is fundamental to all operations...

Command and Control

Command and control is the exercise of authority and direction by a properly designated commander over assigned and attached forces in the accomplishment of a mission.

Elements of Command
- Authority
- Responsibility
- Decision making
- Leadership

Elements of Control
- Direction
- Feedback
- Information
- Communication

Executed through...

Command and Control Warfighting Function

The related tasks and a system that enables commanders to synchronize and converge all elements of combat power.

Tasks
- Command forces
- Control operations
- Drive the operations process
- Establish the command and control system

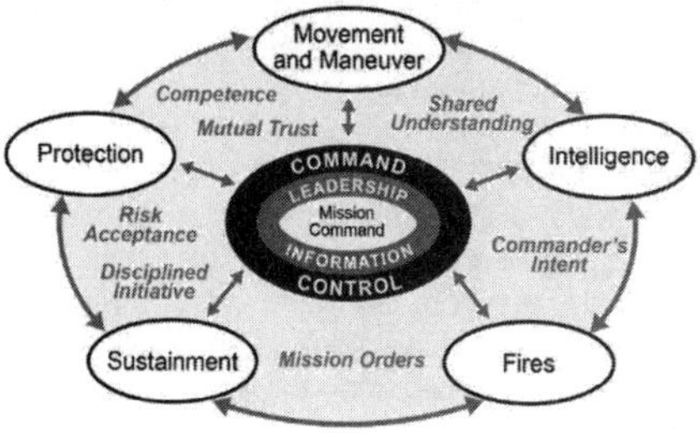

Command and Control System
- People
- Processes
- Networks
- Command posts

Ref: ADP 6-0 (Jul '19), Introductory figure-1. Logic map.

II. Mission Command

> *Never tell people how to do things. Tell them what to do and they will surprise you with their ingenuity.*
>
> *- General George S. Patton, Jr.*

Army operations doctrine emphasizes shattering an enemy force's ability and will to resist, and destroying the coherence of enemy operations. Army forces accomplish these things by controlling the nature, scope, and tempo of an operation and striking simultaneously throughout the area of operations to control, neutralize, and destroy enemy forces and other objectives. The Army's command and control doctrine supports its operations doctrine. It balances coordination, personal leadership, and tactical flexibility. It stresses rapid decision making and execution, including rapid response to changing situations. It emphasizes mutual trust and shared understanding among superiors and subordinates.

Mission command is the Army's approach to command and control that empowers subordinate decision making and decentralized execution appropriate to the situation. Mission command supports the Army's operational concept of unified land operations and its emphasis on seizing, retaining, and exploiting the initiative.

The mission command approach to command and control is based on the Army's view that war is inherently chaotic and uncertain. No plan can account for every possibility, and most plans must change rapidly during execution to account for changes in the situation. No single person is ever sufficiently informed to make every important decision, nor can a single person keep up with the number of decisions that need to be made during combat. Subordinate leaders often have a better understanding of what is happening during a battle, and are more likely to respond effectively to threats and fleeting opportunities if allowed to make decisions and act based on changing situations and unforeseen events not addressed in the initial plan in order to achieve their commander's intent. Enemy forces may behave differently than expected, a route may become impassable, or units could consume supplies at unexpected rates. Friction and unforeseeable combinations of variables impose uncertainty in all operations and require an approach to command and control that does not attempt to impose perfect order, but rather accepts uncertainty and makes allowances for unpredictability.

Mission command helps commanders capitalize on subordinate ingenuity, innovation, and decision making to achieve the commander's intent when conditions change or current orders are no longer relevant. It requires subordinates who seek opportunities and commanders who accept risk for subordinates trying to meet their intent. Subordinate decision making and decentralized execution appropriate to the situation help manage uncertainty and enable necessary tempo at each echelon during operations. Employing the mission command approach during all garrison activities and training events is essential to creating the cultural foundation for its employment in high-risk environments.

Subordinate Decision Making

Successful commanders anticipate future events by developing branches and sequels instead of focusing on details better handled by subordinates during current operations. The higher the echelon, the more time commanders should devote to future operations and the broader the guidance provided to subordinates. Subordinates empowered to make decisions during operations unburden higher commanders from issues that distract from necessary broader perspective and focus on critical issues. Mission command allows those commanders with the best situational understanding to make rapid decisions without waiting for higher echelon commanders to assess the situation and issue orders.

Commanders delegate appropriate authority to deputies, subordinate commanders, and staff members based upon a judgment of their capabilities and experience. Delegation allows subordinates to decide and act for their commander in specified areas. Delegating decision-making authority reduces the number of decisions made at the higher echelons and reduces response time at lower echelons. In addition to determining the amount of decision-making authority they will delegate, commanders also identify decisions that are their sole responsibility and cannot be delegated to subordinates.

When delegating authority to subordinates, commanders strive to set the necessary conditions for success. They do this by assessing and managing risk. Taking risk is inherent at all levels of command. Commanders and staffs assess hazards and recommend controls to help manage risk, rather than forcing unnecessary risk decisions on subordinates. While commanders can delegate authority, they cannot delegate responsibility. Subordinates are accountable to their commanders for the use of delegated authority, but commanders remain solely responsible and accountable for the actions of their subordinates.

Decentralized Execution

Decentralized execution is the delegation of decision-making authority to subordinates, so they may make and implement decisions and adjust their assigned tasks in fluid and rapidly changing situations.

Subordinate decisions should be ethically based and within the framework of their higher commander's intent. Decentralized execution is essential to seizing, retaining, and exploiting the operational initiative during operations in environments where conditions rapidly change and uncertainty is the norm. Rapidly changing situations and uncertainty are inherent in operations where commanders seek to establish a tempo and intensity that enemy forces cannot match.

Decentralized execution requires disseminating information to the lowest possible level so subordinates can make informed decisions based on a shared understanding of both the situation and their commander's intent. This empowers subordinates operating in rapidly changing conditions to exercise disciplined initiative within their commander's intent. Generally, the more dynamic the circumstances, the greater the need for initiative to make decisions at lower levels. It is the duty of subordinates to exercise initiative to achieve their commander's intent. It is the commander's responsibility to issue appropriate intent and ensure subordinates are prepared in terms of education, training, and experience to exercise initiative.

The commander's intent provides a unifying idea that allows decentralized execution within an overarching framework. It provides guidance within which individuals may exercise initiative to accomplish the desired end state. Understanding the commander's intent two echelons up further enhances unity of effort while providing the basis for decentralized decision making and execution throughout the depth of a formation.

Levels of Control

Determining the appropriate level of control, including delegating decisions and determining how much decentralized execution to employ, is part of the art of command. The level and application of control is constantly evolving and must be continuously assessed and adjusted to ensure the level of control is appropriate to the situation. Commanders should allow subordinates the greatest freedom of action commensurate with the level of acceptable risk in a particular situation. The mission variables (mission, enemy, terrain and weather, troops and support available, time available, and civil considerations) influence how much control to impose on subordinates. Other considerations include—

- Enemy disposition and capabilities
- Level of synchronization and integration required
- Higher echelon headquarters constraints
- Level of risk

See following page (p. 5-6) for further discussion.

III. Levels of Control

Ref: ADP 6-0, Mission Command (Jul '19), pp. 1-20 to 1-21 and chap. 4.

Determining the appropriate level of control, including delegating decisions and determining how much decentralized execution to employ, is part of the art of command. The level and application of control is constantly evolving and must be continuously assessed and adjusted to ensure the level of control is appropriate to the situation. Commanders should allow subordinates the greatest freedom of action commensurate with the level of acceptable risk in a particular situation. The mission variables (mission, enemy, terrain and weather, troops and support available, time available, and civil considerations) influence how much control to impose on subordinates. Other considerations include—

- Enemy disposition and capabilities
- Level of synchronization and integration required
- Higher echelon headquarters constraints
- Level of risk
- Level of legal and ethical ambiguity
- Rules of engagement
- Level of unit cohesion
- Level of training
- Level of trust
- Level of shared understanding

← **More control** —— **Less control** →

	Considerations	
• Predictable • Known	Situation	• Unpredictable • Unknown
• Inexperienced • New team	Unit Cohesion	• Experienced • Mature team
• Untrained or needs practice	Level of Training	• Trained in tasks to be performed
• Being developed	Level of Trust	• Established
• Top down • Explicit communications • Vertical communications	Shared Understanding	• Reciprocal information • Implicit communications • Vertical and horizontal communications
• Restrictive	Rules of Engagement	• Permissive
• Optimal decisions later	Required Decision	• Acceptable decisions sooner
• Science of war • Synchronization	Appropriate To	• Art of war • Orchestration

Ref: ADP 6-0 (Jul '19), Figure 1-1. Levels of control.

Different operations and phases of operations may require tighter or more relaxed control over subordinate elements than other phases. Operations that require the close synchronization of multiple units, or the integration of effects in a limited amount of time, may require more detailed coordination, and be controlled in a more centralized manner. Conversely, operations that do not require the close coordination of multiple units, such as a movement to contact or a pursuit, offer many opportunities to exercise initiative.

II. Command & Control Warfighting Tasks

Ref: FM 3-0 (w/Chg 1), Operations (Dec '17), pp. 2-23 to 2-34.

The command and control warfighting function is the related tasks and a system that enable commanders to synchronize and converge all elements of combat power (ADP 3-0). The primary purpose of the command and control warfighting function is to assist commanders in integrating the other elements of combat power to achieve objectives and accomplish missions.

**Editor's Note: FM 3-0 (w/Chg 1), Operations (Dec '17) predates the more recent ADP 6-0, Mission Command (Jul '19) which renamed the "Mission Command Warfighting Function" to the "Command and Control Warfighting Function." For clarity, the following material from FM 3-0 still uses the term "mission command" when discussing warfighting tasks.*

"Mission Command" Warfighting Tasks (from FM 3-0*)

While staffs perform essential functions, commanders are ultimately responsible for accomplishing assigned missions. Throughout operations, commanders encourage disciplined initiative through a clear commander's intent while providing enough direction to integrate and synchronize the force at the decisive place and time. To this end, commanders perform three primary mission command warfighting function tasks. The commander tasks are—

- Drive the operations process through the activities of understanding, visualizing, describing, directing, leading, and assessing operations.
- Develop teams, both within their own organizations and with unified action partners.
- Inform and influence audiences, inside and outside their organizations.

Staffs support commanders in the exercise of mission command by performing four primary mission command warfighting function tasks. The staff tasks are—

- Conduct the operations process: plan, prepare, execute, and assess.
- Conduct knowledge management, information management, and foreign disclosure.
- Conduct information operations.
- Conduct cyberspace electromagnetic activities.

Six additional tasks reside within the mission command warfighting function. These tasks are—

- Conduct CA operations.
- Conduct military deception.
- Install, operate, and maintain the DODIN.
- Conduct airspace control.
- Conduct information protection.
- Plan and conduct space activities.

See following pages (pp. 5-8 to 5-12) for further discussion of these key warfighting function tasks from FM 3-0 (w/Chg 1), Operations (Dec '17).

I. Conduct the Operations Process

Ref: FM 3-0 (w/Chg 1), Operations (Dec '17), pp. 2-24 to 2-26. See also pp. 1-49 and 1-51.

The Army's framework for exercising mission command is the operations process—the major mission command activities performed during operations: planning, preparing, executing, and continuously assessing the operation (ADP 5-0). The operations process is a commander-led activity, informed by the philosophy of mission command. Commanders, supported by their staffs, use the operations process to drive the conceptual and detailed planning necessary to understand, visualize, and describe their operational environment; make and articulate decisions; and direct, lead, and assess operations.

The operations process serves as an overarching model that commanders, staffs, and subordinate leaders use to integrate the warfighting functions across all domains and synchronize the force to accomplish missions. This includes integrating numerous processes such as the intelligence process, the military decision-making process, and targeting within the headquarters and with higher echelon, subordinate, supporting, supported, and adjacent units.

The Operations Process

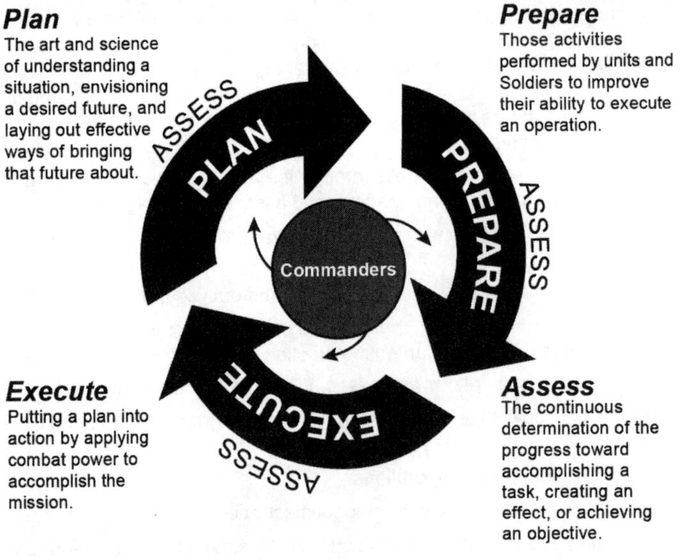
Plan
The art and science of understanding a situation, envisioning a desired future, and laying out effective ways of bringing that future about.
Prepare
Those activities performed by units and Soldiers to improve their ability to execute an operation.
PLAN
PREPARE
EXECUTE
ASSESS
ASSESS
ASSESS
Commanders
Execute
Putting a plan into action by applying combat power to accomplish the mission.
Assess
The continuous determination of the progress toward accomplishing a task, creating an effect, or achieving an objective.

Ref: FM 3-0 (Oct '17), fig. 2-7. The operations process.

The activities of the operations process (plan, prepare, execute, and assess) are not discrete; they overlap and recur as circumstances demand. Planning starts an iteration of the operations process. Upon completion of the initial order, planning continues as leaders revise the plan based on changing circumstances. Preparing begins during planning and continues through execution. Execution puts a plan into action by applying combat power to seize, retain, and exploit the initiative and consolidate gains. Assessing is continuous and influences the other three activities. The operations process, while simple in concept, is dynamic in execution-especially in fast-paced, large-scale combat operations. Commanders must organize and train their staffs and subordinates as an integrated team to simultaneously plan, prepare, execute, and assess operations.

Army operational planning requires the complete definition of the mission, expression of the commander's intent, completion of the commander and staff estimates, and development of a concept of operations. These form the basis of a plan or order and set the conditions for a successful battle. The initial plan establishes the commander's intent, the concept of operations, and the initial tasks for subordinate units. It allows the greatest possible operational and tactical freedom for subordinate leaders. It is flexible enough to permit leaders to seize opportunities consistent with the commander's intent, thus facilitating quick and accurate decision making during combat operations.

Both commanders and staffs have important roles within the operations process. The commander's role is to drive the operations process through the activities of understanding, visualizing, describing, directing, leading, and assessing operations. Commanders balance their time between leading their staffs through the operations process and providing purpose, direction, and motivation to subordinate commanders and Soldiers.

See chap. 1 for full discussion of the operations process from ADP 5-0.

The Commander's Role in Ops Process

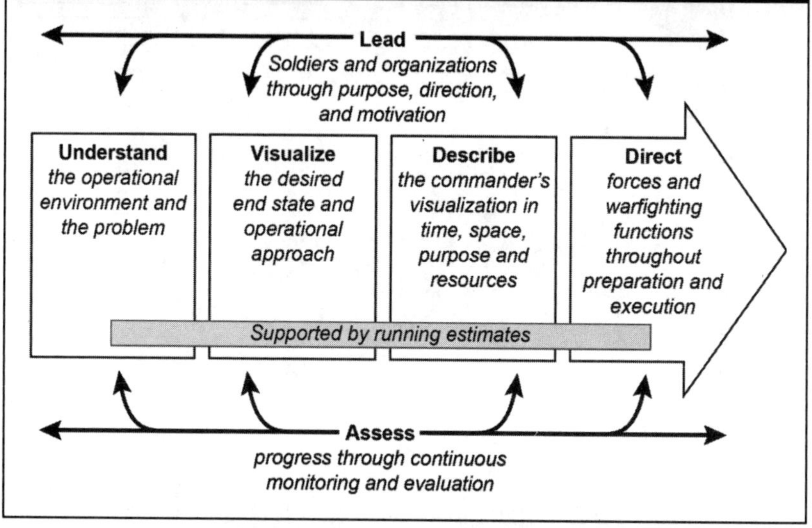
Lead
Soldiers and organizations through purpose, direction, and motivation
Understand the operational environment and the problem
Visualize the desired end state and operational approach
Describe the commander's visualization in time, space, purpose and resources
Direct forces and warfighting functions throughout preparation and execution
Supported by running estimates
Assess
progress through continuous monitoring and evaluation

Ref: FM 3-0 (Oct '17), fig. 2-8. The commander's role in the operations process.

The staff's role is to assist commanders with understanding situations, making and implementing decisions, controlling operations, and assessing progress. Staff members advise and make recommendations to the commander within their area of expertise based on their running estimates. They support the commander in communicating decisions and intentions through plans and orders. While commanders make key decisions throughout the operations process, they are not the only decision makers. Commanders delegate trained and trusted staff members with decision-making authority, freeing commanders from routine decisions. This enables commanders to focus on key aspects of an operation.

See pp. 1-13 to 1-26 for full discussion of how commander's drive the operations process through understanding, visualizing, describing, directing, leading, and assessing operations.

II. Conduct Information Operations

Commanders and staffs synchronize information-related capabilities through information operations. Information operations are the integrated employment, during military operations, of information-related capabilities in concert with other lines of operation to influence, disrupt, corrupt, or usurp the decision-making of adversaries and potential adversaries while protecting our own (JP 3-13). Information operations are commander centric and coordinated as part of planning and targeting. The effects of information operations can be simultaneously observed within an AO and worldwide.

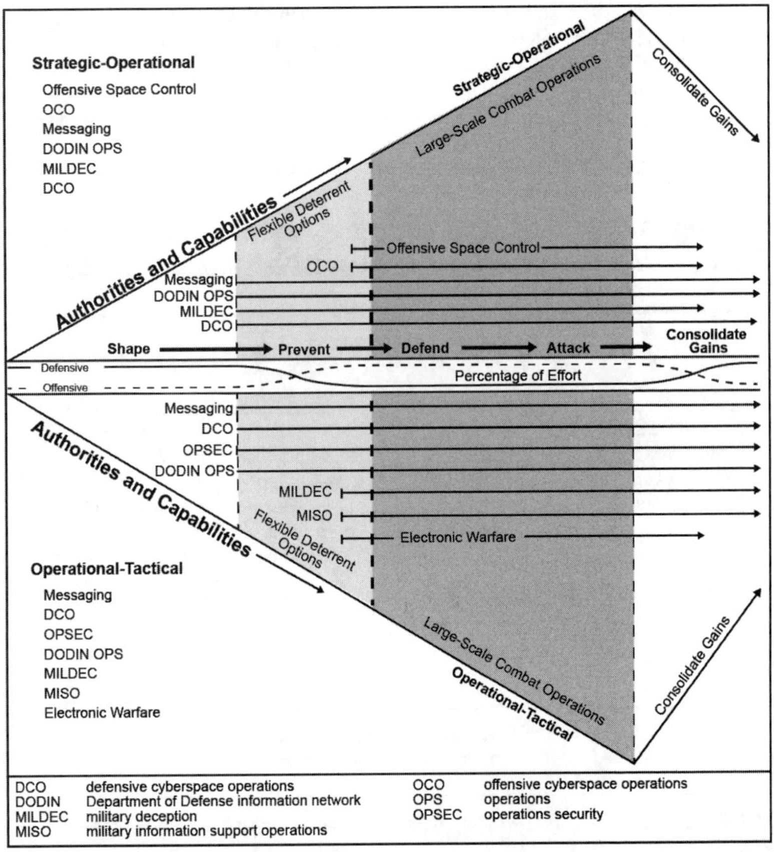

DCO	defensive cyberspace operations	OCO	offensive cyberspace operations
DODIN	Department of Defense information network	OPS	operations
MILDEC	military deception	OPSEC	operations security
MISO	military information support operations		

Ref: FM 3-0 (Oct '17), fig. 2-9. Dynamic continuum of information operations

Figure 2-9 depicts information operations authorities and capabilities in the context of operations to shape, prevent, win, and consolidate gains. As operations move right on the conflict continuum, authorities for the use of information-related capabilities increase. For example, during operations to shape, information operations focus on messaging to inform and influence allies, to deter adversaries, and to conduct defensive cyberspace operations. During large-scale combat operations, information-related capabilities become much more offensively oriented and focused on the support of maneuver commanders. National, joint, and Army capabilities such as offensive space control, offensive cyberspace operations, and EW become available to support ground forces engaging the enemy.

The following sections highlight several of these information-related capabilities. Refer to FM 3-13 for doctrine on information operations.

Information Operations (IO)

Ref: FM 3-0 (w/Chg 1), Operations (Dec '17), pp. 2-26 to 2-28.

Commanders and their units must coordinate what they do, say, and portray. The development of themes and messages in support of a military operation is fundamental to that process. A theme is a unifying or dominant idea or image that expresses the purpose for military action. Themes are tied to objectives, lines of effort, and end state conditions. Themes are overarching and apply to the capabilities of public affairs activities, MISO, and Soldier and leader engagements. A message is a verbal, written, or electronic communication that supports a theme focused on a specific actor and in support of a specific action. Commanders approve and employ themes and messages as part of planned activities designed to influence specific foreign audiences for various purposes that support current or planned operations.

Staffs synchronize information operations throughout the operations process. Information operations specialists must effectively synchronize various information-related capabilities to support the concept of operations. The use of messaging is a critical supporting effort during large-scale combat operations. As in previous wars and conflicts, the message legitimizing why U.S. forces are there and why they fight must be communicated and understood across all echelons and audiences. Commanders must communicate and enforce a positive narrative and be aware that an enemy may lead with information effects and only support them with physical effects.

While all unit operations, activities, and actions affect the information environment, information related capabilities requiring synchronization and coordination as part of information operations include—

- Military deception (MILDEC).
- MISO.
- Soldier and leader engagement, including police engagement.
- CA operations.
- Combat camera.
- OPSEC.
- Public affairs.
- Cyberspace Operations.
- EW.
- Space operations.
- Special technical operations.

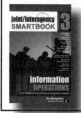

Refer to Joint/Interagency SMARTbook 3: Information Operations (Multi-Domain Guide to IO & Information-Related Capabilities), when published. All military activities produce information. Informational aspects affect the perceptions and attitudes that drive behavior and decision making. The JFC leverages informational aspects of military activities to gain an advantage; failing to leverage those aspects may cede this advantage to others. Leveraging the informational aspects of military activities ultimately affects strategic outcomes.

A. Military Deception (MILDEC)

Military deception is actions executed to deliberately mislead adversary military, paramilitary, or violent extremist organization decision makers, thereby causing the adversary to take specific actions or (inactions) that will contribute to the accomplishment of the friendly mission (JP 3-13.4). MILDEC operations are planned from the top down. Subordinate deception plans must support higher echelon plans.

Tactical deception (TAC-D) is a deception activity planned and executed by, and in support of, tactical-level commanders to cause adversaries to take actions or inactions favorable to the friendly tactical commanders' objectives. TAC-D is conducted to influence military operations in order to gain a tactical advantage over an adversary, mask vulnerabilities in friendly forces, or to enhance the defensive capabilities of friendly forces. TAC-D is unique to the tactical requirements of the local commander and not necessarily linked or subordinate to a greater joint MILDEC plan. In order to ensure that it does not compromise an existing or future MILDEC, TAC-D must be approved two echelons up, not to exceed the combatant command.

The corps echelon is where properly conceived and employed MILDEC is most likely to succeed and mislead enemy commanders as to the true disposition, capabilities, and intentions of friendly forces. Divisions and lower echelons often lack the density of forces and capabilities to successfully deceive a regional peer enemy. Tactical headquarters employ TAC-D measures assigned by a higher echelon headquarters or develop their own measures to support their own concept of operations. These measures must be nested. The tactical headquarters higher echelon headquarters must vet and approve all TAC-D operations. TAC-D requires synchronization across multiple domains and echelons. An enemy is not likely to be deceived when friendly actions do not match the available information. Tactical units assigned to conduct MILDEC activities are often not informed of their mission's true purpose.

It is extremely difficult for BCTs and other types of brigades to employ effective TAC-D because of the lack of resources available at the brigade echelon. Operations security—including effective camouflage, concealment, and the use of decoys—may only delay an enemy from identifying the objective of a BCT operation for short periods. OPSEC may assist in determining the timing for the movement of forces, managing the daily volume of electronic signatures, or the timing of sustainment operations. BCT TAC-D may create only a very short period of time to exploit a position of relative advantage. False insertions, feints, deception fires, smoke screens, decoys, EW and other tactics, techniques, and procedures can create confusion or uncertainty in the mind of an enemy commander which will facilitate friendly maneuver. When possible, TAC-D is used by corps and division support brigades in the close and deep area to add to the dilemmas presented to an opposing enemy commander.

Commanders should assume all ground forces are under continuous observation by enemies and adversaries employing their national space-based capabilities and operate accordingly. Commanders employ camouflage and deception measures to minimize unit exposure and identification for targeting by long-range precision fires or direct action by enemy conventional, special purpose, and irregular forces. The harder it is to identify friendly forces to target, the less likely they will be targeted. Rapidly maneuvering friendly forces also reduces the ability of an enemy to target those friendly forces. The combination of deception, good OPSEC, and enemy limitations are all related. Minimizing the appearance of actual lucrative targets while providing false targets should be a MILDEC goal.

Military Deception

Ref: FM 6-0 (C2), Commander and Staff Organization and Operations (May '15), pp. 11-2 to 11-4.

Modern military deception is both a process and a capability. As a process, military deception is a methodical, information-based strategy that systematically, deliberately, and cognitively targets individual decisionmakers. The objective is the purposeful manipulation of decisionmaking. As a capability, military deception is useful to a commander when integrated early in the planning process as a component of the operation focused on causing an enemy to act or react in a desired manner.

Refer to JP 3-13 for a discussion in information operations and JP 3-13.4 for a more detailed discussion on military deception.

Military Deception Tactics

The selection of military deception tactics and their use depends on an understanding of the current situation as well as the desired military deception goal and objective. (See appendix A for a discussion of operational and mission variables.) As a rule, Army commanders should be familiar with planning and conducting feints, ruses, demonstrations, and displays.

- **Feint**. A feint, in military deception, is an offensive action involving contact with the adversary conducted for the purpose of deceiving the adversary as to the location and/or time of the actual main offensive action (JP 3-13.4).
- **Ruse**. A ruse, in military deception, is a trick of war designed to deceive the adversary, usually involving the deliberate exposure of false information to the adversary's intelligence collection system (JP 3-13.4).
- **Demonstration**. A demonstration, in military deception, is a show of force in an area where a decision is not sought that is made to deceive an adversary. It is similar to a feint but no actual contact with the adversary is intended (JP 3-13.4).
- **Display**. A display, in military deception, is a static portrayal of an activity, force, or equipment intended to deceive the adversary's visual observation (JP 3-13.4).

Common Military Deception Means

Army commanders should also be familiar with some of the more commonly available military deception means that can be employed to support a given military deception. They cover the full scope of units, forces, personnel, capabilities, and resources available to the commander for the conduct of decisive action. In most cases, Army commanders have at their disposal the use of the following six information-related capabilities and other activities to support a planned military deception: :

- Military information support operations (MISO)
- OPSEC
- Camouflage, concealment and decoys
- Cyber electromagnetic activities
- Physical attack and destruction capabilities
- Presence, posture, and profile

B. Military Information Support Operations (MISO)

Psychological factors are an integral part of all operations. MISO include words and actions specifically planned to reduce the combat effectiveness of enemy armed forces and to influence hostile, neutral, and friendly groups to support friendly force operations. However, MISO may take time to achieve a desired change in enemy behavior, depending on the target and the objective. Commanders are responsible for the integration of MISO into military planning. Commanders need to evaluate their plans and operations in view of their psychological impact and alignment with the guidance provided from their higher echelon headquarters. Tactical headquarters at the BCT echelon and below are primarily concerned with MISO designed to produce short-term results to gain a position of relative advantage, such as hastening the surrender of surrounded and isolated enemy forces. Some tactical MISO objectives may achieve goals to consolidate gains. Corps and division headquarters allocate supporting psychological operations companies, platoons, and teams to subordinate units as required.

Corps and divisions facilitate MISO to create periods of relative advantage by providing enemy target audiences information designed for a specific effect that supports friendly operations. Within the constraints of policy, planners and operators creatively erode support for enemy operations, build distrust between adversarial actors, and inform civilian populations of designated evacuation routes or areas that provide sanctuary.

MISO at the tactical level focuses on isolating enemy forces at the division echelon and below. MISO units may also contribute to the deception plans of higher echelon headquarters, and they have the ability to plan and execute TAC-D. MISO planners weigh short-term effects with the impact certain operations may have when a friendly force operates as an occupying force.

Refer to FM 3-53 for additional information on MISO.

C. Cyberspace Electromagnetic Activities (CEMA)

Cyberspace electromagnetic activities is the process of planning, integrating, and synchronizing cyberspace and electronic warfare operations in support of unified land operations (ADP 3-0). Incorporating cyberspace electromagnetic activities (CEMA) throughout all phases of an operation is key to obtaining and maintaining freedom of maneuver in cyberspace and the EMS while denying it to enemies and adversaries. CEMA synchronizes capabilities across domains and warfighting functions and maximizes complementary effects in and through cyberspace and the EMS. Intelligence, signal, information operations, cyberspace, space, and fires operations are critical to planning, synchronizing, and executing cyberspace and EW operations.

CEMA adhere to the joint principles of operations, and of these principles, mass, unity of effort, surprise, and security are the most relevant. Commanders and staffs ensure compliance with relevant authorities and associated legal frameworks before conducting cyberspace and EW operations. When conducting cyberspace operations, the Army acts according to command lines of authority. For example, the Army provides forces for offensive cyberspace operations (OCO), but does not execute these operations except as part of the joint force and as approved by the JFC. OCO and defensive cyberspace response actions are subject to authorities that reside with the President and Secretary of Defense.

Refer to CYBER1: The Cyberspace Operations & Electronic Warfare SMARTbook (Multi-Domain Guide to Offensive/Defensive CEMA and CO). Topics and chapters include cyber intro (global threat, contemporary operating environment, information as a joint function), joint cyberspace operations (CO), cyberspace operations (OCO/DCO/DODIN), electronic warfare (EW) operations, cyber & EW (CEMA) planning, spectrum management operations (SMO/JEMSO), DoD information network (DODIN) operations, and cyber terms.

D. Public Affairs

Ref: FM 3-0 (w/Chg 1), Operations (Dec '17), p. 2-30.

Army public affairs is public information, command information, and community engagement activities directed toward both external and internal populations with interest in the DOD. Public affairs is the commander's responsibility at all echelons of command. Public affairs officers assist commanders and serve on the brigade's special staff and the commander's personal staff (at division through theater army echelons).

The U.S. military has an obligation to communicate with its members and the U.S. public, and it is in the national interest to communicate with international populations. The proactive release of accurate information to domestic and international audiences puts joint operations in context, facilitates informed perceptions about military operations, counters adversarial propaganda, and helps achieve national, strategic, and operational objectives. Effective public affairs help—

- Build partnerships.
- Deter adversaries.
- Enhance allied support.
- Support future U.S. security interests.
- Inform expectations and options.
- Counter inaccurate information, deception, and propaganda.
- Reinforce military success.
- Support military objectives.
- Articulate military capabilities.
- Communicate U.S. actions and policies.
- Support strategic narratives, themes, and goals.

Public affairs is inherent in all military activities, and it is a key enabler for managing and delivering public information through public communication. In Army public affairs, public communication is the communication between the Army and international, national, and local populations through coordinated programs, plans, themes, and messages. It involves the receipt and exchange of ideas and opinions that contribute to shaping public understanding of, and discourse with, the Army. Public communication includes the release of official information through news releases, public service announcements, media engagements, and social networks.

Refer to FM 3-61 for public affairs doctrine.

The abundance of information sources, coupled with technology such as smart phones, digital cameras, video chat, and social media enterprises, allows information to move instantaneously around the globe. Public affairs personnel and units frequently review and analyze media reports at the international, national, and local levels. The results of these analyses are provided to the supported commander on a regular basis. It is imperative for public affairs personnel to rapidly develop themes and messages to ensure that facts, data, events, and utterances are put in context.

Refer to Joint/Interagency SMARTbook 3: Information Operations (Multi-Domain Guide to IO & Information-Related Capabilities), when published. All military activities produce information. Informational aspects affect the perceptions and attitudes that drive behavior and decision making. The JFC leverages informational aspects of military activities to gain an advantage; failing to leverage those aspects may cede this advantage to others. Leveraging the informational aspects of military activities ultimately affects strategic outcomes.

III. Additional Tasks

In addition to command and staff tasks, the mission command warfighting function has several additional tasks, some of which are discussed below.

A. Airspace Control

Airspace control includes the capabilities and procedures used to increase operational effectiveness by promoting the safe, efficient, and flexible use of airspace (JP 3-52). Theater armies, corps, divisions and BCTs require the capability to conduct airspace control. Airspace control increases combat effectiveness while placing minimum constraint upon airspace users. Airspace control relies upon airspace management capabilities provided by joint and Army airspace control elements and often host-nation air traffic control.

See pp. 3-37 to 3-40 for further discussion of airspace control from FM 3-52.

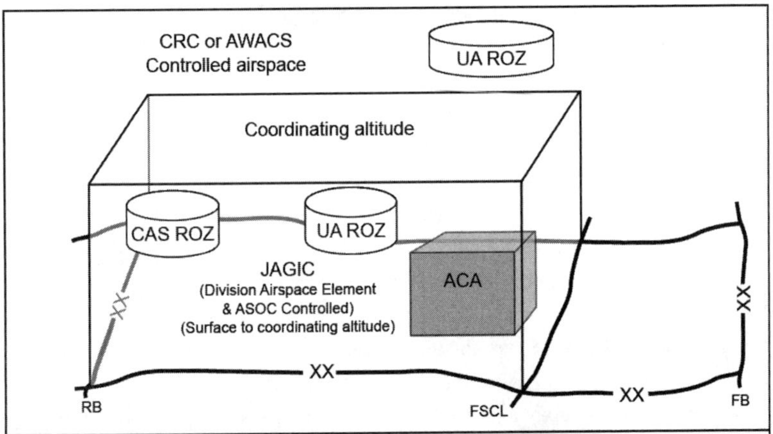

ACA	airspace coordination area	FB	forward boundary
ASOC	air support operations center	JAGIC	joint air-ground integration center
AWACS	airborne warning and control system	RB	rear boundary
CAS	close air support	ROZ	restricted operating zone
CRC	control and reporting center	UA	unmanned aircraft
FSCL	fire support coordination line		

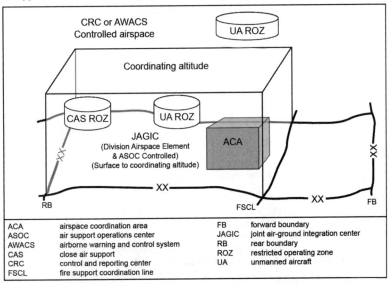

Ref: FM 3-0 (w/Chg 1), fig. 2-10. Example division airspace coordinating measures.

The goal of airspace control at the corps echelon to enable responsive fires and maneuver across the corps AO, and airspace control provides unique coordination challenges in planning and execution with unified action partners. This includes coordination with the land component's BCD as its representative within the air component's air operations center, with the United States Air Force (USAF) theater air-ground system unit in direct support to the corps headquarters and with other theater air-ground system elements executing air operations over the corps AO.

The corps initial airspace control focus is working with higher headquarters to build an airspace control system that supports corps operations. Airspace control procedures for the entire force are set out in the joint airspace control plan published by the joint airspace control authority, developed with input from the functional components. Corps airspace planners working with the joint force land component planners and the BCD, influence the development of the airspace control plan very early in its development to ensure that the eventual airspace control plan and its related airspace control order and special instructions support corps operations with minimal interference. Building the airspace control systems also includes working with USAF to resource required USAF elements. Corps and division airspace control capabilities are significantly enhanced with the addition of aligned direct support

B. Civil Affairs (CA) Operations

Ref: FM 3-0 (w/Chg 1), Operations (Dec '17), p. 2-33.

CA operations are actions planned, executed, and assessed by CA forces that enhance awareness of and manage the interaction with the civil component of the operational environment; identify and mitigate underlying causes of instability within civil society; or involve the application of functional specialty skills normally the responsibility of civil government.

Civil-Military Operations

Unified Action

- **The synchronization, coordination, and integration of the activities of governmental and nongovernmental entities with military operations to achieve unity of effort**
- **Takes place within unified commands, subordinate unified commands, and joint task forces under the direction of these commanders**

Civil-Military Operations

- **The responsibility of a commander**
- **Normally planned by civil affairs personnel, but implemented by all elements of the joint force**

Civil Affairs

- **Conducted by civil affairs forces**
- **Provides specialized support of civil-military operations**
- **Applies functional skills normally provided by civil government**

CA operations consist of three competencies, CA activities, CA supported activities and military government operations. CA forces conduct CA operations to support the commander's concept of operations. These forces are the commander's primary asset to purposefully engage nonmilitary organizations, institutions and populations. CA capabilities establish, maintain, influence, or exploit relations between military forces and civil authorities (government and nongovernment) and the civilian populace in a friendly, neutral, or hostile AO to facilitate military operations and to consolidate operational objectives. CA forces may assist or perform activities and functions that are normally the responsibility of local government.

Refer to FM 3-57 for CA doctrine.

Refer to TAA2: Military Engagement, Security Cooperation & Stability SMARTbook (Foreign Train, Advise, & Assist) for further discussion. Topics include the Range of Military Operations (JP 3-0), Security Cooperation & Security Assistance (Train, Advise, & Assist), Stability Operations (ADRP 3-07), Peace Operations (JP 3-07.3), Counterinsurgency Operations (JP & FM 3-24), Civil-Military Operations (JP 3-57), Multinational Operations (JP 3-16), Interorganizational Cooperation (JP 3-08), and more.

USAF tactical air control system elements, primarily the tactical air control party and the air support operations center.

The corps headquarters understands airspace control guidance published in the airspace control order, air tasking order, area air defense plan, and land component's plan. The corps headquarters takes into account placement of the fire support coordination line and its impact on the operations of other components. Failure to understand these requirements can cause delays in clearing airspace or impact the operations of another component. During planning, the corps headquarters plans airspace use for corps-controlled Army fires, such as Army Tactical Missile System fires and Army aviation strikes.

During execution, the corps headquarters decentralizes airspace control to subordinate elements within their respective AOs for the execution of operations. Enabling subordinate divisions with direct support air support operations centers allows the divisions to form a joint air-ground integration center (JAGIC) and control delegated division assigned airspace by the airspace control authority. Figure 2-10 illustrates some common airspace coordinating measures. The corps authorizes direct liaison between subordinate elements and other theater air-ground system airspace control nodes provided by other Services to minimize risk and maximize effectiveness. However, the corps retains responsibility for policies and for the development of future airspace use even when authorizing direct liaison authorized to subordinate units. The corps airspace element, working with the corps field artillery brigade, enables responsive deep fires by rapidly coordinating airspace for the brigade's rockets and missiles.

The corps headquarters provides airspace control resources to support multinational forces under the OPCON or TACON of the corps commander. Corps airspace control planners support multinational forces with the same resources support as the Army functional brigades working directly for the corps. Airspace management occurs at the lowest levels possible to enable clearance of fires and control low altitude above ground airspace congestion given the threats posed by the enemy's integrated air defense system.

Refer to JP 3-52 for an explanation of joint force airspace control. Refer to FM 3-52 for additional information on Army airspace control and ATP 3-52.2 for multi-Service airspace control techniques and procedures.

C. Space Activities

Space operations influence the conduct of all corps, division, and brigade operations. Space operations enable operations by providing positioning, navigation, timing, satellite communications, space-based intelligence, surveillance, reconnaissance, missile warning, and weather. Army units are consumers of information generated in the space domain and influence space operations by their demands for space-based capabilities. Space operations heavily impact daily operations in Army units. Deliberate planning and targeting processes must request space-based capabilities and effects through the JFC in a timely manner. Commanders who assume short notice responsiveness for space-based capabilities without understanding the limitations of those capabilities increase risk to the mission and their units.

Corps, division, and brigade commanders need to know the potential impact on operations if enemy action or natural phenomena interrupt the provision of those space-based services. Army forces must retain the ability to shoot, move, and communicate during large-scale combat operations when space-based capabilities are denied, degraded, or disrupted. Training and rehearsing combat skills and ensuring the availability of analog alternatives to space (or cyberspace) enabled systems is critical to successfully persisting in the chaos and friction of modern, large-scale combat operations. Units must train to operate with widespread denial, degradation, or disruption of friendly space capabilities.

Refer to FM 3-14 for additional information on space activities.

III. Command Post (CP) Organization/Operations

Ref: FM 6-0 (C2), Commander and Staff Organization and Operations (Apr '16), chap. 1.

This section describes how commanders organize their headquarters into command posts during the conduct of operations. This section defines the different types of command posts and describes their purposes. Next, this section discusses the effectiveness and survivability factors commanders consider when organizing their command posts. This section also describes how commanders cross-functionally organize their staffs within command posts into functional and integrating cells. The section concludes by providing guidelines for command post operations, including the importance of establishing standard operating procedures (SOPs) for the headquarters.

Refer to JP 3-33 for more information on an Army headquarters serving as a joint headquarters.

Command Post (CP)

A command post is a unit headquarters where the commander and staff perform their activities. The headquarters' design, combined with robust communications, gives commanders a flexible mission command structure consisting of a main CP, a tactical CP, and a command group for brigades, divisions, and corps. Combined arms battalions are also resourced with a combat trains CP and a field trains CP. Theater army headquarters are resourced with a main CP and a contingency CP. See appropriate echelon manuals for doctrine on specific CP and headquarters' organization. Each CP performs specific functions by design as well as tasks the commander assigns. Activities common in all CPs include, but are not limited to:

- Maintaining running estimates and the common operational picture
- Controlling operations
- Assessing operations
- Developing and disseminating orders
- Coordinating with higher, lower, and adjacent units
- Conducting knowledge management and information management
- Conducting network operations
- Providing a facility for the commander to control operations, issue orders, and conduct rehearsals
- Maintaining the common operational picture
- Performing CP administration (examples include sleep plans, security, and feeding schedules)
- Supporting the commander's decisionmaking process

I. Command Post Organization

In operations, effective mission command requires continuous, close coordination, synchronization, and information sharing across staff sections. To promote this, commanders cross-functionally organize elements of staff sections in command posts (CPs) and CP cells. Additional staff integration occurs in meetings, including working groups and boards.

See following pages (pp. 5-20 to 5-21) for an overview and discussion of the types of command posts as outlined in FM 3-0.

Types of Command Posts

Ref: FM 3-0 (w/Chg 1), Operations (Dec '17), pp. 2-34 to 2-38.

Main Command Post

A main command post is a facility containing the majority of the staff designed to control current operations, conduct detailed analysis, and plan future operations (FM 6-0). The main CP is the unit's principal CP serving as the primary location for plans, analysis, sustainment coordination, and assessment. It includes representatives of all staff sections and a full suite of information systems to plan, prepare, execute, and assess operations. The main CP is larger in size and in personnel and less mobile than the tactical CP. The chief of staff or executive officer provides staff supervision of the main CP. All units battalion echelon and above are resourced a main CP. Functions of the main CP include, but are not limited to—

- Controlling operations.
- Receiving reports for subordinate units and preparing reports required by higher echelon headquarters.
- Planning operations, including branches and sequels.
- Integrating intelligence into current operations and plans.
- Synchronizing the targeting process.
- Planning and synchronizing sustaining operations.
- Assessing the overall progress of operations.

Contingency Command Post

A contingency CP is a facility tailored from the theater army headquarters that enables a commander to conduct crisis response and limited contingency operations within an AOR. Employing the contingency CP for a mission involves a trade-off between the contingency command post's immediate response capability and its known limitations. These limitations include the scale, scope, complexity, intensity, and duration of operations that it can effectively command without significant augmentation. The contingency CP depends upon the main CP for long-range planning and special staff functional support.

Operational Command Post

An operational CP is a facility containing a tailored portion of a field army headquarters used to control operations for a limited period or for a small-scale contingency. The operational CP provides a field army commander, or designated individual, the capability to form an ARFOR, land component, or JTF headquarters within a JOA. Depending on the situation, the operational CP staff may require additional augmentation, since its design provides minimal essential capabilities. The operational CP may require joint augmentation if it is designated a JTF headquarters or joint force land component headquarters. The operational CP personnel and equipment are deployable by fixed-wing aircraft from their garrison locations into a JOA. However, the operational CP has limited organic transportation once deployed into the JOA and typically occupies a semi-permanent fixed facility. The operational CP relies on the main CP for detailed planning, analysis, and special staff support.

Tactical Command Post

A tactical command post is a facility containing a tailored portion of a unit headquarters designed to control portions of an operation for a limited time (FM 6-0). The tactical CP maintains continuous communication with subordinates, higher echelon headquarters, other CPs, and supporting units. The tactical CP is fully mobile and includes only essential Soldiers and equipment. The tactical CP relies on the main CP for planning, detailed analysis, and coordination. A deputy commander or operations officer generally leads the tactical CP. Corps through battalion commanders employ a tactical CP as an extension of the main CP. Functions of a tactical CP include—

- Controlling the decisive operation or a specific shaping operation.
- Controlling a specific task within a larger operation such as a gap crossing, a passage of lines, a relief in place, or an air assault operation.
- Controlling the overall unit's operations for a limited time when the main CP is displacing or otherwise not available.
- Performing short-range planning.
- Providing input to targeting and future operations planning.
- Providing a forward location for issuing orders and conducting rehearsals.
- Forming the headquarters of a task force with subordinate units task-organized under its control.

When a commander does not employ the tactical CP, the staff assigned to it reinforces the main CP. Unit standard operating procedures should address the specifics for this, including procedures to quickly detach the tactical CP from the main CP. Some multi-functional support brigades and functional brigades and battalions are not resourced with a tactical CP by table of organization and equipment; however, based on the situation, commanders can form a tactical CP from the personnel and equipment authorized from the main CP to assist them with mission command.

Support Area Command Post (SACP)

Depending on the situation, including the threat, size of the support area, and number of units within the support and consolidation areas, division and corps commanders may form a support area command post (SACP) to assist in controlling operations. The SACP enables division and corps commanders to exercise mission command over disparate functionally focused elements operating within the support and consolidation areas that may exceed the effective span of control of the MEB or division and corps main CPs.

The SACP is not a separate section in the units table of organization and equipment. Commanders form a SACP from the equipment and personnel from the main and tactical CPs. The SACP normally co-locates with the MEB, which provides the SACP with signal connectivity, sustainment, security and workspace.

Early-Entry Command Post (EECP)

While not a separate section of a unit's table of organization and equipment, commanders can establish an early-entry command post to assist them in controlling operations during the deployment phase of an operation. An early-entry command post is a lead element of a headquarters designed to control operations until the remaining portions of the headquarters are deployed and operational (FM 6-0).

Based on the situation, an early entry command post normally consists of personnel and equipment from the tactical CP with additional intelligence analysts, planners, and other staff officers from the main CP. The early-entry CP performs the functions of the main and tactical CPs until those CPs are deployed and operational. A deputy commander, assistant division commander, chief of staff, executive officer, or operations officer normally leads the early entry CP.

Command Group

While not a CP, commanders form a command group to assist them in controlling operations when they are not located at a CP. A command group consists of the commander and selected staff members who assist the commander in controlling operations away from a command post (FM 6-0). Command group personnel include staff representation that can immediately affect current operations, such as maneuver, fires (including the air liaison officer), and intelligence. The mission dictates the command group's makeup.

II. Command Post (CP) Organization Considerations

Ref: FM 6-0 (C2), Commander and Staff Organization and Operations (Apr '16), pp. 1-3 to 1-4.

When organizing the CP, commanders must consider effectiveness and survivability. However, effectiveness considerations may compete with survivability considerations, making it difficult to optimize either. Commanders balance survivability and effectiveness considerations when organizing CPs.

A. Effectiveness Factors

CP staff and equipment are arranged to facilitate coordination, information exchange, and rapid decision making. CPs must effectively communicate with all subordinate units. Their organization enables them to quickly deploy throughout the unit's area of operations (AO). Five factors contribute to CP effectiveness: design, standardization, continuity, deployability, and capacity and range.

1. Design and Layout

Many design considerations affect CP effectiveness. At a minimum, commanders position CP cells and staff elements to facilitate communication and coordination. Other design considerations include, but are not limited to:

- Efficient facilitation of information flow
- User interface with communications systems
- Positioning information displays for ease of use
- Integrating complementary information on maps and displays
- Adequate workspace for the staff and commander
- Ease of displacement (setup, teardown, and mobility)
- Effective and efficient power generation and distribution.

Well-designed CPs integrate command and staff efforts. Meeting this requirement requires matching the CP's manning, equipment, information systems, and procedures against its internal layout and utilities. Organizing the CP into functional and integrating cells promotes efficiency and coordination.

2. Standardization

Standardization increases efficiency and eases CP personnel training. Commanders develop detailed SOPs for all aspects of CP operations during all operations. Standard CP layouts, battle drills, and reporting procedures increase efficiency. Units follow and revise SOPs throughout training. Units constantly reinforce using SOPs to make many processes routine. Staffs then effectively execute them in demanding, stressful times.

3. Continuity

Commanders staff, equip, and organize CPs to control and support 24-hour operations without interruptions by enemies, environmental conditions, or actions. However, duplicating every staff member within a CP is unnecessary. Commanders carefully consider the primary role and functions assigned to each CP and resource it accordingly. Internal CP SOPs address shifts, rest plans, and other CP activities important to operating continuously. Leaders enforce these provisions.

Maintaining continuity during displacement or catastrophic loss requires designating alternate CPs and procedures for passing control between them. SOPs address providing continuity when units lose communications with the commander, subordinates, and or a particular CP. Commanders designate seconds in command and inform them of all critical decisions. Primary staff officers also designate alternates.

4. Deployability
CPs deploy efficiently and move within the AO as required. Determining the capabilities, size, and sequence of CPs in the deployment flow requires careful consideration. Commanders can configure modular CP elements as an early-entry command post if needed. They also add or subtract elements to the early-entry command post as needed. CP size directly affects deployment and employment.

5. Capacity, Connectivity and Range
Efficient and effective CP organization allows the commander to maintain the capacity to plan, prepare, execute, and continuously assess operations. CPs require uninterrupted connectivity to effectively communicate with higher and subordinate headquarters. Commanders and staffs must consider various factors that can adversely affect the efficiency of communications systems, such as built-up areas, mountains, and atmospheric conditions.

B. Survivability Factors
CP survivability is vital to mission success. CPs often gain survivability at the price of effectiveness. CPs need to remain small and highly mobile. When concentrated, the enemy can easily acquire and target most CPs. However, when elements of a CP disperse, they often have difficulty maintaining a coordinated staff effort. When developing command post SOPs and organizing headquarters into CPs for operations, commanders use dispersion, size, redundancy, and mobility to increase survivability.

1. Dispersion
Dispersing CPs enhances survivability. Commanders place minimum resources forward and keep more elaborate facilities back. This makes it harder for enemies to find and attack them. It also decreases support and security requirements forward. Most of the staff resides in the main CP; the tactical CP contains only the staff and equipment essential to controlling current operations.

2. Size
A CP's size affects its survivability. Larger CPs ease face-to-face coordination; however, they are vulnerable to multiple acquisitions and means of attack. Units can hide and protect smaller CPs more easily but may not control all force elements. Striking the right balance provides a responsive yet agile organization. For example, commanders require information for decisions; they do not need every subject matter expert located with them.

3. Redundancy
Some personnel and equipment redundancy is required for continuous operations. Redundancy allows CPs to continue operating when mission command systems are lost, damaged, or fail under stress.

4. Mobility
CP mobility improves CP survivability, especially at lower echelons. Successful lower-echelon CPs and those employed forward in the combat zone move quickly and often. A smaller size and careful transportation planning allow CPs to displace rapidly to avoid the enemy.

III. Command Post Operations

Units must man, equip, and organize command posts to control operations for extended periods. Effective CP personnel use information systems and equipment to support 24-hour operations while they continuously communicate with all subordinate, higher, and adjacent units. Commanders arrange CP personnel and equipment to facilitate internal coordination, information sharing, and rapid decisionmaking. They also ensure that they have procedures to execute the operations process within the headquarters to enhance how they exercise mission command. Commanders use the battle rhythm, SOPs, and meetings to assist them with effective CP operations.

A. Standard Operating Procedures

SOPs that assist with effective mission command serve two purposes. Internal SOPs standardize each CP's internal operations and administration. External SOPs developed for the entire force standardize interactions among CPs and between subordinate units and CPs. Effective SOPs require all Soldiers to know their provisions and train to their standards. (Refer to FM 7-15 for more information on the tasks of command post operations.) Each CP should have SOPs that address the following:

- Organization and setup
- Staffing and shifts plans, including eating and sleeping plans
- Physical security and defense
- Priorities of work
- Equipment and vehicle maintenance, including journals and a maintenance log
- Load plans and equipment checklists
- Orders production and dissemination procedures
- Plans for handling, storing, and cleaning up hazardous materials
- Battle rhythm.
- Use of Army Battle Command Systems, such as Command Post of the Future, Advanced Field Artillery Tactical Data System, and Blue Force Tracker

In addition to these SOPS, each CP requires:

- CP battle drills
- Shift-change briefings
- Reports and returns
- Operations update and assessment briefings
- Operations synchronization meeting
- Procedures for transferring control between CPs.

Command Post Battle Drills

Each CP requires procedures to react to a variety of situations. Specific actions taken by a CP should be defined in its SOPs and rehearsed during training and operations.

Shift-Change Briefings

During continuous operations, CPs operate in shifts. To ensure uninterrupted operations, staffs execute a briefing when shifts change. Depending on the situation, it may be formal or informal and include the entire staff or selected staff members. Normally key CP leaders meet face-to-face. The COS (XO) oversees the briefing, with participants briefing their areas of expertise. The briefing's purpose is to inform the incoming shift of:

- Current unit status
- Significant activities that occurred during the previous shift
- Significant decisions and events anticipated during the next shift

Sample Shift-Change Briefing

Ref: FM 6-0 (C2), Commander and Staff Organization and Operations (Apr '16), table 1-1, p. 1-1.

Current mission and commander's intent (COS [XO])

Enemy situation (G-2 [S-2])

- Significant threat or local populace attitudes and actions during the last shift.
- Current enemy situation and changes in the most likely enemy courses of action
- Anticipated significant threat or undesired local populace activity in the next 12/24/48 hours
- Changes in priority intelligence requirements (PIRs)
- Weather update and weather effects on operations in the next 12/24/48 hours.
- Changes to information collection priorities.
- Status of information collection units and capabilities.

Civil Situation (G-9 [S-9])

- Significant actions by the population during the last shift
- Current civil situation
- Disposition and status of civil affairs units and capabilities
- Significant activities involving the population anticipated during the next shift

Friendly situation (G-3 [S-3])

- Significant friendly actions during the last shift
- Subordinate units' disposition and status
- Higher and adjacent units' disposition and status
- Major changes to the task organization and tasks to subordinate units that occurred during the last shift
- Answers to CCIRs and changes in CCIRs
- Changes to reconnaissance and surveillance
- Disposition and status of selected reconnaissance and surveillance units and capabilities
- Answers to FFIRs and changes in FFIRs
- Significant activities/decisions scheduled for next shift (decision support matrix)
- Anticipated planning requirements

Running estimate summaries by warfighting function and staff section —

- Fires
- Air liaison officer
- Aviation officer
- Air and missile defense officer
- G-7 (S-7)
- Engineer officer
- Chemical officer
- Provost marshal
- G-1 (S-1)
- G-4 (S-4)
- G-6 (S-6)

Briefings include—

- Any significant activities that occurred during the last shift
- The disposition and status of units within their area of expertise
- Any changes that have staff wide implications (for example, "higher headquarters changed the controlled supply rate for 120 mm HE, so that means...").
- Upcoming activities and anticipated changes during the next shift

CP operations and administration (headquarters commandant or senior operations NCO).

- CP logistic issues
- CP security
- CP displacement plan and proposed new locations
- Priority of work

COS or XO guidance to the next shift, including staff priorities and changes to the battle rhythm.

Mission Command

IV. Command Post Cells and Staff Sections

Ref: FM 6-0 (C2), Commander and Staff Organization and Operations (Apr '16), pp. 1-5 to 1-8.

Within CPs, commanders cross-functionally organize their staffs into CP cells and staff sections to assist them in the exercise of mission command. A command post cell is a grouping of personnel and equipment organized by warfighting function or by planning horizon to facilitate the exercise of mission command.

CP Cells (Functional and Integrating)

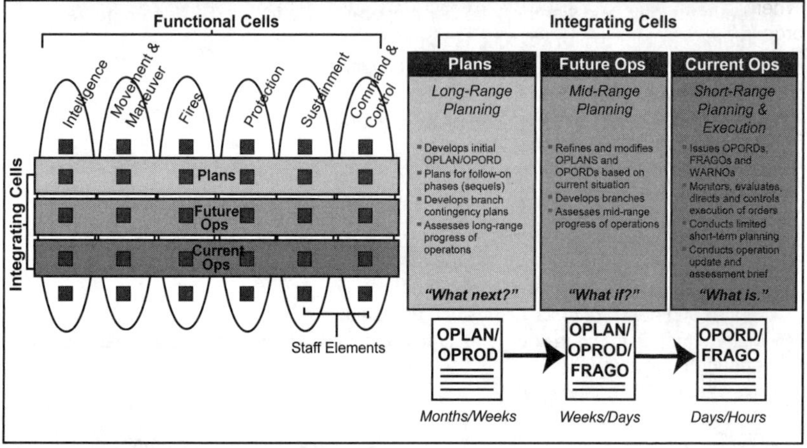
Functional Cells
Intelligence
Movement & Maneuver
Fires
Protection
Sustainment
Command & Control
Integrating Cells
Plans
Future Ops
Current Ops
Staff Elements
Integrating Cells
Plans
Long-Range Planning
Develops initial OPLAN/OPORD
Plans for follow-on phases (sequels)
Develops branch contingency plans
Assesses long-range progress of operatons
"What next?"
Future Ops
Mid-Range Planning
Refines and modifies OPLANS and OPORDs based on current situation
Develops branches
Assesses mid-range progress of operations
"What if?"
Current Ops
Short-Range Planning & Execution
Issues OPORDs, FRAGOs and WARNOs
Monitors, evaluates, directs and controls execution of orders
Conducts limited short-term planning
Conducts operation update and assessment brief
"What is."
OPLAN/ OPROD
OPLAN/ OPROD/ FRAGO
OPORD/ FRAGO
Months/Weeks
Weeks/Days
Days/Hours

A. Functional Cells

Functional cells coordinate and synchronize forces and activities by warfighting function. The functional cells within a CP are intelligence, movement and maneuver, fires, protection, and sustainment. Echelons above brigade are resourced for all five functional cells.

- **Intelligence Cell.** The intelligence cell coordinates activities and systems that help commanders understand the enemy, terrain and weather, and civil considerations. The intelligence cell requests, receives, and analyzes information from all sources to produce and distribute intelligence products. This includes tasks associated with intelligence preparation of the battlefield and intelligence, surveillance, and reconnaissance. Most of the intelligence staff section resides in this cell. The unit's intelligence officer leads this cell.
- **Movement and Maneuver Cell.** The movement and maneuver cell coordinates activities and systems that move forces to achieve a position of advantage in relation to the enemy. This includes tasks associated with combining forces with direct fire or fire potential (maneuver) and force projection (movement) related to gaining a positional advantage over an enemy. Elements of the operations, airspace command and control, aviation, engineer, geospatial information and service, and space staff sections form this cell. The operations officer leads this cell. Staff elements in this cell also form the core of the current operations cell.
- **Fires Cell.** The fires cell coordinates activities and systems that provide collective and coordinated use of Army indirect fires, joint fires, and C2 warfare through the targeting process. The fires cell is comprised of elements of fire support, Air Force (or air component), and electronic warfare staff section. The chief of fires (or fire support officer brigade and below) leads this cell.
- **Protection Cell.** The protection cell coordinates the activities and systems that preserve the force through composite risk management. This includes tasks associated with protecting personnel, physical assets, and information. Elements of the following staff sections form this cell: air and missile defense; chemical, biological, radiological, and nuclear;

engineer; operations security; personnel recovery; and provost marshal. Additionally, safety exists in theater army. The protection cell coordinates with the signal staff section in the C2 cell to further facilitate the information protection task. The chief of protection leads this cell.

- **Sustainment Cell.** The sustainment cell coordinates activities and systems that provide support and services to ensure freedom of action, extend operational reach, and prolong endurance. It includes those tasks associated with logistics, personnel services, and Army health service support. The following staff sections form this cell: personnel, logistics, financial management, and surgeon. The chief of sustainment (or logistics officer brigade and below) leads this cell.

B. Integrating Cells

Whereas functional cells are organized by warfighting functions, integrating cells are organized by planning horizons. They coordinate and synchronize forces and warfighting functions within a specified planning horizon and include the plans cell, future operations cell, and current operations integration cell. A planning horizon is a point in time commanders use to focus the organization's planning efforts to shape future events (ADRP 5-0). The three planning horizons are long, mid, and short (generally associated with the plans cell, future operations cell, and current operations integration cell, respectively).

Planning horizons are situation-dependent and are influenced by events and decisions. For example, the plans cell normally focuses its planning effort on the development of sequels—the subsequent next operation or phase of the operation based on possible outcomes (success, stalemate, or defeat) of the current operation or phase. The future operations cell normally focuses its efforts on branch plans—options built into the base plan that changes the concept of operations based on anticipated events, opportunities, or threats. Planning guidance and decisions by the commander or that of the higher headquarters influence the planning horizons.

Not all echelons and types of units are resourced for all three integrating cells. Battalions, for example, combine their planning and operations responsibilities in one integrating cell. The brigade combat team has a small, dedicated plans cell but it is not resourced for a future operations cell.

- **Plans Cell.** The plans cell is responsible for planning operations for the long-range planning horizons. It prepares for operations beyond the scope of the current order by developing plans, orders, branch plans, and sequels. The plans cell also oversees military deception planning. After completing the initial operation order, the plans cell normally develops plans for the next operation or the next phase of the current operation. The plans cell consists of a core group of planners and analysts led by the plans officer (or the operations officer at brigade and battalion levels). All staff sections assist as required.
- **Future Operations Cell.** The future operations cell is responsible for planning operations in the mid-range planning horizon. It focuses on adjustments to the current operation—including the positioning or maneuvering of forces in depth—that facilitates continuation of the current operation. The cell consists of a core group of planners led by an assistant operations officer (the chief of future operations). All staff sections assist as required. Divisions and above headquarters have a future operations cell. Battalion and brigade headquarters do not. In many respects, the future operations cell serves as a fusion cell between the plans and current operations cells. The future operations cell monitors current operations and determines implications for operations within the mid-range planning horizon. In coordination with the current operations cell, the future operations cell assesses whether the ongoing operation must be modified to achieve the current phase's objectives.
- **Current Operations Cell.** The current operations cell is the focal point for the execution of the operations. This involves assessing the current situation while regulating forces and war fighting functions in accordance with the mission, commander's intent, and concept of operations. The current operations cell displays the common operational picture and conducts shift changes, assessments, and other briefings as required. It provides information on the status of operations to all staff members and to higher, subordinate, and adjacent units. All staff sections are represented, either permanently or on call. *See also p. 1-44.*

See facing page (p. 5-25) for a sample shift-change briefing.

Reports and Returns

A unit's reporting system facilitates timely and effective information exchange among CPs and higher, lower, and adjacent headquarters. An established SOP for reports and returns drives effective information management. These SOPs state the writer, the frequency and time, and recipient of each report. List nonstandard reports in Annex R (Reports) of the operation plan and operation order.

Operation Update and Assessment Briefing

An operation update and assessment briefing may occur daily or anytime the commander calls for one. Its content is similar to the shift-change briefing but has a different audience. The staff presents it to the commander and subordinate commanders. It provides all key personnel with common situational awareness. Often commanders require this briefing shortly before an operation begins to summarize changes made during preparation, including changes resulting from reconnaissance and surveillance efforts.

During the briefing, staff sections present their running estimates. Subordinate commanders brief their current situation and planned activities. Rarely do all members conduct this briefing face-to-face. All CPs and subordinate commanders participate using available communications, including radio, conference calls, and video teleconference. The briefing follows a sequence and format specified by SOPs. That keeps transmissions short, ensures completeness, and eases note taking. This briefing normally has a format similar to a shift-change briefing. However, it omits CP administrative information and includes presentations by subordinate commanders in an established sequence.

Operations Synchronization Meeting

The operations synchronization meeting is the key event in the battle rhythm in support of the current operation. Its primary purpose is to synchronize all war fighting functions and other activities in the short-term planning horizon. It is designed to ensure that all staff members have a common understanding of current operations, including upcoming and projected actions at decision points.

The operations synchronization meeting does not replace the shift-change briefing or operation update and assessment briefing. Chaired by the G-3 (S-3), representatives of each CP cell and separate staff section attend the meeting. The operations synchronization meeting includes a fragmentary order addressing any required changes to maintain synchronization of current operations, and any updated planning guidance for upcoming working groups and boards. All war fighting functions are synchronized and appropriate fragmentary orders are issued to subordinates based on the commander's intent for current operations.

Transferring Control of Operations Between CPs

The employment and use of CPs are important decisions reflected in the operation order. Often, a particular CP may control part or all of the operation for a specific time. Effectively transferring control between CPs requires a well-understood SOP and clear instructions in the operation order. While all CPs have some ability to exercise control on the move, they lose many capabilities they have when stationary. Therefore, CPs normally control operations from a static location. During moves, they transfer control responsibilities to another CP. Transfer of control requires notifying subordinates since many network operations change to route information to the new controlling CP. SOPs establish these requirements to minimize interruptions when transferring control.

B. Battle Rhythm

A headquarters' battle rhythm consists of a series of meetings, briefings, and other activities synchronized by time and purpose. Battle rhythm is a deliberate daily cycle of command, staff, and unit activities intended to synchronize current and future operations. The COS (XO) oversees the battle rhythm. Staffs should logically sequence each meeting, to include working groups and boards, so they have one meeting's outputs available as another meeting's inputs (to include higher headquarters meetings). The COS (XO) balances other staff duties and responsibilities with the time required to plan, prepare for, and hold meetings and conduct briefings. The COS (XO) also critically examines attendance requirements. Some staff sections and CP cells may lack the personnel to attend all events. The COS (XO) and staff members constantly look for ways to combine meetings and eliminate unproductive ones. The battle rhythm enables:

- Establishing a routine for staff interaction and coordination
- Facilitating interaction between the commander and staff
- Synchronizing activities of the staff in time and purpose
- Facilitating planning by the staff and decision making by the commander

The battle rhythm changes during execution as operations progress. For example, early in the operation a commander may require a daily plans update briefing. As the situation changes, the commander may only require a plans update every three days. Some factors that help determine a unit's battle rhythm include the staff's proficiency, higher headquarters' battle rhythm, and current mission. In developing the unit's battle rhythm, the chief COS (XO) considers:

- Higher headquarters' battle rhythm and report requirements
- Subordinate headquarters' battle rhythm requirements
- The duration and intensity of the operation
- Integrating cells' planning requirements

C. Meetings

Meetings are gatherings to present and exchange information, solve problems, coordinate action, and make decisions. They may involve the staff; the commander and staff; or the commander, subordinate commanders, staff, and other partners. Who attends depends on the issue. Commanders establish meetings to integrate the staff and enhance planning and decision making within the headquarters. Commanders also identify staff members to participate in the higher commander's meeting, including working groups and boards. (JP 3-33 discusses the various working groups and boards used by joint force commanders.) The number of meetings and subjects they address depend on the situation and echelon. While numerous informal meetings occur daily within a headquarters, meetings commonly included in a unit's battle rhythm and the cells responsible for them include:

- A shift-change briefing (current operations integration cell)
- An operation update and assessment briefing (current operations integration cell)
- An operations synchronization meeting (current operations integration cell)
- Planning meetings and briefings (plans or future operations cells)
- Working groups and boards (various functional and integrating cells)

Working Groups and Boards

Boards and working groups are types of meetings and are included in the unit's battle rhythm. A board is a grouping of predetermined staff representatives with delegated decision authority for a particular purpose or function. Boards are similar to working groups. However, commanders appoint boards to make decisions. When the process or activity being synchronized requires command approval, a board is the appropriate forum.

A working group is a grouping of predetermined staff representatives who meet to provide analysis, coordinate, and provide recommendations for a particular purpose or function. Their cross-functional design enables working groups to synchronize contributions from multiple CP cells and staff sections. For example, the targeting working group brings together representatives of all staff elements concerned with targeting. It synchronizes the contributions of all staff elements with the work of the fires cell. It also synchronizes fires with future operations and current operations integration cells.

Working groups address various subjects depending on the situation and echelon. Battalion and brigade headquarters normally have fewer working groups than higher echelons have. Working groups may convene daily, weekly, monthly, or intermittently depending on the subject, situation, and echelon. Typical working groups and the lead cell or staff section at division and corps headquarters include the following:

- Assessment working group (plans or future operations cell)
- Operations and intelligence working group (intelligence cell)
- Targeting working group (fires cell)
- Protection working group (protection cell)
- Civil affairs operations working group (civil affairs operations staff section)
- Information operations working group (movement and maneuver cell)
- Cyber electromagnetic activities working group (electronic warfare element)

Sample Working Group SOP

Sample SOP for a division civil-military operations working group.

Purpose/Frequency	Purpose: • Establish policies, procedures, priorities, and overall direction for all civil-military operations projects • Provide update on ongoing civil-military operations projects • Identify needs within the area of operations • Present suggested future projects Frequency: Weekly	
Composition	Chair: G-9 Attendees: • Civil affairs battalion representative • G-2 planner • G-3 operations representative • G-5 planner • G-7 representative • Staff Judge Advocate representative • Military information support planner • Host-nation liaison officers • Engineer planner	• Public Affairs BCT and Marine Corps liaison officer • Military information support element representative • Provost marshal or force protection representative • Special operations forces liaison officer • Surgeon • Chaplain • Project manager and contractor representatives
Inputs/Outputs	Inputs: • Project management status • Information Operations working group (last week's) • Targeting board • Higher headquarters operation order	Outputs: • Updated project status matrix • Proposed project matrix • Long-range civil-military operations plan adjustment
Agenda	• G-2 update or assessment • Operations update • Public perception update • Civil affairs project update • Engineer project update	• Staff Judge Advocate concerns • Discussion or issues • Approval of information operations working group inputs

Ref: FM 6-0 (C2), Commander and Staff Organization and Operations, table 1-2, p. 1-14.

IV. Liaison

Ref: FM 6-0 (C2), Commander and Staff Organization and Operations (Apr '16), chap. 13.

This section discusses liaison fundamentals and responsibilities of liaison officers and teams. It addresses requirements distinct to contingency operations and unified action. It includes liaison checklists and an example outline for a liaison officer handbook.

I. Liaison Fundamentals

Liaison is that contact or intercommunication maintained between elements of military forces or other agencies to ensure mutual understanding and unity of purpose and action (JP 3-08). Liaison helps reduce uncertainty. Most commonly used for establishing and maintaining close communications, liaison continuously enables direct, physical communications between commands. Commanders use liaison during operations and normal daily activities to help facilitate communications between organizations, preserve freedom of action, and maintain flexibility. Effective liaison ensures commanders that subordinates understand implicit coordination. Liaison provides commanders with relevant information and answers to operational questions, thus enhancing the commander's confidence.

Liaison activities augment the commander's ability to synchronize and focus combat power. They include establishing and maintaining physical contact and communications between elements of military forces and nonmilitary agencies during unified action. Liaison activities ensure:

- Cooperation and understanding among commanders and staffs of different headquarters
- Coordination on tactical matters to achieve unity of effort
- Synchronization of lethal and non-lethal operations
- Understanding of implied or inferred coordination measures to achieve synchronized results

A. Liaison Officer

A liaison officer (LNO) represents a commander or staff officer. Laos transmit information directly, bypassing headquarters and staff layers. A trained, competent, trusted, and informed LNO (either a commissioned or a noncommissioned officer) is the key to effective liaison. LNOs must have the commander's full confidence and experience for the mission.

Senior liaison officer rank by echelon	Recommended rank
Multinational or joint force commander[1]	Colonel
Corps	Lieutenant Colonel
Division	Major
Brigade, regiment, or group	Captain
Battalion	Lieutenant
[1]These include joint force commanders and functional component commanders and may also include major interagency and international organizations.	

Ref: FM 6-0 (C1), table 13-1, p. 13-1. Senior liaison officer rank by echelon.

The LNO's parent unit or unit of assignment is the sending unit. The unit or activity that the LNO is sent to is the receiving unit, which may be a host nation. An LNO normally remains at the receiving unit until recalled. LNOs represent the commander and they:

- Understand how the commander thinks and interpret the commander's messages
- Convey the commander's intent, guidance, mission, and concept of operations
- Represent the commander's position

As a representative, the LNO has access to the commander consistent with the duties involved. However, for routine matters, LNOs work for and receive direction from the chief of staff (COS) or the executive officer (XO). Using one officer to perform a liaison mission conserves manpower while guaranteeing a consistent, accurate flow of information. However, continuous operations require a liaison team.

The professional capabilities and personal characteristics of an effective LNO encourage confidence and cooperation with the commander and staff of the receiving unit. In addition to the above discussion, effective LNOs:

- Know the sending unit's mission; current and future operations; logistics status; organization; disposition; capabilities; and tactics, techniques, and procedures
- Appreciate and understand the receiving unit's TTP, organization, capabilities, mission, doctrine, staff procedures, and customs
- Are familiar with:
  - Requirements for and purpose of liaison
  - The liaison system and its reports, documents, and records
  - Liaison team training
  - Observe the established channels of command and staff functions
  - Are tactful
  - Possess familiarity with local culture and language, and have advanced regional expertise if possible

Mission Command

B. Liaison Elements

Commanders organize liaison elements based on the mission variables (known as METT-TC) and echelon of command. Common ways to organize liaison elements include, but are not limited to:

- A single LNO
- A liaison team consisting of one or two LNOs, or an LNO and a liaison NCO in charge, clerical personnel, and communications personnel along with their equipment
- Couriers (messengers) responsible for the secure physical transmission and delivery of documents and other materials
- A digital liaison detachment comprised of several teams with expertise and equipment in specialized areas, such as intelligence, operations, fire support, air defense, and sustainment

Digital Liaison Detachments

Digital liaison detachments provide Army commanders units to conduct liaison with major subordinate or parallel headquarters. Digital liaison detachments consist of staff officers with a broad range of expertise who are capable of analyzing the situation, facilitating coordination between multinational forces, and assisting in cross-boundary information flow and operational support. These 30-Soldier teams are essential not only for routine liaison, but also for advising and assisting multinational partners in conducting planning and operations at intermediate tactical levels. These detachments can operate as a single entity for liaison with a major multinational headquarters, or provide two smaller teams for digital connectivity and liaison with smaller multinational headquarters.

II. Liaison Duties

Ref: FM 6-0 (C2), Commander and Staff Organization and Operations (Apr '16), pp. 13-7 to 13-8.

LNOs also inform the receiving unit's commander or staff of the sending unit's needs or requirements. The LNO's ability to rapidly clarify questions about the sending unit can keep the receiving unit from wasting planning time. During the liaison tour, LNOs:

- Arrive at the designated location on time
- Promote cooperation between the sending and receiving unit
- Follow the receiving unit's communication procedures
- Actively obtain information without interfering with receiving unit operations
- Facilitate understanding of the sending unit's commander's intent
- Help the sending unit's commander assess current and future operations
- Remain informed of the sending unit's current situation and provide that information to the receiving unit's commander and staff
- Expeditiously inform the sending unit of the receiving unit's upcoming missions, tasks, and orders
- Ensure the sending unit has a copy of the receiving unit's SOP
- Inform the receiving unit's commander or COS (XO) of the content of reports transmitted to the sending unit
- Keep a record of their reports, listing everyone met (including each person's name, rank, duty position, and telephone number)
- Attempt to resolve issues within receiving unit before involving the sending unit
- Notify the sending unit promptly if unable to accomplish the liaison mission
- Report their departure to the receiving unit's commander at the end of their mission
- Arrive at least two hours before any scheduled briefings
- Check in with security and complete any required documentation
- Present your credentials to the COS (XO)
- Arrange for an "office call" with the commander
- Meet the coordinating and special staff officers
- Notify the sending unit of arrival
- Visit staff elements, brief them on the sending unit's situation, and collect information from them
- Deliver all correspondence designated for the receiving unit
- Annotate on all overlays the security classification, title, map scale, grid intersection points, effective date-time group, and date-time group received
- Pick up all correspondence for the sending unit when departing
- Inform the receiving unit of your departure time, return route, and expected arrival time at the sending unit

After the Tour

After returning to the sending unit, LNOs promptly transmit the receiving unit's requests to the sending unit's commander or staff, as appropriate. They also brief the COS (XO) on mission-related liaison activities and prepare written reports, as appropriate.

Accuracy is paramount. Effective LNOs provide clear, concise, complete information. If the accuracy of information is not certain, they quote the source and include the source in the report. LNOs limit their remarks to mission-related observations.

- Deliver all correspondence
- Brief the COS (XO) and the appropriate staff elements
- Prepare the necessary reports
- Clearly state what you did and did not learn from the mission

III. Liaison Responsibilities

Ref: FM 6-0 (C2), Commander and Staff Organization and Operations (Apr '16), pp. 13-3 to 13-7.

Both the sending and receiving units have liaison responsibilities before, during, and after operations.

Sending Unit

The sending unit's most important tasks include selecting and training the soldiers best qualified for liaison duties.

Sample Questions

LNOs should be able to answer the following questions:

- Does the sending unit have a copy of the receiving unit's latest OPLAN, OPORD, and FRAGORDs?
- Does the receiving unit's plan support the plan of the higher headquarters? This includes logistics as well as the tactical concept. Are MSRs and RSRs known? Can the CSR support the receiving unit's plan?
- What are the receiving unit's CCIR?
- Which sending commander decisions are critical to executing the receiving unit operation? What are the "no-later-than" times for those decisions?
- What assets does the unit need to acquire to accomplish its mission? How would they be used? How do they support attaining the more senior commander's intent? Where can the unit obtain them? from higher headquarters? other Services? multinational partners?
- How are aviation assets (rotary and fixed-wing) being used?
- How can the LNO communicate with the sending unit? Secure comms?
- What terrain has been designated as key? decisive?
- What weather conditions would have a major impact on the operation?
- What effect would a chemical environment have on the operation?
- What effect would large numbers of refugees or EPWs have?
- What is the worse thing that could happen during the current operation?
- How would you handle a passage of lines by other units?
- What HN support is available to the sending unit? IRs?
- Required reports (from higher and sending units' SOPs)

Packing list

- Credentials
- Forms: DA Form 1594 and other blank forms as required
- Computers and other INFOSYS required for information and data exchange
- Signal operating instructions extract and security code encryption device
- Communications equipment, including remote FM radio equipment
- Sending unit telephone book
- List of commanders and staff officers
- Telephone calling (credit) card
- Movement table
- Admin equipment (for example, pens, paper, scissors, tape, and hole punch)
- Map and chart equipment
- Tent (camouflage net, cots, stove, as appropriate)
- Foreign phrase book and dictionary and local currency as required
- References: Excerpts of higher and sending headquarters' orders and plans, sending unit SOP, sending unit's command diagrams, mission briefings, etc.

The sending unit provides a description of the liaison party (number and type of vehicles and personnel, call signs, and radio frequencies) to the receiving unit:

- Identification and appropriate credentials for the receiving unit
- Appropriate security clearance, courier orders, transportation, and communications equipment
- The SOP outlining the missions, functions, procedures, and duties of the sending unit's liaison section
- Individual weapons and ammunition
- Rations for the movement to the receiving unit

Liaison Checklist-Before Departing the Sending Unit

- Understand what the sending commander wants the receiving commander to know
- Receive a briefing from operations, intelligence, and other staff elements on current and future operations
- Receive and understand the tasks from the sending unit staff
- Obtain the correct maps, traces, and overlays
- Arrange for transport, communications and cryptographic equipment, codes, signal instructions, and the challenge and password-including their protection and security. Arrange for replacement of these items, as necessary.
- Complete route-reconnaissance and time-management plans so the LNO party arrives at the designated location on time
- Verify that the receiving unit received the liaison team's security clearances and will grant access to the level of information the mission requires
- Verify courier orders
- Know how to destroy classified information in case of an emergency during transit or at the receiving unit
- Inform the sending unit of the LNO's departure time, route, arrival time, and, when known, the estimated time and route of return
- Pick up all correspondence designated for the receiving unit
- Conduct a radio check
- Know the impending moves of the sending unit and the receiving unit
- Bring INFOSYS needed to support LNO operations
- Pack adequate supplies of classes I and III for use in transit

Receiving Unit

The receiving unit is responsible for:

- Providing the sending unit with the LNO's reporting time, place, point of contact, recognition signal, and password
- Providing details of any tactical movement and logistic information relevant to the LNO's mission, especially while the LNO is in transit
- Ensuring that the LNO has access to the commander, the COS (XO), and other officers for important matters
- Giving the LNO an initial briefing and allowing the LNO access necessary to remain informed of current operations
- Protecting the LNO while at the receiving unit
- Publishing a standing operating procedure (SOP) outlining the missions, functions, procedures, and duties of the LNO or team at the receiving unit
- Providing access to communications equipment (and operating instructions, as needed) when the LNO needs to communicate with the receiving unit's equipment
- Providing administrative and logistic support

IV. Liaison Considerations

Joint, interagency, and multinational operations require greater liaison efforts than most other operations.

Joint Operations

Current joint information systems do not meet all operational requirements. Few U.S. military information systems are interoperable. Army liaison teams require information systems that can rapidly exchange information between commands to ensure Army force operations are synchronized with operations of the joint force and its Service components.

Interagency Operations

Army forces may participate in interagency operations across the range of military operations, especially when conducting stability or defense support of civil authorities tasks. Frequently, Army forces conduct operations in cooperation with or in support of civilian government agencies. Relations in these operations are rarely based on standard military command and support relationships; rather, national laws or specific agreements for each situation govern the specific relationships in interagency operations. Defense support of civil authorities provides an excellent example. Federal military forces that respond to a domestic disaster will support the Federal Emergency Management Agency, while National Guard forces working in state active duty status (Title 32 United States Code) or conducting National Guard defense support of civil authorities will support that state's emergency management agency. National Guard forces federalized under Title 10 United States Code will support the Federal Emergency Management Agency. The goal is always unity of effort between military forces and civilian agencies, although unity of command may not be possible. Effective liaison and continuous coordination become keys to mission accomplishment.

Some missions require coordination with nongovernmental organizations. While no overarching interagency doctrine delineates or dictates the relationships and procedures governing all agencies, departments, and organizations in interagency operations, the National Response Framework provides some guidance. Effective liaison elements work toward establishing mutual trust and confidence, continuously coordinating actions to achieve cooperation and unity of effort. In these situations, LNOs and their teams require a broader understanding of the interagency environment, responsibilities, motivations, and limitations of nongovernmental organizations, and the relationships these organizations have with the U.S. military.

Multinational Operations

Army units often operate as part of a multinational force. Interoperability is an essential requirement for multinational operations. The North Atlantic Treaty Organization (NATO) defines interoperability as the ability to operate in synergy in the execution of assigned tasks. Interoperability is also the condition achieved among communications-electronics systems or items of satisfactory communication between them and their users. The degree of interoperability should be defined when referring to specific cases. Examples of interoperability include the deployment of a computer network (such as the Combined Enterprise Network Theater Information Exchange System) to facilitate inter-staff communication. Nations whose forces are interoperable can operate together effectively in numerous ways. Less interoperable forces have correspondingly fewer ways to work together. Although frequently identified with technology, important areas of interoperability include doctrine, procedures, communications, and training. Factors that enhance interoperability include planning for interoperability, conducting multinational training exercises, staff visits to assess multinational capabilities, a command atmosphere that rewards sharing information, and command emphasis on a constant effort to eliminate the sources of confusion and misunderstanding.

Chap 6

I. Rehearsals

Ref: FM 6-0 (C2), Commander and Staff Organization and Operations (Apr '16), chap. 12.

Rehearsals allow leaders and their Soldiers to practice executing key aspects of the concept of operations. These actions help Soldiers orient themselves to their environment and other units before executing the operation. Rehearsals help Soldiers to build a lasting mental picture of the sequence of key actions within the operation. Rehearsals are the commander's tool to ensure staffs and subordinates understand the commander's intent and the concept of operations. They allow commanders and staffs to identify shortcomings (errors or omissions) in the plan not previously recognized. Rehearsals also contribute to external and internal coordination as the staff identifies additional coordinating requirements.

Rehearsal Techniques

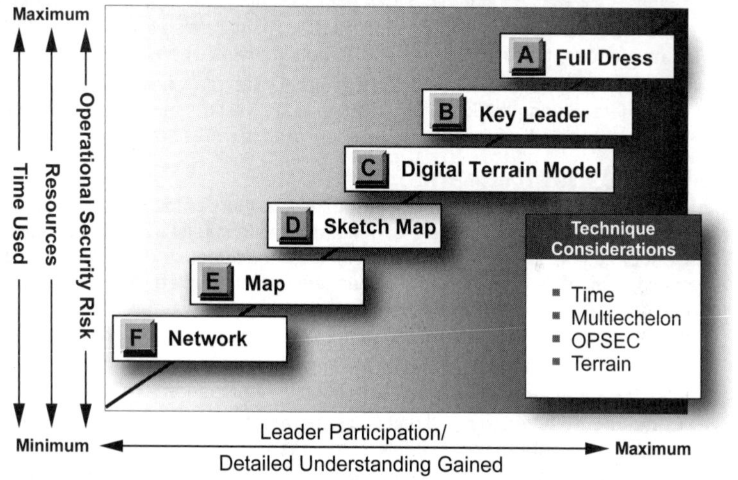

Ref: FM 6-0 (C2), Commander & Staff Organization and Operations, fig. 12-1, p. 12-3.

Effective and efficient units habitually rehearse during training. Commanders at every level routinely train and practice various rehearsal types and techniques. Local standard operating procedures (SOPs) identify appropriate rehearsal types, techniques, and standards for their execution. All leaders conduct periodic after action reviews to ensure their units conduct rehearsals to standard and correct substandard performances. After action reviews also enable leaders to incorporate lessons learned into existing plans and orders, or into subsequent rehearsals.

I. Methods of Rehearsals

Ref: FM 6-0 (C2), Commander and Staff Organization and Operations (Apr '16), pp. 12-2 to 12-6.

Techniques for conducting rehearsals are limited only by the commander's imagination and available resources. Generally, six techniques are used for executing rehearsals.

A. Full-dress Rehearsal

A full-dress rehearsal produces the most detailed understanding of the operation. It involves every participating soldier and system. If possible, organizations execute full-dress rehearsals under the same conditions-weather, time of day, terrain, and use of live ammunition-that the force expects to encounter during the actual operation.

- **Time**. Full-dress rehearsals are the most time consuming of all rehearsal types. For companies and smaller units, the full-dress rehearsal is the most effective technique for ensuring all involved in the operation understand their parts. However, brigade and task force commanders consider the time their subordinates need to plan and prepare when deciding whether to conduct a full-dress rehearsal.
- **Echelons involved**. A subordinate unit can perform a full-dress rehearsal as part of a larger organization's reduced-force rehearsal.
- **OPSEC**. Moving a large part of the force may attract enemy attention. Commanders develop a plan to protect the rehearsal from enemy surveillance and reconnaissance. One method is to develop a plan, including graphics and radio frequencies, that rehearses selected actions but does not compromise the actual OPORD. Commanders take care to not confuse subordinates when doing this.
- **Terrain**. Terrain management for a full-dress rehearsal can be difficult if it is not considered during the initial array of forces. The rehearsal area must be identified, secured, cleared, and maintained throughout the rehearsal.

B. Key Leader Rehearsal

Circumstances may prohibit a rehearsal with all members of the unit. A key leader rehearsal involves only key leaders of the organization and its subordinate units. Often commanders use this technique to rehearse fire control measures for an engagement area during defensive operations. Commanders often use a reduced-force rehearsal to prepare key leaders for a full-dress rehearsal.

- **Time**. A reduced-force rehearsal normally requires less time than a full-dress rehearsal. Commanders consider the time their subordinates need to plan and prepare when deciding whether to conduct a reduced-force rehearsal.
- **Echelons involved**. A small unit can perform a full-dress rehearsal as part of a larger organization's reduced-force rehearsal.
- **OPSEC**. A reduced-force rehearsal is less likely to present an OPSEC vulnerability than a full-dress rehearsal because the number of participants is smaller. However, the number of radio transmissions required is the same as for a full-dress rehearsal and remains a consideration.
- **Terrain**. Terrain management for the reduced-force rehearsal can be just as difficult as for the full-dress rehearsal. The rehearsal area must be identified, secured, cleared, and maintained throughout the rehearsal.

C. Terrain-model Rehearsal (or "Digital" Terrain-model)

The terrain-model rehearsal is the most popular rehearsal technique. It takes less time and fewer resources than a full-dress or reduced-force rehearsal. When possible, commanders place the terrain model where it overlooks the actual terrain of the AO. (reverse slope for OPSEC, though).The model's orientation coincides with that of the terrain. The size of the terrain model can vary from small (using markers to represent units) to large (on which the participants can walk).

- **Time**. Often, the most time-consuming part of this technique is constructing the terrain model.
- **Echelons involved**. Because a terrain model is geared to the echelon conducting the rehearsal, multiechelon rehearsals using this technique are difficult.
- **OPSEC**. This rehearsal can present an OPSEC vulnerability if the area around the site is not secured. The collection of commanders & vehicles can draw enemy attention.
- **Terrain**. Terrain management is less difficult than with the previous techniques. An optimal location overlooks the terrain where the operation will be executed. With today's digital capabilities, users can construct terrain models in virtual space.

D. Sketch-map Rehearsal

Commanders can use the sketch-map technique almost anywhere, day or night. The procedures are the same as for a terrain-model rehearsal, except the commander uses a sketch map in place of a terrain model. Effective sketches are large enough for all participants to see as each participant walks through execution of the operation. Participants move markers on the sketch to represent unit locations and maneuvers.

- **Time**. Sketch-map rehearsals take less time than terrain-model rehearsals and more time than map rehearsals.
- **Echelons involved**. Because a sketch map is geared to the echelon conducting the rehearsal, multiechelon rehearsals using this technique are difficult.
- **OPSEC**. This rehearsal can present an OPSEC vulnerability if the area around the site is not secured. The collection of commanders & vehicles can draw enemy attention.
- **Terrain**. This technique requires less space than a terrain model rehearsal. A good site is easy for participants to find, yet concealed from the enemy. An optimal location overlooks the terrain where the unit will execute the operation.

E. Map Rehearsal

A map rehearsal is similar to a sketch-map rehearsal, except the commander uses a map and operation overlay of the same scale used to plan the operation.

- **Time**. The most time-consuming part is the rehearsal itself. A map rehearsal is normally the easiest technique to set up, since it requires only maps and current operational graphics.
- **Echelons involved**. Because a map is geared to the echelon conducting the rehearsal, multiechelon rehearsals using this technique are difficult.
- **OPSEC**. This rehearsal can present an OPSEC vulnerability if the area around the site is not secured. The collection of commanders & vehicles can draw enemy attention.
- **Terrain**. This technique requires the least space. An optimal location overlooks the terrain where the operations will be executed, but is concealed from the enemy.

F. Network Rehearsal

Units conduct network rehearsals over wide-area networks or local area networks. Commanders and staffs practice these rehearsals by talking through critical portions of the operation over communications networks in a sequence the commander establishes. The organization rehearses only the critical parts of the operation. CPs can also rehearse battle tracking.

- **Time**. If the organization does not have a clear SOP and if all units are not up on the net, this technique can be very time consuming.
- **Echelons involved**. This technique lends itself to multiechelon rehearsals. Participation is limited only by commander's desires and the availability of INFOSYSs.
- **OPSEC**. If a network rehearsal is executed from current unit locations, the volume of the communications transmissions and potential compromise of information through enemy monitoring can present an OPSEC vulnerability.
- **Terrain**. If a network rehearsal is executed from unit locations, terrain considerations are minimal.

II. Rehearsal Responsibilities

Ref: FM 6-0 (C2), Commander and Staff Organization and Operations (Apr '16), pp. 12-6 to 12-9.

This discussion addresses responsibilities for conducting rehearsals. It is based on the combined arms rehearsal. Responsibilities are the same for support rehearsals.

Rehearsal Planning

Commanders and chiefs of staff (COSs) plan rehearsals.

Commander

Commanders provide the following information as part of the cdr's guidance during the initial mission analysis. They re-evaluate it when they select a COA:

- Type of rehearsal
- Rehearsal technique
- Place
- Attendees
- Enemy COA to be portrayed

Chief of Staff (XO)

The COS (XO) ensures that all rehearsals are included in the organization's time-management SOP. COS (XO) responsibilities include:

- Publishing the rehearsal time and location in the OPORD or in a warning order
- Completing any staff rehearsals
- Determining rehearsal products, based on type, technique, and METT-TC
- Coordinating liaison officer (LNO) attendance from adjacent units

Rehearsal Preparation

Commander

Commanders prepare to rehearse operations with events phased in proper order, from start to finish, when time allows:

- Identify and prioritize key events to rehearse
- Allocate time for each event
- Perform personal preparation, including reviews of: task organization, personnel and materiel readiness, and organizational level of preparation

Chief of Staff (XO)

The COS (XO), through war-gaming and coordinating with the commander:

- Prepares to serve as the rehearsal director
- Coordinates and allocates time for key events requiring rehearsal
- Establishes rehearsal time limits per the commander's guidance and METT-TC
- Verifies rehearsal site preparation. A separate rehearsal site may be required for some events, such as a possible obstacle site. A good rehearsal site includes: appropriate markings and associated training aids, parking areas, local security
  - Determines the method for controlling the rehearsal and ensuring its logical flow, for example, a script

Subordinate Leaders

Subordinate leaders are responsible for:

- Completing unit OPORDs
- Identifying issues derived from the parent organization's OPORD
- Providing a copy of their unit OPORD, with graphics, to the parent organization
- Performing personal preparation similar to that of the commander
- Ensuring they and their subordinates bring necessary equip (maps, etc).

Conducting HQ's Staff

- Develop an OPORD and necessary overlays
- Deconflict all subordinate unit graphics. Composite overlays are the first step for leaders to visualize the organization's overall plan
- Publish composite overlays at the rehearsal including, at a minimum: maneuver, fire support, mobility and survivability, and sustainment

Rehearsal Execution

Commander

Commanders command the rehearsal, just as they will command the fight. They maintain the focus and level of intensity, allowing no potential for subordinate confusion. Although the staff refines the OPORD, it belongs to the commander, who uses it to fight. An effective rehearsal is not a commander's brief to subordinates. Its purpose is to validate synchronization - the what, when, and where-of tasks subordinate units will perform to execute the operation and achieve the commander's intent.

Chief of Staff (XO)

Normally, the COS (XO) serves as the rehearsal director. This officer ensures each unit will accomplish its tasks at the right time and cues the commander to upcoming decisions. The chief of staff's (executive officer's) script is the execution matrix and the decision support template. The COS (XO) as the rehearsal director—:

- Starts the rehearsal on time
- Conducts a formal roll call
- Ensures everyone brings the necessary equipment. This equipment includes organizational graphics and previously issued orders.
- Validates the task organization. Link-ups must be complete or on schedule, and required materiel and personnel on hand. The importance of this simple check cannot be overemphasized.
- Ensures sustaining operations are synchronized with shaping operations and the decisive operation
- Rehearses the synchronization of combat power from flank and higher organizations, which are often beyond communication range of the commander and G-3 (S-3) when they are away from the CP
- Synchronizes the timing and contribution of each warfighting function by ensuring the rehearsal of operations against the decisive points, by time or event that connect to a decision.
- For each decisive point, defines the conditions required to: 1) commit the reserve or striking force, 2) move a unit, 3) close or emplace an obstacle, 4) fire planned targets, 5) move a medical station, change a supply route, alert specific observation posts
- Disciplines leader movements, enforces brevity, and ensures completeness. The OPORD, decision support template (DST), and execution matrix are the COS's tools.
- Keeps within time constraints
- Ensures that the most important events receive the most attention
- Ensures that absentees and flank units receive changes to the OPORD. Transmits changes to them by courier or radio immediately.

Asst Chief of Staff, G-3 (S-3)

- Portrays friendly scheme of maneuver
- Ensures compliance with the plan
- Normally provides the recorder

Asst Chief of Staff, G-2 (S-2)

The G-2 (S-2) plays the enemy commander during rehearsals. He bases his actions on the enemy COA the commander selects during the MDMP. The G-2/S-2:

- Provides participants with current intelligence
- Portrays the best possible assessment of the enemy COA
- Communicates the enemy commander's presumed concept of operations, desired effects, and intended end state

Subordinate Leaders

- Effectively articulate their units' actions and responsibilities
- Record changes on their copies of the graphics or OPORD

Recorder

During the rehearsal, the recorder:

- Captures all coordination made during execution
- Captures unresolved problems

At the end of the rehearsal, the recorder:

- Presents any unresolved problems to the commander for resolution
- Restates any changes, coordination, or clarifications directed by the commander
- Estimates when a written FRAGORD codifying the changes will follow

Conducting HQ's Staff

The staff updates the OPORD, DST, and execution matrix.

Rehearsals & AARs

III. Rehearsal Types

Ref: FM 6-0 (C2), Commander and Staff Organization and Operations (Apr '16), pp. 12-1 to 12-2.

Each rehearsal type achieves a different result and has a specific place in the preparation timeline.

A. Backbrief

A back brief is a briefing by subordinates to the commander to review how subordinates intend to accomplish their mission. Normally, subordinates perform back briefs throughout preparation. These briefs allow commanders to clarify the commander's intent early in subordinate planning. Commanders use the back brief to identify any problems in the concept of operations.

The back brief differs from the confirmation brief (a briefing subordinates give their higher commander immediately following receipt of an order) in that subordinate leaders are given time to complete their plan. Back briefs require the fewest resources and are often the only option under time-constrained conditions. Subordinate leaders explain their actions from start to finish of the mission. Back briefs are performed sequentially, with all leaders reviewing their tasks. When time is available, back briefs can be combined with other types of rehearsals. Doing this lets all subordinate leaders coordinate their plans before performing more elaborate drills.

B. Combined Arms Rehearsal

A combined arms rehearsal is a rehearsal in which subordinate units synchronize their plans with each other. A maneuver unit headquarters normally executes a combined arms rehearsal after subordinate units issue their operation order. This rehearsal type helps ensure that subordinate commanders' plans achieve the higher commander's intent.

C. Support Rehearsal

The support rehearsal helps synchronize each war fighting function with the overall operation. This rehearsal supports the operation so units can accomplish their missions. Throughout preparation, units conduct support rehearsals within the framework of a single or limited number of war fighting functions. These rehearsals typically involve coordination and procedure drills for aviation, fires, engineer support, or casualty evacuation. Support rehearsals and combined arms rehearsals complement preparations for the operation. Units may conduct rehearsals separately and then combine them into full-dress rehearsals. Although these rehearsals differ slightly by warfighting function, they achieve the same result.

D. Battle Drill or SOP Rehearsal

A battle drill is a collective action rapidly executed without applying a deliberate decision making process. A battle drill or SOP rehearsal ensures that all participants understand a technique or a specific set of procedures. Throughout preparation, units and staffs rehearse battle drills and SOPs. These rehearsals do not need a completed order from higher headquarters. Leaders place priority on those drills or actions they anticipate occurring during the operation. For example, a transportation platoon may rehearse a battle drill on reacting to an ambush while waiting to begin movement.

All echelons use these rehearsal types; however, they are most common for platoons, squads, and sections. They are conducted throughout preparation and are not limited to published battle drills. All echelons can rehearse such actions as a command post shift change, an obstacle breach lane-marking SOP, or a refuel-on-the-move site operation.

Adequate time is essential when conducting rehearsals. The time required varies with the complexity of the mission, the type and technique of rehearsal, and the level of participation. Units conduct rehearsals at the lowest possible level, using the most thorough technique possible, given the time available. Under time-constrained conditions, leaders conduct abbreviated rehearsals, focusing on critical events determined by reverse planning. Each unit will have different critical events based on the mission, unit readiness, and the commander's assessment.

The rehearsal is a coordination event, not an analysis. It does not replace war-gaming. Commanders war-game during the military decisionmaking process (MDMP) to analyze different courses of action to determine the optimal one. Rehearsals practice that selected course of action. Commanders avoid making major changes to operation orders (OPORDs) during rehearsals. They make only those changes essential to mission success and risk mitigation.

IV. Conducting the Rehearsal

All participants have responsibilities before, during, and after a rehearsal. Before a rehearsal, the rehearsal director states the commander's expectations and orients the other participants on details of the rehearsal as necessary. During a rehearsal, all participants rehearse their roles in the operation. They make sure they understand how their actions support the overall operation and note any additional coordination required. After a rehearsal, participants ensure they understand any changes to the operation order and coordination requirements, and they receive all updated staff products.

Commanders do not normally address small problems that arise during rehearsals. Instead, these are recorded. This ensures the rehearsal's flow is not interrupted. If the problem remains at the end of the rehearsal, the commander resolves it then. However, if the problem can wait until the end of the rehearsal, it may not have been a real problem. If the problem jeopardizes mission accomplishment, the staff accomplishes the coordination necessary to resolve it before the participants disperse. Identifying and solving such problems is a major reason for conducting rehearsals. If corrections are not made while participants are assembled, the opportunity to do so may be lost. Coordinating among dispersed participants and disseminating changes to them is more difficult than accomplishing these actions in person.

A. Before the Rehearsal

Before the rehearsal, the rehearsal director calls the roll and briefs participants on information needed for execution. The briefing begins with an introduction, overview, and orientation. It includes a discussion of the rehearsal script and ground rules. The detail of this discussion is based on participants' familiarity with the rehearsal SOP.

Before the rehearsal, the staff develops an operation order with at least the basic five paragraphs and necessary overlays. Annexes may not be published; however, the responsible staff officers should know their content.

1. Introduction and Overview

Before the rehearsal, the rehearsal director introduces all participants as needed. Then, the director gives an overview of the briefing topics, rehearsal subjects and sequence, and timeline, specifying the no-later-than ending time. The rehearsal director explains after action reviews, describes how and when they occur, and discusses how to incorporate changes into the operation order. The director explains any restraints, such as pyrotechnics use, light discipline, weapons firing, or radio silence. For safety, the rehearsal director ensures that all participants understand safety precautions and enforces their use. Last, the director emphasizes results and states the commander's standard for a successful rehearsal. Subordinate leaders state any results of planning or preparation (including rehearsals) they have already conducted. If a subordinate recommends a change to the operation order, the rehearsal director acts on the recommendation before the rehearsal begins, if possible. If not, the commander resolves the recommendation with a decision before the rehearsal ends.

2. Orientation

The rehearsal director orients the participants to the terrain or rehearsal medium. Orientation is identified using magnetic north on the rehearsal medium and symbols representing actual terrain features. The director explains any graphic control measures, obstacles, and targets and then issues supplemental materials, if needed.

3. Rehearsal Script

An effective technique for controlling rehearsals is to use a script. It keeps the rehearsal on track. The script provides a checklist so the organization addresses all warfighting functions and outstanding issues. It has two major parts: the agenda and the response sequence.

See facing page (p. 6-9) for discussion of the agenda and response sequence.

Special staff officers should brief by exception when a friendly or enemy event occurs within their area of expertise. Summarizing these actions at the end of the rehearsal can reinforce the coordination requirements identified during the rehearsal. The staff updates the decision support template and gives a copy to each participant. Under time-constrained conditions, the conducting headquarters staff may provide copies before the rehearsal and rely on participants to update them with pen-and-ink changes.

4. Ground Rules

After discussing the rehearsal script, the rehearsal director:

- States the standard (what the commander will accept) for a successful rehearsal
- Ensures everyone understands the parts of the operation order to rehearse. If the entire operation will not be rehearsed, the rehearsal director states the events to be rehearsed.
- Quickly reviews the rehearsal SOP if all participants are not familiar with it. An effective rehearsal SOP states:

  - Who controls the rehearsal
  - Who approves the rehearsal venue and its construction
  - When special staff officers brief the commander
  - The relationship between how the execution matrix portrays events and how units rehearse events
- Establishes the timeline; it designates the rehearsal starting time in relation to H-hour. For example, have the rehearsal begin by depicting the anticipated situation one hour before H-hour. One event executed before rehearsing the first event is deployment of forces.
- Establishes the time interval to begin and track the rehearsal. For example, specify a ten-minute interval equates to one hour of actual time.
- Updates friendly and adversary activities as necessary, for example, any ongoing reconnaissance

The rehearsal director concludes the orientation with a call for questions.

The Rehearsal Script

Ref: FM 6-0 (C2), Commander and Staff Organization and Operations (Apr '16), pp. 12-10 to 12-11.

Rehearsal Agenda

An effective rehearsal follows a prescribed agenda that everyone knows and understands.

An effective rehearsal includes, but is not limited to:

- Roll call
- Participant orientation to the terrain
- Location of local civilians
- Enemy situation brief
- Friendly situation brief
- Description of expected adversary actions
- Discussion of friendly unit actions
- Review of notes made by the recorder

The execution matrix, decision support template, and operation order outline the rehearsal agenda. These tools, especially the execution matrix, both drive and focus the rehearsal. The commander and staff use them to control the operation's execution. Any templates, matrices, or tools developed within each of the warfighting functions (for example an intelligence synchronization matrix or fires execution matrix) should tie directly to the supported unit's execution matrix and decision support template.

An effective rehearsal requires the enemy force and other operational environmental factors to be portrayed realistically and quickly without distracting from the rehearsal. One technique for doing this has the G-2 (S-2) preparing an actions checklist. It lists a sequence of events much like the one for friendly units but from the enemy or civilian perspective.

Response Sequence

Participants respond in a logical sequence: either by war fighting function or by unit as the organization is deployed, from front to rear. The commander determines the sequence before the rehearsal. It is posted at the rehearsal site, and the rehearsal director may restate it.

Effective rehearsals allow participants to visualize and synchronize the concept of operations. As the rehearsal proceeds, participants talk through the concept of operations. They focus on key events and the synchronization required to achieve the desired effects. The commander commands the rehearsal. The commander gives orders during the operation. Subordinate commanders enter and leave the discussion at the time they expect to begin and end their tasks or activities during the operation. This practice helps the commander assess the adequacy of synchronization. They do not "re-war-game" unless absolutely necessary to ensure subordinate unit commanders understand the plan.

The rehearsal director emphasizes integrating fires, events that trigger different branch actions, and actions on contact. The chief of fires (fire support officer) or fires unit commander states when fires are initiated, who is firing, from where the firing comes, the ammunition available, and the desired target effect. Subordinate commanders state when they initiate fires per their fire support plans. The rehearsal director speaks for any absent staff section and ensures all actions on the synchronization matrix and decision support template are addressed at the proper time or event.

The rehearsal director ensures that key sustainment and protection actions are included in the rehearsal at the times they are executed. Failure to do this reduces the value of the rehearsal as a coordination tool.

B. During the Rehearsal (Rehearsal Steps)

Ref: FM 6-0 (C2), Commander and Staff Organization and Operations (Apr '16), pp. 12-12 to 12-13.

Once the rehearsal director finishes discussing the ground rules and answering questions, the G-3 (S-3) reads the mission statement, the commander reads the commander's intent, and the G-3 (S-3) establishes the current friendly situation. The rehearsal then begins, following the rehearsal script.

The outline below is based on a generic set of rehearsal steps developed for combined arms rehearsals. However, with a few modifications, these steps support any rehearsal technique. The products depend on the rehearsal type.

1. Step 1 – Enemy Forces Deployed

The G-2 (S-2) briefs the current enemy situation and operational environment and places markers on the map or terrain board (as applicable) indicating where enemy forces and other operationally significant groups or activities would be before the first rehearsal event. The G-2 (S-2) then briefs the most likely enemy course of action and operational context. The G-2 (S-2) also briefs the status of reconnaissance and surveillance operations (for example, citing any patrols still out or any observation post positions).

2. Step 2 – Friendly Forces Deployed

The G-3 (S-3) briefs friendly maneuver unit dispositions, including security forces, as they are arrayed at the start of the operation. Subordinate commanders and other staff officers brief their unit positions at the starting time and any particular points of emphasis. For example, the chemical, biological, radiological, and nuclear officer states the mission-oriented protective posture level, and the chief of fires (fire support officer) or fires unit commander states the range of friendly and enemy artillery. Other participants place markers for friendly forces, including adjacent units, at the positions they will occupy at the start of the operation. As participants place markers, they state their task and purpose, task organization, and strength. Sustainment and protection units brief positions, plans, and actions at the starting time and at points of emphasis the rehearsal director designates. Subordinate units may include forward arming and refueling points, refuel-on-the-move points, communications checkpoints, security points, or operations security procedures that differ for any period during the operation. The rehearsal director restates the commander's intent, if necessary.

3. Step 3 – Initiate Action

The rehearsal director states the first event on the execution matrix. Normally this involves the G-2 (S-2) moving enemy markers according to the most likely course of action. The depiction must tie enemy actions to specific terrain or to friendly unit actions. The G-2 (S-2) portrays enemy actions based on the situational template developed for staff war-gaming.

As the rehearsal proceeds, the G-2 (S-2) portrays the enemy and other operational factors and walks through the most likely enemy course of action (per the situational template). The G-2 (S-2) stresses reconnaissance routes, objectives, security force composition and locations, initial contact, initial fires (artillery, air, and attack helicopters), probable main force objectives or engagement areas, and likely commitment of reserve forces.

4. Step 4 – Decision Point

When the rehearsal director determines that a particular enemy movement or reaction is complete, the commander assesses the situation to determine if a decision point has been reached. Decision points are taken directly from the decision support template.

If the commander determines the unit is not at a decision point and not at the end state, the commander directs the rehearsal director to continue to the next event on the execution matrix. Participants use the response sequence and continue to act out and describe their units' actions.

When the rehearsal reaches conditions that establish a decision point, the commander decides whether to continue with the current course of action or by selecting a branch. If electing the current course of action, the commander directs the rehearsal director to move to the next event in the execution matrix. If selecting a branch, the commander states why that branch, states the first event of that branch, and continues the rehearsal until the organization has rehearsed all events of that branch. As the unit reaches decisive points, the rehearsal director states the conditions required for success.

When it becomes obvious that the operation requires additional coordination to ensure success, participants immediately begin coordinating. This is one of the key reasons for rehearsals. The rehearsal director ensures that the recorder captures the coordination and any changes and all participants understand the coordination.

5. Step 5 – End State Reached

Achieving the desired end state completes that phase of the rehearsal. In an attack, this will usually be when the unit is on the objective and has finished consolidation and casualty evacuation. In the defense, this will usually be after the decisive action (such as committing the reserve or striking force), the final destruction or withdrawal of the enemy, and casualty evacuation is complete. In a stability operation, this usually occurs when a unit achieves the targeted progress within a designated line of effort.

6. Step 6 – Reset

At this point, the commander states the next branch to rehearse. The rehearsal director resets the situation to the decision point where that branch begins and states the criteria for a decision to execute that branch. Participants assume those criteria have been met and then refight the operation along that branch until they attain the desired end state. They complete any coordination needed to ensure all participants understand and can meet any requirements. The recorder records any changes to the branch.

The commander then states the next branch to rehearse. The rehearsal director again resets the situation to the decision point where that branch begins, and participants repeat the process. This continues until the rehearsal has addressed all decision points and branches that the commander wants to rehearse.

If the standard is not met and time permits, the commander directs participants to repeat the rehearsal. The rehearsal continues until participants are prepared or until the time available expires. (Commanders may allocate more time for a rehearsal but must assess the effects on subordinate commanders' preparation time.) Successive rehearsals, if conducted, should be more complex and realistic.

At the end of the rehearsal, the recorder restates any changes, coordination, or clarifications that the commander directed and estimates how long it will take to codify changes in a written FRAGORD.

C. After the Rehearsal

After the rehearsal, the commander leads an after action review. The commander reviews lessons learned and makes the minimum required modifications to the existing plan. (Normally, a FRAGORD effects these changes.) Changes should be refinements to the operation order; they should not be radical or significant. Changes not critical to the operation's execution may confuse subordinates and hinder the synchronization of the plan. The commander issues any last minute instructions or reminders and reiterates the commander's intent.

Based on the commander's instructions, the staff makes any necessary changes to the operation order, decision support template, and execution matrix based on the rehearsal results. Subordinate commanders incorporate these changes into their units' operation orders. The chief of staff (executive officer) ensures the changes are briefed to all leaders or liaison officers who did not participate in the rehearsal.

A rehearsal provides the final opportunity for subordinates to identify and fix unresolved problems. The staff ensures that all participants understand any changes to the operation order and that the recorder captures all coordination done at the rehearsal. All changes to the published operation order are, in effect, verbal fragmentary orders. As soon as possible, the staff publishes these verbal fragmentary orders as a written fragmentary order that changes the operation order.

Rehearsal Assessment

The commander establishes the standard for a successful rehearsal. A properly executed rehearsal validates each leader's role and how each unit contributes to the overall operation—what each unit does, when each unit does it relative to times and events, and where each unit does it to achieve desired effects. An effective rehearsal ensures commanders have a common vision of the enemy, their own forces, the terrain, and the relationships among them. It identifies specific actions requiring immediate staff resolution and informs the higher commander of critical issues or locations that the commander, COS (XO), or G-3 (S-3) must personally oversee.

The commander (or rehearsal director in the commander's absence) assesses and critiques all parts of the rehearsal. Critiques center on how well the operation achieves the commander's intent and on the coordination necessary to accomplish that end. Usually, commanders leave the internal execution of tasks within the rehearsal to the subordinate unit commander's judgment and discretion.

II. The After Action Review (AAR)

Ref: FM 6-0 (C2), Commander and Staff Organization and Operations (Apr '16), chap. 16 and A Leader's Guide to After Action Reviews (Aug '12)

An after action review (AAR) is a guided analysis of an organization's performance, conducted at appropriate times during and at the conclusion of a training event or operation with the objective of improving future performance. It includes a facilitator, event participants, and other observers (ADRP 7-0, Training Units and Developing Leaders, Aug '12). The AAR provides valuable feedback essential to correcting training deficiencies. Feedback must be direct, on-the-spot and standards-based.

After Action Review Steps

1. Plan the AAR
2. Prepare the AAR
3. Conduct the AAR
4. Follow-up (using AAR results)

Ref: FM 6-0 (C2), Commander and Staff Organization and Operations, p. 16-3.

AARs are a professional discussion of an event that enables Soldiers/units to discover for themselves what happened and develop a strategy (e.g., retraining) for improving performance. They provide candid insights into strengths and weaknesses from various perspectives and feedback, and focus directly on the commander's intent, training objectives and standards. Leaders know and enforce standards for collective and individual tasks. Task standards are performance measures found in the respective training and evaluation outlines (T&EO) found on the Army Training Network (ATN) and the Digital Training Management System (DTMS).

Leaders must avoid creating the environment of a critique during AARs. Because Soldiers and leaders participating in an AAR actively self-discover what happened and why, they learn and remember more than they would from a critique alone. A critique only gives one viewpoint and frequently provides little opportunity for discussion of events by participants. The climate of the critique, focusing only on what is wrong, prevents candid and open discussion of training events and stifles learning and team building.

Leaders make on-the-spot corrections and take responsibility for training Soldiers and units. This occurs when leaders understand the commander's intent and the tasks to be trained, and then exercise the principles of Mission Command to improve Soldier, leader, and unit performance. Units that conduct AARs and empower subordinates to make on-the-spot corrections are more effective.

Types Of After Action Reviews

Two types of after action reviews exist: formal and informal. Commanders generally conduct formal action reviews after completing a mission. Normally, only informal after action reviews are possible during the conduct of operations.

Types of After-Action Reviews

Formal Reviews	Informal Reviews
■ Conducted by either internal or external leaders and external observer and controllers (OC)	■ Conducted by internal chain of command
■ Takes more time to prepare	■ Takes less time to prepare
■ Uses complex training aids	■ Uses simple training aids
■ Scheduled - events and / or tasks are identified beforehand	■ Conducted as needed. Primarily based on leaders assessment
■ Conducted where best supported	■ Held at the training site

Ref: A Leader's Guide to After Action Reviews, p. 5.

A. Formal

Leaders plan formal after action reviews when they complete an operation or otherwise realize they have the need, time, and resources available. Formal after action reviews require more planning and preparation than informal after action reviews. Formal after action reviews require site reconnaissance and selection; coordination for aids (such as terrain models and large-scale maps); and selection, setup, maintenance, and security of the after action review site. During formal after action reviews, the after action review facilitator (unit leader or other facilitator) provides an overview of the operation and focuses the discussion on topics the after action review plan identifies. At the conclusion, the facilitator reviews identified and discussed key points and issues, and summarizes strengths and weaknesses.

B. Informal

Leaders use informal after action reviews as on-the-spot coaching tools while reviewing Soldier and unit performance during or immediately after execution. Informal after action reviews involve all Soldiers. These after action reviews provide immediate feedback to Soldiers, leaders, and units after execution. Ideas and solutions leaders gathered during informal after action reviews can be applied immediately as the unit continues operations. Successful solutions can be identified and transferred as lessons learned.

The After Action Review (AAR)

Ref: FM 6-0 (C2), Commander and Staff Organization and Operations (Apr '16), pp. 16-3 to 16-4.

Formal and informal after action reviews generally follow the same format:

1. Review what was supposed to happen

The facilitator and participants review what was supposed to happen. This review is based on the commander's intent for the operation, unit operation or fragmentary orders (FRAGORDs), the mission, and the concept of operations.

2. Establish what happened

The facilitator and participants determine to the extent possible what actually happened during execution. Unit records and reports form the basis of this determination. An account describing actual events as closely as possible is vital to an effective discussion. The assistant chief of staff, intelligence (G-2 [S-2]) provides input about the operation from the enemy's perspective.

3. Determine what was right or wrong with what happened

Determine what was right or wrong with what happened. Participants establish the strong and weak points of their performance. The facilitator guides discussions so that the conclusions the participants reach are operationally sound, consistent with Army standards, and relevant to the operational environment.

4. Determine how the task should be done differently the next time

The facilitator helps the chain of command lead the group in determining how participants might perform the task more effectively. The intended result is organizational and individual learning that can be applied to future operations. If successful, this learning can be disseminated as lessons learned.

Leaders understand that not all tasks will be performed to standard. In their initial planning, they allocate time and other resources for retraining after execution or before the next operation. Retraining allows participants to apply the lessons learned from after action reviews and implement corrective actions. Retraining should be conducted at the earliest opportunity to translate observations and evaluations from after action reviews into performance in operations. Commanders ensure Soldiers understand that training is incomplete until the identified corrections in performance have been achieved.

After action reviews are often tiered as multi-echelon leader development tools. Following a session involving all participants, senior commanders may continue after action reviews with selected leaders as extended professional discussions. These discussions usually include a more specific review of leader contributions to the operation's results. Commanders use this opportunity to help subordinate leaders master current skills and prepare them for future responsibilities. After action reviews are opportunities for knowledge transfer through teaching, coaching, and mentoring.

Commanders conduct a final after action review during recovery after an operation. This after action review may include a facilitator. Unit leaders review and discuss the operation. Weaknesses or shortcomings identified during earlier after action reviews are identified again and discussed. If time permits, the unit conducts training to correct these weaknesses or shortcomings in preparation for future operations.

Lessons learned can be disseminated in at least three ways. First, participants may make notes to use in retraining themselves and their sections or units. Second, facilitators may gather their own and participants' notes for collation and analysis before dissemination and storage for others to use. Dissemination includes forwarding lessons to other units conducting similar operations as well as to the Center for Army Lessons Learned, doctrinal proponents, and generating force agencies. Third, units should publicize future successful applications of lessons as lessons learned.

Step 1. Planning the After Action Review

Ref: FM 6-0 (C2), Commander and Staff Organization and Operations (Apr '16), pp. 16-3 to 16-4.

To maximize the effectiveness of AARs, formal or informal, leaders must plan and prepare to execute AARs. AAR planning is part of each training event. All leaders must understand the unit's mission and the commander's intent for the operation (event).

The amount and level of detail needed during the planning and preparation process depends on the type of AAR to be conducted and available resources. The AAR process has four steps: planning, preparing, conducting, and follow up (using AAR results).

I. Planning the AAR

1. Selecting and training observor controllers (OCs)
2. Reviewing the training and evaluation outline (T&EO)
3. Scheduling stopping points
4. Determining attendance
5. Choosing training aids
6. Reviewing the AAR plan

Commanders are responsible for training their units. They hold subordinate leaders responsible for training their respective organizations. Commanders instill mission command by using orders for events to enable disciplined initiative within the commander's intent to empower agile and adaptive leaders. The AAR helps Soldiers develop a mutual understanding of the unit's strengths and weaknesses. Commanders issue guidance and specify their intent for an upcoming event's AAR.

The AAR plan provides the foundation for successful AARs. Commanders provide their intent and guidance to develop an AAR plan for each training event. Subordinates then determine how to achieve the commander's intent. The guidance applies for formal and informal AARs and should contain—

- Which tasks are trained and are the focus of the AAR
- Which events / phases of the operation are AARs conducted
- Who observes the training and who conducts the AAR
- Who attends
- When and where the AAR occurs
- What training aids are required

Leaders or OCs use the AAR plan to identify critical places and events they must observe to provide the unit a timely and valid assessment; examples include unit maintenance collection points, passage points, and unit aid stations. The AAR plan also includes who (either internal or external to the unit) facilitates the AAR for a particular event. The leader or OC is the individual tasked to observe training, provide control for the training, and lead the AAR.

1. Selecting and Training Observer Controllers (OC)

When planning an AAR, commanders select leaders/OCs who—

- Demonstrate proficiency in the tasks to be trained
- Are knowledgeable of the duties they are to observe
- Are knowledgeable of current doctrine and TTPs

Rehearsals & AARs

When using external OCs, commanders strive to have OCs that are at least equal in rank to the leader of the unit they will assess. If commanders must choose between experience and an understanding of current TTPs or rank, they should go with experience. A staff sergeant with experience as a tank platoon sergeant is a better platoon OC than a sergeant first class who has no platoon sergeant experience.

Commanders are responsible for training and certifying OCs, to include providing training on how to conduct an AAR. Ideally, inexperienced OCs should observe properly conducted AARs beforehand.

2. Reviewing the Training & Evaluation Outline (T&EO)

The commander must specify their intent for the event along with the objectives and tasks to be trained. The commander also states the operational environment that is to be replicated during the event and the focus of the tasks trained. The leaders then review the T&EO which provides the conditions and standards for the respective collective or individual tasks. Leaders use the T&EOs to measure unit and soldier performance.

T&EOs are located on the Digital Training Management System (DTMS) and via the Army Training Network (ATN). Leaders and OCs must review the tasks to be trained as specified in the commander's guidance and intent for an upcoming event. The respective T&EOs are not only provided to remaining OC team members, but also to the Soldiers in the unit. The T&EO states the performance measures and the order specifies the commander's intent. All members of the unit must review these documents to gain a complete and mutual understanding of the critical places and phases to assess task performance.

3. Scheduling Stopping Points

Commanders schedule the time and place to conduct AARs as an integral part of training events. Commanders plan for an AAR at the end of each critical phase or major training event. For example, a leader may plan a stopping point after issuing an OPORD, when the unit arrives at a new position, or after consolidation on an objective, etc.

Commanders plan to allow approximately 30-45 minutes for platoon-level AARs, 1 hour for company-level AARs, and about 2 hours for battalion-level and above. Soldiers receive better feedback on their performance and remember the lessons longer as result of a quality AAR.

4. Determining Attendance

The AAR plan specifies who attends each AAR. At each echelon, an AAR has a primary set of participants. At squad and platoon levels, everyone attends and participates. At company or higher levels, it may not be practical to have everyone attend because of continuing operations or training. In this case, unit and OPFOR commanders, unit leaders, and other key players may be the only participants. Leaders or OCs may recommend additional participants based on specific observations.

5. Choosing Training Aids

Training aids add to AAR effectiveness. Training aids should directly support discussion of the training and promote learning. Local training support center (TSC) catalogs list training aids available to each unit. Dry-erase boards, video equipment, digital maps, terrain models, and enlarged maps are all worthwhile under the right conditions. For example, if reconnaissance reveals there are no sites which provided a view of the exercise area, the AAR facilitator may want to use a terrain table, or digital map if available.

6. Reviewing the AAR Plan

The AAR plan is only a guide. Commanders issue their intent and subordinates determine how to achieve that intent. Commanders, leaders and OCs should review the AAR plan regularly (e.g., training meeting) to make sure it is on track and meets the training needs of the units. The plan may be adjusted as necessary, but changes take preparation and planning time away from subordinate leaders or OCs. The purpose of the AAR plan is to allow OCs and leaders as much time as possible to prepare for the AAR.

Step 2. Preparing the After Action Review

Ref: FM 6-0 (C2), Commander and Staff Organization and Operations (Apr '16), pp. 16-3 to 16-6.

Preparation is the key to the effective execution of any plan. Preparation for an AAR begins before the training and continues until the actual event.

II. Preparing for the AAR

1. **Reviewing training objectives, T&EOs, orders and doctrine**
2. **Identify key events**
3. **Observing the training and taking notes**
4. **Selecting AAR sites**
5. **Collecting observations**
6. **Organize the AAR**

1. Reviewing Objectives, Orders, Plans, and Doctrine

Facilitators review the unit's mission before the after action review. The mission's objectives form the after action review's focus and the basis for observations. Facilitators review current doctrine, technical information, and applicable unit standard operating procedures to ensure they have the tools needed to properly guide discussion of unit and individual performance. Facilitators read and understand all warning orders (WARNORDs), OPORDs, and FRAGORDs issued before and during execution to understand what the commander wanted to happen. The detailed knowledge that facilitators display as a result of these reviews gives added credibility to their comments.

2. Identifying Key Events

Facilitators identify critical events and ensure they collect data on those events or identify personnel who observed them. Examples of critical events include, but are not limited to:

- Issue of OPORDs and FRAGORDs
- Selected planning steps.
- Contact with opposing forces.
- Civil security attacks while conducting stability tasks.
- Passages of lines and reliefs in place.

3. Collecting Observations

AAR Facilitators are either internal (participating in the training) leaders or external (OCs) to the organization. Both have the requirement to make and consolidate observations to facilitate the discussion of what happened. The OCs keep accurate records of what they see and hear, and record events, actions, and observations by time sequence to prevent loss of valuable information and feedback. OCs can use any recording system (notebook, mobile device, prepared forms, 3x5 cards, etc) as long as it is reliable, sufficiently detailed (identifying times, places, and names), and consistent. They include the date-time group (DTG) of each observation so it can be easily integrated with observations of other OCs. This provides a comprehensive and detailed overview of what happened. When the OC has more time, they review the notes and fill in any details not written down earlier.

At times this may be challenging for leaders that are actively participating in the event and also facilitating the AAR. But this can be mitigated through professional discussions, feedback and involvement of all participants in the AAR to develop a clear understanding of the event.

4. Organizing the AAR

Once facilitators have gathered all available information, they organize their notes chronologically to understand the flow of events. They select and sequence key events in terms of their relevance to the unit's mission and objectives. This helps them identify key discussion and teaching points.

An effective after action review leads participants to discover strengths and weaknesses, propose solutions, and adopt a course of action to improve future operations. Facilitators organize an after action review using one of three methods: chronological order of events, warfighting functions, or key events, themes, or issues:

- Chronological Order of Events
- Warfighting Functions
- Key Events/Themes/Issues

5. Selecting After Action Review Sites

After action reviews should occur at or near where the operation occurred. Leaders should identify and inspect the after action review site and prepare a diagram showing placement of aids and other equipment. A good site minimizes wasted time by allowing rapid assembly of key personnel and positioning of aids. For larger units, this might not be possible for the whole operation. However, higher echelon after action reviews may include visits to selected actual sites to provide learning opportunities.

The after action review site should let Soldiers see the terrain where the operation occurred or accurate representations of it. If this is not possible, facilitators find a location that allows Soldiers to see where the critical or most significant actions happened. Facilitators should have a map or other representation of the area of operations detailed enough to help everyone relate key events to the actual terrain. The representation may be a terrain model, enlarged map, or sketch. Facilitators also require a copy of the unit's graphics or recovered displays of the situation from the information systems databases.

Facilitators provide a comfortable setting for participants by encouraging Soldiers to remove helmets, providing shelter, and serving refreshments. These actions create an environment where participants can focus on the after action review without distractions. Participants should not face into the sun. Key leaders should have seats up front. Vehicle parking and equipment security areas should be far enough away from the after action review site to prevent distractions.

6. Rehearse

After thorough preparation, the facilitator reviews the agenda and prepares to conduct the after action review. Facilitators may opt to conduct a walkthrough of the after action review site as well as review the sequence of events planned for the after action review.

Formal AARs - After thorough preparation, the OC reviews the AAR format and gets ready to conduct the AAR. The OC then announces to unit leaders the AAR starting time and location. This allows enough time for the OCs to prepare and rehearse at the AAR site while unit leaders account for personnel and equipment, perform actions which their unit SOP requires, and move to the AAR site.

Informal AARs – Often leaders have minimal time to prepare for AARs and as time permits they identify and prioritize key observations. They then mentally review the training event in light of the observations gathered personally and from subordinates based on one of the three techniques discussed previously. This allows the leader to mentally step through the AAR.

Step 3. Executing After Action Reviews

Ref: FM 6-0 (C2), Commander and Staff Organization and Operations (Apr '16), pp. 16-6 to 16-7.

Facilitators start an after action review by reviewing its purpose and sequence: the ground rules, the objectives, and a summary of the operation that emphasizes the functions or events to be covered. This ensures that everyone present understands what the commander expects the after action review to accomplish.

III. Conducting the AAR

1. **Introduction and rules**
2. **AAR agenda: commander's mission, intent and concept of the operation (what was supposed to happen).**
3. **Summary of events (what happened)**
   - **Identify what was right or wrong**
   - **Determine how the task should be done differently**
4. **Closing comments (summary)**

1. Introduction and Rules

The following rules apply to all after action reviews. Facilitators emphasize them in their introduction.

- An after action review is a dynamic, candid, professional discussion that focuses on unit performance. Everyone with an insight, observation, or question participates. Total participation is necessary to maintain unit strengths and to identify and correct deficiencies.
- An after action review is not a critique. No one—regardless of rank, position, or strength of personality—has all the information or answers. After action reviews maximize learning benefits by allowing Soldiers to learn from each other.
- An after action review assesses weaknesses to improve and strengths to sustain.

Soldier participation is directly related to the atmosphere created during the introduction. Effective facilitators draw in Soldiers who seem reluctant to participate. The following ideas can help create an atmosphere conducive to maximum participation:

- Reinforce the fact that it is permissible to disagree
- Focus on learning and encourage Soldiers to give honest opinions
- Use open-ended and leading questions to guide the discussion
- Facilitators enter the discussion only when necessary

2. Review of Objectives and Intent

After the introduction, facilitators review the after action review's objectives. This review includes the following:

- A restatement of the events, themes, or issues being reviewed
- The mission and commander's intent (what was supposed to happen)
- The enemy's mission and intent (how the enemy tried to defeat the force)

The commander or a facilitator restates the mission and commander's intent. Facilitators may guide the discussion to ensure that everyone present understands the plan and intent. Another method is to have subordinate leaders restate the mission and discuss the commander's intent. Automated information systems, maps, operational graphics, terrain boards, and other aids can help portray this information.

Intelligence personnel then explain as much of the enemy plan and actions as they know. The same aids the friendly force commander used can help participants understand how the plans related to each other.

3. Summary of Events (What Happened)

The facilitator guides the review, using one of the methods to describe and discuss what actually happened. Facilitators avoid asking yes-or-no questions. They encourage participation and guide the discussion by using open-ended and leading questions. Open-ended questions allow those answering to reply based on what they think is significant. These questions are less likely to put Soldiers on the defensive. Open-ended questions work more effectively in finding out what happened.

As the discussion expands and more Soldiers add their perspectives, what really happened becomes clearer. Facilitators do not tell Soldiers and leaders what was good or bad. Instead, they ensure that the discussion reveals the important issues, both positive and negative. Facilitators may want to expand this discussion and ask, "What could have been done differently?" Skillful guiding of the discussion ensures that participants do not gloss over mistakes or weaknesses.

4. Closing Comments (Summary)

During the summary, facilitators review and summarize key points identified during the discussion. The after action review should end on a positive note, linking conclusions to learning and possible training. Facilitators then depart to allow unit leaders and Soldiers time to discuss the learning in private.

The After Action Report

One of the most important collection techniques used in the Army and many other organizations is the after action report. The concept of the after action report can be easily adapted to fit any unit's lessons learned program.

The after action report provides observations and insights from the lessons learned that allow the unit to reflect on the successes and shortcomings of the operation, and share these lessons with the Army.

The reporting unit organizes the after action report in a logical order, usually by operational phase or warfighting function. It should be arranged chronologically when doing so facilitates the understanding and flow of the information reported. Documenting what worked well should receive as much attention as what did not.

Refer to FM 6-0, Table 16-1 for an example of what a commander and staff may elect to cover in their unit's written after action report. This approved brigade after action report template can apply across all echelons.

Step 4. Follow-up (Benefits of the AAR)

Ref: A Leader's Guide to After Action Reviews (Aug '12), pp. 14 to 15.

AARs are the dynamic link between task performance and execution to standard. They provide commanders a critical assessment tool to plan Soldier, leader and unit training. Through the professional and candid discussion of events, Soldiers can compare their performance against the standard and identify specific ways to improve proficiency

IV. Follow-Up

1. **Identify tasks requiring retraining**
2. **Fix the problem**
   - **Retrain immediately (same training event)**
   - **Revise Standing Operating Procedure (SOP)**
   - **Integrate into future training plans**
3. **Use to assist in making commander's assessment**

Leaders should not delay retraining except when absolutely necessary. If the leader delays retraining, the Soldiers and unit must understand they did not perform the task to standard and that retraining will occur later.

The true benefits of AARs come from applying results in developing future training. Leaders can use the information to assess performance and to plan future training to correct deficiencies and sustain demonstrated task proficiency.

Retraining

Time or complexity of the mission may prevent retraining on some tasks during the same exercise. When this happens, leaders must reschedule the mission or training. As part of this process, leaders must ensure that deficient supporting tasks found during the AAR are also scheduled and retrained.

Revised Standing Operating Procedures

AARs may reveal problems with unit SOPs. If so, unit leaders must revise the SOP and ensure units implement the changes during future training.

AAR Fundamentals

- Conducted during or immediately after each event
- Focus is on commander's intent, training objectives and standards
- Focus is also on Soldier, leader, and unit performance
- Involves all participants in the discussion
- Uses open-ended questions
- Encourages initiative and innovation in finding more effective ways to achieve standards and meet training objectives and commander's intent
- Determines strengths and weaknesses
- Links performance to subsequent training

I. Operational Terms & Acronyms

ADP 1-02, Terms and Military Symbols (Aug '18)

ADP 1-02 constitutes approved Army doctrinal terminology and symbology for general use. It builds on the foundational doctrine established in ADP 1-02.

The principal audience for ADP 1-02 is all members of the profession of Arms. Commanders and staffs of Army headquarters serving as joint task force or multinational headquarters should also refer to applicable joint or multinational doctrine concerning the range of military operations and joint or multinational forces. Trainers and educators throughout the Army will also use this publication.

Commanders, staffs, and subordinates ensure their decisions and actions comply with applicable U.S., international, and, in some cases, host-nation laws and regulations. Commanders at all echelons ensure their Soldiers operate in accordance with the law of war and the rules of engagement. (See FM 27-10.)

This publication implements the following international agreements:

- STANAG 1059 (ED. 8). Letter Codes for Geographical Entities. 1 April 2004.
- STANAG 1241 (ED. 5). NATO Standard Identity Description Structure for Tactical Use. 6 April 2005.
- STANAG 2019 (ED. 7)/APP-6 (D). NATO Joint Military Symbology. 16 October 2017.
- STANAG 3680 (ED. 5)/AAP-6 (2017) (2). NATO Glossary of Terms and Definitions (English and French). 7 February 2018.

ADP 1-02 uses joint terms where applicable.

ADP 1-02 applies to the Active Army, Army National Guard/Army National Guard of the United States, and United States Army Reserve unless otherwise stated.

ADP 1-02 is augmented by the Army Dictionary online. Changes to terminology occur more frequently than traditional publication media can be updated. The terminology and symbology database, known as the Army Dictionary, is updated monthly to reflect the latest editions of Army publications. (To access the database, go to https://jdeis.js.mil/jdeis/index.jsp?pindex=207, and log in with a common access card.) This database is an official Department of Defense (DOD) Web site, maintained by the Combined Arms Doctrine Directorate in collaboration with the Joint Staff Directorate for Joint Force Development. The site is part of the Joint Doctrine, Education, and Training Electronic Information System. It includes all Army doctrinal terms and all military symbols in MIL-STD 2525D, including air, land, maritime, space, activities control measures, and meteorological symbols. While the database includes the same joint terms appearing in ADP 1-02, readers should consult the DOD Dictionary of Military and Associated Terms for up-to-date joint terminology.

ADP 1-02 also provides a single standard for developing and depicting hand-drawn and computer-generated military symbols for situation maps, overlays, and annotated aerial photographs for all types of military operations. It is the Army proponent publication for all military symbols, and it complies with Department of Defense (DOD) Military Standard (MIL-STD) 2525D. The symbology chapters of this ADP focus primarily on military symbols applicable to Army land operations. When communicating instructions to subordinate units, commanders and staffs from company through corps echelons should use this publication as a dictionary of operational terms and military symbols.

Combined Glossary (ADP 5-0/6-0)

This glossary -- compiled from both ADP 5-0 The Operations Process (Jul '19) and ADP 6-0 Mission Command (Jul '19)-- lists operational planning and mission command-related acronyms and terms with Army or joint definitions. Where Army and Joint definitions differ, (Army) precedes the definition. Terms for which ADP 5-0 or ADP 6-0 is the proponent are noted as appropriate. The proponent publication for other terms is listed in parentheses after the definition.

Army team building - A continuous process of enabling a group of people to reach their goals and improve effectiveness through leadership and various exercises, activities and techniques. (FM 6-22)

assessment - The determination of the progress toward accomplishing a task, creating a condition, or achieving an objective. (JP 3-0)

battle rhythm - A deliberate, daily schedule of command, staff, and unit activities intended to maximize use of time and synchronize staff actions. (JP 3-33)

branch - The contingency options built into the base plan used for changing the mission, orientation, or direction of movement of a force to aid success of the operation based on anticipated events, opportunities, or disruptions caused by enemy actions and reactions. (JP 5-0)

campaign plan - A joint operation plan for a series of related major operations aimed at achieving strategic or operational objectives within a given time and space. (JP 5-0)

center of gravity - The source of power that provides moral or physical strength, freedom of action, or will to act. (JP 5-0)

chain of command - The succession of commanding officers from a superior to a subordinate through which command is exercised. (JP 1)

civil considerations - The influence of manmade infrastructure, civilian institutions, and attitudes and activities of the civilian leaders, populations, and organizations within an area of operations on the conduct of military operations. (ADP 6-0)

collaborative planning - Two or more echelons planning together in real time, sharing information, perceptions, and ideas to develop their respective plans simultaneously. (ADP 5-0)

combat power - (Army) The total means of destructive, constructive, and information capabilities that a military unit or formation can apply at a given time. (ADP 3-0)

command - The authority that a commander in the armed forces lawfully exercises over subordinates by virtue of rank or assignment. (JP 1)

command and control - The exercise of authority and direction by a properly designated commander over assigned and attached forces in the accomplishment of the mission. (JP 1)

command and control system - (Army) The arrangement of people, processes, networks, and command posts that enable commanders to conduct operations. (ADP 6-0)

command and control warfighting function - The related tasks and a system that enable commanders to synchronize and converge all elements of combat power. (ADP 3-0)

command post - A unit headquarters where the commander and staff perform their activities. (FM 6-0)

Acronyms & Abbreviations

Ref: FM 6-0 (C2), Commander and Staff Organization and Operations (Apr '16), glossary.

ABCT	armored brigade combat team
ACOS	assistant chief of staff
ADCON	administrative control
ADP	Army doctrine publication
ADRP	Army doctrine reference publication
AO	area of operations
AR	Army regulation
ASCC	Army Service component commander
ASCOPE	areas, structures, capabilities, organizations, people, and events
ATTP	Army tactics, techniques, and procedures
BCT	brigade combat team
CBRN	chemical, biological, radiological, and nuclear
CCIR	commander's critical information requirement
CJCSM	Chairman of the Joint Chiefs of Staff manual
CMOC	civil-military operations center
COA	course of action
COP	common operational picture
COS	chief of staff
CP	command post
DA	Department of the Army
EEFI	essential element of friendly information
FFIR	friendly force information requirement
FM	field manual
FOUO	for official use only
FRAGORD	fragmentary order
GSR	general support-reinforcing
IPB	intelligence preparation of the battlefield
JP	joint publication
KMO	knowledge management officer
LNO	liaison officer
MDMP	military decisionmaking process
METT-TC	mission, enemy, terrain and weather, troops and support available, timeavailable, and civil considerations
MISO	military information support operations
MOE	measure of effectiveness
MOP	measure of performance
NCO	noncomissioned officer
OAKOC	observation and fields of fire, avenues of approach, key terrain, obstacles, and cover and concealment
OPCON	operational control
OPLAN	operation plan
OPORD	operation order
OPSEC	operations security
PIR	priority intelligence requirement
PMESII-PT	political, military, economic, social, information, infrastructure, physical environment, and time
RSOI	reception, staging, onward movement, and integration
SBU	Sensitive But Unclassified
SOP	standard operating procedure
TACON	tactical control
TF	task force
TLP	troop leading procedures
TOE	table of organization and equipment
TTP	tactics, techniques, and procedures
U.S.	United States
WARNORD	warning order

commander's critical information requirement - An information requirement identified by the commander as being critical to facilitating timely decision making. (JP 3-0)

commander's intent - A clear and concise expression of the purpose of the operation and the desired military end state that supports mission command, provides focus to the staff, and helps subordinate and supporting commanders act to achieve the commander's desired results without further orders, even when the operation does not unfold as planned. (JP 3-0)

commander's visualization - The mental process of developing situational understanding, determining a desired end state, and envisioning an operational approach by which the force will achieve that end state. (ADP 6-0)

common operational picture - (Army) A display of relevant information within a commander's area of interest tailored to the user's requirements and based on common data and information shared by more than one command. (ADP 6-0)

concept of operations - (Army) A statement that directs the manner in which subordinate units cooperate to accomplish the mission and establishes the sequence of actions the force will use to achieve the end state. (ADP 5-0)

confirmation brief - A brief subordinate leaders give to the higher commander immediately after the operation order is given to confirm understanding. (ADP 5-0)

control - The regulation of forces and warfighting functions to accomplish the mission in accordance with the commander's intent. (ADP 6-0)

control measure - A means of regulating forces or warfighting functions. (ADP 6-0)

coordinated fire line - A line beyond which conventional surface-to-surface direct fire and indirect fire support means may fire at any time within the boundaries of the establishing headquarters without additional coordination but does not eliminate the responsibility to coordinate the airspace required to conduct the mission. (JP 3-09)

culminating point - The point at which a force no longer has the capability to continue its form of operations, offense or defense. (JP 5-0)

data - In the context of decision making, unprocessed observations detected by a collector of any kind (human, mechanical, or electronic). (ADP 6-0)

decision point - A point in space and time when the commander or staff anticipates making a key decision concerning a specific course of action. (JP 5-0)

decision support matrix - A written record of a war-gamed course of action that describes decision points and associated actions at those decision points. (ADP 5-0)

decision support template - A combined intelligence and operations graphic based on the results of wargaming that depicts decision points, timelines associated with movement of forces and the flow of the operation, and other key items of information required to execute a specific friendly course of action. (JP 2-01.3)

decisive point - A geographic place, specific key event, critical factor, or function that, when acted upon, allows commanders to gain a marked advantage over an enemy or contribute materially to achieving success. (JP 5-0)

depth - The extension of operations in time, space, or purpose to achieve definitive results. (ADP 3-0)

end state - The set of required conditions that defines achievement of the commander's objectives. (JP 3-0)

essential element of friendly information - A critical aspect of a friendly operation that, if known by a threat would subsequently compromise, lead to failure, or limit success of the operation and therefore should be protected from enemy detection. (ADP 6-0)

evaluating - Using indicators to judge progress toward desired conditions and determining why the current degree of progress exists. (ADP 5-0)

execution - The act of putting a plan into action by applying combat power to accomplish the mission and adjusting operations based on changes in the situation. (ADP 5-0)

execution matrix - A visual representation of subordinate tasks in relationship to each other over time. (ADP 5-0)

flexibility - The employment of a versatile mix of capabilities, formations, and equipment for conducting operations. (ADP 3-0)

friendly force information requirement - Information the commander and staff need to understand the status of friendly force and supporting capabilities. (JP 3-0)

graphic control measure - A symbol used on maps and displays to regulate forces and warfighting functions. (ADP 6-0)

indicator - In the context of assessment, a specific piece of information that infers the condition, state, or existence of something, and provides a reliable means to ascertain performance or effectiveness. (JP 5-0)

information - In the context of decision making, data that has been organized and processed in order to provide context for further analysis. (ADP 6-0)

information collection - An activity that synchronizes and integrates the planning and employment of sensors and assets as well as the processing, exploitation, and dissemination systems in direct support of current and future operations. (FM 3-55)

information management - (Army) The science of using procedures and information systems to collect, process, store, display, disseminate, and protect data, information, and knowledge products. (ADP 6-0)

intelligence preparation of the battlefield - The systematic process of analyzing the mission variables of enemy, terrain, weather, and civil considerations in an area of interest to determine their effect on operations. (ATP 2-01.3)

key tasks - Those activities the force must perform as a whole to achieve the desired end state. (ADP 6-0)

knowledge - In the context of decision making, information that has been analyzed and evaluated for operational implications. (ADP 6-0)

knowledge management - The process of enabling knowledge flow to enhance shared understanding, learning, and decision making. (ADP 6-0)

leadership - The activity of influencing people by providing purpose, direction, and motivation to accomplish the mission and improve the organization. (ADP 6-22)

levels of warfare - A framework for defining and clarifying the relationship among national objectives, the operational approach, and tactical tasks. (ADP 1-01)

line of effort - (Army) A line that links multiple tasks using the logic of purpose rather than geographical reference to focus efforts toward establishing a desired end state. (ADP 3-0)

line of operations - A line that defines the directional orientation of a force in time and space in relation to the enemy and links the force with its base of operations and objectives. (ADP 3-0)

main effort - A designated subordinate unit whose mission at a given point in time is most critical to overall mission success. (ADP 3-0)

measure of effectiveness - An indicator used to measure a current system state, with change indicated by comparing multiple observations over time. (JP 5-0)

measure of performance - A indicator used to measure a friendly action that is tied to measuring task accomplishment. (JP 5-0)

military decision-making process - An iterative planning methodology to understand the situation and mission, develop a course of action, and produce an operation plan or order. (ADP 5-0)

mission - The task, together with the purpose, that clearly indicates the action to be taken and the reason therefore. (JP 3-0)

mission command - (Army) The Army's approach to command and control that empowers subordinate decision making and decentralized execution appropriate to the situation. (ADP 6-0)

mission orders - Directives that emphasize to subordinates the results to be attained, not how they are to achieve them. (ADP 6-0)

monitoring - Continuous observation of those conditions relevant to the current operation. (ADP 5-0)

multinational operations - A collective term to describe military actions conducted by forces of two or more nations, usually undertaken within the structure of a coalition or alliance. (JP 3-16).

nested concepts - A planning technique to achieve unity of purpose whereby each succeeding echelon's concept of operations is aligned by purpose with the higher echelons' concept of operations. (ADP 5-0)

network transport - A system of systems including the people, equipment, and facilities that provide end-to-end communications connectivity for network components. (FM 6-02)

objective - The clearly defined, decisive, and attainable goal toward which an operation is directed. (JP 5-0)

operational approach - A broad description of the mission, operational concepts, tasks, and actions required to accomplish the mission. (JP 5-0)

operational art - The cognitive approach by commanders and staffs—supported by their skill, knowledge, experience, creativity, and judgment—to develop strategies, campaigns, and operations to organize and employ military forces by integrating ends, ways, and means. (JP 3-0)

operational environment - A composite of the conditions, circumstances, and influences that affect the employment of capabilities and bear on the decisions of the commander. (JP 3-0)

operational initiative - The setting of tempo and terms of action throughout an operation. (ADP 3-0)

operational level of warfare - The level of warfare at which campaigns and major operations are planned, conducted, and sustained to achieve strategic objectives within theaters or other operational areas. (JP 3-0)

operational reach - The distance and duration across which a force can successfully employ military capabilities. (JP 3-0)

operations process - The major command and control activities performed during operations: planning, preparing, executing, and continuously assessing the operation. (ADP 5-0)

parallel planning - Two or more echelons planning for the same operations nearly simultaneously facilitated by the use of warning orders by the higher headquarters. (ADP 5-0)

phase - (Army) A planning and execution tool used to divide an operation in duration or activity. (ADP 3-0)

planning - The art and science of understanding a situation, envisioning a desired future, and determining effective ways to bring that future about. (ADP 5-0)

planning horizon - A point in time commanders use to focus the organization's planning efforts to shape future events. (ADP 5-0)

preparation - Those activities performed by units and Soldiers to improve their ability to execute an operation. (ADP 5-0)

priority intelligence requirement - An intelligence requirement that the commander and staff need to understand the threat and other aspects of the operational environment. (JP 2-01)

priority of support - A priority set by the commander to ensure a subordinate unit has support in accordance with its relative importance to accomplish the mission. (ADP 5-0)

procedures - Standard, detailed steps that prescribe how to perform specific tasks. (CJCSM 5120.01)

rehearsal - A session in which the commander and staff or unit practices expected actions to improve performance during execution. (ADP 5-0)

relevant information - All information of importance to the commander and staff in the exercise of command and control. (ADP 6-0)

risk management - The process to identify, assess, and control risks and make decisions that balance risk cost with mission benefits. (JP 3-0)

route - The prescribed course to be traveled from a specific point of origin to a specific destination. (FM 3-90-1)

running estimate - The continuous assessment of the current situation used to determine if the current operation is proceeding according to the commander's intent and if planned future operations are supportable. (ADP 5-0)

sequel - The subsequent operation or phase based on the possible outcomes of the current operation or phase. (JP 5-0)

simultaneity - The execution of related and mutually supporting tasks at the same time across multiple locations and domains. (ADP 3-0)

situational understanding - The product of applying analysis and judgment to relevant information to determine the relationships among the operational and mission variables. (ADP 6-0)

strategic level of warfare - The level of warfare at which a nation, often as a member of a group of nations, determines national or multinational (alliance or coalition) strategic security objectives and guidance, then develops and uses national resources to achieve those objectives. (JP 3-0)

synchronization - The arrangement of military actions in time, space, and purpose to produce maximum relative combat power at a decisive place and time. (JP 2-0)

tactical level of warfare - The level of warfare at which battles and engagements are planned and executed to achieve military objectives assigned to tactical units or task forces. (JP 3-0)

targeting - The process of selecting and prioritizing targets and matching the appropriate response to them, considering operational requirements and capabilities. (JP 3-0)

task organization - (Army) A temporary grouping of forces designed to accomplish a particular mission. (ADP 5-0)

task-organizing - The act of designing a force, support staff, or sustainment package of specific size and composition to meet a unique task or mission. (ADP 3-0)

tempo - The relative speed and rhythm of military operations over time with respect to the enemy. (ADP 3-0)

tenets of operations - Desirable attributes that should be built into all plans and operations and are directly related to the Army's operational concept. (ADP 1-01)

troop leading procedures - A dynamic process used by small-unit leaders to analyze a mission, develop a plan, and prepare for an operation. (ADP 5-0)

understanding - In the context of decision making, knowledge that has been synthesized and had judgment applied to comprehend the situation's inner relationships, enable decision making, and drive action. (ADP 6-0)

unified action partners - Those military forces, governmental and nongovernmental organizations, and elements of the private sector with whom Army forces plan, coordinate, synchronize, and integrate during the conduct of operations. (ADP 3-0)

unified land operations - The simultaneous execution of offense, defense, stability, and defense support of civil authorities across multiple domains to shape operational environments, prevent conflict, prevail in large-scale ground combat, and consolidate gains as part of unified action. (ADP 3-0)

unity of effort - Coordination and cooperation toward common objectives, even if the participants are not necessarily part of the same command or organization, which is the product of successful unified action. (JP 1)

warfighting function - A group of tasks and systems united by a common purpose that commanders use to accomplish missions and training objectives. (ADP 3-0)

II. Military Symbology Basics

Ref: ADP 1-02, Terms and Military Symbols (Aug '18), chap. 3

This section discusses framed symbols, locations of amplifiers, the bounding octagon, and the locations of icons and modifiers. It also discusses the building process for framed symbols and unframed symbols.

A military symbol is a graphic representation of a unit, equipment, installation, activity, control measure, or tactical task relevant to military operations that is used for planning or to represent the common operational picture on a map, display, or overlay. Military symbols are governed by the rules in Military Standard (MIL-STD) 2525D.

Military symbols fall into two categories: framed, which includes unit, equipment, installation, and activity symbols; and unframed, which includes control measure and tactical symbols:

A. Framed Symbols

A framed symbol is composed of a frame, color (fill), icon, modifiers, and amplifiers. Framed symbols include:

- Unit, individuals, and organization symbols *(see pp. 7-17 to 7-20)*
- Equipment symbols *(see pp. 7-22 to 7-25)*
- Installation symbols *(see p. 7-21)*
- Activity symbols *(see p. 7-20)*

See following page (pp. 7-10 to 7-15) for discussion of the building process for framed symbols.

B. Unframed Symbols

Control measure symbols and mission task verb symbols are unframed symbols. They conform to special rules for their own elements. Unframed symbols include:

- Control measure symbols *(see pp. 7-27 to 7-34)*
- Tactical symbols *(see pp. 7-35 to 7-38)*

See p. 7-16 for discussion of the building process for unframed symbols.

Mission and Operational Task Symbols

The mission and operational task symbols are graphic representations of many of the tactical tasks, tactical enabling tasks, retrograde tasks, and special purpose attacks. However, not all have an associated symbol. Tactical task symbols are for use in course of action sketches, synchronization matrixes, and maneuver sketches. They do not replace any part of an operation order. Mission and operational task symbols should be scaled to fit the map scale and the size of unit represented.

See pp. 7-35 to 7-38.

A. Framed Symbols

Ref: ADP 1-02, Terms and Military Symbols (Aug '18), pp. 3-1 to 3-3.

The frame is the border of a symbol. It does not include associated information inside or outside of the border. The frame serves as the base to which other symbol components are added. The frame indicates the standard identity, physical domain, and status of the object being represented.

Standard Identity

Standard identity reflects the relationship between the viewer and the operational object being monitored. The standard identity categories are unknown, pending, assumed friend, friend, neutral, suspect,and hostile. In the realm of surface operation symbols, a circle or rectangle frame denotes friend or assumed friend standard identity, a diamond frame denotes hostile or suspect standard identity, a square frame denotes neutral standard identity, and a quatrefoil frame denotes unknown and pending standard identity. Table 3-1 shows frame shapes for standard identities for land symbols.

Standard Identity	*Friendly* / *Assumed Friend*	*Hostile* / *Suspect*	*Neutral*	*Unknown* / *Pending*
Unit				
Land equipment and sea surface				
Air				
Space				
Installation				
Activity				

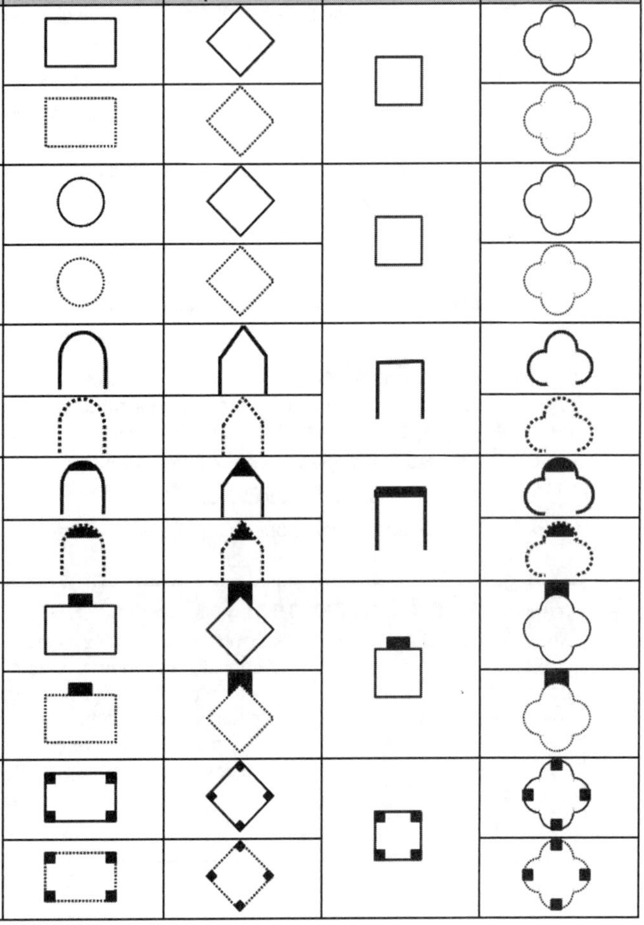

Table 3-1. Frame shapes for standard identities.

Physical Domain

The physical domain defines the primary mission area for the object within the operational environment. An object can have a mission area above the earth's surface (in the air domain or space domain),on the earth's surface, or below the earth's surface (that is, in the land domain or maritime domain). The land domain includes those mission areas on the land surface or close to the surface (such as caves, mines, and underground shelters). Maritime surface units are depicted in the sea surface dimension. Aircraft, regardless of Service ownership, can be depicted in either the air dimension (in flight) or land dimension (on the ground),while air units are depicted as a land unit and facilities as a land installation. Land equipment is depicted in the land dimension. Likewise, landing craft whose primary mission is ferrying personnel or equipment to and from shore are represented in the sea surface dimension. However, a landing craft whose primary mission is to fight on land is a ground asset and is represented in the land dimension.

Continued on next page

Status

Status depicts whether an object exists at the location identified (status is "present" or "confirmed"),will in the future reside at that location (status is "planned" or "anticipated"), or is thought to reside at that location ("suspected"). See table 3-2 for a depiction of friendly frames.

Dimension / *Status*	*Space*	*Air*	*Land Unit*	*Land Equipment and Sea Surface*	*Land Installation*	*Sea Subsurface*	*Activity or Event*
Present or confirmed position		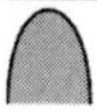					
Anticipated, planned or suspected position							

Table 3-2. Friendly frames in present, planned, or suspected status.

Color (Fill)

In framed symbols, color provides a redundant clue with regard to standard identity. The fill is the interior area in a symbol. If color is not used, the fill is transparent. In unframed symbols (equipment), color is the sole indicator of standard identity, excluding text amplifiers. The default colors used to designate standard identity are blue for friendly or assumed friend, red for hostile or suspect, green for neutral, and yellow for unknown or pending. Affiliation color without the fill may also be used for the frame, main icon,and modifiers.

The Octagon

The octagon serves as a three sector spatial reference for placement of main icons and modifiers in the frame of a symbol. The three sectors specify where main icons and modifiers are positioned and how much space is available for sizing of main icons and modifiers. The vertical bounding octagon allows for effective use of the space when dealing with vertical icons. Figure 3-1 shows an example of a full-frame main icon for all frame shapes.

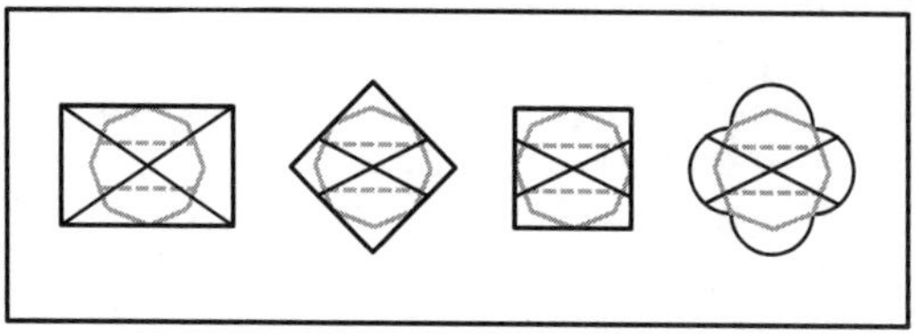

Figure 3-1. Example of full-frame main icons (with octagon sectors).

Continued on next page

Ops Terms & Symbols

The Building Process for Framed Symbols

Ref: ADP 1-02, Terms and Military Symbols (Aug '18), pp. 3-4 to 3-10.

Continued from previous page

ADP 1-02 chapters 4 through 7 provide an extensive number of icons and modifiers for building a wide variety of framed symbols. No attempt has been made to depict all possible combinations. Instead, a standard method for constructing symbols is presented. Once the user is familiar with the prescribed system, any desired symbol can be developed using the logical sequence provided in this chapter. The main icons shown in this publication are adequate for depicting all standard identities for framed symbols. When representing unorthodox framed symbols, users select the most appropriate main icon or modifier contained herein. Soldiers should avoid using any main icon or modifiers or combinations and modifications that differ from those in this publication. If, after searching doctrinal icons and modifiers, it is necessary to create a new symbol, users should explain the symbol in an accompanying legend. Computer-generated systems will have difficulty in passing nonstandard symbols. Table 3-5 shows the steps in the building process for framed symbols.

Step	*Description*	*Example*
1	Choose appropriate frame shape from table 3-1 on page 3-2.	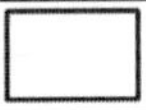
2	Choose appropriate main icon from chapters 2 through 5 and combine it with frame.	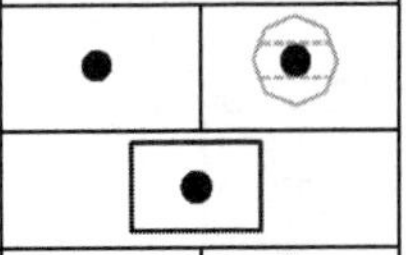
3	Choose appropriate sector 1 modifier from chapters 2 through 5.	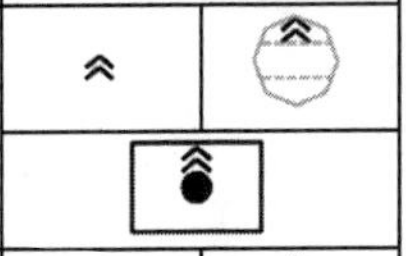
4	Choose appropriate sector 2 modifier from chapters 2 through 5.	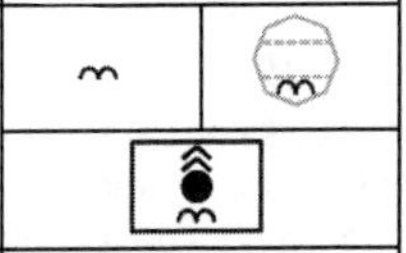
5	Choose minimum essential amplifiers from those listed in table 3-3 on page 3-4.	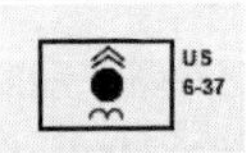

Table 3-5. Building process for framed symbols.

Framed symbols include:

- Unit, individuals, and organization symbols *(see pp. 7-17 to 7-20)*
- Equipment symbols *(see pp. 7-22 to 7-25)*
- Installation symbols *(see p. 7-21)*
- Activity symbols *(see p. 7-20)*

Continued from previous page

Lettering for All Symbols

The lettering for all military symbols will always be upper case. The lettering for all point, line, and area symbols will be oriented to the top of the display (north). In some cases the lettering may be tilted slightly to follow the contour of a line, but it must never be tilted so much that readers must tilt their heads to read it. The lettering for the bounding octagon will be the same as the orientation of the octagon. The lettering for the horizontal bounding octagon will be horizontal from left to right and the lettering for the vertical octagon will be vertical from top to bottom.

Main Icons for Framed Symbols

The main icon is the innermost part of a symbol. The icon provides an abstract pictorial or alphanumeric representation of units, equipment, installations, or activities. This publication distinguishes between icons that must be framed and icons for which framing is optional. This indicator is represented as the center area of field A/AA as shown below in figure 3-2. For better readability, main icons may be "enlarged" to extend into any unused modifier sector.

In general, main icons should not be so large as to exceed the dimensions of the main sector of the octagon or touch the interior border of the frame. However, there are exceptions to this size rule. In those cases the main icons will occupy the entire frame and must, therefore, exceed the dimensions of the main sector of the octagon and touch the interior border of the frame. These are called full-frame main icons and occur only in land domain symbols.

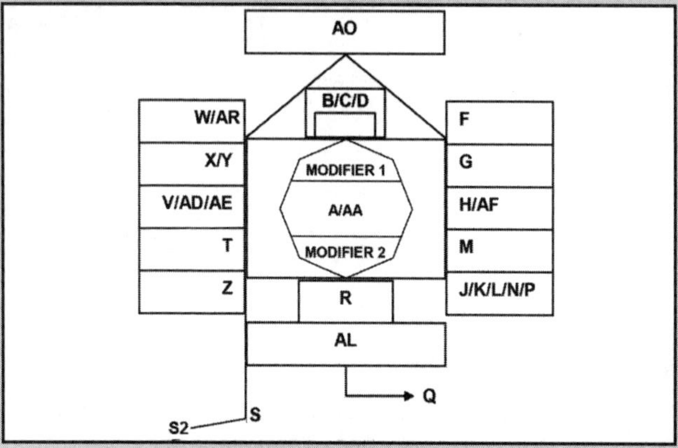

Figure 3-2. Main icon, modifier, and amplifier placement locations

Modifiers for Framed Symbols

A modifier provides an abstract pictorial or alphanumeric representation, displayed in conjunction with a main icon. The modifier provides additional information about the icon (unit, equipment, installation, or activity) being displayed. Modifiers conform to the octagon and are placed either above (in sector 1) or below(in sector 2) the main icon. This indicator is represented as the upper and lower part of field A/AA as defined in fig 3-2 above.

Amplifiers for Framed Symbols

An amplifier provides additional information about the symbol being portrayed and is displayed outside the frame. Figure 3-2 shows the essential amplifier fields around a friendly land unit symbol frame. To avoid cluttering the display, only essential amplifiers should be used. Arabic numerals are normally used to show the unique designation of units. However, Roman numerals are used to show corps echelon units.

The purpose of amplifier placement is to standardize the location of information. Figure 3-2 also illustrates the placement of amplifiers around a frame. The placement of amplifier information is the same regardless of frame shape.

Table 3-4 (following pages) provides a description of amplifiers for framed symbols.

Continued on next page

Continued on next page

Amplifiers for Framed Symbols (Table 3-4)

Continued from previous page

Field	Field Title	Description
A	Main and modifier icons	The innermost part of a symbol that represents a military object and its capabilities (modifiers1 and 2).
B	Echelon	A graphic amplifier in a unit symbol that identifies command level.
C	Quantity	A text amplifier in an equipment symbol that identifies the number of items present.
D	Task force indicator	A graphic amplifier that identifies a unit or an activities symbol as a task force. (See table 4-8 on page 4-27.)
F	Attached and detached (reinforced or reduced)	A text amplifier in a unit symbol that displays (+) for reinforced, (-) for reduced, (+) reinforced and reduced. (See table 4-9 on page 4-28.)
G	Staff comments	A text amplifier for units, equipment, and installations. Content is implementation specific.
H	Additional information	A unique alphanumeric designation that identifies the unit being displayed. ***Note:*** When showing unique alphanumeric designations for combat arms regimental units (air defense artillery, armor, aviation, cavalry, field artillery, infantry, and special forces) the following rules apply: No regimental headquarters: A dash (-) will be used between the battalion and the regimental designation where there is no regimental headquarters (example: A/6-37 for A Battery, 6th Battalion, 37th Field Artillery). Regimental headquarters: A slash (/) will be used between the battalion and the regimental designation where there is a regimental headquarters of an active operational unit to show continuity of the units (example: F/2/11 for F Troop, 2d Squadron/11th Armored Cavalry Regiment).
J	Evaluation rating	A text amplifier for units, equipment and installations that consists of a single-letter reliability rating and a single digit credibility rating. Reliability Ratings: A-completely reliable. B-usually reliable. C-fairly reliable. D-not usually reliable. E-unreliable. F-reliability cannot be judged. Credibility Ratings: 1-confirmed by other sources. 2-probably true. 3-possibly true. 4-doubtfully true. 5-improbable. 6-truth cannot be judged.
K	Combat effectiveness	A text amplifier for units and installations that indicates effectiveness. The entries are— fully operational (FO). substantially operational (SO). marginally operational (MO). not operational (NO). unknown (UNK).
L	Signature equipment	A text amplifier for hostile equipment. "!" indicates detectable electronic signatures.
M	Higher formation	A text amplifier for units that indicates number or title of higher echelon command (corps are designated by Roman numerals).
N	Hostile (enemy)	A text amplifier for equipment. Letters "ENY" denote hostile symbols.
P	Identification, friend or foe Selective identification feature	A text amplifier displaying one or more identification, friend or foe, or selective identification feature identification modes and codes. Display priority is mode 5, mode S, mode 4, mode 2, and mode 3.

Continued from previous page

Field	Field Title	Description
Q	Direction of movement indicator	A graphic amplifier for units and equipment that identifies the direction of movement or intended movement of an object.
R	Mobility indicator	A graphic amplifier for equipment that depicts the mobility of an object. (See figure 5-1 on page 5-1 and table 5-3 on pages 5-12 through 5-15.)
S	Headquarters staff indicator	A graphic amplifier for units, installations, and stability operations that identifies th em as a headquarters. (See table 4-7 on page 4-26.).
S[2]	Offset location indicator	A graphic amplifier used to indicate the offset or precise location of a single point symbol. (See table 4-7 on page 4-26.)
T	Unique designation (track number)	A text amplifier for units, equipment, and installations that uniquely identifies a particular symbol or track number. Prefix = TN: #####. Example: TN: 13579.
V	Type	A text amplifier for equipment that indicates types of equipment.
W	Date-time group	An alphanumeric designator for displaying a date -time group (DDHHMMSSZMONYYYY) or "O/O" for on order. The date - time group is composed of a group of six numeric digits with a time zone suffix and the standardized three-letter abbreviation for the month followed by fo ur digits representing the year. The first pair of digits represents the day; the second pair, the hour; the third pair, the minutes. For automated systems, two digits may be added before the time zone suffix and after the minutes to designate seconds.
X	Altitude or depth	A text amplifier for units, equipment, and installations that displays either altitude, flight level, depth for submerged objects, or height of equipment or structures on the ground. Measurement units shall be displayed in the string. Examples: 1500MSL FL150
Y	Location	A text amplifier for units, equipment, and installations that displays a symbol's location in degrees, minutes, and decimal minutes (or in military grid reference system, global area reference system, or other applicable display formats).
Z	Speed	A text amplifier for units and equipment that displays velocity.
AA	Special headquarters	A text modifier for units. The indicator is contained inside the frame. A named command such as Supreme Headquarters Allied Powers, Europe, United States Pacific Command, United States Central Command, and joint, multinational, or coalition commands such as combined joint task forces or joint task forces.
AD	Platform type	Electronic intelligence notation or communications intelligence notation.
AE	Common identifier	Example: "Hawk" for Hawk surface-to-air missile system.
AL	Operational condition	A graphic amplifier for equipment or installations that indicates operational condition or capacity. Operational condition amplifier, if used, shall be comprised of only one color. Example: Aircraft: Red - damaged, Green – fully capable Example: Missile: Red – imminent threat, Green – no threat
AO	Engagement bar	A graphic amplifier placed immediately atop the symbol. It may denote 1) local/remote status, 2) engagement status, and 3) weapon type. The engagement amplifier is arranged as follows: A: BBB-CC, where A (1 character) denotes a local versus remote engagement, BBB (up to 3 characters) denotes engagement state and CC (up to 2 characters) denotes weapon deployment or asset control.
AR	Special designator	Special track designators such as non-real time and tactically significant tracks are denoted here.

B. Unframed Symbols

Ref: ADP 1-02, Terms and Military Symbols (Aug '18), pp. 3-10 to 3-11.

This section discusses unframed symbols. Control measure symbols and mission task verb symbols are unframed symbols. They conform to rules within their own elements.

Control Measure Symbols

A control measure is a means of regulating forces or warfighting functions. Control measures may be boundaries, special area designations, or other unique markings related to an operational environment's geometry and be necessary for planning and managing operations. Control measure symbols represent control measures that can be graphically portrayed, and they provide operational information. They can be displayed as points, lines, and areas. Control measure symbols can be combined with other military symbols, main icons, and amplifiers to display operational information. Control measure symbols follow the same fundamental building rules as framed symbols, but they are built in accordance with their template. Control measure symbols can be black or white, depending on their display background. Display backgrounds can be blue (for friendly), red (for hostile), green (for obstacles), or yellow (for a chemical, biological,radiological, and nuclear contaminated area fill).

Description, placement, and further discussion of control measure symbols are addressed on pp. 7-27 to 7-34.

Step	Description	Example
1	Choose the appropriate control measure symbol.	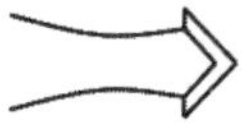
2	Choose the appropriate control measure template that will show the possible amplifiers.	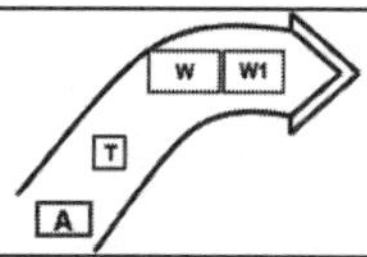
3	Choose the appropriate amplifier information by field.	T | WHITE 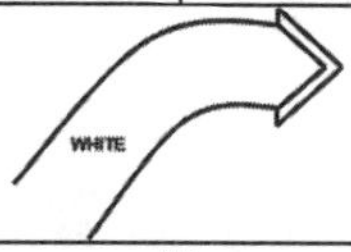
4	Choose the next appropriate amplifier information by field.	W 140600MAR2010 W1 Optional (if required) 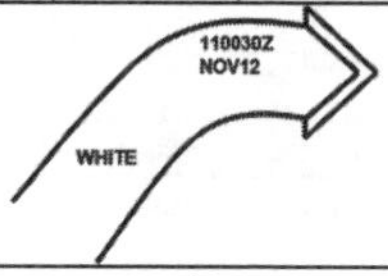
5	Choose the next appropriate amplifier information by field (framed icon).	A 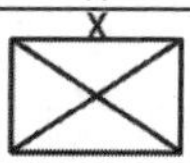 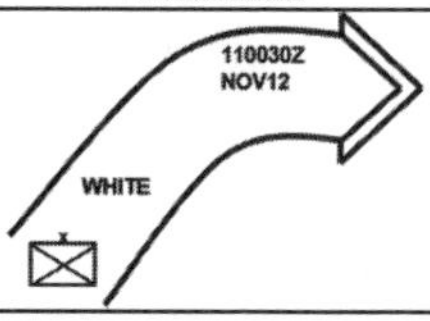

Table 3-6. Building process for control measure symbols.

III. Units, Individuals, and Organizations

Ref: ADP 1-02, Terms and Military Symbols (Aug '18), chap. 4.

A unit is a military element whose structure is prescribed by a competent authority, such as a table of organization and equipment; specifically, part of an organization (JP 1-02). Icons in the main sector of the bounding octagon reflect the main function of the symbol *(see p. 7-13)*.

Main Icons for Units

Icons in the main sector of the bounding octagon reflect the main function.

Function (historical derivation of icon shown in italics)	Icon
Armored (tank track)	
Army aviation or rotary wing aviation	
Chemical, biological, radiological, and nuclear (Crossed retorts)	
Civil affairs	CA
Chaplain (religious support)	REL
Combined arms (modified cross straps and tank track)	
Electronic warfare	EW
Engineer (bridge)	
Explosive ordnance disposal	EOD
Field artillery (cannonball)	
Military intelligence (abbreviation)	MI
Military police (abbreviation)	MP
Missile (missile)	
Mortar	
Ordnance (bursting Bomb)	
Special forces (abbreviation)	SF
Surveillance	
Sustainment (abbreviation)	SUST
Transportation (wheel)	
Water	

Table 4-1. Main icons for units (pp. 4-1 to 4-5).

Examples

Main Icons for Units

Ref: ADP 1-02, Terms and Military Symbols (Aug '18), pp. 4-7 to 4-30.

Full-Frame Icons for Units

Full-frame icons may reflect the main function of the symbol or may reflect modifying information.

Function (Historical derivation in italics)	Icon	Example
Air defense (radar dome)		
Antitank or antiarmor (upside down V)		
Armored cavalry		
Armored infantry (mechanized infantry)		
Corps support		
Headquarters or headquarters element		
Infantry (crossed straps)		
Medical (Geneva cross)		
Reconnaissance (cavalry) (cavalry bandoleer)		
Signal (lightning flash)		
Supply		
Theater or echelons above corps support		

Sector 1 Modifiers for Units

Sector 1 modifiers reflect a unit's specific capability.

Description	Modifier
Attack	A
Armored	
Biological	B
Bridging	
Chemical	C
Command and control	C2
Detention	DET
Maintenance	]—[
Meteorological	MET
Multiple rocket launcher	≈
Nuclear	N
Radar	
Radiological	R
Search and rescue	SAR
Sensor	◆
Smoke	S
Sniper	˙I˙
Unmanned systems	∨
Utility	U
Video imagery	

Examples

Sector 2 Modifiers for Units

Sector 2 modifiers reflect the mobility of the unit or size, range, or altitude of unit equipment.

Description	Icon
Air assault	V
Airborne	⌒⌒
Amphibious	∿∿∿
Arctic (sled)	⌣
Bicycle-equipped	O
Decontamination	D
Heavy	H
High altitude	HA
Light	L
Long range	LR
Low altitude	LA
Medium	M
Medium altitude	MA
Medium range	MR
Mountain	▲
Pack animal	M
Railroad	oo-oo
Recovery	]—[
Riverine	⌐
Short range	SR
Ski	X
Towed	O—O
Tracked/SP	⊂⊃
Wheeled	OOO

Examples

Echelon Amplifiers (Field B)

An echelon is a separate level of command. In addition, there is also a separate echelon known as a command. A command is a unit or units, an organization, or an area under the command of one individual. It does not correspond to any of the other echelons. Table 4-6 shows the field B amplifiers for Army echelons and commands.

Echelon	Amplifier	Example of amplifier with friendly unit frame
Team or crew *Note. This is the smallest echelon and should not be confused with company team and brigade combat team in the next paragraph.*	Ø	ø
Squad	●	•
Section	●●	••
Platoon or detachment	●●●	•••
Company, battery, or troop	I	I
Battalion or squadron	II	II
Regiment or group	III	III
Brigade	X	X
Division	XX	XX
Corps	XXX	XXX
Theater army	XXXX	XXXX
Army group *Note. Used in NATO or multinational military operations.*	XXXXX	XXXXX

Echelon	*Amplifier*	*Example of amplifier with friendly unit frame*
Theater of operations	XXXXXX	
Nonechelon	***Amplifier***	***Example of amplifier with friendly unit frame***
Command	++	

Table 4-6. Echelon amplifier (continued).

Task Force Amplifiers (Field D)

A task force is a temporary grouping of units under one commander formed to carry out a specific operation or mission, or a semipermanent organization of units under one commander formed to carry out a continuing specified task.

Task force amplifier	Example	Example w/ echelon

Table 4-7. Task force and team amplifiers

Reinforced, Detached or Both Amplifiers (Field F)

This amplifier is used at brigade echelons and below. Use a plus + symbol when attaching one or more subelements of a similar function to a headquarters. Use a minus symbol – when detaching one or mores subelements of a similar function to a headquarters. Table 4-8 provides an explanation of attached and detached modifiers.

Description	*Amplifier*	*Example of amplifier with friendly unit frame*
Attached	+	
Detached	–	

Table 4-8. Attached and detached amplifiers.

Operational Condition (Field AL) & Combat Effectiveness (Field K) Amplifiers

Combat effectiveness or operational condition is the ability of a unit to perform its mission. Factors such as ammunition, personnel, fuel status, and weapon systems are evaluated and rated. The ratings are—

- Fully operational (FO) - green (85 percent or greater).
- Substantially operational (SO) – amber (70 to 84 percent).
- Marginally operational (MO) – red (50 to 69 percent).
- Not operational (NO) – black (less than 50 percent).
- Unknown (UNK)

Field AL is used to display the level of combat effectiveness of the unit or equipment symbol (fig. 4-4) .

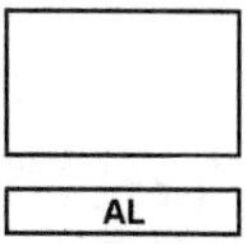

Fig. 4-4. Template for operational condition amplifier.

Field K is used to display the level of combat effectiveness of the unit or equipment symbol using the acronym or abbreviation FO, SO, MO, NO, & UN (fig. 4-5).

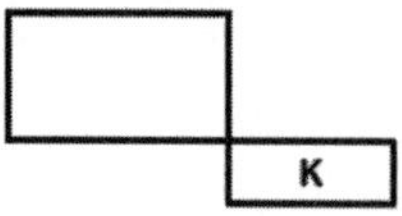

Fig. 4-5. Template for combat effectiveness amplifier.

Offset Locator Indicator Amplifier (Field S^2) and HQs Staff Offset Locator Indicator Amplifier (Field S)

The center of mass of the unit symbol indicates the general vicinity of the center of mass of the unit. To indicate precise location or reduce clutter in an area with multiple units, a line (without an arrow) extends from the center of the bottom of the frame to the unit location displayed as field S^2. The line may be extended or bent as needed.

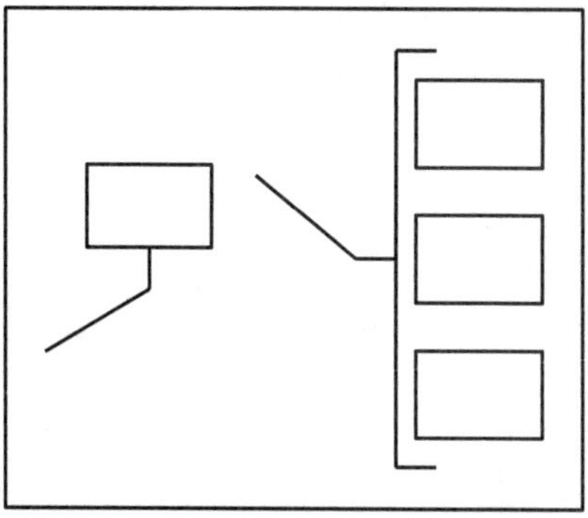

To indicate precise location or reduce clutter of headquarters unit symbols, a staff extends from the bottom left hand corner to the headquarters location displayed as field S.

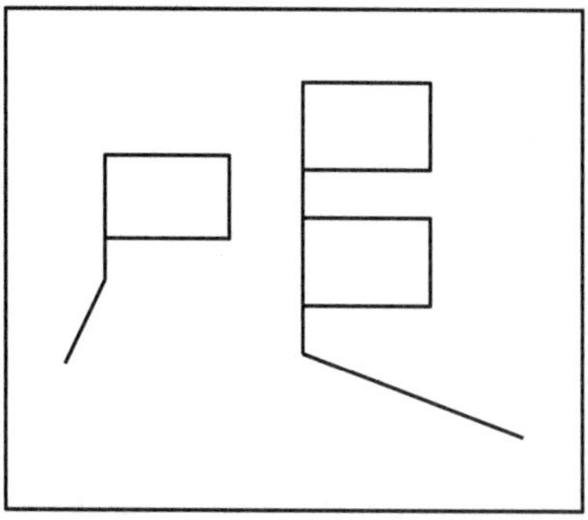

Ops Terms & Symbols

Main Icons for DSCA Individuals and Organizations

Ref: ADP 1-02, Terms and Military Symbols (Aug '18), pp. 4-30 to 4-50.

Symbols for individuals and organizations represent civilians and normally do not have prescribed structures. Organization symbols can reflect civic, ethnic, religious, social, or other groupings. Icons in the main sector reflect the main function of the icon. *(sample)*

Examples

Function	Icon
Fire department	
Governmental	GO
Nongovernmental	NGO
Pirates	
Police department	
Unspecified individual or organization	
Unspecified individual Note: Only this icon uses the vertical bounding octagon. All other icons in this table use the horizontal bounding octagon.	
Unspecified organization	
Criminal activities victim	
Criminal activities victims	
Attempted criminal activities victim	
Attempted criminal activities victims	

Table 4-11. Main icons for DSCA individuals and organizations.

Sector 1 Modifiers

Sector 1 modifiers reflect the function of civilian individuals or organizations. *(sample)*

	Characteristic	Modifier
Types of Killing	Assassinated	AS
	Executed	EX
	Murdered	MU
Criminal Activities	Hijacked	H
	Kidnapped	K
	Piracy	PI
	Rape	RA

Table 4-12. Sector 1 modifiers for defense support of civil authorities individuals and organizations.

Sector 2 Modifiers

Sector 2 modifiers reflect the nature of the relationship of civilian individuals or organizations. *(sample)*

Characteristic	*Modifier*	*Example of modifier with friendly unit frame:* *Note: This does not imply that individuals and organizations are friendly, but only servers as a single frame reference for the symbol.* / *Example of most common usage*
Horizontal bounding octagon		
Vertical bounding octagon		
Types of recruitment		
Coerced	CR	CR
Willing	WR	WR
Leader	L D R	L D R

Table 4-13. Sector 2 modifiers for DSCA individuals and organizations.

IV. Equipment, Installations, Activities

Ref: ADP 1-02, Terms and Military Symbols (Aug '18), chaps. 5, 6 & 7.

Main Icons for Installations

Ref: ADP 1-02, Terms and Military Symbols (Aug '18), chap. 6.

Installations are sites that incorporate permanent, semipermanent, and temporary structures. Icons in the main sector reflect the main function of the symbol.

Examples

Function	Icon
Airport	
Electric power plant	
Mass grave	
Mine	
Sea port	
Telecommunications	

Table 6-1. Main icons for installations.

Sector 1 Modifiers for Installations

Sector 1 modifiers reflect the specific capability of the installation.

	Description	Modifier
Electric power plant fuel source	Coal	CO
	Geothermal	GT
	Hydroelectric	HY
	Natural gas	NG
	Petroleum	
	Description	Modifier
Telecommunications	Radio	RAD
	Telephone	T
	Television	TV

Table 6-2. Sector 1 modifiers for installations.

Sector 2 Modifiers for Installations

Sector 2 modifiers reflect the specific type of installation.

Description	Modifier
Production	PROD
Repair	RPR
Research	RSH
Service	SVC
Storage	STOR
Test	TEST

Table 6-3. Sector 2 modifiers for installations

Main Icons for Equipment

Ref: ADP 1-02, Terms and Military Symbols (Aug '18), chap. 5.

Equipment is all nonexpendable items needed to outfit or equip an individual or organization. Equipment symbols can be used with or without frames. When frames are not used, then standard identity color must be used. Icons in the main sector reflect the main function of the symbol. Equipment can use either the horizontal or vertical bounding octagon depending on the icon.

Description	Icon
Weapon systems	
Note. Weapon systems, missile launchers, and nonlethal weapons use the horizontal bounding octagon and a unique system for indicating size, altitude, or range. Weapons size is indicated by a horizontal line(s) perpendicular to the weapon icon. If an equipment symbol has no lines, it is a basic equipment symbol. Adding one line designates it as light, low altitude, or short-range. Adding two lines designates it as medium, medium altitude, or medium-range. Finally, adding three lines designates it as heavy, high altitude, or long-range. If a weapon system is designated as greater than heavy, high altitude, or long-range, then a heavy, high-altitude, or long-range indicator is used.	
Unspecified weapon	
Flame thrower	
Grenade launcher	
Guns	
Description	Icon
Air defense gun	
Antitank gun	
Direct fire gun	
Recoilless gun	
Howitzer	
Machine gun	
Description	Icon
Missile launchers	
Missile launcher	
Air defense missile launcher surface-to-air missile launcher	
Antitank missile launcher	
Surface-to-surface missile launcher	
Mortar	
Rifle	
Description	Icon
Rockets	
Single rocket launcher	
Multiple rocket launcher	
Antitank rocket launcher	
Description	Icon
Nonlethal weapons	
Nonlethal weapon	
Taser	
Water cannon	

Description	Icon
Vehicles	
Note: Vehicle systems use a unique system for indicating size or range. Vehicle size is indicated by either horizontal or vertical line(s) within the icon depending on the orientation of the symbol. If an equipment symbol has no lines, it is a basic equipment symbol. Adding one line designates it as light or short-range. Adding two lines designates it as medium or medium-range. Finally, adding three lines designates it as heavy or long-range. Note: Armored fighting vehicles, armoured personnel carriers, earthmovers, and tanks use the vertical bounding octagon. All remainin equipment icons use the horizontal bounding octagon.	
Armored fighting vehicle	
Armored personnel carrier	
Armored protected vehicle	
Earthmover	
Tank	
Train locomotive	
Utility vehicle	
Description	Icon
Other equipment	
Bridge	
Chemical, biological, radiological, or nuclear (CBRN) equipment	
Improvised explosive device	IED
Description	Icon
Mines	
Antipersonnel mine	
Antitank mine	
Unspecified mine	
Radar	
Sensor	
Description	Icon
Aircraft	
Note: These are aircraft on the ground. Aircraft in flight use the air domain frame. Change: This brings the land equipment icons in line with air domain icons.	
Helicopter (rotary-wing aircraft)	
Fixed wing aircraft	
Unmanned aircraft	
Description	Icon
Engineer Equipment	
Bridge	
Fixed bridge	
Folding girder bridge	
Hollow deck bridge	
Drill	
Earthmover	
Mine clearing	
Mine laying	

Table 5-1. Main icons for equipment (examples).

Ops Terms & Symbols

Icons & Modifiers for Land Equipment Symbols

This section includes the lists of icons and modifiers for building land equipment symbols. Figure 5-1 shows the placement of land equipment symbol amplifiers around the friend symbol frame. Table 5-1 provides descriptions and formats of each amplifier and modifier. Equipment is all nonexpendable items needed to outfit or equip an individual or organization. Equipment symbols can be used with or without frames. When frames are not used, then standard identity colors must be used.

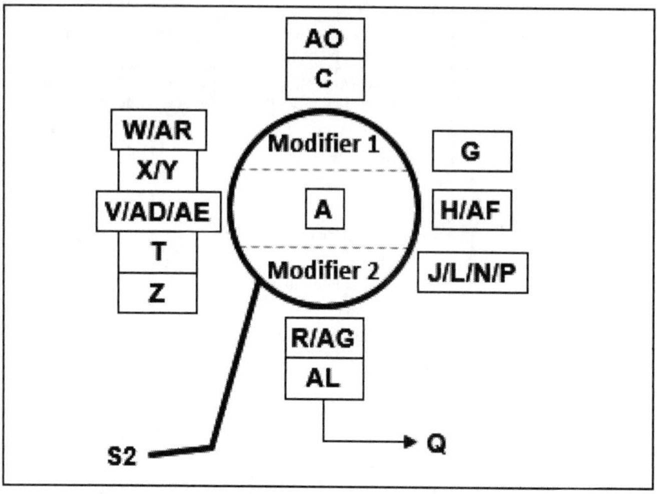

Figure 5-1. Placement of land equipment symbol amplifiers (See table 5-1 on following pages for field descriptions.)

Continued on next page

Sector 1 Modifiers for Equipment *Examples*

This is a change to the previous system.

Description	*Modifier*	*Example of modifier with friendly equipment frame* / *Example of most common usage* / *Icon or symbol without frame*
Horizontal bounding octagon		
Vertical bounding octagon		
Attack	A	
		Attack helicopter

Sector 2 Modifiers for Equipment *Examples*

Description	Modifier
Light	L
Medium	M
Heavy	H

Mobility Indicator Amplifier (Field R) *Examples*

Description	Amplifier
Amphibious	
Barge	
Over snow (prime mover)	
Pack animal	
Railway	
Sled	
Towed	
Tracked	
Wheeled (cross-country)	
Wheeled (limited mobility)	
Wheeled and tracked	

Continued on next page

Ops Terms & Symbols

Land Equipment Symbol Modifiers & Amplifiers

Ref: ADP 1-02, Terms and Military Symbols (Aug '18), table 5-1, pp. 5-2 to 5-4.

Continued from previous page

Field	Field Title	Description
A	Symbol icon and modifiers	The innermost part of a symbol that represents a military object and its capabilities (modifiers1 and 2).
C	Quantity	A text amplifier in an equipment symbol that identifies the number of items present.
G	Staff comments	A text amplifier for units, equipment and installations; content is implementation specific.
H	Additional information	A text amplifier for units, equipment and installations; content is implementation specific.
J	Evaluation rating	A text amplifier for units, equipment and installations that consists of a one-letter reliability rating and a one-number credibility rating: Reliability ratings: A-completely reliable. B-usually reliable. C-fairly reliable. D-not usually reliable. E-unreliable. F-reliability cannot be judged. Credibility ratings: 1-confirmed by other sources. 2-probably true. 3-possibly true. 4-doubtfully true. 5-improbable. 6-truth cannot be judged.
L	Signature equipment	A text amplifier for hostile equipment; "!" indicates detectable electronic signatures.
M	Higher formation	A text amplifier for units that indicates number or title of higher echelon command (corps are designated by Roman numerals).
N	Hostile (enemy)	A text amplifier for equipment; letters "ENY" denote hostile symbols.
P	Identification, friend or foe Selective identification feature	A text amplifier displaying one or more identification, friend or foe (IFF) or selective identification feature (SIF) identification modes and codes. Display priority: Mode 5, Mode S, Mode 4, Mode 3, Mode 2
Q	Direction of movement indicator	A graphic amplifier for units and equipment that identifies the direction of movement or intended movement of an object.
R	Mobility indicator	A graphic amplifier for equipment that depicts the mobility of an object.
S2	Offset location indicator	A graphic amplifier used to indicate the offset or precise location of a single point symbol.
T	Unique designation	A text amplifier for units, equipment and installations that uniquely identifies a particular symbol or track number. Identifies acquisitions number when used with signals intelligence symbology. Prefix = TN:##### Example: TN:13579
V	Type	A text amplifier for equipment that indicates types of equipment.

Continued from previous page

Field	Field Title	Description
W	Date-time group	An alphanumeric designator for displaying a date-time group (DDHHMMSSZMONYYYY) or "O/O" for on order. The date-time group is composed of a group of six numeric digits with a time zone suffix and the standardized three-letter abbreviation for the month followed by four digits representing the year. The first pair of digits represents the day; the second pair, the hour; the third pair, the minutes. For automated systems, two digits may be added before the time zone suffix and after the minutes to designate seconds.
X	Altitude or depth	A text amplifier for units, equipment and installations, that displays either altitude, flight level, depth for submerged objects; or height of equipment or structures on the ground. Measurement units shall be displayed in the string Examples: 1500MSL. FL150.
Y	Location	A text amplifier for units, equipment and installations that displays a symbol's location in degrees, minutes and decimal minutes (or in military grid reference system, global area reference system, or other applicable display formats). Examples: military grid reference system: 38SMB2649083145 global area reference system: 3317.0921N 04412.6332E
Z	Speed	A text amplifier for units and equipment that displays velocity.
AE	Equipment teardown time	Equipment teardown time in minutes.
AF	Common identifier	Example: "Hawk" for Hawk surface-to-air missile system.
AG	Auxiliary equipment indicator	Towed sonar array indicator: A graphic modifier for equipment that indicates the presence of a towed sonar array.
AI	Dead reckoning trailer	A graphic amplifier for units and equipment that identifies where an object should be located at present, given its last reported course and speed.
AJ	Speed leader	A graphic amplifier for units, equipment and installations that depicts the speed and direction of movement of an object.
AK	Pairing line	A graphic amplifier for units, equipment and installations that connects two objects and is updated dynamically as the positions of the two objects change.
AL	Operational condition	A graphic amplifier for equipment or installations that indicates operational condition or capacity. If used, it shall be comprised of only one color. Example. Aircraft: Red - damaged, Green – fully capable. Example: Missile: Red – imminent threat, Green – no threat.
AM	Distance	A numeric amplifier that displays a minimum, maximum, or a specific distance (range, radius, width, and length) in meters.
AO	Engagement bar	A graphic amplifier placed immediately atop the symbol. May denote, 1) local or remote status; 2) engagement status; and 3) weapon type. The engagement amplifier is arranged as follows: A: BBB-CC, where A (1 character) denotes a local versus remote engagement, BBB (up to 3 characters) denotes engagement state and CC (up to 2 characters) denotes weapon deployment or asset control.
AR	Special designator	Special track designators such as non-real time and tactically significant tracks are denoted here.

Activities

Ref: ADP 1-02, Terms and Military Symbols (Aug '18), chap. 7.

Activities symbols are applicable across the range of military operations, but they normally focus on stability activities and defense support of civil authorities' activities. Activities can affect military operations. Activities represented by icons can include acts of terrorism, sabotage, organized crime, a disruption of the flow of vital resources, and the uncontrolled movement of large numbers of people. Many of these icons represent emergency first response activities used in the civilian community. Icons in the main sector reflect the main function of the symbol.

Examples

Function	Icon
Arrest (Change: The stick figure in the center has been changed to the individual icon.)	
Attempted criminal activity against an individual	
Attempted criminal activity against multiple individuals or an organization	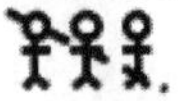
Bombing	BOMB
Demonstration	MASS
Drug related activity (illegal)	DRUG
Explosion	
Extortion (use applicable currency symbol)	$
Graffiti	
Improvised explosive device activity	IED
Infiltration	INFL
Criminal activity victim	
Criminal activity victims	
Poisoning	
Riot	RIOT
Black market	BM

Table 7-1. Main icons for activities.

Sector 1 Modifiers for Activities

Sector 1 modifiers reflect the specific type of activity.

	Characteristic	Modifier
Types of Killing	Assassinated	AS
	Executed	EX
	Murdered	MU
Criminal Activities	Hijacked	H
	Kidnapped	K
	Piracy	PI
	Rape	RA

Table 7-2. Sector 1 modifiers for activities.

V. Control Measure Symbols

Ref: ADP 1-02, Terms and Military Symbols (Aug '18), chap. 8.

A control measure symbol is a graphic used on maps and displays to regulate forces and warfighting functions. Definitions of terms related to control measure symbols are provided in ADP 1-02, chapter 1. Control measure symbols generally fall into one of three categories: points, lines, or areas. The coloring and labeling of control measure symbols are almost identical to framed symbols.

See p. 7-16 for discussion and overview of the building process for control measure symbols (unframed symbols).

Composition of Control Measure Symbols

Control measure symbols can be combined with other symbols, icons and amplifiers to display operational information (see figure 8-1). They do not follow the same building rules as the icon-based symbols but shall be built in accordance with the draw rules specified in the symbol tables.

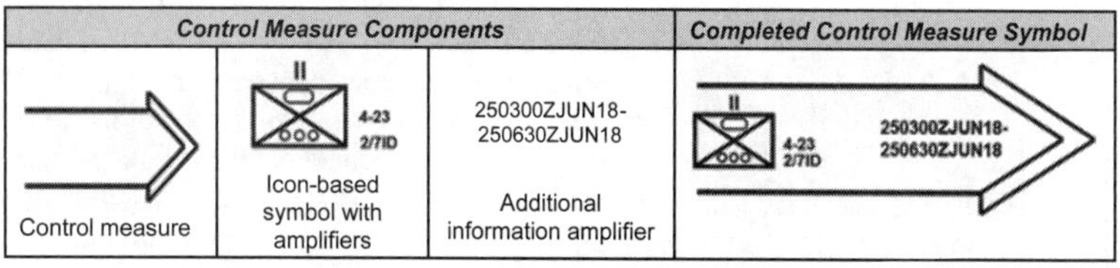

Fig. 8-1. Composition of control measure symbols.

Standard Identity Coloring Control Measures

Friendly graphic control measures will be shown in black or blue when drawn manually or on a color computer-generated display. Hostile graphic control measures will be shown in red. If red is not available,they will be drawn in black with the abbreviation "ENY" placed on the graphic in at least two places. Obstacles as shown in this chapter (friendly, hostile, neutral, unknown or factional) will be drawn using the color green. If the color green is not available, obstacles should be drawn using black. The color yellow will be used for the hatching for chemical, biological, radiological, and nuclear (CBRN) contaminated areas.

Control Measure Acronyms and Abbreviations

Acronyms and abbreviations shown in this chapter are for use with Army control measure symbols,and no acronyms or abbreviations other than those provided in this publication may be used. Acronyms or abbreviations become part of the military symbol language when approved for use as military symbols and are no longer considered an acronym or abbreviation when used within the military symbol construct. The acronyms and abbreviations in this chapter are considered symbols that are part of the military symbol lexicon.

Labeling Control Measures

Make all text labeling in upper case letters. The reader should be able to read the labels for all text labels of modifier or amplifier fields for control measures symbols when the bottom of the overlay is closest to the reader. Labeling written on an angle should be readable to viewers so they do not have to turn their heads.

Status

Status refers to whether a control measure exists at the location identified (status is "present") or will in the future reside at that location (status is "planned", "anticipated", "suspected", or "on order"). If a control measure is on order, the status code shall be specified "A – anticipated or planned" and field amplifier "W"shall be present and specified "O/O". In general, linear control measures (including boundary lines) and area control measures shall be a solid line when indicating present status and a dashed line when indicating anticipated or planned status. There are certain control measures such as counterattack which are drawn in the "present'" status with dashed lines.

Amplifiers

An amplifier provides optional additional information about a tactical symbol. The field identification,field title, description, and maximum allowable display lengths of tactical symbol amplifiers are presented in table 8-2 (facing page). Amplifiers can be defined as either static or dynamic:

- **Static amplifiers** are amplifiers whose size and placement are fixed and remain constant.
- **Dynamic amplifiers** are amplifiers whose size and placement are based on the attributes of an object and can change as these attributes and the scale of the background change.

See facing page for amplifier descriptions for control measure symbols (table 8-2).

The **direction of movement indicator** is an arrow identifying the direction of movement of events. The arrow extends downward from the center of the icon and points in the direction of movement. The indicator is represented in field Q as defined in table 8-2 (facing page) and positioned as shown in figure 8-3 below.

The **echelon indicator** provides a graphic representation of command level and is used to show the element echelon on lines and areas. The indicator is represented in field Q as defined in table 8-2 and positioned as shown in fig. 8-3 (below).

The **offset location indicator** is used when placing an object away from its actual location. The indicator is a line extending downward from an appropriate anchor point on an icon. The actual location (field Y) is given in latitude and longitude. The indicator is represented in field S in table 8-2.

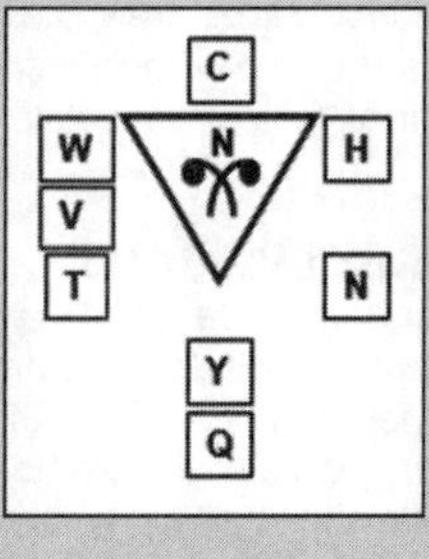

Fig. 8-3. CBRN events composition template

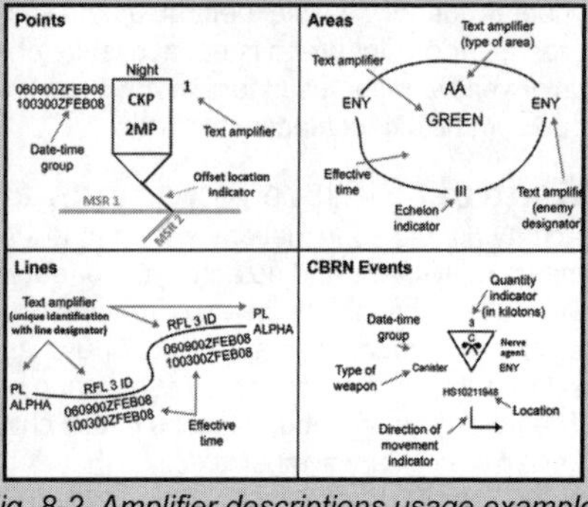

Fig. 8-2. Amplifier descriptions usage examples

*Table 8-2 (facing page) defines the specific content, length and type of each **text amplifier.** Additional information is contained in field H, with the content of this field being implementation specific, provided the maximum number of characters in each field is not exceeded.*

Ops Terms & Symbols

Amplifiers (for Control Measure Symbols)

Ref: ADP 1-02, Terms and Military Symbols (Aug '18), pp. 8-3 to 8-4.

Field Identification	Field Title	Description
A	Symbol icon	The part of a symbol that represents a unit symbol, or object function (modifier).
B	Echelon	A unit symbol that identifies command level.
C	Quantity	Identifies the number of items present.
H	Additional information	Content is implementation specific.
N	Hostile (enemy)	The letters "ENY" denote hostile control measure symbols.
Q	Direction of movement indicator	Identifies the direction of movement or intended movement of an object.
S	Offset location indicator	For points and chemical, biological and radiological (CBRN) events used when placing an object away from its actual location.
T, T1	Unique designation	"T" is used to differentiate points by numbering, lettering or a combination of both. "T1" may be used to include the unit designation. Notes. 1. In some cases, this tactical symbol may require multiple instances of a "T" amplifier to fully create or represent an object. 2. "T1" may be used if field used displayed more than once in a tactical symbol. 3. The unnumbered fields should be filled before the numbered fields
V	Type	Indicates types of equipment or nuclear weapon type.
W, W2	Date and time group (DTG)	"W" identifies the start DTG, and can be displayed alone or in conjunction with "W2" to identify the projected DTG end date. The "W' represents an alphanumeric designator for displaying a date-time group (DDHHMMSSZMONYYYY) or "O/O" for on order. When "W" and "W2" are used in conjunction it identifies the time control measure is in effect. The date-time group is composed of a group of six numeric digits with a time zone suffix and the standardized three-letter abbreviation for the month followed by four digits. The first pair of digits represents the day; the second pair, the hour; the third pair, and the minutes. The last four digits after the month are the year. For automated systems, two digits may be added before the time zone suffix and after the minutes to designate seconds.
X	Altitude or depth	Displays the minimum, maximum or specific altitude (in feet or meters in relation to a reference datum), flight level, or depth (for submerged objects in feet below sea level).
Y	Location	Displays a symbol's location in degrees, minutes, and decimal minutes.
AM	Distance	A numeric amplifier that displays a minimum, maximum, or specific distance (range, radius, width, or length) in meters.
AN	Azimuth	A numeric amplifier that displays an angle measured from true north to any other line in degrees.
AP	Target number	A six character text modifier used in fire support operations to uniquely designate targets where characters 1 and 2 are alphabetic, and characters 3-6 are numeric (for example, AANNNN).
APX	Target number extension	A 2 or 3 character text amplifier. A target number extension is a sequentially assigned number identifying the individual elements in a target, where character 1 is a dash and characters 2 and 3 are numeric, from 1 through 15. It is applicable only to the "point or single target" symbol, is conditional upon the presence of the target designator amplifier, and is visually displayed appended to the target number amplifier.
AS	Country	A 3-letter code representing geographical entity.

Notes.
1. Column headings: P = points, L = lines, A = areas, BL = boundary lines, R/N = radiological or nuclear, B/C = biological or chemical.
2. Numeric entry indicates text amplifier. "G" indicates graphic amplifier. A dash (-) inside boxes indicates non-applicable.
3. Field W: D = day, H = hour, M = minute, S = second, Z = time zone suffix, MON = month and Y = year.

Table 8-2. Amplifier descriptions for control measure symbols.

Boundary, Point, Line & Area Symbols

Ref: ADP 1-02, Terms and Military Symbols (Aug '18), pp. 8-1 to 8-22.

Boundaries

In land warfare, a boundary is a line by which areas of responsibility between adjacent units or formations are defined. Boundaries are composed of—

- Lines.
- The graphics for the highest echelon (field B) unit on lateral boundaries is used for the boundary line. The graphic for the lower echelon (field B) unit on a rear or forward boundary is used for the boundary line. *(See table 8-2, p. 7-29)* When units of the same echelon are adjacent to each other, the abbreviated echelon designator (field T) can be omitted from the alphanumeric designator. *Tables 8-32 and 8-33 on p. 7-34 for a list of abbreviations and acronyms to be used for field T.*
- Numerals, using Arabic numerals to show the numbers of units or Roman numerals to show the number of corps.
- Three-letter geographical entity country codes (field AS) which are shown in parenthesis behind or below the unit designation when the boundary is between units of different countries.

Figure 8-4 provides a boundary composition template that includes orientation of field labels for horizontal (east—west) and vertical (north—south) boundaries.

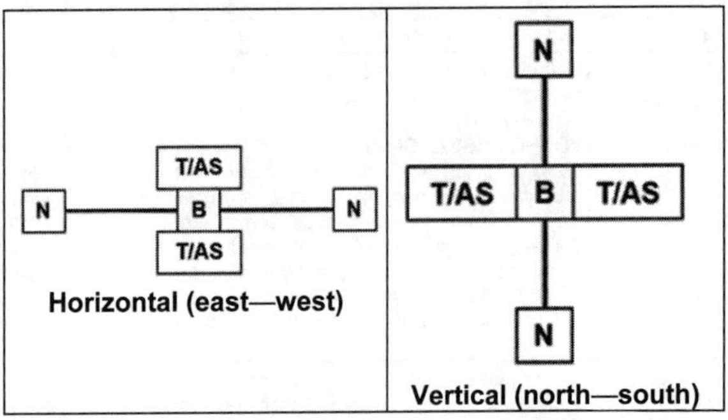

Fig. 8-4. Boundary composition template. (Refer to ADP 1-02, table 8-3 for boundary control measures and table 8-4 for boundary control-line control measures.)

Points

Numerous tables in ADP 1-02, chap. 8 (including sustainment, special supply distribution, and CBRN decontamination) depict point control measure symbols that follow the specific format as shown in figure 8-5 (facing page).

Supply points follow this same format with a modification to the symbol. Supply points use the same icon used for supply units. The supply icon is placed toward the bottom of the box as shown in figure 8-5. The format in figure 8-4 is only used for point and supply point control measures. Other points such as contact, coordination, decision points, and targets are formatted differently. The point type is abbreviated and positioned in field A. For supply symbols this may be a graphic.

Below the abbreviation of the point name, the designation of the unit servicing that point can be included in field T. To differentiate points, they can be identified by a number, letter, or a number and letter combination in field T. Date-time groups can be associated with the point by using fields W and W1. Additional information can be provided in field H. Point symbols cannot be rotated and therefore text will not be written on an angle. Figure 8-5 provides the template for point and supply point control measure symbols.

Ops Terms & Symbols

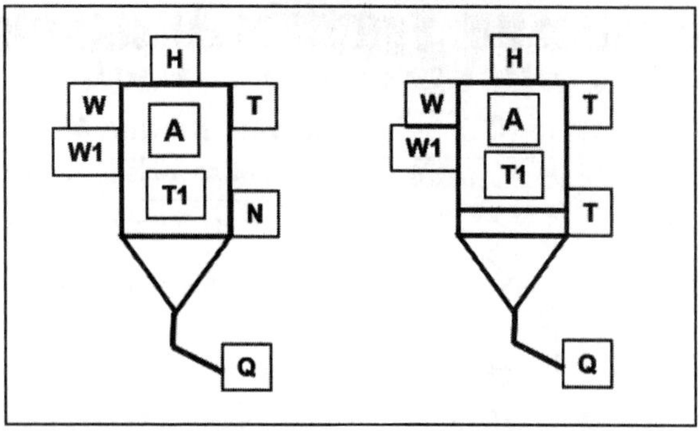

Fig. 8-5. Template for sustainment point (left) and supply distribution point (right) control measure symbols. (Refer to ADP 1-02, table 8-6, point control measure symbols.)

Lines

Most lines are also named as a phase line for ease of reference in orders and during transmissions. Lines that have a specific purpose and are also named as phase lines (such as restrictive fire line [RFL]) should have the primary purpose in the field T1 labeled on top of the line at both ends of the line inside the lateral boundaries or as often as necessary for clarity. The designation of the controlling headquarters for fire support coordination measures is depicted in field T2. The use of phase lines to mark line control measures symbols is not mandatory. Figure 8-6 below provides the template for line control measures symbols.

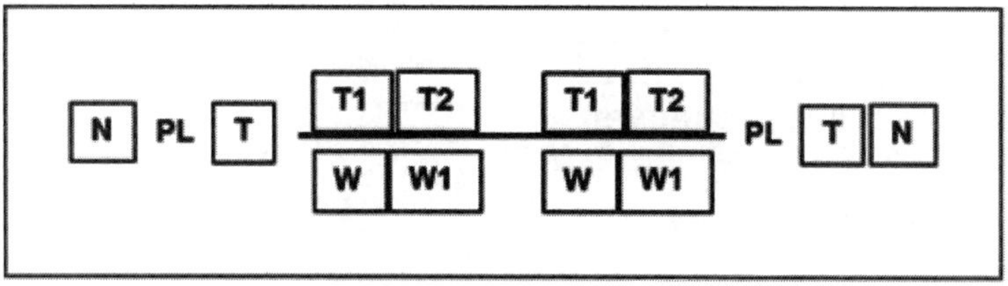

Figure 8-6. Template for line control measure symbols.

Areas

Areas will normally be marked with the abbreviation for the type of area in field A, followed by a name in field T. This labeling should be in the center of the area unless the area is too small or the labeling would interfere with the locating of units. Not all fields are required for each area as some areas may use only one field, while others will use several. Figure 8-7 provides template for area control measures symbols.

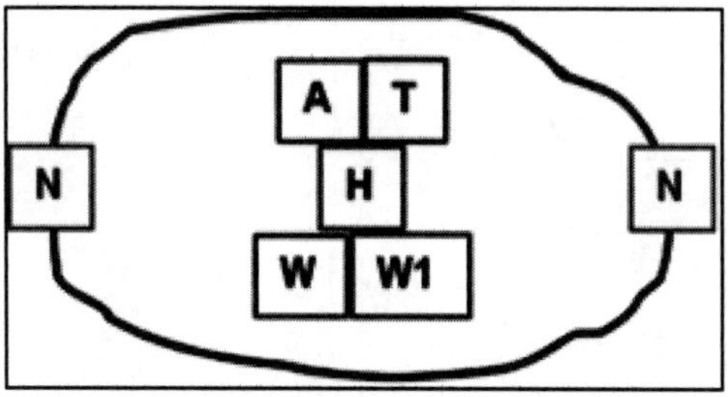

Figure 8-7. Template for area control measure symbols. (Refer to ADP 1-02, table 8-5, area of operations control measures symbols.)

Ops Terms & Symbols

Control Measure Symbols (Examples)

Ref: ADP 1-02, Terms and Military Symbols (Aug '18), tables 8-7 to 8-31.

Mission Command (C2)

Type	Icon
Points	
Coordination point	
Decision point	
Checkpoint	CKP
Linkup point	LU
Passage point	PP
Rally point	RLY
Release point	RP
Start point	SP

Type	Icon
Lines	
Light line	LL

Type	Icon
Areas	
Area of operations	AO
Named area of interest	NAI
Targeted area of interest	TAI

Movement and Maneuver

Type	Icon
General	
Points	
Point of interest	
Lines	
Forward line of troops	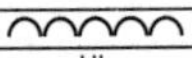
Handover line	HL
Phase line	PL
Areas	
Assembly area	AA
Drop zone	DZ
Extraction zone	EZ
Landing zone	LZ
Pickup zone	PZ
Defensive	
Points	
Combat outpost	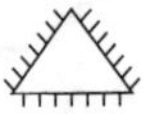
Observation post	
Lines	
Final protective line	FPL
Areas	
Battle position	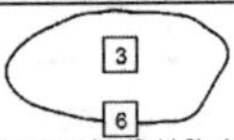 Note:The side opposite (field 6) always faces toward the hostile force.

Movement and Maneuver (cont.)

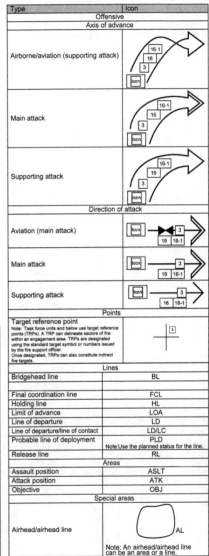

Type	Icon
Offensive	
Axis of advance	
Airborne/aviation (supporting attack)	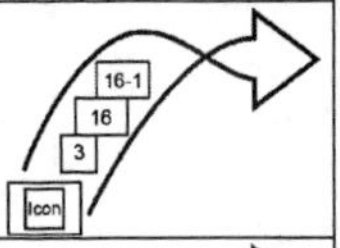
Main attack	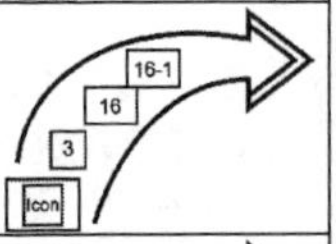
Supporting attack	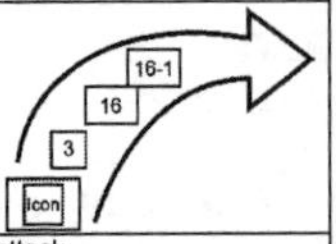
Direction of attack	
Aviation (main attack)	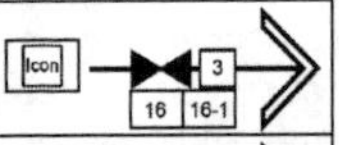
Main attack	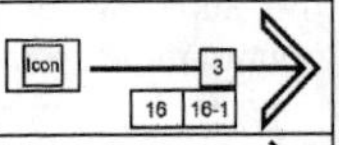
Supporting attack	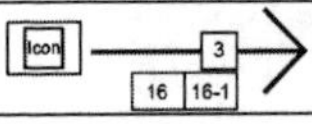
Points	
Target reference point Note: Task force units and below use target reference points (TRPs). A TRP can delineate sectors of fire within an engagement area. TRPs are designated using the standard target symbol or numbers issued by the fire support officer. Once designated, TRPs can also constitute indirect fire targets.	
Lines	
Bridgehead line	BL
Final coordination line	FCL
Holding line	HL
Limit of advance	LOA
Line of departure	LD
Line of departure/line of contact	LD/LC
Probable line of deployment	PLD Note:Use the planned status for the line.
Release line	RL
Areas	
Assault position	ASLT
Attack position	ATK
Objective	OBJ
Special areas	
Airhead/airhead line	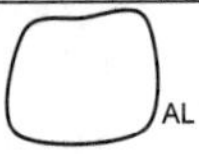 Note: An airhead/airhead line can be an area or a line.

Intelligence

Point, line, or area	
Type	Icon
Decoy/dummy/feint/phoney	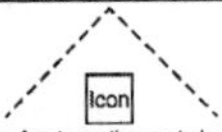 Note: The icon refers to another control measure icon, such as axis of advance, direction of attack, or minefield.

Fires

Type	Icon
Fire support coordination measures	
Points	
Fire support station	
Lines	
Coordinated fire line	CFL
Fire support coord line	FSCL
Restrictive fire line	RFL
Areas	
Airspace coordination area	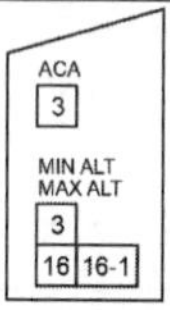
Free fire area	FFA
No-fire area	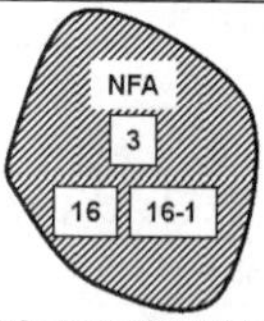 Note: No fire area has black cross-hatching.
Restrictive fire area	RFA

Protection

Type	Icon
Points	
Chemical, biological, radiological, or nuclear (CBRN) events	
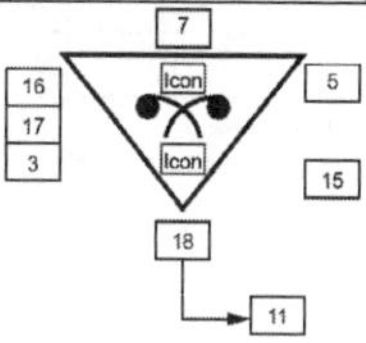	

Type	Sector 1 modifier icon
Biological	B
Chemical	C
Nuclear	N
Radiological	R

Type	Sector 2 modifier icon
Toxic industrial material	T

Displaced Persons, Refugees, and Evacuees	
Type	Icon
Civilian collection point	CIV
Detainee collection point	DET
Enemy prisoner of war collection point	EPW
Areas	
Chemical, biological, radiological, or nuclear (CBRN) contaminated	
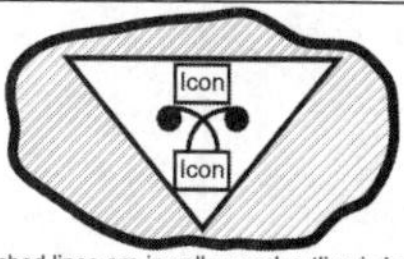 Notes: Cross-hatched lines are in yellow and outline is in black. Use sector 1 and sector 2 modifier icons and fields from CBRN events.	

Displaced Persons, Refugees, and Evacuees	
Type	Icon
Detainee holding area	DET
Enemy prisoner of war holding area	EPW
Refugee holding	REF

Sustainment

Type	Icon
Points	
Ammunition supply point	ASP
Ammunition transfer point	ATP
Rearm, refuel, and resupply	R3P
Refuel on the move	ROM
Class I	
Class II	II
Class III	
Class IV	
Class V	
Class VI	
Class VII	
Class VIII	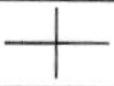
Class IX	
Class X	CA
Lines	
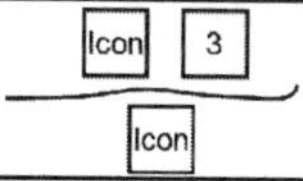	
Alternate supply route	ASR
Main supply route	MSR
Areas	
Brigade support area	BSA
Fwd arming & refuel point	FARP

Airspace Control Measures

Type	Icons
Air control point	
Communications checkpoint	
Air corridor	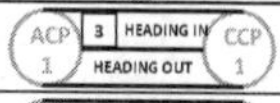
Low-level transit route	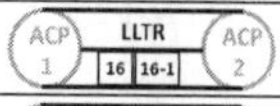
Minimum risk route	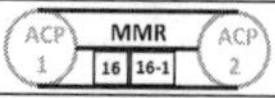
Standard Army aircraft flight route	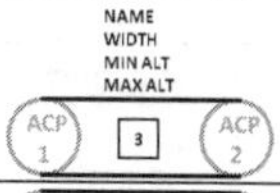
Unmanned aerial vehicle/ unmanned aircraft route	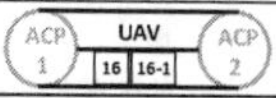
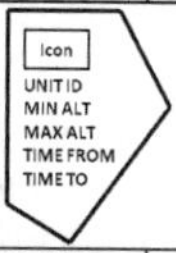	
High-altitude missile engagement zone	HIMEZ
High-density airspace control zone	HIDACZ

Ops Terms & Symbols

Abbreviations and Acronyms for use with Control Measure Symbols

Ref: ADP 1-02, Terms and Military Symbols (Aug '18), pp. 8-119 to 8-120.

Boundaries

Echelon	*Abbreviation or Acronym*
Army group	AG
Army	A
Corps	*Not needed.*
Marine expeditionary force	MEF
Marine air-ground task force	MAGTF
Division	DIV
Air assault division	AAD
Airborne division	ABD
Armored division	AD
Cavalry division	CD
Infantry division	ID
Marine division	MARD
Mechanized division	MD
Mountain division	MTND
Multinational division	MND
Brigade	BDE
Air assault brigade	AAB
Airborne brigade	ABB
Maneuver enhancement brigade	MEB
Multinational brigade	MNB
Naval infantry brigade	NIB
Regiment	REGT
Airborne Regiment	ABR
Marine expeditionary unit	MEU
Group	GP
Battle group	BG
Battalion	BN
Company	COY
Platoon	PLT
Team	TM

Table 8-32. Abbreviations and acronyms for boundaries. (Note. Multinational divisions may use geographical references in parenthesis.)

Unit Functions

Echelon	*Abbreviation or Acronym*
Air defense	ADA
Antitank or anti-armor	AT
Armor	AR
Aviation	AVN
Chem, bio, rad, or nuclear	CB
Civil affairs	CA
Combined arms	CAR
Counterintelligence	CI
Electronic warfare	EW
Engineer	EN
Explosive ordnance disposal	EOD
Field artillery	FA
Infantry	IN
Logistics	LOG
Maintenance	MNT
Medical	MED
Military intelligence	MI
Military police	MP
Naval	NAV
Ordnance	ORD
Quartermaster	QM
Reconnaissance	REC
Signal	SIG
Special forces	SF
Special operations force	SOF
Surveillance	SUR
Sustainment	SUST
Transportation	TPT

Table 8-33. Abbreviations and acronyms for unit functions.

Ops Terms & Symbols

VI. Tactical Mission Tasks (and Symbols)

Ref: ADP 1-02, Terms and Military Symbols (Aug '18), chap. 1 and 9.

A tactical mission task is a specific activity performed by a unit while executing a form of tactical operation or form of maneuver. A tactical mission task may be expressed as either an **action by a friendly force** or **effect on an enemy force**. The tactical mission tasks describe the results or effects the commander wants to achieve. *See following pages (pp. 1-30 to 1-31) for tactical mission tasks.*

Not all tactical mission tasks have symbols. Some tactical mission task symbols will include unit symbols, and the tactical mission task "delay until a specified time" will use an amplifier. However, no modifiers are used with tactical mission task symbols. Tactical mission task symbols are used in course of action sketches, synchronization matrixes, and maneuver sketches. They do not replace any part of the operation order.

A. Mission Symbols

Counterattack (dashed axis)	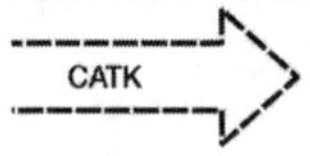	A form of attack by part or all of a defending force against an enemy attacking force, with the general objective of denying the enemy his goal in attacking (FM 3-0).
Cover		A form of security operation whose primary task is to protect the main body by fighting to gain time while also observing and reporting information and preventing enemy ground observation of and direct fire against the main body.
Delay	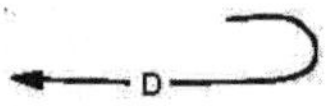	A form of retrograde in which a force under pressure trades space for time by slowing down the enemy's momentum and inflicting maximum damage on the enemy without, in principle, becoming decisively engaged (JP 1-02, see delaying operation).
Guard		A form of security operations whose primary task is to protect the main body by fighting to gain time while also observing and reporting information and preventing enemy ground observation of and direct fire against the main body. Units conducting a guard mission cannot operate independently because they rely upon fires and combat support assets of the main body.
Penetrate	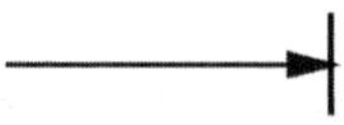	A form of maneuver in which an attacking force seeks to rupture enemy defenses on a narrow front to disrupt the defensive system (FM 3-0).
Relief in Place		A tactical enabling operation in which, by the direction of higher authority, all or part of a unit is replaced in an area by the incoming unit.
Retirement	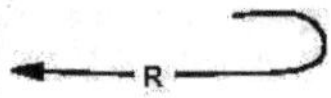	A form of retrograde [JP 1-02 uses *operation*] in which a force out of contact with the enemy moves away from the enemy (JP 1-02).
Screen		A form of security operations that primarily provides early warning to the protected force.
Withdraw	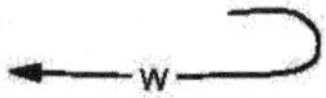	A planned operation in which a force in contact disengages from an enemy force (JP 1-02) [The Army considers it a form of retrograde.]

B. Actions by Friendly Forces

Attack by Fire		*Attack-by-fire* is a tactical mission task in which a commander uses direct fires, supported by indirect fires, to engage an enemy without closing with him to destroy, suppress, fix, or deceive him.
Breach	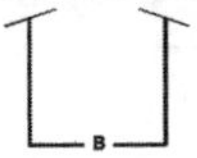	*Breach* is a tactical mission task in which the unit employs all available means to break through or secure a passage through an enemy defense, obstacle, minefield, or fortification.
Bypass	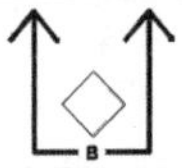	Bypass is a tactical mission task in which the commander directs his unit to maneuver around an obstacle, position, or enemy force to maintain the momentum of the operation while deliberately avoiding combat with an enemy force.
Clear	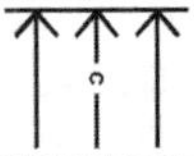	*Clear* is a tactical mission task that requires the commander to remove all enemy forces and eliminate organized resistance within an assigned area.
Control	*No graphic*	*Control* is a tactical mission task that requires the commander to maintain physical influence over a specified area to prevent its use by an enemy or to create conditions for successful friendly operations.
Counterrecon	*No graphic*	*Counterreconnaissance* is a tactical mission task that encompasses all measures taken by a commander to counter enemy reconnaissance and surveillance efforts.
Disengage	*No graphic*	*Disengage* is a tactical mission task where a commander has his unit break contact with the enemy to allow the conduct of another mission or to avoid decisive engagement.
Exfiltrate	*No graphic*	*Exfiltrate* is a tactical mission task where a commander removes soldiers or units from areas under enemy control by stealth, deception, surprise, or clandestine means.
Follow and Assume		*Follow and assume* is a tactical mission task in which a second committed force follows a force conducting an offensive operation and is prepared to continue the mission if the lead force is fixed, attritted, or unable to continue. The follow-and-assume force is not a reserve but is committed to accomplish specific tasks.
Follow and Support		*Follow and support* is a tactical mission task in which a committed force follows and supports a lead force conducting an offensive operation. The follow-and-support force is not a reserve but is a force committed to specific tasks.
Occupy	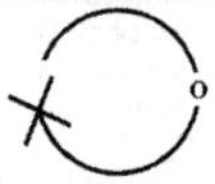	*Occupy* is a tactical mission task that involves moving a friendly force into an area so that it can control that area. Both the force's movement to and occupation of the area occur without enemy opposition.
Reduce	*No graphic*	*Reduce* is a tactical mission task that involves the destruction of an encircled or bypassed enemy force.
Retain	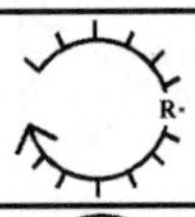	*Retain* is a tactical mission task in which the cdr ensures that a terrain feature controlled by a friendly force remains free of enemy occupation or use. The commander assigning this task must specify the area to retain and the duration of the retention, which is time- or event-driven.
Secure		*Secure* is a tactical mission task that involves preventing a unit, facility, or geographical location from being damaged or destroyed as a result of enemy action. This task normally involves conducting area security operations.
Seize	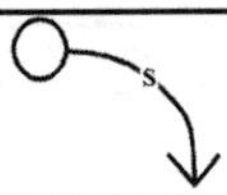	*Seize* is a tactical mission task that involves taking possession of a designated area by using overwhelming force. An enemy force can no longer place direct fire on an objective that has been seized.
Support by Fire	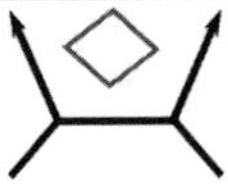	*Support-by-fire* is a tactical mission task in which a maneuver force moves to a position where it can engage the enemy by direct fire in support of another maneuvering force. The primary objective of the support force is normally to fix and suppress the enemy so he cannot effectively fire on the maneuvering force.

C. Effect on Enemy Forces

Block		*Block* is a tactical mission task that denies the enemy access to an area or prevents his advance in a direction or along an avenue of approach.
	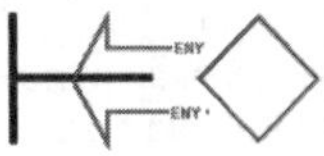	*Block* is also an engineer obstacle effect that integrates fire planning and obstacle effort to stop an attacker along a specific avenue of approach or prevent him from passing through an engagement area.
Canalize	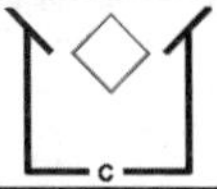	*Canalize* is a tactical mission task in which the commander restricts enemy movement to a narrow zone by exploiting terrain coupled with the use of obstacles, fires, or friendly maneuver.
Contain	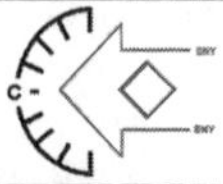	*Contain* is a tactical mission task that requires the commander to stop, hold, or surround enemy forces or to cause them to center their activity on a given front and prevent them from withdrawing any part of their forces for use elsewhere.
Defeat	*No graphic*	*Defeat* occurs when an enemy has temporarily or permanently lost the physical means or the will to fight. The defeated force is unwilling or unable to pursue his COA, and can no longer interfere to a significant degree. Results from the use of force or the threat of its use.
Destroy		*Destroy* is a tactical mission task that physically renders an enemy force combat-ineffective until it is reconstituted. Alternatively, to destroy a combat system is to damage it so badly that it cannot perform any function or be restored to a usable condition without being entirely rebuilt.
Disrupt	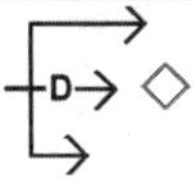	*Disrupt* is a tactical mission task in which a commander integrates direct and indirect fires, terrain, and obstacles to upset an enemy's formation or tempo, interrupt his timetable, or cause his forces to commit prematurely or attack in a piecemeal fashion.
	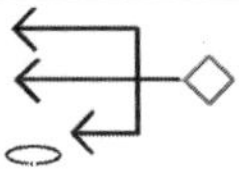	*Disrupt* is also an engineer obstacle effect that focuses fire planning and obstacle effort to cause the enemy to break up his formation and tempo, interrupt his timetable, commit breaching assets prematurely, and attack in a piecemeal effort.
Fix		*Fix* is a tactical mission task where a commander prevents the enemy from moving any part of his force from a specific location for a specific period. Fixing an enemy force does not mean destroying it. The friendly force has to prevent the enemy from moving in any direction.
	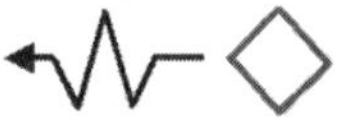	*Fix* is also an engineer obstacle effect that focuses fire planning and obstacle effort to slow an attacker's movement within a specified area, normally an engagement area.
Isolate	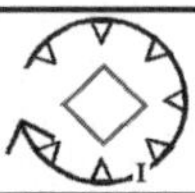	*Isolate* is a tactical mission task that requires a unit to seal off-both physically and psychologically-an enemy from his sources of support, deny him freedom of movement, and prevent him from having contact with other enemy forces.
Neutralize	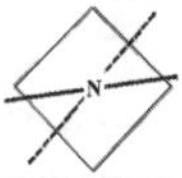	*Neutralize* is a tactical mission task that results in rendering enemy personnel or materiel incapable of interfering with a particular operation.
Suppress		*Suppress* is a tactical mission task that results in the temporary degradation of the performance of a force or weapon system below the level needed to accomplish its mission.
Turn	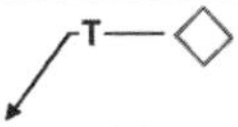	*Turn* is a tactical mission task that involves forcing an enemy element from one avenue of approach or movement corridor to another.
	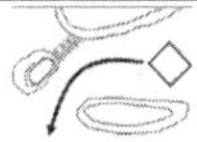	*Turn* is also a tactical obstacle effect that integrates fire planning and obstacle effort to divert an enemy formation from one avenue of approach to an adjacent avenue of approach or into an engagement area.

Ops Terms & Symbols

Tactical Doctrinal Taxonomy

Ref: Adapted from ADP 3-90, Offense and Defense (Jul '19), fig. 2-1, p. 2-3.

The following shows the Army's tactical doctrinal taxonomy for the four elements of decisive action (in accordance with ADP 3-0) and their subordinate tasks. The commander conducts tactical enabling tasks to assist the planning, preparation, and execution of any of the four elements of decisive action. Tactical enabling tasks are never decisive operations in the context of the conduct of offensive and defensive tasks. (They are also never decisive during the conduct of stability tasks.) The commander uses tactical shaping tasks to assist in conducting combat operations with reduced risk.

Elements of Decisive Action (and subordinate tasks)

Offensive Operations

Movement to Contact
- Search and attack
- Cordon and search

Attack
- Ambush*
- Counterattack*
- Demonstration*
- Spoiling attack*
- Feint*
- Raid*

**Also known as special purpose attacks*

Exploitation

Pursuit
- Frontal
- Combination

Forms of Maneuver
- Envelopment
- Frontal attack
- Infiltration
- Penetration
- Turning Movement

Defensive Operations

Area Defense

Mobile Defense

Retrograde
- Delay
- Withdraw
- Retirement

Forms of the Defense
- Defense of linear obstacle
- Perimeter defense
- Reverse slope defense

Stability Operations
- Civil security
- Civil control
- Restore essential services
- Support to governance
- Support to economic and infrastructure development
- Conduct security cooperation

Defense Support to Civil Authorities
- Provide support for domestic disasters
- Provide support for domestic CBRN incidents
- Provide support for domestic law enforcement agencies
- Provide other designated support

Enabling Operations

Reconnaissance Operations
- Area
- Reconnaissance in force
- Route
- Special
- Zone

Security
- Screen
- Guard
- Cover
- Area

Passage of Lines
- Forward
- Rearward

Troop Movement
- Administrative movement
- Approach march
- Road march

Encirclement Operations

Relief in Place
- Sequential
- Simultaneous
- Staggered

Other Enabling Operations (Examples)
- Information Operations (FM 3-13)
- Mobility Operations (ATP 3-90.4)
- Countermobility Operations (ATP 3-90.8)

Tactical Mission Tasks

Actions by Friendly Forces
- Attack-by-Fire
- Breach
- Bypass
- Clear
- Control
- Counterreconnaissance
- Disengage
- Exfiltrate
- Follow and Assume
- Follow and Support
- Occupy
- Reduce
- Retain
- Secure
- Seize
- Support-by-Fire

Effects on Enemy Force
- Block
- Canalize
- Contain
- Defeat
- Destroy
- Disrupt
- Fix
- Interdict
- Isolate
- Neutralize
- Suppress
- Turn

(BSS6) Index

Index

D

E

F

G

H

I

Index

RECOGNIZED AS THE DOCTRINA
REFERENCE STANDARD BY MILITAR
PROFESSIONALS AROUND THE WORLD

THREAT, OPFOR, REGIONAL & CULTURAL

In today's complicated and uncertain world, the military must be ready to meet the challenges of any type of conflict, in all kinds of places, and against all kinds of threats.

HOMELAND DEFENSE, DSCA, & DISASTER RESPONSE

Disaster can strike anytime, anywhere. It takes many forms—a hurricane, an earthquake, a tornado, a flood, a fire, a hazardous spill, or an act of terrorism.

DIGITAL SMARTBOOKS (eBooks)

In addition to paperback, SMARTbooks are also available in digital (eBook) format. Our digital SMARTbooks are for use with Adobe Digital Editions and can be used on up to **six computers and six devices**, with free software available for **85+ devices and platforms—including PC/MAC, iPad and iPhone, Android tablets and smartphones, Nook, and more**! Digital SMARTbooks are also available for the **Kindle Fire** (using Bluefire Reader for Android).

Download FREE samples and SAVE 15% everyday at:

www.TheLightningPress.com

www.TheLightningPress.co

urchase/Order

avings on SMARTbooks! Save big when you order our titles ...ner in a SMARTset bundle. It's the most popular & least expensive way to buy, and a great way to build your professional library. If you need a quote or have special requests, please contact us by one of the methods below!

View, download FREE samples and purchase online:

www.TheLightningPress.com

Order SECURE Online
Web: www.TheLightningPress.com
Email: SMARTbooks@TheLightningPress.com

24-hour Order & Customer Service Line
Place your order (or leave a voicemail)
at 1-800-997-8827

Phone Orders, Customer Service & Quotes
Live customer service and phone orders available
Mon - Fri 0900-1800 EST at (863) 409-8084

Mail, Check & Money Order
2227 Arrowhead Blvd., Lakeland, FL 33813

Government/Unit/Bulk Sales

The Lightning Press is a **service-disabled, veteran-owned small business**, DOD-approved vendor and federally registered—to include the SAM, WAWF, FBO, and FEDPAY.

We accept and process both **Government Purchase Cards** (GCPC/GPC) and **Purchase Orders** (PO/PR&Cs).

15% OFF
RETAIL EVERYDAY

Buy direct from our website and always get the latest editions and the best pricing. Join our SMARTnews email list for free notification of changes and new editions.

www.TheLightningPress.com

VISA MasterCard PayPal